HARVESTS
OF
CHANGE

*These things compose the record of the general life of
civilization for almost the whole period during which men of
my generation were to know it; an immense good fortune to us,
since if the backward vision feeds upon bliss by the simple fact
of not being the immediate, the importunate, or the too
precariously forward, this bliss naturally grows with the
extent of the pasture. I measure the spread as that of half a
century—only with the air turning more and more to the
golden as space recedes, turning to the clearness of all the
sovereign exemptions, the serenity of all the fond assurances,
that were to keep on and on, seeing themselves not only so little
menaced but so admirably crowned. This we now perceive to
have been so much their mistake that as other periods of
history have incurred, to our convenience, some distinctive
and descriptive name, so it can only rest with us to write down
the fifty years I speak of, in the very largest letters, as the
Age of the Mistake.*

*That title might, of course, be blighting to retrospect if one
chose to take it so; it might present the whole time as too
tragically stupid, too deplorably wasted, to be lived over
again critically without sickness and shame. There is, however,
another way of taking it, which is to live it over personally
and sentimentally, exactly to the sought confusion and
reprobation of the forces now preying upon us, exactly to the
effect of saving it at least for the imagination if we may not
save it for the reconciling reason.*

—HENRY JAMES, "The Founding of the *Nation*" (1915)

*And now, therefor, after having been long on the way, we
Argonauts of the ideal, our courage perhaps greater than our
prudence, often shipwrecked and bruised, but, as I say,
healthier than people would like to admit, dangerously healthy,
recovering health again and again—it would seem as if our
troubles were to be rewarded, as if we saw before us that
undiscovered country, whose frontiers no one has yet seen, a
land lying beyond all other known lands and hiding-places of
the ideal, a world so overflowing with beauty, strangeness,
doubt, terror, and divinity, that both our curiosity and our lust
for possession are wrought to a pitch of extreme excitement.
Nothing on earth can satisfy us. Alas! how with such vistas
before us and with our conscience and consciousness full of
such burning desire, can we still be content with the* man of
the present day?

—FRIEDRICH NIETZSCHE, *Ecce Homo*

HARVESTS
OF
CHANGE

American
Literature

1865–1914

JAY MARTIN

Prentice-Hall, Inc., *Englewood Cliffs, New Jersey*

The author wishes to thank the following for their kind permission to quote from their publications: Harvard University Press for *The Mark Twain-William Dean Howells Letters* edited by Henry Nash Smith and William M. Gibson, © 1960 by The President and Fellows of Harvard College, *The Letters of Emily Dickinson* edited by Thomas H. Johnson and Theodora Ward (The Belknap Press), and *The Poems of Emily Dickinson* edited by Thomas H. Johnson (The Belknap Press), poems from which are also reprinted by permission of the Trustees of Amherst College, © 1951, 1955 by The President and Fellows of Harvard College; Little, Brown and Company for *The Complete Poems of Emily Dickinson* edited by Thomas H. Johnson, © 1929, 1957 by Mary L. Hampson; Houghton Mifflin Company for *Life and Letters of Emily Dickinson* edited by Martha D. Bianchi, *Letters of Henry Adams* edited by W. C. Ford, and *Life and Letters of Joel Chandler Harris* edited by Julia Collier Harris; Harper & Row, Publishers, Inc. for *Mark Twain* by Alfred Bigelow Paine, © 1912 by Harper & Row, Publishers, Inc.; Charles Scribner's Sons for *The Letters of Henry James*, *A Small Boy and Others*, and *Notes of a Son and Brother*, all by Henry James; Charles Scribner's Sons and A. Watkins, Inc. for *A Backward Glance* by Edith Wharton, © 1933, 1934 by William R. Tyler, renewed © 1961, 1962 by William R. Tyler; Oxford University Press for *The Notebooks of Henry James* edited by Kenneth Murdock and F. O. Matthiessen; The Book Club of California for *Letters of Frank Norris;* Harvard College Library for an unpublished letter from Henry James to William Dean Howells; and Holt, Rinehart and Winston, Inc. and Laurence Pollinger Limited for "The Mountain," "The Road Not Taken," "Home Burial," "From Plane to Plane," and "The Pasture" from *Complete Poems of Robert Frost*, © 1916, 1930, 1939, 1949 by Holt, Rinehart and Winston, Inc., © 1944, 1958 by Robert Frost.

for my Mother

Preface

I regard the period about which I have written in this book as a time particularly rich with relatedness—assumed, felt, and actual—among people, ideas, convictions, and the institutions of society. Intellectual or social preoccupations, literary or artistic imaginations, visions of hope or despair for American culture— these all intermixed and tended to fertilize the minds and feelings of the men of that age. People went together more frequently and more readily than they went apart.

How this was so during the period from 1865 to 1914 is for my book to say. I want here to express my personal sense that the same has been true for me, and to acknowledge my indebtedness to the kindness, intelligence, and imagination of others.

During a Morse Research Fellowship, awarded to me by Yale University for the academic year 1963–64, I was given the freedom to research for, meditate upon, and to write much of this book. Support for the preparation of the manuscript came from the James Morris Whiton Fund of the Yale Graduate School, administered by John Perry Miller.

I am grateful to Paul O'Connell of Prentice-Hall, Inc., for his support of this book, however long it became, from the beginning. William S. Green showed extraordinary care in the editing and production of the book. Two research assistants, Anthony M. Lavely and David A. Richards, worked faithfully and intelligently for me during my research.

During the later stages of my work, several scholars taught me what the community of learning truly means by their willingness to read individual chapters. Norman Holmes Pearson helped me to solve some of the difficult problems of the first chapter. Gordon S. Haight gave me the benefit of his knowledge of and research upon the tradition of DeForest and Howells, my subject in Chapter Two. Paul Pickrel, my very first reader, commented sympathetically on Chapters Three and Six. W. K. Wimsatt, Jr., pointed out examples of my own myth-making in Chapter Four, and helped me to eliminate them. Richard B. Sewall improved my discussion in Chapter

Seven of Emily Dickinson's poetry during one fine afternoon while we sat in his office surrounded by Emily Dickinson memorabilia.

Four scholars read the entire text. Maynard Mack served as my general reader. R. W. B. Lewis, who first suggested that I write this book, never wavered in his support of it or hesitated to criticize it. Roy Harvey Pearce read the second draft with the humanistic care that his students have come to expect and demand of him. Alfred Kazin went so far in friendship as to *offer* to read my manuscript in a near-final version; and he helped me thereby to make a final version out of it. My gratitude for the generosity of these men is so comprehensive that it must remain inexpressible.

Finally, of my debt in this book to my wife, Helen, I can say only, as Kate Croy does of Milly Theale, "Well, she stretched out her wings, and it was to *that* they reached."

JAY MARTIN

Silliman College
Yale University
New Haven, Connecticut
June, 1966

Contents

A Note on the Text, xv

ONE

The Massing of Forces—
The Forging of Masses   1

THE LOCUS OF CHANGE, 1

> THE RISE OF WEALTH, 2; THE GROWTH OF THE CITY, 3;
> IMMIGRATION, 5; REFORM, 6; EDUCATION, 6;
> THE GROWTH OF SCIENCE AND A NATURALISTIC TEST
> OF TRUTH, 7; TECHNOLOGY, 10

THE SAGES OF SOCIETY, 11

THE RISE AND RELEVANCE
OF MASS LITERATURE, 16

THE TRANSFORMATION
OF NINETEENTH-CENTURY MAN, 21

TWO

The Great American Novel   25

THE IDEA OF NATIONAL IDENTITY, 25

To Be an American: John DeForest, 29

Interoceanic Episodes: William Dean Howells, 35

Howells's Followers, 50

THE IDEA OF NATIONAL IDENTITY—Continued

    Stephen Crane, 55

    Frank Norris, 70

A BRAVE NEW WORLD, 77

        THE DISCOVERY OF EUROPE, 78; THE EXPLORATION
        OF AMERICA, 80

THREE

Paradises Lost   81

SOUTHERN REGIONAL LITERATURE, 88

    Sidney Lanier: The Real and the Ideal, 92

    *Joel Chandler Harris
        and the Cornfield Journalist*, 96

    George Washington Cable, 100

WESTERN REGIONAL LITERATURE, 105

    Edward Eggleston, 111

    Edgar Watson Howe: The Western Nightmare, 116

    The Silent World of Ambrose Bierce, 121

    Hamlin Garland, 124

NEW ENGLAND REGIONAL LITERATURE, 133

    Rose Terry Cooke, 139

    Sarah Orne Jewett, 142

    Mary E. Wilkins, 148

    Edwin Arlington Robinson, 152

    Robert Frost: The Two Roads, 159

FOUR

Mark Twain

The Dream of Drift and the Dream of Delight   165

TWAIN AND HISTORY, 175

TWAIN AND THE IMAGE OF THE CHILD, 184

THE DREAM OF DRIFT, 193

FIVE

Paradises (To Be) Regained   202

CHANGING ASSUMPTIONS, 202

         PHILOSOPHY, 204; THEOLOGY, 204; ECONOMICS, 205;
         JURISPRUDENCE, 206

FRUSTRATION AND COMPENSATION:
THE SHAPE OF UTOPIA, 207

         MATERIALISM, 210; CULTISM, 211; CATASTROPHISM
         AND APOCALYPSE, 213

THE GOOD LIFE: THE MYTH OF SUCCESS
AND THE MESSAGE OF JESUS, 216

Edward Bellamy, 220

William Dean Howells, 226

Ignatius Donnelly, 231

Jack London, 234

SIX

The Visible and Invisible Cities   240

The Continuity of Naturalism—
         Henry Blake Fuller and Frank Norris, 248

Theodore Dreiser, 252

Edith Wharton, 262

THE INVISIBLE CITY, 277

SEVEN

The Apocalypse of the Mind 279

*Walt Whitman's Specimen Man
and the "Genteel Little Creatures,"* 279

Emily Dickinson, 285

Henry Adams, 296

EIGHT

Henry James:
The Wings of the Artist 310

JAMES AND THE AMERICAN QUESTS FOR EUROPE, 317

THE GREAT INTERNATIONAL NOVEL, 322

JAMES'S PORTRAIT OF THE AMERICAN, 329

"THE AGE OF THE MISTAKE," 334

IN THE COUNTRY OF THE BLIND—, 336

—AND THE COUNTRY OF THE BLUE, 339

THE NEW AMERICAN NOVEL, 342

THE "MAJOR PHASE," 350

JAMES'S SUMMING-UP:
THE TWENTIETH-CENTURY SAGE, 258

Index 365

A Note on the Text

In citing sources I have adopted the following practices: (1) At the first mention of any book, or thereafter for particularly important reasons, I give the date of its first publication in parentheses immediately following my reference within the text. (2) Assuming that my readers will be reading or have read the novels and poems that I discuss, I do not cite page numbers or editions for these. In almost every case, I have quoted from the first edition; exceptions are indicated in the text, and occur chiefly in the chapter on Henry James. (3) In my footnotes, I give a full reference for the first citation of any text, including the date of first publication when I use a later or revised edition of the work; thereafter, I give only a short title or brief reference.

ONE

The Massing of Forces–
The Forging of Masses

*"Ah, . . . the name of the good American is as easily given as taken
away! What is it, to begin with, to be one, and what's the extraordinary
hurry? Surely nothing that's so pressing was ever so little defined."*
—Henry James, *The Ambassadors* (1903)

THE LOCUS OF CHANGE

The changes that took place in America between the Civil War
and the First World War were remarkable both for their completeness and
for their rapidity. Institutions, systems of belief, ideological and social
assumptions, ways of feeling at home in the world—in short, the whole scene
of human endeavor and thought—that had existed, as Henry Adams said,
since the Middle Ages, now passed away during this fifty-year period. Confusion, resulting from feelings of personal alienation amid the loss of social
stability, became more and more apparent, particularly in the autobiographies that proliferated at the century's end. Writing autobiography,
James, Adams, Twain, Howells, and their peers in business, law, education,
and science all looked back upon a prewar age now hopelessly lost, and
sought, through their own careers, to discover the locus of change. Henry
James's remark that the members of his family were "such a company of
characters and such a picture of differences, and withal so fused and united
and interlocked" that memory could not separate them[1] is true for the age as
well. Out of the common confusion writers became, as seldom before, public
men: they mixed and mingled, sharing their visions with their contemporaries.
In a period when the needs and demands of culture itself were so overpower-
ing, they seldom attempted to get beyond their time. Rather, the writers
between the wars, immersed in the flowing ocean of consciousness—all that
their culture forced upon them in the way of development and alteration—
these writers, major and minor, undertook the task of preserving culture and
accommodating change to human uses by clarifying, deepening, and intensi-
fying the contents of consciousness for their age. They all were, as Herman

[1] *A Small Boy and Others* (New York, 1913), p. 2.

Melville said of himself in his "Foreword" to *Battle Pieces* (1866), "harp[s] in the wind."[2]

The period thus takes on a fugal quality, in which men of letters, variously mingling with their contemporaries and sharing their concerns, brought new depth to their culture by balancing and assessing the preoccupations, or "themes," of their age, and interweaving them into more complex patterns of understanding and belief. The following list briefly outlines the "themes" that culture could give its men of letters to work upon and out of during this period. By "themes" is meant the forces of change that were massing in the culture itself, forces that men would have to confront and understand in terms of their past if culture were to move forward into a future at all. The characteristics of the period between the wars have been abundantly delineated by contemporary witnesses and the historians who have studied their testimony. A study of them reveals the following as the basic concerns with which the mind, in this age, had to deal.

THE RISE OF WEALTH. Among the best early critics of the age, Henry Adams and Charles Francis Adams, Jr. showed, in their *Chapters of Erie* (1871), that

> the great operations of war, the handling of large masses of men, the influence of discipline, the lavish expenditure of unprecedented sums of money, the immense financial operations, the possibilities of effective co-operation [during the war], were lessons not likely to be lost on men quick to receive and to apply all new ideas.[3]

Wartime needs in meat-packing, transportation, clothing, and weapons had not only created several millionaires, but also soon engendered, as Rebecca Harding Davis lamented, "the disease of money-getting [that]...has infected the nation."[4] The reasons for this astounding growth of wealth are now rather clear. Even before the end of the war, however, Lincoln had expressed his fears for a postwar America that, as Tocqueville had earlier, he now foresaw coming under the domination of a manufacturing aristocracy. To his friend W. R. Ellis, Lincoln wrote prophetically:

> I see in the near future a crisis arising that unnerves me and causes me to tremble for the safety of my country. By a result of the war, corporations have been enthroned, and an era of corruption in high places will follow, and the money power of the country will endeavor to prolong its reign by working upon the prejudices of the people, until all wealth is aggregated in a few hands and the Republic is destroyed.[5]

Not long after, as if in ironic and tragic confirmation of Lincoln's prophecy, Mrs. E. F. Ellet, describing *The Court Circles of the Republic*— itself a revelatory title—noted that despite the recent assassination of President Lincoln, "the fashionable season [in Washington] of 1866 was

2 "Foreword" to *Battle Pieces* (New York, 1866), p. 5.   3 *Chapters of Erie and Other Essays* (New York, 1871), p. 135.   4 *Bits of Gossip* (Westminster, England, 1904), p. 138.   5 Quoted in Sylvia Bowman, *The Year 2000: A Critical Biography of Edward Bellamy* (New York, 1958), p. 74.

almost a carnival"[6] in the splendor of its entertainments. The parade of wealth had begun. From a handful of millionaires before the war, the number grew to over 4,000 by the early '90s.[7] With agrarian control of Congress ended by secession, the government was able to enact a series of laws that gave added power to Northern industrial interests. Railroad subsidies, the National Banking Act, the relaxation of immigration laws, increases in the tariff—these not only helped to achieve victory, but continued, after the war, to provide convenient channels for rapid industrial growth.

To compensate for war years of frustration and loss, men hurried to exploit (and exhaust) the natural and human resources of the country. Sensitive contemporary observers remarked the feverish, almost compulsive, intensity of business activity. So obvious were the symptoms of human exhaustion by the '80s that even Herbert Spencer, whose Social Darwinism American businessmen saw as their *apologia*, ironically proposed a "Gospel of Relaxation" to replace the Gospel of Work in America.

A rapidly increasing passion for frivolous or distracting entertainment also became apparent. Barnum and Beecher and their followers trumpeted their jubilees and hosannas for the populace. Men demanded circuses and popular sermons. They demanded, as well, evidence of increased opulence: palatial architecture—supplied by Richard Morris Hunt and McKim, Mead and White—elegant interiors, the possession of imposing art collections—in short, rich taste. "When the rich man gets good architecture, his neighbors will get it too,"[8] Edith Wharton told her audience in her second book, *The Decoration of Houses* (1897). Increased wealth became the myth of the time, at all levels of society. Citizens of O. Henry's Four Million imagined themselves, like Dreiser's Carrie Meeber, being reborn as denizens of Ward McAllister's Four Hundred.[9]

THE GROWTH OF THE CITY. Between the wars city life—and, of course, the mind it fostered—came to dominate American experience. Like the increase in wealth, the city created new aspirations and new ways of satisfying them. Both helped to shape the new, widened consciousness of the age. Nowhere more than in the city were the contrasts between poverty and wealth so appalling; but nowhere else did they hold such fascination. Particularly in America, where man, in the tradition of Jefferson, Emerson, and Whitman, conceived of American destiny in terms of the regenerative

[6] *The Court Circles of the Republic, Or the Beauties and Celebrities of the Nation... Sold by Subscription Only* (Hartford, 1869), p. 550. [7] See Edward Chase Kirkland, *Dream and Thought in the Business Community* (Ithaca, 1956), p. 6. [8] Edith Wharton and Ogden Codman, Jr., *The Decoration of Houses* (New York, 1897), pp. xxi–xxii. [9] The phrase, "The Four Hundred," was said to have been uttered by McAllister, who, requested in 1892 by Mrs. William Astor to draw up a guest list for her annual ball, replied that there were only four hundred socially acceptable people in New York. The phrase and the assumptions which lay behind it were, of course, immediately criticized. Ignatius Donnelly, the Populist lecturer, called the Four Hundred "a hog-show, where men are rated by their financial weight, because it indicates how many shoats they have butted and bumped away from nature's universal trough." See Donnelly, *The Bryan Campaign for the People's Money* (Chicago, 1896), p. 101. The tensions that would arise from four—or forty!—millions of people aspiring to join a Four Hundred—that is, taking wealth as an ideal—are obvious, and make the subject for scores of novels.

frontier, the city symbolized and seemed to embody evil. (In Christian literature, from Dante's Inferno to Bunyan's Vanity Fair, hell was conventionally represented as a crowded city.) But if the city represented something evil for the American, he seemed to feel as well, like Baudelaire at about the same time, that it offered more intense opportunities for human life than possible anywhere else. Both were seeing, as a later American, T. S. Eliot, would interpret Baudelaire's thought, that "it is better, in a paradoxical way, to do evil than to do nothing: at least, we exist."[10] Eliot would make his Waste Land an "Unreal City"; but it was the city as well that in his poem offered the possibility of regeneration. Americans were willing to face evil that they might experience good. Between the wars, while the rural population of America was doubling, urban dwellers multiplied seven times. From a country that was essentially still agrarian in 1865 and, indeed, still contained large unsettled areas, America became, by 1914, bound to cities and city needs. By the time of the First World War, only about 30 per cent of Americans were involved in agriculture; and those, as Sherwood Anderson's books of the grotesque, *Winesburg, Ohio* (1919) and *Poor White* (1920), suggest, were increasingly enfeebled and ineffectual. While Americans were still conceiving of the Middle West as an aspect of the frontier, Ohio and Illinois now had over a hundred towns and cities, including some of the largest in the country. Even in Missouri and Minnesota, three out of every ten inhabitants were townsfolk.[11]

Clearly, Americans needed to absorb the city into their consciousness—to accommodate, and perhaps compromise, their predilections toward the image of the frontier, with all that this implied, to the actualities of city living. As early as 1870, a critic of American manners noted that "city folks" were the "heroes and heroines" of the time.[12] Writers like James and Howells, followed by Crane, Norris, Dreiser, and Edith Wharton, wrote a literature depicting the delights and dramas of city existence, and helped to shape, by their art, humanly satisfying patterns of urban life. The ways in which they adopted urban actualities to the orders of the imagination allowed Americans widely to accept Richard Harding Davis's assurance in 1892 that "any man who will live in a log house at the foot of a mountain... when he could live at the Knickerbocker Flats, and drive forth in a hansom with rubber tires, is no longer an object of public interest."[13] No longer the cracker-barrel philosopher, but now the sage of the saloon, Mr. Dooley, seemed to hold the cup of knowledge. Surely, then, while Americans were uneasy, all through the period, with the city, they also increasingly found in urban life, as Arthur M. Schlesinger has said, "all those impulses and movements which made for a finer, more humane civilization," including "education, literature, science, invention, the fine arts, social reform, public hygiene, [and] the use of leisure."[14]

---

10 "Baudelaire" in *Selected Essays* (New York, 1950: "New Edition"), p. 380. 11 See Arthur M. Schlesinger, *The Rise of the City, 1878–1898* (New York, 1933), p. 57. 12 George Makepeace Towle, *American Society* (London, 1870), Vol. II, p. 143. 13 Quoted in Gerald Langford, *The Richard Harding Davis Years: A Biography of a Mother and Son* (New York, 1961), p. 122. 14 Schlesinger, p. xiv.

IMMIGRATION. Cities were the first—and most often the last—stop of the waves of immigrants that came to America's shores following the Civil War. Before the War the immigrant was able to adjust to the patterns of rural society with little difficulty. But in the city the problems of adjustment between immigrant and native were more and more intensified. Whitman's multitudinous *Leaves of Grass* and the *Pequod* of Melville's *Moby Dick* (with its English, Dutch, Irish, Portuguese, Sicilian, Danish, Spanish, Negro, and Oriental sailors) had been prophetic of this varied America. Chronicling the march of triumphant democracy in 1885, Andrew Carnegie counted nearly a thousand foreign-language newspapers in the United States.[15] By 1890 a third of all Bostonians were of foreign birth. New York held as many Germans as Hamburg, twice as many Irish as Dublin, and two-and-a-half times as many Jews as Warsaw: it was the greatest immigrant center in the world, with four of every five residents of foreign birth or parentage.[16] The fearful effects of immigration need not be told over. Muckrakers like Jacob Riis and novelists like Stephen Crane vividly portrayed them. It is true that the newcomer to the city was not quite so easily assimilated into American life as, earlier, the Hibernian described in Crèvecoeur's *Letters from an American Farmer* (1782) had been. But immigrants were able, as we can now see, to learn the less obvious patterns of city life almost as readily. It is true as well that the immigrant had in turn decided effects upon the American character. He too, for good or evil, was a force for change. While Immigration Restriction leagues, publicized by Thomas Bailey Aldrich and Henry Cabot Lodge, were lamenting the loss of homogeniety and promulgating a myth of Anglo-Saxon supremacy, immigrants, who for their part, brought with them hopes for a better life, constantly refreshed and revitalized our optimism. The immigrant, who had long used America as a symbol of the Promised Land, helped to produce, as much as the Frontier, the American character. In the period immediately following the Civil War, E. L. Godkin, the Anglo-Irish editor of the *Nation,* embodied the spirit of culture that Lowell, Norton, and Adams were attempting to make American. Later, John Boyle O'Reilly announced that he would run his immigrant paper, *The Pilot,* on "the principles of Democracy as laid down by Jefferson."[17] At the turn of the century, still another immigrant, S. S. McClure, founded the first muckraking magazine, devoted to the analysis and reformation of American industrial and political corruption. "When I came to this country, an immigrant boy, in 1866," he wrote, reflecting his idealism, "I believed that the government of the United States was the flower of all the ages—that nothing could possibly corrupt it."[18] In short, the immigrants to America, along with the

[15] *Triumphant Democracy* (New York, 1886), pp. 344–45. [16] See *ibid.,* pp. 72–3.
[17] O'Reilly created a sensation by the indignation meeting he organized to protest a celebration of the Queen's Jubilee in Boston's Faneuil Hall, where American patriots had spoken during Revolutionary times. To be sure, some of his Irish Anglophobia may have given energy to his indignation; but he protested specifically as an American against this desecration of Revolutionary traditions, and told his audience bitterly: "We must have a hall unpolluted by the breath of Toryism and royalty in Boston." See James Jeffrey Roche, *Life of John Boyle O'Reilly, Together with his Complete Poems and Speeches...* (New York, 1891), pp. 347, 307. [18] *My Autobiography* (London, 1914), p. 265.

American travelers abroad, were making immigration the symbol and occasion for an experience open to the widest and best ideals of culture.

REFORM. Writers had to account not only for the uncontrollable forces of change that were altering American culture, but also for those purposeful visions of change that reformers were proposing and seeking to have realized. The triumph of moral idealism in the War left a heritage of reform that conflicted or coalesced with the other elements that have been listed so far. Certainly America seemed to be a land of both promise and broken promises.[19] In 1865, the holy cause of abolition having been won, William Lloyd Garrison suspended publication of *The Liberator,* and, supported by a gift of $30,000 from his admirers, went to Paris.[20] Few prewar reformers, with the exception of Wendell Phillips, carried over their enthusiasm for reform into the new age. And even Phillips faced postwar problems that required for their solution a knowledge of law, economics, sociology, and political science that he did not possess. As Thomas Wentworth Higginson said: "You could not settle the relations of capital and labor off-hand, by saying, as in the case of slavery, 'Let my people go'; the matter was far more complex. It was like trying to adjust a chronometer with no other knowledge than that won by observing a sun-dial."[21] Questions of reform were no longer just abstract or moral; they involved, and demanded knowledge of, the social body. The old reformers—of whom Miss Birdseye in James's *The Bostonians* is a tenderly ironical representative—had no solution; but they lived on and transmitted their moral idealism to the new generation. William Dean Howells—in his protest over the Haymarket Square executions, for instance —found himself treading where older reformers, John Greenleaf Whittier and his peers, could not.[22] Making a science of reform, clergymen, civic organizations, and men of letters from the '70s onward joined as never before to probe and reveal the diseases of the social body. Before the War Rebecca Harding Davis had criticized the "narrow fury" of the Abolitionists, who, "like Saint George...thought that one dragon filled the world."[23] But after the War it became increasingly true that reformers were noteworthy precisely for the range of their interests, the ways they were envisioning change on all levels and in all aspects of society. Taken together, the multitude of reformers presented a multiple and magnificent image of the Earthly Paradise, which compelled the mind and held the heart. Almost unbelievably, by the time the First World War began, most of their utopias had become realities.

EDUCATION. Part of the program of reform was the argument that increased

---

19 Herbert Croly's *The Promise of American Life* (New York, 1909) summarizes the disillusion of the age in insisting that "the candid reformer can no longer consider the national Promise as destined to automatic fulfillment" (p. 20). 20 Thomas Beer, *The Mauve Decade: American Life at the End of the Nineteenth Century* (New York, 1926), p. 106. 21 *Contemporaries* (Boston and New York, 1899), p. 276. 22 William Dean Howells remarks bitterly in *Literary Friends and Acquaintance: A Personal Retrospect of American Authorship* (London and New York, 1900) that Whittier had not "appreciated the importance of the social movement" (p. 135). 23 Quoted in Langford, p. 11.

education was necessary for intelligent participation in political democracy. Congress created the first Department of Education in 1867 to disseminate the gospel of the free-school. In 1872, when the Supreme Court sustained Kalamazoo's right to establish a free high school, Charles Francis Adams, Jr. wrote in *The North American Review*: "The state, therefore, says to the rich: You shall contribute of your abundance for the education of your poor neighbors' children."[24] Nineteen states had adopted compulsory education laws by 1881, and by the time of the First World War, nearly 90 per cent of American children between seven and thirteen were attending school.

Adult education was booming as well. Andrew Carnegie alone gave over $31 million in support of public libraries; and by 1900 the Commissioner of Education reported over 9000 free circulating libraries in the country. Similarly, the Chautauqua movement evoked an astounding response from the adult population. Founded in 1874 by a Methodist minister, John H. Vincent, it spread rapidly until seventy such assemblies were operating at the century's end. Courses in science, literature, music, religion, and government were given. Six presidents of the United States lectured by the shores of Chautauqua Lake. Vincent claimed in 1886 that there were more than "one hundred thousand readers, who for fifty-two weeks in the year turn the pages of useful books, sing songs of college fellowship, [and] think in a larger world."[25] If the Chautauquan might attend swiftly successive Round Tables on Milton, Temperance, and Geology, the thousands who subscribed to winter "star courses" or lecture series were exposed to an even greater variety of entertainment and experience. John L. Stoddard's "travel talks" (illustrated with his double stereopticon), Russell H. Conwell's inspirational "Acres of Diamonds" speech (delivered 5000 times), Will Carleton's recitation of his ballads, Mark Twain, Bill Nye, the Norwegian violinist Ole Bull, George W. Cable (interspersing his tales with Creole melodies), Henry Ward Beecher, the reformed drunkard John B. Gough, Thomas Nast, Henry M. Stanley—these weekly opened up new ranges of experience for an audience whose craving for knowledge seemed hardly satiable. For the first time, a large part of the mass of people was entering, however tentatively, upon the life of the mind.

THE GROWTH OF SCIENCE AND A NATURALISTIC TEST OF TRUTH. While the public school, the Chautauqua movement, free libraries, and lecture series spread knowledge widely, but often thinly, universities were deepening knowledge, particularly along scientific lines. Whereas before the War the president of every important American college had been a clergyman, now scientists, with John W. Draper's *The Conflict Between Religion and Science* (1874) as their guide, declared war upon religion. In the '60s alone twenty-five scientific schools were founded in a movement which culminated, in 1876, with the establishment of the Johns Hopkins University, which was free from religions obligations.[26] Religion, of course, was not without its cham-

---

[24] Quoted in Don M. Wolfe, *The Image of Man in America* (Dallas, 1957), pp. 130–31. [25] *The Chautauqua Movement* (Boston, 1886), p. 35. [26] See Stow Persons, *American Minds: A History of Ideas* (New York, 1958), p. 241.

pions. One joined in the battle by remarking of Thomas Henry Huxley's address at the opening ceremonies of Johns Hopkins: "It was bad enough to invite Huxley. It were better to have asked God to be present. It would have been absurd to ask them both."[27]

The conspicuous instance of conflict came, of course, in the issue over Darwinism. Between the wars, men were converted—with religious fervor—to the gospel of Darwin. The acceptance of his theory of evolution was part of the general revolt against Calvinism. It assured Americans that Eden was yet to be achieved and that the history of the race was a history of progress. Americans demanded a philosopher of the superman—a Spencer, a Fiske, and later a Nietzsche—to give them a dazzling future, and rejected the philosopher of tragedy like Jonathan Edwards, who offered a glorious, but lost, past. Spencerians, Hegelians, Darwinians, Lamarckians, and catastrophists all spread the excitement, but confused the idea, of evolution. They taught an excited nation how to be modern. In Springfield, Illinois, Lincoln read Darwin and Spencer and "soon grew into the belief in a universal law, evolution." He became, Herndon says, "a warm advocate of the new doctrine."[28] At Yale, President Noah Porter took a volunteer class through Herbert Spencer's *First Principles* with a view toward refuting them; and every member of the class departed a convinced evolutionist.[29] So compellingly did evolution strike the American imagination that, as the Cambridge philosopher Chauncey Wright pointed out, the '70s witnessed the "all but universal" acceptance of a revolutionary doctrine as yet, by rigorous tests of verification, entitled only to be considered a probable hypothesis.[30] No doubt most of the earliest adherents of Darwinism were in the same position as Lady Constance in Benjamin Disraeli's novel *Tancred:*

> "You know, all is development. The principle is perpetually going on. First there was nothing; then there was something; then, I forget the next, I think there were shells, then fishes; then we came, let me see, did we come next? Never mind that; we came, at last. And the next change will be something very superior to us, something with wings."[31]

Nevertheless, Americans had committed themselves to science and were ready to follow where it led. Scientific inquiry had not yet outrun common apprehension; and a young diplomat like Henry Adams could make himself an American disciple of Darwinism by his review of Lyell's *Principles* in *The North American Review* for 1868. Adams could feel at home equally with Whitelaw Reid, editor of the *Tribune,* or Clarence King, director of the United States Geological Survey; with political reformers, or with his

27 Quoted in Richard Hofstadter, *Social Darwinism in American Thought* (New York, 1959: Rev. Ed.), p. 21.   28 William H. Herndon and Jesse W. Weik, *Abraham Lincoln: The True Story of a Great Life* (New York, 1893), Vol. II, p. 148.   29 This is the remembrance of Henry Holt in *Garrulities of an Octogenarian Editor...*(Boston and New York, 1923), pp. 49–50. Herbert Spencer was, without question, the philosopher of Americans between the wars, when his books sold with a rapidity unparalleled in philosophic writing—over 370,000 copies in authorized editions between 1860 and 1903. 30 *Philosophical Discussions*, ed. Charles Eliot Norton (New York, 1876), p. 97. 31 *Tancred, Or the New Crusade* (London, 1847), in *The Works of Benjamin Disraeli* (London, 1927), Vol. X, p. 113.

friends at the Cosmos Club. At the other end of the scale from Adams, John Fiske was defining Darwinism for the masses. His thirty-five Harvard lectures outlining an evolutionary cosmic philosophy were reported verbatim in 1869 to the readers of the New York *World*.[32] In years to come, Fiske's lectures, delivered as far west as Denver, created as much excitement as the arrival of Barnum's circus.

There was, of course, opposition early and late to Darwinism. The theistic objection was propounded most forcefully by the old-school theologian and editor of the *Princeton Review*, Charles Hodge. In *What Is Darwinism?* (1874) he defended the biblical account of creation and pronounced evolutionists "either derationalized or demoralized, or both."[33] The humanist Richard Grant White likewise scorned Darwinism in a satire titled *The Fall of Man: Or, The Loves of the Gorillas: A Popular Scientific Lecture Upon the Darwinian Theory of Development by Sexual Selection. By a Learned Gorilla* (1871). The book is dedicated to Charles Darwin, who convinced the world "that a Shakespeare may be but an oyster raised to the one-thousandth power, or even, a Darwin the cube-root of a ring-tailed monkey."[34] Among scientists, the immensely influential Agassiz argued in the Lowell lectures for a dyamic force of development, an "invisible thread," which was yet not evolutionary.[35]

As Henry Holt reminisced, in those days "people preferred to regard themselves as degenerate rather than as at the highest point in an advance."[36] But scores of theologians and philosophers were very soon actively engaged in the effort to reconcile theism and human distinctiveness with evolution. The argument for compromise between religion and science revolved around the question of whether Adam had fallen conclusively in an unredeemable past or whether man might be evolving toward an ideal which, in the Bible, Adam symbolized. Most Americans, believing above all in progress, tended to choose Adam as their future glory, and lower forms merely as the past from which they had risen. The peppery Lyman Abbott declared, "I would as soon have a monkey as a mud man for an ancestor."[37] John Fiske, Edward Livingston Youmans, John Wesley Powell, Henry Ward Beecher, Joseph LeConte, Minot Savage, and O. B. Frothingham, seeing modern man as "the goal toward which Nature's work has been tending from the first," were all equally as scornful of the good old Adam.[38] Against their arguments and optimistic assumptions, orthodoxy could not prevail. As early as 1871 the Scottish philosopher James McCosh, president of Princeton and leader of American Presbyterians, conceded in *Christianity and Positivism* that God worked though Natural Selection.

[32] In another striking instance of the news value of science, the New York *Tribune* for September 22, 1876 printed in one extra number all of Huxley's addresses in America. [33] (New York, 1874), p. 7. [34] (New York, 1871), p. 3. [35] See Louis Agassiz, *Methods of Study in Natural History* (Boston, 1864), *passim*. [36] Holt, p. 48. [37] *Reminiscences* (Boston and New York, 1915), p. 459. [38] John Fiske, *The Destiny of Man, Viewed in the Light of His Origin* (Boston and New York, 1884), p. 107. Minot J. Savage wrote: "If you accept [evolution], you will have to surrender your belief in 'the fall of man.' Evolution teaches *the ascent of man:* that the perfect Adam is ahead of us, not behind." (*Evolution and Religion: From the Standpoint of One Who Believes in Both: A Lecture* [Philadelphia, 1886], p. 43.)

Following in the wake of Herbert Spencer, John Fiske—particularly in his *Cosmic Philosophy* (1874)—provided the reconciling link between religion and science. On the publication of Fiske's major work Darwin wrote to him: "I never in my life read so lucid an expositor (and therefore thinker) as you are,"[39] and declared that he had not been able before to understand the doctrines of Herbert Spencer. Spencer himself said that he had never heard such "glorious" lectures as when Fiske spoke under Huxley's auspices in London.[40] Like his audience Fiske was interested in history rather than metaphysics. And when Chauncey Wright, C. S. Peirce, and William James discussed *Cosmic Philosophy* with him at a meeting of the Metaphysical Club, he "fell asleep," James says, "under our noses."[41] Discerning a "deep moral purpose" in the universe, Fiske endowed (and thus transfigured) Spencer's "unknowable" final cause with the spirit of New England transcendentalism.[42] (He claimed to have actually seen a horned, hoofed, fiery-eyed devil sitting in his study.) In his hands Natural Selection soon came to exhibit purposes suspiciously similar to Providence. Unlike the rigorously pluralistic Chauncey Wright,[43] he was unwilling to face the uncertainties and vicissitudes of "cosmic weather." But whatever Fiske's fault as a philosopher, he was unequalled as a popularizer of an evolutionary faith that silently dropped the Bible and focused attention upon this world and what Beecher called "the revelation of the rocks."[44] The modern man searching for a cosmic faith found it outlined in Fiske's romance of science.

TECHNOLOGY. In 1874, Mark Twain self-consciously composed a letter on his new $125 typewriter. "I believe it will print faster than I can write," he said proudly. "One may lean back in his chair and work it. It piles an awful stack of words on one page."[45] Inventions were the toys of the age, inventors and industrial promoters its heroes: they seemed to be science incarnate. Technology captured the imagination. Elbert Hubbard's declaration that "a well-appointed factory is a joy" was reechoed in Henry Van Brunt's plea for an architecture of "strict mechanical obedience"; in Washington Gladden's discovery of the "thoughts of God" in "the machine-room of the American Institute " in 1876; in Montgomery Schuyler's analysis of the aesthetics of Brooklyn Bridge; and even in L. H. Morgan's *Ancient Society*, wherein man's progress was measured by invention and discovery, and the railway train thus discovered to be "the triumph of civilization."[46]

39 Quoted in Van Wyck Brooks, *New England: Indian Summer, 1865–1915* (New York, 1940), p. 109. 40 *Ibid.*, p. 263. 41 See Philip P. Wiener, *Evolution and the Founders of Pragmatism* (Cambridge, 1949), p. 130. 42 See Fiske, *Outlines of Cosmic Philosophy* (Boston and New York, 1874). 43 Wright criticized Spencer's and Fiske's "divine agency in creation," and called the Hegelian version of evolution "that fine composition of poetry under the forms of science." In his day Wright alone could see that facts "fall into a dramatic procession in our imaginations. The mythic instinct slips into place of the chronicles at every opportunity.... All cosmological speculations are strictly teleological." (*Philosophical Discussions*, pp. 70–71.) 44 *Evolution and Religion* (New York, 1885), p. 27. 45 Quoted in Albert Bigelow Paine, *Mark Twain: A Biography* (New York, 1912), Vol. I, p. 537. 46Elbert Hubbard, *The Romance of Business* (Aurora, New York, 1917), p. 12; Van Brunt quoted in Wayne Andrews, *Architecture, Ambition and Americans...* (New York, 1955), p. 150; Washington Gladden, *Working People and their Employers* (New York, 1876), p. 15; and Lewis Henry Morgan, *Ancient Society: Or, Research in the Lines of Human Progress from Savagery Through Barbarism to Civilization* (New York, 1877), p. 553.

Earlier, in *Walden,* Thoreau had questioned the value of the telegraph; but now technological innovation became an end in itself and compelled, rather than fulfilled, needs.

In a country ostensibly committed to agrarian visions, technology was bound to generate feelings of anxiety.[47] Most of the fears of technology, however, were allayed by the abundance and luxury which seemed to result from it: the Pullman car, with "sofas and arm-chairs, bulging with soft and velvet-bound cushions,"[48] subdued and tranquilized any thought of menace. With the juncture of the Union Pacific and the Central Pacific in 1869, railroads crossed and crisscrossed the West: the Northern Pacific, the Santa Fe, the Rock Island—all were household words. Before and beyond the natural frontier an industrial frontier was arising that would soon replace it.

THE SAGES OF SOCIETY

Rapidly increasing wealth, the rise of the city, expanding immigration, a widened spirit of reform, mass education, a new scientific point of view, and the acceptance of technology as the American way of life—these were the interests that modified, contradicted, or merged with each other in American culture during the period between the wars. So rapid and wholesale were the changes that these made in American culture that the mind found it difficult to accommodate them. As Henry Adams puts this in his *Education* (1918)—one of the books best depicting the impact of change upon a nine-teenth-century man—in 1865 he was living in a twentieth-century world with eighteenth-century assumptions about order and purpose in change. What principles of stability he and his peers possessed, he hinted in *Mont-Saint-Michel and Chartres* (1904), were inherited from the Middle Ages. Man had to make his beliefs about his world anew, to accommodate his new cir-cumstances. Certainly the old orders of American culture were dissolving. Although the Civil War did not bring about these changes—they had already begun—it did help to accelerate them, and thus for many stood as a symbol of the division between the New and the Old. In a lecture Emerson gave during the early stages of the War, he noted how consciousness tends to break down at critical moments:

> All arts disappear in the one art of war. All which makes the social tone of Europe milder and sweeter than the miner's hut, and the lumberer's camp in America; the ages of culture behind; traditional skills; the slow secular adjust-ment of talent and position; the cumulative outward movement; the potency of experience, is destroyed; and the uncouth, forked nasty savage stands on the charred desert to begin his first fight with wolf and snake, and build his dismal shanty on the sand.

So, similarly, Freud would later say, in times of crisis in a culture—not only of war, but of any variety of critical change—men tend to seek refuge in the past, in various forms of utopianism, or in psychic withdrawal. In short, there is a wholesale collective retreat from the systematization of conscious-ness.

American writers, as men needing to deal with an ordered mind, were

---

[47] These issued into popular myths, such as those of Casey Jones or John Henry, where the individual was destroyed by the machine which he had pitted himself against.   [48] Towle, *American Society,* Vol. II, p. 180.

thus committed during this period to the absorption of the new conditions of
culture into a systematized consciousness. They were obliged not to experiment for the sake merely of a delight in aesthetic advance, but in order to
make a literature that could truly reflect the actualities by which they and
their fellows lived. Emily Dickinson, Howells, James, Twain, Dreiser—all
were, we can now see, deeply experimental writers, endeavoring to give shape,
through imagination, to their chaotic new America. They were the servant-
examples for their race. During this period, then, it was through American
writers that the American consciousness was preserved and slowly began
to evolve.

If we understand the needs that men of letters were obliged to satisfy in a
country otherwise violently separated from stable traditions and possessing
no natural leaders by and through whom security might be guaranteed, we
can begin to account for the extraordinary, popular devotion to the group
of New England writers who, by their very existence, seemed to provide a
beneficent and stable tradition, and thus to compensate for the institutions
of church, aristocracy, and ritual that Americans lacked. In the postwar
devotion to a serious and useful—above all, an ordered—art, Longfellow,
Emerson, Holmes, Whittier, Lowell, and Charles Eliot Norton were both
priests and deities. These men satisfied (and modified) the American need
for objects of secular devotion.

The New England Sages understood and lived up to their obligations to
their fellows. Immediately after the War, in a direct counteractant to the
breakdown of consciousness and the loss of tradition that war always brings,
these writers turned almost as a group to the preservation of the landmarks of
civilization, now in danger of being forgotten or ignored. They insisted upon
the past and tradition by translating its classics. They preserved the past
by putting it in postwar language. Individually they set their work against
particular deficiencies in the society and mind engendered by the War.
Longfellow's and Norton's translations of Dante implied hopeful conclusions
to the inferno through which the United States had recently passed. Bryant's
Iliad put war in a heroic perspective and thus attempted to conciliate both
North and South, as Greeks and Trojans. Against the lack of noble ideals in
the gilded age, C. P. Cranch's Virgil preached the heroic aspiration and the
founding of a great new imperial America. Against the despair and low tone
of the period was Emerson and Channing's *Vita Nuova* or Howells's lectures
on Dante. Finally, counterpoised to the riot of shoddy materialism, the
disintegration of ideals, and the lack of the religious spirit that marked the
postwar period were Higginson's Epictetus, Bayard Taylor's *Faust,* and
Bryant's versions of the Spanish mystical, meditative poets. Homer, Virgil,
Dante, and the others—and such accomplishments of civilization as they
represented—these were preserved and transmitted freshly by the American
pantheon.[49]

[49] We can see in the abundance of translation immediately after the First World War
a parallel to and confirmation of the claim that in the breakdown of consciousness these
sages turned naturally to the inculcation of the past by translation. Moreover these
psychic conditions help to explain why Eliot and Pound would make the characteristic
poetry of the age out of translation, and why such a book about the war mind as
The Enormous Room is bilingual. Again, after the Second World War, and continuing
through the cold war, Americans showed their need for a past by delighting, as never
before, in new translations of the whole past, as if in this way they could possess it.

In their translations as well as in the kind of wisely imitative poetry that they wrote, these men of letters helped to continue the past they could still remember into a future which, to most Americans, was as yet dim. They refused to threaten their culture with the new in literature, since Americans were, as they believed, too distracted by the new in life. Their values and aspirations, in a middle-class American tradition, were consciously conserving, though not necessarily conservative. They were radical enough to be traditional in an age that had spattered tradition with the thin paints of wealth, technology, and science. They were conservators of culture. As André Gide wisely remarked:

> If there were no names in the history of art except those belonging to the creators of new forms there would be no culture. The very word implies a continuity, and therefore it calls for disciples, imitators and followers to make a living chain; in other words, a tradition.[50]

The New England Sages worked self-consciously for a nation that sought to follow in their wise steps. They inspired extraordinary devotion on all levels. Howells has recorded that when he was returning to Ohio from a pilgrimage to Cambridge in the late '60s, he stopped overnight at Hiram with the then Congressman James A. Garfield. Howells began talking about the Cambridge deities, when Garfield excitedly interrupted him:

> He ran down into the grassy space, first to one fence, and then to the other at the sides, and waved a wild arm of invitation to the neighbors who were also sitting on their back porches. "Come over here!" he shouted. "He's telling about Holmes and Longfellow and Lowell and Whittier!" and at his bidding dim forms began to mount the fences and follow him up to his veranda.[51]

Edward Bok tells the story that when somewhat later he visited Cambridge, Oliver Wendell Holmes put him on a bus: "And when the boy had ridden a mile or so with his fare in his hand he held it out to the conductor, who grinned and said: 'That's all right. Doctor Holmes paid me your fare, and I'm going to keep that nickel if I lose my job for it.' "[52] Such testimonies to the awe and affection they inspired suggest their importance as symbols.

To an age committed to new conditions of life—but unable to find objects of devotion or emulation in those who represented the unmitigated New: Jim Fisk, Vanderbilt, Jay Gould—the Sages symbolized the American dream of success and virtue mingled.[53] Emerson and Longfellow lived until 1882,

---

[50] Quoted in Van Wyck Brooks, *The Writer in America* (New York, 1953), p. 51.
[51] *Years of My Youth* (New York, 1916), pp. 204–205. [52] *The Americanization of Edward Bok: The Autobiography of a Dutch Boy Fifty Years After* (New York, 1920), p. 40. [53] Americans liked also to be reminded of the popularity of these poets in England and Europe. E. L. Godkin, the Anglo-Irish founder of the *Nation*, told his readers in 1867 that Longfellow had more readers than any living English poet. Longfellow, R. H. Stoddard claimed, was the one man known all over the world. When Longfellow visited Rome, Franz Liszt set a part of *The Golden Legend* to music. Baudelaire acknowledged that in two passages of *Les Fleurs du Mal* he followed Longfellow, and that in "Calumet de Paix" he paraphrased *Hiawatha*. Longfellow was one of the four American writers whom, Howells said in *Italian Journeys* (1867), all cultivated Italians knew. Emerson was held in nearly as high esteem by foreigners. In 1874, for instance, the students at the University of Glasgow nominated him for lord-rector, an office held earlier by Edmund Burke, Adam Smith, and Macaulay. Shortly thereafter a London publisher asked him to write the Introduction for a book on the Hundred Greatest

Alcott to 1888, Lowell to 1891, and Whittier to the following year; Whittier's final verses were, appropriately, addressed to the last of the group, Oliver Wendell Holmes, who died in 1894. In contrast to an America whose operations seemed entirely new, these grey champions lived on from the past and incarnated traditional values and aspirations.

The change in Walt Whitman is perhaps the best illustration of the role that the man of letters was being forced to assume. In the first edition of *Leaves of Grass* (1855) is a portrait of the hero, bearded, with cocked hat, hand on hip, and shirt unbuttoned at the collar: he is the "rough" whom Walt Whitman proclaims himself and his hero to be. But by the late '80s Whitman had outlived his early persona and had become a good grey poet like his New England contemporaries. In 1889, with his flowing silver hair and beard, his loosely fitting grey suit, with white cuffs turned back over his coat-sleeves, he appeared at the Madison Square Theatre to read a lecture on Lincoln's death. One observer thought that he looked like "an Old Testament prophet."[54] Now he had become one of the group, and Lowell, Stedman, Gilder, and others attended the reading. Andrew Carnegie sent a check for $350 to pay for his box. Appropriately, then, it was Whitman who saw more clearly than anyone else how he and his fellow Sages served their culture. In an essay following the death of Longfellow he wrote:

> [Longfellow] is certainly the sort of bard and counteractant most needed for our materialistic, self-assertive, money-worshipping, Anglo-Saxon races, and especially for the present age in America,—an age tyrannically regulated with reference to the manufacturer, the merchant, the financier, the politician, and the day workman; for whom and among whom he comes as the poet of melody, courtesy, deference,—poet of the mellow twilight of the past in Italy, Germany, Spain, and in Northern Europe, poet of all sympathetic gentleness, and universal poet of women and young people. I should have to think long if I were asked to name the man who had done more, and in more valuable directions, for America.[55]

Through his Fellowship, Whitman had been schoolmaster not of the way

---

Men, saying that only two persons were able to do so—"the two Fathers of the Century, Mr. Emerson and Mr. Carlyle"; he preferred Emerson for his catholicity. In 1882, Herbert Spencer made a pilgrimage to Emerson at Concord—the only time in his life he paid tribute to another thinker. Intellectuals like those in Turgenev's *Fathers and Sons* discussed his work, while at the same time he was, W. T. Stead reported in 1901, the most popular essayist in England. Undoubtedly J. G. Holland was right in saying that "Emerson has a world of honor from men who do not pretend to understand him," for his value was chiefly symbolic: not what he wrote, but what he was, gave him value for a people who needed to have its sense of awe and mystery touched. Quoted and referred to above are the following: Van Wyck Brooks, *New England: Indian Summer*, p. 13; R. H. Stoddard, *Poets' Homes: Pen and Pencil Sketches of American Poets and their Homes* (Boston, 1877), p. 1; Margaret Denny and William H. Gilman, eds., *The American Writer and the European Tradition* (Minneapolis, 1950), pp. 117–18; W. T. Stead, *The Americanization of the World, Or, The Trend of the Twentieth Century* (New York and London, 1901), p. 279; J. G. Holland, *Every-Day Topics: A Book of Briefs* (New York, 1876), p. 32; James Bryce, *The American Commonwealth* (London and New York, 1888), Vol. I, p. 581. [54] W. W. Ellsworth, *A Golden Age of Authors: A Publisher's Recollection* (Boston and New York, 1919), p. 64. [55] *Essays from "The Critic"* (Boston, 1882), pp. 42–3.

of translation, but of Bohemianism—a gentle encouragement of self that contrasted, as strikingly as did the poetry of the New England writers, with the official material ideals of his age. If they taught Americans the past, he had taught them the open road of the future. "The reader of my speculations will miss their principal stress," he wrote in *Democratic Vistas* (1871), "unless he allows well for the point that a new Literature, perhaps a new Metaphysics, certainly a new Poetry, are to be, in my opinion, the only sure and worthy supports and expressions of the American Democracy."[56] The New Englanders conserved the old; Whitman made the values of the past transcend the present and shape the future. Both ways with poetry—in a later context, the ways of Eliot and Pound or of William Carlos Williams and Hart Crane —helped to remake the orders lost in the chaos of the new forces that were entering the life of the nation.

Both groups preserved a vital image of the fine usefulness of mind, sensitivity, and imagination. These they defended against the anticultural values of the period: the emphasis on action over meditation, on material success over personal achievement, specialized over general knowledge, on narrow standards of taste, on forms rather than the spirit of behavior. The importance of that role is suggested by the virtual loss of a lively image of the relevance of the man of letters at the century's end. With Whitman and the New England poets dead, no new "standard" poets were adopted by the nation among such of their followers as Stedman and Stoddard, although Stedman, particularly in his lectures on *The Nature and Elements of Poetry* and in his anthologies, consciously worked for such a position. Poets at the end of the century had difficulty justifying their commitments to mind and art, not only to their audiences, but sometimes even to themselves. Louise Imogen Guiney, Richard Hovey, Bliss Carman, Josephine Preston Peabody —all could take only their jingling technical experiments seriously. George Cabot Lodge, for another, anxious to write poetry, and with obvious gifts, yet compelled to feel guilty over his impulses, wrote his father: "I don't do anything here, nothing tangible. I work five hours a day or six, and what on—a miserable little poetaster. I want to get home and get some place on a newspaper or anything of that kind, and really do something."[57] For Lodge, as for others, the forces—the new themes entering the cultural fugue— seriously threatened the continuance of literary and cultural values, even while they were, at the same time, shaping a new and wider world that would desperately need such values as guides to thought and action.

Gertrude Stein explained in 1918 to the French that America was the oldest country in the world because it entered the twentieth century in the 1880s, ahead of all the other nations.[58] Even earlier, beginning after the Civil War, the new circumstances that would make twentieth-century America were entering the life of the nation, even while men were still acting on their simplistic eighteenth-century educations. The human environment was alter-

---

[56] *Prose Works 1892*, Vol. II: *Collect and Other Prose*, ed. Floyd Stovall (New York, 1964), p. 416. [57] Quoted in Henry Adams, *The Life of George Cabot Lodge* (Boston and New York, 1911), p. 32. [58] *Wars I Have Seen* (New York, 1945), pp. 257–58.

ing drastically: its earlier unity shattered, it was providing the materials for Adams's study of twentieth-century multiplicity. Perhaps the confusingly encyclopedic case of Benjamin R. J. Tucker was the archetypal experience of the age. By the age of eighteen, he says, having read Darwin, Spencer, Mill, Buckle, and Tyndall, he had been successively "an atheist, a materialist, an evolutionist, a prohibitionist, a free trader, a champion of the legal eight-hour day, a woman suffragist, an enemy of marriage, and a believer in sexual freedom."[59] Such was the multiplicity of the period. But the age was marked, as well, by the appearance of a remarkable group of writers who sifted and sorted its disparate elements. Accepting the conditions of the incredibly diverse circumstances of their culture, they sought to give it depth as well. Attempting to write a National Novel or to define the particularities of a region, projecting utopian visions, scrutinizing the permutations and variability of the self as well as the democratic "en-masse," sending their heroes on pilgrimages to new Meccas—to European or American cities—these writers made the themes of their culture part of the music of their poetry and fiction. "How," they asked, as Nietzsche did in *Ecce Homo*, "with such vistas before us and with our conscience and consciousness full of such burning desire, can we still be content with the *man of the present day?"* Argonauts of the ideal, they set sail for the land, and the man, of the future.

THE RISE AND RELEVANCE OF MASS LITERATURE

In this section, we shall examine some of the cultural forces that were directly affecting the distribution and economics of literature itself during this time. The circumstances that influenced literary production between the wars were: (1) the way in which the continuity of literary taste and sales was shattered by the Civil War, (2) the very important development of various kinds of popular media and of new means of distribution on a massive scale, (3) the lack of an international copyright law until 1891, (4) the widespread influence of foreign authors on Americans. These, as shall be shown, altered the context of literary production for the authors of this period.

The influence of the War is obvious. In the South, Merle Curti writes, "almost all the agencies of intellectual life had either suffered materially or broken down completely."[60] Few books were imported through the blockade. Scarcities of paper, ink, and type and the obvious difficulties of distribution, especially the high cost of postage, made a Southern literature virtually impossible. George Cary Eggleston remembered that people were "wholly without" literature in the South; he himself was willing to pay seven dollars for a pamphlet edition of Owen Meredith's *Tannhäuser* bound in coarse wallpaper.[61] Newspapers either failed or were printed on wallpaper and other scraps. The two most famous Southern magazines, *DeBow's Review* and the *Southern Literary Messenger* (once edited by Poe), closed their offices in

[59] Quoted in Arthur Mann, *Yankee Reformers in the Urban Age* (Cambridge, 1954), p. 150. [60] *The Growth of American Thought* (New York, 1943), p. 459. [61] *A Rebel's Recollections* (New York, 1878: 2nd ed.), p. 103.

eliminate the agent's importance,[64] he remained, until the twentieth century, a significant cultural force in many towns where his yearly visits signalized the revival of culture. Even as late as 1905 Charles Scribner persuaded Thomas Nelson Page to allow distribution by canvassers of a collected edition of his work by pointing to the $20,000 received by Richard Harding Davis for the sale of 50,000 sets of volumes whose book store distribution had all but ceased.[65]

As Bryant's case suggests, distribution of books through stores was often haphazard and faulty, for there was no reliable method of merchandising new volumes to retailers. This was done largely through the publishers' auctions in New York. Here, retail buyers crowded into the auction rooms on lower Broadway and bought books on consignment, not at a fixed trade discount. In 1867, for instance, "with good attendance and spirited bidding" only three hundred copies of Whittier's *Snowbound* were purchased for eighty cents a copy, to be sold at one dollar and twenty-five cents.[66] Large retailers, however, were able to buy for extremely low figures and subsequently to sell the books at substantial discounts. This system of "book butchering" caused widespread discontent. Particularly in department stores, books were frequently offered as premiums or used as loss-leaders to attract customers for other articles. A dry-goods store in Los Angeles, for instance, advertised in 1885: "By purchasing 6 pairs lisle thread hose at 49 cents per pair, you may, by paying 10 cents extra, have the choice of our entire stock of novels, or by paying 25 cents, the choice out of the poetical works."[67] Early in 1889, whole sets of books were offered free with the purchase of a fifty-cent bottle of patent medicine.[68] The following year a product appeared called "Book Soap": its manufacturer announced that he had cornered two million novels—among their authors, Dickens, Stevenson, and Scott—for his product and promised "the great unwashed" a different book with each purchase.[69] Despite continued complaints by *Publishers' Weekly* that "this 'bazaar-spirit'. . .has placed an undeserved indignity upon literature,"[70] such salesmanship encouraged a generation to think of literature as ordinary merchandise, and thus stimulated book buying.

Indeed it was an age of books, of print, of oratory, an age of words—"the public mind was," as Constance Rourke observed, "intoxicated by words."[71] From 1875 until 1891, when the International Copyright Law was passed, paperback books were manufactured and distributed at extremely low prices. Literature was meant for the masses. In a centennial oration in 1876, Henry Ward Beecher spoke severely to the laboring man. He "ought to be ashamed of himself," Beecher said, "who has not some books nestling on the shelf."[72]

[64] *American Gazette and Publishers' Circular*, XIII (1869), 249. [65] Donald Sheehan, *This Was Publishing: A Chronicle of the Book Trade in the Golden Age* (Bloomington, Ind., 1952), pp. 191–92. [66] Allan Nevins, *The Emergence of Modern America, 1865–1878* (New York, 1927), p. 237. [67] *Publishers' Weekly*, XXVII (1885), 732. [68] Advertisement for patent medicine in *The American Bookseller*, XXV (1889), 128. [69] Advertisements in *The American Bookseller*, XXVII (1890), 82, and *The Critic*, XVI (1890), 54. [70] *Publishers' Weekly*, XXXVIII (1890), 823. [71] Constance Mayfield Rourke, *Trumpets of Jubilee...*(New York, 1927), p. vii. [72] *Our National Centennial Jubilee: Orations, Addresses and Poems...*(New York, 1876), p. 362. Beecher's oration, delivered at Peekskill, New York, on July 4, 1876, was titled "The Advance of a Century."

1862 and 1864, respectively. Moreover, many of the fine plantatic
and the collections in college buildings—often put to military
destroyed. In the North, of course, the effects of the War were quit
While some publications—*Harper's* and *The Princeton Review*, fc
—suffered by losing their Southern audiences, the enormous deman
of the War brought many new journalistic publications into being a
to alter the character of Northern reading.

Furthermore, those men who for the next fifty years would make
literature came to adulthood sickened and impoverished by the Wa
Lanier, eventually to die from the consumption he contracted in
prison camp; Paul Hamilton Hayne and William Gilmore Simms,
the finanical accumulations of years dissolve; Henry Timrod, st
death after writing some of the best poems of the War—these wer
physically and mentally. Among Northerners, John DeForest,
Bierce, and Walt Whitman, all agonizing over the blind destruction
Adams experiencing pangs of guilt in England; Howells following
anxiously from Venice, doubting the morality of his position there
James nursing the "obscure wound" that prevented him from fight
would haunt him for years—these too were scarred.

Following the War, mass literature entered a period of astonishing
The number of magazines published mounted from 200 in 1860 to
the end of the century.[62] More widely distributed than ever bef
devoted to spreading good taste among the masses, the miscellane
mercurial American popular magazines constituted a significant force
life of the nation. Books, too, were everywhere. New methods of sa
distribution were developed. At the close of the War, books were sold t
the mail, by subscription agents, and in book stores or department
Anticipating the modern book club, Funk and Wagnalls sent a book
other week, for four dollars a year, to 16,000 buyers; Sears, Roebuc
through catalogues.[63] But the subscription plan was the most sens
of postwar sales methods. Publishers found it easy to recruit an ar
traveling book agents from demobilized soldiers. For thousands of
munities, particularly in the South and West, the canvasser was the
link to the increasing allurement of "culture." The agent found the f
in the fields, cornered the men in the barber shop or hotel parlor, and c
and intrigued the housewife in her kitchen, and sold them millions of vo
—Bibles, Encyclopedias, Collected Works, or Memoirs of Presidents
Generals. Appleton had Bryant edit an elaborate two-volume subscriptic
of steel engravings, lovingly entitled *Picturesque America*, which sold n
a million sets, while Bryant's own *Poems* languishingly sold less than
copies in the book stores. All of Mark Twain's work was sold by agents
worked up a ready audience of at least 40,000 for any book he off
Though one periodical claimed in 1869 that the growth of cities w

[62] Robert Spiller *et al.*, *The Literary History of the United States* (New York, 1
Vol. II, p. 805. [63] Frank Luther Mott, *Golden Multitudes: The Story of Best S
in the United States* (New York, 1947), p. 153.

By 1891 books crowded household and library shelves throughout the nation. Perhaps they were ragged, for they were often poorly made—paper, printing, and binding all necessarily became less expensive—but they were read, not merely displayed. Such cheap books were ordinarily produced in series such as the *Lakeside Library* of Chicago or the *Seaside Library* of New York, which included on their lists every popular book not protected by American copyright. As early as the end of 1877, there were fourteen such libraries, often listing over a hundred numbers each and with editions running from 5000 to 60,000, each volume selling for as low as ten cents. Despite fierce competition, these libraries were enormously successful. Technological improvements in bookmaking, the diffusion of education, innovations in merchandising, and the rising standard of living as well as the rising aspirations for culture—these all spilled over into the conditions of literary production.

The staple of the libraries was, of course, the foreign author, who received little or no pay for the sale of his books. An American consul in England was convinced that "the great English writers are quite as familiar in America as in their own country,"[73] while an English traveler found reprints of English authors "in every hotel. . . , in every railroad car, at every book station," from New York to Butte, Cheyenne, and Salt Lake.[74] Fortunately, the age of the pirated book in America coincided with a great period in English and continental fiction, so that, as the *Chicago Inter Ocean* editorialized in 1890, "the trashy novels and machine poetry [of Americans] . . . are largely crowded out by the very cheapness of really classic [European] literature."[75] Following the decline of instruction in Latin and Greek, Dickens, Cooper, Scott and their peers came to be known as "classics." These formed the staple of the popular series. *Lovell's Popular Library* was offering in the '80s, at prices ranging from ten to thirty cents, thirty-three volumes by Carlyle, thirty-two each by Dickens and Cooper, thirteen by George Eliot, twenty by Washington Irving, thirty-five by Ruskin, thirty-one each by Scott and Thackeray, and seventeen by William Gilmore Simms. In short, one could buy, often on a newsstand, the complete works of any standard author for six dollars or less.

The variety of American interest in foreign authors is suggested by the literary essays, frequently in popular magazines, of James, Howells, and Lafcadio Hearn—on George Eliot, Thomas Hardy, Turgenev, Tolstoy, Dostoyevsky, Flaubert, Huysmans, Maupassant, Daudet, Zola. and Anatole France. Far from being known only to an elite, these authors were widely pirated and reprinted in the popular series. Both *Madam Bovary* and *Nana,* published here in the '80s, sold nearly a million copies in cheap editions.[76] Americans, offering prayers for the dying Tennyson and founding endless Browning Societies (one of which was led by Mark Twain), showed astonishing devotion to foreign authors. In the '90s an American could, as Stuart Merrill did, become a French symbolist poet, praised by Mallarmé himself.

[73] Towle, *American Society*, Vol. II, p. 230. [74] Quoted in Raymond Howard Shove, *Cheap Book Production in the United States, 1870 to 1891* (Urbana, Ill., 1937), p. 28. [75] Quoted in *ibid.*, p. 46. [76] Mott, *Golden Multitudes*, p. 248.

Richard Hovey was translating Verlaine and Mallarmé, and articles on the symbolists were appearing in such popular journals as the *Cosmopolitan,* the *Nation, Living Age,* and *Scribner's.* The book by Arthur Symons which fired T. S. Eliot's imagination when he discovered it in 1908 in the library of the Harvard Union, *The Symbolist Movement in Literature,*[77] had been originally published in *Harper's* for 1893.

This kind of lively popular association with foreign literature was largely terminated by the International Copyright Law of 1891. To be sure, there had been considerable opposition to the law—from the pirates, the Harpers and Henry Carey Baird, and from paper makers and businessmen concerned with book manufacture, who feared that a law protecting foreign authors would multiply the number of imported books. Even Mark Twain, though suffering financially through lack of copyright, felt that

> I can buy a lot of the great copyright classics, in paper, at from three cents to thirty cents apiece. These things must find their way into the very kitchens and hovels of the country. A generation of this sort of thing ought to make this the most intelligent and the best-read nation in the world. International copyright must becloud this sun and bring on the former darkness and dime-novel reading.[78]

But strongly emotional currents of literary nationalism won the day. The *Boston Globe* reported that "the extent to which... popular series are steeping our people in English thoughts... is considered with apprehension in many quarters."[79] Edward Eggleston, one of the strongest advocates of copyright, wrote of the "barbaric state" of the law: "The whole American people are inestimably losers because of this thing. They are deprived of all chance of a national literature, reflecting the life of our country, its ideas, its inspirations, and its aspirations."[80] Eggleston's *The Faith Doctor* was the first book published under copyright. By 1894, for the first time, more American than foreign novels were published in the United States.

The years between 1875 and 1891 had been the age of cosmopolitan publishing in America, and the cheap reprinters had been the vehicles for widening the American's contact with world literature. Before the age of pirating, the most popular books in America had been those written by natives and appealing, as Lizette Reese said, "to that type of romantic, poorly educated

[77] In *The Criterion* for 1930, Eliot wrote: "I myself owe Mr. Symons a great debt: but for having read his book, I should not, in the year 1908, have heard of Laforgue or Rimbaud; I should probably not have begun to read Verlaine; and but for reading Verlaine, I should not have heard of Corbiere. So the Symons book is one of those which have affected the course of my life." The study was originally titled "The Decadent Movement in Literature." The other poet who had a considerable influence upon Eliot and his contemporaries, John Donne, had long been popular in New England; Emily Dickinson knew his work. The first modern edition of Donne anywhere was edited by James Russell Lowell and published by the Grolier Club.   [78] Quoted in Paine, *Mark Twain,* Vol. II, p. 687.   [79] Reprinted in *Publishers' Weekly,* XXIII (1883), 522.   [80] Quoted in George Cary Eggleston, *Recollections of a Varied Life* (New York, 1910), pp. 233–34. This somewhat misrepresents even the obvious situation of American authorship. Paperback series of American authors, by Houghton, Mifflin and others, sold widely. In May of 1887, for instance, Ticknor and Company began issuing weekly the *Ticknor Paper Series* of American novels for fifty cents each. Both new books and those successful in higher-priced editions were included. This series, containing titles by Howells, E. W. Howe, Edward Bellamy, Henry James and Joel Chandler Harris, became very popular, and many titles went into editions of eight or nine thousand copies in a few months.

woman...who at that time filled the position now held by the average female frequenter of the movies."[81] In 1872, a report by the managers of the Boston Public Library listed Mrs. E. D. E. N. Southworth, Caroline Lee Hentz, and Mary J. Holmes as the most popular authors.[82] But in 1893, after twenty years of pirating, a canvass of leading libraries showed that Dickens was the most widely read novelist, with Scott, Cooper, Eliot, Alcott, Hawthorne, O. W. Holmes, Bulwer-Lytton, and Thackeray as his rivals. Twain held thirteenth and Howells twenty-sixth place.[83] Even then, however, the effects of copyright were already being felt; for the public had not kept pace with emerging currents of foreign literature, and Hardy, Meredith, and Stevenson failed to appear on the lists. By 1900 the literary situation had changed drastically. Charles Scribner, requested by the Department of Commerce and Labor to answer a series of questions about the effects of the copyright law, replied:

> The American author has been benefited...in that there is more encouragement for the publisher to pay the American author when he cannot take for nothing the works of English authors. It is an interesting fact that since the law was passed, books which have the greatest sale in America are by native authors, such as Churchill's "Richard Carvel," Westcott's "David Harum," Major's "When Knighthood was in Flower," Ford's "Janice Meredith," Page's "Red Rock," etc., whereas a few years ago such a list would be made up almost entirely of books of foreign authorship.[84]

The kinds of books which achieved popularity in 1872 and those listed by Scribner in 1900 are strikingly similar in their appeal to the romantic and nostalgic. Between these two dates lay buried a remarkable thirty-year renaissance during which the American popular imagination was briefly touched—and thus shaped and guided—by the enduring and permanent in the composite imagination of the Western world.

THE TRANSFORMATION OF NINETEENTH-CENTURY MAN

Opened to new varieties of experience; undergoing enormous changes in population and social patterns; perplexed and dazzled by increased wealth; delighted by science, the American mind wavered and, unable to control the rush of experience, lost a firm hold on tradition. The nineteenth-century mind was fragmented by the knowledge violently thrust upon it.

Erich Kahler has spoken of the unique character of the modern world as

> a crowding of events in the domain of our vision and consciousness, an oppressive closeness and overwhelming shiftiness of events, an excess of details and complexities in every single event—in short, what I would call an *overpopulation of the surfaces*.[85]

Out of contrast and contradiction our daily lives are shaped. This overpopulation of surface experience first began seriously to transform America

---

[81] Lizette Woodworth Reese, *A Victorian Village: Reminiscences of Other Days* (New York, 1929), p. 206. [82] Nevins, *The Emergence of Modern America*, p. 234. [83] Schlesinger, *The Rise of the City*, p. 251. [84] Sheehan, *This Was Publishing*, p. 99. [85] *The Tower and the Abyss* (New York, 1957), pp. 95–6.

after the Civil War. The new demands of the machine, the city, and widened knowledge resulted, on the one hand, in an insensitivity to conflicting values; and, on the other, in a new sensibility consisting of a receptivity to fact and detail. The decline of the traditional value-governed mind, that is, was accompanied by the corresponding growth of a peripheral mind open to a torrential rush of experiences precisely because it no longer discriminates among them.

The loss of a sense of contrast between values was everywhere apparent in American life after the War. Indeed, such a consciousness is, as the German philosopher Ernst Jünger has written, a necessary condition for modern war. First introduced in the Civil War, it remained an aspect of the mind that could not quite face the confusions of the peace which followed. Grant wrote in his *Memoirs* that "while a battle is raging one can see his enemy mowed down by the thousand, or the ten thousand with great composure." Grant's aide, Adam Badeau, remarked that even "after the fiercest fighting and the most awful destruction, [Grant] still...gave orders grimly."[86] Yet, in civilian life he had not been able to stay through a hurdle race because he could not bear "to see men risk their necks needlessly." In one of the bloodiest battles of the war, it is reported, while he generously poured troops into their graves, Grant became incensed at the sight of a man beating a horse, had him severely punished, and muttered about it for the remainder of the day.[87]

Such confusion of values was not confined to wartime. The dulling of values and the absence of discrimination that characterizes the wartime consciousness anticipated the mind to come in peace. In every area of American life postwar critics began to comment upon the alteration in the American consciousness. All the while Henry Ward Beecher was on trial for his alleged intimacy with Mrs. Tilton in 1876, his congregation was listening to his sermons with rapt attention, and even sent flowers to decorate the courtroom—"like placing wreaths," Godkin said, "about the open manhole of a sewer."[88] Most of the participants in the Crédit Mobilier scandal could not be convinced that they had done anything wrong; and in 1876, a large number of Americans, supporting Blaine for President, could not see that his railway transactions, even if admitted, discredited him: he was, they insisted, "just the smart man we want."[89] In the 1872 election Thomas Nast caricatured Greeley, Schurz, and Sumner with the same virulence he had devoted to Tweed and Tammany Hall, which clearly, as the editor of *Harper's* said, showed "a lack of moral perception."[90] Brooks Adams commented on the fact that people "are no longer even conscious of shame at profaning the most sacred of ideals" in decorating

[86] Quoted in Edmund Wilson, *Patriotic Gore: Studies in the Literature of the American Civil War* (New York, 1962), p. 150; see also Ulysses Simpson Grant, *Personal Memoirs* (New York, 1885), Vol. I, p. 521.   [87] General Horace Porter, *Campaigning With Grant* (New York, 1897), pp. 164–65.   [88] E. L. Godkin, "This Week," *The Nation*, XX (1875), 71.   [89] See the letter to the editor, "Blaine's Popularity in the West," deploring the low standards of the West and citing this as evidence, in *The Nation*, XXII (1876), 413.   [90] J. Henry Harper, *The House of Harper. A Century of Publishing in Franklin Square* (New York and London, 1912), p. 303. Harper is quoting a letter from George William Curtis to Thomas Nast concerning his satirical cartoons.

warehouses and railway stations with designs copied from abbeys and altars.[91] A traveler who heard a "good-natured series of songs" delivered in a Western hotel parlor commented:

> no one in the room except myself seemed to find it in the least incongruous or funny that he sandwiched "Nearer, my God, to thee" between "The man who broke the bank at Monte Carlo" and "Her golden hair was hanging down her back," or that he jumped at once from the pathetic solemnity of "I know that my Redeemer liveth" to the jingle of "Little Annie Rooney."[92]

The chief prophet, promotor, and publicizer of this sensibility dulled to contrast, but receptive to details, was P. T. Barnum. Popular both before and after the War, Barnum (1810–1891) stands as a symbol of the character and diversities of his age. In his Museum, as well as in his later circuses, he combined a succession of art, freaks, oddities, and morality with pure illusion, sensation, and proclaimed fake. The changing charlatanry of the exhibits reduced the public to a neutral receptivity. Successively amused, annoyed, puzzled, terrified, astonished, and inspired, the beholder ceased to distinguish between the real and illusive and merely wandered among the explosions of his sensations. The gaudy exterior of Barnum's Museum—which contrasted strikingly to the gloom within—cajoled the public to come and see "the great picture of Christ Healing the Sick in the Temple, by Benjamin West, Esq., The Albino Lady, and 500,000 curiosities." A brilliant transparency of a mermaid turned out to be a withered joining of a monkey's head with a fish's tail. Barnum made Tom Thumb a sensation and offered Brigham Young $200,000 a year to exhibit him as a curiosity in the East. He reveled in being denounced as a humbug, for this "brought grist to his mill" by keeping his name before the public; and he rejoiced to learn that visitors would give more to see the proprietor of the Museum than its curiosities. Sheer size and number had captured the American mind. Barnum's tent contained four rings in which three full circus companies gave different performances simultaneously; in the ring running around these he exhibited the Roman Hippodrome. He had two white whales captured for exhibition that, he thought upon inspection, looked like porpoises. It was necessary for Agassiz of Harvard to inspect and endorse them as genuine. When they were killed in a fire, they appeared to him among the ruins only to be "the worst specimens of baked and boiled fish." One has only to contrast this kind of qualitative sensibility to the imaginative vitality of an earlier age in which a *Moby Dick* could be written to realize the dramatic shift in sensibilities that had occurred.[93]

Yet at the same time, Barnum was a shrewd critic of the illusions that beset his (and even our) time. His *Humbugs of the World* (1865) exposed adulterations of food and drugs, medical fraud, stock swindles, and even scientific and literary humbug. Much of his life combined charlatanry

[91] *The Law of Civilization and Decay: An Essay on History*, "Introduction" by Charles A. Beard (New York, 1943 [1895]), p. 349.   [92] James Fullarton Muirhead, *America, the Land of Contrasts: A Briton's View of His American Kin* (London and New York, 1898), p. 22.   [93] This discussion of Barnum is drawn from P. T. Barnum, *Struggles and Triumphs: Or, The Life of P. T. Barnum, Written by Himself*, ed. George S. Bryan (New York and London, 1927), 2 vols.

with a strong moral strain. He became a Bible salesman at the Vauxhall Saloon; he organized the city of East Bridgeport, where he sold model houses to people who would forswear drinking and smoking;[94] he lectured widely on temperance and during the War spoke for the preservation of the Union and against slavery. After the war he spent a session in the Connecticut legislature as a critic of railroad monopoly and political corruption. His circus was always advertised as "Barnum's Great Moral Show"; clergymen received free passes. Then too, in the Lecture Room he presented moral and romantic dramas—viewed by little Henry and William James who were permitted to spend their Saturday afternoons at the Museum. Fifty years later Henry would pronounce these afternoons "flushed with the very complexion of romance" and declare that they embodied "the very flower of the ideal."[95]

The moral structurelessness that Barnum's career exemplifies paralleled less imaginative qualities in the vast audience he attracted. The American mind had been violated and transformed by knowledge—not of good and evil, but of a world that was for the first time photographed, measured, explored, described, analyzed, and counted. "We mostly put faith in our statisticians," Lowell wrote in 1886, while the older "celestial computations are gone somewhat out of fashion."[96] Like Melville in *Battle Pieces,* the writers of the age responded or reacted to the increased rush of objective experience rather than to "celestial computations." In understanding the opportunities that the fragmentation of the modern mind offered them to reshape it, give it a new and more fruitful order, American writers of the later nineteenth century began to create the twentieth-century mind. Beginning with a consciousness opened by knowledge and incredibly widened, they deepened and justified man's new view of the world. In the evolution of the consciousness of modern man as American, they were the finders and makers.

94 John Fiske's first book was a rebuke to Barnum's plan. 95 *A Small Boy and Others,* pp. 155, 165. 96 James Russell Lowell, "The Progress of the World" in *Latest Literary Essays and Addresses, Prose Works* (Boston and New York, 1900), Vol. VII, p. 160.

TWO

The Great American Novel

He declared that he was above all an advocate for American art. He didn't see why we shouldn't produce the greatest works in the world. We were the biggest people, and we ought to have the biggest conceptions. The biggest conceptions, of course, would bring forth in time the biggest performances. We had only to be true to ourselves, to pitch in and not be afraid, to fling imitation overboard and to fix our eyes upon our National Individuality. "I declare," he cried, "there's a career for a man, and I have twenty minds to embrace it on the spot— to be the typical, original, aboriginal, American artist! It's inspiring!"
—Henry James, *Roderick Hudson* (1875)

THE IDEA OF NATIONAL IDENTITY

Between showcases, often in strikingly incongruous places, sat the living monstrosities and curiosities of Barnum's Museum—giants, fat men, midgets, albinos. To these Barnum added a bizarre set of living representatives of various races—there were Indians, Chinese, Gypsies, and even, as his advertisement declared, a "live Yankee."[1]

From the conclusion of the War until the rise of regional literature in the '80s, the local identities and allegiances of Americans—as Yankee, Rebel, or Westerner—were looked upon as antique remnants, perhaps fit for exhibition to the curious, but inadequate to sustain the new national unity and purposes which Americans were claiming as their destiny. Reacting against the sectional impulses which, resulting in war, had caused astonishing suffering, and responding as well to other causes, Americans minimized their basic differences and spoke of their national identity as consisting of a harmony of regions.

The notion of a uniform American identity resulted in part from a realistic recognition of the multitude of circumstances which were actually drawing the country more closely together. But it reflected as well the hopes which men had for a peaceful future free from sectional contests. Americans were demanding, and out of their needs making a myth of, unity. Whitman's war poems envisioned not merely Union victory—and the name whereby the North defined itself is revelatory—but a victory

[1] Quoted in Rourke, *Trumpets of Jubilee*, p. 395.

25

of unity. Samuel Bowles, traveling west only six weeks after Appomattox, mistook his wishes for facts and found a "mysterious but unmistakable homogeneity of [American] people."[2] The vision of unity tantalized even men like Grant, who in concluding his *Personal Memoirs* felt that "we are on the eve of a new era, when there is to be great harmony between the Federal and Confederate."[3] As early as 1878 George Cary Eggleston could ask a Northern reader to "put himself in the place of the Southerners and look at some things through their eyes."[4] Charles Dudley Warner too recorded his amusement in his novel *Their Pilgrimage* (1887) at a rich woman's cry: "I'm provincial. It's the most difficult thing to be in these levelling days."[5] Except during the mid-'80s, when a regional again temporarily replaced a national point of view, Americans made such anti-sectional leveling their ideal. Popular novels like Winston Churchill's *Richard Carvel* (which sold more than a million copies) and plays like David Belasco's *The Heart of Maryland* (1895) and Bronson Howard's *Shenandoah* (1888) showed love triumphant over sectional barriers. Eminent historians like Frederick Jackson Turner suggested that "the thing to be avoided...is the insistence upon the particular interests and ideals of the section in which we live."[6] Even in the twentieth century Theodore Roosevelt could use the long outworn phrase, "New Nationalism"—which he said, "puts the national creed before sectional or personal advantage"[7]—as a slogan to attract and entrance voters.

The need would help to make the actuality. In fact, despite the eventual resurgence of sectional points of view, the most striking difference between the America of 1865 and 1914 was its increased unity. Technological, economic, and social, as well as strongly emotional factors helped to make this true. The discussion of these factors will be divided into two groups.

(1) Of the technological innovations, those improving communication were most important. Earlier, the steamboat and the telegraph had loosely allied the West with the North and South. The new transcontinental railroad with its multitude of trunk lines, the organization of Western Union, the consolidation of news services into the Associated Press, and the appearance of the telephone—all in the late '70s, bound the sections together. Northern machinery not only supplied the West and South with manufactured necessities, but its machine-made products imposed similar tastes everywhere. The flow of Northern industrial capitalism into the South drew these sections together by similar ties of economic interest. Atlanta, Chattanooga, and Durham were Northern ideological outposts. The New Industrialism they preached was a subtle form of the New Nationalism. The vast productivity of McCormick's reaper made both East and South

2 *Across the Continent: A Summer's Journey to the Rocky Mountains, The Mormons, and the Pacific States* (New York, 1865), p. 159. 3 Vol. II, p. 553. 4 *A Rebel's Recollections* (New York, 1878), p. 2. 5 New York, p. 216. 6 *Frontier and Section: Selected Essays of Frederick Jackson Turner*, ed. Ray Allen Billington (Englewood Cliffs, N.J., 1961), p. 135. 7 In an address titled "The New Nationalism" delivered at Osawatomie on August 31, 1910; printed in *The New Nationalism* (New York, 1910), p. 28.

dependent upon the West for food. Then too, the increased mobility afforded by railroads made for accelerated emigration. In the ten years following 1873 more than two million Americans, from North and South, migrated beyond the Mississippi. Northerners like Albion W. Tourgée settled in the South for health or business reasons; Southerners entrained for the North. Those who did not actually migrate were sufficiently curious about other regions to take such a tour as the one Kipling met at Yellowstone Park. A clergyman informed him there that "the tourists included representatives of seven of the New England States." They believed, Kipling says, that "this running to and fro upon the earth, under the auspices of the excellent Rayment, would draw America more closely together."[8] Such mobility, for whatever of these reasons, meant not merely the interchange of men, but the migration of their ideas and institutions as well.

In response to this mobility, federal agencies—the Departments of Agriculture, Commerce, and the Interior—expanded and multiplied; national laws like the Interstate Commerce Act (1887) were passed. National authority was so markedly asserted against the notion of regional autonomy that when President Cleveland ignored the traditional reading of the Constitution by sending troops into Chicago during the Pullman strike of 1894, Governor Altgeld needed to remind him that "the principle of local self-government is just as fundamental in our institutions as is that of Federal supremacy."[9] The Pullman walkout itself, like the widespread and bloody railroad strikes of 1877, was a sign that labor was recognizing its growing national interdependence.

(2) As important as technological, social, and economic conditions were, emotional factors were no less relevant in promoting unity. Following the War all sections of the country were sympathetically united in grief and, to some extent, self-accusation. Novels with a consolingly religious tone (like Elizabeth Stuart Phelps's *Gates Ajar* [1869]) were best sellers in all sections. This spirit of tolerance grew as Northerners became convinced that Reconstruction had worked badly. Even James Russell Lowell would declare: "The whole condition of things in the South is shameful, and I am ready now for a movement to emancipate the whites."[10] When he and such a formerly radical abolitionist as Higginson began praising the South for its education of Negroes, the North showed itself ready to let the South manage its own race relations. A friend of Henry Adams, Senator Don Cameron of Pennsylvania, spoke for many Republicans when he rejected the proposed Force Bill of 1890 as disturbing the community of interests between North and South. Henry's brother, Charles Francis Adams, Jr., brigadier-general for the North, became "a very popular character"[11] in Virginia for his laudatory addresses on Lee. Revived in the '80s, the songs of Stephen Foster, with their romantic pictures of happy plantation

---

[8] *American Notes* (New York, 1889), p. 133. [9] Quoted in Schlesinger, *The Rise of the City*, p. 415. [10] Quoted in Wilson, *Patriotic Gore*, p. 477. [11] Charles Francis Adams, Jr., *1835–1915: An Autobiography* (Boston and New York, 1916), p. 45.

life, and Harris's tales of Uncle Remus—rather than the suffering figure of Stowe's Uncle Tom—gave Americans their sense of the lost South. Publishers of history textbooks who sought national adoptions were wise, in the light of this spirit of tolerance, to present the war as "a careful balance of right on both sides."[12]

George Washington Cable would explain the basis of reconciliation in *The Negro Question* (1890), by contending that while the North ostensibly fought for slavery, it was really union which it sought; the South took up arms for the slavery which appeared vital to it, but legitimized its contentions under the banner of state sovereignty. Victory for the Union, combined with the end of Reconstruction (which allowed slavery to slip back under new forms) in his sense, then, removed all barriers to reconciliation.

But several other factors were also in operation. A common language united Americans. Where else, as Montgomery Schuyler asked, could one travel for three thousand miles "and find everybody, not merely intelligible, but in no sense strange, in his speech?" Humorists like Artemus Ward, Orpheus C. Kerr, and Josh Billings sported with a speech funny precisely in proportion to its deviation from an assumed national norm.[13] Not until the '80s would regionalists take dialect seriously.

Furthermore, all sections were united by a common historical heritage and similar dreams of the future. The Centennial Exposition of 1876, coinciding with the end of Reconstruction, was a national reminder of a glorious Revolutionary heritage shared by all Americans. It was also magnificently prophetic of the national future. The seven main buildings and the scores of annexes erected by the States of the Union and foreign exhibitors had cost nearly $10 million to construct. The biggest exposition ever held up to that time, it was, according to its organizers, America's tribute to "the unparalleled advancement in science and art, and all the various appliances of human ingenuity for the refinement and comfort of man."[14] In Machinery Hall stood the Corliss engine. Nearby, visitors could see tacks, carpets, clothing, and bricks manufactured, or watch the mysterious operations of the new typewriter and pneumatic tube and see the New York *Herald*'s plant turn out its newspapers.

But it was the fine-arts exhibit—the largest ever assembled in America—that attracted the greatest crowds. The establishment of national patterns of taste was extremely important, for Americans of all sections were busy

---

12 Henry F. May, *The End of American Innocence: A Study of the First Years of Our Own Time* (New York, 1959), p. 44. 13 Schuyler, *Westward the Course of Empire: "Out West" and "Back East" on the First Trip of the "Los Angeles Limited"* (New York and London, 1905), p. 164. The national magazines were extremely influential in establishing a standard of language. "It is well known," Ezra Pound wrote in 1913, "that in the year of grace 1870, Jehovah appeared to Messrs. Harper and Co. and to the editors of 'The Century,' 'The Atlantic,' and certain others, and spake thus: 'The style of 1870 is the final and divine revelation. Keep things always just as they are now" (*Patria Mia* [Chicago, 1950 (written 1913)], p. 42). 14 Quoted in Russell Lynes, *The Tastemakers* (New York, 1955), p. 112. See also Louis Hartz's argument that the South, which had originated the notion—basically a romantic one—of American nationalism, was now free, with the end of slavery, to assert this theory strongly once more. (*The Liberal Tradition in America: An Interpretation of American Political Thought Since the Revolution* [New York, 1955], p. 165).

restoring or establishing "culture." The three million visitors to the Exposition took back to their various sections similar guides for a national taste. Perhaps the best symbol of the national and cosmopolitan character of the Exposition was its music: the "Grand March" was written by Richard Wagner "especially for the occasion"; the hymn was composed by the abolitionist Whittier, and the cantata written by a former Confederate soldier, Sidney Lanier.

American magazines were the literary equivalents of the impulses of nationalism implicit in the Centennial Exposition. Edited by Josiah Gilbert Holland, *Scribner's* was, in fact, established on the principles, and for the purpose, of reconciliation between sections. The articles which Holland commissioned Edward King to write in 1873 on *The Great South* ingratiated Southerners, enlightened Northerners, and helped to increase good feeling between the sections. Even after the Century Company purchased *Scribner's* and changed its name in 1881, its editors continued to work for reconciliation: Holland's successor, Richard Watson Gilder, invented the series which symbolized for many the very essence of mutual tolerance: the "War Series." Issues of *The Century* paired accounts of the same event or battle of the war as seen by a Northerner and Southerner: a Virginian's view of John Brown's raid, for instance, was accompanied by Frank Sanborn's "Comment by a Radical Abolitionist"; General Beauregard's analysis of Bull Run stood beside a Union private's account of the same battle. For the series Mark Twain wrote "The Private History of a Campaign that Failed." In time, every living general contributed to this series which, one observer said, "did more to bring together North and South than anything that had happened since they were torn apart in 1861."[15]

To Be *an American: John DeForest*

Out of their sense of a national identity Americans had long demanded a national literature. The Hartford Wits, and especially the poets and critics who followed in the aftermath of the War of 1812, had felt the influence of these demands. As early as 1847, Duyckinck's *Literary World* commented that if all the documents relating to "this prolific text...of a native authorship" were collected, they would make "a very respectable library."[16] In the '70s and '80s Americans again demanded that their literature make an image of the national felicity for which they yearned. To satisfy the new needs of the postwar period, this demand was put into new terms. Critics ceased to seek the American Epic, and began to demand the Great American Novel. Americans asked, how represent *the* American? or, Where locate the typical America? What is this American

[15] Ellsworth, *A Golden Age of Authors*, p. 233. The popular response to the War Series is suggested by *The Century's* almost immediate increase in circulation from 137,000 to 225,000 copies monthly; after two years when the series was issued in four volumes, 75,000 sets were subscribed at $20 and $30 each. [16] On the background to the search for a national literature see Ben T. Spencer, *The Quest for Nationality: An American Literary Campaign* (Syracuse, 1957).

like? What does it mean, as James put it, to *be* an American? And where does he live? What *is* his America? In asking and seeking to answer such questions, writers went far toward creating in the popular mind the assumption and image of a national identity that would steadily make Americans more resemble each other.

Early in 1868 a writer in the *Nation* confessed that although a "literature truly American" had been frequently called for, the phrase had been used in several different senses—to mean: the depiction of the physical character of the land; the effects of democracy; the delineation of a particular area, especially New England; the superiority of America to Europe; the substitution of Tecumseh for Lancelot as an appropriate hero in a work that merely carried over the old epic or romantic forms and conventions; or the celebration of the national heritage. Rejecting these, he approved as the basis for a distinctively American literature the aspirations expressed in the preface to Whitman's *Leaves of Grass* and concluded that "a literature that should reflect Mr. Whitman's hope" could be called American, and would presently appear. Such difficult questions as what that literature would be like—how, and in what forms it would "express America"—the writer was content to leave to the happy inspiration of the individual poet.[17]

In the next number of the *Nation*, however, John DeForest took up these problems in an article estimating the presence and possibility of the "Great American Novel."[18] "The task of painting the American soul within the framework of a novel," he argues, "has seldom been attempted and has never been accomplished farther than very partially." Irving and Cooper, he says, cautiously avoided the attempt; Paulding, Brown, Kennedy, and Simms "are ghosts, and they wrote about ghosts, and the ghosts have vanished utterly." Great as Hawthorne undoubtedly was, DeForest insists, his characters are shadowy and fail even to represent New England; Holmes, according to DeForest's account, was hampered by his theories and lack of sympathy; Henry Ward Beecher, C. Weir Mitchell, and Bayard Taylor he rejects conclusively. This article, quite clearly, is the voice of a kind of critical busk that burns away the refuse of the past in preparation for the birth of the New. Wanting to write a National Novel himself, DeForest was here preparing his audience for a literature that would reflect the new conditions of fact and desire that were shaping a national identity. He would teach his fellows how to make and read the Great American Novel. Only *Uncle Tom's Cabin*, he argues at last, approaches successfully the broad, true, and sympathetic representation of American life—with a "national breadth to the picture, truthful outlining of character, natural speaking, and plenty of strong feeling"—necessary to make the Great American Novel. How, DeForest asks in conclusion, can the novelist represent American multiplicity without sundering the unity of his work?

DeForest himself had already begun to set forth his answer to this

17 "Literature Truly American" (an anonymous letter), *The Nation*, VI (1868), 7–8.
18 The following remarks are from John DeForest, "The Great American Novel," *The Nation*, VI (1868), 27–9.

question in his version of the National Novel. *Miss Ravenel's Conversion from Secession to Loyalty* (1867) established the pattern for his books: they abound with conflict and contrast; their drama and satisfactions arise from the ways strife is resolved into harmony. North, South, and West—Americans, Mexicans, Europeans, and Orientals; Negroes, immigrants, Indians, Whites; Democrats and Republicans, both honest and corrupt; Puritans, Catholics, rationalists, and debauchees; millennialists and free lovers; the innocent and the experienced; heroes and desperados, saints and sinners, scientists and sensualists, prophets and clowns, lovers and fierce antagonists—all these and more mingle together in DeForest's novels to be mixed and, by being mixed, to be transformed and reconciled. By bringing such characters, representing conflicting persuasions, together, DeForest shows how contact, understanding, and, perhaps, love could unite a nation. The America he portrays is defined by diversity driving towards harmony. By making a National Novel, DeForest helped to make a Nation.

Ironically, the growing unity of the nation would eventually efface the personal and social contrasts that make the National Novel dramatic. Writing of "The Great American Novel" in the *Yale Review* for 1927, Edith Wharton suggested that the new novel would have to abandon the old formulas. "It is because we have chosen to be what Emerson called 'mixed of middle clay' that we offer, in spite of all that patriotism may protest to the contrary, so meagre a material to the imagination," she remarked. "It is not because we are middle-class but because we are middling that our story is so soon told."[19] She herself modified the formula by making it picaresque and subjecting her characters to the varieties and multiplicities of international experience. DeForest, Howells, and their followers, by helping to make Americans "middling" destroyed the possibilities of their way with the novel, and made her way inevitable. Between DeForest's *Miss Ravenel's Conversion* and the rise of regional literature in the '80s (when Americans first reacted against a middling character), is the great age of the aspiration to write the chimerical National Novel.

Miss Ravenel's Conversion is DeForest's allegory of the tragedy and horror of conflict and, as well, his image for the happy synthesis and harmony of the dialectical contraries which make strife. The Civil War is itself virtually a character—the spirit of evil—stalking through the book. DeForest has been praised for the realism of his battle-scenes. For him, however, realism was a means of depicting vividly the horrors of war so as to inculcate in his audience a lively sense of the felicities of peace. He is not, in this sense, so much a realist as antiromantic. He wants to show how far from glorious war is:

> A dozen steps away, rapidly blackening in the scorching sun and sweltering air, were two more artillerists, stark dead, one with his brains bulging from a bullet hole in his forehead, while a dark claret-colored streak crossed his face, the other's light-blue trousers soaked with a dirty carnation stain of life-blood drawn from the femoral artery.

[19] *Yale Review*, New Series XVI (1927), 650–51.

This is his portrait of death. His depiction of suffering in the field hospital is even more grotesquely Goyaesque:

> It was simply an immense collection of wounded men in every imaginable condition of mutilation.... In the center of this mass of suffering stood several operating tables, each burdened by a grievously wounded man and surrounded by surgeons and their assistants. Underneath were great pools of clotted blood, amidst which lay amputated fingers, hands, arms, feet and legs, only a little more ghastly in color than the faces of those who waited their turn on the table. The surgeons, who never ceased their awful labor, were daubed with blood to their elbows....

Such nightmarish scenes lie at the heart of the book. Like Melville's *Battle Pieces*—the collection of poems that appeared the previous year—*Miss Ravenel's Conversion* primarily depicts not the antagonism of North against South, but of Union against Section, of harmony against conflict, love against fierce pride, society against willful selfhood. North and South stand as the book's chief historical symbols and represent all that these contraries imply, socially, politically, emotionally, and intellectually. DeForest's version of the Great American Novel thus accepts the diversity of American conditions, but shows difference made harmonious. The ways Dr. Ravenel summarizes the War's meaning suggests some of the varieties of meaning in the apocalyptic allegory of the novel: "In these days," he says, "—the days of Lincoln, Grant, Sherman, and Farragut—faith in the imagination—faith in the supernatural origin of humanity—becomes possible. We see men who are demoniacal and men who are divine....I have beheld heaven fighting with hell." He can see the conflict in economic and political terms as well: "The victory of the North," he adds,

> is at bottom the triumph of laboring men living by their own industry, over non-laboring men who wanted to live by the industry of others.... Slavery meant in reality to create an idle nobility. Liberty has established an industrious democracy.

In these and a variety of other ways the war and the individual responses of the characters to it symbolize a test of America itself. What, they ask, is the America that will prevail? The quality of the individual American is tested in Lillie Ravenel and John Colburne.

At the beginning of the book Lillie Ravenel and her father arrive in New Boston (i.e., New Haven), exiles from New Orleans, where Dr. Ravenel's political and religious convictions threatened his safety. Miss Ravenel, depicted as still childish and, of course, unconverted to the Union cause, remains, unlike her father, "strictly local, narrowly geographical in her feelings and opinions." Loved by two young men, a New Englander and a Virginian, Lillie symbolizes the American mind divided between all that each represents. Lillie, who will first incline toward and soon marry Colonel Carter, the Virginian and a West Point patrician, must learn, after Carter dies, how to love Colburne in order that the book can end, as its last word has it, in "victory." Thus the book proposes at first Lillie's choice between allegiance to North and South. As Carter puts it to Colburne, "you and I will go [to New Orleans] some day, and reconquer her patrimony, and put her in possession of it, and then ask her which she will have." Lillie, to be sure, is converted from secession to loyalty; but she also comes at last to possess—as both Carter and Colburne, in somewhat lesser ways do—the lessons of North and South. She saw herself, the narrator says, "in double: the one figure widowed and weeping, seated amid the tombs of perished hopes: the other also widowed in garb, but about to put on bridal garments." It is impossible, DeForest is suggesting, to have one properly, as an American, without having the other.

Colburne, similarly, changes. Unlike one of his New England contemporaries—a "pale bit of human celery"—Colburne retains in his character (and name) not only the heritage of Puritanism ("cold"), but also a natural exuberance of animal spirits ("burn"). While his moral training restrains his energy, his natural liveliness refreshes his morality and keeps it from becoming narrow and sour. Like the balanced New England house, Lillie tells him in the beginning, he is square. "But how," he asks, "shall we become triangular, or circular, or star-shaped, or cruciform?" He learns, in the course of the book, to reshape himself both through his contact with the "picturesque ins and outs of [Carter's] moral architecture" and in his association with the Southern devotee of the *divin sens* and the *sainte passion*, Mrs. Larue. From both he learns what it means to be triangular or cruciform.

The adopting of various parts is precisely Mrs. Larue's nature. She wears many masks: in politics she is "as double faced as Janus," a Federal at home and a secessionist abroad; she is "a most forgiving, cold-hearted, good-natured, selfish, well-bred little creature." Wearing her hair *à la Madone* she so impresses a minister with her sanctity that he dedicates a work on moral reform entitled *St. Mary Magdalen* to her; at the same time she recommends Don Juan as a model man to Colburne and succeeds in seducing Carter, to whom she writes a playful letter signed "Ste. Marie Madeleine." A chameleon, she plays the *femme raisonnable* for Dr. Ravenel and *femme savante* for Colburne. But beyond these surface contraries, beneath the mask, she has no self whatsoever; she is, as the imagery suggests, a reptile, a spider, a witch, a fiend, or a Circe. Under her spell, Colburne is metamorphosed not into a swine, but into a man. He too is converted by experience. He puts aside his Latin and Greek and takes up French; the "child of Puritanism" comes to take account of "Balzac's moral philosophy."

"Those days are gone by, and there will be no more like them forever, at least not in our forever," the narrator writes.

Not very long ago, not more than two hours before this ink dried on the paper, the author of the present history was sitting on the edge of a basaltic cliff which overlooked a wide expanse of fertile earth, flourishing villages, the spires of a city, and, beyond, a shining sea.... From the face of another basaltic cliff two miles distant, he saw a white globule of smoke dart a little way upward, and a minute afterwards heard a dull, deep pun! of exploding gunpowder.

Quarrymen there were blasting out rocks from which to build lives of industry and happy family homes. But the sound reminded him of the roar of artillery....

In the midst of peace and abundance, the narrator is led to think of war. Like his later descendants, the narrators of *The Remembrance of Things Past* and Allen Tate's *The Fathers*, DeForest's narrator is suddenly plunged, by imagination, into the past: through his characters, symbols for him of aspects of himself, he relives his own reactions. The book that results is thus essentially a meditation on history made concrete in character.

Neither Lillie nor Colburne, then, are free from the history which they symbolize. The kind of National Novel that DeForest envisioned refused to be Adamic, to project characters free from space and time, ever rejuvenating and celebrating themselves in moving from civilization to the Free Territories. Ironically, it was innocence—and its corollaries in narrowness, sectional or individual prejudice, and forgetfulness—DeForest knew, that had kept men apart and so led to war. DeForest rejoiced in experience and opened the lives and minds of his characters to it. He celebrates the self expanded by knowledge, and the nation whose sections are combined into "a grand, re-united, triumphant Republic."

The reconciliation of such personal, geographical, and political diversities in the novels following *Miss Ravenel's Conversion* obsessed DeForest's mind and ruined his art. More and more this basic pattern of his imagination stood out from the fiction, until at last it stood alone. The *structure* of his successive novels so overrides ordinary verisimilitude that his characters are reduced to mere positive and negative forces through which a play of attraction and repulsion works. His novels approach a mathematics of ideology, a school for the writers of the National Novel. The heroine of his second novel, *Overland* (1871), for example, Clara Muñoz Garcia Van Diemen, is forced to choose between her two lovers, Coronado and Ralph Thurstane, and thus between the two aspects of herself—Spanish and Nordic, Catholic and Protestant, Southwestern and Northeastern. Making a moral and symbolic pilgrimage across the Great American Desert, at the end of her journey she is regenerated, not by innocence, but in her experience of conflict. The narrator concludes:

> When she entered on this journey she resembled the girl faces of Greuze; now she is sometimes a *mater amabilis,* and sometimes a *mater dolorosa;* for her grief has been to her as a maternity.... Her countenance has had a new birth, and exhibits a more perfect soul.

Kate Beaumont (1872), which Howells considered a successful novel, shows no less the structure of conflict. Writing a modern parallel to *Romeo and Juliet*, DeForest allows Frank McAllister and Kate to attempt, in loving each other, to end the feud of their South Carolina families. Between the English Puritan and the French Chevalier, the Unionist McAllisters and the Calhounist Beaumonts, the Saxon and the Latin, their love effects reconciliation. Such patterns of conflict as make *Overland* and *Kate Beaumont*, DeForest translated into the moral struggle between good and evil in his fourth novel, *Honest John Vane* (1875). This novel, a lesser version of *The Gilded Age* or Henry Adams's *Democracy,* alludes to the Crédit Mobilier scandal in portraying a Congress more interested in special (and profitable) legislation than in the national well-being. The conflict of good against evil, dramatized as personal profit versus national interest, makes the book into a bloodless morality play in which evil triumphs.

In *Irene the Missionary* (1879) DeForest translated the National Novel into international terms, as Howells and James were doing, by sending his Americans to Syria. Here, the predictable characters—Irene Grant, the inexperienced daughter of a conservative minister, and Hubertson DeVries, a cosmopolitan archaeologist familiar with all kinds of experience—predictably, fall in love. The "Student of the Scriptures" and the "Student of Balzac" are married. So obvious is DeForest's concern with working out a complex structure of contraries and resolutions in *The Bloody Chasm* (1881), that his structure itself may be said to form the novel's subject. DeForest, who first announced the need for, and described the nature of, the Great American Novel, was its victim. After *Miss Ravenel's Conversion,* his novels became worse the more he needed to make them, in his sense, American. But with that first novel he was, in 1867, as Howells said, "really the only American novelist" working at the forefront of consciousness. Following after him, Howells and James would find that he had begun a tradition by making a form for the National Novel—one that they could invest with life as he, but once, could not.

Interoceanic Episodes : William Dean Howells

Quite in contrast to the way in which the First World War would touch the idealism of Americans and lead sensitive young men, craving for experience—Hemingway, Dos Passos, and Faulkner among them—to enlist even before America's entry into the war, no major novelist of the '70s and '80s except John DeForest served in the Civil War. James's obscure wound prevented him from enlisting; Twain's brief service in the Confederate cavalry convinced him that the Nevada territory would be both safer and more profitable: their versions of the National Novel could not involve the war. Between DeForest and Stephen Crane, whose *Red Badge of Courage* (1895) marks the culmination of the Great American Novel, we have no great dramatization of the war. Another author, William Dean Howells, destined to be the leading innovator in this way with fiction, wrote the campaign biography of Lincoln and took as his spoils the consulship of Venice. There, having already visited the sages of Boston and Cambridge and having seen Whitman in New York, he prepared himself, quite consciously and intently, to inherit their position in American Letters. He sought to combine in his own work the traditions of both New England and the Whitman fellowship. Before the War he had been publishing his poems alternately in the New Englander's *Atlantic* and the New York Bohemian paper, *The Saturday Press.* His pilgrimage in 1860 to the Cambridge and Concord sages was inevitably coupled with a stop in New

York at Pfaff's bar, where Walt Whitman daily presided. If this young man from Ohio had pleased and flattered the New Englanders by knowing their works intimately—and so reassured them that their message was being heard nationally—he had also been following the activities of the New York group. By the time he appeared in Pfaff's to meet Whitman, he had read the 460 pages of the third edition of *Leaves of Grass* (1860) and had reviewed it in "A Hoosier's Opinion of Walt Whitman." In this piece Howells announced his reaction against the genteel tradition by espousing Whitman and scorning "the Misses Nancy of criticism," who, at the name of Whitman, "hastened to scramble over the fence and on the other side stood shaking their fans and parasols...and shrieking, 'Beast! Beast!'"[20] Already Whitman had called loudly for a literature national in scope and sympathy. And while Howells never fully accepted *Leaves of Grass*—as he could never fully comprehend it—Whitman's lesson of nationality provided Howells with the basic premises that would shape his literary career. He could not have failed to add Whitman's insistence on nationality in literature to the ideals he was adopting from the New England writers, or to remember that Emerson had greeted Whitman as his heir. Howells made himself the heir of both.[21]

Venice was for Howells, as James Russell Lowell said, "the University in which he has fairly earned the degree of Master."[22] Through the essays which Howells wrote for the *North American Review* on Italian literature he began to make a name for himself in Cambridge, where Dante was held in particular esteem. His travel impressions, recorded in *Venetian Life* (1866), were serialized in the *Boston Advertiser*. Dealing thus with Italy, he was following in the tradition of Hawthorne, Longfellow, and Norton, as well as of Bayard Taylor, the New York author already well known as America's leading travel writer. When he returned from Venice at the close of the War it was in New York that his future seemed to be. In 1866 he commenced a journalistic career with the *Nation* and claimed, in a column for that journal, the literary supremacy of New York over Boston. "Don't despise Boston!" James T. Fields, publisher of the *Atlantic*, said to him at a gathering in Bayard Taylor's house. "Few are worthy to live in Boston,"[23] Howells suavely replied. Howells knew that he was worthy, and not long after accepted the assistant editorship of the *Atlantic*.

[20] Quoted in Edwin H. Cady, *William Dean Howells: The Road to Realism* (Syracuse, 1956), p. 86. This entire discussion of Howells owes much to Cady's two-volume study of Howells, *The Road to Realism* and *The Realist at War*. [21] Whitman everywhere proclaimed his intent to embody national experience. For instance, in a self-adulatory book which he himself wrote (but which John Burroughs obligingly signed) entitled *Notes on Walt Whitman* (1867) Whitman declared of *Leaves of Grass*: "The Nationality of the book seems to me perfect. Its treatment and consideration of the States of this Union as so many equal brothers, of exactly average right and position, each the peer of the other, is of the greatest value...but [includes] not the States alone; it expands from them, and includes the world. Out of it, in these poems, flow countless analogies, illustrations and noble lines connecting an American citizen with the citizens of all nations" ([New York, 1867], p. 337). [22] Lowell, reviewing *Venetian Life* in "Critical Notices," *The North American Review*, CIII (1866), 612. [23] Howells, *Literary Friends and Acquaintance*, p. 111.

In Cambridge Howells's fluency in Italian gained him entry into Longfellow's Dante nights, devoted to the perfection of his translation of *The Divine Comedy*. Oliver Wendell Holmes even presented himself at Howells's temporary apartment. And when he purchased a house on Sacramento Street—with money advanced by Charles Eliot Norton—Lowell and Longfellow duly called privately, and Lowell told President Andrew A. White of Cornell that Howells was "almost the only one of our younger authors in whom I have faith."[24] Publicly, Lowell called Howells "an artist worthy to be ranked with Hawthorne in sensitiveness of observation, with Longfellow in perfection of style."[25]

Very much like Henry James, Howells approached fiction tentatively, through criticism and travel writing. At the same time that he was lecturing at Harvard and the Lowell Institute on "The Italian Poets of Our Century," he was serializing the articles in the *Atlantic* that would make up *Italian Journeys* (1869) and *Suburban Sketches* (1871). Only after long preparation did the traveler write the novels that would thus be informed by the pleasures and conditions of merely circulating. "At last I am fairly launched upon the story of our last summer's travels," he wrote as he began *Their Wedding Journey,*

which I am giving the form of fiction so far as the characters are concerned. If I succeed in this—and I believe I shall—I see clearly before me a path in literature which no one else has tried, and which I believe I can make most distinctly my own.

This novel would be, as he described it, "a sort of narrative—half-story, half-travel sketch."[26]

T. W. Higginson was the earliest critic to understand what Howells's version of the National Novel would be. Lamenting in 1879 that Howells had as yet provoked no serious criticism, Higginson set about distinguishing him from James. Howells has been, he said:

far less anxious to compare Americans with Europeans than with one another. He is international only if we adopt Mr. Emerson's saying, that Europe stretches to the Alleghenies. As a native of Ohio, transplanted to Massachusetts, he never can forego the interest implied in this double point of view. The Europeanized American, and, if we may so say, the Americanized American, are the typical figures that re-appear in his books.... Mr. James writes "international episodes": Mr. Howells writes interoceanic episodes: his best scenes imply a dialogue between the Atlantic and Pacific slopes.[27]

It is important to remember that while Howells began with sketches of Boston and Europe, he concluded his career with stories recalling his youth in the West, with *A Boy's Town* (1901), *New Leaf Mills* (1913) and *Years*

24 *New Letters of Lowell*, ed. Mark A. DeWolfe Howe (New York, 1932), p. 153. 25 Lowell, reviewing *Suburban Sketches* in "Critical Notices," *The North American Review*, CXII (1871), 237. 26 Quoted in Cady, *The Road to Realism*, p. 158. 27 "Short Studies of American Authors: Howells," *The Literary World: Choice Readings from the Best New Books and Critical Reviews*, X (1879), 249.

of My Youth (1917). His last novel, *The Leatherwood God* (1920), is a
fable of frontier Ohio. Between Boston, Europe, and frontier Ohio; East
and West; culture and anarchy; society and self, the lines of force were
drawn. Upon them he played for fifty years the varied symphony of the
American experience, now slight and melodious, now harsh and abundant,
as it seemed to be to him and to the audience which followed him faithfully
through this devastatingly rapid period of change in American life and letters.

In his first attempt to mingle travel and fiction, "fiction got the best of
it."[28] For while *Their Wedding Journey* (1871) is based in fact, it rapidly
assumes a meaning and relevance that real life seems to embody only
upon reflection. Basil and Isabel March, who have met in Europe, marry
in America and decide to take the inevitable wedding journey to Niagara
Falls. As a realist, committed from the outset to the "foolish and insipid
face" of actual life, Howells attempts to treat their typically American
romantic, clichéd wedding journey seriously and thus use it as a symbol
of national life. In the open-minded innocence with which they embark upon
their journey, the two lovers gain a regenerated Adamic insight into
America, and become "the first man and the first woman in the garden of
the new-made Earth." Recognizing this—"they were both very conscious
people"—they set about to observe, and to sympathize with (and so to
renew in themselves), American life. The continent itself thus becomes,
through them, "a larger Arcady" in "a golden age," where they "want very
little of being a nation of shepherds and shepherdesses."

The scenes which Howells arranges on the string of his travel narrative
are contrived so as to present to the observation of Basil and Isabel the
multiplicities of American life. Repeatedly Howells is able to discover the
appropriate action whereby to condense and symbolize the multiform character of the nation. Basil has said that "as this was their first journey together
in America, he wished to give it at the beginning as pungent a national
character as possible." In their own marriage—Basil is a committed Ohioan
and Isabel a Bostonian fierce in her local pride—they suggest the very
amalgamation which they variously observe: in the waiting rooms of train
stations, in the variety of racial mixture and classes in New York, in the
rural and urban types who ride the Albany night boat, in the through train
from East to West, in the various bridal couples seeing the Niagara sights,
in the lobbies of hotels, and in restaurants and dining rooms. Even in
their own names, Basil and Isabel are anagrams of each other, harmonizing
opposites. Youth and age, city and country, East and West, the established,
the new rich, and the slum-dwellers—all swim into the watchful ken of
Basil and Isabel as they march across their changing America. Observed
sympathetically and wisely, any one aspect of America, Howells knows, may
represent all. The narrator thus chooses revelatory symbols to define the
harmonious mixture of things making America—for example, the train station:

> The ticket-seller's stamp clicked incessantly as he sold tickets to all points
> South and West: to New York, Philadelphia, Charleston; to New Orleans,

---

[28] Quoted in Cady, *The Road to Realism*, p. 159.

Chicago, Omaha; to St. Paul, Duluth, St. Louis; and it would not have been hard to find in that anxious bustle...an image of the whole busy affair of life.

While DeForest nearly always embodies his sense of strife and reconciliation in a romantic plot convention, Howells writes the National Novel—more successfully than DeForest—by bringing the acute consciousnesses of his characters to bear upon diverse experience and thus achieves reconciliation through the sense and sensibilities within them. His version of the Great American Novel is essentially naturalistic and psychological.

Using the scenic materials in Parkman's histories for much of the background to *Their Wedding Journey*, Howells expanded the travel book by giving the Marches a double sense—of Europe, and of the past in America—with which they give depth to their sense of the present. They recapture history by letting their imagination play upon the present. As they leave Quebec at the end of their journey, for instance, "it seemed to them that they looked upon the last stronghold of the Past" and "could hear the marching hosts of the invading Present." Indeed, throughout their journey they measure the retreating past against the invading present. These "absurdly sentimental people" cast a poetry over the landscape and "invite themselves to be reminded of passages of European travel by it," even while they reconstruct the American past of the Mohawk Valley and St. Lawrence River region. America and Europe, as well as the "Past" and the "Present," are fused in the fancies of the wedding journeyers and thus also filtered through their sensibilities. In Howells's concern to make a novel out of the mental adjustment to the varieties of human and national life, he made *Their Wedding Journey* his first attempt at writing what he called "the ante-natal phantom, pleading to be born into the world, the American novel."[29]

Howells's mind characteristically built upon his experience. Among the people Basil and Isabel meet on their journey are Colonel Ellison of Milwaukee, his wife, and Miss Kitty Ellison of Eriecreek, in western New York, who had come to Niagara with her cousin and his wife hoping, perhaps somewhat tentatively, now to touch briefly the face of romance. In his second novel, *A Chance Acquaintance* (1873), Howells imagined the possibility that on the Saguenay boat from Quebec, Kitty, "expectant of the joys its departure should bring," should encounter the romance she hoped for. In *Their Wedding Journey*, she had been fascinated by the Marches, who, in their personal warmth and cosmopolitan experience, seemed to confirm the ideal view of Boston and the East which she had learned from her western uncle: he lived "for an ideal Boston," and had "a never-relinquished, never-fulfilled purpose of some day making a journey to Boston." But Howells was intent on counterpointing this second novel to his first, and thus he replaces the kind Marches with the cold, Europeanized Bostonian Miles Arburton. Miles, who had "often been mistaken for an Englishman," boards Kitty's boat, and quickly gives her "a glimmer of cold dismissal." Lacking the Marches' willingness to find poetry in the common things about them, he

---

29 Quoted in Van Wyck Brooks, ed., *Their Wedding Journey* (Greenwich, Conn., 1960), p. vii.

has only a rigid sense of etiquette; lacking their sympathy, he is selfishly imperious. Her uncle's surrogate, Kitty encounters Boston in Miles's person. The natural and the conventional, the Westerner and the Easterner—in these two persons, the diversities of America come together and join momentarily. Briefly touched by a passion which breaks through his conventionality, he confesses to Kitty the beginnings of love for her. But almost instantly Miles's conventionality reasserts itself and the two lovers are driven apart.

Curiously, Howells returned to the problems set forth in these two novels many years later. In 1899 he issued a revised edition of *Their Wedding Journey*, with an added chapter entitled "Niagara Revisited, Twelve Years After Their Wedding Journey." Basil has given up his literary ambitions and established a moderately profitable insurance agency. His marriage has been happy, but has meant, inevitably, compromised hopes and ideals. As Isabel puts it, "had not the commonplace, every-day experiences of marriage vulgarized them both?" Yet they still manage to invest their experiences with poetry and are now taking their two children on a trip into the past. Their earlier consciousness of past and present is duplicated and doubled; for their children know by heart all the details of the earlier trip. When finally the family arrives at Niagara Falls, Kitty Ellison fills Isabel's thoughts. What has become of her? "It seemed to [Isabel] a hard world that could come to nothing better...for the girl whom she had seen in her first glimpse of it." Then, incandescently, a face in a train window flashes briefly before them— Kitty Ellison's. So, as it seemed, nothing had changed very much; probably she still lived in the nearby Eriecreek with Uncle Jack. Here was the tragedy of the commonplace real.

Howells had not been entirely content with his treatment of the inconclusive separation of Kitty and Miles. In *An Open-Eyed Conspiracy* (1897) he presented a similar situation of the young, innocent, rural girl arriving at Saratoga in search of romance. But now the Marches remain to bring the romance to a successful conclusion. The love match which they supervise is appropriately placed against the background of Saratoga, where various regional types—"the Southern dark, as well as the Northern fair complexion"—gather, and where even its hotels, the Grand Union and the United States, symbolize national harmony. The same theme recurs in *Their Silver Wedding Journey* (1899), where Basil and Isabel observe and direct a pair of quarreling lovers across Europe, and accomplish their reconciliation at last in America. In Burnamy and Agatha, Basil and Isabel review their youth—they find themselves, as Basil prophesies, "coming upon our former selves over there [in Europe], and travelling round with them—a wedding journey *en partie carrée*."

The Marches appear in two other Howells novels, *A Hazard of New Fortunes* and *The Shadow of a Dream*, both published in 1890. Clearly Basil March held a particular fascination for the writer who used him in novel after novel. We can understand the reasons for this by comparing March's and Howells's literary careers. In each of the novels in which Basil appears, Howells tells us that after his marriage Basil "had been forced to forego the distinctly literary ambition with which he had started in life." In Basil's compromises, his weaknesses, his evasions, Howells created a profound, heuristic image of his fears and hopes for his own career. Henry James revealed in 1886 that Howells had long believed himself to lack "the faculty of the novelist" and had even showed James "certain unfinished chapters... in triumphant support of this contention." Howells believed particularly that he had no skill for dialogue. "Only step by step," James says, did he work his way cautiously into the novel.[30] In *Their Wedding Journey* Basil is for Howells an image of the failure which he might possibly become. In Basil, who settled for secure positions, and who would eventually become an insurance agent, Howells reminded himself of the opposite risk he was running in beginning to write fiction. In 1871, the same year that *Their Wedding Journey* appeared, Howells had become editor of the *Atlantic Monthly*. Should he not, like March (he might well have asked himself at this critical point in his life), be content with this secure position?

A second critical period in Howells's life culminated in 1886, the year of the famous Chicago Haymarket Square riot. By this time he had in his troublings about problems of ethics come under Tolstoy's influence, which in curious ways revitalized the Swedenborgian idealism of his early Christian training and thus at last allowed him to accept his father's utopianism. Tolstoy, as Howells wrote, "gave me new criterions, new principles, which, after all, were those taught us in our earliest childhood, before we came to the evil wisdom of the world."[31] Under this influence Howells wrote *The Minister's Charge* (1887) and *Annie Kilburn* (1888). And when eight anarchists were singled out for trial and convicted of the Haymarket Square bombing—even though no one of these was suspected or accused of actually throwing the bomb—Howells was convinced that both American and universal principles of justice had been violated. In a letter to a Chicago poet he described the "horror and the shame of the crime which the law is about to commit against justice,"[32] and sent a plea for clemency to Whitelaw Reid's *Tribune*. Eventually, in 1893, the new governor of Illinois, J. P. Altgeld, would pardon the three surviving anarchists; but at the moment the terrified country was dedicated to their destruction. At this moment, Howells stood virtually alone among Americans of national reputation in protesting the original verdict. Older reformers like John Greenleaf Whittier joined in the general hysteria; younger ones like Debs and Washington Gladden were strangely silent. "Howells' heroism in this moment," as Edwin Cady has written, "...has almost never been adequately recognized."[33] He could not be a Basil March. Instead, he risked his reputation and invited the abuse which followed upon his defense of the anarchists.

So complete had been Howells's sudden awakening to the abuses of justice in human society that, as he told Henry James, he hardly dared "to trust pen and ink with all the audacity of my social ideas." He had come to abhor civilization "and [to] feel that it is coming out all wrong in the end, unless

---

[30] Henry James, "William Dean Howells," *Harper's Weekly*, XXX (1886), 394. [31] Quoted in Cady, *The Realist at War*, p. 9. [32] *Ibid.*, p. 71. [33] *Ibid.*, p. 80.

it bases itself anew on a real equality."[34] Defending the Chicago anarchists, he had genuinely risked the loss of his popular following, and even of his editorial position. Therefore, he again used Basil March as his hero and mask when, in 1889, he began a novel that was profoundly derived from his feelings about the injustice of the Haymarket Square convictions. This book he called *A Hazard of New Fortunes*. Hazarding his own fortunes in the figure of Basil, Howells turned him out of his Boston insurance agency and brought him to an editorial post in New York. There, in the city the Marches had gone through on a midsummer day's nightmare seventeen years earlier, they wander anew—searching for an apartment, visiting acquaintances, riding the elevated—observers and critics of the modern city. By 1890 New York had become the acknowledged center of taste and intellect, of business and speculation in America. "There's only one city that belongs to the whole country, and that's New York," Fulkerson, business manager of March's periodical, declares flatly. Coming from the less energetic Boston, and ultimately from the agrarian West, March is forced to confront and understand America's incredible diversity: in quick succession he encounters different representatives of the West in Fulkerson and the owner of the magazine, Dryfoos; of the South in Colonel Woodburn and his daughter; of rural New England in the Leightons; of Europeanized America in the artist Beaton; of the aesthete in Kendricks; and of the social climber in Christine Dryfoos. Basil (who reminds one somewhat of Howells's friend Thomas Bailey Aldrich) is Western-plated, Europe-plated, and Boston-plated. Having been gilded by various environments, he shares a part of all the American diversities he encounters. In his sensibility the tensions of modern America are seen and sorted. So far as they may be resolved, he brings them together in his final vision of social justice.

Generally speaking, four versions of the American mind offer themselves to him for consideration. Dryfoos typifies the American ideal of success Howells had earlier studied in *The Rise of Silas Lapham* (1885).[35] The old man, until recently a simple farmer, has become a power on the Exchange and seems to embody the American Dream. But March is not misled by Dryfoos's rise. Although March recognizes readily enough that such a success (in Dryfoos's case, the discovery of oil on his property) is "the ideal and ambition of most Americans," he sees also that Dryfoos has "undergone a moral deterioration in succeeding. All of his generous instincts have been turned toward mere money-making." His inability to recognize any longer the principles of human justice is best suggested in the pitiless Social Darwinism which he advocates. He assumes the necessity for antagonistic competition between capital and labor. What will this mean for America?— Howells is asking. In the crucial banquet scene, where the various points of

---

[34] *Ibid.*, p. 91. [35] Even Francis Parkman, though somewhat troubled and uncertain about the meaning of *Silas Lapham,* showed how far Americans unconsciously assumed the premises of the dream of success by interpreting Lapham's rise "as the achievement of social recognition." Howells's disappointment was hardly concealed in the irony of his comment: "I did not think it my part to point out that I had supposed the rise to be a moral one." For an autobiographical account of this conversation see Howells, *Literary Friends and Acquaintance*, p. 141.

view of the novel clash, the sugar-candy derrick which represents Dryfoos's business is knocked in fragments on the table in a striking symbol of the way America "will look after labour and capital have fought it out together."

The opposite ideal is not so much formulated as acted out by Conrad, Dryfoos's son, who works for a millennial "kingdom of heaven upon this earth." The Social Gospel movement, which arose essentially from the assumption that man should be happy on earth as well as regenerated in heaven, was centered largely in Boston and New York. As early as 1878 Henry Adams's cousin, Octavius Brooks Frothingham, announced that "the faith in the glory of the hereafter is waning. The poor are impatient now and will not wait for the hereafter. They must have consolation in the present."[36] When Frothingham moved to New York to preach the Religion of Humanity, Howells, Stedman, and other sensitive New York contemporaries became his parishioners or co-workers. Howells himself became a member of the Church of the Carpenter, founded directly upon Social Gospel principles. Moreover, he was familiar with Social Gospel theory through the work of the well-known minister Washington Gladden. In Howells's home town of Columbus, Ohio, Gladden had made a reputation for his work in effecting peaceful cooperation between capital and labor. His *Working People and Their Employers* (1876) laid down a sensible program for arbitrating industrial disputes and tempering the "iron-laws" of Malthusian economics with Christian principles. Dying in a transportation strike that climaxes *A Hazard of New Fortunes*, Conrad Dryfoos, who represents the growth of Christian justice in America, appears to be a figure suggesting both Earthly Paradise and Christlike Atonement. "It wasn't only in healing the sick and going about to do good" that Conrad was important, March says, "it was suffering for the sins of others."

Conrad dies trying to protect the German anarchist Lindau, who is also killed in the riot. Lindau too is a martyr to American injustice. He represents a political version of the Earthly Paradise. As an artist's model, he had been painted as "the Law and the Prophets in all [of Beaton's] Old Testament pictures, and he's Joseph, Peter, Judas Iscariot, and the Scribes and Pharisees in the New." In his vision of the Earthly Paradise, not God, but the State is Providence: "The men who voark shall have and shall eat," he says; "and the men that will not voark, they shall sdarfe. But no man need sdarfe. He will go to the State, and the State will see that he haf voark." The fourth vision of the ideal state is represented by the feudalism of Colonel Woodburn. To Lindau's vision Colonel Woodburn replies: "You are talking paternalism, sir"; and the German retorts: "And *you* are dalking feutalism." Woodburn's feudalism is truly antithetical to Lindau's socialism; other visions of the good life occupy intermediate positions between them. The Colonel advocates an enlightened serfdom as the only solution to the "great problem of labour and poverty." In a paper he writes for *Every Other Week* he argues that if slavery had not been destroyed it would eventually have made the perfect state. Like Lindau and Conrad, he opposes the competitive commercialism

36 *The Rising and the Setting Faith and Other Discourses* (New York, 1878), p. 82.

which the elder Dryfoos represents. Not upon competition, but on responsibility he will raise up his utopia:

> The enlightened, the moneyed, the cultivated class...shall be responsible to the working-classes.... The working-class shall be responsible to the leisure class for the support of its dignity in peace.... The rich shall warrant the poor against planless production.

Throughout this clash of opposites, March is silent; for most of the book he is the reflector strangely unwilling to reflect. Yet after the riot in which Conrad and Lindau are killed, his vision of ideal justice coalesces. Early in the book Lindau has explained that he had taken a room in the poorest section of town to burn poverty into his consciousness:

> Andt you must zee it all the dtime—zee it, hear it, smell it, dtaste it—or you forget it.... I thought I was nodt like these beople down here...and zo I zaid I better take myself in time, and I gome here among my brothers—the beccars and the thiefs.

Challenged by this insistence on the need to confront real life, Basil adjusts his perspective. The fancy with which, in *Their Wedding Journey,* he had transformed life into an aesthetic construct, a series of artifacts satisfying the imagination, he gives up for a naturalistic acquiescence to the facts of real life, however unsatisfying. Wandering alone through the New York streets he now understands as striving and suffering life what he had earlier seen only as spectacle; Basil moves, like Howells, from aesthetics to ethics. In the critical moment immediately before the riot—at which March, too, is present—he begins "to feel like populace," as his sense of humanity struggles with "his character of philosophical observer." It is he who descends from his horse-car to discover Conrad and Lindau lying together and thus to move from meditation to action. Refusing to indulge in utopian daydreams, he sifts the sense in all of those he has encountered and arrives at the essential coin of justice struck from them. He tells Isabel in the general, concluding, impartial vision of the book:

> It ought to be a law as inflexible in human affairs as the order of day and night in the physical world, that if a man will work he shall both rest and eat, and shall not be harassed with any question as to how his repose and his provision shall come.

Like Howells in his defense of the Chicago anarchists, March endangered his new fortune—the renewal of his literary hopes—in defending Lindau against the plutocracy represented by Dryfoos. But each man, every day, Howells was saying, gambles haphazardly in this world of chance. To Conrad fortune, and to Lindau Fortune, brings death; to Dryfoos and Beaton, alienation and moral deterioration. Basil March alone is transformed and dignified by his hazard, for he alone risks his fortunes, fully recognizing both the possibilities of loss and his commitment to truth.

In praise of *A Hazard of New Fortunes*, William James wrote to Howells: "The year which shall have witnessed the apparition of your 'Hazard of New Fortunes,' of Harry's 'Tragic Muse,' and of my 'Psychology' will indeed be a memorable one in American Literature!!"[37] Unlike many critics who see in *A Hazard* only one of Howells's "economic novels," William James, who was unsympathetic to Howells's Tolstoyanism, recognized that the book centers not in economics but (as Howells would say later of *Through the Eye of the Needle* [1907]), in "the personal equation"—the effect of economic and other conditions upon various people. Howells's version of the National Novel here, as elsewhere, was primarily psychological, concerned with the way conflicting ideas lodge in the mind and clash mentally: it was the individual person and the quality of his mind that Howells was interested in. Indeed, *The Shadow of a Dream* (1890), the novel which Howells began immediately upon completing *A Hazard,* suggests how completely his fiction resides in the exciting permutations of the individual consciousness. The transformed, sensitized Basil—who Howells found growing under his hands as he concluded *A Hazard* and was planning his new novel—reappears as the narrator of this tragedy of an American *ménage à trois.* William James might well have named *The Shadow of a Dream* as a fourth to the triad he proposed, for Howells's handling of his psychological tragedy suggests Henry's method. Moreover, Howells had been learning his psychology from Ribot's and William James's studies of personality, as his perceptive and thoughtful review of James's *Principles of Psychology* would show in the following year.[38]

Howells based *The Shadow of a Dream* upon Ribot's theory (stated in *Diseases of Personality*) that dreams sometimes prophesy coming physical maladies. Adapting Ribot's theory to suit his own forebodings, Douglas Faulkner, a wealthy Westerner and early friend of Basil's, contends that dreams of moral evil may portend evil to come. He himself has had a persistent dream which is endangering his sanity. At the moment of his death from a heart attack the dream seems to have taken complete possession of him. Staring fixedly at Rev. James Nevil, he pushes his wife away "with a look of fierce rejection." Obviously, his dream has to do with the unfaithfulness of his wife with Nevil. Out of the recesses of his suffering Faulkner casts the shadow of his dream upon his wife and friend—and upon Basil, who observes and reflects the unfolding tragedy.

Howells depicts Faulkner in association with clusters of imagery of darkness and decay. The decaying garden in which he discusses his dream with Basil is grotesquely un-Edenic:

> The pear-trees...bore on their knotty and distorted scions, swollen to black lumps, crops of gnarled and misshapen fruit that bowed their branches to the ground; some peach-trees held a few leprous peaches, pale and spotted with the gum that exuded from their limbs and trunks.

Faulkner, about to die in this garden, draws away from the old flower-beds, which appear to him as graves. In his young manhood, he had made a complete collection of all the engravings of Murillo's Madonna, and of "all the Madonnas of the Parmesan school," a hint concerning his absurdly sentimental conception of purity and innocence. Now, having used his illness to

[37] *The Letters of William James* ed., Henry James (Boston, 1920), p. 299. [38] In "Editor's Study," *Harper's,* LXXXIII (1891).

persuade Nevil to accompany him and Hermia to Europe, he is possessed by an equally strong—and repulsive—vision of evil. He dreams recurrently that Hermia and Nevil are lovers waiting for him to die. The same ceremony—with Nevil presumably officiating at both, and Hermia as both bride and widow—celebrates their marriage and solemnizes his funeral.

Only much later, when Hermia and Nevil actually do fall in love does the shadow of his mad dream fall upon them. As in *Hamlet,* from which Howells took his title, the dream is the ghost that drives them to a tragic end. For both lovers now attribute significance to the dream which no one but the manic Faulkner had accepted earlier. They too enter the world of dreams. March feels that he must appear to be "like something in a dream" to Hermia. Even he has nightmares in the train on which he takes her back home. The malevolent presence of Faulkner and his dream hangs ominously over them all. In the study which, Faulkner's mother says, "we keep aired every day," March detects "a ghostly scent of tobacco, as if from the cigars that Faulkner kept on nervously consuming."

Nevil is crushed by the accusation implied in the dream. When March goes to his church with him (in a parallel to Basil's trip with Hermia), Nevil cannot fit his key into the church door. Thus Howells symbolizes Nevil's feelings of guilt and alienation. March opens it for him and in Nevil's study—"a kind of Protestant confessional"—reverses positions with him and hears from Nevil his penitential confession of "our weakness, perhaps our sin!" Their psychological dilemma remains unresolved; Nevil is killed accidently, and Hermia dies quietly a year later. The world of chance intervenes to leave them in the shadow of the dream. Theirs, Basil declares, was the tragedy of innocence. The dream had "power over the hapless pair...only because they were so wholly guiltless of the evil imputed to them." But in a fine concluding ambivalence, Howells has March resift the various possibilities and also consider the opposite possibility "that the dream was a divination of facts; that Hermia and Nevil were really in love while Faulkner lived, and were untrue to him in their hearts which are the fountains of potential good and evil." Brilliantly suggestive and richly ambiguous, *The Shadow of a Dream* showed how skillfully Howells could handle the direct presentation of the "personal equation."

Howells felt, as he would remark in reviewing James's *Principles,* that the human mind "was not yet explored or mapped except at a few points."[39] In his careful study of Howells's realism, Gordon Haight has shown that in Howells's novels the realistic point of view is inextricably mingled with the romantic action; the mundane and commonplace are silvered by a romantically fanciful imagination; details and desire, motion and emotion, combine.[40] "There are two kinds of fiction that I like almost equally, a real novel and a fine romance," Howells wrote in 1897.[41] The realistic and naturalistic Howells frequently demonstrated an interest in the supernatural. Björnson would tell Howells: "[You are] one of the greatest psychologists of your own age,...perhaps the greatest now living in the sphere where

39 *Ibid.,* 314.   40 "Realism Defined: William Dean Howells," in Spiller, *et al., Literary History...*, Vol. I, pp. 885–98, *passim.*   41 Quoted in Van Wyck Brooks, *William Dean Howells: His Life and World* (New York, 1959), p. 219.

you have your kingdom and realm."[42] As a realist Howells distrusted and tended to discredit the supernatural, but he was drawn irresistibly toward the mysterious. Psychology gave him a way of remaining a naturalist while entertaining apparently supernatural phenomena as varieties of mental experience. "The new psychology," as Henry Adams defined it, "split personality not only into dualism, but also into complex groups."[43] Howells was fascinated by psychology and, understanding how it could give depth to the naturalistic novel, studied it assiduously in medical books and magazines. In two books—*Questionable Shapes* (1903) and *Between the Dark and the Daylight* (1907)—he would construct short stories around the "filmy shapes that haunt the dusk."[44] These, he told S. Weir Mitchell, novelist and specialist in nerve diseases, were thinly fictionalized records of his own mental history. This partial surrender of the realist to the mystic was a curious characteristic of the period in which not only Howells, but other realists like Ibsen, Hauptmann, Maeterlinck, Strindberg, and Henry James all evinced unmistakable interest in the strange and apparently supernatural. Even a philosopher of science like the apologist for Darwin, John Fiske, could feel the power of this tendency. In 1872 he published *Myths and Myth-Makers,* and dedicated it to Howells, "in remembrance of pleasant Autumn evenings spent among Werewolves and Trolls and Nixies."[45]

Howells, then, was a writer who left his mind (and thus his novels) open to the wide sweep and swing of the winds of doctrine, and knew, at his best, that they blow all ways at once. He was prepared to accept and dramatize ambiguity. Here we have let his several projections of novels through Basil and Isabel March typify his method and mode in its various aspects.[46] Often Howells was able to deepen his sense of a theme or situa-

---

[42] In this interest he again resembles James. Together they virtually invented the naturalistic ghost story, based on the kind of work that William James was doing in preparation for *The Varieties of Religious Experience*. It seems hardly accidental that the fathers of Howells and the Jameses were both Swedenborgians. (Björnson quoted in Van Wyck Brooks, *Howells: His Life and World* [New York, 1959], p. 170.) [43] *The Education of Henry Adams: An Autobiography* (New York, 1907), p. 433. [44] Part of this phrase Howells used for the title of an anthology which he edited with H. M. Alden, *Shapes that Haunt the Dusk* (New York, 1907). He concluded in his introduction to this volume that Americans, "who seem to live only in the most tangible things of material existence, really live more in the spirit than in any other.... It is something that has tinged the nature of our whole life" (pp. v–vi). [45] *Myths and Myth-Makers: Old Tales and Superstitions Interpreted by Comparative Mythology*, Boston, p. iii. [46] Other characters besides the Marches appear and reappear in his books, or are referred to recurrently in the American world which Howells creates. In its coherence and complexity, it is a world not unlike Faulkner's. Some of these occurences are: Clara Kingsbury (*A Modern Instance, A Women's Reason, An Imperative Duty*); Evans (*The Minister's Charge, A Woman's Reason*); Bromfield Corey (*The Minister's Charge, Silas Lapham, April Hopes*); Charles Bellingham (*The Minister's Charge, Silas Lapham, April Hopes, Out of the Question*); Florida Vervain and Ferris (*A Foregone Conclusion* and *A Fearful Responsibility*); Mr. and Mrs. Kenton (*At the Sign of the Savage, A Fearful Responsibility, The Kentons*); Brice Maxwell (*The Quality of Mercy, The Story of a Play*); Kendricks (*A Hazard, Open-Eyed Conspiracy*); Bartley Hubbard (*Silas Lapham, A Modern Instance*); Denton (*The World of Chance, A Traveler from Altruria*); Wetmore (*A Hazard, The Coast of Bohemia*). Such recurrent characters weave Howells's novels together and impart to any one book a sense that it shares the larger meanings and relevance of the work taken as a whole. Like Curtis Jadwin, the capitalist in Norris's *The Pit*, many a person liked Howells because he "knows all the Howells people."

tion in other novels after he has filtered these through the Marches' sensibilities, but the Marches truly represent his main interests. It would help, however briefly and almost diagrammatically, to indicate the kinds of novels Howells wrote.

(1) *A Foregone Conclusion* (1875) and *The Lady of the Aroostook* (1879) are perhaps deeper extensions of the contrast between the innocent American and the Europeanized American that Howells had attempted to make earlier in *A Chance Acquaintance*. In *A Foregone Conclusion,* Howells contrasts the American South (in his heroine Florida Vervain) to the European South, Italy. In order to understand Florida, the Howells-like American consul at Venice, Ferris, must return to America and be re-Americanized by fighting in the War Between the States. Similarly, Staniford, the Europeanized American in *The Lady of the Aroostook*, shows in his suspicions of the "lady," Lydia Blood, that his years of European experience have hardened his moral sense and corrupted his simple American ethics. These books appeared, of course, almost simultaneously with *Daisy Miller* and the other books in which James was working out his international theme. Somewhat later, in *Indian Summer* (1885), Howells returned to a similar theme. Here, however, the tale ends happily, as Theodore Colville manages, in Florence, to reconcile the desires of middle-age with the memories of youth, his past innocence with his middle-aged experience.

(2) Similar to *Their Wedding Journey* are novels like *Mrs. Farrell* (originally "Private Theatricals," serialized in 1875), *Dr. Breen's Practice* (1881), and *The Landlord at Lion's Head* (1897). These novels, similar in form, group traveling Americans together—in all of their geographical, social, political, and personal diversity—at seaside resorts, hotels, and mountain farms. The same device is used in *A Traveler From Altruria,* where Mr. Homos describes his country to a group that gathers at a summer resort hotel. Beginning with his first novel Howells arranged to have his Americans slowly grope their way to a national character by meeting at such points of convergence. Everywhere in his work, up through *The Minister's Charge* (1887), *The Story of a Play* (1898), and *The Kentons* (1902), hotels, watering places, and resorts would emerge as the *mise en scene* for the mixing and matching of the "personal equation."

(3) In *A Modern Instance* (1882), *The Rise of Silas Lapham* (1885), *Annie Kilburn* (1888), *The Quality of Mercy* (1892), and *The Son of Royal Langbrith* (1904), Howells wrote some of the earliest novels to assess seriously and deeply the general effect of industrial modernism upon the American mind. These raise and dramatize, from other perspectives, the problems of *A Hazard of New Fortunes.* Basil March gives way to other characters who each solve or fail to solve the problems of the modern mind by testing their individual sensibilities and moralities in the new condition of society.

Howells's particular kind of greatness is, of course, at best only partially suggested by such lists. His skillful participation in American life as a novelist consisted in his ability to make similar themes serve quite different purposes by filtering them, in action, through freshly conceived sensibilities. His concern with the aspects of the individual psyche emerges not only in *The Shadow of a Dream* and in his short stories, but also in his autobiographical fiction. Using similar materials in all of these, he writes quite different books. In six volumes largely drawn from his Ohio youth—fiction like *The Flight of Pony Baker* (1902) or *New Leaf Mills* (1913), reminiscence such as *My Year in a Log Cabin* (1893) or *Years of My Youth* (1916) —Howells clearly demonstrates that his achievement lies not alone in his ability to remember or invent suitable literary materials to express memory, but to focus upon whatever material comes his way an enormous number of different sensibilities, and thus to disperse or metamorphose similar materials into multifarious forms. No one book represents Howells. To read him at all one must read him completely. During his life he published over a hundred volumes and he was always afraid that he was running out of material. Yet few writers have been less guilty of repeating themselves. In an unpublished letter to Howells, James advised him to "continue to Americanize and to *realize* that is your mission."[47] Howells did Americanize. He helped to teach his contemporaries what the American really was by writing of him in all his guises. Learning from Whitman and drawing upon his Protestant sense of self, his commitment to the "personal equation," he demonstrated the largeness of mind which Whitman said the Americans of the future would possess. In his hundred volumes, he wrote as many chapters of the Great American Novel.

The writer who could thus understand the varieties of American life, and portray them both lovingly and shrewdly, was himself, as his audience came to believe, the man who best symbolized America. By 1900, when the New England Sages and Whitman were all dead, it was Howells who, combining their traditions, stood alone as the American Sage, preserving the idea of culture and transmitting a sense of its relevance. Westerner, and heir to Whitman and New England, he was the archetypal American. In *Literary Friends and Acquaintance* (1900), Howells tells the story that when he made his pilgrimage to the wise men of the East he was invited to dinner at the Parker House by James T. Fields (editor of the *Atlantic*), Lowell, and Holmes. "Well, James," Holmes said to Lowell for Howells to hear, "this is something like the apostolic succession; this is the laying on of hands."[48] By the middle '90s Howells had succeeded to their roles as Sages and, when they died, he alone replaced them. At Longfellow's death Howells made the selection of poems to be published posthumously; he was asked to write the official biographies of Lowell and Whittier; he preserved the Pharaohs in the spices of *Literary Friends* and *My Literary Passions* (1895). Championing Emily Dickinson after the posthumous

---

[47] Unpublished letter of Henry James to William Dean Howells, dated "22 July [1879]" in the Harvard University Library.   [48] *Literary Friends and Acquaintance*, pp. 36–7.

publication of her *Poems* (1890, 1891), he was the first to understand the whole history of the American imagination. He carried the history of American culture in his consciousness. As he said at his seventy-fifth birthday dinner—attended by the President of the United States:

> If I missed the personal acquaintance of Cooper and Irving, of Poe and Prescott, I was personally acquainted with all the others in whom the story of American literature sums itself. I knew Hawthorne and Emerson and Walt Whitman; I knew Longfellow and Holmes and Whittier and Lowell; I knew Bryant and Bancroft and Motley; I knew Harriet Beecher Stowe and Julia Ward Howe; I knew Artemus Ward and Stockton and Mark Twain; I knew Parkman and Fiske.[49]

All these were dead. Among the younger writers he had greeted and often promoted single-handedly Abraham Cahan, Harold Frederic, Henry Blake Fuller, Robert Herrick, Frank Norris, and Hamlin Garland. In 1915 at the age of seventy-eight, his critical discrimination as bright as ever, he announced the renaissance in American poetry and singled out as its leaders: Edgar Lee Masters, Edwin Arlington Robinson, Vachel Lindsay, John Gould Fletcher, and Conrad Aiken. He was "very much pleased" with Pound's translations from the Greek.[50] Above all, he recognized and praised the "distinctive power" of Robert Frost. But he did not forget the past. He preserved all. In 1919, two years before Weaver's life of Melville, when few people knew Melville's name, Howells wrote that all the living romancers were "as nothing, in the presence of one such romancer as Herman Melville." Howells was, as Van Wyck Brooks admirably says, "the one American writer who was aware of all the others."[51] When he died in 1920 he was writing an essay on "The American James." Succeeding the Fireside Poets as Sage, Howells presided over the generation that followed the one they served. His task was different from theirs, for his generation had had to alter its sensibility to accommodate the new circumstances altering the American environment. Changes in the American scene meant, inevitably, changes in the American mind. Howells changed with America and, by writing the National Novel that the New Englanders had not needed to write, helped his America to change with him.

Howells's Followers

In the hands of DeForest, Howells, and James (who will be discussed in detail in Chapter Eight), the Great American Novel achieved definable form. Based on the fact and condition of travel—of Americans in America or Americans in Europe or in the Orient—it measured emotional, racial, and intellectual contraries against each and all others. In this dialectic of expanding (and deepening) consciousness, opposites attract, and the Southerner comes to ask, What does it mean to be an American?; the Puritan

---

[49] Howells, "Literary Recollections," *North American Review*, CXCV (1912), 551–52. Originally a speech given on March 2, 1912. [50] So Ezra Pound reports in *Patria Mia*, p. 45. [51] Quoted in Van Wyck Brooks, *William Dean Howells*, p. 24.

experiences and understands passion; those who hate, those who are separated, come to recognize and declare the beneficence of love. Into the bright circle of consciousness new shapes come bulging, until the self-contained consciousness is obliterated and remade.

Lesser writers than those just considered also attempted to bring about this kind of metamorphosis in their work. Albion W. Tourgée, Constance Fenimore Woolson, and Richard Harding Davis each, for the time and audience they understood, wished to write the National Novel. During the war, Tourgée was an officer in the Union army. He was wounded at Bull Run and Perryville and was a participant (like Ambrose Bierce) in the actions of Chickamauga and Lookout Mountain. He moved to Greensboro, North Carolina in 1865, convinced that the South would soon make giant economic advances. As one involved in Reconstruction politics, he served as Superior Court judge for six years. Finally, in 1879, he took his family back north. In that year *A Fool's Errand: By One of the Fools* appeared and was an immediate sensation. Widely thought to be partially auto-biographical, *A Fool's Errand* excitingly revealed Southern conditions and used the contrast between North and South that would form the substance of Tourgée's later books. Betwen 1879 and 1883, five other novels appeared. These, added to *A Fool's Errand*, Tourgée shaped into a series which he called the "American Historical Novels." The novels cover the period from 1840 to 1876 in this order: *Hot Plowshares* (1883), *Figs and Thistles* (1879), *A Royal Gentleman* (1874), *A Fool's Errand* (1879), *Bricks Without Straw* (1880), and *John Eax* (1882). In his preface to *Hot Plowshares* Tourgée summarized his attempt in the series. History, he says, is concerned with the collective, with "nouns of multitude," taking "no heed of the individual save when he becomes connected with the general result." Biography, on the other hand, "covers the whole area of History with private landmarks." Fiction, he Whitman-like concludes, makes the nature and actions of collective democracy meaningful by dramatizing its effects upon the simple, separate person. Then, as to his subject:

> Twenty-two years ago a great nation was broken in twain in an hour. There was no splintering of the parts, no strain, no lesion.... The mutually repellent forces within the respective sections had completed their work.... Many years ago the author conceived the ideal that he might aid some of his fellow-country-men and country-women to a juster comprehension of these things by a series of works which should give...the effects of these distinct and contrasted civilizations upon various types of character and during specific periods of the great transition.[52]

Earlier, in the preface to *A Royal Gentleman,* he had commented on the myths which the sections accept of each other—the Northern man "has made up a South for himself," and vice-versa.[53] Now, emphasizing that the "years of [my] boyhood and youth were almost equally divided between the East and the West,"[54] and that his manhood has been spent in the

[52] *Hot Plowshares* (New York, 1883), pp. 1, 2–3. [53] (New York, 1884), p. viii. [54] *Hot Plowshares*, p. 3.

South, Tourgée offered himself and his novels as examples of the drama of division ending in harmony.

Across New York factory towns, Southern cities and farms, New England seminary villages, on the Western Reserve, in Washington, Tourgée's fiction roams restlessly, accusing the nation of a conspiracy of contrast. But reconciliation comes, and in the last novel of his series, *John Eax*—a story of the "New South"—he could finally conclude: "If the North and South are contrasted, it is but to show the fusing potency of love."[55]

Even more interesting, perhaps, is the instance of Constance Fenimore Woolson. She and William Dean Howells were, Henry James wrote in 1884, the only two novelists writing in English that he read. James wrote discerningly of her novels and, indeed, in at least one of his books, *The Wings of the Dove*, relied upon one of her plots. Like James's and Howells's, her work was subject to the various impulses of regional America and the European South. Her earliest writings were travel sketches realistically, but also romantically, describing the Great Lakes region, particularly around Mackinac Island; the title of one, "Lakeshore Relics," describes them all. These she worked finally into fiction in *Castle Nowhere: Lake Country Sketches* (1874), published, characteristically, not before she had removed from that region. Settling in St. Augustine, Florida, she again turned to travel writing. In 1880, the year after she moved to Italy, her collection of ten Southern stories, *Rodman the Keeper*, appeared, followed by three Southern novels. In a library in Florence she would chance upon her granduncle's—"Uncle Fenimore's"—*Excursions in Italy* (1838) and again repeat her tentative approaches to fiction through travel 'impressions" sent back to the American magazines. By now she had, indeed, lent her distinctive character to the travel form in inventing a party of tourists who comment on the sights. With these imaginary innocents she traveled, much like Twain's innocents, as far East as Cairo.

Inevitably for one who so strongly felt the fascination of the American South,[56] Italy provided materials for her fiction. Some of her best work was done against a European background, where, necessarily, the American claimant appeared and reappeared, in willy-nilly adjustment to the European *milieu*. "The Front Yard," for instance, has a New England spinster marry a young, worthless Italian. "A Transplanted Boy" studies the effect of long

---

[55] *John Eax and Mamelon, Or The South Without the Shadow* (New York, 1882), p. ix.
[56] For instance, in "The South Devil": "Great vines ran up the palms, knotted themselves, and came down again, hand over hand, wreathed in little fresh leaves of exquisite green. Birds with plumage of blush-rose pink flew slowly by; also, some with scarlet wings, and jeweled paroquets. The great Savannah cranes stood on the shore, and did not stir as the boat moved by. And, as the spring was now in its prime, the alligators showed their horny heads above water, and climbed awkwardly out on the bank; or else, swimming by the side of the canoe, accompanied it long distances, no doubt moved by dull curiosity concerning its means of locomotion, and its ideas as to choice morsels of food. The air was absolutely still; no breeze reached these blossoming aisles; each leaf hung motionless. The atmosphere was hot and heavy with perfumes. It was the heart of the swamp, a riot of intoxicating, steaming, swarming, fragrant, beautiful, tropical life, without man to make or mar it. All the world was once so, before man was made" (*Atlantic Monthly*, XLV [February, 1880], 192).

residence in Italy upon a boy of American parentage, who becomes indistinguishable from his Italian associates. *Jupiter Lights* (1889) is her experiment in bringing together the National and International Novel. The scene begins in Florida, shifts to the Mackinac Lake Country, and then moves to Italy as Miss Woolson tests her varied characters not—as Tourgée was doing—against history, but against the varying impulses and possibilities within themselves, objectified by the varying qualities of the changing background. Discussing her novels, James noted her kind of complex consciousness—a lesser version of his own—that held these various characters in suspension. "It would not be hidden from a reader of 'Anne' or 'East Angels,' " he wrote,

> that the author is a native of New England, who may have been transplanted to a part of country open to some degree to the imputation of being "out West," and may then have lived for a considerable time in the South, and who meanwhile may constantly have retained as a part of her essence certain mysterious and not unvalued affinities with the State of New York.[57]

She made her novels a testimony to the wideness and varieties of experience possible to an American—herself—in the later nineteenth century. Speaking of Constance Woolson as a "thoroughly American" author, her (and Howells's) publisher, J. Henry Harper, remarked that "the war for the Union was the great romance of her life," and found it curious that Constance Woolson spent her last years abroad.[58] But for her, as for Howells, DeForest, and James, the European experience was one particularly American. In that ultimate war for Union in the American consciousness all regions and local allegiances were at odds and provided the realistic materials for a romance called the Great American Novel.

In 1886 Richard Harding Davis appeared in Camden to interview Walt Whitman for *The Philadelphia Press*.[59] Afterward Whitman expressed surprise to Horace Traubel in learning that the young reporter—"I thought him an Irish boy," he declared[60]—was the son of Rebecca Harding Davis, one of the earliest and best of the American realists. Her first story, "Life in the Iron-Mills," published in the *Atlantic* in 1861, grimly described the debased lives of the Welsh puddlers in the Wheeling mills. "If I had the making of men," a character comments, "these men who do the lowest part of the world's work should be machines—nothing more—hands."[61] Beginning to write only a few years after Whitman, she helped to shape the patterns of the kind of national fiction that DeForest and Howells would perfect, and her son, in a sense, debase.[62] As for Richard, he tried to remember in interviewing Whitman that his mother considered the poet a seer. He assiduously attempted to get Whitman's opinion on politics

[57] Henry James, "Miss Woolson" in *Constance Fenimore Woolson*, ed. Clare Benedict (London, 1930), p. 2. [58] J. Henry Harper, *The House of Harper*, p. 226. [59] This scene Christopher Morley later dramatized in *Walt*. [60] Horace Traubel, *With Walt Whitman in Camden (July 16, 1888–October 31, 1888)* (New York, 1908), Vol. II, p. 34. [61] *Atlantic Monthly*, VII (1861), p. 439. [62] Her *Silhouettes of American Life* (New York, 1892), for instance, was praised for including and balancing "types taken from North as well as South, East as well as West." Quoted in Langford, *The Richard Harding Davis Years*, p. 124.

and literature; but he was dismayed and distracted by the fact that the great man's fingernails were dirty. He was concerned more with manners—in the narrowest sense—than with morals—in the widest. But he was the coming man. When he visited Boston after the striking success of his book of stories, *Van Bibber and Others* (1892)—which sold 4,000 copies by the second day after publication—he was welcomed enthusiastically. Howells "went so far out of his way to be as kind and charming as an old man could be," Richard wrote to his mother. Dr. Holmes, "who never goes any-place," came to visit him; and when Richard called on Julia Ward Howe he heard her recite "The Battle Hymn of the Republic." A year later, his mother visited Boston and discovered several reading clubs there devoting most of their programs to her son's stories.[63]

America, was changing. It was, as it neared the century's end, redefining its cultural basis. Boston drifted into Indian Summer, a tired acquiescence to an often oversensitive gentility. Howells, sensitive to the changing center of culture, moved to New York. But Richard Harding Davis exemplified literature and symbolized culture for the mass of Americans preparing to enter the twentieth century. He was, for the generation of H. L. Mencken, "the hero of our dreams." Like one of Sinclair Lewis's characters, the young man of the '90s entertained a "vision of himself as a Richard Harding Davis hero." In 1916 Booth Tarkington would remember Davis as the "beau ideal of jeunesse dorée." "Of all the great people of every continent," Tarkington wrote,

> this was the one we most desired to see.... [Young] men and young women have turned to him ever since his precocious fame made him their idol.... He bade them see that pain is negligible, that fear is a joke, and that the world is poignantly interesting, joyously lovable.[64]

As the model for Charles Dana Gibson's drawings of the young man about town in *Life*, he shaped a generation's ideal of athletic masculinity. As a model for the new American rich—those who, as Harry Thurston Peck put it, had "not gone much further in the attainment of distinction than the possession of money"[65]—he sported English tweeds and invented characters like Courtland Van Bibber who embodied or supplied their ideals of cosmopolitan refinement.

Replacing Bayard Taylor as the American traveler, Davis sallied forth on excursions to the "mild West" (as he called it) and to the Mediterranean. For Americans newly curious about their English heritage, he descanted on *Our English Cousins* (1894). For Americans intrigued and embarrassed by the delights of Paris he wrote *About Paris* (1895). Yvette Guilbert, whose naughty songs he censured, offered to teach him French. In *Three Gringos in Venezuela and Central America* (1896) and *The Congo and the Coasts of Africa* (1907)—most of all, in the six wars in which he starred—he followed and reestablished a tradition of the romance of travel that would be continued, after Davis's death, by the work of Ernest Hemingway.

63 Langford, *The Richard Harding Davis Years*, pp. 113ff.   64 Quoted in *ibid.*, pp. 101–102.   65 Quoted in *ibid.*, pp. 108–109.

Hemingway not only followed Davis by traveling to and writing about countries Davis had romanticized, but he also assumed as his own the romantic, athletically masculine persona which Davis had projected. Making the National Novel into the Romance of Nation in such books as *The Princess Aline* (1895) and *Soldiers of Fortune* (1897), Davis wrote a debased form of the Great American Novel that Hemingway could give life to only by the skill of great reserve. By instinct he would give new life to the form. But in the '90s, the materials of Howells came to seem too common, and those of James too fine for popular taste. DeForest, Tourgée, and Miss Woolson were utterly forgotten. By the time Van Wyck Brooks, Lewis Mumford, and other critics emerged in the second decade, it seemed that between the great golden prewar romantics and themselves there had been only brown decades. And so they set out to establish an American tradition, while just under the glittering surface broadcast by Davis and his followers, a fertile and usable past waited to be rediscovered.

Stephen Crane

The tradition of the National Novel that DeForest, Howells, and James had established was continued briefly by Stephen Crane and Frank Norris. The early deaths of both writers ironically symbolized the way that this tradition was dying. Crane died prematurely in 1900 and Norris in 1902. We must remember that Crane was but fourteen years older than Ezra Pound and only four years older than Robert Frost. Had he lived and continued to write in the tradition of the National Novel he would have been regarded—like Edwin Arlington Robinson, two years older than Crane—as only a slightly older contemporary of those writers who made a renaissance in American literature during the second decade of the twentieth century. The same is true, of course, of Frank Norris. After their deaths, Howells lived nearly two decades, without eminent disciples to represent his tradition freshly.

While Norris might well have developed, along with Dreiser, the naturalistic aspects of Howells's program for realism, Crane was the legitimate successor to Henry James and the more Jamesian aspects of Howells, in his concern to delineate the character of the American sensibility. Like Howells, Crane chose for his subject matter places or circumstances that gave occasion for the mixing and mingling of diversities. The first of these is, of course, the obvious one—war, particularly the Civil War, which DeForest had so early seen as offering an image of the nation blending and changing. In wartime, men from different sections meet, fighting or aiding each other. There is, both DeForest and Crane suggest, a breakdown of local identity. The Cheery Soldier in *The Red Badge of Courage* declares:

> There was shootin' here an' shootin' there...in th' damn darkness, until I couldn't tell t' save m' soul which side I was on. Sometimes I thought I was sure 'nough from Ohier, an' other times I could a' swore I was from th' bitter end of Florida. It was th' most mixed up dern thing I ever see.

Crane finds his image of national blending not only in war, but also on New York's Tenderloin or its Bowery (*Midnight Sketches*); by placing different kinds of men in closely confined situations (a life boat in *The Open Boat,* or in a blizzard-swept hotel in *The Blue Hotel*); in bringing them together, as Howells does, in a summer resort hotel (*The Third Violet*); by making deliberate fictive excursions into extreme social situations (*An Experiment in Misery* and *An Experiment in Luxury*); and by testing, as James did, Americans against Europe (*Active Service*). He wrote about Western resorts like Hot Springs, Arkansas, where he found an "absence of localism,"[66] or cities like New Orleans at Mardi Gras time, and Galveston, Texas, where many diversities mixed. Indeed, his comments concerning Galveston are one of the best defenses of the National Novel against the popularity of the regional point of view. "There has been a wide education in distinctions," Crane writes. "It might be furtively suggested that the American people did not thoroughly know their mighty kinship, their universal emotions, their identical view-points upon many matters."[67] At his death, he was planning a novel which has some of the marks of the kind of National Novel Mark Twain might have written—one dealing with a carnival wandering about the United States, to be called either "The Merry-go-Round" or "Tramps and Saints." He was gathering, in addition, material for a novel on the Revolutionary War.[68]

Like the other writers of the National Novel, Crane traveled extensively. His first published article dealt with the explorer Henry M. Stanley. Eager to see the Mississippi, watch a cowboy ride, and experience a blizzard on the plains,[69] he made an arrangement with the Bacheller Syndicate to write articles about the West and Mexico. When Crane died he was, like Norris, planning a trip around the world. He had, of course, covered the Greco-Turkish War and the Spanish-American War; he had occupied a crumbling mansion at Brede, England, not far from James. Traveling feverishly to the very end, he died abroad in Germany.

Crane early declared himself the disciple of Howells and Hamlin Garland in the propagation of realism. At first, he wrote,

> I developed all alone a little creed of art which I thought was a good one. Later I discovered that my creed was identical with the one of Howells and Garland, and in this way I became involved in the beautiful war between those who say that...we are the most successful in art when we approach the nearest to nature and truth, and those who...don't say much, but they fight villainously and keep Garland and I out of the big magazines.[70]

A year later, in 1895, inscribing a copy of *The Red Badge of Courage* to Howells, Crane spoke of the "many things he has learned [from Howells]

---

[66] *Stephen Crane: Uncollected Writings,* ed. Olov W. Fryckstedt (Uppsala, Sweden, 1963), p. 133. [67] *Ibid.,* p. 146. [68] Two years before Crane died, Robert Barr predicted that he "was most likely to produce the great American novel." Indeed, Ben Hecht more recently declared that in *Maggie* and *George's Mother* he had already succeeded in doing so. [69] See *The Collected Short Stories of Stephen Crane,* ed., Thomas Gullason (Garden City, N.Y., 1963), p. 22. [70] Stephen Crane, *Stephen Crane's Letters,* ed., R. W. Stallman and Lillian Gilkes (New York, 1960), pp. 30–31.

of the common man and, above all, for a certain re-adjustment of his point of view victoriously concluded some time in 1892."[71]

Crane is referring, obviously, back to his first great triumph, the novel which brought him the friendship of Howells and Garland: *Maggie: A Girl of the Streets* (1893). In many ways, the inspiration for this book—one which John Berryman says "initiated modern American writing"[72]—came from Howells, who was deeply concerned with the problems of urbanization. Howells had suggested to Garland that he use Bowery materials. "It isn't my field," Garland told Crane, who made it his.[73] Moreover Crane, as he reported in one of his earliest "specials" for the New York *Tribune,* had heard Garland's lecture on Howells at Avon-by-the-Sea, New Jersey in 1891. " 'A Hazard of New Fortunes,' " he reports Garland as saying, "is the greatest, truest, sanest study of a city in fiction."[74] Crane would also have found in Howells's essay "An East-Side Ramble" (1890) an accurate characterization of the squalor and compensatory illusions of slum life. Howells responded enthusiastically to *Maggie,* calling it "Greek"[75] in its stark tragic power, and later declaring that among Crane's books it was his "first love"—a better book, he thought, "than all the Black Riders and Red Badges."[76]

The story of the first publication of *Maggie,* at Crane's expense, is well known. It appeared in 1893 without a publisher's imprint under the pseudonym of "Johnston Smith" ("Johnson"—similar to "Johnston"—and "Smith" were the two names most listed in the city directory). That Crane masked his narration and directed it, as it were, through this composite, anonymous man, suggests that he was attempting to give his vision of Maggie's tragedy universality through the multicellular, impersonal, anonymous mass man—the Johnsons and Smiths who observe and indifferently record her career. Originally, indeed, Crane had refused to give his characters names at all, thus further emphasizing their essential anonymity and the ironical inconsequence of such real suffering as he depicts.

Near the beginning of *The Red Badge* Crane has Henry Fleming meditate on the possibility of heroism in the machine age: "He had long despaired of witnessing a greeklike struggle. Such would be no more, he had said. Men were better, or more timid. Secular and religious education had effaced the throat-grappling instinct." But in *Maggie* he had already proved that men in the present are no less savage than in the past: they are rather worse than better. Like Twain, Crane relied on the recapitulation theory of human development for his irony. Apparently confirmed in the '90s by embryological experiments, this theory suggested that the human embryo, from the fertilization of the cell through to birth, recapitulated all the stages of human development. Generalizing this sequence, psychologists saw

---

71 *Ibid.,* p. 62.   72 Quoted in John Berryman, *Stephen Crane* (New York, 1950), p. 52.
73 Hamlin Garland, "Stephen Crane: A Soldier of Fortune," *Saturday Evening Post,* CLXXIII (July 28, 1900), 17.   74 "Howells Discussed at Avon-by-the-Sea," unsigned report appearing in New York *Tribune* (August 18, 1891), p. 5, in Fryckstedt, *Stephen Crane: Uncollected Writings,* p. 9.   75 *Prefaces to Contemporaries, 1882–1920,* ed. George Arms, William M. Gibson, and Frederic C. Marston, Jr. (Gainesville, Fla., 1957), p. 62.
76 *Letters,* p. 102.

childhood as the savage stage of the race. Thus, in the beginning of *Maggie,* Crane presents his young savages engaged in a mock-Homeric battle—one, however, totally devoid of the Homeric virtues. Like the heroes before Troy, Jimmie throws stones in defense of his gravel heap. He too delivers great war-crys—but they are only curses. He too fights for honor—but only for that of Rum Alley against the equally grotesque Devil's Alley. His opponents are "barbaric," "true assassins"—yet they are only the children of the slum. The Achilles who comes to Jimmie's aid, called Pete, wears a "chronic sneer" and tilts his cigar "at an angle of defiance" as proofs of his manhood. Entering the conflict with his battle oath—"Ah, what d' hell,"—he "smites" (in the cliché of chivalry) a boy on the *back* of the head. All this is to say that in *Maggie* Crane superimposes a vague memory of the heroic past upon a savage present. The heroic world has given way to the slums. This novel is his *Maggie Agonistes.*

Crane's modern world, then—in *Maggie* no less than in *The Red Badge*—is ruled by war. A sense of fear and trembling, the stunned receptivity of the soldier, hangs over it. Crane's irony, however, cuts both ways. By recalling the Homeric world he reveals us to ourselves as savage and cowardly. But at the same time, his satire, like most forceful satire, criticizes the romance and chivalry of his heroic world as well. His vision is contrary—set against itself. He is comfortable with neither the ideal nor the real, but alienated from both. The conventional ideal that he uses to illustrate the decline of modern man he must, therefore, expose as hopelessly idealistic. In *Maggie,* then, he parallels his mock-heroic satire against the slum world with three other ironically treated themes: (1) the mock-chivalric satire on the courtly lover; (2) the mock-sentimental satire on the happy American family; and (3) the mock-genteel satire on the angelic-child figure.

Pete, of course, with his elaborately "oiled bang," his checkered pants, his "red puff tie," and his patent leather shoes, is a grotesque mockery of the courtier. He had been the warrior; soon he becomes the lover. Helen (Maggie) becomes Guinivere. Pete's manners are now ridiculously sophisticated: he surveys the world with "valor and contempt," and pronounces his judgment upon it. "Rats!" he says gloriously. He had, after all, "seen everything." Maggie thinks him "a very 'elegant' bartender"—a detail that Dreiser would borrow to attribute to Hurstwood. To Maggie, Pete looks "aristocratic," "as if he might soil." In short, he is her "ideal man." Ironically, Crane spells out the tragedy of the "Ragged Girl" about which Howells had wanted to write a happy novel. Although Maggie is uncontaminated by her environment, she is deficient in knowledge. And the very innocence which allows her to flourish into womanhood is then the reason for her betrayal. Although Pete can court no more elegantly than to announce, "Say Mag, I'm stuck on yer shape. It's outa sight," and to boast of his victories in street fights like the childish courtiers in *A Connecticut Yankee,* still, in her innocence, Maggie concludes: "He was a knight."

Crane develops his other mock-conventional themes in a similar fashion. The theme of the happy American family had been popularized by several well known writers, among them Louisa May Alcott, in *Little Women* (1868), *Little Men* (1871), and *Jo's Boys* (1886). In this convention, the family usually is threatened with not only a series of minor disappointments, but also with dissolution. At the end, however, the family is joyfully unified. This literary convention, to be sure, had strong emotional appeal in an America that was undergoing a significant breakdown in family relations. With transportation making all parts of the country more accessible and familiar, with the cities draining the countryside of its sons, the family dissolved. The year after *Maggie* appeared, tramp armies marched across the country. The family was obviously breaking down. Howells, Twain, Dreiser, Norris, Edith Wharton, Crane—all felt strong compulsions to reject their fathers.

Refusing to allow his novels to compensate for life's losses, Crane, in *Maggie*, violently shatters the literary convention of the happy family. Maggie's mother is hardly more than an animal, characterized by red fists, tossing hair, curses, massive shoulders, huge arms, immense hands, grunts or screams of hatred, and muddled sentiments. Her home is always spoken of as "gruesome." Crane ironically concludes this theme by making the half-witted mother wish hysterically to possess Maggie's corpse so that she might put her baby booties on her adult feet. Thus Crane symbolizes the foolish hope for miracles in the conventional theme. For Maggie there is *no* redemption. Her betrayed adulthood can never be renewed. As Jimmie says to her mother, "Dey [the booties] won't fit her now, yeh fool."

Crane's satire on the innocent-eye theme of childhood occupies the early part of the story and is an aspect of his narrative of Maggie's growth to maturity. Several books portraying childhood as ways of reviving the past had appeared after the war—from Aldrich's *The Story of a Bad Boy* (1870) to Twain's *Huckleberry Finn* (1885). These had formed the convention of the child making mischief because of his romantic adventurousness. Tom and Becky lost in the cave, the discovery of buried treasure, and the discovery of Injun Joe are all really illustrations of how appealingly devilish the American Boy was. Add to this the book that was sensationally popular shortly before *Maggie* appeared, Frances Hodgson Burnett's *Little Lord Fauntleroy* (1886). Crane was so violently antagonized by this book that he refused to attend a dinner at which Mrs. Burnett was present. Beginning with *Maggie*, Crane satirized the genteel child, writing a series of tales about Maggie's young brother, Tommie, including two brilliant ones, *An Ominous Baby* and *A Dark Brown Dog*, about the savage cunning of a child. And even as late as his *Whilomville Stories* (1900)—describing his own youth and insisting, by his title, that this was a stage of existence to which he could never return—he portrayed brilliantly a diabolical young girl called the "angel-child."

In an interview with Howells which Crane reported in 1894 for the New York *Times*, Howells expressed the fear that realism would have to wait still longer for general acceptance. But Crane refused to wait for the currents of romanticism to subside. Instead, in a second New York novella, *George's Mother* (1896); in a series of war tales—*The Red Badge of Courage* (1895),

The Little Regiment (1895), and *Wounds in the Rain* (1900); and in a series of tales, sketches, and poems touching on almost every aspect of American life, he satirized the romantic pretensions of the American imagination.

We have forgotten how deep and serious Crane's involvement with American life was, preferring to follow H. G. Wells's notion that he was an inexperienced genius who "could sit at home and, with nothing but his wonderful brain and his wonderful induction from recorded things, build up the truest and most convincing picture of war."[77] Although critics have occupied themselves with the "recorded things" that might have served as source materials for *The Red Badge,* we should remember that Crane had learned, not from Tolstoy, Zola, Hinman, the *Century* "War Series," or Joseph Kirkland, but from American society itself what the feeling of war was like. We must remind ourselves of what he knew of America.

Contrary to Wells's views, Crane was an experienced and excellent journalist, particularly of "specials" and feature articles. Representative of Crane's journalism is a series of articles he wrote during 1894, the same year that *The Red Badge* was serialized in a shortened version by the Bacheller Syndicate. In April, in a piece called "A Night at the Millionaire's Club," Crane dramatized the concern which people were then feeling over the conspicuous consumption of the wealthy classes, and their aping of foreign manners, concerns which would be studied more scientifically by Thorstein Veblen, but no less exactly by Crane. The members of the Millionaire's Club, including William C. Whitney and Chauncey Depew, each occupy a chair which stands on "two thousand dollars worth of floor" while gazing at ceiling decorations which cost "seventy-four dollars per square inch." Suddenly—as Crane adapts the literary jokes of Twain's "Whittier Birthday Dinner Speech" to his purpose of social satire—an attendant announces to the club: "Sirs, there is a deputation of visitors in the hall who give their names as Ralph Waldo Emerson, Nathaniel Hawthorne, George Washington, and Alexander Hamilton. They beg the favor of an audience." Crane can be a master humorist, and he makes the most of this situation. Confusion reigns in the hall until one Erroll Van Dyck Strathmore settles the question: "Where are they from?" he asks. Told they are from America, and assured that they appear respectable, he concludes:

> "You will tell them that as we know no one in America, it is not possible that we have had the honor of their acquaintance, but that nevertheless it is our pleasure to indulge them a little. . . . You will say to them that if they will repair quietly to any convenient place, wash their hands and procure rubber bibs, they may return and look at the remains of a cigarette which I carelessly threw upon the door-step. . . . Afterward, you will sponge off the front steps and give the door-mat to one of the downtown clubs."[78]

On the day after this article appeared in *Truth,* another article by Crane,

77 "Stephen Crane: From An English Standpoint," *North American Review,* CLXXI (August, 1900), 236. 78 *Uncollected Writings,* p. 43.

An Experiment in Misery, was published in the *New York Press.* In this
tale a young man is initiated into the nature of suffering on the Bowery
by taking a kind of Dantean journey into the inferno of poverty. In the end
"he confessed himself an outcast" from the life of capitalism. Two companion sketches to this followed: *An Experiment in Luxury* and *The Men
in the Storm.* In the first, published less than a month later, the same
innocent visits a rich college friend. Here Crane's essential vision of the
savagery of modern society gave him the power to anticipate Veblen's
anthropological analysis of the leisure class. The rich woman he sees as

> a savage, a barbarian, a spear woman of the Phillistines, who fought battles to
> excel in what are thought to be the refined and worthy things in life; here was
> a type of the Zulu chieftainess who scuffled and scrambled for place before the
> white altars of social excellence.[79]

In *The Men in the Storm,* Crane again swings in the opposite direction to
analyze, as coldly and impersonally as possible, a group of men waiting
for a cheap bed—a scene whose power to compel is confirmed by Dreiser's
own use of it in *Sister Carrie.*

Another sketch of the same period is *Billy Atkins Went to Omaha,* a
thickly detailed study of riding the rails. *Mr. Binks' Day Off* is, as Crane
describes it in his subtitle, "A Study of a Clerk's Holiday." Here he
delineates the lower-middle-class clerk who, managing to get into the country
once each year, is speechless with wonder. At the top of a hill watching
the sun set, he can say only, "I wonder why....I wonder why the dickins
it—why it—why—."[80] But what unexpressed suffering there is in that
inarticulate moment of joy; what a passionate denunciation there is in
that unformulated question. Crane was far more direct in a report he
wrote on the Scranton mines, *In the Depths of a Coal Mine,* for *McClure's
Magazine* in August, 1894. He sees the miners, no less than his literal soldiers,
as "symbols of a grim, strange war that was being waged in the sunless
depths of the earth." Like the slums, battle, or nature, the mines are fearsome prisons: "Man is in the implacable grasp of nature. It has only to
tighten slightly, and he is crushed like a bug."[81] Again, in another tale,
innocuously titled *A Christmas Dinner Won in Battle,* Crane vividly dramatizes the conflict between capital and labor, luxury and poverty. As in
John Hay's *The Breadwinners* (1887), which Crane here satirizes, there is
a national railway strike and a riotous attack on the mansion of a railroad

---

[79] *Ibid.,* p. 50.   [80] *Ibid.,* p. 65.   [81] *Ibid.,* p. 72. Crane's denunciation of the operation of
the mines was too strong for even the muckraking *McClure's,* and was deleted. But
Corwin Linson, the artist who illustrated Crane's article, gives it as follows: after
telling of a recent accident which endangered some visiting coal-brokers in the mine,
Crane wrote, "I confess to a dark and sinful glee at the description of their pangs; a
delight at for once finding coal-brokers associated in hardship and danger with the
coal-miner....If all men who stand uselessly and for their own extraordinary profit
between the miner and the consumer were annually doomed to a certain period of
danger and darkness in the mines, they might at least comprehend the misery and
bitterness of men who toil for existence at these hopelessly grim tasks" (Corwin
Linson, *My Stephen Crane* [Syracuse, 1958], p. 70).

official. Crane recognized, as few other Americans could, how brutalized the American lower classes were becoming. In the rioting crowd are

> women—gaunt and ragged creatures with inflamed visages and rolling eyes. . . .
> They had emerged from the earth. . .to engage in this carousal of violence. And
> from this procession there came continual threatening ejaculations, shrill cries
> for revenge, and querulous voices of hate, that made a sort of barbaric hymn,
> a pagan chant of savage battle and death.[82]

As well as Jacob Riis, E. A. Ross, and the other social analysts of his time, Crane knew who the people of the abyss were and what they portended for the future of America.

Crane here touched upon the theme of urban degradation which Jack London would later stress in *The Iron Heel*. But Crane knew more than London. An article which he wrote during 1895, when he was traveling in the West, shows that his sense of agrarian degradation was no less keen than Hamlin Garland's. In the *Nebraskans' Bitter Fight for Life* Crane wrote of the drought then gripping parts of Nebraska:

> The farmers, helpless, with no weapon against this terrible and inscrutable
> wrath of nature, were spectators at the strangling of their hopes. . . . It was as
> if upon the massive altar of the earth their homes and their families were being
> offered in sacrifice to the wrath of some blind and pitiless deity.[83]

He understood, in city and country, that the cry of rage and frustration was the human condition—that life was not simply, as the older Americans had it, earnest; but savage. Well aware of the economic desolation of many Americans, Crane was still no socialist. "I was a Socialist for two weeks," he said once, "but when a couple of Socialists assured me I had no right to think differently from any other Socialist and then quarrelled with each other about what Socialism meant, I ran away."[84] He knew that the condition of suffering lay at the heart and end of existence. At the same time that William James was declaring what disaster might lie at the end of human endeavor, Crane was dramatizing disaster and declaring that for man thus fated only "the absence of excitement, fright, or any emotion. . .of a man intent upon his business"[85] would suffice, though indeed even this might not prevail. For Crane there was none but secular salvation; and, as the Puritan clergymen in his family would have proclaimed, there was very little salvation at all.

It was what Crane learned from American society, then, rather than what he learned from Zola, Tolstoy, and others, that was the essential source of his ability to evoke war and the bewildered and pretentious reaction to war in *The Red Badge*. War, he understood, was merely an intensification of the general human condition. "An artist," he said, ". . .is nothing but a powerful memory that can move itself at will through certain

---

[82] *Uncollected Writings*, p. 108. [83] *Ibid.*, p. 122. [84] Quoted in Beer, *Stephen Crane*, pp. 205–206. [85] I quote from "Marines Signalling Under Fire at Guantanamo," *The War Dispatches of Stephen Crane*, ed. R. W. Stallman and E. R. Hagemann (New York, 1964), p. 150. Crane was fascinated with the signalmen in the Spanish-American War, seeing in them a symbol of man's courage, "wigwagging into the gulf of night" (p. 150).

experiences sideways."[86] Crane moved sideways through American society by translating it into the Civil War and himself into Henry Fleming. Essentially *The Red Badge* is a study of the fears and illusions of Henry. He joins the army in the first place because of his pretentious illusions about his own worth. What he learns, however, is, as Crane repeatedly writes early in the tale, that he was "merely a part of a vast blue demonstration." All the evidences of war work against his romantic view of himself— the sight of dead soldiers, the way men in battle drop "here and there like bundles," the mass, collective life of the military, the death of Jim Conklin. These all teach him that he is merely an aspect of the collective—not community, but—chaos. The simple, secure world of romantic pretentions is sundered by the sublime confusion of the universe.

The world of Stephen Crane is conveyed by general or fragmentary impressions. Correspondingly, the human beings who inhabit it are either undifferentiated members of a collective mass or partial, incomplete individuals. What world there might be between these—of relevant communities and groups or of genuine individuals—is wholly absent from his work. The battle-scenes of *The Red Badge,* of course, provide occasion for numerous portrayals of the man undifferentiated from the mass. Lifting his rifle and "catching a glimpse of the thick-spread field, [Henry Fleming] blazed at a cantering cluster." Later, the enemy seems to be a "flaming opposition"; elsewhere the troops are merely "forms" or "figures." Henry discerns forms that "begin to swell in masses out of a distant wood." He casts an ironical eye over the collective activities of the army, in which "whole brigades grinned in unison and regiments laughed." In the morning the army awakes and trembles with eagerness; after battles it lies "heaving from its hot exertions," bleeding, complaining, or jesting. At nightfall, "the column broke into regimental pieces, and the fragments went into the fields to camp." Here, the mass begins to disintegrate into its component parts, although these still remain undifferentiated within. Elsewhere, Crane uses successive impressions—from further observation—to redefine his original impressions. A brigade ahead of Henry's lay "stretched in the distance behind a long grey wall, that one was obliged to look twice at to make sure that it was smoke." His first impression—that the brigade is positioned behind a wall— is altered by his second. As the enemy attacks, the "walls of smoke" dissolve into "a mob-like body of men." Willing to guarantee only his impression, Crane insistently offers only a blurred world. In "Horses—One Dash," for instance, the sleepy Richardson seems to see "some low houses... squatting amid the bushes. The horseman rode into a hollow until the houses rose against the sombre sundown sky, and then up a small hillock, causing these habitations to sink like boats in the sea of shadow."

On the other hand, men are elsewhere defined in Crane's work in terms of single features and emerge as partial and distorted beings. When the focus is not blurred, it is intensely concentrated. In *The Red Badge,* for instance, Henry sees not troops, but only their heads, "floating upon a pale sea of smoke." When Maggie's brother Jimmie is sent for a pail of beer, we are limited to his impressions: "Straining on his toes he raised the pail

86 Quoted in Berryman, *Stephen Crane,* p. 6.

and pennies as high as his arms would let him. He saw two hands thrust down to take them. Directly the same hands let down the filled pail, and he left." In the bar "an odour of grasping, begrimed hands and munching mouths" represents its customers. "Eyes strangely microscopic" peer at Maggie from dark doorways. Maggie's mother is spoken of merely in terms of her angrily tossing fists on several occasions. Hands reach out to grasp, and disembodied voices call in this fragmentary world which Crane gives us.

Crane uses several other devices of narrative, imagery, and verbal structure to make this partial world vivid. Frequently in his narrative he freely renders and reports the thoughts or speech of his characters without actually guaranteeing (sometimes not even suggesting) that his rendition is accurate. He reduces the vitality of even the characters he has created by substituting the narrative voice for theirs. For instance, at the conclusion of *George's Mother,* as the "woman without weapons" dies, "Kelcey began to stare at the wallpaper. The pattern was clusters of brown roses. He felt them like hideous crabs crawling upon his brain." Or there is Henry Fleming's rationalization for his fleeing the battle: "There was the law, he said. Nature had given him a sign. The squirrel, immediately upon recognizing danger, had taken to his legs without ado." Not what his characters actually say or think, but only his impression of what it might be is important for Crane. When his characters do become articulate, they either have nothing of consequence to say, or else define their limitations by what they take to be significant statements. In his supreme moment of sentiment, all Maggie's brother is able to say is, "Deh moon looks like hell, don't it?"

Further, Crane's imagery itself tends to degrade his characters. He regards most, as those in *George's Mother,* "like animals in a jungle." The opposing army charges "like wild horses," the veterans dig at the ground "like terriers," the colonel scolds "like a wet parrot," and Henry runs "like a rabbit." When not animal-like, the characters are often merely foolish. As the soldiers shoulder their equipment in preparation for an attack, "it was as if seven hundred new bonnets were being tried on." Later, a wounded man "hopped like a schoolboy in a game." The men in *The Open Boat* are sailing in a boat smaller than a bathtub. His characters are weakened and dehumanized. Crane orders his verbal structure so as to reflect their passivity. His language, a European critic has said, is characterized by "a weakening of the verb through a substitution of adjectives and prepositional phrases for adverbs; a predominance of verbs of perception throughout his work; and a frequent use of verbs like 'to seem' and 'to appear' " as witness of a basic passive attitude.[87]

Caught in this chaotic world, Henry vacillates between fear and pretention. Eventually, as Charles C. Walcutt has well shown, he succeeds in convincing himself that his pretentions are true reflections of reality. He ends up essentially as Pete ends up in *Maggie*: childish, selfish, and self-congratulatory. "If there is any one point that has been made," Walcutt

[87] Orm Overland, "The Impressionism of Stephen Crane: A Study in Style and Technique," *Americana Norvegica*, ed. Sigmund Skard and Henry H. Wasser (Philadelphia, 1966), p. 279.

writes in *American Literary Naturalism,* "it is that Henry has never been able to evaluate his conduct. He may have been fearless for moments, but his motives were vain."[88] Crane emphasizes this self-delusion by using the imagery of fairy tales to characterize Henry's self-understanding: the "gigantic figure of the colonel on a gigantic horse"; the images of monsters and dragons, a sky the color "of fairy blue," soldiers who appear imp-like, campfires "like red, peculiar blossoms," fences that appear like "gold thrones or pearl bedsteads"—these all are instances of the ways in which Henry deludes himself by seeing the real romantically. Self-assured by his temporary assertion of anger and passion, he at last convinces himself that "he would no more quail before his guides wherever they should point. He had been to touch the great death, and found that, after all, it was but the great death. He was a man." Henry has learned only how .to explain away death, whereas true gentlemen, Crane told Nellie Crouse, "know how to stand steady when they see cocked revolvers and death comes down and sits on the back of a chair and waits."[89] Henry never learns this in *The Red Badge.*[90] As in *Maggie* and *George's Mother,* Crane satirizes the traditional American novel of initiation. He proves better than any earlier writer Melville's axiom: "All wars are boyish and are fought by boys."[91]

"Crane's whole dark view of existence," Philip Young has said, "of man damaged and alone in a hostile, violent world, of life as one long war which we seek and challenge in fear and controlled panic—it is all an amazing forecast of Hemingway."[92] Hemingway himself has written that he inherited three good writers as an American—Twain, James, and Crane; and of Crane's tales he prefers *"The Open Boat* and *The Blue Hotel.* The last one is the best." These along with *The Bride Comes to Yellow Sky* are Crane's finest short stories. We have been concentrating on Crane's bowery tales and *The Red Badge* in an attempt to define the character of his style and vision. We shall now conclude this discussion of Crane's fiction by briefly considering the particularities of each of these three short stories.

In the background of *The Bride Comes to Yellow Sky* (1898) were two recent books and an institution. First was Richard Harding Davis's account of his Western journey in 1890 in which he debunks the Wild West myth, calling it "the mild west."[93] Nobody, he discovers, but Texas Rangers, is allowed to tote a gun. Second, on a more scholarly level, is Frederick Jackson Turner's report, in 1893, on *The Significance of the Frontier in American History.* This famous paper—Frank Norris also responded to it— announced the filling up of the apparently limitless American West with settlers. Turner announced, in effect, that the frontier which had imparted to American institutions their particular character, had passed. The institution referred to is Buffalo Bill's Wild West Show—phenomenally successful

---

[88] *American Literary Naturalism: A Divided Stream* (Minneapolis, 1956), p. 81.
[89] *Letters,* p. 114.   [90] The point of Crane's later tale, "The Veteran," seems to be that much later in life, in far less spectacular circumstances, Henry finally asserts true heroism. But the price of this success is, of course, his death.   [91] In "The March Into Virginia, Ending in the First Manassas (July, 1861)," *Battle Pieces and Aspects of the War* (New York, 1866), p. 22.   [92] *Ernest Hemingway* (New York, 1952), p. 163.
[93] *The West from A Car-Window* (New York, 1892), p. 6.

both here and in England. Cody's show was the institutionalized version of the Old West, fitted up with modern gimmicks—advertising, revolver blanks, public relation agents. These make for the parable of Jack Potter's capitulation to marriage. Crane's early emphasis on the couple's train trip, their stiff concern with clothes and appearance—sitting "as in a barber shop"—their thoughts about the train itself, its luxuriousness, its "cultured" parlour car; their proud acquiescence to metapersonal time orders ("We are due in Yellow Sky at 3:42"), their concern with monetary systems, Jack's concern with treating the porter properly—these all suggest that Jack's consciousness has already surrendered to civilization. The traveling salesman will later reinforce and generalize this, for Yellow Sky as a whole is about to surrender to him. The drummer—and the civilization he represents—is, as well as the woman, the Bride who comes to Yellow Sky.

The Frontier is about to wed Civilization. Only Scratchy Wilson remains, a wonder with a pistol—"the last of the old gang that used to hang out along the river here." Appropriately, in a final mad defense against the real and symbolic weddings, Scratchy goes on his tear. Jack, of course, is caught between two worlds—of past and future. Unaware of how far Yellow Sky has capitulated, and feeling in his position as Marshal a particular responsibility to maintain the Wild-West image of the dime novels, he fears the civilized institutions which he has wed; he flees from the dining car with a "sense of escape." Denying his part in the Western ritual by marriage, he feels suddenly as if he "had committed an extraordinary crime." He fears a brass band; the station master terrorizes him. He speaks as one "announcing death." In the Western ritual, of course, he now deserves death as he goes sacrificially, symbolically and literally, to meet Scratchy, unarmed—symbolically, that is, unarmed against the savage frontier, with its "Apache scalp music"—by his capitulation to civilization. True to the ritual pattern, the wife sees herself in the confrontation of Jack and Scratchy as "a slave to hideous rites." Betraying his "code," his myth, it is appropriate for Jack to die. But even Scratchy himself has been contaminated, and this is Jack's salvation. His shirt, we recall, was made "by some Jewish women on the East side of New York"; his western boots— probably made in Lowell, Massachusetts—"had red tops with gilded imprints, of the kind beloved in winter by little sledding boys on the hillsides of New England." It is not Jack who has betrayed Yellow Sky, it is history— transportation, factories, the sweat system, the telegraph, the drummer. Now no longer a badman, merely a drunk, swaying from side to side, Scratchy retreats, leaving his funnel-shaped marks in the sand.

The Blue Hotel (1898) again works on the theme of the Western myth of the Frontier. Possessing a romantic name—the Palace Hotel—and an incredible color, the blue hotel assumes surreal, nightmarish qualities. Immediately it comes to assume the character of a trap. In choosing his paints, Pat Scully was "a master of strategy" who "worked his seductions," Circe-like, upon arriving travelers. He "practically made them prisoners," and they feel that they cannot escape. Later, in the blizzard, the blue hotel resembles an "island of the sea." Prevented by Scully from leaving the hotel, the Swede "had the step of one hung in chains"; his room becomes as "hideous as a torture chamber." Alien in race and in his fears, the Swede sees "the existence of man as a marvel, and conceded a glamour of wonder to these lice which were caused to cling to a whirling, fire-smitten, ice-locked, disease-stricken, space-lost bulb." The world itself becomes a trap, an absurd prison.

The Swede, of course, as the Easterner says, believes in the Western myth of violence. "It seems to me," he comments, "that this man has been reading dime novels, and he thinks he's right out in the middle of it—the shootin' and stabbin' and all." Meanwhile, Scully has been trying to convince the Swede that Fort Romper, like Yellow Sky, has made its compromise with civilization. "Why man," he says, "we're going to have a line of ilictric street cars in this town next spring." A new railroad is coming to town; and four churches, a big brick schoolhouse, and a factory are already there. He shows the Swede a picture of his lawyer-son. "Why," he concludes, "in two years Romper'll be a met-tro-pol-is." There is no more West, everyone tries to say; only the Swede still clings to the myth of its violence. Even the town gambler has "a real wife and two real children in a neat cottage in a suburb, where he led an exemplary home life. He was so just, so moral, that, in a contest, he could have put to flight the consciences of nine-tenths of the citizens of Romper." In *The Blue Hotel* Crane seems to be satirizing, as in *The Bride Comes to Yellow Sky,* the Western myth of violence; but this is only apparent, for in this surreal world of the blue hotel, appearances are stripped bare by the Swede's *imagination* of violence: by believing in violence, he bares the essential violence in man. His civilization falls away—and it is not the Western myth, but the essentially savage character of man himself that is revealed. In the Swede's fear, Scully had resembled a murderer; ironically, he comes to actually resemble one. Just as the cowboy under tension suddenly reveals his own savagery—"kill him! kill him! kill him!" he cries—so Scully suddenly and for the first time bursts into a more primitive brogue and shouts: "I'd loike to take that Swede...and hould'im down on a shtone flure and bate 'im to jelly wid a shtick!" At this point he and the cowboy break into a savage chant of destruction; and later, the exemplary gambler, slightly provoked, proves to have a knife handy, which he slides into the Swede, piercing his body "as if it had been a melon."

And so the Swede was right, if in the wrong way. It is not the Western myth of violence which he has read about, but the essential savage, primitive violence existing just below the civilized surface of man that confirms his fears. The Swede—in the final ironical cash-register image—has proved himself essentially right. As the sacrifice that Jack Potter almost became, the Swede finds that death is the paradoxical purchase of his wisdom. Over this ritual Scully has presided as the witch-doctor. His front room in the hotel seems a "proper temple" for a stove which hums with "god-like violence." His appearance is "curiously like an old priest." With him the rest are involved; for like Johnnie, they were all figuratively cheating—pretending that the Swede's myth was groundless. The Easterner's final recognition that "the Swede might not have been killed if everything had been square" suggests this. All, as the Easterner sees, denied their civilization, thus, all shared in the grim purchase. "The essential American soul," as D. H. Lawrence said, "is hard, isolate, stoic, and a killer."

In *The Open Boat* (1897) it is the savagery of the universe—the seven mad gods of the sea—which requires a sacrifice. Not the weak correspondent, or the maimed captain, or the ineffectual cook, but the oiler, the man who by his endurance saves the other three, is thus the one singled out for destruction. While the captain clings helplessly to the plunging boat, the cook paddles himself as if he were in a canoe, and the correspondent is caught in a deadly current, the oiler swims strongly. He was "ahead in the race." But the land requires its sacrifice. Remaining alive in the midst of a sinister sea of waves and sharks, the oiler dies at the water's edge; between waves his forehead is clear of the water. The others are welcomed by blankets; but for him it is a shroud—the only welcome of the land is in the "sinister hospitality of the grave."

The sense of land, of course, to double the irony, has been in the men's minds all during their hours at sea. Here Crane's impressionism changes to psychoanalytic delineations of the unrecognized yearnings toward the land that, to their tired minds, means rest. The imagery is domestic: "Many a man ought to have a bathtub larger than the boat which here rode upon the sea," Crane remarks of the collective sense of the boat's inadequacy to sustain life; consequently, it will come later to resemble a grave, and perhaps a coffin. The water that should be in a bathtub they desperately try to keep out. If water on land is life-giving—even here, they all take a drink of water from a jar—now it is death-dealing. The waves so steadily threaten annihilation that the men all watch with anxious fear the endless succession of danger, never looking to the sky, knowing that it was dawn or dusk only, as it were, by the color of the waves. Above the water are vicious gulls threatening their heads and consequently almost causing them to overturn the boat. Under the surface are sinister denizens of the sea, paradoxically flaming—diabolically—in the water.

Their bathtub-boat becomes a bronco, prancing and rearing far inland. Riding this "wild colt," they resemble "circus men." The foam of the waves recalls to their minds "tumbling snow"; the waves become inland hills. Three of the men are, in a family metaphor, the captain's "children." Thoughts of home make the succession of waves with seaweed now seem "like carpets on a line in a gale." The gulls—who also suggest freedom from the sea—resemble "a covey of prairie-chickens a thousand miles inland." As the men try to shift positions, this metaphor becomes: "it is easier to steal eggs from under a hen than it was to change seats in a dinghy." They think, ironically, of people who row boats for pleasure on Sundays at home. Wearied, the correspondent feels that he could "tumble out upon the ocean as if...it was a great soft mattress." The sea-water in the bottom of the boat makes a couch. Two lights on the horizon are the "furniture of the world." The wind rages like "a mountain cat." When the correspondent finally does plunge into the water he rides waves as if he were "on a hand-sled," or performs gymnastics.

Through such metaphors Crane defines the mental state of his characters. Out of their anguish the men mentally overleap the sea and translate it into inland, domestic metaphors in order to relieve their anxieties. Here impressionism—the domestic perspective they give to their sea—becomes the symbolism of their inexpressible hopes for life in the face of death. For above all stands not only the sea, but the ominous images of an indifferent universe. The refrain accusing the seven mad gods of the sea runs almost hysterically through the story. The signals from the shore are meaningless. The wind-tower, above all, resembles a "giant, standing with its back to the plight of the ants. It represented...the serenity of nature amid the struggles of the individual....[She] was indifferent, flatly indifferent." Accepting death, the helplessness of the individual, the correspondent reveals here what Crane had been able to suggest in no other story—that in the true community of the "subtle brotherhood of men" lies the salvation from death. The correspondent recognizes that this experience of family, order, community, "was the best experience of his life," even though it comes only at the risk of death. This is Crane's better version of Hemingway's *The Old Man and the Sea*—of the triumph over nature that the brotherhood of men facing death represents. The central turning point of *The Open Boat*, occurs when the correspondent can feel sympathy even for the faraway, unknown, imaginary dying soldier in Algiers. Even before the correspondent is saved literally—by a man who, thus blessed, appears to him to be a saint—he is saved psychologically. The coherence of inland society has transcended the natural disorder of the mad sea gods. Saved psychologically, he can be saved in actuality. But the real testimony of his salvation is in the story we are reading. For the final certitude is that the story, the artistic consequence of experience, exists—that Crane, like his correspondent, has learned to be an interpreter by experiencing sympathy lovingly. Thus Crane depicts not the tragedy, but the triumph of man set in a cold universe.

One of Crane's friends has described how "when he was not working, he would sit writing his name—Stephen Crane—Stephen Crane—Stephen Crane—on the books, magazines, and loose sheets of paper about the studio."[94] Stephen Crane—Stephen Crane—this is the inquiring "I," the focus of sensibility at the center of the stories. It is the "I" testifying to its engagement—sometimes ironic, but at last sympathetic—with experience. It is, as Whitman put it, the "simple, separate person" seeking its image in the democratic en-masse. "Stephen Crane—Stephen Crane—Stephen Crane"—it is the artist himself, his ultimate affirmation. In his emphasis on the "I" Crane was repeatedly accused of Whitmania. But in detaching his simple person from the democratic en-masse, more than Whitman ever did, and defining the novel *scenically* as "a series of sharply

94 Quoted in Berryman, *Stephen Crane*, p. 73.

outlined pictures which pass before the reader like the panorama, leaving each its definite impression,"[95] Crane resembles no author so much as Henry James. Like James, Crane draws his readers into the life of his fiction by making them experience a sequence of sensations. By pretending to be, like his reader, merely a spectator of the life he dramatizes, he appears to pass on this life to the reader without distortion. Author and reader, he insists, can each make his separate judgment of it.

The intense concentration of Crane's fiction fulfilled James's notion of what American fiction should be—direct, subtle, brief, and concerned with the sensibility of man and so with the inner sense rather than the outward plot of the novel.[96] It was no accident that when Crane moved to England he settled near Henry James and Joseph Conrad. For, as Ford Madox Ford said of these writers, "the approach to life is the same with all. . . three: they show you that disillusionment is to be found alike at the tea-table, in the slum, and on the tented field."[97] After Crane's death, James himself declared with feeling: "My relation to Crane was. . .unblemished in cordiality. The difference in our ranges of habit and experience was terrific," for, as James added, Crane "had lived with violence."[98] But James knew, no less than Crane, the essential violence underlying human relations. And the Master (from whose criticism Crane learned most of what he first knew of French literature) brought the dying twenty-seven-year-old author five manuscripts for his opinion. Even such a weak work of Crane's as *The Third Violet* (1897) James could speak of as representing "the right thing" in fiction. It is recorded on good authority that at a party Crane and James went off alone to discuss questions of style. Unlike Twain, Crane was enthusiastic about James's fiction. He pronounced *The Portrait of a Lady* a "masterpiece," and said of James's difficult novel *What Maisie Knew* that it was "alive with all the art. . .at the command of that great workman."[99] In short, each writer deeply respected and understood the other's delineation of the modern sensibility. Crane, Ford Madox Ford said, had "a deep reverence and a great affection" for James, while the Master "constantly alluded to Crane as 'that genius,' and I have heard him say over and over again, 'He has great, great genius.' "[100] It is the deepest of testimonies by the best critic of the age to the kinship of art which the two men shared. Like James, Stephen Crane wrote his name across the art of an age.

Frank Norris

Crane apparently, however, did not impress a confident young man named Frank Norris. By 1898, when the Spanish-American War was declared,

95 Quoted in Robert Wooster Stallman, ed., *Stephen Crane: An Omnibus* (New York, 1961), p. 190.   96 Crane declared himself opposed to long novels that, like Zola's and Tolstoy's, "go on like Texas."   97 *Return from Yesterday* (London, 1931), p. 217. 98 This and the following quotations are taken from the account of James and Crane given by Eric Solomon, *Stephen Crane In England, A Portrait of the Artist* (Columbus, Ohio, 1964), pp. 80, 88.   99 Quoted in Beer, *Stephen Crane*, p. 166.   100 "Stevie & Co." in *New York Essays* (New York, 1927), pp. 24, 26.

Crane was world-famous for *The Red Badge of Courage* and for the filibustering expedition off the Cuban coast which he dramatized in "The Open Boat." In Key West, awaiting the arrival of Cervera's fleet off Cuba, Crane went out daily with the dispatch boat *The Three Friends,* which delivered messages to the blockading fleet. On one of these expeditions the as-yet-unknown Norris, one year Crane's senior and a minor correspondent for *McClure's,* was allowed to go along. Describing Crane, in an article which *McClure's Magazine* never published, he wrote, "The Young Personage [Crane] was wearing a pair of duck trousers grimed and fouled with all manner of pitch and grease and oil. His shirt was guiltless of collar or scarf....His hair hung in ragged fringes over his eyes. His dress-suit case was across his lap and answered him for a desk. Between his heels he held a bottle of beer...."[101] Undoubtedly Norris was envious of Crane's earlier success in carrying on Howells's tradition. He would, in fact, always speak scornfully of Crane's work—he even parodied *The Red Badge of Courage* in a sketch called "The Green Stone of Unrest." Even more desperately than Crane, Norris wanted to write the Great American Novel. But he would choose his own way to do it.

Undoubtedly Crane disappointed Norris in literature as well as in life; for Norris, much the same as the hero of his autobiographical novel *Blix,* had "suffered an almost fatal attack of Harding Davis."[102] Norris began by following Davis's, rather than Crane's, version of Howells's tradition. Norris (himself an earlier Hemingway) had followed Davis's romantic trail to Africa whence he (predictably) had sent back travel letters to the *San Francisco Chronicle.* Like his predecessors in the tradition of the National Novel, Norris was a traveler. At the time of his death he was trying to persuade Gilder of *The Century* to take the "descriptive articles" which he planned to write in order to defray expenses for the trip he was to take around the world gathering material for the last volume of his "Epic of the Wheat," to be called *The Wolf: A Story of Europe.*

Norris's version of the National Novel is essentially a romantic one. Although he is frequently called a naturalist, and does show some acquaintance with Zola in *McTeague,* where he attempts naturalistically to define city life, his other novels celebrate the romance of force. In them Norris made the battle for food or justice modern equivalents for the chivalric contests of the Middle Ages. This parallel was one of the familiar metaphors of the period, and appears in such different works as Sidney Lanier's projected *Jacquerie* and Henry Adams's *Mont-Saint-Michel and Chartres* (1904).[103] Norris's interest in things chivalric is well documented. *Yvernelle*

[101] *The Letters of Frank Norris,* ed. Franklin Walker (San Francisco, 1956), pp. 16–17. [102] *Blix* (New York, 1899), p. 19. [103] Both of these writers were, like Norris, acquainted with the work of Zola—Lanier referring to him in the lectures that made up his book *The English Novel* (1883) and Adams calling him "the amiable Zola" in a letter of 1898. One must recall that in addition to his better-known works, Zola published a triad (*Rome, Lourdes,* and *Paris*) in which was implicit the metaphor superimposing the medieval past upon the present. Norris, significantly, was not influenced by Zola while he studied in France, but only after he returned to America. Then, he ostentatiously carried about a copy of Zola, offering to defend him against all comers. This was plainly

(1892), a jingling romance of chivalry in octosyllabic couplets, was his first book, the product of several years of interest in Froissart's *Chronicles* and other chivalric literature. His first published essay concerned medieval armament. As an art student in Paris he had decided to make his master-work an enormous canvas of the Battle of Crécy. His last book, *The Pit* (1903), he would dedicate to his brother, "in memory of certain lamentable tales of the round (dining-room) table heroes; of the epic of the pewter platoons, and the romance cycle of *Gaston le Fox,* which we invented, main-tained, and found marvellous at a time when we both were boys."[104] Chancing upon some of these episodes of Gaston le Fox, Norris's father, outraged that his son should be wasting his time so, called him back from Paris. No longer an art student, he would become a writer—one who, however, carried a sense of the epic grandeur of Froissart's battles into his portrayals of modern life.

Even in his acquired naturalism Norris sifted Zola through the evolutionary historical transcendentalism of Spencer, Fiske, Sumner, and others who insisted that the cosmic plan worked, however cruelly, for progress and good. Norris inherited this Social Darwinism from his father (the hero of *The Pit,* Curtis Jadwin, was modeled after him), who, converted by the evangelist Dwight L. Moody, organized and taught Sunday school. Like Jadwin, he probably took pride in running his school on business principles and preaching the Social Darwinism which, identifying the human and divine orders, had become the code of the American businessman. When the official philosopher of Social Darwinism, Herbert Spencer, visited America in 1882, businessmen were delighted to feast him at Delmonico's. Henry Ward Beecher, who earlier had declared that "God has intended the great to be great and the little to be little," spoke warmly of Spencer on this occasion.[105] Riches and godliness seemed to be in league. The elder Rockefeller addressed this parable to his Sunday School:

> The growth of a large business is merely a survival of the fittest.... The American Beauty rose can be produced in the splendor and fragrance which bring cheer to its beholder only by sacrificing the early buds which grow up around it. This is not an evil tendency in business. It is merely the working-out of a law of nature and of God.[106]

Implicit in all this is a refurbished Calvinism (Norris's father was a Presbyterian) which insists that the process of election is the key to under-standing the beneficence of God in history.

A romantic attitude influenced by Richard Harding Davis, a dose of

---

a gesture of protest, both against his evangelistic father and against the restrictions he felt being imposed upon him in the America—specifically the campus of the University of California—to which he returned. In California he frequently called himself "The Boy Zola"—with an accurate emphasis on "Boy." In this, moreover, he was assuming a mask no less than when he signed his name over a drawing of a six-shooter.   104 New York, p. v.   105 See the account of this dinner in Henry Holt, *Garrulities of an Octogenarian Editor,* pp. 50–51.   106 Quoted in Stow Persons, ed., *Evolutionary Thought in America* (New Haven and London, 1950), p. 163.

Zola's naturalism, a popular updating of the chivalric ideal, and the ethic of Social Darwinism—these are the basic ingredients of Norris's romance of force. Again and again in his books, Norris would celebrate the romance of universal history as it transcends the debris of personal failure. His conclusion to *The Octopus* (1901) is well-known:

> Falseness dies; injustice and oppression in the end of everything fade and vanish away. Greed, cruelty, selfishness and inhumanity are short-lived; the individual suffers, but the race goes on. Annixter dies, but in a far-distant corner of the world a thousand lives are saved. The larger view always and through all shame, all wickednesses, discovers the Truth that will, in the end, prevail, and all things surely, inevitably, resistlessly work together for good.

Chronicling and applauding the triumph of impersonal forces, Norris nevertheless found the drama for his novels in characters whose greatness is measured precisely in terms of their ability to compete with immutable laws. Magnus Derrick and his subordinates struggling against the iron coils of the Octopus (the encroaching railroad); or Curtis Jadwin attempting to corner the wheat—these must inevitably be defeated; yet the strength of mind and will which makes their personal victory seem almost possible reflects their almost superhuman heroism. Thus Norris reaffirms the traditional American emphasis on the individual (his full name was Benjamin Franklin Norris) by writing novels of success in which *great* failure comes to suggest the highest human attainment. When Jadwin is finally beaten, passing dazedly out of the pit amid cheers exulting over his failure, his chief opponent proclaims: "They can cheer now, all they want. *They* didn't do it. It was the wheat itself that beat him; no combination of men could have done it—go on, cheer you damn fools! He was a bigger man than the best of us." So strongly does Norris's romance of the individual assert itself that, contrary to the conventional naturalist formula which called for a concluding tragedy, Jadwin, who in his success was losing his wife, now in his failure succeeds in regaining her love and looks forward to "[their] future, which is to be happier than any years [they] have ever known."

On the one hand, then, force is all-powerful, overwhelming characters who are not even individuated by first names—Vandover, Annixter, McTeague, Osterman, Vanamee. On the other hand, Norris as a novelist suggests, it is only through the epic greatness of the characters who are placed in conflict with natural law that the power of its immutability can be recognized. Far from conflicting, these two tendencies point equally to Norris's romantic glorification of power. Though he swore allegience to Zola, he was never a scientific materialist; though he sat, in the office of *McClure's Magazine*, near the desks of Ray Stannard Baker, Ida Tarbell, and Lincoln Steffens, he was not a muckraker. Basically concerned with the elemental romance of life in all its varying multiplicity, Norris used the concepts and clichés of naturalism or reform that his age made available as metaphors in portraying the vitality of that life. In his essay "The Novel With a 'Purpose'" he argued that the writer is indifferent as writer to whatever social or intellectual ends his work serves, and "the moment...that the writer becomes really and vitally interested in his purpose his novel fails." As an artist he may have sympathy for the characters he creates, though not necessarily for their prototypes in reality:

> It does not at all follow that the same artist would be moved to tears over the report of parallel catastrophes in real life. As an artist, there is every reason to suppose he would welcome the news with downright pleasure. It would be for him "good material." He would see a story in it, a good scene, a great character. Thus the artist. What he would do, how he would feel as a man is quite a different matter.[107]

Not only in this essay, but in several others collected posthumously in *The Responsibilities of the Novelist* (1903), Norris made clear that in his widely publicized "Epic of the Wheat" he hoped to use the neglected materials of the Western expansion to write, as he said in a letter, "the big American novel."[108] By the time Norris wrote his essay on "A Neglected Epic," Frederick Jackson Turner had already announced the significance of the closed frontier. Like Turner, Norris insisted that the conquering of the West was "the last great epic event in the history of civilization," completing as it did the westward march of civilization that began centuries earlier in the Orient. Yet while earlier and less noble westward migrations produced their *Iliad*s and *Aeneid*s and *Roland*s, our American frontier had, he lamented, inspired no literature better than the dime novels, produced no hero nobler than Buffalo Bill. Striving to make the character of our epic clearer, he insisted that "our heroes died that the West might be subdued, that the last stage of the march should be accomplished, that the Anglo-Saxon should fulfill his destiny and complete the cycle of the world."[109] The American epic, he said, would necessarily be based on characteristic American aspirations, and must deal with business: the modern businessman is the equivalent of the Epic Warriors of earlier ages. Arguing from the precepts of Social Darwinism, Norris contended that in trade there is the same kind of spirit of competition as earlier was expressed in war. Had the crusaders been alive in America, they would have headed steel companies; Carnegie, in the Middle Ages, "would have been first on the ground before Jerusalem," he contends in "The Frontier Gone at Last."[110] Finally, in another essay he considered the possibility of "The Great American Novelist." Finding only regional writers, he declared the Great American Novel to be "mythical like the Hippogriff"[111]—though in a later essay, "An American School of Fiction?," he recognized that "of all the producers of American fiction [Howells] has had the broadest vision, [in being] at once a New Englander and a New Yorker, an Easterner and—in the Eastern sense—a Westerner.... Mr. Howells," Norris concluded, "has had no successors."[112]

Norris, of course, was already laying ambitious plans to succeed Howells,

107 Frank Norris, "The Novel With a 'Purpose'" in *Responsibilities of a Novelist and Other Literary Essays* (New York, 1903), pp. 28, 30–31. 108 *Letters*, p. 35. 109 "A Neglected Epic" in *Responsibilities of the Novelist*, pp. 61–65. 110 *Ibid.*, p. 74. 111 *Ibid.*, p. 89. 112 *Ibid.*, p. 196. The heroine of *The Pit*, Laura Dearborn, reads only Howells among American novelists. Jadwin, although culturally her opposite, also finds his "abiding affinity" in Howells. Norris saw Howells as his model, representing (and appealing to) all classes.

to whom he first announced his plan for the "Epic of the Wheat." "I think a big Epic trilogy *could* be made out of such a subject," he wrote Howells early in 1899, "that at the same time would be modern and distinctly American."[113] In a distinct sense, Norris was clearing the way in the essays of *The Responsibilities of the Novelist* for the kind of fiction he hoped to write. Finding all American literature past and present hopelessly provincial, shortsighted, degenerate, or blighted by imitating the standards of Europe, Norris offered his own way with fiction as the American way: he alone would be the truly national American novelist whose absence he lamented in his essays. Disposing of Cooper, Hawthorne, James, and Twain—even of Howells —he left himself in sole possession of the field. Writing for *The Boston Evening Transcript* in 1902 an essay entitled "The National Spirit as it Relates to 'The Great American Novel,' " he contended again that "we should have found our national Epic in the 'Winning of the West.' "[114] Coincidentally, *The Pit* was ready to appear. Denying in public that any one else had written the Great American Novel, he himself, as he told Ernest Peixotto, was doing something "B. I. G."[115] Always ready to further his tradition, Howells himself had earlier thundered a Jovian nod in Norris's direction from his "Editor's Easy Chair" and pronounced *The Octopus* "a prodigious Epic."[116]

Although epic similitude is directly stressed more frequently in *The Pit*,[117] in conception and execution *The Octopus* is obviously Norris's chief attempt at the Great Heroic Novel. Indeed, the *raisonneur* of the book, Presley, is himself searching for an epic theme. In one sense, the subject of the novel is the way the epic can be brought into being. Presley is a writer preparing, at the conclusion of the novel, to write the epic he has lived; the novel is in a sense hung upon his growing insight into the nature of an American epic, as he has lived through it. During the book, he rejects most of the genteel notions of the epic. A graduate of "an Eastern college," he stays at Magnus Derrick's ranch in California in hopes of finding the great subject for his poem; for he "was determined that his poem should be of the West, that world's frontier of Romance." But Presley has entered an action quite devoid of the sort of romance he was seeking; for it was one that Norris modeled after the well-known Mussel Slough affair—in which an actual conflict between ranchers and the Southern Pacific Railroad over freight rates and land prices ended in a bloody battle in the San Joaquin Valley. Presley at first finds this conflict irritating and distracting, for "in the picture of that huge romantic West that he saw in his imagination, these dissensions... [were] material, sordid, deadly commonplace." As Norris sums up Presley's problem, but also, of course, his opportunity, "he searched for the True

---

[113] Mildred Howells, ed., *Life in Letters of William Dean Howells* (Garden City, New York, 1928), p. 103. [114] *The Boston Evening Transcript*, February 5, 1902, p. 17. [115] *Letters*, p. 37. [116] "Editor's Easy Chair," *Harper's*, CIII (1901), 824. [117] "Down there in the muck and grime of the business district raged the Battle of the Street, and therein he was a being transformed, case-hardened, supremely selfish, asking no quarter; no, nor giving any. Fouled with the clutchings and grapplings of the attack, besmirched with the elbowing of low associates and obscure allies, he set his feet toward conquest, and mingled with the marchings of an army that surged forever forward and back; now in merciless assault, beating the fallen enemy underfoot, now in repulse, equally merciless, trampling down the auxiliaries of the day before, in a partial dash for safety; always cruel, always selfish, always pitiless."

Romance, and, in the end, found grain rates and unjust rate tariffs." Presley was forced to learn to redefine the epic for modern times.

Eventually, he forgets his unwritten "Song of the West," along with the galloping romanticism it implies, by reinterpreting the chivalric encounter. He now understands the conflict between Magnus Derrick and the Octopus —the railroad—"that great monster, iron-hearted, relentless, infinitely powerful." Always the Octopus "had issued triumphant from the fight; always S. Behrman, the Corporation's Champion, remained upon the field as victor." Here it is obvious that Norris's diction is designed to evoke epic battles or chivalric jousts. Much later, envisioning his role anew, Presley would even be able to declare himself "the champion of the People." Cedarquist, the manufacturer, had suggested that Presley's epic should deal with the way the farmer and manufacturer are crushed by the Trust. Blindly angered by the social and economic tyranny of the railroad, Presley abandons his hope for an epic and begins to read Bakunin, Malthus, and Henry George. Thus equipped, and newly inspired, he writes a poem—not a "Song of the West," but one called "The Toilers,"—obviously recalling Markham's "Man with a Hoe" in its character and in the cirumstances of its publication. Now preaching an epic of involvement, he insists that he had not been able to write before, since "his convictions had not been aroused."

But, in keeping with Norris's argument in "The Novel With a 'Purpose,'" such convictions interfere with his art. Indeed, Presley soon loses the calm perspective necessary for art and plunges even more deeply into emotional involvement. After the bloody climax, declaring himself "a Red," he tries to assassinate Behrman, the railroad's agent, by throwing a bomb through his window. He was to learn the weakness of his position and his art. Even Shelgrim, the railroad president (modeled after Collis P. Huntington), tells Presley that since his poem is inferior to the picture that inspired it, it is superfluous. Only at last, in the concluding passage already quoted, does Presley achieve the supreme detachment necessary to the artist in his contemplation of the primordial power of the wheat. Neither the railroad nor the farmers are responsible for that power. Even the great Shelgrim is himself helpless before the wheat's power, he tells Presley:

> "Mr. Derrick, does he grow his wheat? The Wheat grows itself. What does he count for? Does he supply the force? What do I count for? Do I build the railroad?...The Wheat is one force, the Railroad another.... Complications may arise, conditions that bear hard on the individual—crush him maybe—*but the Wheat will be carried to feed the people* as inevitably as it will grow."

Thus, at the conclusion Presley has arrived at the stage of understanding where he might begin the true Epic of the West. But, of course, Norris has already written it for him: *The Octopus* is a demonstration of the epic which Presley had been searching for. The quest for the epic becomes the subject of the epic. On the one hand the ranchers have failed; on the other, in a melodramatic anticlimax Behrman, representative of the railroad, is buried in the wheat as it pours into a ship's hold. The principals in the conflict both fall before force. Only Norris, the author who chronicles, understands, and interprets all this, succeeds, for he shapes his understanding into a book. Out of the reality of destruction he builds the artifice of success.

In an article written shortly after Norris's death in 1902, Howells mourned both his loss and Crane's two years earlier. Of the two who would in different ways have carried on and completed Howells's tradition—now ended by their deaths—he preferred Norris for "the full music of his...aspiration, the rich diapason of purposes securely shaping themselves in performance."[118] Certainly, when he died, Norris's epic aspirations were singing and seething within him. He was preparing to start his researches for *The Wolf,* the third book in his "Wheat" trilogy. Already he was speaking to his brother of another epic trilogy in which each novel would detail a day of the Battle of Gettysburg. He would suggest through this crucial struggle, he said, the overriding power of the national identity and the destiny of a unified America. Perhaps, like Stephen Crane, he had read *Miss Ravenel's Conversion.* Howells would certainly have encouraged him to do so, and Norris had read Howells's praise for DeForest in *Heroines of Fiction* (1901). Of course, Norris had read *The Red Badge*: he was working his way through the epics and the epic tradition of the Great American Novel. Whitman-like, Norris wished to contain multitudes—to be a DeForest, a Howells, a James, a Crane. Then in 1902, two years after Crane, Norris died. Standing alone, his own best work completed, Howells was alienated from the younger men of the second decade whom he might have influenced through Crane and Norris. With their deaths the tradition of the National Novel that we have traced ended. Howells could only listen silently to the critics who would later contend that there had never been one.

A BRAVE NEW WORLD

With the emergence of the United States as a "modern" culture appeared also its first lost generation. The kind of expansion of consciousness that has been described here included the possibility of alienation—a sense of being lost in this fearsome, large new world. At the very least, it tended to mean and cause discontent with familiar places and with traditional patterns of thought and belief. Soldiers returning from the Civil War were of course restless. They found their homes, North and South, inevitably changed. In the South, nearly 750,000 men came home, but were able to find work only on land that had formerly been cultivated by their slaves. Soldiers returning to the West, as John Hay, Lincoln's secretary, did, found "poverty everywhere." "A man can live for almost nothing here," Hay wrote of Warsaw, Illinois in 1867, then added: "But he...makes nothing."[119] Easterners were equally discontented, and were preparing to leave backwater New England for the fortunes they anticipated finding in the South or West. Men migrated restlessly from one region to another. Those with enough money left America

[118] "Frank Norris," *North American Review*, CLXXV (December 1902), 777. [119] Quoted in Tyler Dennett, *John Hay: From Poetry to Politics* (New York, 1934), p. 63.

for Europe, there to establish or repopulate the colonies of Americans abroad that James would describe in *The American, The Portrait of a Lady,* and *The Golden Bowl.* Southerners—like those in John DeForest's *The Bloody Chasm*—refought the war or lived *la vie Bohème* in Paris, Venice, and Rome. Northerners like Christopher Newman escaped the intensified demands of industrialism in the same cities. The American, who thought of himself, Henry Adams says, as a "pushing, energetic, ingenious person," was in reality a "quiet, peaceful, shy figure, . . . somewhat sad, sometimes pathetic," and "bored, patient, [and] helpless."[120] The mass of men, of course, could hardly wander about Europe; but many did drift about America. Former soldiers resumed a kind of camp life, forming, by 1870, a conspicuous tramp class that would grow until 1894, when the tramp armies of Coxey, Kelly, and Fry marched to Washington. Among those who took up again the tasks of business or farming in all sections of the country there was, Carl Schurz reported to the President shortly after the war, "a nervous anxiety to repair broken fortunes," which imprinted "a morbid character" upon "all the movements of the social body."[121] Restless, nervous, lacking a sense of place or a commitment to work, this was indeed a generation lost. The American mind seemed to be divided, as will again be pointed out in the discussion of James, between dissatisfaction with American actualities and utopian visions of either European civilization or of the Western Virgin Land.

THE DISCOVERY OF EUROPE.   The discontent with place in the '60s and '70s was in part a reflection of the widened contact which Americans were having with Europe. The last Virgin Lands were being discovered and explored. If the earth diminished in glamor and mystery, that was because its strangeness had been reduced by the advance of knowledge. One technological innovation is symbolic of the effect of many along these lines. After Cyrus W. Field laid the first trans-Atlantic cable in 1866, American bankers and brokers expected to find the opening quotations for London securities on their desks in the morning. By the same cable, William of Prussia's speech to his parliament was transmitted to America almost immediately (at the cost of $5,790) and Napoleon III communicated with Maximilian. Thus, as Allan Nevins has concluded, "in the broad fields of business, of news, and of diplomacy, the new link with the old world instantly proved itself invaluable; and men within a few years instantly accepted as a matter of course the intimate contact with European events."[122] By 1872, Howells and Aldrich were only slightly exaggerating when they facetiously remarked:

> A pleasure trip to Europe has become commonplace; the highways and byways are worn smooth by the feet of many pilgrims; there is no longer a space left on sacred statue or medieval column for the noble American to scratch his name.[123]

---

120 *Education,* p. 297.   121 Quoted in *American History Told By Contemporaries,* ed. Albert Bushnell Hart (New York and London, 1901), Vol. IV (*Welding of the Nation: 1845–1900*), p. 455.   122 Nevins, *The Emergence of Modern America,* p. 86.   123 William Dean Howells and Thomas Bailey Aldrich, eds., *Jubilee Days: An Illustrated Daily Record of the Humorous Features of the World's Peace Jubilee* (Boston, 1872), p. 22. I quote from the issue of June 22, 1872.

Americans were beginning to claim their European inheritance, as a story like James's "The Passionate Pilgrim" (1875) suggested. Not merely Easterners, but Westerners as well, a writer in the *Nation* for 1873 declared, wanted "to hear Froude lecture, would like a chance of listening to Lucca, and wonder what the Emperor of Austria will think of the Illinois schoolhouse at the Vienna exhibition."[124]

Americans had discovered Europe.[125] There they sought a contemporaneous posterity which they could exploit without being responsible for. They used Europe as a means of escape from American conditions. They sought to possess—through travel or, vicariously, through travel writing—the history, the romance, and the experience or knowledge that, idealizing innocence, they had foresworn, but nonetheless needed. As a shrewd critic of American contradictions observed:

> The American who, in his own country, is in feverish haste to improve conditions, when he sets foot in Europe, becomes the fanatical foe of progress. The old world, in his judgment, ought to look old. . . . He is enchanted with the thatched cottages which look damp and picturesque. He detests the model dwellings which are built with a too obvious regard for sanitation. He seeks narrow and ill-smelling streets.[126]

Europe became part of the American dream. By 1898, even Edmund Clarence Stedman, temporary dean of American poets, had prepared a *Complete Pocket-Guide to Europe,* and was telling his readers: "A voyage across the Atlantic is today such a common undertaking that most travellers make as brief preparation for it as if they were going by train from New York to Chicago."[127] It was this kind of lively association with Europe, then, that

---

124 *The Nation,* XVII (July 31, 1873), 69. 125 In the discussion of the attractions which Europe, on the one hand, and the unsettled West, on the other, had for Americans no consideration is given—since there was no major writer who made this his basic theme —to the way in which Americans were compelled to see their destiny bringing them to China and Japan. This interest appears everywhere in American life. The Centennial Exposition of 1876 inspired a vogue for oriental art and decoration that showed up in houses as different as Longfellow's and William H. Vanderbilt's. Bayard Taylor and Thomas Bailey Aldrich wrote polished oriental and Arabic lyrics. John Hay reported hearing Omar Khayyam's *Quatrains* "quoted once [by Henry Adams or Clarence King?] in one of the most lonely and desolate spots of the Rockies." The painter Elihu Vedder, whose illustrations inevitably accompanied Omar's sayings, pronounced himself "an abject admirer of all things in Japanese art." In the summer of 1886, Henry Adams arrived in Japan where he studied Buddhism with his cousin Sturges Bigelow, the author of *The Soul of the East,* and Ernest Fenollosa. Adams's interest in the East has been memorialized in the famous Saint-Gaudens Rock Creek statue—a kind of archetypal Kuan Yin—and his book reconstructing the life of a Tahitian queen, *The Memoirs of Arii Taimai* (1901). The paintings of John LaFarge, who also accompanied Adams across the Pacific, established a tradition in the western interpretation of the South Seas that Gaughin would follow. Fenollosa, of course, would stimulate Ezra Pound's interest in China and Japan, and teach him the theory of the ideogram that lies at the heart of the *Cantos.* It is probably Ezra Pound who represents best, among our major writers, how the dream of the Far East dazzled the American imagination and could, like Europe or the Virgin Land, become symbolic of all that Americans aspired for, but found lacking in their own country. Referred to above are the following: R. H. Stoddard, *Poets' Homes,* p. 13; *Mr. Vanderbilt's Home and Collection: Described by Edward Strahan* (Boston, New York and Philadelphia, 1883–84), 4 vols., *passim*; John Hay, *Addresses* (New York, 1890), p. 48; Elihu Vedder, *The Digressions of V. . . .* (London and New York, 1910), p. 316. 126 Samuel McChord Crothers, "The Toryism of Travelers" in *Humanly Speaking* (Boston, 1912), p. 116. 127 Edmund C. Stedman and Thomas L. Stedman, eds., *The Complete Pocket-Guide to Europe* (New York and London, 1898), p. x.

gave Henry James the material for the particular version of the Great American Novel that will considered separately in the concluding chapter.

THE EXPLORATION OF AMERICA. For Howells, of course, it was the transcontinental dialogue that was most important, though it should not be forgotten that he too frequently wrote the International Novel, usually attributed to James alone. Howells made his central excitement the discovery of American variety. For Americans were rapidly discovering America. In the mid-'60s, Americans turned with disgust from the waste of the war to envision the abundance of their future in the dream of the Western Eden. Mountain men, scientists, engineers, and settlers began in earnest the staking out of the continent. As late as 1865, one must remember, the West remained mysterious in the popular mind, though it dazzled the imagination. Samuel Bowles, influential editor of the *Springfield Republican*, reminded his readers in the preface to his book of American travel, *Across the Continent* (1865): "You know how strange it seemed to us that our party was almost the first who had ever travelled across the Continent simply to see the country."[128] But by the early '70s a summer's excursion to the West, "living in the wild backwoods style,"[129] became fashionable, and Clarence King, head of the first U. S. Geological Survey, was tormented by nightmarish visions of tourists swarming "up and down our Sierras, with perennial yellow gaiter, and ostentation of bath-tub."[130] The mysterious West soon dissolved into a mythical West. This is merely the most striking aspect of American self-exploration, however; for no less were the mysteries of the separate American regions made the subject of exploration and fiction after the War. Americans came to know each other. On the dialogue that thus resulted, DeForest, Howells, and the writers who followed them built their separate versions of the National Novel.

---

128 *Across the Continent*, p. iii. The interest in the West was enormous. Playing upon it, Bowles made the *Springfield Republican* famous. Representative Schuyler Colfax, who accompanied Bowles on his journey, was afterward much in demand as a lecturer on the wonders of the continent. The popular following he won secured him the Vice-Presidential nomination under Grant in 1868. 129 Towle, *American Society*, Vol. II, p. 76. 130 Clarence King, *Mountaineering in the Sierra Nevada*, 6th ed., "With Maps and Additions" (Boston, 1879 [1871]), p. 81.

THREE

Paradises Lost

> *He wanted the unimaginable accidents, the little notes of truth for which the common lens of history, however the scowling muse might bury her nose, was not sufficiently fine. He wanted evidence of a sort for which there had never been documents enough, or for which documents mainly, however multiplied, would never be enough.... Recovering the lost was at all events on this scale much like entering the enemy's lines to get back one's dead for burial; and to that extent was he not, by his deepening penetration, contemporaneous and present? "Present" was a word used by him in a sense of his own and meaning as regards most things about him markedly absent. It was for the old ghosts to take him for one of themselves.*
>
> —Henry James, *The Sense of the Past* (1917)

The authors of the National Novel based their books on the multiplicity of modern life. They made their novels epic by showing the heroism necessary to win harmony from the clash of polarities. Unwilling to minimize regional differences—the central excitement in their books arises from the striking contrasts in America—these writers helped to formulate the images of distinctive sections that would emerge as full-fledged stereotypes in regional literature. In this sense, the creation of a series of conscious and articulate regional points of view was, paradoxically, in part the consequence of that growth of national uniformity described in the previous chapter. As political barriers and antagonisms eased, North and South were able to recognize and resolve their cultural differences. No longer likely to bring war about, these differences became subjects in and of themselves. And as a result, between 1880 and the end of the century regional writing predominated in American literature, especially in the magazines.

The prewar suspicions had, in many ways, made the sections foreign to each other. When Whitelaw Reid toured the South immediately after the war, for example, he encountered a States' Rights advocate who insisted that if the "Government" were going to grant Negro suffrage, "then I wouldn't live under the Government. I'd emigrate, sir. Yes, sir, I'd leave this Government, and go North." He seemed to imagine, as Reid wrote, "that going North was going under another Government, and spoke of it as one might speak of emigrating to China."[1] The same provincial attitude prevailed in the West. George Cary Eggleston described the prewar West as cherishing "its own ways of living, its own overweening self-consciousness of superiority to all the rest, its own narrow bigotries, and its own suspicious contempt of everything foreign to itself."[2] But after the War, in each section there appeared under the influence of the national spirit a large body of readers interested in the sectional pecularities of the others. Americans began to take pride in the breadth and diversity of their culture as they began to define it all as American.

At the same time, however, each region was emphasizing its own myth, a fact tending to indicate collective psychic retreat from historical actuality. Uncomfortable with the powerhouse of history, men made myths of the past. Fearing the dynamo, they embraced the Virgin. Certainly, Americans insisted on progress, but they lamented as well the innocence they had lost.[3] There was widespread disillusion with modern industry and politics. The common man was becoming a mere statistic, the "average man," in an age, as Emerson said in 1878, "of the omnibus, of the third person plural, of Tammany Hall."[4] Workers felt caught between the image of degradation in Markham's "Man with a Hoe" and its alternate, the factory man ruled by engineers and specialists like F. W. Taylor. Would man imitate the beast or the machine?

Industry and political corruption, the Captain of Industry and the Ward Boss, appeared simultaneously and seemed to work in league with each other. Business was built, it seemed, upon the foundation of government; and, as Bryce said, nowhere was government so corrupted as in America. Tammany Hall symbolized American politics. During a brief investigation of Boss Tweed, six of the richest men in New York—including John Jacob Astor—were asked to look over his books and subsequently certified them "correct and faithful."[5] When Tweed was finally arrested, his million-dollar bond was supplied by the financier Jay Gould. State and national governments were no less infested with corruption. In 1867 the New York *Tribune* exposed the fact that votes in Albany were openly bought and sold. And in 1872, after Grant had appointed eleven relatives to office, Charles Sumner elegantly expressed the general revulsion in alluding to "a dropsical nepotism swollen to elephantiasis."[6] A war had been fought for industrial progress. A war had been fought to reestablish a pure, moral government. But by the '80s men were saying that modern industry and politics meant cities filled with

---

1 *After the War: A Southern Tour* (New York, Cincinnati, and London, 1866), p. 27.
2 *Recollections of a Varied Life*, p. 6. 3 Americans were beginning to learn that evolution did not guarantee progress; Spencer and Fiske had been false leaders. Charles Sanders Peirce distinguished evolutionary change from progress by insisting that all change is novel and that no general laws can completely explain development. Moreover, there was the consummate irony that the co-discoverer of evolution, Alfred Russell Wallace, announced that man had not progressed in intellect or morals since the Egyptians. Wallace declared himself a Socialist, and insisted that man had to *work* for progress. Thus, the notions of automatically unfolding progress were being undercut. No longer certain, the future began to issue forth its terrors. 4 Ralph Waldo Emerson, *The Fortune of the Republic: A Lecture Delivered at the Old South Church, March 30, 1878* (Boston, 1878), p. 36. 5 Quoted in Washington Gladden, *Recollections* (Boston and New York, 1909), p. 198. 6 Quoted in Dixon Wecter, *The Hero in America: A Chronicle of Hero Worship* (New York, 1941), p. 329.

the physically and morally diseased, degraded homes, ward politics—in short, the life of Devil's Row and Rum Alley that Crane portrayed in *Maggie* and Brand Whitlock in *The Thirteenth District* (1902). Progress meant Poverty. No wonder that as men had enthusiastically celebrated progress, they now, with disgust equal to their enthusiasm, turned from it.

Progress seemed unworthy of the past it had lost for men. In such a difficult time, Americans longed for simpler conditions, and made a mythical past embody their collective fantasies. Thus, the emphasis on regionalism beginning in the '80s was essentially a retreat to the past and a defense of past points of view, due largely to the fact that the traditional assumptions of American culture were in conflict with new circumstances of American life.

The most important of these new phenomena was the repudiation of the Jeffersonian, agrarian notion that the farmer was the exemplar of American virtue.[7] The ideal of a morally superior farming community—as its spokesmen put it, of "Attic Simplicity"—no longer seemed tenable in the '80s and '90s. Tied to railroads and city markets, farming became similarly mechanized. The farmer was merely an adjunct to the metropolis. In the West, South, and Northeast alike, rural slums blotched the countryside. In *Kate Beaumont* (1872) DeForest early portrayed the spiritless, bestial lives of Southern tenant farmers. In all sections, the migratory class of rural workers that Steinbeck and others would treat was taking form. With the mechanization and dispossession of the farmer and exhaustion of available land, the real possibility of an agrarian future abruptly ended.

Both metropolitan and rural life were compiling encyclopedias of stunted lives that read very much the same. City or country—it seemed man had nowhere to go after 1880. Essentially this meant that man would resort to the substitute consolations offered by the past. There, in the past, was the Paradise they had lost. There they might refind their ways into psychic stability. Beginning with the celebration of the Centennial of Independence in 1876, each year marked another jubilee: America became the land of memorials. By official proclamation the past was a national treasure.[8] The

---

[7] For instance, a popular Grange Song of the '70s:

> The farmer's the Chief of the nation,
> The oldest of nobles to be;
> How blest beyond others his station;
> From want and from envy how free;
> His patent was granted in Eden
> Long ages and ages ago;
> O, the farmer, the farmer forever,
> Three cheers for the plow, spade, and hoe.

As late as 1895, this notion was still serving as the basis of Brooks Adams's *The Law of Civilization and Decay*. [8] The Revolutionary period in particular provided an image of energy and purpose which the later nineteenth century otherwise lacked. The popularity of historical novels reflected the appeal of the Revolution. S. Weir Mitchell's *Hugh Wynne: Free Quaker*; Paul Ford's *Janice Meredith*; and Winston Churchill's *Richard Carvel* each sold in the hundreds of thousands. Another evidence of interest in the Revolutionary past is in the proliferation of ancestral societies in the '80s—for example, the Sons of the American Revolution, the Colonial Dames, and the Society of Colonial Wars. There was surely, as James Bryce pointed out in 1888, "a passion among Americans for genealogical researches." See *American Commonwealth* (London and New York, 1888) Vol. I, p. 602.

paradox of progress and regress that we have been examining is finally best symbolized by such elaborate restorations as Henry Ford's Greenfield Village, where relics of pre-industrialism were laboriously reconstructed on a tract situated next to the Edison Institute of Technology—a juxtaposition of pastoral and modern that would have delighted Henry Adams.

Retreat into the past did not cease with the Revolutionary period, but continued headlong—like the historic leap of Twain's Connecticut Yankee—into the Middle Ages. In the unity of the thirteenth century Americans found substitutes for twentieth-century multiplicity. Fra Elbert Hubbard, following Ruskin and Morris, taught his Roycrofters the beauty of handicraft, and lovingly hand-illustrated his gentle, aphoristic books. Under Phillips Brooks, the "Anglo-Catholic" replaced the "Unitarian" Church in Boston. There, indeed, the flight from the present was perhaps most emphatic. At Harvard, Charles Eliot Norton revered the age of Giotto as profoundly as he despised the Age of our Ford, telling his students in Italian 4 that "it were better for us had we never been born in this degenerate and unlovely age."[9] Josephine Preston Peabody, a pupil of Norton's, was reading Condivi's life of Michelangelo and declaring that stories of New England irritated and depressed her. Like many New Englanders ("the only thing I wanted in life was to be made a cardinal," Henry Adams wrote in 1899[10]), Josephine Peabody lived half-in, half-out of the Middle Ages. On Michaelmas she ate goose, invoking Saints Gregory and Catherine; she celebrated the memory of obscure saints chronicled in Chambers's *Book of Days* and spent vigils in memory of Keats. In Boston Vida Scudder wrote her "imaginary biography" of a disciple of Saint Catherine; while Agnes Repplier, lamenting the "hardship of being born too late,"[11] wrote biographies of Junipero Serra and Mere Marie of the Ursulines.

The New England version of the retreat to medievalism is characteristic of response elsewhere—one might point equally to the South or West. In fact, the book which popularly defined the whole character of the impulse was by an Indiana author, Charles Major, and was entitled *When Knighthood was in Flower* (1898).

This retreat, it should be reemphasized, was not to a historical, but to a mythical past. It was a yearning, as James dramatized it in *The Sense of the Past,* for the "truth for which the common lens of history...was not sufficiently fine."[12] One may be tempted to see this retreat from the demands of history to the consolations of myth as a backward turning in the evolution of American culture[13]; yet the student of American history must recog-

9 *The Diary and Letters of Josephine Preston Peabody,* ed. Christina Hopkinson Baker (Boston and New York, 1925), p. 73. 10 Quoted from a letter to John Hay, dated May 31, 1899 in *Letters of Henry Adams 1872–1918,* ed. Worthington Chauncey Ford (Boston, 1938), p. 232. 11 Quoted in Van Wyck Brooks, *The Confident Years: 1885–1915* (New York, 1952), p. 33. 12 *The Sense of the Past* (London, 1917), p. 48. 13 Earlier Americans had been able, as Henry James Sr. could, to see society, in time and space, as the regenerate form of man. That man was saved by the knowledge he added to his innocence was the assumption, basically, of the writers in the tradition of a National Novel as has been defined here. Whitman, their seer, wrote, for instance, that his aim was "to produce Personalities not merely as full as those of primitive times, but which will have, in addition, all that the long train of knowledge, science, inventions and commerce, have accumulated since." Culture—consciousness—was to perfect natural innocence. See David Noble's *The Paradox of Progressive Thought* (Minneapolis, Minn., 1958).

nize that Americans have always delighted in inventing mythologies—
legends of Sleepy Hollow or of the Gloomy Woodlands of Weir. Uneasy
with history, knowledge, and experience, Americans, particularly in the later
nineteenth century, retreated to a mythical past that provided them no bridge
whereby to reenter the present. Lacking a past, Americans had to invent
one; but having invented one, they became restless in it also. They knew
what it meant to be Hank Morgans, neither in nor out of time, dreaming of
past *and* present.

This myth-making facility was to a large part a reflection of the fact that
America, as the psychologist G. Stanley Hall has said, is "an unhistoric land."
Our constitution is fiat law, not the result of historic precedent; our literary
history, the origins of customs, fashions, institutions, and religion lie in
foreign countries. "We have had," Hall said, "neither childhood nor
youth. . . . No country is so precociously old for its years."[14] Americans had
always cherished and made a myth of their lack of an encumbering past.
The Democratic Review of 1842, for instance, insisted that "no other
civilized nation has. . . so completely thrown off its allegiance to the past."[15]
Even as late as 1875, when John Fiske inquired of a Lyceum manager about
the potential popular appeal of lectures on "America's Place in History,"
he was told: "The subject is one that would interest very few people."[16]
Ezra Pound—who would make the myth of American history his epic subject—spoke of "America of the Instant,"[17] and dated the beginnings of
America as recently as 1870.

In an absolute sense, of course, Americans had a fixed and definite historical
past, whose nature historians had begun to understand and reveal before
the Civil War. But by and large they felt, as a character in Cable's *Grandissimes* says, that "tradition," or myth, "is much more authentic than
history." Americans have steadfastly denied whatever historical past they
possessed because they have conclusively derived greater satisfactions from
a mythical one. To be sure, the myths whereby Americans have made their
universe meaningful are psychologically lively actualities and provide transpersonal systems characteristic of mythical behavior. There is nothing strange
about living in accordance with myth; on the contrary, the interest in
history is a recent development in the life of humanity.[18] Archaic man
defended himself against the irreversibility that history entails by asserting
the primacy of archetypal patterns. As recently in the history of philosophy
as Hegel, man has been comforted by the affirmation that nature eternally
repeats itself. For the myth-directed mind, reality is stable by virtue of
its lack of novelty—by its repetition of exemplary patterns. In the '70s,
however, the theory of evolution began to create severe difficulties for the
myth-directed mind. When Darwin introduced temporal relatedness into
the previously timeless Aristotelian biological classes, he implicitly rejected

---

[14] G. Stanley Hall, *Adolescence: Its Psychology and Its Relations to Physiology,
Anthropology, Sociology, Sex, Crime, Religion, and Education* (New York, 1904), Vol. I,
p. xvi. [15] Quoted in R. W. B. Lewis, *The American Adam: Innocence, Tragedy and
Tradition in the Nineteenth Century* (Chicago, 1955), p. 159. [16] Quoted in Brooks,
New England: Indian Summer, p. 173. [17] Pound, *Patria Mia*, p. 22. [18] See Mircia
Eliade, *The Myth of the Eternal Return*, trans. Willard R. Trask (New York, 1954),
p. 48. See also Eliade, *Myths, Dreams and Mysteries: The Encounter Between Contemporary Faiths and Ancient Realities*, trans. Philip Mairet (New York, 1960), pp. 30ff.

the immortality of universals. According to Darwin and his followers, man was cast out, unsheltered, into the temporal novelty of "cosmic weather," as Chauncey Wright called it. If exemplary patterns were not repeated, if change were genuinely novel, then man seemed truly lost in a universe that he could not hope to comprehend.

It is understandable, then, why the celebration of progress brought with it a corresponding loss in man's sense of stability; why the novelty of change led to a terror of the future; why the beginnings of modernism were inevitably accompanied by a return to archaism. The "disinclination to face historic time," Mircea Eliade has said,

> together with an obscure desire to share in some glorious, primordial, total time, is betrayed, in the case of modern people, by a sometimes desperate effort to break through the homogeneity of time...and re-enter a time qualitatively different from that which creates, in its course, their own history.[19]

Nineteenth-century Americans sought escape from historic time in a bewildering series of mythic substitutes, chiefly in distractions that "killed time." Thoreau had wittily said that one could not "kill time" without injuring eternity; but it was precisely by avoiding change that Americans preserved their sense of eternality. In the museums that placed new and old objects side by side; in the "concentrated time" of ritualistic athletic events,[20] circuses, and other public spectacles; in the annual repetitions of political contests that so bewildered Europeans; in periodic revivals (as with Moody and Sankey or General Booth) of religious excitation—in all of these the concept of normal time was denied. Sometimes these activities would merge, as, for instance, in the person of Billy Sunday, who was famous equally as a baseball player and a fiery revivalist preacher; or in William Jennings Bryan, who made politics a religion and argued the fundamentalist side in the Scopes trial. Less and less able to escape time in their daily activities, Americans organized or invented an incredibly diverse number of escapes.

Literature, of course, provided the most easily available and most satisfying substitute for the lost paradise of archetypes. There were several reasons for this. Mass literature of the printing press replaced oral folk traditions

---

[19] Eliade, *Myths, Dreams, and Mysteries*, p. 34. [20] The ritualistic origins of sports are well established. Baseball, for instance, first became popular in the Civil War camps, for it provided the soldiers with an involvement in coherent patterns of competition that did not seem present in the war itself. In the first championship game, on October 1, 1866, played in Philadelphia between the Atlantics and Athletics, 30,000 spectators so crowded the enclosure that there was no room left for the players to field and the game ended after one inning. By 1867, there were fifty-six teams formed in Illinois alone, and forty-two in Iowa. As Cap Anson said, "the craze was spreading like wildfire across the country." This and the series of later athletic crazes which frenzied the country are understandable only in terms of their values as substitutes for the traditional mythic patterns that were being threatened. In the twentieth century, with the aid of the insights of anthropologists, Ernest Hemingway would be able to use athletic events—fishing, bull-fighting, and so on—in their ritualistic senses as symbols of the traditions that man had lost, but needed to refind. (Referred to above are Nevins, *The Emergence of Modern America*, p. 219, and Adrian C. [Cap] Anson, *A Ball Player's Career, Being the Personal Experiences and Reminiscences...* [Chicago, 1900], p. 27.)

while still preserving their basic patterns of order and meaning. The story of *Tarzan*, for instance, which Edgar Rice Burroughs based upon information in Stanley's account of his search for Livingstone, has the same structure and story as several North American initiation rites in which one learns to communicate with the animals. Moreover, in its plot and character conventions, popular literature tends to fulfill expectations preestablished by the predictable outcome of plot-situations, and so asserts the principle of repetitive order. Finally, literature in general establishes its own temporal duration and so offers a brief modification of our daily time-schemes. Escaping our history by living the fictive hero's myth, we romantically reconstruct the past and thus spiritualize the present.

American regional literature from about 1880 to 1900 essentially involved the idealization of a past time—usually real, but almost always exaggerated into a myth—when the particular region enjoyed certain advantages, benefits, or the presence of great men. Now missing, these, the regionalist believed, were never to be restored. What may be called the "daydream" of the regionalist was derived from his celebration of this faultless past. Each region, to be sure, projected a different myth—shaped from its past history and its present needs. But all had in common, as their basis, the idealization of a heroic past, such as has been described here as a general tendency or aspect of American culture from 1880 to 1900. The regionalists simply gave their audiences the ideal materials whereby to romantically reconstruct the past felicity of a paradise now lost.

"The 'great American novel' for which critics yearned so fondly twenty years ago," Edward Eggleston declared in the 1892 preface to *The Hoosier Schoolmaster*, "is appearing in sections." Only the creation of a distinctively regional point of view, he and his followers said, "has made our literature really national."[21] In opposition to DeForest, Howells, James, and their followers, Eggleston led many writers in insisting that our literature should, at best, delineate single, separate aspects of American life. By 1898, even John DeForest returned specifically, in *A Lover's Revolt*, to the romance of the New England past—the subject forty-two years before of his first book, *Witching Times* (1856). DeForest's defection was symptomatic of the shift in American taste from the National Novel to regional writing. Increasingly, in popular taste, as Hamlin Garland remarked, "the similarities do not please, do not forever stimulate and feed as do the differences."[22]

Regional writing—daydreams of a sort—seemed the answer to this general malaise; but regional writers had their nightmares, as well as their daydreams. This, as shall be pointed out, was literally the split in the life and writing of such regionalists as Joel Chandler Harris and Edgar Watson Howe. The nightmare of regionalism superimposes the present upon the past and proves, by insisting that only a defective past could have produced a present so incomplete and unsatisfying, that the daydream is mythical.

---

[21] Edward Eggleston, *The Hoosier Schoolmaster: A Novel. Revised, with an Introduction and Notes on the Dialect* (New York, 1892), pp. 6–7. [22] Hamlin Garland, *Crumbling Idols: Twelve Essays on Art and Literature,* Introd. by Robert E. Spiller (Gainesville, Fla., 1952 [1894]), p. 57.

The nightmare shadows and shatters the daydream. The joyous, sunshiny world of John Esten Cooke or Thomas Nelson Page stands out against the violent, dark world of Ambrose Bierce. The daydream sings of the idyllic past-in-the-present; the nightmare, of the heritage of depravity. The daydreamer insists that the golden age lies just behind the veil of reality and might break through at any moment. The writers of nightmare find the past irretrievable and the present irredeemable.

Romantically reconstructing myth or realistically destroying it—these are the two ways of regional literature. The best of the regional writers— Sidney Lanier, George Washington Cable, Hamlin Garland, Rose Terry Cooke, Mary Wilkins, and Sarah Orne Jewett—embody, in different degrees, both tendencies. They are compelled to dramatize the nightmare version of the daydream they yearn to accept. In the best of regional writers we can detect the presence and force of the need to reconstruct a glorious past, along with a simultaneous recognition that such a paradise never existed and could not, even if it had, be regained. Generally, then, the best regional writing is intensely ironic; the regionalists are tormented by the gulf between myth and reality. Committed by their inherited training to myth-making, they are driven by their art to critical assessments of the glittering images of hope or memory foisted upon them. The terrible pressures of this tension are suggested by the fact that most of the regionalists were forced to leave the regions they wrote about, chiefly in order to relieve the daily pressure of this irony in their lives, and so concentrate it fully in their art. George Washington Cable wrote of New Orleans in Northampton, Massachusetts; Hamlin Garland composed his most bitter stories of the Midwest in Boston; Bret Harte spent most of his artistic life in England and Germany; Twain lived in Hartford, Vienna, or Baden-Baden, self-exiled in Europe for nine years. All looked simultaneously with irony and love upon the regions from which they had driven themselves. Inveterate wanderers, alienated men, they celebrated and analyzed the particular regions to which they could never go home again. The body of literature to which these writers managed to give permanent form remains part of the significant history of their age and provided a means, for the next age, of transcending the need of an eternal return.

SOUTHERN REGIONAL LITERATURE

The Southern myth of a Lost Paradise revolved around the "feudal" image of the plantation. Because tobacco, cotton, rice, and sugar were all grown for export in the South, the directors of large planting interests (rather than the commercial tradesmen of the town, as in the North) became, early in colonial times, the central social and economic figures—the ideal men—of Southern culture. The literature that cultured Southerners made and read reflected the kind of hero and the state of society created under these conditions. Even before the War, William Gilmore Simms of South Carolina and John Esten Cooke of Virginia used the idealized Old Dominion as their subject. ("Old Dominion" was the Virginians' term for their *ancien régime*; it is used here to refer to the idealized pasts of other Southern states as well.) The most famous of all the novels idealizing the Old Dominion, Cooke's *Virginia Comedians* (1854), depicts Virginia ten years before the Revolution, when that state contained, as Cooke says again in *Stories of the Old Dominion* (1879), "some of the greatest men who have lived in America."[23] During a long career, Cooke memorialized and romanticized this age. For him and his readers, it was the lost, golden age, of which the modern age was but a pale replica. When he at last wrote his *Virginia: A History of the People* (1883), he devoted only 38 of 510 pages to the period from the Revolution to his time. In his myth of the lost Golden Age, the Old Dominion was Eden. But it had been violated and depraved by history—the modern age—and had become merely Virginia.

But for others—with historical senses less discriminating than Cooke's—the Old Dominion began subtly to expand in chronology and significance. Writing his best books before the Civil War, Cooke had looked back on a lost age of felicity and placed it seventy-five years earlier, in Revolutionary times. Forty years after Cooke began writing, however, people became convinced that *his* age had embodied a paradise, now lost to them. It is characteristic of regional writing that with the passage of time, the idealized age is also moved forward, not only because old-timers tend to idealize their generation, but also because no one wants the lost age to be irremediably separated from the present that is contrasted to it. For the '80s, then, the golden age came to include the whole period that had been abruptly—and tragically, as people North and South now came to think—ended by the Civil War. For obvious reasons, this was especially true in the South. In a fanciful attempt to imaginatively "reinstate" a benevolent feudalism which had never existed, save in imagination, young Southerners after the War began to call themselves "disinherited knights" and gathered together to hold what they styled "tournaments," modeled after the jousts in *Ivanhoe*. (One of these is well described as symbolic of the Southern mind in Allen Tate's novel of 1938, *The Fathers*.) Clothed in medieval garb, they tilted for prizes offered by aristocratic women conventionally styled "queens of love and beauty."[24] The organizations they invented and joined, like the Klan—with a governing body including a Grand Cyclops, a Grand Magi, and a Grand Turk—and the Knights of the White Camelia, were replete with medieval trappings. They read Scott—a practice which Twain half-seriously claimed had caused the Civil War—and Thackeray, remembering that in their heritage was the blood that Henry Esmond transmitted to his Virginia descendants. When the Northern-oriented, industrialized New South threatened their daydreams, they moved further South, to Mexico with Maximillian at first, then to the European Souths, Rome and Venice. F. Hopkinson Smith, who created the image of the Southern squire in *Colonel Carter of*

---

[23] John Esten Cooke, *Stories of the Old Dominion* (New York, 1879), pp. 7–8. [24] Nevins, *Emergence of Modern America*, p. 208.

Cartersville (1891), flitted from Mexico to Venice. In Venice he could be content, for, as he said in *Gondola Days* (1897): "In this selfish, materialistic money-getting age, it is a joy to live...in a city the relics of whose past are the lessons of our future."[25] Born in New Orleans, America's greatest architect, H. H. Richardson, more subtly preserved the relics of this medieval imagination, in modern buildings like Trinity Church, by turning—contrary to his *beaux arts* training—to the architecture of Provençal France for his inspiration and models. His famous wish—to design a steamboat and a railroad station—arose from his desire to subdue these modern, industrial objects to the shapes and traditions of the medieval ideal. It is no accident that he designed the house of the historian—Henry Adams—who would write *Mont-Saint-Michel and Chartres* and was one of his closest friends. Even as late as 1910, writers like James Branch Cabell retreated to the even deeper Souths of the imagination; and, by dwelling in their Poictesmes— Cabell's name for his idealized past—escaped "that daily workaday life which is to every man abhorrent."[26]

In 1888, commenting on the virtual domination of the magazines by Southern writers, Albion Tourgée defined the Southern myth with understanding since unsurpassed. Around "the myriad of deposed sovereigns," he said, "will cluster the halo of romantic glory, and the epoch of their overthrow will live again."[27] More successfully than anyone else, Thomas Nelson Page defined for the '80s a blissful Old Dominion which had continued to exist until the Civil War cruelly shattered it. His most famous story, "Marse Chan: A Tale of Old Virginia,"[28] consists of an ancient Negro's recollections, in 1872, of the life of pastoral plantation days, an age when "distance was nothing...[and] time was of no consequence." Particularly the Negro remembers with pride and continues to be devoted to his former master, "Marse Channin'," killed in the War. He describes the age past in terms which Page derives from the Southern sweet dream of peace:

> "Dem wuz good ole times, marster—de bes' Sam uver see! Dey wuz, in fac'! Nigger didn' hed nothin' *it all* to do—jes hed to 'ten to de feedin' an' cleanin' de hosses, an' doin' what de marster tell 'em to do; an' when dey wuz sick, dey had things sont 'em out de house, an' de same doctor come to see 'em whar 'ten to de white folks when dey wuz po'ly, 'an all. Dyar warn' no trouble nor nuttin'.

In the '80s, Page's version of the myth so completely took hold in the imaginations not only of Southerners but of Northerners as well that even such a formerly fervent abolitionist as Thomas Wentworth Higginson—an officer in a Negro regiment during the war—was reduced to tears by Sam's melancholy recollections of a dead age. Page taught a generation that though the prewar South had some social faults, it offered "the purest, sweetest life

---

25 Quoted in Spiller, *et al.*, p. 832.   26 Quoted in Brooks, *The Confident Years*, p. 343.
27 Albion W. Tourgée, "The South as a Field for Fiction," *The Forum*, VI (1888), 412.   28 "Marse Chan" is collected, along with other stories by Page, in a volume titled *In Ole Virginia* (New York, 1887).

ever lived," and he prompted several generations to mourn this age, now gone with the whirlwind of change.[29]

Even before the war, such emphasis as Page's upon the chivalric myth of the *ancien régime* had been countered and counterpoised by such realistic accounts of Southern violence and brutality as Harris's *Sut Lovingood* (sketches, first published in 1854, book form 1867) and Longstreet's *Georgia Scenes* (1835). It was not surprising, then, that the renewed insistence on the myth after the war—the result of psychic withdrawal caused by the shock of defeat—should have led eventually to a reaction by some South-erners in the opposite direction: to the insistence that the Old South was responsible for the War, and must be wiped away. The nightmare of the present, of the War, dimmed the glitter of the Golden Age. Whether one proposed a reorganization of Southern life in accordance with democratic ideals, as Lanier did; or proselytized for an industrial New South, as Joel Chandler Harris for a time did; or showed that the old South merely fore-shadowed the chaotic state of the new, as Cable did, they all showed how the daydream, uncontrolled, could create the nightmare.

Deriding, then, the romantic appeal of the Old South, a group of Southern progressives promulgated their vision of a South reborn and reconstituted. The South after the War, of course, demanded a remaking, a new beginning in the literal sense. The War had reduced large areas to frontier conditions. Although previously a well-established society, the South now failed to show the great accumulations of property and stable political power ordinarily found in settled cultures. Formerly prosperous, the South's investments in securities and slaves were now worthless; the best land lay vacant, or was sold at prices from three to five dollars an acre—prices corresponding to those on the Western frontier. Houses, public buildings, and wartime factories were destroyed. "In short," as one historian has said, "there was in the South after 1865 a return to the primitive...seldom met with any-where except on the frontier, and rarely on so large a scale even there."[30] Unquestionably, many Southerners after the war felt the sense that the weight of the past had been lifted from them, and, acknowledging the paradox of a fortunate fall in the destruction of the Old South, prepared to make a future. Sidney Lanier ended his essay on "The New South" with a vision of the land, "virgin to plough, pillar, axe, or millwheel," and of Edenic complete-ness, where "a neighborly congregation [of] soils, minerals, and vegetables" would supply man "with all the necessaries, most of the comforts, and many of the luxuries, of the whole world."[31] His was one version of the future for the South—a vision modeled on the Western ideal of the yeoman farmer and celebrated by Lanier in his "Psalm of the West" (1876). Another version

---

[29] Hopelessly driven by such puerile fantasy, Page, when he did not use the Southern myth, turned naturally to the Santa Claus myth of Christmas in such stories as "Charles Whittier's Christmas Party" (1894); "Polly: A Christmas Recollection" (1887); *Santa Claus' Partner* (1889); *A Captured Santa Claus* (1902); and *Tommy Trot's Visit to Santa Claus* (1908). Sidney Lanier, on the other hand, wrote a magnificent satire on the Santa Claus myth in "Hard Times in Elfland." [30] John D. Hicks, *The Populist Revolt: A History of the Farmer's Alliance and the People's Party* (Minneapolis, 1931), p. 37. [31] "The New South" in *Retrospects and Prospects* (New York, 1899), p. 135.

of the "New South," formulated by Henry W. Grady, editor of the *Atlanta Constitution,* was a South remade in the image of the triumphant North, complete with cotton mills, railroads, Northern factories, investment, and emigration—accompanied and supported by scientific farming, popular education, and economic reform. For Grady and other spokesmen of this reborn South, the truly heroic age—the age of steel—was yet to come. They hoped, as the hero of Cable's *Lover of Louisiana* (1918) put it, that the Old South, symbolized by the landed squire, would be "industrialized, capitalized, commercialized, modernized out of existence."[32]

Sidney Lanier : The Real and the Ideal

The best of the Southern writers were caught between the ideals of an Old South that had never been and a Utopian New that had not yet come into being. Sidney Lanier presents a remarkable instance of an imagination pressed by the conflicting demands of these opposing forces. Lanier is often spoken of in critical histories as one of the poets of ideality, and clearly he was concerned with envisioning and embodying in his work the highest of traditional ideals. His imagination was deeply involved with the chivalric past. A revelatory newspaper account tells of such a chivalric tournament as described earlier, which took place at McGaheysville, Virginia in 1879, and in which Lanier took part indirectly: from the veranda of a cottage, Lanier charged the Knights to abandon evil, follow good, and ever to live nobly in the service of their queens. Also pertinent is that four of Lanier's uncles had been named after characters in Scott. Moreover, his friend, the Southern poet Paul Hamilton Hayne, tells us that the medieval romance was Lanier's "daily mental food,"[33] Geoffrey of Monmouth, Malory, Gower, Chaucer, and Langland being among his favorites. Attempting near the end of his life to establish sound finances, he edited four volumes of a prospective series to be called "The Boy's Library of Legend and Chivalry." These were the chivalric tales in which he delighted—*The Boy's Froissart* (1878), *The Boy's King Arthur* (1880), *The Boy's Mabinogion* (1881), and *The Boy's Percy* (1882). "Pot-boilers all," he called them. Yet, in his introductions and annotations he went far beyond commercial necessities by including examples of Old French, analyses of the development of English, quotations from Chaucer, and disquisitions upon the downfall of chivalry in the development of trade. He was, in fact, attempting quite consciously to recreate the atmosphere and attitudes of the age of chivalry for his young audience.

For an age, as Lanier saw it, that had lost the power of its ideals, he attempted to reinvigorate the best ideals of the chivalric past. He recognized, as Howells, James, Twain, and Emily Dickinson also did, that his was a secular age and needed an order based—as chivalry was—upon honor and decency in human affairs. He would make a secular defense against chaos. Here and there in his boy's books he directly expresses his intent, as in the *Froissart,* when he advises his boy audience "to speak the very truth; to

32 (New York, 1918), p. 263. 33 Henry W. Lanier, ed., *Letters of Sidney Lanier: Selections from His Correspondence, 1866–1881* (New York, 1899), p. 220.

perform a promise to the uttermost; to reverence all women;...to be constant to one love; to be fair to a bitter foe; to despise luxury; to preserve simplicity, modesty, and gentleness in heart and bearing."[34] That he was driven to create a heroic myth for his own age is strikingly suggested by the emendations he made in his medieval chronicles. All in the chivalric narratives that he considered unchivalric he ruthlessly excised—that Galahad was illegitimate; that Arthur and his sister produced Modred; that Tristram and Iseult were lovers. In short, he idealized even medieval romance itself, quite unlike English writers—for instance, Bulfinch in his *The Age of Chivalry* (1858)—who were under no similar compulsion to create a myth of myth, and so could be faithful to their texts. Lanier adored these chivalric writers, because, as he said in *Shakspere and His Forerunners* (1902), "they have enlightened us with...celestial revelations of the possible Eden which the modern Adam and Eve may win back for themselves by faithful and generous affection."[35] Using medieval materials to recreate his Eden, he was compelled to make even these mythical, finer than they were. He would write a new Genesis in which—through their human grace—the American Adam and Eve might restore Eden.

Trade, as might be expected, is the diabolic force of dishonor in Lanier's myth. His epic poem, to be called "The Jacquerie" and which he worked on intermittently, was based on the "strange uprising" of peasants in fourteenth-century France, and was to describe, Lanier wrote,

the first time that the big hungers of *the People* appear in our modern civilization, and it is full of significance. The peasants learned from the merchant potentates of Flanders that a man who could not be a lord by birth, might be one by wealth; and so Trade arose, and overthrew Chivalry. Trade has now had possession of the civilized world for four hundred years.... Thus in the reversals of time, it is *now* the *gentleman* who must rise and overthrow Trade. That chivalry which every man has...in his heart...must in these latter days organize its insurrections and burn up every one of the cunning moral castles from which Trade sends out its forays upon the conscience of modern society.[36]

Although he never completed "The Jacquerie," Lanier in his writings as a whole presents a unified and powerful critique and condemnation of trade— "the old spider that has crawled all over our modern life, and covered it with a flimsy web that conceals the Realities."[37]

In "The Symphony" (first published in 1875) this Reality reemerges through the power of art, here symbolized in the various musical instruments of the orchestra, which, singly and in unison, speak out against trade. Violins, strings, the flute, the clarinet, the horn, hautboys, and bassoons oppose their several versions of love against the selfishness implied in merely commercial enterprise:

[34] *The Boy's Froissart: Being Sir John Froissart's Chronicles of Adventure, Battle, and Custom in England, France, Spain, etc., Edited for Boys, With an Introduction* (New York, 1879), p. ix. [35] *Centennial Edition of the Collected Works of Sidney Lanier*, ed. Kemp Malone (Baltimore, 1945), Vol. III, p. 6. [36] In a letter to Judge Logan E. Bleckley dated November 15, 1874, in *Centennial Edition*, Vol. IX: *Letters, 1874–1877*, pp. 121–22. [37] Letter to Hayne dated April 17, 1872 in *Centennial Edition*, Vol. VIII: *Letters, 1869–1873*, p. 224.

How piteous false the poor decree
That trade no more than trade must be!
Does business mean, *Die, you—live I?*
Then "Trade is trade" but sings a lie:
'Tis only war grown miserly.
If business is battle, name it so.

Against the pitiless competition implied by the commercial code of trade, Lanier places the testimony of love variously interpreted: as charity for the poor; in Christ's message that man cannot live by bread alone; in the primacy of intuition over rationality and of child-like innocence over commercial experience; in the love of women; and in the ideals of chivalry. His famous conclusion that "Music is Love in search of a word" suggests that in the harmony and order of Art—such as in the poem he has written— modern man may find the clearest means of understanding the principle of Love.

It is clear, of course, that this poem, quite unlike the proposed "Jacquerie," originates not in a nostalgia for the medieval, but in a penetrating vision of the defects of modern life to which, perhaps, his knowledge of the medieval has given him an advantageous perspective. "The Symphony," and, indeed, a dozen other poems by Lanier, far from avoiding contemporary conditions by embracing chivalric idealism, are among the earliest accurate analyses of the problems posed by the rapid development of industrial capitalism after the War. We tend to forget, because we are largely guided at present by the social sciences in our understanding of social problems and have relegated poetry to nonsocial areas, that American poets—Whittier, Lowell, and Lanier, for example—at least briefly led in the development of social awareness. Richard Hofstadter insists that Lester Ward, for instance, "was the first and most formidable of a number of thinkers who attacked the unitary assumptions of social Darwinism and natural law laissez-faire individualism."[38] Certainly, when Ward's *Dynamic Sociology*, criticizing the business ethic, appeared in 1884, Social Darwinism—the policy of noninterference in the crushing "evolutionary" competition of business—was being widely defended: in sociology by Sumner, and in practice by Carnegie, Gary, Hill, and others. The tradition of American economists—of McVickar and Wayland, for instance— looked back to Adam Smith's pronouncement that "greed and universal competition" were necessary to good management and progress. But Lanier's poem anticipated Ward's book by nearly ten years in its vision of the inadequacies of the notion of the survival of the fittest. Lanier emphasized, first, that modern man's possession of Christian culture, his heritage of its traditional ideals, freed him from following the laws of biological change. Indeed, in his emphasis on the element of cooperation in nature itself, rather than on the element of conflict, which the Darwinists stressed, Lanier anticipated Kropotkin's *Mutual Aid* (1902). In short, alone among Americans in

38 *Social Darwinism in American Thought* (New York, 1959: rev. ed.), p. 68.

the 1870s[39] Lanier emphasized (as Veblen would characterize the development of social thinking in the '80s and '90s) the importance of "peace, good will, and economic efficiency, rather than a life of self-seeking, force, fraud, and mastery."[40] His artistic vision was as accurate and complete as Ward's social version of the mistakes of modern economics.

Perhaps, then, "The Jacquerie" remained fragmentary because it did not sufficiently participate in the double vision of Lanier's mind. The poetry that came from that mind inextricably mingled the real and the ideal. In an outline for a poem that remained unwritten at his death Lanier wrote a Blakean parable on the creative act:

> Youth, the circus-rider, fares gaily round the ring, standing with one foot on the bare-backed horse—the Ideal. Presently, at the moment of manhood, Life (exacting ring-master) causes another horse to be brought in who passes under the rider's legs, and ambles on. This is the Real. The young man takes up the reins, places a foot on each animal, and the business now becomes serious.
>
> For it is a differing pace of these two, the Real and the Ideal.
>
> And yet no man can be said to make the least success in life who does not contrive to make them go well together.[41]

Asked what age he preferred, this lover of chivalry replied, "the Present."[42] His long "Psalm of the West" (1876), recounting, *Columbiad*-like, the settlement of America, leaves out altogether the settlement and glories of the Old Dominion. Intellectually in the Southern tradition, he yet read Wordsworth and Keats rather than Scott, and German as well as French literature; he preferred George Eliot to Thackeray and wrote a book on the English novel justifying his preference. Living in a society that generally mistrusted science and even drove out well-known scientists like the LeConte brothers, Lanier nevertheless spoke of scientific progress as one of the highest achievements of the nineteenth century. "Today," he said, "science bears not only fruit, but flowers also." He read Tyndall and Darwin, studied "science, biology, chemistry, evolution and all," he told a friend in 1880,[43] and wrote a shrewd critique—resembling Henry Adams's—of Huxley. Idealizing the old, he yet wrote an essay calling for a "New South." In the varied recognitions of the claims of past and present, which all of these imply, he truly rode the double horses of his parable. He was the poet whose role, as he describes it in "Corn" (1875), was to bring together, and in his own being transform and reconcile, contraries:

---

[39] The one exception to this—and with Lanier, he makes a curious couple—is Chauncey Wright, the realistic philosopher who influenced Peirce and James. Criticizing Spencer's notion of the survival of the fittest in 1875, Wright wrote: "But he would leave out of the category of natural agencies in politics the paternal care of the rulers of mankind .... This gains him a popular hearing, especially with the youth of democratic America." (*Philosophical Discussions*, p. 57.) [40] Quoted in Joseph Dorfman, *Thorstein Veblen and His America* (New York, 1934), p. 190. [41] *Poem Outlines* (New York, 1908), p. 58. [42] Quoted in Edwin Mims, *Sidney Lanier* (Boston, 1905), p. 311. [43] These remarks are quoted from Mims, pp. 312–13 and 316.

So thou dost mutually leaven
Strength of earth with grace of heaven;
So thou dost marry new and old
Into a one of higher mould;
So thou dost reconcile the hot and cold,
The dark and bright,
And many a heart-perplexing opposite....
Thou took'st from all that thou mightst give to all.

Joel Chandler Harris and the Cornfield Journalist

Visiting the South in 1887, Charles Dudley Warner pronounced it "wide awake to business."[44] A group that centered around the publicity and oratory of Henry Grady had helped to create this condition. Among Grady's friends and co-workers, Joel Chandler Harris was the one most largely responsible for the editorial defense of the New South in Grady's *Atlanta Constitution*. From 1876 until the first decade of the twentieth century, Harris was the editorial paragrapher and then chief editorial writer for this paper. When Grady died in 1889, Harris wrote his biography. Grady was, Harris insisted, "the very embodiment of the Spirit that he aptly named 'the New South'... that, reverently remembering and emulating the virtues of the old... turns its face to the future."[45] Harris, too, seemed to have turned his face to the future, along with the stock speculators, railroad interests, and textile manufacturers who had wrested control of the state from the planting aristocracy and were bent on keeping it from the rural population. From 1876 until Grady died in 1889, Harris's editorials, widely reprinted in the North, spread an unalloyed gospel of the New South.

One of Harris's closest editorial advisers in the North, Walter Hines Page, spoke of the difference he felt between "Joe Harris" the journalist, and "Joel Chandler Harris" the author.[46] He was sure that the journalist did not appreciate what the author had achieved. Certainly it is true that Harris spoke consistently of his *Uncle Remus* stories as "accidents" and even as "the 'Remus' trash." He claimed in public print that he was merely the editor of the tales he gathered, although he had written and rewritten some of them as many as sixteen times.[47] He seemed uncomfortable with the stories he had written. Although he wrote to J. W. Burlinghame, editor of *Scribner's*, "I wish I were out of newspaper work so I could devote my

---

[44] Warner's visit was in 1887, and the quotation is taken from an article, "The South Revisited," *Harper's*, LXXIV (1887), 638. It was later reprinted in *Studies in the South and West*...(1889), in *The Complete Writings of Charles Dudley Warner* (Hartford, 1904), Vol. VIII, p. 123. [45] *The Life of Henry W. Grady, Including His Writings and Speeches, A Memorial Volume Compiled By Mr. Henry W. Grady's Co-Workers on "The Constitution," and Edited by Joel Chandler Harris (Uncle Remus)* (New York, 1890), p. 59. [46] Page's remarks in an interview, "The New South," in the *Boston Post* (September 28, 1881), quoted in Julia Collier Harris, *The Life and Letters of Joel Chandler Harris* (Boston and New York, 1918), pp. 177–78. [47] It is interesting to note that one of Theodore Roosevelt's uncles had earlier taken down some Brer Rabbit stories from an old Negress's dictation, and published these verbatim in *Harper's* where, as Roosevelt testifies, "they fell flat." Only with much labor did Harris give them permanent life.

whole time to stories and magazine work," he turned down an offer from Gilder and The Century Company whereby he would have received a fixed and adequate income for creative work.[48]

He himself was well, even painfully, aware of the distinction between his two selves. Alluding to the unexpected popularity of his novel *Sister Jane: Her Friends and Acquaintances* (1896), which he considered "poor stuff," he attributed it to the appeal of "the brother" in the book, William Wornum. "No doubt," he wrote,

> that's because the brother represents my inner—my inner—oh well! my inner spezerinktum; I can't think of the other word. It isn't 'self' and it isn't—oh, yes, it's the other fellow inside of me, the fellow who does all my literary work while I get the reputation, being really nothing but a cornfield journalist.[49]

Editors were continually irritated by his doubts—those of the skeptical, practical cornfield journalist—of the literary work that the "other fellow" had submitted; on occasion Harris even withdrew work that had already been accepted. In a letter of 1898 to his daughters he again took up the theme of the double self:

> As for myself—though you could hardly call me a real, sure enough author— I never have anything but the vaguest ideas of what I am going to write; but when I take my pen in my hand, the dust clears away and the "other fellow" takes charge. You know all of us have two entities, or personalities. . . . I have often asked my "other fellow" where he gets all his information, and how he can remember, in the nick of time, things that I have forgotten long ago; but he never satisfies my curiosity. He is simply a spectator of my folly until I seize a pen, and then he comes forward and takes charge.
>
> Sometimes I laugh heartily at what he writes. . . . [It] is not my writing at all; it is my "other fellow" doing the work and I am getting all the credit for it. Now, I'll admit that I write the editorials for the paper. The "other fellow" has nothing to do with them, and, so far as I am able to get his views on the subject, he regards them with scorn and contempt.[50]

Much like Edgar Watson Howe, Harris the jovial cornfield journalist kept a firm hand on his literary self, allowing him only the nights, after a day's work had tired the journalist, for his creative riot. He regularly avoided discussions of literary matters. Asked by an editor, for instance, to contribute to a symposium on the historical novel, he characteristically replied: "Now, if you had asked me something about the different brands of pot-liquor, whether that made from collards has a finer flavor than that made from cabbages, . . . you would have found me at home, as the saying is."[51] Lionized in New York in 1882, he refused to make speeches, and even ran into his hotel in a panic. Not long thereafter he would refuse—at the last moment—an offer of $10,000 to lecture with Mark Twain. He was never known to read his Uncle Remus tales in public. Indeed, he even refused

---

[48] *Life and Letters*, pp. 310, 214. [49] *Ibid.*, p. 345. [50] *Ibid.*, pp. 384–85. [51] *Ibid.*, pp. 565–66.

to read them to his children. Throughout life, he stuttered or was speechless in the presence of strangers. Characteristically of the psychic complex that underlies stuttering, he avoided novel situations, even (like Charles Lamb, also a stutterer) refusing to change the style of his clothes as he grew older, and so coming to appear slightly antiquated.[52]

But the "other fellow" took his revenge on the journalist of the New South by insisting upon his own, autonomous vision. Gradually—and particularly after the death of Henry Grady, an alter-ego support for the journalist—the publicist of the New South, the journalist himself, was transformed by the insistent energy of his literary self. This transformation came in the Uncle Remus tales, beginning in the late '70s, while Harris was deeply involved in spreading Grady's vision of the New South. In the December, 1877 issue of *Lippincott's* Harris had read an article on Negro folklore which, he later said, "gave me my cue, and the legends told by Uncle Remus are the result."[53] Only a few days later he wrote an essay on "The Old Plantation," the myth stirred up in association with the folktales. Here he declared that "the memory of the old plantation will remain green and gracious forever."[54] The Ideal began to encroach upon the Real. This was the work of the "other fellow," and it resulted three years later in *Uncle Remus: His Songs and Sayings: The Folklore of the Old Plantation* (1880). For the next decade the journalist and the writer would run side by side. During the week the journalist celebrated the industrial, progressive New South; but in Harris's tales, songs, and legends, and in the rural, pastoral Nature editorials which regularly appeared on Sundays, the "other fellow" celebrated the epic of the primitive, Edenic world of Uncle Remus.

Announcing in the preface to *Uncle Remus* that his book was to be catalogued with humorous publications, Harris also insisted, contrariwise, that his intention was "perfectly serious": "to give to the whole a genuine flavor of the old plantation" as a "sympathetic supplement" to Harriet Beecher Stowe's *Uncle Tom's Cabin*. Uncle Remus—having "nothing but pleasant memories"[55] of the discipline of slavery—replaces Uncle Tom, as dream replaces reality and the Old South replaces the New. In the stories Uncle Remus—the Negro who serves as a father-figure—initiates the white child—who is the product of the postwar "practical reconstruction"—into "the mysteries of plantation lore," revealing the secret mysteries and rituals of an age now passed. The image of initiation appears regularly. In "The Night Before Christmas," the last and one of the best stories in *Nights with Uncle Remus: Myths and Legends of the Old Plantation* (1883), Uncle Remus takes the boy to the Negro cabins and, in a marvelously ambiguous rite, like a priest announces: "Less go back ter ole times":

52 *Ibid.*, pp. 57–8, 178.   53 "An Accidental Author," *Lippincott's Monthly Magazine of Popular Literature and Science*, N.S. XI (1886), 419.   54 The quotations from Harris's essays in this chapter are in *Joel Chandler Harris, Editor and Essayist: Miscellaneous Literary, Political, and Social Writings*, ed., Julia Collier Harris (Chapel Hill, N.C., 1931). This quotation, from "The Old Plantation," is found on p. 91.   55 "Introduction" to *Uncle Remus* (New York, 1880) p. vi.

"Now, den," Uncle Remus went on, "dey's a littel chap yer dat you'll all come ter know mighty well one er deze odd-come-shorts, en dish yer littel chap ain't got so mighty long fer ter set up 'long wid us. Dat bein' de case we oughter take'n put de bes' foot fo'mus fer ter commence wid."

He then leads a hundred voices in a Christmas dance song from the old times, keeping time by striking his breast; and as the little boy drifts into sleep "the song seemed to melt and mingle" into his dreams. It is Christmas day and he has been born anew.[56]

The world into which the boy is initiated is, of course, far from comic. It has the seriousness of the ideal. When one character complains that Uncle Remus never smiles, he replies "with unusual emphasis": "Well, I tell you dis, Sis Temply, . . . ef deze yer tales wuz des fun, fun, fun, en giggle, giggle, giggle, I let you know I'd done drapt um long ago. Yasser, w'en it come down ter gigglin' you kin des count ole Remus out."[57] Furthermore, in the world of Uncle Remus, ordinary values are transformed. The weak Brer Rabbit regularly wins over the strong fox, wolf, cow, and bear; ultimately all the strong animals die violent deaths: the rabbit ruthlessly murders the wolf, for instance, early in the series. Harris had hinted in his preface to *Uncle Remus* that it was "to a certain extent allegorical" that "it is not virtue that triumphs, but helplessness; it is not malice, but mischievousness."[58] Certainly it is clear that the stories are largely allegorical assertions of the superiority of the weak against the strong—of the power of the Old Plantation against the New Industry; of the primacy of the primitive over the modern, of wisdom over power. "The Story of the Deluge," which Uncle Remus tells, rejects the Noah myth and insists that in a congress of animals the crayfishes became so angry when the elephant stepped on two of their family that they bored down until they made holes for the fountains of the earth to "squirt out" and flood the earth. The weakest animals always, these tales assert, have primary strength. Such tales, of course, originally gave the slave society particular satisfaction by implicitly asserting the superiority of the weak slave over his powerful master. In them Harris found a subtle way of expressing his psychic need to rebel against the industrial program to which, as a journalist, he had been committed by Grady.

After Grady's death, new characters emerged in Harris's world. The persona that Harris the journalist first adopted, Billy Sanders—the "philosopher of Shady Dale"—is a rustic critic of the industrial politics that Grady had promoted. In "Mark and Mack, and the Philosophy of Trusts" (1900), Billy satirizes the way McKinley and Hanna have promoted big business. He dislikes reformers, editors, railroad men, and in general "the scramble after the bright dollar."[59] Another persona, "the Sage of Snap-Bean Farm"— a new Horace, reviving the pastoral Sabine Farm—also

[56] "The Night Before Christmas" in *Nights With Uncle Remus* (Boston and New York, 1883), pp. 412, 413, 415. [57] *Ibid.*, p. 338. [58] "Introduction" to *Uncle Remus*, p. xiv. [59] "Mr. Billy Sanders Discourses on the Negro Problem" in *Joel Chandler Harris, Editor and Essayist*, p. 216.

emphasizes the kind of agrarian rejection of the new industrialism that was being voiced politically by Tom Watson. Harris's friend and leader of the Southern Populists, Watson had been violently criticized by Grady and the *Atlanta Constitution*. But as the Sage of Snap-Bean Farm, Harris takes Watson's ground. The Farmer refuses to regard science seriously, and insists that "all the political principles that are worth remembering. . .could be placed on one page of a very small book."[60] One of his most critical disquisitions is entitled "The Philosophy of Failure." In this piece, the Sage, finding the modern standards of commercial success unsatisfactory, elevates "the old Colonel, whose history is in decided contrast to everything that stands for. . . success," above the modern businessman, and so implicitly rejects the new industrial values.[61] As in *Uncle Remus*, the primitive conquers the modern, the failure becomes the true success, the weak is the only strong. It is appropriate, then, that Billy Sanders, the Sage, and the old Negro all appeared together as various personae for Harris in *Uncle Remus's Magazine*, which he wrote for the last two years of his life. At last, his other self had become his only self. Defending "things unseen" in his last Christmas editorial, Harris wrote that he "hopes that Santa Claus will come to [children] while they sleep, and that real Fairies will dance in their innocent dreams!"[62] He was living in the world of the "other fellow's" fantasies. Just before he sank into a final unconsciousness preceding death, Harris was asked how he felt. "I am about the extent of a tenth of a gnat's eyebrow better," he replied.[63] No cornfield journalist would have said that. It was the final triumph of the "other fellow."

Perhaps, then, Harris's "other fellow" had indeed been his true self and had taken on the guise of the liberal progressive merely as a mask, in order to continue writing in a South where the literal satirist might be in physical danger. Harris was well aware of the tender sensibilities of his Southern audience. A writer such as Thackeray, Harris wrote in an essay entitled "As to Southern Literature" (1879), "took liberties with the people of his own blood and time that would have led him hurriedly in the direction of bodily discomfort if he had lived in the South."[64] Masked as a cornfield journalist, a harmless darky, and a jovial farmer, Harris satirized the South emerging in his time by questioning all of the values it was developing. Fearing the results of writing direct satire, he adopted personae who could transmute and suppress the satirical into the allegorical impulse.

George Washington Cable

In an editorial written in 1881, two years after Harris had assessed the possibilities of Southern literature, he was able to offer as evidence of the South's sensitivity to criticism the bitter attacks made upon George Washington Cable's novel of the same year, *The Grandissimes*. Beginning

---

60 "Shakespeare of Modern Business" in *ibid.*, p. 389.   61 "The Philosophy of Failure" in *ibid.*, p. 300.   62 "Santa Claus and the Fairies" in *ibid.*, p. 335.   63 *Life and Letters*, p. 588.   64 *Editor and Essayist*, p. 44.

with the publication of this book and steadily mounting as Cable proposed a series of drastic civil-rights reforms, violent criticism was heaped upon Cable. The region eventually expelled the writer who could not mask his nightmare as its daydream. Finally, Cable would write to his wife: "The South makes me sick, the West makes me tired, the East makes me glad," and then move his family East, from New Orleans to New England, feeling "as though I had never been home till then."[65]

Before finally settling in Northampton, Massachusetts, however, Cable had attempted to define and preserve the integrity of the man of letters in the South. "Literature in the Southern States," an 1882 commencement address at the University of Mississippi, is Cable's remarkable effort to assure—or reassure—himself of the critical freedom that could allow him to remain in the South as a critic of the South. He traces the dissolution of Union into the sectional rivalry of North and South to their divergent ideas of popular liberty. The North continued in and expanded the Western European tradition of human rights while Southern thought, Cable says, failed to fit any of the basic categories of Western social theory—a notion recently repeated and defended by Louis Hartz—and so, Cable concludes, "Our life had little or nothing to do with the onward movement of the world's thought." Reverting to and cherishing pre-Revolutionary ideas in literature, the Southern audience and its writers merely imitated the old and thus lost touch with the revolutionary, progressive heritage that as Americans they swore allegiance to, but that was supported only in the North. Southern literature provided a means of escaping from the contradictions of slavery into antique fantasy: "It was to uphold the old. It was to be cut by the old patterns. It was to steer by the old lights." Cable demands, in conclusion, the destruction of provincial distinctions by the elimination of the constraint of civil liberties wherein separation first originated. We want, he says, neither the Old South *nor* the New South, but "What we want—what we ought to have—is the No South," the dissolution altogether of the idea of sectional distinctiveness.[66] A year later, addressing the graduating class of the University of Louisiana on "The Due Restraints and Liberties of Literature," he suggested that the breakdown of sectionalism could best be accomplished by literature. Thus he called for literary independence—"that we throw our society, our section, our institutions, ourselves wide open to [writers'] criticism and correction, reserving the right to resent only what we can refute."[67] Clearly, he was already feeling the conflict between his vision of social justice and the failure of Southerners to support his efforts to enact his vision in fiction.

By 1884, Cable had decided simultaneously to move North and campaign for Negro rights. In a series of essays—"The Freedman's Case in Equity" (1885), "The Silent South" (1885), and "The Negro Question" (1888)—he brilliantly attacked and exposed the contradictions of actual and practical

[65] Quoted in Arlin Turner, *George Washington Cable* (Durham, N.C., 1956), pp. 152, 222.   [66] "Literature in the Southern States" (1882) in *The Negro Question* (New York, 1888), pp. 41, 42–3, 44.   [67] "The Due Restraints and Liberties of Literature" in *ibid.*, p. 48.

slavery. These essays were aspects of the same historical clarity which had enabled him to write his best novel, *The Grandissimes* (1881), in which he constructed a shimmeringly ambiguous myth of the conflicts and contraries in the mind and body of the South. The very structure of this novel, with its dialectical logic similar to DeForest's and Howells's, is based upon the paradox of the regional dream and nightmare. As the book begins, a New Orleans *bal masque* is nearly over and the dancers are ready to unmask. In a significant grouping, two men—costumed as Epaminondas Fusilier and his Indian queen Lufki-Humma, progenitors of the illustrious Grandissime-Fusilier line—are accompanying two women—one dressed as a monk, the other as a *Fille à la Cassette,* in imitation of an ancestor of the De Grapions, a family which has traditionally been engaged in Montague-Capulet-type strife with the Grandissimes. Indeed, as we penetrate the masks—several chapters later—these disguises have accurately defined this conflict and have brought together in disguise the actual leading representatives of the two families. Furthermore, these living representatives symbolize the past in representing the way their family traditions impinge upon them in the present. The action of the book pushes ever toward unmasking principles and prejudices as well as people. Cable so arranges his symbolism that the world itself becomes an affair of masks, to be stripped away patiently. Some time after finishing *The Grandissimes* he wrote: "It is not sight the story-teller needs, but second sight. . . . Not actual experience,. . .but the haunted heart."[68] Haunted by the masks of divisive reality, Cable drives through them; puzzled and frustrated by sight, he restores the unity of moral truth by second sight.

The true unmasking in the novel is the unmasking, by historical change, of the vain attempt to save the past ideal unchanged. The events of the book begin in 1803, just after the Louisiana cession, when the personal and social as well as the political orders are violently changing. As French control gives away to American—an American governor suddenly appears and old land titles are brought into question—so Joseph Frowenfeld ("an American by birth, rearing and sentiment") arrives in New Orleans, where he soon becomes friends with both Honoré Grandissime and Aurore Nancanou *née* De Grapion. Thus the North and South, innocence and tradition, the democratic and the aristocratic notions of liberty, science and superstition, all meet, conflict, and join. The frequency with which Cable draws upon military imagery in his descriptions suggests the clash of opposites—"Wars in the Breast," as one chapter title has it. After reading his outline for *The Grandissimes,* the critic and realistic novelist H. H. Boyesen wrote to Cable that the book would be a *Kulturroman*—"a novel in which the struggling forces of opposing civilizations crystallize and in which they find their enduring monument."[69] No doubt he thus helped to sharpen Cable's sense of the possibilities in his plot to portray conflict and resolution—not merely of opposite civilizations, but also of contrary families and individuals struggling

---

68 Quoted in Newton Arvin, ed., *The Grandissimes* (New York, 1957), p. x.   69 Quoted in Turner, p. 90.

toward the truth revealed in clash. Verbally, the cultural conflict is dramatized as the difference between Frowenfeld's scientific English, the Parisian French of Honoré Grandissime, the Ciceronian rhetoric of Agricola, and the African patois. In all senses, men here speak different languages. (It was natural that New Orleans would suggest this dramatic use for language; indeed, Lafcadio Hearn's first book, *Gombo Zhebes* [1885], was a study of Creole language and proverbs.)

The clash of culture, then, is not only between the new and old, but also between the Negro and white. There are—we discover when another mask is removed—really two Honoré Grandissimes, half brothers, equally loved by their father. But one—ironically, in this aristocratic society, the elder one—is partially Negro; and, though handsome by Creole standards, lighter than his brother, and educated in Paris, he is rebuked when he dares to appear in Creole society. The ironies are manifold. Toward the end of the book, the free man of color says to his brother:

"You are the lawful son of Numa Grandissime; I had no right to be born." But Honoré quickly answered:

"By the laws of men, it may be; but by the laws of God's justice, you are the lawful son, and it is I who should not have been born."

Finally, language is again employed to symbolize clash and reconciliation: Honoré, taking Honoré f. m. c. into his merchantile house, breaks all traditions for the sake of truth in renaming it "Grandissime Brothers."

The quadroon Honoré, however, is no critic of the shams and evasions in his society. It is left for the story of Bras-Coupé—forming the central episode of the novel—and for Clemence, the *marchande des calas*, to emphasize the strife between black and white, slave and master, the conflict between bondage and freedom. Bras-Coupé, an African prince, has been captured in battle and sold into slavery. Noble, proud, and rebellious by nature, he strikes his master and escapes to a swamp. Finally captured, lashed, multilated, and hamstrung, he dies, a tragic symbol of the degradation of man in slavery. Even in his assumed name, meaning "the Arm Cut Off," he makes himself, Cable says, "a type of all Slavery, turning into flesh and blood the truth that all slavery is maiming." Clemence, on the other hand, formulates, in her criticism of Southern society, a psychological explanation of why slave-holders insist that their slaves are free of cares. "Dey wants us to b'lieb we happy," she says, "dey 'bleeged to b'lieb it—fo' dey own cyumfut." Caught bringing voodoo charms into Agricola's house, she is taken to the swamp where Bras-Coupé hid himself and is shot in the back.

Inevitably, the book is filled with the conflicting images of brilliant light and impenetrable darkness. What Frowenfeld gravely calls "the shadow of the Ethiopian" falls across the bright gaiety of New Orleans society. Honoré, indeed, with a heightened sense of tragic possibility, understands the shadow as "the *Némésis* w'ich, instead of coming afteh, glides along by the side of his morhal, political, commercial, social mistake! It blanches, my-dé-seh, ow whole civilization!" Of course, it is a nemesis which has particularly pursued the Grandissimes, for their old land titles are dubious under the new administration, and economic ruin threatens them. Just as the lands of Bras-Coupé's master become sterile under his curse, so the holdings of the House of Grandissime are crumbling and becoming worthless, cursed by the false conventions and pride of white society. Drawing parallels between his characters and the Greek epic heroes, Cable chronicles the fall of the House of Grandissime by as real a nemesis as any that pursued the Atridae. The parallel is obvious in Cable's catalogue-like account of the gathering of innumerable Grandissimes:

> ...the first-comer, the great-grandsire—the oldest living Grandissime—Alcibiade, a shaken but unfallen monument of early colonial days. . . . Gallant crew! . . . That is Colonel Agamemnon Brahmin de Grandissime, purveyor to the family's military pride. . . .Achille Grandissime. . . .Alphonse Mandarin. . . .Valentine [Menelaus?] Grandissime. . . .He is a large, broad-shouldered, well-built man.

Like the South in general that Cable criticized in his commencement address, the House of Grandissime is embracing the old, the traditional, the mythical. For them, as Agricola declares, "tradition is much more authentic than history" That venerable incendiary—the "aged high-priest of a doomed civilization"—writes an essay on the "Insanity of Educating the Masses." Dying, he warns Frowenfeld against "the doctrine of equal rights—a bottomless iniquity." On his tomb the family carves his last two words—"Louisiana Forever"—but they come more and more distinctly to recognize, "as years went by, that Forever was a trifle long for one to confine one's patriotic attention to a small fraction of a great country."

Honoré is the Apollo—so Aurore thinks of him—to the "shadow of the Ethiopian." The novel is the exhibition of his manifestation of light and his consequent ability to save the House of Grandissime—economically and morally—by transforming it into "Grandissime Brothers," eliminating, by absorbing, the shadow. The novel that thus exhibits Honoré's moral education, of course, suggests the kind of moral growth that Cable believed was necessary in the '80s. It is the imaginative counterpart to his sociological analysis of the "Silent South," as he called it. *The Grandissimes,* he wrote in his diary, "contained as plain a protest against the times in which it was written as against the earlier times in which its scenes were set."[70] He was describing, of course, as James said Venice was, a "visitable past," since much of the architecture of the Creole district in his day dated from the times he was describing. Lafcadio Hearn even wrote an article—illustrated by Joseph Pennell—identifying the houses to which Cable referred in his story. And, of course, the basic dualities remained the same in 1880 as in 1803, as the narrator repeatedly suggests. In short, Cable understood in *The Grandissimes* what a generation of later Southerners would have to discover for themselves. He knew that the past, however ideal it seemed, was the nightmare of the present. Only in that recognition could one go on, he believed, to cut loose from the past and make the ideal future.

---

70 Quoted in Arvin, ed., *The Grandissimes,* p. viii.

Despite Cable's great work in historical and sociological analysis as well as in literature, the myth of the South persisted until the First World War. At the eve of the conflict, Ellen Glasgow published *Virginia* (1913)—an attack, like her earlier novels beginning with *The Descendant* (1897), upon the Virginia Old Dominion. Even then a typical Southern women said to her:

> If only I had your gifts, I should devote them to proving to the world that the Confederacy was right. Of course, I know that even the best novelists are not so improving as they used to be; but I have always hoped in my heart that either you or Annie Cabell's son would write another *Surrey of Eagle's Nest*.[71]

But there would be no new *Surrey*; Cooke, its author, was dead. And only after the war would there be another *Grandissimes*. Then novelists discovered that the myth represented not reality, but a profound projection of Southern needs. As Allen Tate said of himself and his contemporaries, they realized that the myth of the South, the epic of "defeat and heroic frustration" of the Lost Cause, could be "converted into a universal myth of the human condition."[72] For instance, William Faulkner's Yoknapatawpha saga began with his third novel, *Sartoris* (1929), the balancing of a heroic, ante-bellum past with a (therefore) tragic present. This book helped to make Faulkner one of our major novelists by forcing him to discover the omnipresence of a usable past. *Sartoris* begins:

> As usual, old man Falls had brought John Sartoris into the room with him, had walked the three miles in from the county Poor Farm, fetching, like an odor, like the clean dusty smell of his faded overalls, the spirit of the dead man into that room where the dead man's son sat and where the two of them, pauper and banker, would sit for half an hour in the company of him who had passed beyond death and then returned.[73]

Fifty years earlier Cable had made a similar discovery and produced a novel better than all but Faulkner's greatest. Refusing to seek refuge in the comforting paradise of a lost past, Cable projected its contradictions, frustrations, and solutions upon the present. Like the Southern writers who would follow him forty years later, he made a myth of myth.

WESTERN REGIONAL LITERATURE

The myth of the West involved essentially the notion of a revived Eden, not of a past, an *ancien régime*, but of one in the land itself. The land seemed to promise a renewal of the abundance of the lost Garden. Man was to be perfected by Prosperity—a vision shared by Franklin and Jefferson and transmitted to their intellectual descendants; prosperity was mistaken for Paradise. In the West, as the author of *The Eden of Labor* (1876) wrote, "there would be abundance for all mankind."[74] The myth of the earthly paradise—associated with Eden, which was never reported destroyed by God

---

[71] Ellen Glasgow, "Preface" to *Virginia* in "The Old Dominion Edition of the Work of Ellen Glasgow" (Garden City, N.Y., 1929 [1913]), p. viii. [72] "A Southern Mode of the Imagination" in *Collected Essays* (Denver, Colo., 1959), p. 568. [73] (New York, 1929), p. 1. [74] T. Wharton Collens, *The Eden of Labor; Or, The Christian Utopia* (Philadelphia, 1876), p. 116.

or man—has a long history in Western European thought. Usually placed to the West of the known world in the Middle Ages, Eden seemed to have been rediscovered with the discovery of America. On his third voyage, writing in the Gulf of Paria, Columbus announced his discovery of the Garden, "the spot of the earthly Paradise, whither no one can go but by God's permission."[75] Just before the settlement of Jamestown, Chapman was pronouncing Virginia "Earth's only Paradise" in *Eastward Ho*. The early separatist settlers of America regarded themselves as carrying history forward into a Virgin Land, concealed from Europeans until the Reformation. This myth of renewal was reinvigorated by the emphasis of European romanticism upon the noble savage and the primitive in general: Chateaubriand sought the noble man in the savage of the American wilderness. And while Americans, like Melville, were familiar with "The Metaphysics of Indian Hating,"[76] European romantics were beginning to convince us that the savage was the noble anarch.

Thus the myth of the West was the dream of Europe, and later, of the Eastern seaboard, which inherited the European tradition. In the West mankind was, as the American, divinely granted a second chance. After the Revolution, patriots insisted that democracy would preserve American innocence by preventing the corruption of the natural man in degrading or artificial institutions. It would take an acute English critic, Henry Maine, to point out much later that this conception of democracy "bears the credentials of a Golden age, nonhistorical and unverifiable."[77] Americans themselves blithely insisted on the reality of their renewal. Emerson turned his hopes for the nation westward and, aiding the advance of culture, himself lectured as far west as Wisconsin. Whitman announced that in appearance he was one of "the Beginners, the Adamic men,"[78] perpetually going forth like a child, ever starting out on the road, passing to India, ever singing himself and thus singing a renewed creation into being.

The West glittered in the imagination of the East. Not only Whitman and Emerson, but Americans in general, believed the West to be, Bryce said as late as 1888, "the most distinctively American part of America," as promising opportunity, freedom, and purity—in short, renewal.[79] In the early '70s tours of the West became fashionable, and Bostonians thronged the dance halls of Dodge and Abilene. The Grand Duke Alexis of Russia toured the plains and participated in a buffalo hunt organized by Generals Custer and Sheridan and Buffalo Bill. After the hunt several tribes of Indians performed "a grand war dance in honor of the distinguished visitor."[80] Some of these

75 Quoted from another interesting book on the subject, William F. Warren (President of Boston University), *Paradise Found: The Cradle of the Human Race at the North Pole* (Boston and New York, 1885), p. 4. 76 See Herman Melville, *The Confidence Man*, 1857. 77 *Popular Government: Four Essays* (New York, 1885), p. viii. 78 Whitman is writing of himself in a book signed by John Burroughs, entitled, *Notes on Walt Whitman, as Poet and Person* (New York, 1867), p. 85. "As near as I can make it out" Sidney Lanier wrote wryly, "Whitman's argument seems to be that, because a prairie is wide, therefore debauchery is admirable and because the Mississippi is long, therefore every American is God." (Quoted in T. W. Higginson, *Contemporaries* [Boston and New York, 1899], p. 97.) 79 *American Commonwealth*, Vol. II, p. 271. 80 Buffalo Bill (pseudonym for W. F. Cody), *Story of the Wild West and Campfire Chats*...(Philadelphia, 1888), p. 620.

same Indians later took part in the Custer massacre. But Alexis probably saw only the child of nature: myth makes eyes for men.

There is no better example of the ability of the newly revivified myth of Eden to change men's past ways of seeing, while reality remains unchanged, than the reversal of the myth of the Great American Desert. Before the Civil War the notion that a Great American Desert lay just beyond the Missouri widely prevailed. Having himself taken the sea route to California in 1849, Bayard Taylor reported the difficulties that emigrants had faced in crossing the "scorching and sterile"[81] desert. When Taylor traveled to Colorado in 1867, however, he found that a distance of forty miles "embraced all we had seen of the Desert," and declared: "I am fast inclining to the opinion that there is *no* American Desert."[82] In addition, the railroads were conducting extensive publicity campaigns against the notion of the Desert. Having received extensive land grants from the government, the railroads sought to attract settlers to these lands and thus establish freighting business along their routes. They therefore inculcated the reverse of the Desert myth: the notion of a Paradise Valley in the West. Leaflets from the Union Pacific, for instance, called the potential settlers' attention to "a flowery meadow of great fertility clothed in nutrious grasses, and watered by numerous streams."[83] In general, as a contemporary adviser to emigrants warned them, agents rendered "the country a perfect paradise.... The crops are grown without labor, the houses are builded without effort, the live stock takes care of itself, the rain irrigates thoroughly the long-parched soil, so soon as the immigrant plants his foot on it."[84] But the warning was unheeded. The hard times following the panic of 1873 swelled the westward stream of settlers to a torrent. It did indeed seem an Eden, where even the desolate Rockies became the Big Rock Candy Mountains.

It is not surprising, moreover, that almost all of the writers who romanticized the West after the war were transplanted Easterners. Bret Harte from Albany, New York; Artemus Ward from Watertown, Maine; Edward Rowland Sill from Windsor, Connecticut; and Charles Warren Stoddard from Rochester, New York all went West to exploit materials which they knew primarily through the myth that the East had made. As late as the twentieth century Easterners were still teaching Westerners what the West meant. In 1899, Theodore Roosevelt, then governor of New York, read a lecture to the men of Chicago's Hamilton Club. To these Westerners, who, he said, "distinctly embody all that is most American in the American character," Roosevelt, a native New Yorker, preached "the doctrine of the strenuous life."[85] He taught them what it meant to be a cowboy.

On the other hand, Western writers were greeted enthusiastically in an East that was ready to see the West as the next step in the march of Empire

---

[81] *Eldorado, or Adventures in the Path of Empire*...(New York and London, 1850), p. 47. [82] *Colorado: A Summer Trip* (New York, 1867), pp. 32, 41. [83] Quoted in John D. Hicks, *The Populist Revolt*, p. 6. [84] L. P. Brockett, *Handbook of the United States of America and Guide to Emigration; Giving the Latest and Most Complete Statistics*...(New York, 1884), p. 118. [85] "The Strenuous Life" in *Citizenship, Politics, and the Elemental Virtues, Works of Theodore Roosevelt*, ed. Herman Hagedorn (New York, 1925), Vol. XV, p. 267.

and Western writers as the natural heirs of the East. To a large extent, Howells's rapid rise from a journalist in Columbus, Ohio to editor of the *Atlantic* was due to the power this assumption held over Easterners. James Russell Lowell made a particular point of questioning Howells about Ohio. Lowell said that "he had always fancied that human nature was laid out on rather a larger scale there than in the East."[86] Mark Twain was taken into the distinguished Langdon family, and then into the select Nook Farm community of Hartford, Connecticut; all along the seaboard he found his lecture halls jammed and editors anxious to take whatever he might offer; and when he traveled to England, such different men as Darwin, Browning, and Turgenev showed him high respect—all for much the same reasons.

Immediately after the Civil War the largely unknown West did indeed seem a Promised Land. Travelers spoke untiringly of the "boundless mineral and agricultural wealth of the Territories."[87] Western farming came decisively to dominate the national agricultural economy, while mining towns like Virginia City were dotted with magnificent palaces. The ranch came to replace the plantation as the symbol of the expansive life. Railroads sent back bulky testimonials to the success of agriculture, while periodical mining crazes swept California and Nevada. The American imagination projected, as Henry Nash Smith has said, "two quite distinct Wests." On the one hand, the image of the farmer with his sacred plow suggested "fecundity, growth, increase, and blissful labor in the earth." On the other, the free inhabitants of a wilder West implied a rejuvenation of man himself: "Its heroes bore none of the marks of degraded status. They were in reality not members of society at all, but noble anarchs owning no master, free denizens of a limitless wilderness."[88] Typically of the noncontradictory appeal of myth, these two notions frequently amalgamated to form an image of the noble savage in a blissfully civilized agrarian society.

So long as there was available land Americans could experience the hope, as Frederick Jackson Turner put it, of "perennial re-birth."[89] But the nightmare of the real was soon shadowing the myth. Soon after the war, John Hay of Illinois admonished an Eastern myth-maker: "In spite of the praise which you continually lavish upon the West, I must respectfully assert that I find only a dreary waste of heartless materialism, where great and heroic qualities may indeed bully their way up into the glare, but the flowers of existence inevitably droop and wither."[90] As early as 1875 Charles Nordhoff was anticipating with anxiety the exhaustion of these lands as "a serious calamity to our country." "Our cheap and fertile lands," Nordhoff said, "have acted as an important safety-valve for the enterprise and discontent of our non-capitalist population." Lacking these lands, cut off from the

[86] Reported in Howells, *Literary Friends and Acquaintance*, p. 27. | [87] A. K. McClure, *Three Thousand Miles Through the Rocky Mountains* (Philadelphia, 1867), pp. 3–4. [88] *Virgin Land: The American West as Symbol and Myth* (Cambridge, Mass., 1950). Quotations on pp. 52, 123, 52, respectively. [89] *Frontier and Section: Selected Essays of Frederick Jackson Turner*, p. 38. [90] *The Life and Letters of John Hay*, ed. William Roscoe Thayer (Boston and New York, 1908), Vol. I, p. 56.

"limitless" bounty of nature, America would be, Nordhoff wrote, in the same position as the Europe whose ills Americans gloried in describing and despising.[91]

After the '70s, by which time the best lands had all been claimed, this fear was more and more widely expressed. Nature's bounty had been closed not only by the unavailability of productive land, but also by the railroads, which had transformed the farming economy in Iowa, Minnesota, Kansas, and Nebraska. The railroad made the farmer dependent upon national and even international markets. This yeoman found a whole new group of creditors, shippers, and merchants between himself and his purchaser. His sacred plow was manufactured by John Deere in Moline, Illinois. He was no longer a pioneer. As one rural editor wrote, "There are three great crops raised in Nebraska. One is a crop of corn, one a crop of freight rates, and one a crop of interest."[92] In 1883 an embittered social reformer, William Godwin Moody, summed up the transformation of the farmer since the war in a book called *Land and Labor.* "Within the last twenty years," Moody declared, "we have taken immense strides in placing our country in the position in which Europe is found after a thousand years of feudal robbery."[93] Disillusioned, Moody watched the heavily mortgaged lands of the small farmer fall into the hands of railroads and bankers, then reunited as large bonanza farms organized on mass-production principles, where the farmer was merely a seasonal tenant. Even when the farmer managed to hold a land title, W. J. Ghent claimed in 1902, he was really "the joint tenant of the farm implement trusts, the new harvester trust, of the produce trusts which fix the rate of transportation, . . . [and] of the water trusts."[94] Like any medieval peasant, serving the new religion of commerce, he paid his tithes.

"The shattering of the myth by economic distress," Smith writes, "marked . . . the real end of the frontier period."[95] Unable to deal, in terms of the myth, with the tragic cessation of abundance, Americans responded in various ways. Some merely returned East, to cities where an increasingly high standard of living and culture made pioneering seem to have been drudgery. Between 1888 and 1892 half the people of western Kansas come eastward with "In God we trusted, in Kansas we busted" chalked on their wagons. Parts of Nebraska, Colorado, Nevada, California, Ohio, and Michigan declined in population.[96] The restless frontiersman who had earlier been idealized in the legends of Daniel Boone and Davy Crockett now became the rootless vagrant—"these chronic emigrants whose broken-down wagons and weary faces greet you along the dusty highways of the far West"[97]—who Clarence King satirically portrayed in his "Newtys of Pike." Shortly after the

[91] *The Communist Societies of the United States: From Personal Visit* and *Observation: Including Detailed Accounts of the Economists, Zoarites, Shakers, the Amana, Oneida, Bethel, Aurora, Icarian, and Other Existing Societies, Their Religious Creeds, Social Practices, Numbers, Industries and Present Condition* (London, 1875), p. 12. [92] Quoted in Hicks, *The Populist Revolt*, p. 83. [93] *Land and Labor in the United States* (New York, 1883), p. 63. [94] *Our Benevolent Feudalism* (New York, 1902), p. 57. [95] *Virgin Land*, p. 188. [96] Hicks, p. 32. [97] Clarence King, *Mountaineering in the Sierra Nevada* (Boston, 1871; 6th ed., with maps and additions, 1879), p. 3.

frontier closed, in 1893, Coxey's "Army" of vagrants began shuffling its way toward Washington.

Others—those who remained—began to organize in defense of their economic and political interests. The Grange, founded in 1867, grew rapidly and succeeded in procuring government legislation regulating the railroads. As the farmers' burdens seemed to ease, the power of the Grange diminished. But in its wake followed a succession of similar farmer-inspired organizations: the Greenback party, the Farmers' Alliance, and the People's Party (Populists). One party engendered another, as if the mere existence of party organization and rhetoric provided a cushion for the impact of reality upon myth. Certainly Ignatius Donnelly's famous preamble for the People's Party's first national platform suggests, in its shrill cynicism, the pain involved in the shattering of the myth: "A vast conspiracy against mankind has been organized on two continents," wrote Donnelly. "If not met and over-thrown at once, it forebodes terrible social convulsions, the destruction of civilization, or the establishment of an absolute despotism."[98] Donnelly's cry takes on the imagery of the apocalyptic religious crusades. The candidate of Democrats and Populists in 1896, William Jennings Bryan, was called by one of his admirers "the new Christ of Humanity."[99] Westerners formed political organizations with evangelistic overtones in order to legislate the Eden they had lost back into existence.

The image of Eden that lay at the center of the Western myth was, as Arthur K. Moore has well stated, "a structure of irrational expectations."[100] The impossibility of fulfilling the contradictory and fantastic hopes implied by it did not, however, prevent attempts to realize the myth, but only increased the frustration following upon the ultimate failure of those attempts. There is no better picture of the way the myth drove men restlessly and fruitlessly across the continent than Robert Louis Stevenson's in *Across the Plains* (1892):

> Where were they to go? Pennsylvania, Maine, Iowa, Kansas? These were not places for immigration, but for emigration, it appeared, . . . and it was still westward that they ran. Hunger, you would have thought, came out of the east like the sun, and the evening was made of edible gold. And, meantime in the car in front of me, were there not half a hundred emigrants from the opposite quarter? Hungry Europe and hungry China, each pouring from their gates in search of provender, had here come face to face. The two waves had met; east and west had alike failed; the whole round world had been prospected and condemned; there was no El Dorado anywhere; and 'till one could emigrate to the moon, it seemed as well to stay patiently at home. Nor was there wanting another sign, at once more picturesque and more disheartening; for, as we continued to stream westward toward the land of gold, we were continually passing other emigrant trains upon the journey east; and these were as crowded as our own. Had all these return voyagers made a fortune in the mines? Were they all bound for Paris, and to be in Rome by Easter?[101]

98 "St. Louis Platform, February, 1892," quoted in Hicks, p. 436. 99 Quoted in Dixon Wecter, *The Hero in America: A Chronicle of Hero Worship* (New York, 1941), p. 368. 100 *The Frontier Mind: A Cultural Analysis of the Kentucky Frontiersman* (Lexington, Ky., 1957), p. 6. 101 *Across the Plains: With Other Memories and Essays* (Leipzig, 1892), pp. 62–3.

Stevenson's personal Eden was not yet closed; for him it lay peacefully beckoning in the South Seas. But for the Western regionalists, Paradise had been irrevocably lost. Disillusioned with the myth of the Garden, they wrote fiction which rejoiced bitterly in the fall of man. They were realists because they had lost the myth whereby to be idealists, though in everything they wrote they proved how longingly they wished to reinstate a system of romance. Ordinarily these realists are presented in literary histories as consciously seeking to reform literary fashions. On the contrary, and despite their occasional protestations, these writers who are spoken of as the fathers of realism—Eggleston, Howe, Kirkland, Garland—like the Southern writers who have been discussed, were realists only because their myths had been shattered by experience. As soon as the shock of their disillusion was dissipated, they usually either reoriented their value-schemes in accordance with new systems of myth and romance, or eliminated the personal shock of repeated recognition by resorting to the objectivity of historical research and writing. Like Cable, for example, who turned after *The Grandissimes* to writing romance (like *The Cavalier* [1899]) and history (like *Strange True Stories of Louisiana* [1889]), these writers went in one of two directions, both of which veered away from contemporary reality. Essentially idealists yearning to celebrate the myth of their region, they were forced by the real circumstances of economic poverty, moral degradation, and mental desperation in their West to become critics of myth. Only briefly each one of these writers dramatized the nightmare of the grotesque real. Then, in each case, they sought new myths to live by. They "ate" their past, but needed to "have it" too.

Edward Eggleston

In 1850 the Reverend E. O. Neill delivered the sermon for the first official day of Thanksgiving in the Minnesota territory. In it he contended that "the country so far has been as near an El Dorado as any ever found beneath the skies, and its fountains are as renovating as any that are not fountains of eternal life." Three years later J. Wesley Bond, lauding his state in *Minnesota and its Resources,* set up Minnesota *"against the rest of the world and all the other planets,"* yielding to none in fertility of soil, salubrity of climate, and power to rejuvenate morally and physically.[102] To this new Eden Edward Eggleston, then twenty years old, migrated in 1857. During his youth, his family had wandered all over the state of Indiana, living at Vevay (where he was born), New Albany, and Madison, and visiting relatives in such primitive backwoods towns as Clifty, the prototype for Flat Creek in *The Hoosier Schoolmaster.* In 1854 he had visited relatives in Virginia, remaining over a year. In 1856 he made his first trip to Minnesota, returned to Indiana briefly as a circuit rider, then finally settled in Minnesota for nine years. There he would race through a variety of occupations—none successful in this land of plenty, where success was assured: agent for sub-

[102] Quotes from Neill and Bond in Bond, *Minnesota and Its Resources* (New York, 1853), pp. 52, 60.

scription book sets, soap-maker, showman for a "grand stereopticon dissolving view exhibition," and, in between each of these, itinerant preacher. Insatiably restless, Eggleston yielded alternately to compulsions to roam and spells of despondency when away from home. Revisiting Indiana in 1860 only confirmed his sense of alienation: "This was my home," he cried, "but here I had no home. I knew not where I was going or who I was going to see. I walked on. I read the signs and wept! No mother on earth—brothers and sisters in distant lands—no home here."[103]

He only returned home by remaking, in his books, the home he had lost in his youth. The gestation of his first novel, *The Hoosier Schoolmaster* (1871), is instructive. In 1863 Eggleston jotted down some "Hoosierisms"— " 'Outsider,' 'Pison Head,' and 'Ole Hoss.' " He had heard the Hoosier dialect spoken in the backwoods of Decatur County, where he had spent only three months, and he proves that he had sufficiently forgotten the dialect by adding to his notes the (misspelled) name of the Maine humorist, "Artemas Ward," whom he called a "Hoosier classic."[104] Eggleston himself had never spoken the Hoosier dialect. He had seen the backwoods life, his brother said, "in perspective. He always had something better in his own home and associations, by which to measure the rudeness that showed itself all about him."[105] Indeed, as George Cary Eggleston says elsewhere, their parents, fearing contamination of their children's speech, "were more than usually strict in exacting correct usage" from the boys.[106] This background helps to explain what kind of book *The Hoosier Schoolmaster* is. Regularly failing in his business ventures in Minnesota, which he had thought to be an earthly paradise, discontented and alienated as an adult, Eggleston revisited the childhood from which he had been cut off—the primitive childhood which, indeed, he had never had—through the medium of the Hoosier dialect.

In 1870 Eggleston resurrected his list of Hoosierisms and sent them to Lowell, whose *Bigelow Papers* (1848) pointed out Eggleston's way in literature and who encouraged him to collect more such dialectal peculiarities before they disappeared. But by then Eggleston had not been to Indiana for nearly two decades; he had been living in Chicago for four years, and was soon to move even further east, to Brooklyn and New York, where he would spend the rest of his life. As early as 1869 he wrote: "I begin to wish I was a Yankee. I think I should like to be a Pilgrim Father. . . . I begin to think that Puritanism is Tip-topism."[107] Becoming a Yankee, he intensely felt the loss of his simpler, rural past, and so became the Hoosier he had never been. His Hoosierisms he recollected not in tranquillity, but in the hurry of large cities, harassed by the weekly deadlines of the publications for which he now worked. His collection of Hoosierisms, far from reminiscent, were, like his mind and his novels, the result of what he called a sense of "comparative sociography."

103 Quoted in William Pierce Randel, *Edward Eggleston, Author of* The Hoosier Schoolmaster (New York, 1946), p. 61.   104 Quoted in *ibid.*, p. 79.   105 George Cary Eggleston, *The First of the Hoosiers: Reminiscences of Edward Eggleston and of that Western Life Which He, First of All Men, Celebrated in Literature and Made Famous* (Philadelphia, 1903), p. 14.   106 *Recollections of a Varied Life* (New York, 1910), p. 8.   107 Quoted in Randel, p. 100.

He produced *The Hoosier Schoolmaster* for *Hearth and Home,* a dying periodical he was trying to revive. A decade before, he had denied novels a place in his home and, indeed, in 1870 owned only one novel. But his book flowed quickly and spontaneously; and when the first three installments raised the magazine's circulation, he continued and finished his novel in ten weeks. The book tells, essentially, the fable of initiation. Ralph Hartsook arrives, as the book opens, in Flat Creek to apply for the new schoolmastership. "He had lived a bookish life," Eggleston tells us. But now, he has "a delightful sense of having precipitated himself into a den of wild beasts." Like a raccoon which he sees a pack of dogs violently destroy, he feels that among the people of Flat Creek he is in "the midst of a party of dogs who would rejoice in worrying his life out." From the civilized town of Lewisburg (the Vevay of Eggleston's birth, where the Swiss townsfolk spoke English and French), which now seems "like Paradise," he is plunged into the savage, primitive hell of Flat Creek. But this, he says, is "what he needed." In the course of the book Ralph succeeds by learning to be animal-like, imitating a bulldog, "quiet but invincible."

The world of savage violence is paralleled by the evil that momentarily seems to dominate the universe. A child advises Ralph: "Better get away from Flat Creek. You see God forgets everybody down here." Here the countryside has a gnarled, diabolical aspect which suggests a wasteland. Even the inhabitants of Flat Creek are degraded and hopelessly grotesque. Squire Hawkins, for instance, is a mere man of patches and separable parts— a coat too small, a dirty wax-colored wig, dyed whiskers, spectacles that fall off regularly, a set of badly-fitted false teeth, and a ghastly glass eye "perpetually getting out of focus by turning in or out." As the language of Flat Creek is a corruption of human speech, so the bodies of its inhabitants are caricatures of the human form. As Ralph's civilization is measured by the extent to which it survives exposure to savagery in Flat Creek, so good comes violently into contact with evil. That which Saint Paul called the "Old Adam," Eggleston says, "Darwin would call the remains of the wild beast." It seems briefly to Ralph "that the final victory of the Evil, the Old Adam, the Flesh, the Wild Beast, the Devil, was certain." But finally, in this morality scheme, the "good angel" wins out over "the demon" and Ralph's justification, socially and morally, is complete. The story proves—contrary to one of the characters' embittered conviction—that "God has not forgot" and that the universe runs ultimately on moral principles. Ralph has been transformed and strengthened in transcending savagery and evil and, "like the knights who could only find the Holy Grail in losing themselves,...[he] found the purest happiness."

Eggleston's response to the Western myth is a violent exposure, as he says in his preface, of "the unreal world to which Cooper's lively imagination had given birth."[108] His own men of nature are neither noble nor pure, but strangely distorted. In a long series of Indian tables which he wrote for magazines and which curiously parallel and complement his studies of white

108 "Preface" to *The Hoosier Schoolmaster* (New York, 1871), p. 5.

savagery, Eggleston insisted on distinguishing between the noble savage of poets and "the wild and brutal savages themselves."[109] Still, he returned again and again to his primitive life for his fiction. Like Hartsook, he seeks to escape from savagery by being initiated into it. He writes a modified Grail myth in which Eden is restored only after one passes through the wasteland of evil. When Albert Charlton, in Eggleston's *The Mystery of Metropolisville,* first arrives in Minnesota, he "cried out that it was a paradise." "Mebbe tis," his companion sneers, "but anyway, it's got more'n one devil into it." In each of his novels Eggleston manages to sift the evil out until only the essential paradise remains. In *The End of the World* (1872), the sequel to *The Hoosier Schoolmaster,* the lovers August and Julia are poised between the excitement of a Millerite announcement that the millennium is about to arrive catastrophically, and the eccentric medievalism of a "backwoods philosopher" who is equally convinced that the world has been in decline ever since the Middle Ages. Both of these myths, Eggleston implies, were ways of avoiding the commonplace drudgery of Western life— "day-dreaming" that "unfits us for duty in this world of tangible and inevitable facts."[110] Yet true happiness is neither in a New Jerusalem to come nor in an *ancien régime,* but only, as the lovers learn, in this world.

In *The Mystery of Metropolisville* (1873), Eggleston portrays the unsettled society of a 1856 Minnesota boomtown, with its host of self-seeking speculators, swindlers, "land sharks," and town projectors. Albert Charlton has been east to college and picked up progressive ideas along with a feeling of intellectual superiority that make him as selfish as any Metropolisville land shark. Only after a year in prison does he realize the need for *caritas.* The book ends as he marries and becomes the leading citizen of a town he founds—Charlton—the symbol of his transformation into a community man.

Similarly, Mort Goodwin, hero of *The Circuit Rider* (1874), becomes the modern equivalent to the Knights Templar through the spiritual conversion that transforms him from a backwoodsman into a circuit rider who "obliterated his dialect." Like all of Eggleston's characters he moves, as Eggleston describes it, through "a melange of picturesque simplicity, grotesque humor and savage ferocity, of abandoned wickedness and austere piety." To regain Eden—as these characters do—one has to cast out the devils which threaten it. Eggleston's books consist of attacks on the Garden; but at his paradoxical conclusions his characters and the readers are left firmly in possession of their Earthly Paradises. He regains the Garden by sending forth heroes who prove their goodness in a world of evil. At the conclusion of their journeys through the Western Wasteland they (like T. S. Eliot's Tiresias) intone "Datta Dayadhvam Damyata," and Eden appears.

After he had begun *The Hoosier Schoolmaster,* Eggleston seized upon Hippolyte Taine's *Philosophy of Art in the Netherlands* as providing justification for his use of commonplace materials in his "humble, homely, Hoosier

---

[109] "Little Crow, The Sioux Chief" in *The Little Corporal, Fighting Against Wrong, and For the Good, the True and the Beautiful,* I (1865), 51. [110] *The End of the World* (New York, 1872), p. 278.

story"—although earlier, in 1870, he had reviewed the book for *The Independent* in a perfunctory manner. For the preface to *The Mystery of Metropolisville* he adapted parts of Taine's critical theory to his own uses and claimed that

> the work to be done just now...is to represent the forms and spirit of our own life....I have wished to make my stories of value as a contribution to the history of civilization in America....Of the value of these stories as works of art, others must judge....I have at least rendered one substantial though humble service to our literature, if I have portrayed correctly certain forms of American life and manners.[111]

As the myth of Eden ceased to drive him after years of living in cities, he stopped writing novels wherein to re-create Edenic conditions and situations. He had written four novels in three years; but now four years would pass before *Roxy* (1878) appeared. During this time he was increasingly attracted by historical studies, and soon after the publication of *Roxy* announced his plan to give up fiction altogether and to write a series of volumes on the history of American civilization. While he would write three more novels, those were very different from his earlier fiction: one was for children; another took place in Illinois; and the third, *The Faith Doctor* (1891), was a story of New York, somewhat resembling Howells's *The Undiscovered Country*.

When Eggleston, himself a former circuit rider, finished *The Circuit Rider,* he became pastor of a Church of the Christian Endeavor, oriented along the lines of the Social Gospel movement, in the Williamsburg section of Brooklyn. His membership grew steadily. He was especially good at dealing with young people—the Sunday School of 1200 was one of the largest in the country. The Paradisal myth retained its hold upon him still, but he eventually replaced religion with history. Four years later in 1878, coincidentally with his turning from fiction to history, he grew weary of his Church and resigned the pastorate, saying that he had not "a shred or a raveling of belief in the supernatural."[112] Now he kept Thomas á Kempis "on the highest shelf," preferring to "walk in wide fields with Charles Darwin." Moving from supernaturalism to naturalism, Eggleston freed himself from the tensions arising from his disillusion with the myth of Eden, which he had implicity sought to revitalize, by criticizing, in his novels. Freed from the myth, he no longer sought entry into the primitive life and consciousness where the myth flourished. If he had earlier wanted to become a Yankee, he was now a confirmed New Yorker, a distinguished member of the Century Club, and had traveled frequently to Europe. When his *Beginners of a Nation* (1896) was published after two decades of work, one reviewer charged Eggleston with Anglophilic views in giving the impression that England alone spawned

---

[111] *The Mystery of Metropolisville* (New York, 1873), p. 7. It is both curious and instructive that a later Indiana writer would independently discover in Dutch art a justification for his own practices in fiction. This was Theodore Dreiser, whose early career as journalist in Chicago and New York is also a remarkable reproduction of Eggleston's. [112] Quoted in Randel, p. 259. See also p. 166.

American culture. His well-known essay, "Wild Flowers of English Speech in America," barely mentions the condition of the language anywhere but in the East. Now he found satisfaction in the romance of the past. While writing *The Graysons: A Story of Illinois* (1888) in Venice, he told his brother, he was delighted,

> after living all day in the atmosphere of the great primitive West, where the scene of the story was laid, to pass almost instantly into the historic surroundings of Venice, which he could do merely by throwing down his pen and going out of doors.[113]

The pen which he had used to gain access to the primitive life of his novels he now cast aside for the warm glow of a Venice evening, where no shadows of discontent played along the solemn canals.

Edgar Watson Howe: The Western Nightmare

Eggleston, said Hamlin Garland in speaking for Edgar Watson Howe, Joseph Kirkland, and himself, "was the father of us all."[114] Of the writers in the tradition which Eggleston fathered, Howe made the earliest impact upon the American consciousness. In 1883, after *The Story of a Country Town* had been refused by several publishers, Howe himself set his book into type and printed it on his Atchison, Kansas newspaper job press. It was an immediate sensation, and within two years was reprinted twenty-five times. In his novel Howe vividly expressed the tensions that many sensitive American writers felt, and so evoked an immediate response from them: the copies he mailed—out of "violent enthusiasms" for *A Modern Instance* and *Roughing It*—to Howells and Mark Twain brought equally enthusiastic reactions. Howells reviewed the book in *The Century* while Twain responded by commenting—the first time, he said, that he had ever thus commented— that Howe's "picture of the arid village life is vivid, and what is more, true. I know, for I have seen and lived it all."[115] In a Chicago periodical Joel Chandler Harris pronounced the novel "the most characteristic American story that has thus far been written." George Washington Cable, who listened as Mark Twain read him passages of the book, shouted, "Superb! He is colossal!"[116] Several other critics suggested that *The Story of a Country Town* was the closest an American had come to writing a novel defining, by dramatizing, the American experience.[117] Despite its defects of sentimentality, conventionality, and artificiality in plot and characterization, the "constant note of sadness"[118] that Henry Nash Smith finds in the novel gives it a remarkable power. Better than any other novel of the period, it suggests how

---

[113] George Cary Eggleston, *The First of the Hoosiers*, p. 362.   [114] *My Friendly Contemporaries: A Literary Log* (New York, 1932), p. 131.   [115] Quoted in C. E. Schorer, "Mark Twain's Criticism of *The Story of a Country Town*," *American Literature*, XXVII (1955), 110. Howells's review was in *The Century*, XXVIII (1884), 632–33. [116] Quoted by Claude Simpson, ed., in *The Story of a Country Town* (Cambridge, Mass., 1961), p. x.   [117] In *Plain People* (New York, 1929), Howe himself well expressed the regionalist theory that "in every town there is material for the great American novel" (p. 184).   [118] *Virgin Land*, p. 245.

the agrarian dream had been shattered and left only an embittered vision of futility.

The critical response to Howe's novel strikingly illustrates the way in which literate Westerners rejected the myth that Easterners had made of the West. Westerners saw in its disillusion a true reflection of Western life. Twain insisted upon its fidelity to bitter fact; while in his letter to Howe, Howells called the novel "a very remarkable piece of realism." In his subsequent review Howells added that whoever has lived in a country town "must recognize the grim truth of the picture," and praised Howe for refusing to portray the West's "rough and rude traits as heroic." On the other hand, Horace Scudder, reviewing the novel in the *Atlantic Monthly,* conceded its power while insisting that it was "a nightmare without the customary self-conviction of the nightmare"—or a fantasy "spun from the brain of the writer" that seems "to turn the very moon to green cheese."[119] An Easterner, Scudder was not able to understand the intensity of Howe's disillusioned book as a reflection of real conditions in the West. Hamlin Garland, a transplanted Westerner, standing confusedly between the two positions, called the book "real yet unreal." As we can now see from the evidence of later books by Howe—especially *Country Town Sayings* (1911), *The Anthology of Another Town* (1920), and his autobiography, *Plain People* (1929)—virtually every detail in the novel is drawn from fact, except for some of the romantic elements that Howe incorporated into his story in imitation of the reigning formulas for fiction. His mood of despair and futility is derived from the juxtaposition of the real with an ideal society. Thus the "real" elements are transformed by the intensity of emotional response to the hero's failure. Howe's intensity can be measured only by the fantastic expectations that the myth allowed and even encouraged. Howe, very much like Joel Chandler Harris, wrote the book, he says in his preface, "entirely at night," when he was exhausted from "a hard day's work as editor and publisher of a small evening newspaper." Like Harris's, Howe's "other fellow" was released at night when the consciousness was wearied by a day of newspaper routine. This is reflected in the fact that although he had originally intended to write a romantic, conventional novel about the eccentric Damon Barker, certain inward compulsions forced him to dramatize the tragedy of Jo Erring. It is the expression of his deepest nightmares of a dark world that the daylight and daydreams had denied. By the time Howe finished his novel he had so little understanding of its point that he claimed, "If it proves a success or a failure, I shall not be surprised, for I have no opinion of my own on the subject."[120]

The object of the book, narrated ten years after Jo's death by Ned Westlock, is to depict the grim, degraded lives of farmers in Kansas by retelling the Garden of Eden story—a second fall from grace, complete with the conventional characters of the morality drama. Jo Erring, the erring or sinning central character, plays Everyman to the contending spirits of

[119] "Recent American Fiction," *The Atlantic Monthly,* LV (1885), 126–27. [120] "Preface" to *Story,* p. 3.

familial joy in The. (Theodore) Meek and of selfishness in Clinton Bragg;
a humanitarian minister named Goode Shepherd offers, as a title chapter
says, "A New Dispensation"; a lazy, particularly curious farmer named
Big Adam cultivates an overgrown garden, "the worst-looking place on
earth."

"Ours was the prairie district out West, where we had gone to grow up
with the country," Ned begins. "The dusty tramp of civilization westward, . . ." he continues, "seems to have always been justified by a tradition
that men grow up by reason of it." The hopeful first settlers named their
town Fairview. But ironically, Fairview centers in "the bleakest point in
the country," its citizens are "miserable and discontented," and instead
of growth, the West that the narrator knows means only sterility in crop
failures, disillusionment in bankruptcy, and disappointment in systems of
credit and railroad rates. The hopeful "fair view" is blighted by economic
disaster: reality cannot support the myth. Thus the novel is littered with
broken wasteland images of sterility, death, and evil. Even commonplace
circumstances assume ominous significances: a graveyard, where Ned had
played as a child, surrounds the church, where the steeple bell rings fitfully
in the wind "as if the ghosts from the graveyard had crawled up there"
to toll it. Ned's white house "looked like a ghost at night," and after ten
years he remembers Fairview as wholly enveloped in shadow—"because the
free air of Heaven had deserted them [the townspeople] as a curse."
Another town in which Ned lives, Twin Mounds, is situated on the site of
former burial grounds; and the novel's third dismal town is appropriately
named Smoky Hill. Instead of the Earthly Paradise, indeed, Fairview and
these other Western towns are portrayed as hell-like. In his dying breath
Dr. Tremaine—with whose wife the Rev. Westlock runs away—"referred
to his wife as a snake, and to his neighbors as devils." Westlock himself,
Ned says, was a "worthy man driven by a fiend with whip and lash."
Clinton Bragg, whose sullen presence destroys Jo's happiness, is evil incarnate. Jo observes that he "looks like one of the Devil's sons." His room,
people say, reconstructs the Earthly Hell—"it was full of stuffed snakes,
lizards, bats, and other hideous things; . . . his match-safe was a human
skull; and . . . a grinning skeleton hung against the wall. . . . [It] was quite
generally believed that the Devil called on him every bad night." Surrounded
by decay, death, and evil, the people who came west to "grow up with
the country" are merely degraded by it. The Garden of Eden becomes the
Garden of Evil.

This shift is recorded dramatically in Jo's passage from hope to despair.
In the beginning of the book he believes in the conventions of the Protestant
Ethic. "I am very happy here," he says, "but after all there is nothing
like a fairy story in it; nothing unreal, and nothing that is likely to
melt away. . . . I am simply in a place where if I work hard, I shall get
something for it." For him, the universe morally corresponds to the worth
of an individual. By the end of the novel, after a marriage made bitterly
unhappy by his jealously, he has come to believe "that unhappiness attends

every condition in life." He had "offered to sell [himself] to the Devil to be married to Mateel"; but by the time of his marriage his hopes have already been shadowed by his discovery that his wife had once loved Clinton Bragg. His innocence is debased by experience: "She had the experience which I should have had," he says of Mateel, "while I had the innocence and faith in marriage which a wife should possess." He dreams repeatedly of a cave in which a "delicious symphony" is drowned in "coarse uproar and laughter, as if the Devil and his imps were flushed with wine at a banquet, and were telling each other of the follies of men." This remarkable dream becomes so oppressively real that he enters it daily, even while awake, and seems to hear a voice crying for help from the cave. Against the grim darkness of the cave is presented the dazzling light of "the eternal city," against the diabolical discord plays the "delicious symphony," through which the voice in pain cries. Hope and memory offer themselves, but Jo comes to believe that it is he who cries for help from the cave, where he is irretrievably lost. Thus he has "passed into [the Devil's] possession body and soul" and, dumbly hoping for a release from pain in oblivion, ends his tragedy in the only way he can imagine, by committing suicide.

While Jo's disillusionment dramatizes the helpless decline of the Western myth of human possibility, Lytle Biggs is consciously the shrewd critic of that myth. A professional politician and publicist, he has no illusions about the Great West, but preys upon the farmers who have been, like Jo, blinded by agrarian clichés. "The pretense that a man cannot be honest except he plow or sow for a living, is not warranted by the facts," he tells Ned in confidence, "...but because politicians who occasionally have use for them have said these things, the farmers go on accepting them." He organizes and harangues meetings of the Farmers' Alliance, and commands a good fee, "for I never fail to relate how honest, how industrious, how intelligent, and how oppressed [farmers] are." He has observed that "when a Western man gets a considerable sum of money together, he goes East to live," and has drawn the inevitable conclusion. Picking up the theme of the book, which all the characters refer to, he concludes that the West is essentially debased, its population made of those "who came here to grow up with the country, having failed to grow up with the country where they came from."

Biggs is clearly in the aphoristic tradition of Western humor, which with its cynicism and disillusionment, perhaps better than any other popular form, confirmed the widespread repudiation of the Adamic ideal. H. W. Shaw, under the name of Josh Billings, annually sold as many as 127,000 copies of his *Farmers Allminax* for ten years (1870–79). Bill Nye sold nearly 500,000 copies of his *Comic History of the United States* (1894) John Phoenix (G. H. Derby), G. W. Peck, and Petroleum V. Nasby (David Ross Locke) all sold rapidly during and immediately after the war. Howe shares this tradition: Biggs's comment, "A man with a brain large enough to understand mankind, is always wretched, and ashamed of himself," is echoed by all of the Western humorists—by Josh Billings's observation that "Every man has a weak side, and some have two or three"; by Bill Nye's remark that "Our church sociables and homicides in the West will compare favorably with those of the effeter cities of the Atlantic slope. Our educational institutions and embezzlers are making rapid strides"; or by Petroleum V. Nasby's prefatory warning: "I didn't put these thoughts uv mine upon paper for amoozement. There hern't bin anythin amoozin in Dimocrisy for the past five years."[121]

After *The Story of a Country Town*, Howe's work went in two directions. His subsequent novels are romances extraordinarily different from the anti-romantic *Story*. They are the kinds of novels Howe had intended to write in the first place, before his "other fellow" took over. He had rid himself of his personal agony in his first novel, and wrote only romantic compensation for that agony thereafter. On the other hand, disillusioned still with his West, he become an aphoristic satirist in his journalism. He emerged the most famous paragrapher in the United States, in a sense making himself into a Lytle Biggs by exorcising the Jo Erring from his consciousness. He would finally say in *Plain People* that "as a literary critic, I am compelled in old age to desert poor 'Jo Erring.' "[122] But he remained the cynical critic of reform, idealism, and progress. "Faith may have removed mountains way off somewhere, a long time ago," he wrote in *Country Town Sayings*, "but it won't remove a wart at home this week."[123] In *The Blessings of Business* (1918) he wrote: "In our public affairs we attempt to put into effect the programme of every braggart, providing he will brag of education, patriotism, gallantry, religion, human brotherhood, Christianity, liberty, and kindred subjects."[124] A year later, in a volume of *Ventures in Common Sense* (1919), edited and introduced by H. L. Mencken, who admired and resembled Howe, the Kansan insisted that "pessimism is always nearer the truth than optimism."[125] He even subsequently turned against literature and frequently declared that "the less you think about the poetic sort of things the better off you are"; for he had come to think of writers as "mere entertainers, as are strolling players, circus performers, and musicians."[126] When he retired after thirty years from the editorship of the Atchison, Kansas *Globe* he followed Lytle Biggs's advice and went east, spending his last years—minutely recorded in four books—traveling restlessly around the world. Like Joel Chandler Harris, Howe managed to destroy his alter ego. But in submerging Jo Erring's agonizingly personal experience of defeat beneath the indifferent "Sayings" of Lytle Biggs, he made peace with reality only by surrendering his sensitivity to the conditions that drove him to cynicism.

121 Henry W. Shaw, *The Complete Works of Josh Billings* (Sydney, 1919), p. 448; Edgar Watson Nye, "Our Forefathers" in *Bill Nye's Remarks* (Chicago, 1893), p. 203; David Ross Locke, *"Swingin Round the Circle"* (Boston and New York, 1873), p. 7. 122 Howe, *Plain People*, p. 217. 123 *Country Town Sayings: A Collection of Paragraphs from the Atchison Globe* (Topeka, Kan., 1911), p. 38. 124 *The Blessings of Business* (Topeka, Kan., 1918), p. 76. 125 (New York, 1919), p. 270. 126 *Country Town Sayings*, p. 26; *Ventures in Common Sense*, p. 124.

The Silent World of Ambrose Bierce

Ambrose Bierce was another writer whose simple and perhaps even sentimental idealism was inverted into misanthropic cynicism. Born in Ohio in 1842, he served with distinction in the War, then moved to California. There he would remain for most of his life—except for four years when he lived in London and wrote for satirical periodicals; and for a brief period when he was stirred by the mining fever that occasionally inspired vague hopes of wealth in even the most embittered Westerner, serving as general manager of a mining company near Deadwood, South Dakota. Even near the end of his life, at the age of seventy, after years of bitter, cynical writing, he still felt the conventional attractions of the Western myth. "In the West," he wrote to a friend, "is room enow to expand the mind and heart. *Even at my age* I feel the 'call of it,' and it is among the probabilities that I shall not 'return to civilization' when I again get out of it."[127] As, of course, he did not.

Yet the picture of Bierce as an egotistical, malign journalist drawn by Josiah Royce in his novel of California, *The Feud of Oakfield Creek* (1887), is reasonably accurate. He was a fierce and stern moralist living in what he believed to be an age of moral looseness. For three decades he exposed, with apparently perverse relish, the rottenness of American life, its political corruption, its moral debasement, its economic chicanery. Heading the news staff of the Hearst *San Francisco Examiner* in Washington for the struggle against Collis P. Huntington's proposed Funding Bill in 1896, Bierce sent back headlines like: "Bierce on the Funding Bill. He Tells How Huntington in Washington is Fighting Fiercely, Like a Cornered Rat, With His Old Familiar Weapons, a Paid Press and a Sorry Pack of Sleek and Conscienceless Rogues." When Huntington confronted Bierce and demanded pointedly: "Well, name your price; every man has his price," Bierce's reply was headlined across the country. "My price," he answered, "is about seventy-five million dollars, to be handed to the Treasurer of the United States."[128] His price was unfailing honesty, devotion to duty, fidelity—a combination of inherited puritan virtues (he was descended from William Bradford, the Pilgrim leader, through his mother) and the military virtues that the army had instilled in him. So stern was his morality that it was everywhere unsatisfied. He criticized every aspect of American life. *The Devil's Dictionary* (1906) is his demonstration that the whole thesaurus of American life had been depraved. In his journalism he recorded his revelation of the decline of American ideals. The National Anthem Americans had come to sing, he said in *The Wasp*, was "A Rational Anthem," which begins: "My country, 'tis of thee, sweet land of felony." "Patriotism" he defined as "combustible rubbish ready to the torch of anyone ambitious to illuminate his name."[129]

---

[127] Quoted in Paul Fatout, *Ambrose Bierce: The Devil's Lexicographer* (Norman, Okla., 1951), p. 306. [128] Quoted in *ibid.*, pp. 214, 215, 219. [129] *The Devil's Dictionary* in *Collected Writings*, ed. Clifton Fadiman (New York, 1946), p. 323.

To his essentially puritanical ideals the morals of contemporary Christianity could not measure up. In his *Devil's Dictionary* he defined "Christian" as "one who believes that the New Testament is a divinely inspired book admirably suited to the spiritual needs of his neighbor. One who follows the teachings of Christ in so far as they are not inconsistent with a life of sin."[130] Rejecting the Christianity of his times, he proclaimed in *The Devil's Dictionary* and *The Fiend's Delight* what he called "the True Creed of Satanic Obsession," in an elaborate illustration of how the degraded American faith was far less pure than his diabolical counterpart. In these he writes the American, regional nightmare version of William Blake's *The Marriage of Heaven and Hell*. Following Emerson's "Self-Reliance" to its extreme, and feeling that his morality came not from the corrupted Christianity that he knew, he as much as echoed Emerson's "If I am the Devil's child, I will live then from the Devil." Like Whitman, he chanted the square deific, one in which the Trinity formed a minority. Like Mark Twain, his illusions were dispelled by the Mysterious Stranger. Like Thoreau, he found his virtue where and as he could: "If not good, why then evil," Thoreau had written—"If not good god, good devil." Finding no good god, Bierce made the best of the devil. Failing, too, to find the good life, in scores of stories and sketches he made the best of violent death.

In the modern wasteland, only violent death has the intensity of life, a discovery that Hemingway, somewhat in Bierce's manner, would later make the subject of his own fiction. Bierce's stories repeat again and again the cycle of dull life and violent death. Earlier, in Chapter One, mention was made of the kind of new mind emerging in the later nineteenth century, one characterized by a highly developed sensitivity to detail without a corresponding sensitivity to moral discrimination. Bierce's stories perfectly reflect this psychic condition. In the presence of death, his characters are intensely observant, often witty, sometimes ironical, occasionally even absurdly gleeful. Their souls are summed up in the intensity of their sensations—but beyond these they have nothing. All the traditional values evoked by life and death are entirely absent, leaving only the insistent report, as in a newspaper, of their curious existence. Consider the beginnings of some of his stories: *Oil of Dog*: "My name is Boffer Bings. I was born of honest parents in one of the humbler walks of life, my father being a manufacturer of dog-oil and my mother having a small studio in the shadow of the village church, where she disposed of unwelcome babies"; *An Imperfect Conflagration*: "Early one June morning in 1872 I murdered my father—an act which made a deep impression on me at the time"; *One Summer Night*: "The fact that Henry Armstrong was buried did not seem to him to prove that he was dead: he had always been a hard man to convince." In these stories, as in others, Bierce uses characters whose consciousness refuses to go below the surface of events, behind facts. Only the mechanical motions of fact, never the values or emotions that lie behind facts, are recorded.

130 *Ibid.*, p. 211.

Moreover, Bierce's leading characters are remarkably inarticulate. This is perhaps the chief feature of the grotesque world he creates. It is a world of silence, a world without values and therefore only dimly understood. In "The Affair at Coulter's Notch," for instance, Captain Coulter obeys his orders to bomb enemy forces near a plantation house—his own, it turns out—without remonstrance. Downing Madwell, victim of "The Coup de Grâce," meditates over the body of a dying friend, kills him out of mercy, and is caught—no doubt, to be himself executed, all without speaking. The most remarkable instance of Bierce's use of the inarticulate is in "Chickamauga." A child who falls asleep in the forest after playing out his childish game of war wakes to find the forest alive with weird, distorted shapes—men crawling, stumbling, dragging themselves through the woods toward the brook:

> He moved among them freely, going from one to another and peering into their faces with childish curiosity. All the faces were singularly white and many were streaked and gouted with red. Something in this—something too, perhaps, in their grotesque attitudes and movements reminded him of the circus clown whom he had seen last summer in the circus, and he laughed as he watched them. But on and ever on they crept, these maimed and bleeding men, as heedless as he of the dramatic contrast between his laughter and their own ghastly gravity. To him it was a merry spectacle. He had seen his father's Negroes creep upon their hands and knees for his amusement—had ridden them so, "making believe" they were his horses. He now approached one of these crawling figures from behind and with an agile movement mounted it astride. The man sank upon his breast, recovered, flung the small boy fiercely to the ground as an unbroken colt might have done, then turned upon him a face that lacked a lower jaw—from the upper teeth to the throat was a great red gap fringed with hanging shreds of flesh and splinters of bone. The unnatural prominence of nose, the absence of chin, the fierce eyes, gave this man the appearance of a great bird of prey.... And so the clumsy multitude dragged itself slowly and painfully along in hideous pantomine—moved forward down the slope like a swarm of great black beetles with never a sound of going—in silence profound, absolute.

Resuming his game, the child runs ahead and, waving his sword, becomes the general of this ghastly band. Not until he arrives at a flaming plantation is it clear that while he slept the battle of Chickamauga has been fought; for he is a deaf-mute who has heard nothing. When he finds his mother, blown apart by a shell, he stands "motionless, with quivering lips, looking down upon the wreck." In the lips, quivering, yet ever unable to express their burden of anguish, Bierce concentrates the tragedy of the inarticulate. Ultimately, Bierce is suggesting, life is meaningless when it can express or attach no meaning to death. Man can say nothing because he knows nothing.

By the complete obiteration of value-discrimination in his stories, Bierce provokes the reader himself into responding emotionally and so bringing to consciousness the values which the rush of daily fact and detail has buried beneath their surface accumulation. His stories, then, are therapeutic. The stories so violently deny all meaning to existence that the reader is forced to assert, from what values he may possess, a meaning for it. Bored by life, the reader is shocked back into it by the terror of death. Bierce's world is so incomplete and biased that the reader must make it whole. Scorning and abusing, above all, traditional values based on hope, faith, love, family, innocence, and sympathy, he forces the reader to commit himself to a morality and a moral view of reality so pure as to be beyond Bierce's fierce satire. For on the summit of the ideal Bierce himself stands. Dramatizing the nightmare, he ever had the daydream in sight. At the end of four decades of unyieldingly harsh criticism, he wrote to a friend of an "enchanted forest...to which I feel myself sometimes strongly drawn as a fitting place to lay down my weary body and my head":

> The element of enchantment in that forest is supplied by my wandering and dreaming in it forty-one years ago when I was a-soldiering and there were new things under a new sun. It is miles away, but from a near-by summit I can overlook the entire region—ridge beyond ridge, parted by purple valleys full of sleep. Unlike me, it has not visibly altered in all these years, except that I miss, here and there, a thin blue ghost of smoke from an enemy's camp. Can you guess my feelings when I view this Dream-land—my Realm of Adventure, inhabited by memories that beckon me from every valley? I shall go; I shall retrace my old routes and lines of march; stand in my old camps; inspect my battlefields to see that all is right and undisturbed. I shall go to the Enchanted Forest.[131]

Still lingering after forty-one years, this Edenic vision of the Happy Valley, of nature uncorrupted by civilization, beckoned to Bierce. Shortly after, in 1914, Bierce disappeared into Mexico, and was never heard from again.

Hamlin Garland

Hamlin Garland and Ambrose Bierce illustrate, in their differences, the polarities of literary temperament. Bierce ridiculed "Miss Nancy Howells and Miss Nancy James," who were, for him, "two eminent triflers and cameo-cutters-in-chief to Her Littleness the Bostonese small virgin"[132]; Garland spoke of both Howells and James with veneration. Dubious about most collective reforms, Bierce spoke of the Populist as "a fossil patriot of the early agricultural period," while Garland threw his energy into reform and lectured to Populist and Nationalist organizations. Bierce's matter-of-fact style, his fidelity to surface realism, is so intense that his work becomes like the "magic realism" in the painters of the *Neue Sachlichkeit:* surreal; Garland's *veritism*—his term for realism true to the perceptions of the artist—always verges toward the impressionistic, and even, in his middle period, becomes unalloyed romanticism. Yet Bierce spoke of his stories as romances, while Garland declared himself Howells's disciple in the battle for realism. Bierce spoke viciously of the regional writers as "that pignoramus crew of malinguists, cacephonologists and

131 *The Letters of Ambrose Bierce*, ed. B. C. Pope (San Francisco, 1922), p. 204.   132 Quoted in Fatout, *Ambrose Bierce: The Devil's Lexicographer*, pp. 131, 146.

apostrophographers who think that they get close to nature by depicting the sterile lives and limited emotions of the gowks and sodhoppers."[133] Garland made his earliest and best reputation by writing prairie songs and regional stories in which emotional and mental action is conveyed by the kinds of speech it prompts. Yet, despite these differences, in his work Garland shows, like Bierce, the characteristic tension of the regional writer —between his sense of a lost past and a present so debased that it shows no resemblance to that heroic past from which it has been severed. Garland thus, by nature and training, wrote two kinds of stories. In the one, he asserts that the present is corrupted, but, hypothesizing progress and amelioration, writes fiction of a strongly reforming character. In his other kind of writing, he rejects the present (and thus the future) in reverie for a golden day long past. With the one hand he is a realist, with the other a romanticist. These are aspects of the double vision of all regional literature. The depth of the writer's romanticism drives him to realism, in a rage to reorder his antiromantic age. Contrary to the claims of many critics that Garland fell into romance after an earlier realistic recognition of social problems in the West, it is clear that from the very beginning of his career both impulses are present and operate sometimes simultaneously, sometimes separately, in his work.

Garland's earliest reputation, of course, was as the rugged naturalist, a lieutentant of Howells in the campaign for realism—one of the Rocky Mountain toughs whom Emerson, Whitman, and others had prophesized would come out of the West. Whitman greeted Garland impulsively as such a Western man: "I always seem to expect the men and women of the West to take me in—what shall I say?—oh! take me in one gulp," he commented after reading an admiring letter from Garland.[134] Henry Blake Fuller, who would long remain Garland's friend, fictionally described Garland as this kind of rugged realist in a story called "The Downfall of Abner Joyce." In the contrast between the aesthete Adrian Bond (Fuller himself) and the "veritist" Joyce, Fuller reveals his understanding of Garland's blunt realism:

"The world is only a big coral for us to cut our teeth upon [says Bond], a proving-ground, a hot-bed, from which we shall presently be transplanted according to our several deserts. . . . I know I ought to shut my eyes to all this and start in to accomplish something more vital, more indigenous—less of the marquise and more of the milkmaid, in fact—"
"Write about the things you know and like," said Abner curtly.
"If to know and to like were one with me, as they appear to be with you! A boyhood in the country—what a grand beginning. . . ."
Abner tossed his head with a suppressed snort.[135]

To some extent, no doubt, Garland self-consciously accepted and assumed the guise of a realist. In 1886, although he had not yet published a book, Garland wrote to Edgar Watson Howe that they two stood together "in

---

[133] *The Devil's Dictionary*, p. 329.   [134] Quoted in Horace Traubel, *With Walt Whitman in Camden* (New York, 1908), Vol. II, p. 163.   [135] In *Under the Skylights* (New York, 1901), pp. 39, 41.

solitary grandeur" in the literature of the great West.[136] His book of essays, *Crumbling Idols*, was intended to be a violent and sensational literary repudiation of the genteel, sentimental, Europeanized East. "Shall we sit down and copy the last epics of feudalism, and repeat the dying Echoes of Romance?"[137] he asks there, and in reply celebrates the spirit of change, creation, vitality—in short, of "veritism." To some extent he became the kind of Westerner that he learned the East expected him to be.

But Garland was also genuinely shocked into realism when, after studying in Boston for three years, he returned west in 1887 to be with his family in Ordway, South Dakota. At Osage, Iowa he stopped to revisit scenes of his youth, but found that the gold had tarnished: "All the gilding of farm life melted away," he recollected later. The "hard and bitter realities" overwhelmed him as he observed "the gracelessness of these homes, and the sordid quality of the mechanical daily routine of these lives."[138] "Why lie about it?" he asked himself, and shortly began writing the score of stories— "Mrs. Ripley's Trip," "Under the Lion's Paw," "A Prairie Heroine," and "Up the Coulee" among others—in which he would tell the truth by rejecting the myth of the West. His actual reconfrontation of daily life in the West of Osage and Ordway hurried him back to Boston to "put on the garments of civilization once more."[139]

In the preface to *Main-Travelled Roads* (1891) he wrote that in this visit "rural life presented itself from an entirely new angle. The ugliness, the endless drudgery, and the loneliness of the farmer's lot smote me with stern insistence." He became "the militant reformer." Other writers had for a century idealized the frontier in writing of man's escape in the territories from the artificial conventions imposed by civilization upon the natural man. But Garland saw and said that the frontier man was even more rigidly caught in the entangling web of conventions. Poverty-ridden; tied to the dulling drudgery of unprofitable farms; disliking the alien Dutchmen and Norwegians who formed cultural pockets about them; hating and fearing the bankers, politicians, and manufacturers who seemed to oppress them; forgetting the culture of New England from whence they migrated—Garland's farm people, stripped of civilization, are terrible, almost subhuman beings, much like Eggleston's Hoosiers—hollow men who have abandoned hope, memory, and desire. Commending Garland's stories, Howells wrote in his "Editor's Study" of *Harper's Magazine*:

> If any one is still at a loss to account for that uprising of the farmers in the West...let him read *Main-Travelled Roads*....The stories are full of those gaunt, grim, sordid, pathetic, ferocious figures...whose blind groping for fairer conditions is so grotesque.[140]

---

[136] Quoted in Jean Halloway, *Hamlin Garland* (Austin, Tex., 1960), p. 24. [137] *Crumbling Idols: Twelve Essays on Art and Literature*, Introd. by Robert E. Spiller (Gainesville, 1952), p. 3. [138] *A Son of the Middle Border* (New York, 1917), p. 355. [139] *Ibid.*, p. 373. [140] Howells's review, which appeared modified as an "Introduction" to the 1893 edition of *Main-Travelled Roads*, is reprinted in Howells, *Prefaces to Contemporaries*, pp. 35–40; the quotation is from p. 38.

Certainly, Garland's return to the West had violently shattered the dream of his youth and of the grandeur of his region. Back in Boston, feeling "acute self-accusation" because his parents and sister remained in the West while he could escape to the cultured East, Garland was shocked into the realistic depiction of Western conditions.[141]

In two volumes of loosely related stories, *Main-Travelled Roads* and *Other Main-Travelled Roads* (1910), as well as in *Praire Folks* (1893) and *Roadside Meetings* (1930), Garland symbolized life—the "via," the way—as a road which "has a dull little town at one end, and a home of toil at the other."[142] Each of his stories traverses part of this wearying road, which only occasionally crosses a rich meadow. The image of the road forms the basic metaphor of his books. Indeed, the main action of most of the stories involves a journey. "Mrs. Ripley's Trip" (1888)[143] was the first story in which Garland reflected his disillusionment with Western conditions. After constant work on an Iowa farm "where poverty was a never-absent guest," sixty-year-old Jane Ripley announces that she is going to return to "Yaark State" to visit her family. Quite simply, she takes her trip, and then returns to her burden, "never more thinking to lay it down." The very lack of incident, the absence of emotional contact between Mrs. Ripley and her husband, the depth of unexpressed yearning indicated in the years of saving dimes to make the trip all suggest the dehumanizing, repetitive toil that enslaves the almost inarticulate characters of the story. This story and the one Garland published in 1889, entitled "Under the Lion's Paw," were both reprinted in Henry George's *Standard* as evidence supporting George's land theories. "Under the Lion's Paw" is built on the back-trailing return east of Tim Haskins and his family from Kansas, where their farm has been ruined by grasshoppers. Tim's dreams are agitated by memories of the malevolent insects: "They jest set around waitin' f'r us to die t' eat us, too. My God! I ust t' dream of 'em sitt'n' 'round on the bedpost, six feet long, workin' their jaws." This is Garland's literal depiction of the Western nightmare. Next Tim rents a farm and, hopeful that he will be able to improve and buy it, endures a daily "ferocity of labor": "No slave in the Roman galleys could have toiled so frightfully and lived, for this man thought himself a free man, and that he was working for his wife and babies." When he discovers that the improvements he has made have doubled the cost of the farm, he recognizes and at last sullenly submits to the numbing weight of the lion's paw—economic inequity—not killing him, but slowly crushing his humanity away.

Again, in "The Return of a Private," written the following year, a soldier returns wearily homeward shortly after the war to a farm that has been wasted and impoverished during his absence. Now, as a farmer—"the epic figure which Whitman had in mind," Garland sardonically remarks—

---

[141] *A Son of the Middle Border*, p. 373. [142] "Preface" to *Main-Travelled Roads* (Boston, 1891), p. xi. [143] Of the stories mentioned here and below, all are collected in *Main-Travelled Roads* except "A Prairie Heroine" (retitled "Sim Burns' Wife"), which is collected in *Other Main-Travelled Roads*. Where stories were originally published earlier, the date of that publication is indicated.

he and his wife "are fighting a hopeless battle, and must fight till God gives them furlough." In these and other stories the conventional symbol of the journey as a moral progress spiraling upward—as in *The Divine Comedy* or *Pilgrim's Progress*—is altered by the recognition that there is no progress possible for the Western man. His journey merely repeats the same dull round of work, from birth to death. His life, and the birth and death that frame it, have lost its meaning. Although various reformist groups enthusiastically greeted Garland as their literary spokesman, he himself formulated no economic or political utopias. "I aimed to show," he wrote, "...not that free-trade was right, not that the single-tax was a panacea and right—...but to show that the whole condition of the average American farmer was wrong."[144] Garland's gaze at Western conditions is steady and pitiless. No longer the open road, but the interminable road he sang. In his stories, beauty is debased, love irrelevant, vitality sapped, and freedom limited. Only human sympathy, flickering briefly in "A Day's Pleasure" and "God's Ravens," suggests the possibility of a higher life, one nowhere realized.

"Up the Coulee" and "A Prairie Heroine" are the stories that perhaps best record both the loss of the agrarian myth and the consequent yearnings for a better life that these Westerners believed existed in the cultured, affluent East. It was a curious reversal, as actuality drove the West to create the myth of an East that might, it imagined, fulfill its vague aspirations for physical and emotional ease. In "Up the Coulee," Howard McLane, a successful actor and playright, returns to the West after a ten-year absence. After a decade of "electric lights, painted canvas, hot colors, creak of machinery, mock trees, stones, and brooks"—the burden of "artificial" civilization—he is impressed with the incredible beauty of Western nature. But this natural beauty merely makes more appalling the revelation of the mean life of farming, "with all its sordidness, dullness, triviality, and its endless drudgeries." As Howard's prematurely aged brother complains, "anything under God's heavens is better'n farmin'," and several people in the story think of Howard as proof of the easy affluence possible in urban and Eastern life. Howard alone comes to understand the hopelessness of life in both city and country, East and West.

As Howard is a sensitive observer who gives this story conceptual significance, so in "A Prairie Heroine" (first printed in *Prairie Folks* in 1893, but in later editions called "Lucretia Burns" or "Sim Burns' Wife") Dougles Radbourn and the young schoolteacher, Lilly, articulate the mute suffering of Lucretia Burns, the "Prairie Heroine." Radbourn has repudiated the Western myth in whose snare the lives of Sim Burns and his wife are twisted and deformed. He tells Lilly:

> Writers and orators have lied so long about 'the idyllic' in farm life, and said so much about the 'independent American farmer,' that he himself has remained blind to the fact that he's one of the hardest-working and poorest-paid men in America.

144 Quoted in Halloway, p. 49.

Although Radbourn offers several radical solutions, the actual circumstances of Lucretia's suffering defy and mock abstract theorizing, and Lilly can at last suggest to her only resignation. Ironically, Lucretia becomes a Prairie Heroine only by resuming the empty, unheroic life of an automaton. Like Lilly, Garland sponsors no solution in his work. Faced with a life so bleak, he sees it only as a nightmare to be experienced, not as a problem to be solved. Perhaps he best expresses his need merely to reveal the hopeless conditions of agrarian suffering, and so ease their mental burden in "Altruism," one of his *Prairie Songs* (1893):

> Thou shalt not rest while these my kind
> Toil hopelessly in solitude;
> Thou shalt not leave them out of mind—
> They must be reckoned with. The food
> You eat shall bitter be,
> While law robs them and feedeth thee.[145]

But such stories and poems as these, written between about 1888 and 1891, form only a small part of Garland's work. In 1893 he told his publisher: "I am ready to send out purely literary books. . . .I shall not repeat either my economic writing or this literary and art reform [i.e., *Crumbling Idols*]. Having had my say I shall proceed on to other things."[146] Garland, as it happened, was a realist for only three years. First and last, he was a maker and follower of myth and romance. Indeed, his first book, *Boy Life on the Prairie*, written in 1885, was a "purely literary book" romantically detailing events from his youth—"in a mood of homesickness," he says in his introduction—two years before he made the trip home that precipitated in him a romantic disillusionment making him briefly appear to be a militant reformer. *Boy Life on the Prairie* constituted his wish to return to a mythically benign Western world "where time did not exist." In the conclusion of this idyll, the boy-hero, Lincoln Stewart, returns to the Prairie as Garland would do. But in 1885, Lincoln, Garland's daydream persona, concludes his return to the West by affirming—unlike Garland— the continuing actuality of the Virgin Land—"those splendid prairie lands,/ Far in the West, untouched of plough and harrow,/Unmarked by man's all-desolating hands."[147] He is able to embrace the myth of a Western Eden, existing in the pioneer past and, only temporarily closed for the present, to be recreated in a golden agrarian future. This indeed was Garland's feeling at the time. His brief, but agonizing, disillusionment after his return home was intense in proportion to his previous emotional commitment to the Western myth.

Both before and after this "realistic" interlude Garland wrote from an essentially romantic viewpoint, although his style remained uniformly realistic in fidelity to fact and detail. One should remember that romantic novelists had been led by Scott into faithful depictions of human speech,

---

145 *Prairie Songs* (Cambridge and Chicago, 1893), p. 78.   146 Quoted in Halloway, p. 98.
147 *Boy Life on the Prairie* (Boston and New York, 1926 [1899]), p. 319.

nature, and society in order to lend plausibility to their romances. By Garland's time, realism in style had become a convention of romance. His literary preferences prove his essential romanticism. Although he was later to admire Howells, in 1880, chancing on *The Undiscovered Country,* he was "irritated and repelled by [his] modernity." At about the same time, however, he was, contrariwise, attracted by the cosmological justifications of optimism offered by John Fiske.[148] Now, in the '90s, after his brief realistic period, he returned to these preferences. In a series of novels—beginning with *Rose of Dutcher's Coolly* (1895), continuing through *The Eagle's Heart* (1900), *Her Mountain Lover* (1901), *The Captain of the Grey Horse Troop* (1902), and *Hesper* (1903), and ending with *Cavanagh, Forest Ranger* (1910), Garland learned how to impose a romantic plot upon what he came to call "sociological background"—like the Indian problem or the need for conservation of natural resources. Being "quite outside the controversial belt," Garland exulted, these novels were very popular, *The Captain of The Grey Horse Troop* selling more than 100,000 copies.[149]

In these novels of the Rockies he used, as Walter Fuller Taylor has accurately noted, the conventional themes established by the Waverly romance—"flight and pursuit, courage and chivalric love, daring deeds of knights and other adventurers costumed as cowboys and ranchmen and soldiers and Indians."[150] After *Rose of Dutcher's Coolly* he moved the locale of his fiction to the far West and rapidly lost fictive contact with the scenes familiar to him from his youth. Disillusioned by and seeking release from wearisome "main-travelled roads," he swung out joyfully on the high trails of adventure. "From the plains, which were becoming each year more crowded, more prosaic," he wrote, "I fled in imagination...to the looming silver-and-purple summits of the Continental Divide."[151] Avoiding the present and having ceased to aspire for the future, he celebrated the past. "The truth is," he wrote in his journal in 1896, "I am beginning to take a delight in the glory of days gone by."[152]

When the Yukon gold fever spread across America in 1898, Garland, a thirty-eight-year-old established author, compulsively packed for the Klondike. "I was not a goldseeker," he wrote in *The Trail of the Goldseekers* (1899), "but a nature hunter." In Alaska he hoped once more to recapture the frontier vitality that he believed he could remember from his youth. Predictably, he found the savannas of British Columbia as he imagined "the prairies of Indiana, Illinois and Iowa...were sixty years ago." He needed to have the past restored. The Alaskan trail revived his sense of a heroic past and gave him "blessed release from care and worry and the troubled thinking of our modern day. It has been a return to the primitive and the peaceful."[153] This romantic realist now had kind words even for Joaquin Miller, the flamboyantly romantic poet of the high Sierras. Back in America after five months in the Yukon, he began a tour giving

---

148 *A Son of the Middle Border,* p. 227.   149 See Halloway, p. 174.   150 *The Economic Novel in America* (Chapel Hill, N. C., 1942), p. 179.   151 *A Daughter of the Middle Border* (New York, 1921), p. 21.   152 A journal entry dated February 14, 1896, quoted in Halloway, *Hamlin Garland,* p. 129.   153 (New York and London, 1899), p. 8.

a lecture called "The Joys of the Trail." For the rest of his life he would ride the trail of the past.

After the turn of the century, when there were no new Alaskas to conquer, the frontier seemed to live only in the minds of those who could remember it. Addressing a convocation at the University of Chicago in 1905, Garland spoke on "Vanishing Trails":

> A whole world, an epic world, is vanishing, fading. . . . The land of the log cabin, the country of the cayuse, the province of the trapper, the kingdom of the cow-man, are passing, never to return. All this hardy and most distinctive life will soon be but a dim memory, enduring only faintly in romance. . . . I cannot but feel that something brave and buoyant, something altogether epic, is passing.[154]

He had turned away from the degraded "main-travelled road" of endless toil, now to symbolize life, in his essays and novels, as the open trail— brave, epic, and ennobling. As an Oklahoman who heard a lecture of his in 1922 would call him, he was a "professional pioneer."[155] In that same year he sailed with his family for England, where he gained—as he told Fuller upon returning—a cosmopolitan outlook that wholly erased his former interest in American social problems. Abner Joyce was rapidly becoming Adrian Bond. Now, in a dozen volumes of autobiography, he frankly created an epic youth for himself to match the epic of pioneer life which he had dreamed. For a twentieth-century audience, cut off irrevocably from the revitalizing frontier, Garland made new versions of the Western myth. "Some say it is all an illusion, this world of memory or imagination," he wrote in *Back-Trailers from the Middle Border* (1928), "but to me the remembered past is more and more a reality, a joyous, secure reality." Rejoicing in the law of memory which "softens outlines and heightens colors," he recorded only the "poetic phases" of this era.[156] In *My Friendly Contemporaries* (1932) he told his readers how he replied to G. B. Shaw's question about the location of his Middle Border: "In a sense it does not exist and never did."[157] But in the minds of thousands of Americans— for his *Middle Border* series was enormously popular—the West that Garland celebrated represented an era whose greatness only he remained alive to sing. Garland, in short, committed himself to keeping alive the myth he had once, briefly, been compelled to reject. When Sinclair Lewis's *Main Street* appeared in 1920, reiterating some of Garland's criticisms of Mid-western life three decades earlier, Garland found it a "disturbing and depressing book," and was annoyed by the bitter, vengeful tone which he detected in it. *Main Street* "fails to convince," he insisted (ironically echoing the criticism genteel critics in the '90s leveled at his *Main-Travelled Roads*), "simply because the writer is not quite large enough, not quite generous enough, to fuse the minute, distressing details into something noble."[158] For Lewis, who in writing *Main Street* clearly had *Main-Travelled Roads* in the

---

154 Quoted in Halloway, p. 195. 155 Quoted in *ibid.*, p. 269. 156 (New York, 1928), p. 378. 157 *My Friendly Contemporaries* (New York, 1932), p. 519. 158 *Ibid.*, p. 337.

back of his mind—and relied on the same life-street metaphor for his satirical vehicle—this must have been a surprising criticism.

But Garland had long before 1920 committed himself to the epic revivification of the myth of the West, and could never return to the criticism in *Main-Travelled Roads*, whose tradition Lewis continued. Sadly, Howells, still consistent in his realism, advised Garland in 1910:

> One day, I hope you will revert to the temper of your first work, and give us a picture of the wild life you know so well on the lines of *Main-Travelled Roads*. You have in you greater things than you have done.... "Be true to the dream of thy youth"—the dream of an absolute and inspiring "veritism."[159]

But the dream of Garland's youth—the dream, for instance, of *Boy Life on the Prairie* and of his autobiographies—was of a Western Garden, the idyllic vision that briefly he had been shocked into criticizing. To that first dream he was true.

By the end of his life, then, he had transformed his history into myth and lived in a world of spirits and shadows. When the American Psychical Society was formed in Boston in 1892 Garland was one of its six officers, chosen because his skepticism, it was thought, would counterbalance the enthusiasm of its founders, Minot Savage and B. O. Flower. Almost immediately, however, Garland began to report inexplicable phenomena. In a novel, *The Tyranny of the Dark* (1906), and in a nonfictional dialogue, *The Shadow World* (1908), Garland weighed the claims of spiritualism and science. The shadow world of spiritualism was one that he entered more and more deeply as the edges of reality were frittered away by his myth-making. In 1936, after Garland had completed *Forty Years of Psychic Research,* he testified that a Spanish priest from the early settlement of California, Father Junipero Serra, appeared to him as his spiritualistic guide. Along with Father Serra, several of Garland's deceased friends seemed to materialize—Lorado Taft (the sculptor, Garland's brother-in-law), Arthur Conan Doyle, W. T. Stead, and Henry Blake Fuller. They led him on expeditions into the California desert in search of buried crosses as testimonies to the immanence of the spirit world. Fuller, dead for seven years, provided (Garland said) suggestions for the book he wrote about this experience— *The Mystery of the Buried Crosses* (1939). In concluding that book, he dimly sensed the way in which his spiritualism was the mystic counterpart to his celebration of a heroic West:

> Psychic mysteries still allure me, as distant mountain ranges allured me in my youth. As a mental pioneer, I am still moved to cultivate unknown valleys and tunnel unnamed ranges.
>
> Unlike the true frontiersman, few of us who seek the borderlands of human life are able to overtake the forms which flee, or touch the hands which beckon. Perhaps it is better so—the never-ending joy of the seeking remains.[160]

No doubt when he died in 1940, crossing into the deeper world of shadows and out of the tyranny of light, he stepped lightly.

[159] Quoted in Halloway, pp. 207–208.   [160] *The Mystery of the Buried Crosses* (New York, 1939), pp. 313–14.

NEW ENGLAND REGIONAL LITERATURE

The myth of New England has roots in the ideologies and utopias of precolonial Europe and England. Elaborating upon the Elizabethan empire-builders' notion that England had a holy and national destiny to fulfill in colonizing and exploiting the New World, Pilgrims and Puritans saw America as a land blessedly set aside for them until after the Reformation. There God manifested His intention to people an uncorrupted wilderness with His holy elect. The New World, then, constituted a renewed hope for abundance, both material and spiritual. Immigrants to an England made New and purified by divine ordination regarded themselves as instruments in the establishment of a promised land. No longer old England, but "God's American Israel" was the source of all virtue and hope for a regenerated future. In this structure of belief was established the essential independence of America from, as Americans would come to call it, the Old World; an independence asserting itself politically in the Revolution, economically in laws restricting trade, and intellectually in the call for the fiat creation of a distinctively American culture. The original colonial charters gave the colonies pre-emptory rights to the continent—a right ending only at the Pacific Ocean as their western boundaries. The states along the Atlantic seaboard thus became the contractual progenitors of those which would be established in their westward paths. In these terms, the Northwest was quite literally a mere extension of the New England states, progressively refined as the course of empire moved further away from the Europe whose sun had passed its zenith. New England said and seemed to see confirmed—in its statesmen, authors, and merchants—that in its matrix a nation was conceived, born, and matured, then sent forth on its perpetually resumed errand into the wilderness. With the abolition of slavery, it seemed to New Englanders as if the one great remaining burden of evil had been lifted from the country, and that it could now go on to its sanctified destiny in making America in the image of New England. This idea of Mission, as Frederick Merk has said, "was present from the beginning of American history....It was idealistic, self-denying, hopeful of divine favor."[161] In periods of crisis it became insistent and compelling. For New England it held the particular power of traditional sanctions. Both the apocalypse of the Civil War and the success New Englanders seemed to have achieved in purging the country of slavery appeared to guarantee that the New England Mission was about to be fulfilled.

But although a revival of moral enthusiasm swept New England after the Civil War, it was curiously short-lived. Instead of increasing, religious fervor, it began to seem, was on the decline. People began to remember that even before the War, New England analysts had noted the surprising, and even alarming, effects that the decline of devotional Puritanism had had upon New Englanders. Novels like *The Scarlet Letter* (1850) and Harriet Beecher Stowe's *The Minister's Wooing* (1859), the first set in

[161] *Manifest Destiny and Mission in American History: A Reinterpretation* (New York, 1963), p. 261.

colonial and the second in post-Revolutionary times, both emphasized the incredible pressures which Puritanism put upon its Saints as well as its Sinners. In her chapter entitled "Views of Divine Government," Mrs. Stowe explains that New England life is tied rigidly to notions of the sublime and eternal. In her version of New England's psychological history, the original Puritans were epic investigators into the nature of divine government; their society, deeply engaged in theological questions, boldly evolved a religion potent in its picture of both the grandeur of God and the insignificance of man. Coming into existence under God's wrath and "with a nature so fatally disordered that, although perfectly free agents, men were infallibly certain to do nothing to Divine acceptance until regenerated," mankind possessed sufficient freedom to be morally responsible, though insufficient goodness to hope for sanctification or to know how to earn it. The Puritan way was indeed hard. And, she says,

> if we add to [these conditions]...the fact that it was always proposed to every enquiring soul, as an evidence of [personal] regeneration, that it should truly and heartily accept all the ways of God thus declared right and lovely, and from the heart submit to Him as the only just and good, it will be seen what materials of tremendous internal conflict and agitation were all the while working in every bosom.

This heroic self-abnegation dignified the moral or mental hero, but left his weaker brethren morbidly sensitive, introspective, and confused. While the ancestors of Emerson rose to noble heights of self-reliant individualism, others were lost in the shadows of tragic solitude. Melville, commenting in 1851 on "the frightful poetic creed" in Hawthorne's "The Unpardonable Sin," wrote that "the cultivation of the brain eats out the heart," and announced that "in those men who have fine brains and work them well, the heart extends down to hams."[162] But for the thousands of Ethan Brands isolated on the lonely farms, in decaying seaports, or in the dismal hill-towns of rural New England, the brain had eaten into the hams. Hawthorne was right in telling Howells that the suppression of emotion had so debilitated the New England soul that its apparent insensibility was real. Following Hawthorne and Mrs. Stowe, other writers after the Civil War chronicled the decline of New England. The tortured heroines of Elizabeth Stuart Phelps—like herself, all brought up on the strictly Calvinist doctrines of the Andover argument—Harriet Prescott Spofford's New England legends, Whittier's "Among the Hills," Elizabeth Stoddard's *The Morgesons* (1862)—whose nun-like heroine, Veronica, T. W. Higginson saw as an analogue to a real recluse, Emily Dickinson—Holmes's *Elsie Venner* (1861)—these all hinted at the results of a Puritanism that had ceased to ennoble and was beginning to degrade.

The psychological problems of the individual were compounded and intensified by the Puritan myth of Mission. New Englanders were required

---

162 Melville concludes: "I stand for the heart. To the dogs with the head! I had rather be a fool with a heart than Jupiter Olympus with his head." *The Letters of Herman Melville*, ed. Merrell R. Davis and William H. Gilman (New Haven, 1960), p. 129.

by their Puritanism to be self-abnegatory; but, by their belief in their destiny or mission, to be successful. But again, after the War especially, it became clear that economically many areas of New England were in decline. Its population was decreasing. At least four causes accounted for the depopulation. First, the gold rushes of the '40s and '50s lured forth many young men. Later, when the railways connected isolated villages with urban and manufacturing centers, these drew off a further portion. "The running of the first train over the Eastern Road from Boston to Portsmouth —it took place more than forty years ago," wrote Aldrich in *An Old Town by the Sea* (1893), ". . . was attended by a serious accident. . . . The catastrophe was followed, though not immediately, by death. . . . [This] initial train, freighted with so many hopes and the Directors of the Road, ran over and killed—Local Character."[163] So also, in the Civil War the ablest men—those most likely to prosper and raise families—were often among the first killed; those remaining migrated, in many cases, south or west after the War, while the maimed and ill returned to linger in their New England towns. Last, in the '70s and '80s the West, glittering with promises, attracted still more of the energetic male population.

The New Englanders whom Rebecca Harding Davis found on Cape Cod in 1895 were "a few stooped, full-eyed old men and lean old women." "The young men and their wives," she wrote, had "gone to Idaho or Kansas," since with the completion of the continental railroad, prairie farmers could ship and undersell New England farmers even in their own markets. Three-fifths of the counties in Connecticut, three-fourths in Vermont, and nearly two-thirds in New Hampshire and Maine declined in population. In Massachusetts, Judge C. C. Nott said in 1889, there were 1500 abandoned farms. He wrote to *The Nation* that between Brattleboro and Williamstown he had found a deserted village—its church abandoned, its academy dismantled. Only two farmers remained, living in solitude at opposite ends of town: "All of the others had gone—to the manufacturing villages, to the great cities, to the West. Here had been industry, education, religion, comfort, and contentment, but there remained only a drear solitude of forsaken homes." Another commentator, A. F. Sanborn, drew a picture of agrarian New England mirroring Garland's critique of the West. In this desolate New England the houses were weather-beaten, showing hardly a trace of paint, the farmers were over-burdened by debts they could never hope to pay, and discontented over their exhausted soil. Its women, Sanborn said, "are pale, haggard, prematurely old, shrill, ill-tempered, untidy, and inefficient in their housekeeping." As their dull husbands found pleasure in hard cider—though foreswearing beer—these women took refuge in "floods of unwholesome patent medicine, and in the nostrums of quacks." Likewise, in a report on "Rural Degeneracy," R. L. Hartt described the inbreeding, drunkenness, bastardy, and idiocy that were beginning to prevail in New England. While defenders of New England were quick to blame the merging of foreign elements in its population for the decline in the Protestant Yankee

163 (Boston and New York, 1893), p. 259.

character, such a study of depravity as Richard Dugdale's showed that criminal families, like the Jukes, could trace their lineage to colonial times. Now, Hartt asked rhetorically of a New England fair, "that loathsome rabble,—gathered from twenty decadent hill towns,—are they not, every soul of them, descended from the Puritans?"[164]

The psychological effects of Puritanism, then, were accentuated by economic decline. While earlier settlers had exercised their wills upon great issues, to their rural descendants no significant issues remained to be settled. Will had degenerated into willfulness; self-reliance had become mere selfishness; noble resolution had declined into unreasoning stubbornness. As Mrs. Davis wrote, the New Englander "has given up the lofty Puritan faith, and has kept the objectionable Puritan temperament."[165] All of the Puritan virtues had been transformed—thrift into niggardly economy, hard work into needless toil, self-denial into narrowed lives—as the lack of opportunity for the exercise of those virtues dwindled; as Robert P. Tristram Coffin has remarked, "the New England philosophy of the Superior and Improving Man is a philosophy founded on prosperity."[166]

Nevertheless, the myth of the East persisted, as we have seen, in the work of Garland and others who backtrailed east. To the Western Mrs. Ripleys the East suggested luxury, refinement, and attainment. This myth, of course, persisted in New England as well. New Englanders in decline found obvious consolations in reviving the myth of Mission and viewing their destinies as still central for American development. Mrs. Davis, in 1895, still found the myth strong enough to attack. Americans, she insisted,

> think, apparently, that the old-time Yankee of Lowell and the Puritan of Hawthorne are still living in their farms and villages, producing brain-force for the whole country. They neglect to look into the effect which a century of insufficient food, narrow interests, hard economy, and superfluous education has produced in them.[167]

New Englanders looked back to that golden previous century, when Lowell's Yankee or Hawthorne's Puritan created a schema of expectations that, though not to be fulfilled, yet suggested the vitality of their own accomplishments and dreams. This backward glance is suggested, as Van Wyck Brooks has written, by the vogue for antique-hunting which began in the '80s, "as if the race were truly dying and one had to gather the relics before they vanished."[168]

Indeed, the race *was* dead, as mythical races always are. Only a few writers remained in whose tortured consciousnesses its declension was shaped

---

[164] The following analyses of the New England decline are referred to: Rebecca Harding Davis, "In the Grey Cabins of New England," *The Century*, XLIX (1895), 620–23; C. C. Nott, "A Good Farm for Nothing," *Nation*, XLIX (1889), 406; A. F. Sanborn, "The Future of Rural New England," *The Atlantic Monthly*, LXXX (1897), 74–83; Rolin L. Hartt, "A New England Hill Town," *Atlantic Monthly*, LXXXIII (1899), 573; and Richard Dugdale, *The Jukes: A Study in Crime, Pauperism, Disease, and Heredity* (New York and London, 1877), p. 8.   [165] "Grey Cabins," 621.   [166] *The New Poetry of New England* (Baltimore, 1938), p. 11.   [167] "Grey Cabins," 620.   [168] *New England: Indian Summer 1865–1915*, p. 330.

into art. J. Henry Harper has told how his publishing house received a remarkable manuscript:

> The pictures of horror were too terrible for a normal mind to gaze upon; one instinctively revolted at this glimpse into an actual hell. There was but one thing to do—to skim it over rapidly, and get the dreadful thing out of the place. But it was literature, and great literature too. It was the kind of book that the devil himself might have written, and it came in the ordinary way by express from a dull and decorous New England town.[169]

It is a provoking hint. One wonders how many New Englanders, tormented into speech, wrote stories and novels that were hurriedly returned by the genteel publishers of Boston and New York. Nevertheless, a remarkable group of writers began after the war to delineate the New England character, to reassess and deflate its myths. Harriet Beecher Stowe, Rose Terry Cooke, Sarah Orne Jewett, and Mary E. Wilkins set forth their individual versions of the contrast and continuity between New England's idyllic and heroic past and its diseased present. Following out the basic pattern of regional writing that we have been tracing, all show attachments to the romance of the past. Like Cable in the South and Garland in the West, Stowe, Wilkins, and Jewett would write historical romances. At the same time, in their best work the past is investigated and questioned by its culmination in an unsatisfactory present. All thus seek to balance the claims of past and present. C. H. Foster has spoken of the "New England doubleness"—the balancing of introspection and humor, the serious and mirthful—in Emerson, Thoreau, and Stowe.[170] "Mirth is the Mail of Anguish," Emily Dickinson, who shared this "doubleness," writes. Such "doubleness" is the stylistic vehicle of the regional writers in their ambivalent balancing of past and present. In their dialectic of satisfaction and discontent they seek to reweave the historic garment and so envision a past culminating not in a sullen present, but in a golden future.

In her preface to *Oldtown Folks* (1869), Mrs. Stowe explains her object: "to interpret to the world the New England life and character in that particular time of its history which may be called the seminal period." "I will endeavor," she continues, "to show you New England in its *seed-bed,* before the hot suns of modern progress had developed its sprouting germs into the great trees of today." Horace Holyoke, in whose persona the "Preface" is written, says that he "tried to make my mind as still and passive as a looking glass...and then to give you merely the images reflected there." But Mrs. Stowe's retelling of history in his voice is far from an objective mirroring of the New England past. History is refracted in his multifaceted glass. Mrs. Stowe's need to modify rigorous Puritanism—an impulse clear in *The Minister's Wooing*—compels her to misrepresent the character of seminal New England. Through Horace Holyoke she argues the thesis—without, of course, assuming personal responsibility for it—that the original Puritan theology and ecclesiastical polity had been seriously

[169] *The House of Harper,* p. 273. [170] *The Rungless Ladder: Harriet Beecher Stowe and New England Puritanism* (Durham, N. C., 1954), pp. 3–11.

altered and impaired by Jonathan Edwards and his followers. These later Puritans, Holyoke says, limited their congregations to only a portion of Christians, those who gave evidence of regeneration; whereas earlier settlers and founders like Governor Winthrop or Thomas Dudley refused to be separatists and included all Christians in their view of the church—in short, they "were in all but political opinion warmly attached to the Church of England." Thus for Horace, Edwards and his followers transformed and ruined the Church that the founders had established. The "seed-bed" itself remained pure, while the Edwards interlude, as Horace now sees it, was merely a temporary aberration, responsible for the psychological suffering that Mrs. Stowe analyzes in *The Minister's Wooing*.

Certainly, as C. H. Foster has said, she "knew better than she wrote"[171]; she possessed information that showed how completely and brilliantly Edwards epitomized and clarified the tendencies of Puritanism. But she makes Edwards the demon with a flaming sword so that she can keep seminal New England an essential Eden, without devils. Horace Holyoke, a man of wide, almost universal religious tolerance, a "Calvinist, Arminian, High-Church Episcopalian, and simple believer," lets all persuasions speak, and so, in his own intellectual universality, sets up the dialectic of truth and error. Harriet, too, had become an Episcopalian in 1864, and now justified her conversion as an aspect of the Great Circle of historical return. The era of evil—of sin and suffering—was over, as Edwards' day was over. In the symbolic action of the novel, the New England "seed-bed" was ready to emerge once more.

Mrs. Stowe was generally governed by emotional compulsions and wrote largely under their power—as witness her confusion in trying to explain her composition of *Uncle Tom's Cabin* (1852)—first with her *Key* (1853), then with her repeated insistence that "God wrote it." Waiting for her emotions to drive her, she took ten years to finish *The Pearl of Orr's Island* (1862), while in the meantime she completed several other books that briefly interested her. Beginning in *Oldtown Folks* (1869) and continuing through *Sam Lawson's Oldtown Fireside Stories* (1872) and *Poganuc People* (1878), the myth of the past possessed her increasingly. In a writer such as Mrs. Stowe, whose emotions spill over from turmoil into art, myth and fiction are virtually one. For a culture that, already in the '60s, felt its power diminishing, Harriet recreated the myth of the past. The last two books of this group she wrote from her Florida home. At that distance New England was increasingly silvered with romance. Sending a copy of her *Poganuc People* to Dr. Holmes, she wrote: "As I get old I do love to think of those quiet simple times, when there was not a poor person in the parish." One of the chapters of *Oldtown Folks* is entitled "We Begin to be Grown-Up People." It is the tragedy of experience and the end of innocence[172]

---

171 *Ibid.*, p. 182. 172 For instance, see Chapter **XXX**: "We begin to be grown-up people. We cannot always remain in the pleasant valley of childhood. I myself, good reader, have dwelt on its scenes longer, because, looking back on it from the extreme end of life, it seems to my weary eyes so fresh and beautiful; the dew of the morning-land lies on it, that dew which no coming day will restore."

that Mrs. Stowe delineates—the tragedy of Time passing. But if Time is inexorable, so too is art. "Come, Sam, tell us a story," *Oldtown Fireside Stories* begins. Like Sam Lawson she revives the past—the stories are based on Calvin Stowe's recollections of his childhood in Natick—by fixing it in fiction. In writing novels, she balances the passing with the eternal and thus creates an enduring contemporaneous past. That past still remains for us briefly to hold and have in the books wherein she so lovingly recreated it. For many of her contemporaries, no doubt, it was more real and enduring than the desolate wasteland present they daily faced.

Rose Terry Cooke

Rose Terry Cooke had attended the Hartford Female Seminary, which Catherine Beecher, Harriet's sister, founded and organized on the principles she had derived from her conversion to a personal religion based on love rather than sin. There Miss Terry was influenced by the Rev. John Pierce Brace, who had been Harriet's instructor at Litchfield Academy and appears as Jonathan Rossiter in *Oldtown Folks*. Like Mrs. Stowe, she was, as Harriet Prescott Spofford said, "of undoubted and undiluted Puritan blood, which is to be found nowhere bluer than in Connecticut." Like Harriet, too, her writing is governed largely by the ebb and flow of emotions long suppressed and then impulsively overflowing. She is said to have composed easily and rapidly, writing on her knee and seldom revising. "She would be," a friend said of her, "as good a hater as lover should occasion rise, for indifference is impossible to her and all her emotions are strong ones."[173] Swift composition under the influence of emotions is a characteristic of all regional writing. Sarah Orne Jewett, whom we shall consider shortly, was also a woman whose work was strongly determined by her emotions. Despite her reputation for careful craftsmanship she too wrote rapidly, often without revising. As early as 1873 she told Horace Scudder: "I always write impulsively—very fast and without much plan." Later she would tell Annie Fields that she had written a story in a half-hour. "Who does it?" she asked—a question Joel Chandler Harris was also asking—"For I grow more and more sure that I don't."[174] By writing impulsively, the regionalists were able to break through the later nineteenth-century backwater of genteel conventions, and in exploring directly the emotional flood which compelled them to write they produced a body of literature peculiarly free of time and place and so of continuing relevance to our age.

Subject to the various emotions that successively possessed her, Mrs. Cooke's work falls into three fairly distinct groups. She began her career with idealistically religious sketches and poems—her tales of New England Saints. Her first novel, *Happy Dodd; Or, "She Hath Done What She Could"* (1878), is perhaps the most interesting of her celebrations of New England

173 Harriet Prescott Spofford, "Rose Terry Cooke" in *Our Famous Women* (Hartford, 1884), pp. 175, 191. The whole selection, interesting for including autobiographical material, is on pages 174 to 206.   174 Quoted in F. O. Matthiessen, *Sarah Orne Jewett* (Boston and New York, 1929), pp. 44, 81.

Sainthood. Here she studies the figure, at once piteous and heroic—a mood Mrs. Cooke attempts again and again to evoke—of Happilonia Dodd from childhood to death. Some of the sketches in *Rootbound* (1885), published by the Congregational Sunday-School and Publishing Society, are successful along similar lines: "The Deacon's Week," for instance, relates the heroic failure of a man's attempt to live for a week as Christ would have—the theme that would, a decade later, make *In His Steps* a sensational best-seller. Others, the "Saint the First" and "Saint the Second" pair, "Clara's Question," and "John Carter's Sin" describe New Englanders who become saint- or martyr-like in devoting themselves to others. Secondly, Mrs. Cooke wrote stories for children. Perhaps the best of these moralizing tales is the novel *No* (1886), which attempts to show boys the virtue of self-denial. In the "Preface" to this book she refers to a childhood amusement called "The Game of Human Life," in which the players moved their pieces about a board whereon were painted the various types of humanity. The severest penalty came to the player who landed on the "Complaisant Man," for he had to go back to the beginning. "I never understood this then," she writes, "but I know now what it meant: the man who yields,…who cannot say 'No!' never succeeds, is never respected, is a failure in both worlds."

Her third and best kind of fiction revolves about flinty New Englanders who say No! in thunder—in fire and brimstone, too—characters who refuse love, kindness, and beauty out of habit and their long, irrevocable traditions of emotional repression and psychological introspection. These are Mrs. Cooke's New England Sinners. If on the one hand she describes the saintly uses of self-denial, she knows likewise that these virtues can fritter away into mere self-will and selfishness. Her women are stunted and her men brutalized by the heritage of a Puritanism which once produced noble characters.

Mrs. Cooke's work has been unjustly ignored by historians of American literature. In the great first issue of *The Atlantic* in 1857, hers was the lead story; and from then until her death in 1891, she was its foremost contributor of short stories.[175] More clearly and astutely than Mrs. Stowe and long before Garland or Howe, she treated the story of rural decline, the tragedies of heroic characters whose brand of heroism no longer has any function and so sours into incredible meanness. She calls such people, in the title of one of her most striking sketches, "The Sphinx's Children" (1886). This special race possesses, she says in her parable, "intellect and will" along with "hearts of flint." Such men were needed to create and preserve moral law when the world was threatened by "rank and miasmatic civilization—its hot-beds of sin and misery—its civil corruptions and its social lies—its reeling rotten principalities—its sickly atmosphere of effeminate luxury." The Puritans, who had to be "stony and strong," were descendants of the pitiless sphinx; but their children—the characters of whom she writes—needed love and pity, moral relaxation. For like Parson Robbins,

---

175 See Ima Honaker Heron, *The Small Town in American Literature* (Durham, N. C., 1939), p. 80.

in "Cal Culver and the Devil," they magnify sin—and so live lives of fear and trembling—in order that their virtue will seem to have a purpose.

Her analysis of the tragedy of New England character was shrewd and decisive, establishing the conventions to be followed by Sarah Orne Jewett, Mary E. Wilkins, and even Edwin Arlington Robinson and Robert Frost. In a brilliant sketch called "West Shetucket Railway," she writes of the New Englander:

> Born to an inheritance of hard labor, [and fighting]...against a climate not only rigorous but fatally changeful, a soil bitter and barren,...without any excitement to stir the half-torpid brain, without any pleasure, the New England farmer becomes in too many cases a mere creature of animal instincts...— hard, cruel, sensual, vindictive. An habitual church-goer, perhaps; but none the less thoroughly irreligious. All the keener sensitiveness of his organization blunted with over-work and under-feeling till the finer emotions of his soul dwindle and perish for want of means of expression.... And when you bring this same dreadful pressure to bear on women...—when you bring to bear on these poor weak souls, made from love and gentleness and bright outlooks,...the daily dullness of work, the brutality, stupidity, small craft, and boorish tyranny of husbands to whom they are tied beyond escape, what wonder is it that a third of all the female lunatics in our asylums are farmers' wives, and that domestic tragedies even beyond the scope of a sensation novel, occur daily in these lonely houses, far beyond human help or hope?

From her stories emerges a procession of stunted, frustrated, betrayed lives —old maids living "on a small amount of money carefully invested," like Miss Lucinda or Miss Beulah; women growing old in their prim houses waiting for lovers to return from the West or the sea; Hetty Buels, putting on their widows' rings when at last they know their Eben Jacksons are dead; men whose obstinacy has become so strong that, like Freedom Wheeler's, it is inverted and set against Providence itself; characters like Thomas Tucker who are too honest to live; and "vine-covered and grass-strewn volcanos" like Hannah Blair, who allow their strong emotions to errupt only at the moment of death, after emotionally devastating years of suppression.[176] Such characters are at once pitiable and noble. They believe, as one of them says in "Cal Culver and the Devil" (1881), that "energy, force, *Sturm und Drang,* make the world go round, not soft strokes."

Again and again, however, to this New England degradation Mrs. Cooke says the "Paradisiac Amen," as she calls it in "The Sphinx's Children." Acknowledging the irrelevance—even the malevolence—of the old virtues in the circumstances she depicts, she yet seeks to retain, by reinterpreting and somewhat softening, the Puritan Ethic. In the "faithless faith" of the Puritans, she writes in "Mrs. Flint's Married Experience" (1881), lay "elements of wonderful strength.... However we may sneer at Puritanism, it had its strong virtues; and its out-growth was honesty, decency, and

---

[176] The following stories by Mrs. Cooke are referred to: "Miss Lucinda"; "Miss Beulah's Bonnet"; "Eben Jackson"; "Freedom Wheeler's Controversy with Providence" from *Somebody's Neighbors;* "Some Account of Thomas Tucker"; and "Too Late" from *The Sphinx's Children.*

respect for law. A share of such virtues would be worth much to us now."
Clearly, then, Mrs. Cooke's stories are—ambivalently, but not ambiguously
—all of a piece. In the one kind she writes the episodes of the Puritan Book
of Saints; in the other, those of saintly virtues made diabolical by circumstance. Venerating the holy past, she yet recognizes that it is closed to the
profane present. To the strong breast of the sphinx's children she seeks to graft
a living heart. At the conclusion of *No*, Jack Boyd has an oak shield "with
NO carved on it in elaborate and quaint letters." But he has also, in the
course of the book, learned how to say—the last chapter's title—Yes! to
affection, kindness, and understanding. By learning about the heroic denial
of the Puritan faith, one is able to make the blessed affirmation of the new
dispensation.

Sarah Orne Jewett

Like Mrs. Cooke and, later, Mary Wilkins, Sarah Orne Jewett wrote
stories for children early in her career. *Play Days* (1878) she wrote con-
temporaneously with her first important book, *Deephaven* (1877), while
the children's book, *Betty Leicester's Christmas* (1894), preceded her
acknowledged masterpiece, *The Country of the Pointed Firs*, by only
two years. Like Mrs. Cooke's and Miss Wilkins's, Miss Jewett's children's
stories dramatize the conventional virtues of the weakened, later nineteenth-
century Protestant Ethic: self-reliance, individualism, honesty, thrift, hard
work, and prudence. Essentially, they were idealizing the lost youth of New
England in writing of the simpler virtues of childhood, a characteristic of
regional writers in all sections. When one brings to mind that Lanier and
Harris both produced several books for children; that Eggleston spent years
editing Sunday-school publications and that his *Hearth and Home* spawned
the most famous later nineteenth-century children's periodical, *St. Nicholas:
An Illustrated Magazine for Young Folks*, edited by Mary Mapes Dodge;
that Garland's first book was *Boy Life on the Prairie;* and that the New
England writers often wrote for the children's market, it is obvious that the
regional literary impulse was emotionally connected to the knowledge, attitudes, and emotional attachments of childhood, a world now irrevocably
eliminated by what Miss Jewett called (in an early sketch, "River Driftwood")
"the destroying left hand of progress." To be sure, the regionalists lamented
the loss of a childhood that had never been precisely the same as the heroic
past which they celebrated. It provided, rather, a matrix for nostalgia
toward the epical history which had only recently (so it seemed) ended in
decline. At the age of forty-eight, in 1897, Miss Jewett wrote to Sara
Norton: "This is my birthday, and I am always nine years old." Discussing
her children's stories, she peevishly told Howells that "everybody is distress-
ingly grown up and I have 'nobody to play with.'" As her friend Annie
Fields wrote, "she never put her dolls away."[177]

177 Quoted in Matthiessen, pp. 106, 38; and in Richard Cary, *Sarah Orne Jewett* (New
York, 1962), p. 19.

For Sarah Orne Jewett the New England past was intimately associated with her childhood. Accompanying her doctor father on his rounds instead of attending school—for she was sickly—the young Sarah felt herself a part of his, instead of her own, generation. "I look upon that generation," she would say later, "as the one to which I really belong—I who was brought up with grandfathers and granduncles and aunts for my best playmates."[178] To preserve her childhood, therefore, she chronicled the New England past, and vice-versa. Mrs. Stowe's Sam Lawson had obviously been a projection of Calvin Stowe's reminiscences of his youth. Between Mrs. Stowe and Sarah Orne Jewett there were curious affinities. Annie Fields and Celia Thaxter assured Sarah that she was Sam Lawson's spiritual daughter, and both affectionately addressed her as "Pinny Lawson" in letters and conversation.[179] Sarah Jewett frequently recalled that *The Pearl of Orr's Island* had first inspired her to write of New England. She once told Willa Cather that her head was full of old women and old houses, and when the two came together in her brain with a click, she knew a story was under way. She was concerned with preserving for people, as she said, "the separateness and sanctity of the front yard of their grandmothers." And she added the conservative defense that "we Americans had better build more fences than take any away from our lives."[180]

In this aspect of her work, then, she built a fictive fence about the flourishing past of her birthplace, South Berwick, Maine, once a prosperous seaport and shipbuilding town rivaling Portsmouth and Boston for economic and cultural leadership. Certainly the kind of cosmopolitanism fostered by international trade instilled in Berwick and other New England shipping centers amazing cultural vigor. In "The Queen's Twin," Miss Jewett remarks that along the coast of Maine "one may see plain, contented old faces at the windows whose eyes have looked at faraway ports and known the splendors of the Eastern world."

> They shame the easy voyager of the North Atlantic and the Mediterranean; they have rounded the Cape of Good Hope and braved the angry seas of Cape Horn in small wooden ships.... The sea captains and the captains' wives of Maine knew something of the wide world, and never mistook their native parishes for a whole instead of part thereof. They knew not only Thomaston and Castine and Portland, but London and Bristol and Bordeaux, and the strange-mannered harbors of the China Sea.

But Jefferson's Embargo Act of 1807 destroyed the affluence of Berwick along with that of several other New England towns, including Hawthorne's Salem. By Sarah Jewett's time, only a memory of that better world survived to haunt a present that envisaged no future. In the essential dignity of her loss and grief, the leading character of *The Country of the Pointed Firs*, Mrs. Todd, "might have been Antigone alone on the Theban plain." Other characters who live in Deephaven or Dunnet Landing gently bring out relics of that heroic age: "an old flowered-glass teacaddy," brought "to my

---

[178] Quoted in Matthiessen, p. 30.   [179] John E. Frost, *Sarah Orne Jewett* (Kittery Point, Me., 1960), p. 69.   [180] Quoted in Matthiessen, p. 31.

mother from the island of Tobago"; or "a beautiful coral pin from a port...
somewheres up the Mediterranean"; or china "bought...in the port of
Bordeaux."

In Sarah Jewett's time, as Captain Littlepage says in an early part of
The Country of the Pointed Firs, "shipping is a very great loss." Cut off
from the world, the community has narrowed and become ignorant. The
old sea-captain's agonized vision, like Yeats's vision in "The Second Coming," is of a world in decline: "the worst have got to be best and rule
everything; we're all turned upside down and going back year by year."
From this angry, chaotic, drifting world of the present, Miss Jewett, like
her fellow New Englanders, looked toward the coherent world of the past, in
her case symbolized by Dunnet Landing. This affection for the past was
unquestionably in Lowell's mind—for it was an affection he shared—when
in his last letter before his death he called Sarah Jewett's stories "idylls
in prose." "The life they commemorate," he wrote, "is as simple in its main
elements, if not so picturesque in its setting, as that which has survived for
us in Theocritus."[181]

The title story of *A White Heron* (1886) is perhaps the best example of
Sarah Jewett's version of the New England idyll. The heroine of this tale
is a "little maid who had tried to grow for eight years in a crowded manufacturing town," but who now thrives on the upland farm where her grandmother has brought her. Regenerated, Sylvia becomes a child-of-nature
in the best Wordsworthian tradition. (Miss Jewett repeatedly wrote of
her admiration for both Dorothy and William Wordsworth.) "The wild
creatures counts her one of themselves," her grandmother tells an ornithologist
who has come from the city in search of a white heron for his collection.
Sylvia, who has seen the bird, is "vaguely thrilled by a dream of love" and
determines to discover its nest for him. As Sylvia climbs a gigantic landmark
pine, from where she will see the bird emerge from its nest, Miss Jewett
suggests the dangers of this betrayal of nature: "the sharp dry twigs caught
and held her like angry talons" as she proceeds upward. But the tree—
suddenly personified as a masculine force in nature, a natural counterpart
of the urban visitor—also accepts, loves, and finally protects the tiny being
ascending it. She can find romance in nature rather than with man. Discovering
the bird's secret, she is finally—without knowing why—true to Nature, and
does not reveal the location of the nest. Instead, in her mystic communion
with the idyllic, pastoral world she finds her substitutes and consolations
for the money and romantic love that civilization offered. She earns her
name and fate.

But Lowell was only partially right. Like Harriet Stowe's and Rose
Cooke's, Sarah Jewett's work is driven by the Yes and No of New England
"doubleness"—the vitalizing principle of all regional writing, which forces
an objective, impersonal, and critical gaze to accompany the affectionate
backward glance (see pp. 87–88). Needing to write and believe in idylls, the
regionalists had to justify them by casting a cold eye on both the life and

181 Quoted in *ibid.,* p. 89.

death of their cultures. Against the consoling parable of "A White Heron" one would have to set the bitter and bleak desolation of other stories, like "The King of Folly Island" (1888), in order properly to understand the vital ambivalence of Sarah Jewett's work. The story this time is drawn through the point of view of the summer visitor Frankfort, a successful businessman, who is escaping the city. Arriving on an offshore island, he feels "as if he had taken a step backward into an earlier age. . . . He had really got to the outer boundary of civilization." On the curiously named Folly Island—the outermost island—he feels himself "as far away as he could get from city life and the busy haunts of men." So far the story follows the usual romantic pattern: natural, as opposed to civilized, life is idealized; the past is more comforting than the present; country is set against city. But it is the urban point of view speaking here; for Frankfort, who reads Wordworth's poems, hopes to find in the country all that his urban existence lacks.

Miss Jewett intimates from the first that this idyllic countryside is a myth created by the summer visitor. Jabez Pennel, the storekeeper and postmaster of St. John's Island, and the men who gather along the shore, pitiably eager to see the mail—briefly to touch civilization—all live pinched, mean lives, suggesting that, separated from the culture of the mainland, they lack the elements essential for human growth. Moreover, in George Quint, the King of Folly Island, Miss Jewett created the best of her New England solitaries: the New England will perverted into antihuman willfulness. A trivial argument has resulted in his vowing that he will never set foot on any land but his own again. He is an Ancient Mariner who has cursed himself to wander forever on the sea, away from human habitation. But his willfulness has implicated his daughter Phebe as well, condemning her to a solitary life for which she has neither will nor desire.[182] Both are casualties of the New England will superbly developed, but, left with no occasion for exercise. Like the Pilgrims—Miss Jewett herself makes this analogy— Quint has asserted his contractual freedom; but, lacking their high mission, he becomes, in his folly, not a pilgrim but merely an exile. In the persons of Frankfort and Quint, alienated urban existence and isolated rural life come together; in the measurement, both are found empty. Both men are hollow. "The truth is," Frankfort says, "I don't belong to my neighbors any more than you do." In his business, he too is a King of Folly. Phebe dying of consumption, Quint and Frankfort each isolated in his own folly—this is the No! in thunder of which the regionalists speak.

The triumph of *The Country of the Pointed Firs* (1896) is that it simultaneously affirms and denies the world of Dunnet Landing. The life there is to be seen not from the outside—as Kate and Helen, two Boston girls, saw it in *Deephaven*. Instead, the narrator of *The Country of the Pointed Firs* begins where they remained. At first, she slightly condescends to the

---

[182] The story is modeled after the life of the poetess of the Isle of Shoals, Celia Thaxter —like Sarah Jewett, a close friend of Whittier's, to whom "The King of Folly Island" is dedicated.

antique-village quaintness of Dunnet Landing; but she is progressively initiated into its manners and morals. In the best sense the stories are tentative sketches—never completed stories—in which the narrator becomes increasingly aware that the world of Dunnet Landing is neither idyllic nor antique, and certainly not quaint, but vibrantly alive to hope, frustration, contentment, and suffering. In "Amandar," Rose Terry Cooke had written of "the dreadful reticence that underlies all New England character, and forbids it to blossom in expression, though like some abnormal plant, it may bear fruit abundantly in deeds." Similarly, as the narrator of *The Country of the Pointed Firs* penetrates the convention of reticence, she understands the signs, smiles, tones, and gestures of the Dunnet people, who never say the important things they manage in other ways to communicate. "There, it does seem so pleasant to talk with an old acquaintance that knows what you know, . . ." Susan Fosdick, a visitor much sought after by the Dunnet townspeople, says; "Conversation's got to have some root in the past, or else you've got to explain every remark you make an' it wears a person out."

As the book progresses the narrator gradually gains entry into that root in the past. Leaving a local funeral after the services but before the burial, she is reminded early in the book "that I did not really belong to Dunnet Landing." Yet, already undergoing initiation, she does her work in the empty schoolhouse and begins to feel "as if I were a small scholar." Captain Littlepage, who comes to the schoolhouse, becomes her first master, Mrs. Todd having already told her something of town history. He enters quoting *Paradise Lost,* and moves from a dissertation on the intellectual and psychological effects of the loss of shipping to his own mad proof of the truth of his criticisms. Later, on Green Island, where Mrs. Todd's mother lives, the narrator expresses the desire to be initiated into the world of Dunnet Landing—"to be a citizen of such a complete and tiny continent and home of fisherfolk." The mother, Mrs. Blackett, in turn, tells her, "I shan't make any stranger of you." Mrs. Todd shows her secret places where she had never taken anyone before. Mother and daughter take her to their family-reunion festival where, at last, she "felt like an adopted Bowden." But the summertime within the great time of past and future has been moving resolutely through the book, and as fall approaches—the Fall is suggested—the summer visitor must return to the outer world. Now initiated, she suddenly begins to fear "to find myself a foreigner" away from Dunnet. As her parting gift Mrs. Todd gives her a coral pin, long before bought for Joanna, the recluse of Shell-Heap Island, implying that in some sense the narrator will now likewise be a hermit in the world to which she is returning, cut off from the relevant community of Dunnet Landing. "So we die before our own eyes," the narrator concludes. From the schoolhouse scholar, the innocent, to experience and her symbolic death back in the world she has come full circle.

From spectator she has become participant, thus understanding the double impulses of the New England world, which contains both an Edenic

Green Island and a desolate Shell-Heap Island; both the sociable Mrs. Blackett—though even she, on her island, is isolated socially—and shy recluses like William Blackett, Joanna, and the two farming families who, though sharing a small island, have not spoken to each other for three generations, "even in times of sickness or death or birth." Joanna, whose total isolation counterbalances Mrs. Blackett's social instincts, illustrates the "singular turn" to harshness that emotional energy had taken in the decline of New England. She confides to Mrs. Todd, "I have committed the unpardonable sin" (never revealed) and so withdraws from society "like one of the saints in the desert"—but without their social justification and without Ethan Brand's tragic suffering. Understanding her tale, the narrator is brought to the abrupt recognition that "in the life of each of us...there is a place remote and islanded," while she is yet able to accept the joy in the "gay voices and laughter from a pleasure-boat that was going seaward full of boys and girls" past Shell-Heap Island at that moment.

Sant Bowden is another whose talent has been buried by circumstance. His heritage is from the militant Norman spirit that Miss Jewett depicted in her history book, *The Normans* (1898). But he has had no chance to be a military hero. Rejected for service in the Civil War, he is now a frustrated old man who incessantly plans military strategies and maneuvers that can never be carried out.

The very title of the book conveys its essential ambivalence; for the *Pointed Firs* are, on the one hand, an obvious analogue to Whitman's *Leaves of Grass,* and like grass suggest endurance, continuing fertility, and masculine strength. At the same time, the forests of pointed firs visually suggest the fleets of ships whose endless masts once forested the harbors of Berwick: the last sight the narrator has of Dunnet is of "the tall masts of its disabled schooners in the inner bay," rotting at the wharves. The image of pointed firs referred to, at the very beginning, in the title of the book, and suggesting the dual possibilities of fertility or decadence, is thus seized upon at the very end by the narrator as the essential symbol for her experience of New England doubleness. The islands she has found represent both prison and paradise; and she is committed to accepting and rejecting both. Held by the hopes and promises of the New England Mission, she had yet to reject it and face sternly the crumbled relics of its ruin.

On her secretary in the upper hall of her house Sarah Orne Jewett pinned a slip of paper on which she had written two critical maxims by Flaubert— for she, revering her French ancestry, worked as much with a sense of the European tradition as Cable or Kate Chopin in cosmopolitan New Orleans, Henry James, and Howells. The first of Flaubert's injunctions echoes her father's literary advice ("Great writers don't try to write *about* people and things, they tell them just as they are") by insisting on the historicity of realism: "Écrire la vie ordinaire comme on écrit l'histoire." The second goes further: "C'est ne pas de faire rire, ni de faire pleurer, ni de vous mettre à fureur, mais d'agir à la façon de la nature, c'est à dire de faire rêver." The portrayal of common life as history or history-becoming-dream— these are the possibilities that in her best work Sarah Jewett simultaneously realized. The characters in her work who mean the most to us are those who dream their history, but, in so doing, help to incorporate into history-in-the-making part of the heroism of their dreams.

Mary E. Wilkins

Charles Miner Thompson, in pointing to her largely suppressed romanticism, called Mary E. Wilkins a disguised idealist.[183] For nearly a decade Mary E. Wilkins made a career of producing stories and poems for children. But with *A Humble Romance* (1887) and *A New England Nun* (1891), she abruptly turned about to criticize New England decadence more sternly and comprehensively than any of her peers had dared. Although she could tell an interviewer in 1890, "I didn't even know I was a realist until [critics] wrote and told me," her preface to the 1890 Edinburgh edition of *A Humble Romance* made the basic assumptions that Howells had long before set forth as the realist's faith. Her stories, she wrote, "were studies of the descendants of the Massachusetts Bay colonists, in whom can still be seen traces of the features of will and conscience, so strong as to be almost exaggerations and deformities, which characterized their ancestors." Rejecting the remnants of the Puritan village tradition that for Harriet Stowe and Rose Cooke still remained viable material; unconcerned with the consolations that Sarah Jewett found in nature or memory; unwilling to sentimentalize the fading and yellowing antique, as Lucy Larcom, Celia Thaxter, Annie Trumbull Slosson, and others did; uninterested in the Concord idealism these others inherited, Mary E. Wilkins delineated in full the humorless, vacant, mindless, narrow New Englander who had appeared as only one aspect of the work of her predecessors.

Six years after *A Humble Romance*, in 1893, Stephen Crane would shock his readers by depicting city life truthfully in *Maggie*. But in the American mind city slums had, of course, long been the repository of evil. Earlier than Crane and with more conscious artistry than the western regionalists showed, Mary Wilkins depicted the essential misery of rural life. The first paragraph of *A Humble Romance* well suggests the kind of critical force of that story:

> She was stooping over the great kitchen sink, washing the breakfast dishes. Under fostering circumstances, her slenderness of build might have resulted in delicacy or daintiness; now the harmony between strength and task had been repeatedly broken, and the result was ugliness. Her finger joints and wrist bones were knotty and out of proportion, her elbows, which her rolled-up sleeves displayed, were pointed and knobby, her shoulders bent, her feet spread beyond their natural bounds—from head to foot she was a little discordant note.

[183] "Miss Wilkins—An Idealist in Masquerade," *The Atlantic Monthly*, LXXXIII (May 1899), 665–75.

With her "red, sodden fingers" and speechless despair, Sally stands as mutely pathetic as any of the defeated figures in Crane, Norris, or Dreiser. Farm and village life, she was saying four years earlier than *Main-Travelled Roads,* is merely the rural version of the urban ghetto.

Another story in her first volume, "A Conflict Ended," suggests the stylistic and tonal paradoxicalness at which Miss Wilkins ordinarily aims. Ten years before the story begins, Marcus Woodman has objected to the investiture of a new pastor and, in a burst of stubborn self-assertion, vows never to set foot in the church again. For ten years each Sunday he has sat on the church steps—while, with an equally self-assertive vow, his betrothed has refused to marry him so long as he continues his folly. Even though the story ends happily, Miss Wilkins insists on the tragedy of ten years made dull and painful; with all the villagers we feel, as the narrator says, "the pathos in the comedy." Mary Wilkins's characters would be comic if they were not so hopelessly pathetic. For many years the secretary of Oliver Wendell Holmes, Sr., she learned well from the mock-seriousness of his New England poems and novels how to handle pathetic comedy, turning often into tragedy. Like him, she writes, as she said in a preface to her novel *Pembroke* (1894), "of the human will in different phases of disease and abnormal development." The wills of her characters are diseased by exaggeration and incongruity and betrayed into ludicrous commitments.

In "Gentian," for instance, a farmer refuses to let his wife cook for him because she secretly gave him medicine in his tea when he was dangerously ill. When she returns home after leaving him for nearly a year, he sends her away again—then appears at her sister's house to ask her to come home, as he had been intending to do when she first appeared. He surrenders his self-will in one direction even as he asserts it in another. In "A New England Prophet" Miss Wilkins delineates the pathetic absurdity of the Millerite craze, much as Eggleston had done in *The End of the World.* As in that novel, a shrewdly skeptical critic reveals the high comedy in the absolutely serious millennial conviction. Similarly, Candace Whitcomb in "A Village Singer" revolts against being displaced as choir soloist by playing her own organ and singing loudly from her house next to the church. David and Maria, in "Two Old Lovers," have been keeping company together for twenty-five years. Certainly, as Miss Wilkins says, "There was something laughable, and at the same time rather pathetic, about [their]...courting," for David has never overcome his reticence so far as to ask her to marry him. In "The Revolt of 'Mother,' " too, emotional contraries intermingle. After living for forty years in a shack, Sarah Penn watches incredulously and sullenly the construction of a new barn—a second barn—by her husband. Pleading and expostulation having failed, she revolts against her flinty New England husband and moves her furniture and family out of the house and into the new barn. She has lived an animal existence for forty years, the symbolism suggests, and now she insists on living at least as well as the stock.

In her best stories Mary Wilkins has an admirable control of her art. She was accomplished enough that her English publisher could confide to her in 1891 "that Mr. Henry James who is a dear friend of mine has lately been taken with an enormous enthusiasm for your stories. He has been reading them all one after another...and has the greatest opinion of them."[184] Howells, too, was warmly enthusiastic about her fiction, seeing in her a disciple for his realism. Her best story is undoubtedly "A New England Nun." Louisa Ellis, the "New England Nun" who has been waiting fourteen years for her lover, Joe Dagget, to return from making his fortune in Australia, is shocked by his masculine presence—which now seems crude to her—when he finally comes back to claim her hand. For, in the intervening years, she has "turned into a path...so straight and unswerving that it could only meet a check at her grave": unwittingly she has become another in the tradition of New England solitaries. Her path is described by the adverbs modifying her unconscious modes of action—"peacefully sewing," "folded precisely," "cut up daintily." She distills essences—ignoring, as Yeats would say in "All Soul's Night," the "whole wine"—and wears at least three aprons, which she dons or discards for various roles. Into this delicately ordered world, Joe comes bumbling and shuffling, bringing dust into Louisa's house and consternation into her heart. Whenever he enters her house, Louisa's canary—the symbol of her delicacy as well as of her imprisonment—awakes and flutters wildly against the bars of his cage. Joe's masculine vigor is symbolized by a great yellow dog named Caesar, which Louisa has chained in her back yard for fourteen years, and fed corn mush and cakes. Joe threatens to turn him loose, which suggests to Louisa a picture of "Caesar on the rampage through the quiet and unguarded village." At last, accidentally overhearing Joe and Lily Dyer confess their love for each other—while yet Joe sadly but sternly remains true to Louisa—she gently rejoices that she can release him, and herself, from his vows. In contrast to the wild, luxuriant fertility—the fields ready for harvest, wild cherries, enormous clumps of bushes—surrounding the scene between Joe and Lily stands the gently passive sterility of Louisa's life, who looks forward to "a long reach of future days strung together like pearls in a rosary." In contrast to the fervid summer pulsating with fish, flesh, and fowl, is Louisa's prayerful numbering of days in her twilight cloister.

Beginning with the comic stereotype in New England literature of the aging solitary—someone like Rose Cooke's Miss Lucinda—Mary Wilkins transmutes Louisa into an affectionately pathetic but heroic symbol of the rage for passivity. Much like Nicholas Gunn in "A Solitary," she consecrates her whole being to acquiescence. Nicholas, whose stony self-denial Wilkins compares to a Buddhist monk's, also shows the paradoxical tropical intensity of the cold New England character in the sudden dawning in him of passionate sympathy for a sick man. The same intensity is to be found in the other characters mentioned here: the various revolts of

---

184 Quoted in Edward Foster, *Mary E. Wilkins Freeman* (New York, 1956), p. 89.

"Mother," Candace Whitcomb, Narcissa Stone (in "One Good Time"), of Delia Caldwell (in "A Conquest of Humility"), or of Marcus Woodman are documents of the smoldering violence in the New England character, recalling the energy which once subdued a wilderness and settled a land. Now, not what they do, but what they essentially are in their passionate commitments—though they have no purpose worthy of commitment—suggests the true measure of their heroism. Lacking a heroic society, Mary Wilkins's heroes are debased; noble in being, they are foolish in action. Seen thus, Mary Wilkins is in her best work—as Louise Imogen Guiney said—"a sort of sordid Aeschylus."

Briefly exploring this paradox in *A Humble Romance, A New England Nun,* and *Pembroke,* Mary Wilkins then began to turn more and more to romance and mysticism. It is only at first surprising that in replying to Sarah Jewett's praise of her first volume, Mary Wilkins wrote: "I never wrote any story equal to your 'White Heron.' I don't think that I ever read a short story...that so appealed to me. I would not have given up that bird any more than you would if he had come back."[185] Following out the line of pantheistic nature mysticism that Sarah Jewett had opened in that story, Mary Wilkins would write the romantic stories of *Understudies* (1901), *The Wind in the Rose Bush* (1903), and *Six Trees* (1903). The last volume she would speak of as her best book. Almost simultaneously with Miss Jewett's *The Tory Lover* (1901) she published her own historical romance of colonial Virginia, *The Heart's Highway* (1900). Now, a decade after her realistic delineations of the paradox of the New England decline, she could write:

> The most of my work is not the kind that I myself like. I want more symbolism, more mysticism. I left that out [of the early stories] because it struck me people did not want it, and I was forced to consider selling qualities.[186]

Hamlin Garland's transformation from realistic skeptic to romantic mystic provides an interesting parallel to this metamorphosis. He likewise acknowledged in 1893, that "realism or Americanism *pays.* . . . And even Mr. Howells ...contrives to live on $10,000 or $15,000 a year." Eugene Field was saying just then in the *Chicago Daily News* that "Howells is the only bad habit Garland has," for away from Howells's influence, Garland

> really becomes quite civilized and gets imbued with orthodoxy; and then he, too, begins to see fairies and flubdubs, and believes in the maidens who have long golden hair and cannot pail the cow; and his heroes are content to perspire instead of sweat, and they exchange their cowhide peg boots for silk hose and medieval shoon.[187]

Field's playful satire was extraordinarily prophetic. As soon as Garland discovered that the romance of the West paid equally as well as realism, he followed the tendency common in all regional writing to celebrate the myth which he had earlier rejected. In common not only with Garland, but also with Harris, Cable (in *The Cavalier* [1901]), Grace King (who begins

185 Quoted in Matthiessen, p. 84. 186 Quoted in Foster, *Mary E. Wilkins Freeman,* p. 162. 187 Quoted in Halloway, *Hamlin Garland,* pp. 86, 85.

her *Memories of a Southern Woman of Letters* [1932]: "The past is our only real possession in life"), Eggleston, Howe (in *A Moonlight Boy* [1886] and later novels), Harriet Stowe, and Sarah Jewett, Mary Wilkins turned alternately toward a glorious—but, alas, lost—past and a romantic present. Even her novel of the relations between capital and labor, *The Portion of Labor* (1901), ends in the fireworks of love triumphant. One of her characters in *Jerome: A Poor Man* (1897) had insisted: "Everything on this earth means somethin' more'n itself. . . .They're symbols, that's what they be, and we've got to work up from a symbol that we see to the higher thing that we don't see." Frustrated by the environment that necessarily limited and degraded the characters in her early stories, Mary Wilkins soon passed to environments that "we don't see," and in *By the Light of the Soul* (1906) sketched consolations like those Garland was finding in spiritualism. It was both appropriate and ironical, then, that in 1926 Garland should be chosen to present to her the Howells Medal for Fiction. The event seemed to him to resemble "the ceremony of pinning a gold cross on the bosom of a disabled soldier in a forgotten war."[188] Perhaps by then they had both forgotten what that long battle had been for; but certainly, in her early stories, Mary Wilkins had achieved some of its firmest victories.

Edwin Arlington Robinson

Late in 1896, Edward Eggleston, still remembered as the author of *The Hoosier Schoolmaster* but having recently achieved renewed popularity with his history, *The Beginners of a Nation* (1896), wrote in an enthusiastic letter to a young author:

> I don't thank you for sending me a book, for I get books of poetry until I haven't shelf-room for them. But you have given me a rare sensation: you have sent me a book that I can read, and for that I thank you. . . . Let a total stranger hail you with admiration, putting aside all flattering words.[189]

On February 6, 1897, Eggleston commented on modern literature for *The Outlook,* and, finding Hardy and Meredith "trying too hard to be unusual," he added "that a man in Gardiner, Maine, has written lately some delightfully original little bits of verse and printed them in a little blue pamphlet. . . . He calls it 'The Torrent and the Night Before.' His name is Edwin Arlington Robinson."[190] Between Eggleston, who in 1871 was inspired by Taine and the Dutch masters to write one of the first truly regional novels, and Robinson, who under the influence of the French would reunite American regionalism with European traditions, are the two decades which transverse the rise and fall of the American regional genre. Eggleston, often spoken of as our first regionalist, writing to Robinson, in some ways our last, suggests both the brevity of our history and the continuity of our literature.

[188] Hamlin Garland, *Afternoon Neighbors: Further Excerpts From a Literary Log* (New York, 1934), pp. 318–19.   [189] Quoted in Emery Neff, *Edwin Arlington Robinson* (New York, 1948), pp. 78–9.   [190] Quoted in Randel, *Edward Eggleston,* p. 219.

Indeed, Robinson's list for complimentary copies of *The Torrent and the Night Before* sums up the age he culminated. Among recipients were Swinburne, Hardy, Gosse, Aldrich, Gilder, Stedman, Whitman's disciple Horace Traubel, and S. Weir Mitchell. Gosse wrote approvingly; and Stedman, preparing to formulate his sense of the American tradition in his *American Anthology* (1900), requested permission to include in it "Luke Havergal" and four other poems from the volume. Encouraged, Robinson sent copies of *Captain Craig* (1902) to Howells, R. H. Stoddard, and T. W. Higginson. Of this volume, William James wrote that parts were "fully as good as anything of the kind in Wordsworth."[191] These eminent Victorians admired Robinson's achievement, although perhaps they would have wanted to alter his intentions. Contrary to the image critics later formed of Robinson as a rebel willfully shouldering his leviathan way through the scattered ruins of a twilight party, he, in turn, frequently expressed his admiration for them. He quoted and praised those poets—Aldrich, Stedman, and Gilder —who are usually grouped as the leaders in the idealistic or genteel reaction to the conditions of modernism. To Gilder he wrote in 1908 that thirty or forty of his poems were "not only interesting but exciting." He read not only Dickens and Thackeray, but also the horde of popular romancers— F. Marion Crawford, Richard Blackmore, and William Black—who followed them. Certainly, he was indiscriminate in assessing the value of the sentimental drama which cluttered the stage. His favorite poets were Crabbe, Cowper, Wordsworth, and Tennyson. Although he read French and, indeed, admired Zola, his favorite was apparently Daudet—perhaps guided in this by Henry James's praise—while he nowhere mentions Mallarmé, Rimbaud, or Baudelaire. By training and taste, he was the common critic and acquiescent reader of his age.[192]

There was a difference, however, in the kinds of poems he produced. For in his temperamental inclination—"he was cast," Frost wrote, "in a mold of sadness"[193]—as well as from the experience of disaster in his personal, family, and community life, he moved away from the fluent confidence or charming doubt that frequently characterized the work of his fellows. They had taken to heart or mind Howells's comment that the smiling aspects of life were the more American. Robinson's experience of disaster centered around Gardiner, a town—much like Sarah Jewett's Berwick—in which lingered a sense of a heroic past now irrevocably lost. Located on the Kennebec River, once a harbor for New England's prosperous sea-going ships and an important fishing ground for the Pilgrims, Gardiner had steadily increased in prosperity up to the early '80s. Robinson's father became a leading citizen of the town. He sent his first son, Dean, to medical school and prepared his second, Herman, for business. His third, Edwin, presented an embarassing problem, one, however, that could be side-stepped

191 Quoted in Neff, p. 129. 192 The discussion of Robinson's reading is drawn from Neff and from *Untriangulated Stars: The Letters of Edwin Arlington Robinson to Harry DeForest Smith, 1890–1905*, ed. Denham Sutcliffe (Cambridge, Mass., 1947). 193 "Introduction" to Edwin Arlington Robinson, *King Jasper* (New York, 1935), p. viii.

by the family affluence. Then, in 1887, Dean returned to Gardiner from his medical practice, hopelessly addicted to drugs. And despite his early apparent brilliance, Herman's business collapsed in 1893 along with the national economy and the family fortune—which was tied up in Western real estate—while he turned to alcohol for solace. Three years later Robinson's mother died of black diphtheria, a disease then so feared that Dean had to momentarily revive his medical skill to attend her. Edwin, fearful of the responsibilities that were pressing upon him, believed he could not live beyond thirty-five. He was virtually deafened by a neglected mastoid infection and came so close to losing his sight that for a period of six months in 1893 he could not read for longer than ten minutes.

As with his personal and family fortunes, so with his community: Gardiner's economy dramatically crumbled in 1893 and in the years that followed steadily declined further. These are the circumstances, inner and outer, that he depicts in his poetry. Adopting the villanelle from the genteel writers, he used its refrain and repetitive rhyme in "The House on the Hill" to suggest the repetitiveness of Failure. Published in the same year as Sarah Jewett's *Country of the Pointed Firs*, "The House on the Hill" (from *The Torrent and the Night Before*) describes the decline of a rural community. As Theodore Roosevelt accurately pointed out in the *Outlook* review which made Robinson famous, he knew "the grey, empty houses from which life is gone" in rural New England.[194] All the poet can do is reiterate his denial of meaning:

> They are all gone away,
>   The House is shut and still,
> There is nothing more to say.
>
> Through broken walls and gray
>   The winds blow bleak and shrill:
> They are all gone away
>
>   *   *   *
>
> There is ruin and decay
>   In the House on the Hill:
> They are all gone away,
>   There is nothing more to say.

In another poem in the same volume, "The Dead Village," he portrayed a town where only "the ghosts of things" lingered—"No life, no love, no children, and no men." Sharing with Mary Wilkins the tragic sense of the New England decline, he wrote around 1895 "The Chorus of Old Men in Aegeus"—the subject of lost tragedies by Sophocles and Euripides—as the companion poem to "Luke Havergal," and so pointed up the relation between his theme of failure and the traditional theme of the vanity of human wishes. "Things have been going so like the devil with me," he

[194] "The Children of the Night," *The Outlook*, LXXX (August, 1905), 913.

wrote to a friend in summing up his experience of disaster, "...that nothing short of idealism would have kept me together."[195]

But the idealism he now achieved—he called it "a kind of optimistic desperation"[196]—was hard won and would consequently be kept cautiously hidden in the poems tracing the problem and character of personal and collective failure. He was saved from the graceful ideality of Stedman and the others by seeing his own failure nationalized in the apparent degradation—which another New Englander, Henry Adams, was also recording—of American progressivistic assumptions. Like his older peers, Hawthorne, Harriet Stowe, Rose Cooke, Sarah Jewett, and Mary Wilkins, he faced as his central problem the resolution of solitude, the problem particularly of the artist, but actually of any individual, to find meaning in the sterile societal deadend of a now fruitless tradition. "Solitude," he wrote Harry Smith, "...sharpens [one's] sympathy with failure where fate has been abused and self demoralized." Certainly, in describing Gardiner to a friend in 1893 he resolutely attacked the American myth of success:

> Gardiner...has been a frozen hell to me. Here I am, shut in by myself with only one or two people in town that I care two snaps of my finger for (and who, in turn, care about as much for me) with no prospects.... [If] I end up a penniless *gent* full of golden theories of fame and riches, I shall not lay all the blame, if there be blame in the matter, to myself; I shall not feel that it all might have been different, had I changed my opinions and actions a little when my mind was young and flexible. My philosophy does not swallow this teaching of our good old grandfathers who worked sixteen hours and sang psalms and praised heaven that a life is what we make it. And let me beg here that you may not permit any of your ambitious pupils to write essays on "Every man the architect of his own fortune."[197]

Robinson's heroes were bound to be antiheroes, like Captain Craig (or his heir, John Crowe Ransom's "Captain Carpenter") and the scores who followed him out of Tilbury Town or those in the Arthurian cycle—misfits and alienated men whose moral heroism is paradoxically made possible by the fact of their irredeemable failure. "I shall never be a Prominent Citizen," Robinson wrote in 1895, "and I thank God for it, but I shall be something just as good perhaps and possibly a little more permanent." Exploring personal alienation and social failure, he achieved success; setting forth the actuality of despair, he secured hope ("I suppose I'm the damnedest optimist that ever lived,"[198] he wrote in 1913); dramatizing the reign of the antihero, he defined and made relevant a hero for the modern world.

Santayana was undoubtedly right in telling William Lyon Phelps that the poets of Robinson's generation—Trumbull Stickney, George Cabot Lodge, and others—failed because they lacked an alternative to an en-

---

[195] Letter of December 7, 1896, *Untriangulated Stars,* p. 264. [196] Letter of April 4, 1896, *ibid.,* p. 244. [197] Unpublished letter, in Harvard College Library, to George W. Latham, dated December 20, 1893. Quoted in Lawrence Thompson, "Introduction" to *Tilbury Town: Selected Poems of Edwin Arlington Robinson* (New York, 1953), p. xv. [198] Letters of August 20, 1895 and December 15, 1913, *Selected Letters of Edwin Arlington Robinson* (New York, 1940), pp. 11, 80–1.

feebled and now imitative Brahminism. But in the tradition of New England regionalism reaching back to Hawthorne in the '50s, Robinson possessed both a literary tradition and a scheme of values which his contemporaries lacked.[199] It was by adapting this tradition of prose conventions and assumptions to his verse that he managed to avoid the sterile conventions of the poetry of his decade. In his first volume, he claimed, "there is not a red-bellied robin in the whole collection. When it comes to 'nightingales and roses' I am not 'in it' nor have I the smallest desire to be."[200] Following the methods and conventions of nineteenth-century prose regionalists, he became our first twentieth-century poet.[201]

Captain Craig (1902), as Robinson wrote Harry de Forest Smith, "is a rather particular kind of 20th century comedy."[202] Not for eight years after this would he publish another volume, and never again, perhaps, would he show the same experimental elasticity as in the epic comedy of the errant clown and sage, Captain Craig. Among the critics, however, only Trumbull Stickney—who died a year later—felt or acknowledged the power of the poem. Writing in *The Harvard Monthly* he praised Robinson's "honesty and simplicity of...mind, the pathos and kindness of his heart, above all the humor with which his imagination is lighted up continually."[203] For the rest, bewilderment, anger, irony, and polite ignorance passed for criticism. *Captain Craig* explores the comedy of alienation and failure. His true individuality fettered by the Puritan conventions of Tilbury Town—where men like Aaron Stark, with "eyes like little dollars in the dark," promote the Puritan ethos—this antihero is truly a failure, having become only "whatever he was not." He cannot find a society that will allow him to be all that he is. As a consequence, like Melville's confidence man, he adopts various disguises—becoming a hobo, a deadbeat, a poet, and a clown —in order to protect his true inwardness against the alterations New England society would make in it.

As a mark of his masquerade, he assumes the mock-title Captain Craig.

[199] Like Sarah Orne Jewett, who, Willa Cather says, always called her writings sketches —never stories—Robinson detested the very name of the short story, but determined to write the "sketch" (as he too called it) after the manner of the French *contre*. Apparently attempting to follow in Miss Jewett's tradition, he labored on a volume of prose fiction and considered the urge to write poetry "my worst and most persistent enemy." His biographer, Emery Neff, has suggested that from these unpublished sketches came the populace and stories of Tilbury Town, in poems like "Charles Carville's Eyes," "Cliff Klingenhagen," "Fleming Helphenstine," "Reuben Bright," and "Richard Cory." Even after his first volume he told a Harvard classmate it would be his last verse, for "I am full to the muzzle with prose ideas." Of course, he would alter the direction of American poetry by putting these prose ideas into verse sketches (Neff, pp. 44, 86, 13). [200] Letter of October 28, 1896, *Selected Letters*, p. 13. [201] One should recognize the difficulty of transforming the poetic conventions by prose formulas. Rose Terry Cooke (*Poems* [1888]), Mary E. Wilkins (*Decorative Plaques* [1883] and *Once Upon a Time* [1897]), and Sarah Orne Jewett (*Verses* [1916]), all wrote poetry, most of which is unreadable today. None of these was able to adapt her prose methods to poetry. Before Robinson, only Whittier, perhaps, had been able to match realism in poetry ("Among the Hills" [1868]) with realism in prose (*Leaves from Margaret Smith's Journal in the Province of Massachusetts Bay,* 1678–89 [Boston, 1849]). [202] Letter of June 2, 1900, *Untriangulated Stars,* p. 306. [203] Quoted in Neff, p. 128.

He is a captain by becoming, more truly than the persona of W. E. Henley's *Invictus*, the captain of his soul. Recognizing that his worldly failure is utterly complete—for he cannot even beg—he begins to explode the balloons of Tilbury conventions. He mocks the world that has mocked him. Thus, by having discovered his alienation from commercial, genteel, and Puritan life he learns to assert his individuality. Then, laughing loudly, he proclaims his new vision:

> "No penitential shame for what had come,
> No virtuous regret for what had been,—
> But rather a joy to find it in his life
> To be an outcast usher of the soul
> For such as had good courage of the sun
> To pattern Love."

His auditors flee "like brokers out of Arcady," while the narrator alone remains, as he begins his education under Craig's redefining rebellion against Tilbury standards. His work, Craig says, is nonutilitarian, like a sonneteer's, a clown's, or a clergyman's. As the poem progresses he assumes even further disguises: he sees himself as a child, a knight-errant, Christ, Hamlet, and, finally, Socrates. He praises characters like Count Pretzel von Würzburger, *dit L'Obscene,* "a vagabond, a drunkard, and a sponge./But always a free creature with a soul."

Such are the ideals he sets against Tilbury town. Metaphorically Craig's power is characterized by an enormous number of varied images of light— light dazzling bright, pale, and cold, and even light filtered through Craig's "unwashed attic window." Equally defining him are references to music of similarly various kinds. He is, as a Platonic hero of the Ideal, defined by light and music. But in his discourses Craig insists continually on the dissonance and darkness through which he has achieved his recognition. He has known men "...on foul floors, like starved outrageous lizards,/Made human with paralysis and rags"; or bodies of wounded soldiers filled with maggots; or women, "Flat-breasted miracles of cheerfulness/Made neuter by the work that no man counts"; and ruined children. Optimism and pessimism he finds but two of "fifteen-thousand ways to be one-sided."

Thus, dying, he gathers his five or six disciples—he is himself a disciple, "an Usher in the Palace of the Sun," and has been sending them epistles— to read his last will and testament. Though at first he sought riches, like his disciples did before he came, he can now leave his disciples more:

> "I, Captain Craig, abhorred iconoclast,
> Sage-errant, favored of the Cosmic Joke,
> And self-reputed humorist at large,
> Do now, confessed of my world-worshipping,
> Time-questioning, sun-fearing, and heart-yielding,
> Approve and unreservedly devise
> To you and your assigns for ever more,
> God's universe and yours."

Briefly in the delirium of his death-throes he returns to Athens and calls again as Socrates for the cup. Then, in his last, emphatically ironical insistence on his role as humorist, he utters his final word—"Trombones." Unsaddened that he is dying, he rejoices, rather, that he has truly lived. That night his transformed disciples in The Chrysalis—their prophetically named club—play the victorious march from *Löhengrin,* and, gathering for his funeral the next day, have trombones and brass aplenty, as the Tilbury Band blares its way triumphantly, joyously, and indiscreetly—followed by children—to Captain Craig's grave. The antihero, having become a genuine hero by redefining values, has earned the title he had assumed.

In *The Town Down the River* (1910) Robinson abandoned the experimentation which marked *Captain Craig,* to develop the themes of his first volume. Later volumes continued along these lines. Robinson's interest in consciousness and its needs—unsatisfied in the society he knew—began to be expressed in ode and omniscient narrative, rather than dramatically, as in *Captain Craig.* Although the title poem of *The Man Against the Sky* (1916) has been highly praised, it is a poem too much given over to rhetoric. Poems in that volume that, like "Flammonde," resemble *Captain Craig* testify conclusively to the decline in Robinson's energy; for such characters as Flammonde and Benwick Fenzer—representing contraries that had interacted in the drama of *Captain Craig*—now require separate poems for the poet who now lacks the elasticity to combine (and so modify) contraries in one. By 1917 Robinson had begun to turn to the kind of allegorical reconstruction of the past that he had earlier criticized in William Vaughan Moody's poetry. In *Merlin* (1917), *Lancelot* (1920), and *Tristram* (1927), he established the rhetorical formulas and attitudes that would affect even his more lyrical work. He now found that he, unlike Captain Craig, could be popular. *Tristram,* shrewdly promoted—but also lacking the complexity and experimentation of *Captain Craig*—sold 57,475 copies in its first year. During these years even his best poems, like "Rembrandt to Rembrandt' 'and "John Brown," were cast in the myth of the past, while the long narratives, *Roman Bartholomew* (1923), *Cavender's House* (1929), and those that followed were increasingly Gothic in incident and setting. This pattern, of course, repeats the familiar shape of regional careers: after the writer's violent reassessment of the outworn myths of conventional society—similar in *Main-Travelled Roads,* or *A New England Nun,* and *Captain Craig*—he later seeks refuge in the reconstructed past to which he has emotionally been tied all along, and thus produces new *ancien régimes,* Colonial sketches, romances of Virginia or of the primeval West, epics of a past whose greatness (as the writer comes to see it) makes the present intolerable, for life as well as for literary material. Robinson, of course, could turn savagely upon himself and his tendency to make a myth of the past—for instance, in "Miniver Cheevy." But that poem was written in 1910, while the vision of *Captain Craig* still lingered as a possibility in his consciousness. Better than most of the other regionalists, Robinson could make a genuine literature out of his sense of the past; poetry, perhaps, more easily accommodates and even thrives on myth than the short-story form, which most of the other regionalists employed. Much of his later work has a finish and even a kind of psychological complexity which *Captain Craig* lacks. But in that earlier volume he created a hero— or antihero—who stands as a culmination of the whole critical tradition of New England regionalism, a vivid representation of the terrible alternatives to which modern man has been driven by his past.

Robert Frost: The Two Roads

"What I like is griefs and I like them Robinsonianly profound," Robert Frost wrote in his introduction to Robinson's posthumous *King Jasper* (1935). "His theme was unhappiness itself," Frost continues,

> but his skill was as happy as it was playful.... [The] style is the way the man takes himself; and to be at all charming or even bearable, the way is almost rigidly prescribed. If it is with outer seriousness, it must be with inner humor. If it is with outer humor, it must be with inner seriousness.[204]

Frost's description of Robinson is, of course, a characterization of his own way with poetry. By 1935 he had been a professional poet for over forty years, having first published a poem, "My Butterfly, An Elegy," in *The Independent* for November, 1894. Born nineteen years earlier, during Grant's presidency, Frost is as much a part of the nineteenth-century tradition as Robinson. As early as 1915, William Dean Howells praised and sought to characterize the thrust of Frost's work by shrewdly defining it as "the quality of Sarah Orne Jewett and Miss Mary Wilkins and Miss Alice Brown finding metrical utterance."[205] Like these seekers after a lost Eden, Frost finds consolation by humorously or ironically rejecting the idea of myth altogether. George Nitchie has attributed the melancholy in Frost's poems to the irretrievability of the lost Garden. This is undoubtedly true. But it is true as well, in more general ways, that even his humor testifies to the depth of his melancholy. As Frost said with regard to Robinson, inner seriousness must find expression in outer humor. Captain Craig always laughs at his most melancholic reflections. Thus, it is in the quality of Frost's humor, which he shares with nearly all of the regional writers, that his essential seriousness becomes clear. The poet, like the speaker in "Directive," is unwilling to give unambivalent directions, having "only...at heart your getting lost." The alternating (and sometimes simultaneous) acceptance and rejection characteristic of regional writing consists of a stoical acceptance based on the recognition that whatever is, is right; and a rejection of the present nostalgically derived from the vision of a golden past in which whatever was, was more right. From this Yes-and-No comes the rapid movement from humor to sentiment, anguish to mirth, and the unwillingness to decide between seriousness and jest that defines Frost's style and attitude. Having only, as earlier New Englanders had, the Grey Cabins of New England, he

---

[204] (New York, 1935), pp. viii, xii–xiii. [205] "Editor's Easy Chair," *Harper's*, CXXXI (September 1915), 635.

nonetheless yearns to transform them by a vision of the green shadows of Eden.

As has been said before, by the '90s the themes and methods of New England regional writing had become stereotyped and conventionalized. Within the tradition of these conventions Frost works; he perfects what in other hands would have been merely cliché. He treats the regional themes in their extreme implications for the isolation of man. His rural solitaries thus become symbolic of the alienated condition of modern man. Frost's is only ostensibly an early nineteenth-century New England—including no immigrants, no cities, no racial or religious minority problems, a New England so simplified that it excludes even the tensions in nineteenth-century village life between the individual and his community, like those depicted by Mrs. Cooke or Mary Wilkins. In Frost's bleak vision, there is seldom a cure for isolation, resolution for solitude. Elemental in their loneliness, Frost's characters can thus mean more than they are. Frost strips bare the regional clichés, revealing the archetypes of loneliness and despair beneath them. It is not without significance that Frost first made his reputation in England and that among his earliest admirers were Pound and Yeats. Frost knew, through his particular experience with the New England decline, what Yeats learned from his particular experience with Ireland. Both understood how an effective center of value and judgment had dropped out of modern life. Joanna's Shell-Heap Island has no nearby Dunnet community in Frost's poems. Things fall apart. For the Captain Craigs or Mr. Floods of Frost's poetry there are not even rural Tilbury towns to ease the irreducible and irremediable loneliness of self which his characters feel. Frost's New England is archetypal rather than historical. A farmer in "The Mountain" tells the narrator, in a typical scene, "There is no village—only scattered farms./We were but sixty voters last election./ We can't in nature grow to many more." Rejecting the industrial system in "The Lone Striker," the hero makes his decision easy because he imagines the only alternative to be a life of freedom in nature—although, as Mary Wilkins knew, the life of the industrial worker (as in *The Portion of Labor*) was no more dehumanizing than life in a decaying village. Between the sterile lives of country and city lay the New Englander's tragic choice. Frost's conventionalized New England is one that combines the seventeenth-century colonial organization of society—by individual or family units—with the way in which nineteenth-century industrialism, transportation, and expansion decreased New England's economic and intellectual importance, and so produced the strange, isolated, or self-willed characters in "An Old Man's Winter Night," "The Witch at Coös," "The Pauper Witch of Grafton," "The Black Cottage," "The Hill Wife," "Snow," "The Self-Seeker," "A Servant to Servants," and "The Subverted Flower." Frost's subject matter, this is to say, derives from the stock of literary conventions established by the regionalists we have considered (and such of their followers as Lucy Larcom, Arlo Bates, Alice Brown, Rowland Robinson, Sally Pratt McLean, and Anne Trumbull Slosson).

So many of Frost's critics have spoken about his poetry as if it represented a series of reports on an existing reality that it is important to emphasize the way in which his New England is fundamentally mythical, a literary construct from which he derives images and themes whereby to convey in verse his sense of the human condition. Unwilling to tie his poetry to social issues—he repeatedly indicated in the '30s how these seemed to threaten his vision—he constructed an idyllic New England brought to ruin inexplicably (though he, like his regional predecessors, knew the reasons) and so providing tragic material for a poetry of grief and disaster. In the same way that earlier poets could write endlessly out of the matter of Troy, so Frost produced a dozen volumes by reaching variously into the established matter of New England. In one of his earliest poems, "Ghost House," the narrator dwells "in a lonely house I know/That vanished many a summer ago," and finds its ghosts "As sweet companions as might be had." His poems commune with ghosts, while his particular New England is best symbolized by the poignant and desolate cellar hole, netted with twining grapevines and wild raspberries, which appears repeatedly in his verse. Remembrances of an idyllic past, on the one hand—those of childhood (for instance, in "Birches") or of bucolic nature (in "A Winter Eden" and "A Drumlin Woodchuck")—may console the poet. But, on the other hand, he also rehearses the moral and physical wrecks of the present: the woodpile left to decay in a swamp; the hill (in "The Birthplace") once cleared by man but now filling up with trees again; or the sullen terror of guilt-ridden lives like the woman's in "The Fear."

Using "The Pasture" as the epigraph to the last several editions of his *Complete Poems,* Frost invites the reader to enter momentarily his pastoral world:

> I'm going out to clean the pasture spring;
> I'll only stop to rake the leaves away
> (And wait to watch the water clear, I may):
> I shan't be gone long.—You come too.

> I'm going out to fetch the little calf
> That's standing by the mother. It's so young
> It totters when she licks it with her tongue.
> I shan't be gone long.—You come too.[206]

Entering the pasture, one enters Frost's book; for Frost attempts to give it the easy appearance of nature itself. Into that nature, with him, we grope our way. The poems mark stages of the reader's initiation. But, of course, even in the invitation one senses the dangers of that pastoral world, where pure nature (the spring) is muddied, and childlike innocence

[206] The following poems of Robert Frost are quoted: "Ghost House" (*A Boy's Will* [London, 1913]), "The Pasture" (*North of Boston* [London, 1916]), "The Road Not Taken" (*Mountain Interval* [New York, 1916]), "For Once, Then, Something" (*New Hampshire* [New York, 1923]), "Acquainted With the Night" (*West-Running Brook* [New York, 1928]), "Home Burial" (*North of Boston*), and "From Plane to Plane" (*Complete Poems* [New York, 1949]), all in *The Complete Poems of Robert Frost* (New York, 1949).

(the calf) totters in its contact with the world of adulthood; both (and so, we too) must be saved by the poet.[207] In his ultimate unwillingness to insist upon either the past or the present, the rural or the urban, the garden or the machine, Frost has been called, by Yvor Winters and others, a "spiritual drifter." But it is precisely in the richness of his uncompromising ambivalence that he proves valuable. For twentieth-century man he provides alternate sets of seventeenth- to nineteenth-century values; against the proletariat collective he offers a vision of a highly personal rural order; against the hasty energy of technology he sets the equally forceful patience of nature; against economic or political utopias he urges the persistence of the real and the possible. He is useful precisely because in every possibility he recognizes an alternative and so refuses to close his mind and art with social, psychological, or economic dogmas. He has made drift the principle of his mastery.

His world is perhaps the closest version in American poetry to William James's *Pragmatism* (1907) or John Dewey's instrumentalism. Both James and Frost were deeply affected by the tendencies of the Progressive Era. As has been abundantly shown, the Progressives attacked or reassessed traditional doctrines—particularly in politics and economics—in order to free the individual from older absolutistic systems. But, as Dewey insisted, merely this was not enough: "The fundamental defect in the present state of democracy," he said, "is the assumption that political and economic freedom can be achieved without first freeing the mind."[208] James, in *Pragmatism,* sought to free the individual mind from the collectives and absolutes of thought that he shrewdly detected in traditional philosophy: his pragmatism cut through fixed laws, large units or massive categories of thought, and slavish adherence to dogmatic systems. For him, the chance world—the world of intellectual frontiering—was the true democratic counteractant to the intellectual totalitarianism of rationalism or monism. Not a comfortable system of knowledge or belief, but individual creativity, is made responsible for choice. Every act was, for James, an experiment the outcome of which was more or less uncertain. Thus through James's optimism runs a tough-minded pessimism, which recognizes the dangers as well as the romance of an experimental universe. "Is the last word sweet?" he asks in *Pragmatism.*

> Is all "yes," "yes" in the universe? Doesn't the fact of "no" stand at the very core of life?...I find myself willing to take the universe to be really

---

[207] In his discussion of Frost's pastoralism, John Lynen writes of "the decay of the Arcadian myth": "the pastoralism of tradition had long since gone—disappeared with a finality which defied the most strenuous efforts of the nineteenth century to revive it." Although this is largely true, one should remember that Sarah Jewett, for example, had consciously played on the conventions in "A Dunnet Shepherdess," and in her repeated point that sheep are wandering over the island hillsides around Dunnet harbor. New Englanders had not forgotten the pastoral image. Conrad Aiken, of course, used it in *Brownstone Eclogues,* and the pastoral image is played upon by William Carlos Williams in *Paterson.* See John Lynen, *The Pastoral Art of Robert Frost* (New Haven, 1960), pp. 14–15. [208] See Dewey, *Democracy and Education: An Introduction to the Philosophy of Education* (New York, 1937), pp. 94–116, 372, and *passim.*

dangerous and adventurous, without therefore backing out and crying "no play."...I am willing that there should be real losses and real losers, and no total preservation of all that is.[209]

In this epic, chance universe Robert Frost also lives and, like James, ever insists on keeping his scheme of possibility uncertified—willing to choose wrongly, if need be, but needing, in any event, to choose. One thinks, for instance, of the poem "The Road Not Taken," where the choice is purely arbitrary, a Jamesian experiment. For although Frost tries to reassure us:

> Two roads diverged in a wood, and I—
> I took the one less traveled by,

the truth is, he soon says, "as for that, the passing there/Had worn them really about the same." He could have chosen either—or both—with equal reason. This is a kind of celebration of the Epic of the Will. Similarly, in "For Once, Then, Something," Frost wrote his answer to the critics who were dissatisfied with his unwillingness to look through a chance universe to a comforting system of absolutes. All he sees is the "Me myself" in a universe that only reflects the desires he invests it with. For sixty years he was, as he said in "Acquainted With the Night," "unwilling to explain," though heroically manipulating and sifting the varieties of poetic experience.

Such ambivalence provides the drama for the best of Frost's poems. In the well-known "Home Burial," two kinds of sensibilities rage in conflict. Inconsolable in her grief over the death of her child, Amy is shocked by what she takes to be her husband's callousness in resuming normal life after digging the grave in his ancestors' graveyard. He, working within tradition and so accepting—but with no less sensitivity—the necessity of death and decay, feels as cursed as she in their mutual misunderstanding. Separated by a flight of stairs, and by the character of their respective individual- and tradition-bound griefs, they are yet held together by their love. Such simultaneous contact and separation make up the internal drama in which Amy and her husband are forever suspended—separate but connected, immobilized, like the lovers on the Grecian Urn, at the moment of crisis:

> "*You*—oh, you think the talk is all—I must go—
> Somewhere out of this house. How can I make you—"

> "If—you—do!" She was opening the door wider.
> "Where do you mean to go? First tell me that.
> I'll follow and bring you back by force. I *will!*—"

So, also, in "The Death of the Hired Man," Mary and Warren struggle to assess the question of their responsibility toward Silas, whose death leaves their debate permanently unresolved. Both poems have, however, authoritative finality in suggesting to the reader how richly complex and rewarding the human debate is. In the last poem of the *Complete Poems*, "From Plane

[209] (New York, 1955 [1907]), pp. 190, 191.

to Plane," Frost is still working in a vigorously multifarious, dramatic world. He begins:

> Neither of them was better than the other.
> They both were hired. And though Pike had the advantage
>
> Of having hoed and mowed for fifty years,
> Dick had of being fresh and full of college.
> So if they fought about equality
> It was on an equality they fought.
>
> "Your trouble is not sticking to the subject,"
> Pike said with temper. And Dick longed to say,
> "Your trouble is bucolic lack of logic,"
> But all he did say was, "What *is* the subject?"

By a series of tacks and compromises the college man and the farmhand (despite his bucolic logic) manage to reach similar positions. Man works from plane to plane. The drama of the poem, as always, consists in the dance of alternatives as the characters and their ideas shift and change in confronting possibility. The "subject" is not the question of work, or of grief, as in "Home Burial," or of responsibility, as in "The Death of the Hired Man." Rather, the subject is the conversation itself: man talking, deciding, alternatingly alienated from and relating to his fellows in the community of ideas. The subject is the poem itself: the figure a poem makes.

A suggestive story, "The Monarch of Dreams," by Thomas Wentworth Higginson, begins: "He who...goes wandering through the hill-country of New England, must adopt one rule as invariable. When he comes to a fork in the road, and is assured that both ways lead to the desired point, he must simply ask which road is the best; and, on its being pointed out, must at once take the other.... The passers-by will always recommend the new road, which keeps to the valley and avoids the hills; but the old road, deserted by the general public, ascends the steeper grades and has a monopoly of the wider views."[210] This passage of Higginson's is, of course, specifically important to Robert Frost's "The Road Not Taken," but in a larger sense it well describes, as Frost's poem also does, the two ways that regional writers have needed to go in this period. For them, as modern men, only the main-traveled road exists, the new road, of life-in-the-present; yet from that middling path, the "steeper grades" or "wider views" of the past become all the more attractive. Thus, as the traveler cannot, they take both ways at once, imaginatively, the new and old roads. These I have called the nightmare and daydream of regional writing; for needing to take both ways, they can have neither. Like the characters of Frost's dramatic dialogues, they remain ever suspended between them, in the divine discontent of creativity.

---

[210] *The Monarch of Dreams* (Boston, 1886), pp. 7–8.

FOUR

Mark Twain

The Dream of Drift
and the Dream of Delight

> *"Well, I mean to have a good time, whether or no," said Newman.*
> *"I am not cultivated, I am not even educated; I know nothing about*
> *history, or art, or foreign tongues, or any other learned matters. But*
> *I am not a fool either, and I shall undertake to know something about*
> *Europe by the time I have done with it. I feel something under my*
> *ribs here...that I can't explain—a sort of mighty hankering, a desire*
> *to stretch out and haul in."*
>
> *"Bravo," said Mrs. Tristram, "that is very fine. You are the great*
> *Western Barbarian, stepping forth in his innocence and might, gazing*
> *awhile at this poor effete Old World, and then swooping down on it."*
>
> *"Oh, come," said Newman. "I am not a barbarian, by a good deal....*
> *I am a highly civilized man....I stick to that. If you don't believe it,*
> *I should like to prove it to you."*
>
> —Henry James, *The American* (1877)

Many years after collaborating with Mark Twain on *The Gilded Age* (1872), Charles Dudley Warner argued in *The Relation of Literature to Life* (1895) that "all genuine, enduring literature is the outcome of the time that produces it, is responsive to the general sentiment of its time."[1] However simplistic and inaccurate, Warner's conviction well represents the view of authorship held by most of the writers of his age. Perhaps even more than his peers, Mark Twain needed to understand his audience in order to write at all; in each of his books he was more led to ponder the relation of his own to the collective mind. Enormously successful from the beginning—his first book, *Innocents Abroad* (1869) sold 67,000 copies in its first year—Twain always showed intense interest in the details of printing and distribution.

All of his major books were sold by subscription. Although he encouraged Howells and Aldrich also to prepare books suitable for distribution by canvassers, the book they planned together following his advice, "Twelve

---

[1] *Complete Writings of Charles Dudley Warner,* Vol. XV, p. 47.

Memorable Murders," was fortunately never written; for subscription selling required a particular talent in an author for sensing mass needs, a talent which Twain alone, among major American writers, possessed. With an assured sale of 40,000 copies for almost any book he offered, he could declare: "Why, any other means of bringing out a book is privately printing it."[2] But to keep his books selling "just like the Bible" he was obliged to accurately assess the character of his audience. If he aspired to become wealthy,[3] he had to respond nimbly to the permutations and diversities in public taste.

In an age when literary business was far less complex than today, Twain was absorbed in commercial considerations. He moved to Hartford partially to be near his publishers, the American Publishing Company, and freely offered advice on book design, illustrations, and sales publicity or practices. Eventually, of course, these concerns would so occupy his mind that he would himself become a subscription publisher—of Grant's *Memoirs* and *Huckleberry Finn* among others—as well as the sponsor of a spectacularly unsuccessful typesetting machine and of a kaolatype process for engraving illustrations. Deeply interested, moreover, in politics, business, and invention; returning repeatedly to the lecture platform to replace the money that he lost in speculation; committed personally and socially to literature as a remunerative profession; and ever in demand as a speaker at public occasions, Twain actively undertook a personal, direct study of the American audience. He was engaged in making and seeing the history of his age. He sought to turn this engagement into profit with his books. But his ability to measure and control his own ego by setting it against the collective mind inevitably caused Twain anxiety and frustration. Eventually, his deepened sense of the complexity of the mind of his age immobilized him as a writer. He frequently declared himself to be a representative, archetypal man. Even as late as 1907, the year following the appearance of his study of the damned human race, *What is Man?*, he announced: "I am the whole human race, without a detail lacking; I have studied the human race with diligence and strong interest all these years in my own person; in myself I find in big or little proportion every quality and every defect that is findable in the mass of the race."[4] But in an age changing so swiftly that man himself seemed in the process of transformation, who was the Representative Man? Incredibly sensitive to the shifting, unpredictable mass mind, Twain shows

---

[2] Quoted in Albert Bigelow Paine, *Mark Twain: The Personal and Literary Life of Samuel Langhorne Clemens* (New York and London, 1912), Vol. I, p. 503. In this chapter the quotations from Twain's works, except as noted, are from *The Complete Works of Mark Twain*, "American Artists Edition" (New York, n. d.), 26 vols. [3] As early as 1867 Twain wrote: "Honest poverty is a gem that even a King might feel proud to call his own, but I wish to sell out. I have sported that kind of jewelry long enough. I want some variety. I wish to become rich, so that I can instruct the people and glorify honest poverty a little, like those good, kind-hearted, fat, benevolent people do." He would always be of two minds about wealth, of course; his "Open Letter to Commodore Vanderbilt" brilliantly shows his suspicions of wealth. See Franklin Walker and G. Ezra Dane, eds., *Mark Twain's Travels With Mr. Brown* (New York, 1940), p. 236. [4] Quoted in *Mark Twain in Eruption*, ed. Bernard DeVoto (New York, 1940), p. xxix.

in his work the confusions and contradictions of an unsteady time. The life of his art was the life of his audience made subtle, but nonetheless showing the same hesitancies, false starts, and derangements.

It is easy to forget how little of Twain's work was in fiction. Like Howells and DeForest, he was (so Howells put it of himself) a "traveler" before he was a "noveler," and his fiction was informed by the fact and condition of travel. Like his age, he seemed to have been born on the move. After the war, Twain replaced Bayard Taylor as the American Traveler, his first book, *Innocents Abroad,* appearing, appropriately, in the same year as Taylor's last travel book, *By-Ways of Europe* (1869). Until Twain learned from Cable to read publicly from his own work, his lectures detailed his travel experiences. His talk at Cooper Union in 1867 (where Lincoln had appeared seven years earlier), billed as "A Serio-Humorous Lecture Concerning Kanakadom Or, The Sandwich Islands," was typical of the subjects of his platform efforts for a decade. The restlessness mirrored in his writing was a reflection of his early life. Leaving Hannibal at the age of eighteen, he worked in the composing room of the *St. Louis Evening News* only long enough to earn railroad fare to New York. He was drawn to the metropolis, like thousands of his fellows, by the World's Fair of 1853. To his sister he wrote glowingly of the marvelous Crystal Palace, "the lofty dome, glittering jewelry, gaudy tapestry, etc., with the busy crowd passing to and fro— 'tis a perfect fairy palace—beautiful beyond description."[5] (Theodore Dreiser would later make a similar journey to the Columbian Exposition of 1893 and show strikingly similar feelings.) After leaving New York for Philadelphia, he paused at Washington, and then returned home briefly, only to wander back to St. Louis, and on to composing rooms in Muscatine and Keokuk, Iowa, and Cincinnati. Even at this time, in 1856, he was dreaming of traveling to the headwaters of the recently surveyed Amazon River, there to establish his fortune with a vast cocoa plantation.[6] He even took passage on the *Paul Jones* to New Orleans, thence to depart for the Amazon. Only at this crucial point did he change plans and convince Horace Bixby to take him on as an apprentice pilot. Still he was on the move. After his four years of piloting Mississippi steamboats, rendered autobiographically in the first half of *Life on the Mississippi* (1883), he served briefly as an officer in the Missouri militia, an experience he burlesqued in "The Private History of a Campaign that Failed." In 1861 he went to the Nevada Territory as assistant to his brother Orion, recently appointed secretary to the territorial governor. In his eight years since first leaving Hannibal he had wandered restlessly all over the country. "All I do know or feel is that I am wild with impatience to move—move—move!" he would write in 1867, early naming and cursing the restlessness that drove him throughout life.[7]

But he was not long in turning his personal wanderlust to the uses and

[5] Paine, Vol. I, pp. 94–5. [6] Part of the Southern myth of mission involved establishing a tropical empire embracing the Mississippi and Amazon basins and controlling the Pacific trade. Moving West and then East, Twain would later identify his ideals with the Eden myth. But it is important to note that his earliest impulses allied him with the myth of the manifest destiny of the South. See Henry Nash Smith, *Virgin Land,* p. 154. [7] Quoted in Paine, Vol. I, pp. 321–22.

orders of art. Whitman had written in 1860 of travel as a metaphor for experience:

> On journeys through the states we start,
> (Ay, through the world, urged by these songs,
> Sailing henceforth to every land, to every sea,)
> We willing learners of all, teachers of all, and lovers of all.

Twain was gathering material as he wandered, finding in his rootlessness a root in art. Learning from all, he would soon make himself a teacher—though never a lover—of all. His first reputation was as the Great Western Barbarian, the backwoods humorist. In 1865 Henry Clapp's *Saturday Press*—the official paper of Whitman's New York Bohemians—printed "Jim Smiley and His Jumping Frog." Twenty years later, Twain would call himself a member of "the Pfaff gang," perhaps seeing himself in Whitman's tradition. But in 1865 he referred to the frog story as "a villainous backwoods sketch,"[8] and feared it would obscure his serious work. Reacting against the regional sketch as a sign of his "backwoods" origin, he sought to establish himself as a man of taste and culture by arranging with the *Sacramento Union* to write a series of Sandwich Island travel letters. These he remade into an article for *Harper's*. Between the regional sketch and the cosmopolitan letter, between the Bohemian New York of Whitman and the genteel metropolis of Harper Brothers, the lines of Mark Twain's career were to run.

But for the moment, the literature of travel prevailed. The announcement of the Quaker City Holy Land Excursion—the first guided pleasure tour from America—stirred Twain's imagination. At once he could play both the Western Barbarian and the Civilized American. The excursion was to be, he wrote, "a picnic on a gigantic scale"; its "select company" of passengers would "hob-nob with nobility and hold friendly converse with kings and princes, Grand Moguls, and the annointed lords of mighty empires!" Guiding the curious traveler nearly around the world, the Quaker-City steamboat excursion was the answer to the postwar American's prayer. And Twain was its chronicler.[9]

As Twain's revisions of his *Alta Californian* and *Tribune* letters show, in *Innocents Abroad* he was concerned not merely with the crowded details of travel, but also, and more deeply, as the background for his humor, with the moral relevance and significance of the journey to the Holy Land.[10] If the Western humorist in Twain satirized tradition—insisting that "the informa-

8 Quoted in *ibid.*, Vol. I, p. 278. 9 The quotations above are from Twain's comments in *Innocents Abroad*. Both Henry Ward Beecher and General Sherman were originally signed for the trip, though each withdrew at the last moment. Replacing them as a representative of the new American mind was John Greenwood, agent for P. T. Barnum, who "travelled 17,735 miles and brought back several interesting relics from the Holy Land, which were duly deposited in the Museum." (See P. T. Barnum, *Struggles and Triumphs...*, Vol. II, p. 643.) 10 Paine provides an interesting biographical detail: Mark Twain probably did not now [on the Quaker City excursion] regret those early Sunday-school lessons; certainly he did not fail to review them exhaustively on that journey. His note books fairly overflow with Bible references....The little Bible he carried on that trip, bought in Constantinople, was well worn by the time they reached the ship again at Jaffa. (Vol. I, p. 338.)

tion the ancients didn't have was very voluminous"—the imagination of the traveler saw the discovery of Europe and the Near East as a ceremony of initiation to knowledge. Mark Twain worked naturally in mythical patterns. To his archetypal mind, the theme of journeying naturally suggested and symbolized the wandering of the questing pilgrim toward regeneration. Writing largely under the influence of unconscious impulses, Twain worked very closely to the archetypal experience of Americans and the older European imagination in which they share. This helps to explain his great success in understanding and anticipating the desires of his audience. Evidence that his mind, like the collective mind, moved in archetypal patterns is plentiful. As early as 1869 he was planning what he called a "Noah's Ark Book" as a sequel to *Innocents Abroad*. Detailing the cruise of the ark in diaries kept by its passengers, this project would eventually be transformed into the diaries of Adam and Eve, sections of which he worked on during four decades. With the Rev. Thomas K. Beecher he seriously proposed in 1881 to erect a memorial to Adam. Later, in 1888, Twain developed a plan even more closely resembling the myth of pilgrimage in *Innocents Abroad:*

> Dress up some good actors as Apollyon, Greatheart, etc., & the other Bunyan characters, take them to a wild gorge and photograph them—Valley of the Shadow of Death; to other effective places & photo them along with the scenery; to Paris, in their curious costumes, place them near the Arc de l'Etoile & photo them with the crowd—Vanity Fair; to Cairo, Venice, Jerusalem, & other places (twenty interesting cities) & always make them conspicuous in the curious foreign crowds by their costume.... It would take two or three years to do the photographing & cost $10,000; but this stereopticon panorama of Bunyan's *Pilgrim's Progress* could be exhibited in all countries at the same time & would clear a fortune in a year. By and by I will do this.[11]

Twain's conception of *travel* in *Innocents Abroad* rapidly comes to take on its root meaning of *travail*—to suffer and labor spiritually. Twain's pilgrims make the archetypal journey on the *via,* the way of life toward death. They are symbols of what men must go through—the confusions and disorders—on their way toward grace and salvation. If Twain's sense of salvation remains a secular one, it shows, nonetheless, the same form as the traditional journey toward grace. Traveling, Twain's characters earn not grace, but knowledge. They are "saved" by coming to consciousness. *Innocents Abroad* was originally entitled, and was eventually subtitled, *The New Pilgrim's Progress*. Twain takes the world's most recent pilgrim—the American Innocent—upon the journey to Jerusalem. His quest is no less serious for being delightfully masked in a good deal of humor and parody. Twain's recognition of the pastness of the past—of the difference between Europe and America—leads both to high comedy and high tragedy. At the very beginning of the cruise, the expedition photographer brings out his lantern exhibition to "show the passengers where they shall eventually arrive." But "by a funny accident the first picture that flamed out upon the

---

11 Quoted in Paine, Vol. II, p. 872.

canvas was a view of Greenwood Cemetery." Thus the pilgrims' journey is toward death; their excursion is merely the modern equivalent—as the *New* Pilgrims—to the journey of Everyman. Toward the end of the book, Twain comments: "I have given...information for people who will not read Bible history until they are defrauded into it by some such method as this. I hope that no friend of progress and education will obstruct or interfere with my peculiar mission." His role is to keep the diary of the mission of modern man.

Twain's pilgrims, moreover, march in a straggling procession from America, through Europe, to the Holy Land. They are, he suggests, like one of the wandering tribes of Israel moving through the desert of European corruption in search of the original Promised Land. Entering Damascus, Twain recalls "an honoured old tradition that the immense garden which Damascus stands in was the Garden of Eden"; "the sacred river Jordan" is "a grateful vision, after so much desert." Particularly as an American writer Twain is able to make use of journey symbolism in comparing specifically to his own pilgrims the journey of the seventeenth-century Pilgrims to America. These Pilgrims possessed and promulgated their own particular version of the American destiny and of America as the promised land of regeneration. Now Twain's New Pilgrims resail that journey and reassess that hope. They sing from "the Plymouth Collection of Hymns"; their devotions are satirized as synagogical by "the unregenerate" aboard; and they are a "select"—i.e., in the separatist version, an "elected"—group. Twain, who keeps the journal for the expedition, is its William Bradford.

The book ends in a hymn and prayer, as, returning to America, "the glad pilgrims...joined hands again and the long, strange cruise was over. Amen." But their moral accomplishments remain inconclusive. The material, nineteenth-century world intrudes on and limits moral possibility. At the climax of their journey, at the Sea of Galilee, the pilgrims bargain with a boatman to ferry them in the seapaths of Christ—only to conclude, as prudent nineteenth-century businessmen, that the fare is too high. Even "after coming half around the globe to taste that pleasure" of following after Christ on land and sea, they betray the principles of the moral journey by at last asserting the material considerations of the gilded age. In Twain's discovery in Jerusalem of "the grave of a blood relation," Adam, is the central irony of the book—at once mirthful and anguished. "I deemed it no shame to have wept over the grave of my poor dead relative," Twain writes. "Noble old man—he did not live to see me—he did not live to see his child. And I—I—alas, I did not live to see *him*." The present is irretrievably severed from the past. Eden remains closed. Beginning as Innocents these New Pilgrims are thus projected into experience. Going forth like Whitman's child, they return like Melville's Ishmael, reborn into the knowledge of good and evil.

In an attempt to repeat and expand the success of *Innocents Abroad,* Twain naturally continued to work in the genre of travel literature. As part owner of the Buffalo *Express* in 1870, he ran a series called "Around the World," for which a substitute traveler, D. R. Ford, sent back factual reports that Twain remade into his own first-person narratives. He proposed to write a book of travels to African diamond mines on a similar plan, with a surrogate traveler, and was frustrated only by the death of his correspondent. In *The Galaxy* for 1870 he found that he could use the travel form to write social criticism. Imitating Oliver Goldsmith's *Letters from a Citizen of the World* in a series called "Goldsmith's Friend Abroad Again" (purportedly written by a Chinese immigrant to San Francisco), Twain satirized political and social corruption.

He was, in all of these, of course, casting about to repeat the success of his first book by writing of his travels. Not for some time did he hit upon the idea of using his travels to the West as material. No doubt he still thought of this as providing only backwoods material. Finally, however, he began a book which he called at first *The Innocents at Home*. In his earlier chronicle he had used the journey eastward to the Eden of the Holy Land as an analogue to the westward journey, to the American Eden. In *Innocents Abroad* he declares that French railroads are lesser Eastern stagecoach lines; the elegant gold statuary of Milan reminds him of the crude bullion of Nevada; Lake Como hardly measures up to the Mississippi; Venice appears to his American eyes to be merely "an overflowed Arkansas town"; St. Peter's is neither as large nor as beautiful as the Capitol in Washington. The Old Eden was closed. The restless search of the book is for a New Eden. Now, in his new book, he reverses this process and sends his Innocents on a journey to the New American West. If the Eastern Eden was closed— by corruption—perhaps the Western Eden, as the regionalists were saying, was all the more open.

This book was retitled and published as *Roughing It* (1872). Although in the book Twain draws upon his Nevada experiences, *Roughing It* is far from a nostalgic memory of his life ten years earlier. He does not so much realistically recreate as literally remake his sense of the West, by sifting fact through his imagination. Certainly *Roughing It* should be read not as a report on the West, but as a report on Twain's state of mind and art ten years later. Indeed, when he began planning the book he wrote in query to his brother, Orion: "Have you a memorandum of the route we took, or the names of any of the stations we stopped at? Do you remember any of the scenes, names, incidents, or adventures of the coach trip?—*for I remember next to nothing about the matter.* Jot down a foolscap page of items for me."[12] *Roughing It* is clearly experience not only ordered but made by a conscious craftsman. And yet Twain had known enough of the West not to fall into the conventions of Western myth-making. He casts a cold eye on the scene no less than in *Innocents Abroad*. Fundamentally Twain reverses all of the expectations implicit in the myth of the Virgin Land. The Eden of the West stands ever before his hero—Twain himself as an Innocent— as the New Jerusalem glittered before the Pilgrims. And it is equally elusive.

From the very first, Twain reacted against the assumptions of the Western

12 Quoted in Paine, Vol. I, p. 421. Italics added.

agrarian myth. A sense of the importance of civilization and culture; an awareness of the limitations of man and human life; and a suspicion of utopian speculation and social panaceas were part of his conservative heritage. His father, true to his given name, John Marshall Clemens, was an austere Whig, emotionally attached to the East. Mark Twain himself was born only three decades after the distintegration of Marshall's Federalism, and he was clearly influenced by his father's beliefs (via Marshall) in restricted suffrage, in the Constitution and courts as bulwarks against majority tyranny, and in the rights of property. Twain was never touched, as Easterners like Hawthorne were, by Jacksonianism. He was early delighted in Federalist Philadelphia[13] and disgusted with Jacksonian Hannibal, thus symbolizing his heritage of attachment to Federalist rather than Jeffersonian institutions and assumptions. He would spend his life not in nature, but in cities, in America and Europe. His first sketch, "The Dandy Frightening the Squatter," was published in 1852 not in the Hannibal *Journal,* but in *The Carpet Bag* of Boston. His Federalism, moreover, directed his sense of American politics in the Gilded Age. In the '60s and '70s, he frequently spoke of "this wicked ungodly suffrage" and commented: "We know there is Unrestricted Suffrage, we *think* there is a Hell: but the question is, which do we *prefer?*"[14] His short utopian sketch, "The Curious Republic of Gondour" (1875), which Howells printed anonymously in the *Atlantic,* gave his answer to this question. In Gondour, "Brains and property managed the state. A candidate for office must have marked ability, education, and high character, or he stood no sort of chance of election. If a hod-carrier possessed these, he could succeed; but the mere fact that he was a hod-carrier could not elect him, as in previous times."[15] Similarly, in a lecture on "Universal Suffrage" he had already anticipated this solution—adding weight to the vote of education and property—by pointing out to his Monday Evening Club the fallacy of weighing the vote of "a consummate scoundrel" as heavily as that of "a president, a bishop, a college professor, a merchant prince."[16] Even as late as 1901, he outlined a plan for a "casting-vote party," whose purpose would be to "compel the two great parties to nominate their best man always."[17] Moreover, his repeated exposures of the moral rot beneath an apparently idyllic Jeffersonian village life (as in "The Man That Corrupted Hadleyburg") suggest the way his opinions directly entered his art.

In *Roughing It,* then, the narrator, deliberately obscuring the time-sequence, sets two "poor innocents," Orion and the narrator's own younger self, on the journey to Nevada. Although Twain was twenty-six-years old when he made the actual trip, here he makes his persona an innocent who

---

13 He wrote in 1853: "I like this Philadelphia amazingly, and the people in it. There is only one thing that gets my 'dander' up—and that is the hands are always encouraging me: telling me 'it's no use to get discouraged—no use to be downhearted, for there is more work here than you can do!' 'Downhearted' the devil! I have not had a particle of such a feeling since I left Hannibal." (See Paine, Vol. I, p. 99.) 14 Quoted in Louis J. Budd, *Mark Twain: Social Philosopher* (Bloomington, Ind., 1962), p. 59. 15 Twain, *The Curious Republic of Gondour and Other Whimsical Sketches* (New York, 1919), p. 8. 16 Quoted in Walter Blair, *Mark Twain and Huck Finn* (Berkeley, 1960), p. 132. 17 Quoted in Paine, Vol. III, p. 1147.

"had never been away from home," and was going to explore "the curious new world." He appears so young at one point that Brigham Young remarks to Orion, " 'Ah—your child, I presume? Boy or girl?' " Unlike Twain, this Innocent had lived for years "in the close, hot city [St. Louis], toiling and slaving." Feeling emancipated "from all sorts of cares and responsibilities" as soon as he leaves the States, he renews the search for Eden. The incidents of Western travel are now analogues, for the narrator, of his trip to the Holy Land; and his trip to the West continually reminds him of his trip to the East, for he comes to learn that both are the same, both Edens are closed. Seeking an Eden of ease, he is repeatedly confronted with the necessity for labor and the actuality of pain. In his experience of the difficulties of overland travel, the frustration of mining, the boredom of newspaper work, the violent dangers of half-civilized life, his expectations dwindle. Driven by the dream of Eden ever westward, from Nevada to California, he sails the historic American journey to the Pacific and still further west, to the Sandwich Islands. There, for a moment, he seems to have reached his blessed isle: "I breathed the balmy fragrance of jasmine, oleander, and the Pride of India. . . . I moved in the midst of a summer calm as tranquil as dawn in the Garden of Eden," he says. But the "perfumed air" immediately becomes filled with mosquitoes; and the narrator discovers that American missionaries, with their gospel of the Fall, have invaded the Garden. Eden dissolves again, and he is driven restlessly back to San Francisco, then to New York, whence, still an innocent, he will take the Quaker City excursion and continue his eastward pursuit of the Promised Land. He comes, inconclusively, full circle. At the end of the book, the narrator speaks in his own person to point out the realistic "Moral" which he appends: "If you are of any account, stay at home and make your way by faithful diligence." East and West, Eden is closed.

Similar contrasts between desire and performance run through all of Twain's travel writing.[18] Here we shall follow out the history of Twain's career by briefly examining his other travel books; for these, at their best, show him directly facing an unsatisfactory world, one that he needs both to castigate and remake. He travels at the tips of his nerve-endings, and continually exposes himself in his responses. The narrator of *A Tramp Abroad* (1880), for instance, explains that he determined to go to Europe for three reasons: to travel familiarly about the country by foot; to study art; and to learn the German language. But in fact, he and his companion fail to do any of these: the travelers seldom walk, engaging an incredible variety of conveyances at any opportunity; Twain's specimen drawings are execrably bad, and his appreciations of European art are pitched even lower than his burlesques of the old masters in *Innocents Abroad;* finally, his famous essay

[18] His writing is energized by the pain of disillusion. This is well suggested by the fact that although he filled hundreds of stylographic pages with memoranda of his trip to England in 1872, he could not write the travel book with which he planned to follow *Roughing It.* From England he wrote to his mother: "I have had a jolly good time, and I do hate to go away from these English folks: they make a stranger feel entirely at home." (Paine, Vol. I, p. 470.) As Paine summarizes his trip, "All his impressions of England had been happy ones." Thus he could make no book from it. (*Ibid.*, Vol. I, p. 470.)

on "The Awful German Language" indicates the outcome of his third line of endeavor.[19] In short he has *been,* as the punning title suggests, a tramp abroad—no longer with the excuse of innocence—wandering vaguely, purposelessly in a land where he remains alien. William Dean Howells was sensitive to this tension between innocence and experience in Twain's mind and art. In his review of *A Tramp Abroad,* Howells wisely observed: "His wit is turned upon matters that are out of joint.... His opinions are no longer the opinions of a Western American newly amused and disgusted by European differences, but the Western American's impressions on being a second time confronted with things he has had time to think over."[20] In *A Tramp Abroad* Twain made the discovery that both his search and himself are out of joint in a world where expectation never ends in satisfaction.

Similarly, in *Following the Equator* (1897) Twain takes the tropical journey that ever intrigued Northern travelers. The cynical aphorisms attributed to the fictive *Pudd'nhead Wilson's New Calendar* that head each chapter, however, focus Northern realism upon the tropical dream, and suggest the disillusion involved in the Edenic search. "Let us be grateful to Adam our benefactor. He cut us out of the 'blessing' of idleness and won for us the 'curse' of labor," Wilson says. Twain knew that the fall from illusion to actuality was fortunate. But he was also tormented by the pain caused by that fall. In *Following the Equator,* then, Twain sets his persona on the reiterated journey searching for ease. Inaccurately remembering the Honolulu he saw twenty-nine years earlier as "a Paradise which I had been longing all these years to see again," he finds that an onshore cholera epidemic will confine him to his ship. Restlessly, and more rapidly than in any earlier book, he moves around the world, finding Paradise ever closed. Bombay appears momentarily to be "the Arabian Nights come again." But even there, seeing a burly German strike a native servant, he is overwhelmed by the tragedy of slavery, and by memories of his youth:

> For just one second, all that goes to make the *me* in me was in a Missourian village, on the other side of the globe, vividly seeing again these forgotten pictures of fifty years ago...and in the next second I was back in Bombay, and that kneeling native's smitten cheek was not done tingling yet! Back to boyhood—fifty years; back to age again, another fifty; and a flight equal to the circumference of the globe—all in two seconds by the watch!

Like Edith Wharton's Lily Bart, whose seal is a flying ship with the motto *Beyond!,* Twain finds that world travel merely follows the great circle back to self. In his own ego is enacted the drama of youth and age, promise and disillusion. After *Following the Equator* Twain published very little. There

---

[19] These are, of course, narrative, not autobiographical, strategies. He exaggerates both the magnitude of his intentions and the smallness of his accomplishments in order to sharpen the contrast between desire and performance. The satire on the pedestrian journey is based only upon a walk from Hartford to Boston which Twain and Twichell attempted in 1874. Twain studied German carefully and read it easily. And the satire on art appreciation follows a long tradition in Western humor. [20] "Mr. Twain's New Book," *The Atlantic Monthly,* XLV (May 1880), 687.

was nothing much to say. There was nothing much to do. And there was no place left to go.

TWAIN AND HISTORY

Howells—and DeForest, and Henry James—by adapting the travel narrative to fiction in order to write novels in which contraries mix and resolve conflict into harmony, made the National Novel, the Great American Novel. Twain commented to Howells in 1885, "you are really my only author; I am restricted to you; I wouldn't give a damn for the rest." He reserved a kind of praise for Howells that he would give to no one else. *A Hazard of New Fortunes* he thought "a great book." In *A Foregone Conclusion* he found "absolute perfection of character-drawing."[21] Convinced beyond question of the power and permanence of Howells's work, he wrote:

> ...only you see people & their ways & their insides & outsides as they *are*, & make them talk as they *do* talk. I think you are the very greatest artist in these tremendous matters that ever lived. There doesn't seem to be anything that can be concealed from your awful all-seeing eye. It must be a cheerful thing for one to live with you & be aware that you are going up and down in him like another conscience all the time. Possibly you will not be a fully accepted classic until you have been dead a hundred years, ... but *then* your books will be as common as Bibles. ... In that day *I* shall be in the Cyclopedias, too,—thus: "Mark Twain; history & occupation unknown—but he was personally acquainted with Howells."[22]

But while Twain, like Howells, was engaged in an adaptation of the travel narrative to the writing of novels, he would never write comfortably or long in the Howells tradition. Twain went his own way with the novel. Driven, like Howells and his peers, to *seek* harmony, he looked so shrewdly that he found only chaos behind the appearance and promise of harmony. His books thus work toward reversing all of the expectations of Howells's National Novel.

As we have seen, Twain's travel narratives discover, rather than dissolve, barriers. Their common theme is the way the sensitive, innocent individual

[21] *Mark Twain–Howells Letters: The Correspondence of Samuel L. Clemens and William D. Howells, 1872–1910,* ed. Henry Nash Smith and William Gibson, with the Assistance of Frederick Anderson (Cambridge, Mass., 1960), Vol. II, pp. 533, 579; Vol. I, p. 17.
[22] Lest this sound like falsely extravagant praise, one should remember that in 1879 Howells was a much more highly respected writer than Twain. Even as late as 1897, when J. K. Bangs polled the readers of *Literature,* Howells led Twain as most popular author for three consecutive months. Earlier, in 1882, Howells had placed fifth, behind the New England sages, while Twain was far down the list, placing fourteenth, in the estimation of readers of *The Critic.* Twain's best piece of literary criticism, written in 1906, was a study of the continuity and development of Howells's style over four decades. From his editorship of *The Atlantic,* in his "Editor's Study" in that magazine, and later on his "Editor's Easy Chair" in *Harper's,* Howells, for his part, championed Twain. Beginning in a *Century* article of 1882, he repeatedly advised the public to take Twain seriously, reminding them that "his humor is, at its best, the foamy break of the strong tide of earnestness in him." As early as 1873, Howells drew a character (in *A Chance Acquaintance*) who "had read one book of travel, namely, *The Innocents Abroad,* which he held to be so good a book that he never read anything else about the countries which it treated." Forty years later, *My Mark Twain* (1910) showed how deeply Howells's admiration for Twain continued to run. (Referred to above are *Letters to Howells,* Vol. II, p. 538; Paine, Vol. II, p. 732; *Letters to Howells,* Vol. I, p. 13.)

is defeated and alienated in seeking to incarnate his ideals. Repeatedly the individual is shut out from all that he considers valuable. The narrative of travel in Twain's hands is, then, a vehicle for rejecting experience. It mocks the world which it cannot embrace. In Twain's inability to write the National Novel to which by personal inclination and social encouragement he might have turned naturally, we can see the pressure that his acute sense of history put upon him. If he early (as he puts it) "worshipped" the epic, romantic historian Francis Parkman,[23] he later came to rely on such avowedly scientific, skeptical historians as Voltaire, Paine, John Draper, and Andrew D. White as his authorities for the history of human decline. More than Howells—perhaps more than any contemporary but Henry Adams— Twain was conscious of the push of history against human ideals.

This, to be sure, was the discovery that Henry Adams insisted upon as his own in several books, best of all in his *Education*. It is no accident that Twain's career strikingly parallels Adams's. Both Twain and Adams drifted aimlessly in and out of a variety of occupations before the War—Twain in Western towns, Adams in the University of Berlin and on the European tour. Twain's early journalism is matched by Adams's European letters to the Boston papers, including an account of his interview with Garibaldi that he sent from Palermo. With the beginning of hostilities in the Civil War, Orion Clemens and Charles Francis Adams, both Lincoln appointees, were sent to their foreign posts, one in the Nevada Territory, the other as Minister to England. With them, as private secretaries, went their two younger relatives. In later life both would feel, along with Henry James, a sense of exile in having thus avoided participation in the War. For a time, both wrote anonymously—Twain for the Virginia City *Territorial Enterprise*, Adams as London correspondent for the New York *Times*. From 1867 to 1868 Twain was in Washington, D.C. as secretary for William Stewart, Senator from Nevada. At the same time, he was writing feature material for several papers on the congressional session and discovering, to his disgust, that the "whole city was polluted with peculation and all other forms of rascality— debauched and demoralized by the wholesale dishonesty that prevails in every single department of the Washington Government, great and small."[24] Similarly, conducting his Washington experiment as a free-lance journalist for the *North American Review* and the *Nation* during 1868–69, Adams discovered in the so-called gold conspiracy a scandal "which smirched executive, judiciary, banks, corporate systems, professions, and people, all the great active forces of society, in one dirty cesspool of vulgar corruption." To express his sense of the corruption enveloping the American Government, he formulated the conundrum: "If a Congressman is a hog, what is a Senator?"[25]

The essays which Adams collected in *Chapters of Erie* (1871) appeared two years earlier than the indictment of corruption whereby Twain and

---

[23] Quoted in Paine, Vol. I, p. 284.   [24] Quoted in Budd, p. 35.   [25] *The Education of Henry Adams*, pp. 271–72, 261.

Warner gave a name to their era, *The Gilded Age*.[26] Fevered by speculation, the Washington of Twain and Warner is a microcosm of the moral and mental confusion in postwar America. Two incidents occurring near the beginning of *The Gilded Age,* symbolizing the brutality and deceptive hollowness of the new era, introduce the two main themes of the novel. Twain analyzes and satirizes the first theme—the corruption of the American government in a race for wealth—by dramatizing the rise and fall of Laura Hawkins as a lobbyist in Washington. Twain symbolizes this theme in his account of a steamboat race. Ending in senseless disaster, the race suggests that the frantic race for wealth is equally as senseless, and results only in tragedy. Laura Hawkins, of course, is the chief casualty in the Washington race. Saved from the exploded boat, she is consumed by her passion for money and power. Like the heroine, Madeleine Lee, of Adams's *Democracy* (1880), Laura goes to Washington (as she herself puts it) "to find out what I am." She arrived "in a state of grievous uncertainty as to what manner of woman she was." Her action is thus an aspect of her self-knowledge. But unlike Mrs. Lee she devotes her intelligence merely to the exploitation of others in the pursuit of wealth. Instead of knowledge, she gains only cunning and so is really not a forerunner of Adams's heroine so much as of DeForest's scheming lobbyist, Josephine Murray, in *Playing the Mischief* (1875). At the end of the book, prematurely aged, Laura wills her own death.

The second theme of the book has to do with the way illusion corrupts the mind. This theme Twain symbolizes in his depiction of Colonel Sellers's fantastical substitutes for the real essentials of life. A warm glow in the stove's isinglass door proves to be produced only by a lighted tallow candle within. "What you want is the *appearance* of heat, not the heat itself," the colonel says. Sellers's sumptuous banquets turn out to consist wholly of raw turnips and water. His fantasy turns his poverty into opulence. The wealth which Sellers, the Hawkinses, Dilworthy, and others pursue is equally chimerical. It leads only to their moral and intellectual bankruptcy. Not until Washington Hawkins recognizes how the promise of wealth has ruined the lives of everyone he has known, and so lets his Tennessee lands go for taxes, is the curse of illusory wealth ended. From speculative fantasy he returns to the gospel of work. Perhaps after all, the book concludes, honesty (Mr. Noble) and hard work (Philip Sterling) will inherit the country.

Twain was inclined to view the vagaries of American politics coldly and ironically. The epigraphs that head each chapter of *The Gilded Age*—taken

26 It should be noted, however, that *Mark Twain's (Burlesque) Autobiography* satirized Gould, Fisk, and others involved in the Erie raids with cartoons strung above a parody of "The House that Jack Built," and appeared in the same year as Adams's book. Even earlier, in 1869, Twain had written "An Open Letter to Commodore Vanderbilt," suggesting in conclusion: "All I wish to urge you now, is that you crush out your native instincts and go and do something worthy of praise....Go, boldly, proudly, nobly, and give four dollars to some worthy charity." Much later, in *A Connecticut Yankee,* he made Jay Gould serve pointedly as his model for the slave driver. (Buffalo *Express,* [February 29, 1869]. See Henry Duskis, ed., *The Forgotten Writings of Mark Twain* [New York, 1963], pp. 10–12.)

from the Anglo-Saxon, Chippeway, Choctaw, Eskimo, Egyptian, Chinese, Assyrian, Latin, Danish, French, Arabic, and other languages and cultures—focus the composite culture of the world upon the paltry foolishness of this Gilded Age. But to that age, all wisdom remains untranslated and incomprehensible. The modern America which Twain was satirizing was rootless rather than free; it lacked, rather than transcended, a tradition. It suggested to Twain not the beginning, but the end of freedom. In 1874, only two years after *The Gilded Age* appeared, Twain wrote his wife a burlesque letter looking sixty-one years ahead. He envisioned an apparently utopian society blessed with technological innovations—including the telephone and the airplane—but, more closely inspecting this state, rapidly dissolved it into a dystopia. American democracy had returned to oligarchy. Twichell had become the Archbishop of Hartford, Howells the Duke of Cambridge, Aldrich the Marquis of Ponkapog, and Twain himself the Earl of Hartford in a monarchical, Jesuitical realm established some years earlier by one O'Mulligan the First. The chaos of democracy had dissolved into the injustice of aristocracy. With Adams, Twain watched public and government indifference to corruption sap national strength. Essentially a reformer, as his journalism shows, he hoped for a government engaged in the realization of political ideals. Rejecting the traditional Lockean-Jeffersonian concept of contractual, negative government, he wrote: "That government is not best which best secures mere life and property—there is a more valuable thing—manhood."[27]

Soon after finishing *The Gilded Age*, Charles Dudley Warner, commenting on Froude's pessimistic analysis of progress, expressed his confidence in the American future, wishing not to look backward to the crudities of an earlier age, but forward to "this country a century from now."[28] It was precisely the question of progress—essentially a question of historical teleology—that tormented Twain. Whereas Warner could go on to write utopian novels, Twain more and more inclined to a view of history denying progress. *A Connecticut Yankee in King Arthur's Court* (1889) testifies to the growing hold upon Twain of a dark view of history. It is a novel that simultaneously entertains the opposite views of history as decline and history as progress. Published a year after Bellamy's utopian novel, *Looking Backward: 2000–1887*, when the books responding to Bellamy were just beginning to appear, *A Connecticut Yankee* appears at first to be a utopian book. In the beginning Twain appears to look back to the brutal and degraded past of the sixth century in order to look forward with new perspective to the redeemed nineteenth-century present and thus, presumably, to a future similarly marked by universal progress. Certainly it is clear, however, that while Twain was attracted to Bellamy's vision of a twenty-first-century utopia, he would have been at the same time almost as strongly persuaded by Ignatius Donnelly's predictions of the catastrophe that would soon wipe out civilization. His hope for utopia was merely the social version of his search for Eden. Was

27 Quoted in Budd, p. 137.   28 "Thoughts Suggested by Mr. Froude's 'Progress' " in *Complete Writings*, Vol. XV, p. 205.

the Golden Age, Eden, before man, or was all his glory behind him, and history the record of his fall through time into eventual chaos? Twain's double vision had it both ways: he could criticize his utopia even while asserting it. Twain spoke of *Looking Backward* as "the latest and best of all the Bibles," and referred to Bellamy as "the man who has made the accepted heaven paltry by inventing a better one on earth."[29] Through Howells, an early member of Bellamy's Boston Nationalist Club, Twain was in contact with many of Bellamy's promoters. Sylvester Baxter, for one, wrote to him as a fellow traveler, and extended an invitation to address a Nationalist meeting in 1888 on the same program as Bellamy himself. Twain was apparently known as a sympathizer with Nationalism. Hamlin Garland reported widely to his Nationalist friends that "Mark Twain was profoundly touched by *Looking Backward*."[30] Momentarily persuaded by the current of utopian optimism, Twain himself wrote, in an essay called "On Progress, Civilization, Monarchy, etc.," that progress was apparently inevitable, and that "there was no limit to human possibilities as regards human betterment."[31]

In *A Connecticut Yankee,* however, he dramatized both the progress and the poverty of history. The novel ostensibly dramatizes and celebrates the historical change from past to present as the transformation of chivalry into reason, savagery and brutality into kindness, slavery into freedom, a degraded populace into a well-clothed, well-educated one, fear into joy. This transformation is accomplished by the Yankee mechanic who represents the modern mind. He is "a Yankee of the Yankees—and practical; yes, and nearly barren of sentiment, I suppose—or poetry, in other words." Transported into the sixth century, Hank Morgan soon comes to understand his historical opportunity. To the "dark land" he bears the light of nineteenth-century technology, freedom of religious belief, and the American scorn of inherited titles. Soon, he has "the civilization of the nineteenth century booming under its very nose." With knights riding bicycles or playing baseball and saints used as "manufactories," he transforms the institutions and, as he believes, the assumptions of feudalism. Incarnating the spirit of modernism, he projects his utopia:

> First, a modified monarchy, till Arthur's days... [are] done, then the destruction of the throne, nobility abolished, every member of it bound out to some useful trade, universal suffrage instituted, and the whole government placed in the hands of the men and women of the nation, there to remain.

But, of course, Twain deliberately chose and portrayed a historical situation in which modern progress could not begin. Arthur's realm, as Twain's sources told him, had plunged into Eddaic chaos and the darkness of centuries. Hank could not, in any event, make his utopia against history: for the history of Arthur's kingdom was all past, fatally conclusive. The moment of light had crumbled into the dark ages. It is man himself—human evolu-

---

[29] *Letters to Howells,* Vol. II, pp. 579, 622. [30] Quoted in Arthur E. Morgan, *Edward Bellamy* (New York, 1944), p. xii. [31] Quoted in Roger Salomon, *Mark Twain and the Image of History* (New Haven, Conn., 1961), p. 28.

tion—that Hank has neglected to consider. Following immediately upon his affirmative dream of a republican utopia, Hank momentarily acknowledges that "there are times when one would like to hang the whole human race and finish the farce." Brutally degraded, only in moments does the manhood of the populace assert itself; only the best of the nobility—Arthur and Launcelot—are better than children or savages. At the end of the book only fifty-three young men—all trained in Hank's "Man-Factory"—stand by him. And these, like Hank, are now committed not to the joys but the terrors of civilization. Utopia, in apocalypse, becomes the frightful dystopia of the dark ages, as Hank destroys the civilization he has envisioned and created. His technology is devoted to war, death, and destruction; thus his triumph is his inevitable defeat. Surrounded by the bodies of electrocuted knights, he is trapped by his own victory. Proclaiming his doctrine of mechanical energy without correspondingly increasing consciousness—as Adams would put it—Hank initiates not civilization but inertia. It is Hank himself, then, symbol of the nineteenth-century, who brings about the decline of history. The final victor is therefore Merlin, symbol of the most primitive superstition, who casts a thirteen-century spell over the sleeping Hank.

A Connecticut Yankee, then, cuts both ways: against the age of chivalry, of course; but also against the machine society of the '80s. Reaching a conclusion very similar to the lesson of Adams's *History of the Administrations of Jefferson and Madison,* Twain was deciding, as he put it much later, that "whenever man makes a large stride...he is sure to think that *he* has progressed whereas he has not advanced an inch; nothing has progressed but his circumstances.... [Circumstances] are stronger than he and all his works."[32] Innocence and experience are both inadequate to control the movement of historical change. The knights are as helpless as children before Hank's knowledge. But essentially, as a man, he is no less childish than they. He too struts and frets and devotes his energy to getting up startling "effects." Equally as foolish, finally, as their chivalry, his modernism is merely more deadly. Like the personae of Twain's travel books, Hank fails to discover and is powerless to legislate his utopian fantasies. Like them, he becomes merely an alien—from both past and present, chivalry and modernism. Wandering vaguely, out of space, out of time, he revisits the castles which still stand as relics of the past. He names his manuscript account of his history "The Tale of the Lost Land." Dreaming a dream within his dream he simultaneously affirms and denies his affiliation to past and present, but he can have neither. He dies "getting up his last 'effect.' "

A Connecticut Yankee was Twain's first book in five years. Yet shortly before its publication he spoke of it to Howells as "my swan-song, my retirement from literature permanently."[33] No doubt several reasons lay behind his compulsion to retire from literature. One was that he was confident at the moment that the Paige Typesetter would make him rich. But there were deeper reasons than this. In his next letter to Howells he hinted at the chief

---

[32] Quoted in *Mark Twain in Eruption,* ed. Bernard DeVoto, p. 66. [33] *Letters to Howells,* Vol. I, 610–11.

reason: "Well my book is written—let it go. But if it were only to write over again there wouldn't be so many things left out. They burn in me; & they keep multiplying & multiplying; but now they can't ever be said. And besides, they would require a library—& a pen warmed up in hell."[34] Questions of literary form and social convention had tormented him in *A Connecticut Yankee*. Attempting to create an adult narrator whose consciousness could reflect more widely and penetrate more deeply than Huckleberry Finn's and still maintain the vernacular wisdom and the moral perception of the innocent, Twain envisioned the figure of the hardheaded Yankee mechanic as his solution. But in *A Connecticut Yankee* the wanderer disintegrates into the clown. Hank becomes the victim of his technological jokes. An adult Huck Finn, he is beseiged by history. He is lost rather than freed. Time has no Virgin Land, history no Eden, to save Hank from himself. Moreover, the totality of Twain's criticism in the book, the suggestion of a pen warmed up in hell, threatened to break through literary convention and so alienate the audience whose continuing favor Twain seemed to require—as an emotional, even more than as a financial, support. Much like Henry James, who was going through a crisis in popularity during these same years, Twain needed the assurance that he was popular. But now his deepest impulses were pulling him away from his audience. He would more and more scorn all that the collective mind affirmed, and consequently would lose the popular following which he seemed so much to need. He began his career in mass subscription selling, and ended it by printing his books anonymously or privately, or even leaving them in manuscript. Eventually the skeptical tendencies of *A Connecticut Yankee* would issue into Twain's "Eddypus Cycle," in which he traced the rise and dissolution of American civilization itself. In this parable, Christian Science establishes a new religious totalitarianism with Mary Baker Eddy as presiding deity. (The "Eddypus Cycle" was one of those pieces that remained unpublished.)

Twain's imagination, then—to adapt Melville's phrase—spins against the way it drives. His act is ever in friction with his intent. Seeking an elusive Paradise in his travel books, he is repeatedly compelled to celebrate the drama of expulsion. Although he needed to discern teleology in history in order to fall in with the current popularity of utopian optimism and the traditional American faith in inevitable progress, he nonetheless depicted a nightmare of progress ending in retrogression; he affirmed only a history of decline. Even the limited faith he expressed in American democracy in *A Connecticut Yankee*, furthermore, he burlesqued and scorned in his very next book, *An American Claimant* (1892). Here he adopted Howells's technique of using the boardinghouse as a microcosm for America, and satirized not only the young British nobleman who plays at republicanism, but also the Americans, who turn out to have developed a set of social and political hierarchies as wickedly antidemocratic as any Europeans could possess. Furthermore, whereas Twain had written affirmatory fables of democratic, natural nobility in *The Prince and the Pauper* (1882) (and to some extent in the episode of

---

[34] *Ibid.*, Vol. I, p. 613.

Hank and Arthur wandering in disguise), in *The Personal Recollections of Joan of Arc* (1896) he set forth the story of a noble being caught and destroyed by history. In this book, which Twain himself described as a companion to Tom Cantry's tale, *The Prince and the Pauper,* Joan is presented as "the most extraordinary person the human race has ever produced." Essentially an innocent—indeed, a child like Tom—she has a range and relevance more serious than his. Yet whereas his innocence is preserved in history, Joan exemplifies innocence betrayed and destroyed by it. She is Twain's equivalent to Adams's Virgin; but in her spinning fall she simultaneously makes for Twain the further point (Adams's point in the chapter, "The Virgin and the Dynamo" in his *Education*) that history sunders unity into multiplicity, pretended order into chaos. Eventually Twain would name one of his commentators on history the "Mad Philosopher" to express the pain that a sense of history occasions.

In order to understand history imaginatively, at its roots—the germ theory of history was then popular—Twain tried to imagine what the diaries or journals of Adam and Eve and their children would be like. He invented what he called the "papers of the Adam family." But even while figures in Twain's mythical papers of the Adam family—such as the "Professor of the Science of Historical Forecast," or the "Father of History"—stressed the rigidity of historical laws, Twain personally yearned for an escape from time into the Paradise of archetypes. Tormented by history, he sought to escape from it. He looked backward, therefore, to regain lost innocence by locating it outside of history altogether. He would write of Adam himself. Like Henry Adams, Twain saw that the notion of uniform evolution seemed to break down when applied to man's development:

> There is one thing that always puzzles me: as inheritors of the mentality of our reptile ancestors we have improved the inheritance by a thousand grades; but in the matter of the morals which they left us we have gone backward as many grades. *That evolution* is strange & to me unaccountable & unnatural. Necessarily we started equipped with their perfect and blemishless morals; now we are wholly destitute; we have no *real* morals, but only artificial ones—morals created and preserved by the forced suppression of natural & healthy instincts. Yes, we are sufficiently comical inventions, we humans.[35]

In the early '70s Twain began his "translations" from the archives of the Adam family. Casting himself as the "Father of History," he drew together the scattered, fragmentary testaments of the oldest human family. For nearly forty years he pretended to work at his cipher, "translating" the last papers as late as 1908. The first of the "Adam Family" papers is an "extract from Methuselah's Diary." Writing 747 years after the Creation, Methuselah observes the growing corruption of Adamic society and speculates about the possibilities of its destruction, as foretold by the prophets. As Father of History, it is clear, Twain was paralleling the rise and fall of Adamic society with the signs of decay and portents of destruction observable in his own

---

[35] Quoted in Paine, Vol. III, p. 1363.

time. In both, as Bernard DeVoto comments, "a great civilization had reached the point when the destructive forces it contained were beginning to dominate. He [Twain] appreciated its greatness; he also appreciated the inevitability of its collapse."[36]

A passage from "Eve's Autobiography: Year of the World, 920" continues the observations of decadence noted by Methuselah. Like the signs of chaos in the early twentieth century, overpopulation, war and the uncontrolled use of science for destruction, all mark the end of Eve's world. At this point there appears in the archives Reginald Selkirk—the Mad Prophet who "merely builds prognostications...out of history and statistics, using the facts of the past to forecast the probabilities of the future." Observing the social rot in all aspects of Adamic life—in "money-fever, sordid ideals, vulgar ambitions"—he foresees the flood. But he introduces as well his "Law of Periodical Repetition." As described in a lecture by the Professor of the Science of Historical Forecast on which Selkirk reports, this law implies not only destruction but also, thereafter, the rise of man in a renewed Adamic state: "Will this wonderful civilization of today perish? Yes, everything perishes. Will it rise and exist again? It will—for nothing can happen that will not happen again." The "Papers of the Adam Family" ends as Shem, in the midst of moral, political, and social rot, awaits the flood and, with the dissolution of the old, the promise of the renewed.

The character of the new Adamic society is suggested by one of Eve's reminiscences: "Love, peace, comfort, measureless contentment—that was life in the Garden," she writes. "Pain there was none, nor infirmity, nor any physical signs to mark the flight of time; disease, care, sorrow.... never came. All days were alike, and all a dream of delight." After the apocalyptic destruction of corrupt Adamic society, the true Adamic age would come again. Twain uses historical determinism to free him from history. In Twain's historical scheme, then, optimism lights the underside of darkness. For the corruption and portents of world dissolution that he saw in his own time suggested to him how near renewal hovered. His well known satirical "Greeting from the Nineteenth to the Twentieth Century" is marked not only by cold fury, but also by a kind of hysterical joy in the recitation of degradation. Just as Twain's analysis of determinism in *What Is Man?* (1906) is shown clearly by its disclaimers of personal responsibility to be really a "plea for pardon,"[37] so also his observation of historical decline is an inverted affirmation of man's chance for regeneration.

---

[36] Bernard DeVoto, ed., Mark Twain, *Letters from the Earth* (New York, 1962), p. 57. The quotations from this volume below are on pp. 84, 88, 91, 71. [37] Bernard DeVoto, *Mark Twain at Work* (Cambridge, Mass., 1942), p. 116. Such inversion is a commonplace of psychology. To Twain's, compare the experience of George Cary Eggleston:

  After a deal of psychological suffering I found peace by reconciling myself to the conviction that I was foreordained to be damned in any case, and that there was no use in making myself unhappy about it. In support of that comforting assurance I secretly decided to accept the Presbyterian doctrine of predestination instead of the Methodist theory of free will in which I had been bred.
  (*Recollections of a Varied Life,* pp. 22–3.)

TWAIN AND THE IMAGE OF THE CHILD

Spurred on by the interest that evolutionary theory had aroused in the origin and early development of man, Twain dramatized his vision of Eden best in terms of childhood. He was deeply concerned in knowing exactly what the child was, and in variously depicting childhood and primitiveness he touched upon most of the conventional views of the child promulgated in his era. Twain worked close to the assumptions of contemporary psychology. Early studies in embryology in the later nineteenth-century seemed to confirm the notion psychologists taught that the individual, in growing, passes through the main stages of his race's development.[38] The older faculty-psychology had been interested chiefly in the adult mind of civilized man. But Darwinism, adorned by romanticism, reversed this outlook, and, emphasizing a genetic approach, proclaimed the child father to the man and the savage the progenitor of civilization; and the child was the only noble savage left. John Fiske, turning this assertion into a historico-philosophical principle, theorized that the long extrauterine period of infancy in human offspring provides the key to understanding man's primacy in the evolutionary struggle. Man's childhood is, as Fiske put it, "the whole explanation of the moral and intellectual superiority of men over dumb animals." Beginning in the '70s, the child rapidly became the center of American cultural life. Americans began to celebrate and protect the child.[39]

Childhood, moreover, seemed to be the phase in which one could study man free from the dull round of getting and spending that he would enter in adulthood. Still free from the materialism of adult life, the child, as James Mark Baldwin wrote in 1895, "has not learned his own importance, his pedigree, his beauty, his social place, his religion, his parental disgrace; and he has not observed himself through all these and countless other lenses of time, place, and circumstance."[40] Antiquity knew the noble savage as the Scythian or the Arcadian; the Enlightenment and the romantics discovered him in the American Indian or Polynesian; but for the Gilded Age he was

38 Stephen Crane used this same theory loosely in "An Ominous Baby" and *Maggie: A Girl of the Streets,* on the assumption that childhood parallels the cruel, savage stage of race development.   39 Boys were less often encouraged to "Look labor boldly in the face;/Take up the hammer or the spade"; rather, laws restricting child labor were being proposed. With the shift of population to cities, fears were expressed that youth would be deprived of a heritage of nature and so have its natural impulses restrained. In 1880, G. Stanley Hall—whose *Adolescence* (1904) would later summarize the genetic theory—then a lecturer in psychology at Harvard, showed that over half the children entering Boston schools had never seen a plow, spade, robin, squirrel, or snail. Already in 1877, the Rev. Willard Parsons of Sherman, Pennsylvania had devised the plan of "country week" for poor children, which led directly to the "fresh-air funds" of metropolitan newspapers and charities. Four years later, the first summer camp—at Squam Lake, New Hampshire—was opened, chiefly for city boys who wanted to adventure in the now mysterious nature. The supposed needs of the child were casting doubts on the value of civilization. See the following: Philip P. Wiener, *Evolution and the Founders of Pragmatism,* p. 146; John Fiske, *A Century of Science and other Essays* (Boston and New York, 1899), pp. 108–109; Richard D. Mosier, *Making the American Mind: Social and Moral Ideas in the McGuffey Readers* (New York, 1947), p. 101; Schlesinger, *The Rise of the City,* p. 128.   40 *Mental Development in the Child and the Race* (New York and London, 1895), p. 4.

the America Child. As G. Stanley Hall put it, "the child revels in savagery."[41]

The impact of the new idealization of childhood upon the age is well mirrored in its literature. In the *St. Nicholas Magazine* (founded in 1873), *Harper's Young People* (founded in 1879), and a score of imitators, ephebic literature, or literature dealing strictly with the child, was established as a distinct class and force in American writing. In *Little Women* (1868) and *Little Men* (1871), Aldrich's *Story of a Bad Boy* (1869), Charles Dudley Warner's *Being a Boy* (1878), Lucy Larcom's *A New England Girlhood* (1889), Howells's *A Boy's Town* (1890), and *Years of my Youth* (1916), E. E. Hale's *New England Boyhood* (1893), and Hamlin Garland's *Boy Life On the Prairie* (1899), fiction rapidly became recollection, as writers felt a deep personal necessity to recall (and so preserve) the innocence of the pre-Civil War era, for which their own uncorrupted childhood seemed like the most appropriate symbol. As civilization and history became oppressively complex, they sought the simplicity of their origins; when they saw beneath the gilding on their age, they sought the fresh optimism of their youth. We have seen earlier that regional writing hovers about such a constellation of feeling and attitude, and that all of the regional writers wrote occasionally, and some frequently, for children. These writers thus asserted their continuing contact with the innocent child mind as an aspect of their strength as writers concerned with revisiting the past.

Twain's mind has deep affiliations with that of the other regionalists. In 1880, Twain wrote to a young admirer that he would like to be and remain a "cub pilot" on the Mississippi, where there was

> summer always; the magnolias at Rifle Point always in bloom so that the dreary twilight should have the added charm of their perfume; the oleanders on the "coast" always in bloom, likewise the sugar cane always green, never any "bagasse" burnings, the river always bank-full, so we could run all the chutes—how heavenly that would be![42]

It is a vision of perfect and perpetual contentment, a hymn of ease associated with the River and with Childhood. Working, as most regional writers did, mainly from impulse, and so creating literature by turning loose his unconscious drives, Twain repeatedly turned to similar images in expressing his dream of felicity. In 1874, he had told Howells that the regional story "is rather out of my line," and even declared: "I like history, biography, travels, curious facts and strange happenings, and science. And I detest novels, poetry, and theology."[43] Both of these statements, as the next decade would prove, were part of Twain's mask as an artist—identical to his desire but antithetical to his natural character. Early a wanderer, insistently denying his frontier background to embrace Eastern civilization, he nonetheless turned more and more frequently to recollections of his childhood. Recognizing and insisting on his nurture in culture, he longed all the more

---

[41] *Adolescence: Its Psychology and Its Relations to Physiology, Sociology, Sex, Crime, Religion and Education*, Vol. I, p. x. [42] Quoted in Blair, *Huck Finn*, p. 256. [43] Quoted in Paine, Vol. I, pp. 514, 512.

strongly for his lost life in nature. His artist's mask, then, drove him into hateful contraries. This world traveler, this Father of History, thus also became the loving chronicler of childhood. It was no frivolity that his wife and friends like Mrs. Stowe familiarly called him, not Mark, the traveler, or Sam, the historian, but "Youth"—the regionalist.[44]

Twain's brief first attempt at recalling his childhood, his "Boy's Manuscript" recollecting his youthful love-making, was written shortly after his marriage, in 1870. But his first important use of his childhood occurred in a series written for the *Atlantic* called "Old Times on the Mississippi." In 1874, Howells had urged Twain to write something for his January *Atlantic* —an issue always carefully planned as a strong number—but Twain had replied, "it's no use. . . . My head won't go." Two hours later, after a reminiscent talk with Twichell, Twain suddenly found his "inspiration tank" full and suggested to Howells a series "about old Mississippi days of steamboating glory and grandeur as I saw them."[45] Now, with his consciousness spilling into recollection, he wrote his seven *Atlantic* papers rapidly, the first three within ten days.

The chivalric and romantic traditions which Twain ridiculed in *A Connecticut Yankee* were, Paine says, "the very things which he in his happier moods cared for most."[46] His *Atlantic* series, "Old Times on the Mississippi," which formed the first half of *Life On the Mississippi* (1883), found him in one of these happier moods; for in these sketches Twain invested the river and his youth with the images of adventure, rest, and contentment which suggest the full indulgence of his primitivistic inclinations. "Learning the river," as a cub-pilot does, means, in a clear sense, unlearning civilization's conventions. Twain several times makes the point that pilots are interested in nothing but the river. Loosed from the shore they become one with nature, in intuitive rapport with the least of nature's hieroglyphics. In a famous passage Twain compares the response of the passenger and that of the pilot to a sunset. The passenger senses only the romance, the beauty of the scene; but the pilot, reading the river and understanding its dangers, has lost "the grace, the beauty, the poetry" of the scene. The passenger's, of course, are merely the conventional, adult responses to the scene, the product of a romantic conception of landscape. The pilot reads nature unobstructed by stereotyped responses to scenery. His is the truly innocent eye, boring into nature itself. Free from stereotypes of mind, the pilot is also above social conventions. He is, Twain says, "the only unfettered and entirely independent human being that lived in the earth." The true American hero, the pilot alone has no master; like the snow that surrounded Thoreau's cabin, the knowledge and position of the pilot protects his freedom and projects him out of the usual categories of time and space. He is the Adamic demigod, and his the archetypal state, that Twain was seeking.

This contrast between conventional pieties and natural responses is the

---

[44] "Youth. . .was always [Olivia's] name for him," Paine says (p. 395). J. H. Twichell records in his diary Mrs. Stowe's use of the curiously appropriate nickname. (See Paine, Vol. I, pp. 566, 395.)   [45] Quoted in Paine, Vol. I, p. 531.   [46] Paine, Vol. II, p. 891.

subject of *The Adventures of Tom Sawyer* (1876). After a hesitant beginning in "A Boy's Manuscript," Twain worked on *Tom Sawyer* in 1872, then
put it aside for a further "call" until 1874, and finally finished it in 1875.
The years of its gestation and composition thus surround his meditations,
in "Old Times," on his own youth. Working from the assumptions of the
genetic psychology described above, Twain suggests in his preface that
although *Tom Sawyer* is a children's entertainment, "part of my plan has
been to try to pleasantly remind adults of what they once were themselves."
Father to the man, the boy, Tom Sawyer, is all that the adult will be, while
he yet retains an innocent eye. The adventures, thoughts, and emotions of
the boys in *Tom Sawyer* thus become emblematic of a stage both in the
growth of civilization and in the life of any one man. As Twain understood
human development, the two grand archetypes which contend with social
mores for the adulthood of man are romantic conventions and natural religion
(i.e., superstition, or magic). These are respectively represented, of course,
in Tom Sawyer and Huck Finn. Both essentially orphans, they are cut free
to find their new fathers in either society or nature, Tom choosing civilization while Huck chooses nature. Their different choices are contrasted early
in the book. Tom swaps his trinkets—"lickrish," a fishhook, and marbles—
for the colored tickets which children earn in Sunday School for memorizing
biblical passages. For memorizing two thousand verses, the student would
be rewarded with a Bible. Winning his by trickery, but nonetheless earning
"the glory and éclat that came with it," Tom remains, both in method and
object, within the conventions of his pseudo-Christian society. When Huck
first enters swinging a dead cat, on the other hand, we learn that he has
swapped for it a blue Bible ticket (and a bladder). He disposes of the
symbolic tickets; Tom assiduously collects them. Moreover, Huck is planning on using the cat as part of a magical ritual—to be performed in the
graveyard—with which to drive away warts. His worship and devotion
involve nature; Tom's are fastened to society.

So it continues throughout the book. In his romantic melancholy, his
affected death-wish, his fantasy career as Robin Hood or as the Black
Avenger of the Spanish Main, and as a gentleman highwayman, Tom remains
within the confines of social, chivalric myth. His actions are governed by
knowledge, learned from books. "You'll see that in any book," Tom
repeatedly says in explaining the intricacies of chivalric lore. Tom rules his
life by the books. He lives in the fantasies of his society. But Huck reads
no books and, in fact, does not even attend school. For Tom he is a "romantic
outcast." Moving on the verges of society—afraid only of adults and groups,
as he shows at the end—Huck is the noble savage:

> Huckleberry came and went, at his own free will. He slept on doorsteps in
> fine weather and in empty hogsheads in wet; he did not have to go to school
> or to church, or call any being master or obey anybody; he could go fishing or
> swimming when and where he chose, and stay as long as it suited him; nobody
> forbade him to fight; he could sit up as late as he pleased; he was always the
> first boy that went barefoot in the spring and the last to resume leather in the

fall; he never had to wash, nor put on clean clothes; he could swear wonder-
fully. In a word, everything that goes to make life precious, that boy had. So
thought every harassed, hampered, respectable boy in St. Petersburg.

Tom escapes momentarily from respectability in his fantasy, though still
remaining within convention. Huck, on the contrary, lives a perpetual
escape, following the codes of nature and self rather than those of society.

The adventure of the two boys along with Joe Harper on Jackson's Island
is again instructive of their essential differences. Initially presiding over
what they call their "Evasion" (of society), Tom speaks of it in mythical
terms—as a pirate's life. But although in their first night Huck falls rapidly
into "the sleep of the conscience free," the two other boys feel society reaching at them from within, through their consciences. "They said their prayers
inwardly," and began to feel "that they had been doing wrong to run away"
and in stealing food from their homes. Twain, as has been suggested, was
deeply and permanently influenced by environmentalist psychology. Rejecting the older notion that conscience was an a priori moral guide, the environ-
mentalists followed Darwin's lead in *The Descent of Man* in developing
a naturalistic theory of mind. Conscience was thus seen as a deceptive,
mischievous guide, the product—as William Graham Sumner would try to
demonstrate anthropologically in *Folkways*—of historical circumstance only.
Early in 1876, six months before *Tom Sawyer* was published, Twain read
a story to his Monday Night Club called "The Facts Concerning the Recent
Carnival of Crime in Connecticut." Here he explained that he had surprised and killed his conscience—a grotesque dwarf—and had then, following his natural impulses, gleefully gone on a rampage of crime. "Nothing in
the world," he concluded, "could persuade me to have a conscience again."
More flatly and dogmatically than he would do in fiction, Twain told the
young Kipling: "Your conscience is a nuisance.... Perhaps it's best when
it's dead."[47] But in portraying the similarly "conscience-free" Huck, he
creates an unfettered demigod, free because unentangled by social imperatives. Because he is unprotected from the terrors of nature by culture, Huck,
it is true, suffers deeply from intermittent fears; but, hindered by culture,
Tom suffers from unrelenting guilt.

After Tom and Huck find their buried treasure—as romance is translated
into social actuality—Huck is inevitably captured by society—"dragged
into it, hurled...into it—and his sufferings were almost more than he
could bear." He loses his freedom by gaining wealth and respectability. He
suffers from the fate always poised before Henry James's characters; by
possessing the coin of society, he becomes possessed by it. Tom, wise in
worldly ways, promises to "take care" of him.

Twain could not have failed to recognize how much this fable was a
parable accurately summarizing his own career. Although astonishingly
successful as a writer, he resisted the society that rewarded him. He spoke
of himself as a "scribbler of books" and, as early as 1868, declared his
intention of giving up "literature and all other bosh—that is, literature

---

[47] Quoted in Rudyard Kipling, *American Notes* (New York, 1889), pp. 261–62.

wherewith to please the general public."[48] He told Howells that piloting was the only career in which he had been entirely happy: only on the river had he been entirely free. As a natural child, Huck, of course, was the pilot while Tom represented the civilized passenger. Both were aspects of Twain; but it was the free Huck whom he wanted most to be. In the cub-pilot whom he placed at the center of "Old Times on the Mississippi," Twain remembered himself as a Huck-like being who had run away from home (as he himself had not done), and, escaping from the shore, had become the free and easy apprentice.

But this escape existed only in memory, from a distance of twenty-one years. And as Twain found when he revisited the river in 1882, there was no escape but in memory. Howells had advised him to complete his meditative Mississippi papers by giving a factual historical account of the river and a realistic description of its character and condition in the present. Thus he drove Twain into history—into seeing himself as a part of a time sequence. This would have been painful in any event for Twain's consciousness. But two decades had so drastically altered the river that Twain's return to it was history with a vengeance. Traveling with his publisher, James R. Osgood, and with a stenographer to take his notes down, Twain was now writing as the professional author, determined to make a book, not allowing one to come from the "inspiration tank." From the first he found that [the pilot's] occupation is gone, his power has passed away, he is absorbed into the common herd." His river has been subjected to the machine culture: barges, the railroad, and bridges have made steamboat traffic obsolete; the government has mechanized even nature itself, by tearing out snags and enlarging channels. The pilot has become a mere functionary in a well-regulated system of transportation. Having created a myth in his first twenty chapters of *Life on the Mississippi* (i.e., "Old Times"), then, Twain destroyed it in the next twenty; his hymn to nature was balanced by the chant of the dynamo. The freedom of the child or savage—in this context both the half-horse, half-alligator keelboatman and the cub-pilot—had been subdued by technological advance. The lazy air of expectation in Hannibal had been superseded by the "progress, energy, [and] prosperity" of St. Louis or the "newness, briskness, swift progress, wealth, intelligence, fine and substantial architecture, and general slash and go and energy of St. Paul." As the symbol for America, the growing cities—Chicago and New York above all—replace the unchanging river. Uneasily holding the two halves of his book together— preserving unity, for instance, by finding Horace Bixby unchanged and Hannibal essentially the same—Twain managed a shaky affirmation of the values of both the garden and the machine. This was in 1883, while Twain was still optimistic enough to hold what David Noble has called the "paradox of progressive thought"—the belief that the natural man would be perfected by machine society. It would be six years yet before *A Connecticut Yankee* would prove that he could no longer affirm wholeheartedly either nature or

---

[48] Quotations are from *Life on the Mississippi*, in *Works,* Vol. VII, p. 185; and in Paine, Vol. I, p. 360.

the machine. Six years before *A Connecticut Yankee,* when both would turn nightmarish, he could optimistically accept both.

Toward the end of *Life on the Mississippi* Twain found in Hannibal a striking symbol of the simultaneity of past and present. "I woke up every morning," he writes, "with the impression that I was a boy—for in my dreams the faces were all young again, and looked as they had looked in the old times." Stimulated momentarily into a blissful dream of youth—and so declaring the continued possibility of a free existence—he daily watched his dream dissolve in reality. "But I went to bed," he immediately adds, "a hundred years old, every night—for meantime I had been seeing those faces as they are now." In Hannibal he found realized his own diverse allegiances: to youth and adulthood, to nature and technocracy, to the free creature as well as to the astute businessman, to the loving husband and father and to the professional scribbler of books—to the Huck Finn that he admired and to the Tom Sawyer whom he resembled.

The hero of *The Adventures of Huckleberry Finn* (1885) shares with Twain his richly ambiguous personality, even in name. While Huck's surname was derived, appropriately, from the actual Hannibal town drunkard, Jimmy Finn, "Huckleberry" is the name of a fruit stictly New England in origin, one Twain had not seen in the West.[49] Like Twain himself, Huck is both the anarchical Westerner and the conservative New Englander. In the fictive time which elapsed between *Tom Sawyer* and this novel, Huck's character has shifted. Under the supervision of the widow Douglas and Miss Watson, he has begun to absorb and assume the conventions of his society. He has become his own Tom Sawyer. No longer "conscience-free," he finds, in the course of the novel, that his conscience follows him like a "yaller dog," as theirs had earlier pursued Tom and Joe. Drawn into acquisitive society by his accidental acquisition of wealth at the end of *Tom Sawyer,* his problem is how to reachieve and retain his earlier Adamic state.

In this novel, then, the pressure of society is all the more imperative. Huck learns both Presbyterian and Methodist versions of Heaven and Hell; in a slaveholding house he absorbs the assumptions of slavery. In school he learns to spell, read, and write; he wears new clothes and sleeps in a bed. In short, after three or four months, Huck finds that although

> I liked the old ways best, . . . I was getting so I liked the new ones, too, a little bit. The widow said I was coming along slow but sure, and doing very satisfactory. She said she wasn't ashamed of me.

Tom, too—now even more obsessed than earlier with chivalric fancies— initiates Huck into the rituals of romance. As slavishly as others follow the formal rules of Christian culture, Tom relies upon his "pirate books. . . and robber books" for their unimpeachable (though frequently incompre-

---

49 Rose Terry Cooke, who was intimate with the Twichell family and whose stories— particularly "Freedom Wheeler's Controversy with Providence"—Twain admired, named her last collection of tales *Huckleberries: Gathered from New England Hills,* explaining: "I have called this latest collection of New England stories by the name of a wild berry that has always seemed to me typical of the New England character."

hensible) codes of behavior. Still being shaped by this environment, Huck begins to be affected by both Christianity and romance: on the one hand he prays; on the other, he attempts to raise a genie by rubbing an old tin lamp. But when, shortly, Pap arrives and forces Huck to live with him, he soon reverts, ostensibly, to his conscience-free existence.

Nevertheless, the impressions exerted on him by culture, however briefly, have altered the state of his mind. Now that he is no longer the innocent his only alternative to social acquiescence, we are made to realize, is to become bestial and brutal like Pap. Unless he is innocent he cannot escape society without degradation. His father, for instance, although alienated from society, a vagrant and a hopeless drunk, still carries with him a guilt-ridden conscience and a full measure of social prejudices. His delirious hallucination of the Angel of Death and his disquisition on the free Negro able to vote show him to be, in his ignorance, not free from society, but merely the lowest, most vicious form of it. Now tainted with convention like Pap, and invested with a conscience, Huck, the innocent of *Tom Sawyer,* threatens to sink into barbarianism in *Huckleberry Finn.* In *Roughing It* and *Following the Equator* Twain described how, touched by the knowledge of good and evil—the civilizing effect of Christian missionaries—the noble Hawaiian islanders soon disintegrated into a shiftless, diseased, ignoble, rapidly dying race. Huck stands perilously on the edge of a similar transformation.

His salvation comes, of course, through Jim. A slave, and therefore never a part of the dominant conventional society, Jim revives in Huck an immediacy of response to nature—a response outer and inner—undistorted by stereotyped social patterns of belief or action. Terrorized in slavery by the vagaries of the white society over which he has no control—his ultimate terror is of being sold down the river—Jim is, in society, merely the grotesque darky who tells tall tales for psychic self-protection. But when he is free upon the river, Jim becomes, as Daniel G. Hoffman has written, "a magus,...a magician in sympathetic converse with the spirits that govern —often by malice or caprice—the world of things and men."[50] Helplessly impotent as magician and prophet in the slave huts, he becomes an infallible guide in the natural world. For the brutal, half-civilized father Huck has lost, he is given a surrogate in Jim. (It is Jim, significantly, who finds and conceals Pap's body.) Continuing the theme of initiation from the first part of *Life On the Mississippi,* in his novel Twain removed all traces of the technology that threatened joyous life in the second part of that book by substituting, in this new fable, a raft for the steamboat, Jim for the river-wise pilot, and Huck for the cub who has run away from home. The child and savage drive through the adult, civilized mask. By the conclusion of the novel Twain has understood society through Huck and Jim in ways that he could not understand it in his own person in *Life on the Mississippi.* And in this respect *Huckleberry Finn* is a more nearly perfect *Life on the Mississippi.*

[50] *Form and Fable in American Fiction* (New York, 1961), p. 332.

But their river remains an Eden infested with serpents. Ever touched and invaded by the life of the shore, it provides only moments of true freedom. Tricked by nature, Huck and Jim drift past Cairo, Illinois, in a fog and so lose their opportunity to mount the Ohio to freedom. Once their chance for freedom is lost, they are immediately beset by the serpents of civilization. The troublesome conscience which Huck has acquired now asserts itself. At Jim's joy over the likelihood of literal freedom, Huck meditates:

> He *was* most free—and who was to blame for it? Why, *me*. I couldn't get that out of my conscience, no how nor no way.... It hadn't ever come home to me before, what this thing was that I was doing. But now it did; and it staid with me, and scorched me more and more. I tried to make out to myself *I* warn't to blame...but it warn't no use.

Driven by conscience, Huck prepares to betray Jim by paddling ashore. He fails because, he says significantly, "I warn't man enough." Rather, he is child enough to follow his natural impulses.

Immediately thereafter civilization reenters upon the river even more ominously: a steamboat runs over their raft and drives Huck to shore. The Shepherdson-Grangerford feud that Huck witnesses there and, later, Colonel Sherburne's murder of Boggs and the deception of the Wilks girls present Huck with testaments concerning the essential brutality of a society that pretends to be chivalric, law-abiding, and Christian. Jim, shaman of nature, is subjugated and replaced by the Duke and Dauphin, who, assuming a sequence of disguises, duping an ignorant and degraded populace, are the magicians of civilization. Pretending to be exiled royalty, repeating the chivalric formulas, playing heroic scenes from Shakespeare, disguising Jim as an Arab, or playing a multiplicity of other fantastic roles, these two are adult versions of Tom Sawyer, refashioning his romantic fantasies as devices in their confidence game.

Huck, too, assumes disguises, chiefly of a protective variety, the natural expression of his fear of discovery by society. Nowhere are his psychic fears better demonstrated than in the roles he spontaneously assumes. In all of his deceptions he imagines his isolation. As "Sarah Williams" ("my father and mother was dead, and the law had bound me out to a mean old farmer,...so I...cleared out"); in his tale of the shipwreck and disaster of the *Walter Scott* to the ferryboatman; in the account of his family tragedy to the Grangerfords ("my sister Mary Ann run off and got married and never was heard of no more, and Bill went to hunt them and he warn't heard of no more, and Tom and Mort died, and then there warn't nobody but just me and Pap left, and he was just trimmed down to nothing...so when he died I took what there was left,...started up the river,...and fell overboard, and that was how I come to be here"); with the King and the Duke ("my folks was living in Pike County, in Missouri,...and they all died off but me and pa and my brother")—in all of these he naturally hints, in the kind of masks he assumes, at his fears about his own alienation and death. Unlike the deceptions of the confidence men, these guises are the spontaneous, unconscious expression of his essential being. Of the tales he tells, he himself says: "I went right along. . .just trusting to Providence [i.e., intuition] to put the right words in my mouth, . . . for I'd noticed that Providence always did put the right words in my mouth, if I let it alone."

Thus conceiving of himself as a spy in society, he can pierce the ultimate guise of conventional society itself—the notion of slavery and the mask of color that veneer Jim's essential manhood. Thus he can learn that Jim is "white inside." Surrendering only for a moment to his social conscience in his ultimate moral self-confrontation, Huck finally decides: "All right, then, I'll *go* to hell," and sets out to free Jim. Heroically accepting the alienation from society that he so deeply fears, he resolves to follow the impulses of intuition. W. H. Auden well calls this a pure act of "moral improvisation."[51] But in returning to the shore Huck is once more immersed in social convention. Although he has resolved to be an outlaw in a literal sense, he is mistaken by Aunt Sally, in the book's sternest irony, for Tom Sawyer. True to his final identity, he plays out the mannered "Evasion" of setting Jim free according to the conventional plot of romantic escape. He identifies as wholly with his new role as with his earlier ones, and reassumes the mores of the shore. Explaining to Aunt Sally why he is late, for instance, he says:

> ". . .We blowed out a cylinder-head."
> "Good gracious! Anybody hurt?"
> "No'm. Killed a nigger."
> "Well, it's lucky; because sometimes people do get hurt."

Up to the end of the book he remains Tom Sawyer. Only at the very end, with the Evasion concluded happily within social convention, is he free from this role and able to "light out for the territory ahead of the rest," where he hopes thenceforth to be free from civilization. On the river or in the territory, we know, Huck can never return into the Eden of innocence; even if the Tom Sawyers of the world did not pursue him, he carries his sense of them within him. It is appropriate, then, that the numbers of *The Century* that serialized *Huckleberry Finn* also carried Thomas Nelson Page's idealization of the slaveholding Old Dominion, "Marse Chan."

THE DREAM OF DRIFT

After *Huckleberry Finn,* the regional and nostalgic promise of Eden implied in "Old Times on the Mississippi" was dissipated in Twain's imagination and his work. Twain would move, in *Pudd'nhead Wilson* (1894), rather, to even more ambiguous problems of morality and personal identity, in a world even more confused and fearsome. Through neither the omniscient eye of the travel narrative, nor the penetrating eye of the utopian historian, nor the reminiscent eye of the regionalist historian could Eden be regained.

Yet Twain had continued to evoke images of rest and satisfaction, beginning with his earliest writing, through three decades. The central image for

---

51 "Huck and Oliver" in *Mark Twain: A Collection of Critical Essays,* ed. Henry Nash Smith (Englewood Cliffs, N. J., 1963), pp. 113–14.

peace in his earliest writing is that of drift. Walter Blair has observed: "From the start, and more and more as time passed, the river and the raft had come to mean to Twain happy escape from what hurt and harassed him in civilization."[52] Writing to Olivia soon after their engagement, Twain himself revealed that his vision of happiness "always takes one favorite shape—peace, & quiet—rest, & seclusion from the rush & roar & discord of the world. You & I apart...."[53] What the River and the Raft essentially meant was the condition of drift: physical inertia or even undisturbed sleep, a loss of the time-sense, a denial of experience, images of nakedness and dawn, and emotions of companionability. These are all associated with the rest and seclusion for which he yearned. The drifting excursion of *Innocents Abroad* was conceived of as "a picnic on a gigantic scale," recorded by an "inexperienced eye." The youthful Twain of *Roughing It* makes a raft out of his stagecoach. "Stripping to [his] underclothing," he luxuriates upon the "lazy bed" of mailbags while the stagecoach drifts easily across the prairie. On Lake Tahoe he spends his time "drifting around in the boat" instead of laboring for the fortune he claims to be seeking. "So empty and airy did all spaces seem below us," he comments, "and so strong was the sense of floating, ... that we called these boat excursions 'balloon voyages.' " (Two decades later, he would employ this very balloon image, as an alternative to the drifting raft, in *Tom Sawyer Abroad* [1894]. There Huck remarks, as of his raft, "Land, I warn't in no hurry to git out and buck at civilization again.") Floating down the Neckar in *A Tramp Abroad,* Twain and Harris, in nightshirts, find that their rafting "calms down all feverish activities, ... soothes to sleep all nervous hurry and impatience, ... and existence becomes a dream, a charm, a deep and tranquil ecstasy." In 1877, Twain and Twichell went to Bermuda, and Twain reported the trip in four *Atlantic* essays entitled "Some Rambling Notes of an Idle Excursion." Twain found Bermuda "like Heaven," free "from the triple curse of railways, telegraphs, and newspapers." So, likewise, in *Tom Sawyer* he celebrated the idle excursion of the boys on Jackson Island, "shedding clothes as they went, until they were naked," and playing Indian—not imitating Injun Joe, debased by civilization, but being primitive noble savages. Images of the fresh new dawn, suggesting regeneration, run throughout *Tom Sawyer,* as well as *Life on the Mississippi* and *Huckleberry Finn.*

For financial and personal reasons, Twain himself had been drifting aimlessly—as he came to see it—around the world for ten years beginning in 1891. In January of 1900, he wrote to a friend: "I am tired to death of this everlasting exile." "The poor man is willing to live anywhere if we will only let him 'stay put,' " wrote his wife.[54] The dream of vagrant, morally free drift had dissolved into a nightmare of feverish wandering. The first indications of this change came in his abortive attempts to revive Tom and Huck for further adventures. Huck, after all, had ended his book committed to wandering. But where would he go and what would his wandering mean?

---

[52] Blair, *Huck Finn,* p. 346.   [53] *The Love Letters of Mark Twain,* ed. Dixon Wecter (New York, 1949), p. 70.   [54] Quoted in Paine, Vol. III, p. 1102.

Twain began a sequel to *Huckleberry Finn* called *Huck Finn and Tom Sawyer Among the Indians,* and even set the first nine chapters on his Paige Typesetter. Arising from Tom's notion of going to the Injun country for adventures and Huck's retreat to the territory, this book rapidly becomes a recitation of well-worn Wild West escapades. *Tom Sawyer Abroad,* originally titled *New Adventures of Huckleberry Finn,* was actually completed, along with *Tom Sawyer, Detective* (1896); but these two stories were hardly more successful than the Western adventures promised to be. Another story was suggested to Twain by his conclusion to *Tom Sawyer.* There he had promised "to take up the story...and see what sort of men and women they [the main characters] turned out to be." In 1902 he found what he believed to be a "matchless chance" in a plan to bring the "old fellows" back to Hannibal after fifty years of wandering. His notebook description of the plot in 1891 reads: "Huck comes back, 60 years old, from nobody knows where— & crazy. Thinks he is a boy again, & scans every face for Tom & Becky. Tom comes at last, 60, from wandering the world & tends Huck, & together they talk the old times; both are desolate, life has been a failure, all that was lovable, all that was beautiful is under the mould. They die together."[55] Growing into adulthood, the boys would, it seems clear, become mere tramps, aimlessly drifting in a civilization they did not create but cannot deny. Another unfinished manuscript related to these attempts to revive Huck is "Tom's Conspiracy," which DeVoto describes as "a maze of romance and rank improvisation that is trivial to begin with and speedily becomes disheartening."[56]

DeVoto, furthermore, has described a cycle of manuscripts which show how fully the image of luxuriant drift had become fraught with anxiety and frustration—even terror—in Twain's mind. Among a number of sketches of ships marooned in the Antarctic is one, according to Bernard DeVoto, of an "enchanted sea wilderness...where ships were caught in a central place of calm."[57] In another tale a happy family man dreams that he and his family are on a mysterious ship, sailing in the "Great Dark of Antarctica" toward a terrible "Great White Glare." A strange being aboard the ship, the "Superintendent of Dreams," convinces the passengers that their horrible dream of living death is the true reality. In the various narrative alternatives whereby Twain tried to complete and make this story meaningful, he brings in episodes of discovered treasure, mutiny, a lost child, madness, and apocalyptic destruction. At last he leaves alive only the narrator (an adult Huck) and his loyal Negro companion (a later Jim), helpless and imprisoned in the merciless glare. The drifting raft is now the ship moved aimlessly by a malevolent fate. Hope for freedom changes into the fear of endless servitude; dawn is replaced by the pitiless White Glare, naked warmth by incredible cold, joy by hysteria, contentment by mutiny. Freedom from responsibility is revealed as moral purposelessness. Like their creator, Twain's heroes live in the terrible glare of the fact that release is only exile; individuality is actually alienation.

55 Quoted in *Letters to Howells,* Vol. II, p. 748n.   56 *Mark Twain at Work,* p. 113.
57 *Ibid.,* p. 121.

Representing this emerging view of the loneliness of the human condition is the figure of the stranger in Twain's work, among whom Hank Morgan and David Wilson are early anticipations. In the late '90s Twain began to experiment with the figure of Satan, the archetypal stranger. To Satan Twain addressed a series of fictive letters; he began working on an interview with Satan; he wrote episodes in the life of a "Young Satan." Satan, Twain apparently came to feel, was an appropriate symbol of man made heroic by asserting himself futilely against the determinism of the universe. In one manuscript, a young Satan appears in Tom's and Huck's St. Petersburg as a kind of Hank Morgan who gets up spectacular effects for the admiring rustics. This story, with the scene shifted to Eseldorf, Austria, became *The Mysterious Stranger* (1916), written between 1897 and 1900. Rather than the therapeutic effect which DeVoto believes this tale to have had upon Twain's mind, *The Mysterious Stranger*, composed during the depth of Twain's despair, is his final capitulation to the Great Dark. The allegory begins with a village perfect in its quiet restfulness—"a paradise for us boys," Theodor remarks. Drowsing in the peace and warmth of perpetual summer, dreaming, "infinitely content," the village is suddenly invaded by a stranger, who soon reveals that he is young Satan, nephew to the fallen angel. Granting all, even unexpressed, wishes, and unfettered by time and space, he seems ready to make a paradise on earth.

The name Satan takes—Philip Traum—is German for "dream," and the boys' dream of paradise soon dissolves. Man's conscience, the "moral sense" of scholastic philosophy, is revealed as essentially debased and cruel. The civilizations it has raised have been marked (like the "Stupendous International Procession" in which Twain satirized the twentieth century) by wars, injustice, suffering, and barbarity. Far from free, man is imprisoned, not by divine will or foreordination, but by his own environment and circumstances. Finally, Satan strips away the ultimate mask of Eden to reveal that all existence is a dream—that *"Nothing exists save empty space—and you!"* The dreaming self, it turns out, drifts helplessly through space and time, imagining both, peopling its fancy with worlds and hopeful, joyous beings. In fact man is "alone in shoreless space, [condemned] to wander its limitless solitudes without friend or comrade forever." In *The Mysterious Stranger*, then, Twain's hope for peace is momentarily revived. But in the end the questing self has no goal and merely lives on without companions, imprisoned in its own perpetual dream. That self is only, as Satan concludes, "a vagrant thought, a useless thought, a homeless thought, wandering forlorn among the empty eternities." The malevolent figure of the Satanic stranger darkens by his presence the later manuscripts described above and finally turns Twain's quest for peace into the desire for death.

Entangled in the fantasies of his despair, tormented by feelings of responsibility for the death of his eldest daughter in 1896, shaken by the loss of his fortune through speculation, and troubled both by years of exile and a feverish compulsion to publish in order to prove his continuing popularity, Twain ceased to write books of major importance. Although he had been a professional writer for over two decades, he found, after watching both past and present sour in *A Connecticut Yankee,* that try as he might he could complete satisfactorily only a small fraction of the projects he began. Desperate in his need to pay off debts, he could do no better than *Pudd'nhead Wilson.* For the rest, he published *Joan of Arc* anonymously and *What Is Man?* privately, perversely insisting that these were his best books. *Following the Equator* he toiled through without any hope but that it would sell. Indeed, he could no longer be sure even of his sales; for, five years earlier in 1892, *The American Claimant* had been his first book in twenty years that had not paid. He needed the money: the Paige Typesetter had consumed the fortune he had made from his early books. During the decade 1890–1900 he was dependent on literature for the first time in his life, and this seemed to paralyze his creativity. He began to have ·doubts about his skill as a writer. His fear for his literary potency even struck at his body. For years after 1890 he was plagued by psychosomatic pains in his arm—he called it rheumatism—whenever he attempted to write: "The moment I take up my pen my rheumatism returns,"[58] he wrote a friend. His vast number of incomplete manuscripts shows how often he took up his pen—and with what frequency he laid the result aside.

These failures as an artist struck sharply at his failure as a man and, as a result, turned Twain seriously to autobiography. Hitherto he had been able to rely upon a popular public reception. By writing he had earlier continued to assert his connections with his public and so continued to feel himself a vital part of the American community of values, beliefs, and aspirations. More and more, however, he seemed to be estranged from that community, even though he turned desperately to his old formulas and personae—particularly those connected with Hannibal, Huck's St. Petersburg, and Pudd'nhead Wilson's Dawson's Landing. His false starts and mounting pile of unfinishable manuscripts showed him how insecure was his identification with the public. He was led deeply to question himself. His very writing became a source of terror, rather than assurance, to him. At the same time it was, financially, his only support and, emotionally, his only solace. If the fear of impotency as a writer haunted him, the mere act of writing sustained him in his worst times. To Howells, whose daughter Winifred had died horribly, Twain wrote after the blow of his own daughter Susy's sudden death:

> [I am] indifferent to nearly everything but work. I like that; I enjoy it, I stick to it. I do it without purpose & without ambition; merely for the love of it.... [It] puzzles me to know what it is in me that writes, & that has comedy-fancies & finds pleasure in phrasing them.[59]

Twain had not completed his tale of the tragic failures of Huck and Tom. Now, however, he began to write freely of his own dismal failures of sixty years in an enormous manuscript, which he called *Mark Twain's Autobiography.* This was not his first experiment in autobiography. In the '70s

---

[58] Quoted in Paine, Vol. II, p. 945.   [59] *Letters to Howells,* Vol. II, p. 664.

he had written an elaborate burlesque of his family history in an unpublished sketch, "The Autobiography of a Damn Fool." Still, he had not seriously pondered the problems of the autobiography. In 1877, when Howells wrote to him for suggestions for the series of *Choice Autobiographies* (1877–78), which he was editing, Twain replied: "I didn't know there were any but old Franklin's & Benvenuto Cellini's."[60] But in the '90s he began to conceive of an autobiographical form that would define the character and essence of the artist-as-man. This self-revelation would by its nature, he soon decided, be a private utterance from the grave. This decision freed Twain from the fear of public disapproval that had prevented him from finishing other projects he had conceived. He expressly commanded from the beginning that the book not be published until he had been dead a hundred years. With that public block to creativity removed he wrote with energy greater than he had possessed for twenty years.

It was his purpose, he declared in 1906, "to extend [his] notes to 600,000 words, and possibly more." He told Howells that he intended to make a library of his life in an autobiography so detailed that "the set of volumes could not be contained merely in a city, it would require a state, and that there would not be any multi-billionaire alive. . .who would be able to buy a full set, except on the installment plan."[61] Released by the scheme of entirely writing for himself alone, Twain's energies were in full flow, spilling consciousness upon the page in great waves of creativity. For a writer who had feared that his creative potency was gone, this was a joyous awakening and fresh reassertion of self. Twain so obviously reveled in this restoration of his creative powers, feeling in it a renewal of self, that he made no artistic attempt to control his outpourings. He spoke with such freedom that even today, although portions of his autobiographical dictation have been published by Albert Bigelow Paine (two volumes), Bernard DeVoto, and Charles Neider, still a fourth of Twain's dictation remains unpublished.

When Howells learned that Twain had undertaken an autobiography, he advised and dared him to tell "the black-truth, which we all know of ourselves in our hearts."[62] Abandoning his public persona, Twain wrote his book as from the grave, "for a good reason: I can speak thence freely."[63] His self-revelations, he says, are as intimate as those in a love letter. This well defines the essential character of his book. It is a love letter of the ego to itself, proclaiming itself by the act of richly setting down its memories. And simultaneously it is a love letter in which Twain celebrates his glorious acceptance of a world that can prompt such a flood of reminiscences and be the scene of a life so ultimately rich. The earliest sections of the book, recollections of his Hannibal boyhood, were written in Vienna during 1897–99, simultaneously with *The Mysterious Stranger*. It is these recollections which allowed him to emerge from his despair. From 1900 until his death he was occupied and sustained by his self-exploration.

60 *Letters to Howells,* Vol. I, p. 180. 61 This and other remarks by Twain on his autobiography are quoted from Charles Neider's "Introduction" to *The Autobiography of Mark Twain* (New York, 1959), pp. ix–xxiii. 62 *Letters to Howells,* Vol. II, p. 781. 63 "Preface" to *Mark Twain's Autobiography* in *Complete Works,* Vol. XXV, p. xi.

Twain based his autobiography upon the values he had earlier associated with the freedom of drift; and the form of the *Autobiography* consists of Twain's making his theme of luxurious, vagrant drift into a principle of narration. Intending in his book, as he remarked, "to wander whenever I please and come back when I get ready," Twain felt his way toward the systemless system of free association. The "right way to do an Autobiography," he said, was: "Start it at no particular time in your life; wander at your free will all over your life; talk only about the thing which interests you at the moment; drop it the moment its interest threatens to pale, and turn your talk upon the new and more interesting thing that has intruded itself into your mind meantime." He had turned the terror of drift back into a principle of pleasure, and, in a literary way, thus managed to justify to himself the incompleted manuscripts which had led him to question his ability as an artist. "The only thing possible for me," he said in 1906, "is to talk about the thing that something suggests at the moment—something in the middle of my life, perhaps, or something that happened only a few months ago." Into this loosely flowing autobiographical narrative he put the articles, stories, and fragments which he had lain aside. Even books like *Is Shakespeare Dead?*, *The Death of Jean,* and *Captain Stormfield's Visit to Heaven*[64] were dropped into the *Autobiography*. The symbols of his failure became the testaments to his success.

Attempting to provide a collective, historical background to his private meditations, he hit upon the idea—one later developed by John Dos Passos, among others—of scattering newspaper clippings throughout his book. These, he said, would be inserted in later editions, after the history of his times had been forgotten. Like Henry Adams, whose *Education* Twain probably had not seen, he conceived of his narrative as providing the tailoring with which to clothe the manikin of self. "Biographies are but the clothes and buttons of the man," he wrote in his epigraph to the *Autobiography*.[65] Even more than Adams's, Twain's book marks a new stage in the autobiographical form. This has gone too long unrecognized. The post-Civil War generation was the first to truly feel the new conditions of consciousness that would come to restructure mental process and shape the modern mind. The rising new science of psychology—Freud's first article was published in 1879, and William James's and Dewey's treatises appeared in the '80s—occasioned an interest in mental processes for their own sake: men, for the first time, simultaneously thought and thought about their thought. Men became interested in wayward thoughts as well as ordered ones; neurotic more than rational behavior; lying as well as truth. During this time anthropology, too, was winning converts away from history to studies of the myths and symbols of modern man. Lewis Henry Morgan's pioneering anthropological treatise, *Ancient Society* (1878), wrote the professor of Medieval History at Harvard, Henry Adams, "must be the foundation of all future work in American his-

---

[64] *Captain Stormfield* may be termed Twain's ultimate failure among his attempts to rewrite his personal visions to make them publically acceptable. Except for an extract, this book remained unpublished even though he worked on it for thirty years. [65] *Autobiography* in *Complete Works,* Vol. XXV, p. 2.

torical science."[66] Moreover, writers were reflecting the sense of lostness that these changes produced and were proclaiming the predicament of Everyman by delineating their own alienation.

To all of these impulses Twain responded in his *Autobiography*. Joseph Frank has shown, in his well-known essay, "Spatial Form in Modern Literature," how the twentieth-century writer has responded to the new content and structure of consciousness by portraying a world built on isolated events and blurred sequences. Interested in archetypes rather than instances, in symbolism rather than history, modern writers have abrogated the conventional time schemes of literature to follow, instead, the shifting postures of the mind in flux. "Instead of depicting natural appearances in all their overwhelming vitality," Frank writes, "the will-to-art turns toward spiritualization; it eliminates mass and corporeality and tries to approximate the eternal, ethereal tranquillity of otherworldly existence."[67]

This describes exactly the intent and form of Twain's self-exploration. Growing up as a writer at the same time as the rise of American naturalism— with its leader, Howells, as his best literary friend—Twain was the first writer able to reflect the structure of the modern mind, his own, in literature. In this sense, his book is far more modern than the much later autobiographies of Theodore Dreiser or Edith Wharton. Not until Conrad Aiken's *Ushant* (1952) would Twain's form be reattempted and perfected. Twain was primarily concerned with his method—the exploration of himself as an artist—not with the mere revelation of himself as man or the detailing characteristic of literary memoirs. "I intend that this autobiography shall become a model for all future autobiographies," he wrote, "...and I also intend that it shall be read and admired...because of its form and method— a form and method whereby the past and the present are constantly brought face to face." He insisted to Paine, accordingly, that the sections be printed exactly in the order written, regardless of chronology. Not the order of the writer's life, but the arrangement of his consciousness as autobiographer was the principle of the form and method. Rejecting time sequences, Twain further obscured the facts of his life by deliberately confusing dates, inventing "facts," rearranging events, and thus emphasizing the true importance of creation above memory. He insisted that inventions "will do just as well as the facts." His deliberate obscuration of fact and distortion of sequence are, of course, only apparently systemless. Understanding the *Autobiography* better than any other of his books, Twain shrewdly described its systemlessness as "a system which follows no charted course, and is not going to follow any such course. It is...a complete and proposed jumble...[which] can never reach an end while I am alive."

In this manner Twain reasserted his potency as an artist to the last. His revelation of creativity preserved the man—perhaps from the madness that in the late 1890s Twain hovered near. Making the failure of the man to successfully order his experience the principle merit of his method as a

66 Quoted in B. J. Stein, *Lewis Henry Morgan* (New York, 1931), p. 190. 67 Joseph Frank, *The Widening Gyre* (New Brunswick, N. J., 1963), p. 54.

writer, the artist justified his life. He illustrated its value by showing how it served the purpose of art. Seeking his sweet dream of peace in world travels, utopian fancies, or regional nostalgia, Twain had drifted toward despair. But at last, within himself as an artist—in the art which he had practiced for forty years—he made his drift a dream of delight.

FIVE

Paradises (To Be) Regained

"There it was waiting for you. Isn't it an ivory tower, and doesn't living in an ivory tower just mean the most distinguished retirement?"
—Henry James, *The Ivory Tower* (1917)

CHANGING ASSUMPTIONS

Returning from the war, Colonel Charles Francis Adams, Jr., happened upon John Stuart Mill's essay on Comte, which "revolutionized in a single morning," he said, "my whole mental attitude." "My intellectual faculties," he explained, "had then been lying fallow for nearly four years, and I was in a most recipient condition."[1] The way that ideas suddenly took violent hold of Adams after years of war was characteristic of the time. Ideas were the new weapons. Henry Holt, similarly, had his "eyes opened to a new heaven and a new earth" by reading Spencer's *First Principles* in 1865.[2] For these, as for Americans in general, the war had enforced an intellectual hiatus for four years, a long time in the life of a rapidly developing culture. Fact had sped ahead of mind, motion ahead of emotion. With the resumption of normal life, it seemed that the old ideas had lost their power to move or convince—simply by virtue of having been so long ignored. Now, men rushed to replace the Old—as it were, by force—with the "tradition" of the New. As Dewey wrote in 1910 of intellectual progress, it "usually occurs through sheer abandonment of questions together with both of the alternatives they assume. . . . We do not solve them; we get over them."[3] Only two decades before the War, men had universally and unhesitatingly rejected the evolutionary proposals of Robert Chambers's *Vestiges of the Natural History of the Creation* (1844). In the mid-'60s, they so eagerly embraced Darwinism that the scientific evidence for the hypothesis was scarcely weighed.

As with Darwinism, so elsewhere. Not since the Revolutionary period had the life of the mind been so exciting and thought so stimulated. The period between the Civil and First World Wars was an age of ideas—ideas so passionately held that they even seemed adequate substitutes for ideals. It

---

[1] *1835–1915: An Autobiography* (Boston, 1916), p. 179. [2] Quoted in Nevins, *The Emergence of Modern America*, p. 231. [3] John Dewey, *The Influence of Darwin on Philosophy and Other Essays in Contemporary Thought* (New York, 1910), p. 19.

202

was an age, as suggested earlier, in which traditional assumptions about the nature of society, God, morality, politics, economics, history, and law were replaced by new convictions. It was an age of investigation and analysis, but also of confusion; for, as Santayana observed, never before had men known so many facts while being masters of so few principles.[4] Each man embraced his own version of Newness; and so while he might be committed to Ward's dynamic sociology, for example, in other areas of human concern his allegiance might go to Emersonian Transcendentalism, Witherspoon's or McCosh's Scottish Common-Sense epistemology, Wayland's economics, Spencerian psychology, the reliance upon natural law in jurisprudence, and so on, even though the assumptions underlying all these (and the various popular versions of thought drawn from them) were essentially conflicting and contradictory. One could find defenders aplenty for each of these positions, but no one who would (for none could) reconcile them into a coherent philosophy. Instead, men like Ward—who had originally entitled *Dynamic Sociology* "The Great Panacea"—preserved intellectual unity by devoting themselves to single causes. Even the comprehensive systems adumbrated by Spencer, Fiske, and others not only were wooden, but were riddled with contradiction. Above all, then, it was an age of change, of ideas in vigorous movement. "My generation," wrote James H. Tufts, a colleague of Dewey, "has seen the passing of systems of thought which had reigned since Augustus.... Principles and standards which had stood for nearly two thousand years are questioned."[5]

The utopianism which marks the age can be satisfactorily explained only in this context of the expansion of ideas. To start with, men's minds and opinions were so rapidly changing that only a kind of ultimate confusion could have resulted. Anything seemed possible, so revolutionary did the new ideas (and the new conditions of life) seem. Utopianism during the period from 1865 to 1914, then, was not so much the breakdown of logic as the abrogation of the old logics. Where existence meant change, the only logic that men could accept freely was a logic of possibility. In short, the logic of the age was one readily accommodating utopian impulses.

Change was the only certainty. Altered economic, social and political conditions had rendered conventional assumptions obsolete. The circumstances of urbanization and industrialization discussed earlier raised questions the answers to which the older absolute, agrarian, or personalistic frameworks could not supply. With the metamorphosis of institutions, therefore, came the transformation of ideology. Eighteenth-century Enlightenment philosophy and early nineteenth-century romanticism and Transcendentalism had each proposed a set of absolutes—the first, a mechanistic absolute; the other, an absolute of intuition. Faith in reason and natural law characterized the one, faith in truths that make reason superfluous the other. Such faiths were largely complementary, not contradictory, aspects of a belief in human certitude. Both the Enlightenment philosopher Jefferson and the Transcendentalist Emerson, for instance, as Henry Steele Commager has observed,

4 See Commager, *The American Mind*, p. 48. 5 Quoted in *ibid.*, p. 106.

assumed a universe governed by law and intelligible to reason; both taught that God, or Providence, was benevolent, Nature beneficent, Man and Society perfectible. To both, Man was the focus of the universe, and to both, the laws that controlled Nature and Society guaranteed, in the end, the infinite happiness of mankind.[6]

However different otherwise, both believed in the existence of absolutes and the possibility of certitude. Now, however, Nature, God, Society, and Law were to be written in lower case, and to become biology, chance, social statics, and due process. Rejecting their inherited system of absolutes, philosophers, historians, and social scientists began to follow the lead of the biologists and physicists[7] in declaring life basically experimental, self-determining, and open-ended. Confusion was engendered by changing assumptions in several areas that had previously shown near-unanimity of opinion.

PHILOSOPHY. Learning the theory of probabilities from his father, who was a famous mathematician at Harvard, Charles Sanders Peirce was among the first philosophers to insist on the random design of the universe. "Try to verify any law of nature," he argued, "and you will find that the more precise your observations, the more certain they will be to show irregular departures from law."[8] Thirty years earlier Tocqueville had reported that no civilized country paid less attention to philosophy than America. But from the mid-'60s to the end of the century the enormous vitality of American philosophy reflected the deep engagement of Americans with ideas. The first journal in English devoted entirely to philosophy was founded by W. T. Harris in St. Louis. Peirce's pragmaticism and James's pragmatism, Dewey's instrumentalism, and Harris's Hegelianism all combined on the forefront of intellectual advance to undermine both idealism—like that of James's father —and the Scottish Common-Sense philosophy made academically official at Princeton by James McCosh, at Yale by Noah Porter, and elsewhere by their fellow professors of "moral philosophy" or "natural theology." Perhaps the new problems of philosophy still resembled the old ones but, as James Mark Baldwin pointed out, the new ways philosophers talked about them suggested the changes in the answers they would be offering. "Instead of the problem of 'design,' " he wrote in 1909,

> we now have discussions of "teleology"; instead of the doctrine of "chance," we now have the "theory of probabilities"; instead of "fatalism" and "freedom," we now have "determinism" and "indeterminism,". . .instead of "God," we hear of "absolute experience"; instead of "Providence," of "order" and "law"; instead of "mind" and "body," of "dualism" and "monism."[9]

THEOLOGY. Traditional theism had been weakened even before the war by biblical criticism and comparative study of religions. Now, books on these subjects multiplied and people began to assume comparative or anthro-

6 *Ibid.,* p. 86.   7 Einstein's "Special Theory of Relativity," demonstrating the inadequacy of Newtonian concepts of absolute space and absolute time, was published, one should remember, in 1905.   8 Quoted in Morris R. Cohen, *American Thought: A Critical Sketch,* ed. Felix S. Cohen (Glencoe, Ill., 1954), p. 274.   9 *Darwin and the Humanities* (Baltimore, 1909), pp. 81–82.

pological points of view. Washington Gladden's most popular book was *Who Wrote the Bible?* (1891); and James Freeman Clarke's *Ten Great Religions* (1871) went through ten editions in fifteen years. Although not to have a really popular impact until later, James G. Frazer's *Golden Bough,* revolutionizing the concept of faith through the comparative study of mythology, was published in 1890. Proclaiming a Religion of Humanity, and drawing upon the fruits of comparative scholarship, O. B. Frothingham preached the gospel by excerpting his own from the sacred scriptures of all religions, as well as from the poetry of Longfellow, Whittier, and others. Traditional ethics were also shifting. William Graham Sumner, himself an ordained minister, demonstrated in *Folkways* (1906) that ethical codes shift with time and place, and that "mores can make anything right and prevent the condemnation of anything." Once thought to be the "voice of God," conscience became in Sumner's naturalistic critique merely the behavioral product of learning processes, "the rules of the game of social competition which are current now and here."[10] Moreover, conceptions of religious belief were changing. In 1840, Henry James, Sr. had written to an American scientist, his friend Joseph Henry, requesting scientific evidence of the eternal moral and religious truths of the universe.[11] By the twentieth century, his son William had thoroughly abandoned the attempt to logically establish the validity of traditional religion, and instead offered psychological justification for the beliefs he collected. By working a revolution in the older dualistic views of mind, such books as Dewey's *Psychology* (1887), Baldwin's *Senses and Intellect* (1889), and James's *Principles* (1890) provided the background against which James worked. Rejecting metaphysics and viewing consciousness functionalistically, these men were among the first to understand ideas as plans of action and mind as the instrument with which man adjusted to his environment.

ECONOMICS. In the fundamental assumptions of economic thought similar shifts occurred. The textbook that had retained its official hold upon academic economics long after its publication in 1837 was Francis Wayland's *Elements of Political Economy.* "Political Economy," Wayland—President of Brown University—declared early in the text,

> is the Science of Wealth.... By Science...we mean a systematic arrangement of the laws which God has established.... It is obvious, upon the slightest reflection, that the Creator has subjected the accumulation of the blessings of this life to some determinate laws.[12]

Following Adam Smith, Malthus, and Ricardo, Wayland taught his students that man is motivated by a self-interest which the mechanism of competition transforms into socially good results. To profit man, therefore, competition must be allowed to operate freely, without state intervention. William Graham Summer, who was taught from Wayland's text, would update Wayland's terms by using Darwin's and Spenser's. But he would not essentially

---

[10] (New York, 1906), p. 52 and *passim.* [11] Wiener, *Evolution and the Founders of Pragmatism,* p. 98. [12] (New York, 1837), p. 3.

change it. No less than Wayland's, his economics derives from a conception of society as largely static.

Inevitably, the expansive postwar period would modify this position. If classical economics in England had been called (with good reason) "the dismal science," American optimism reacted from its doleful prognostications. Even before the war, Henry C. Carey had begun his economic speculations with the conviction that a divine harmony of interests made high wages and high returns on land and capital concomitant with increased productivity.[13] To this formulation Henry George added the factor of rapid increase in population, and thus strikingly reversed Malthusian economics. "In any given state of civilization," he wrote in *Progress and Poverty* (1879), "a greater number of people can produce a larger proportionate amount of wealth, and more fully supply their wants, than can a smaller number."[14] In the last quarter of the century Ely, Seligman, and others returned from Germany and, under the influence of the historicism of Schmoller and Wagner, insisted that state control of industrial strife was indispensable to human progress.

In 1890, Francis Walker, whose conservative text had replaced Wayland's among academics and who had dismissed the Single Tax as "a project steeped in infamy," told the American Economic Association: "The bounds of tradition, the barriers of authority have...been swept away. Everything once settled in economic theory is audaciously challenged, the most venerable and well approved of our institutions are rudely assailed."[15] Of all the economic antichrists that Walker feared, Thorstein Veblen, who redefined economics in terms of the two fundamental institutions of the engineers and the price-system, was the most formidable. Economists had turned from a dismal to an optimistic science; from a belief in absolute law to faith in the beneficence of rapid change; from a static to a dynamic conception of the movement of society. The changes, then, in economic assumptions, were enormous.

JURISPRUDENCE. If the state was the outcome of a slow process of accumulation, as the new German-schooled economic historicists taught, then its laws were the instruments whereby men adjudicated conflicting desires in the struggle for existence and not, as enlightenment jurists assumed, the static reflections in society of rationality or eternal natural laws. No country had so made its constitutionalism sacred or so venerated its judiciary as America. Law was an American faith. For this reason legal theory, among all formal systems of thought, withstood longest the impact of the "realism" affecting natural and social sciences. For several decades after the war, while political and economic experimentalism became ways of thought, legal

13 Morris Cohen, commenting on the curious difference between American and European assessments of American intellectual achievements, has noted that "Histories of political science written by Europeans pay scant attention to any of our political theorists. But hardly any history of economic thought fails to mention a relatively large number of American economists." At his death in 1879, Carey was regarded abroad as the best-known citizen of the United States. One of the reasons Marx had so little influence in the United States was the strength of American economists like Carey, L. H. Morgan, Henry George, Veblen, and Charles Beard. (*American Thought*, p. 86.) 14 *Progress and Poverty: An Inquiry into the Cause of Industrial Depression and of Increase of Want With Increase of Wealth* (New York, 1929: "Fiftieth Anniversary Edition" [1879]), pp. 149–50. 15 Quoted in Dorfman, *Thorstein Veblen*, pp. 72–73.

thought remained static. Courts repeatedly rejected the kinds of laws based on the new dynamic assumptions of sociology and economics: "The political field lay strewn with the corpses of social welfare laws struck down by judicial weapons."[16] Legal thought was weighted down by the theory of natural rights. Of his famous pioneering work in the historical approach to traditional legal theory in *Ancient Law* (1861), Sir Henry Maine retrospectively wrote:

> At the outset...I found the path obstructed by a number of a priori theories which, in all minds but a few, satisfied curiosity as to the past and paralyzed speculation as to the future. They had for their basis the hypothesis of a Law and State of Nature antecedent to all positive institutions.[17]

Maine's historicism—his view that law derived from and changed with culture—would prevail. Trained at Peirce's Metaphysical Club, Oliver Wendell Holmes pre-eminently brought to lawmaking a pragmatist functionalism which asserted that good laws were those which worked best for society, and must therefore develop with changing social needs. Law must be tested, he insisted, not by a hypothetical system of Rights and Duties, but in the context of Experience. Perhaps this realistic approach was most grandly voiced by Woodrow Wilson in *The State* (1898):

> Spoken first in the slow and general voice of custom, Law speaks at last in the clear, the multifarious, the active tongues of legislation. It cannot outrun the conscience of the community and be real, it cannot outlast its judgments and retain its force. It mirrors social advance.[18]

In law, as in economics, politics, psychology, sociology, theology, and philosophy, the shifts in assumptions were so various, so often only partial and seldom drastic, that few people in the second half of the nineteenth century could fully comprehend their nature; no one, perhaps, could understand their total implications. Thus, the changes in intellectual assumptions and emotional attachments outlined here offered equally confusion and illumination, caused despair as well as confidence, brought fragmentation of consciousness along with its widening, and made men grasp for seeming panaceas as well as for a new but still only potential unification of mind. The hopes and fears of Americans exploded passionately into the vacuum created by the disappearance of their old world-view. In some ways, then. this was a stepping backward in the inevitable march forward. Or, it was a leaping forward—into visions of utopia.

FRUSTRATION AND COMPENSATION: THE SHAPE OF UTOPIA

The hopes and fears of Americans were largely channeled into institutions which could satisfy aspects of the utopian need—institutions of protest, of fraternity, or of labor brotherhood, and finally into the institution of the utopian novel. As early as 1873, Westerners met to hear read "The Farmers' Declaration of Independence," which called upon the government to end

16 Commager, *The American Mind,* p. 372. 17 *Popular Government: Four Essays* (New York, 1886 [1885]), p. v. 18 *The State: Elements of Historical and Practical Politics* (Boston and New York, 1918 [1898]), p. 92.

the "tyranny of monopoly," as that document put it.[19] In 1877, Peter Cooper, speaking with a moral enthusiasm for reform, warned the newly elected President Hayes that millions of Americans, "thrown out of employment, or living on precarious or inadequate wages, have felt embittered with a lot, in which neither economy nor industry, nor a cheerful willingness to work hard, can bring an alleviation."[20] That same year marked the first national strike in American history, after four years of repeatedly reduced wages. The following year the Greenback-Labor coalition polled more than one million votes—the largest number for any third party since early Republican days—and seated fourteen members in Congress. Thereafter, significant third parties of protest—the Populists, the Socialists, the Nationalists—would regularly demonstrate the extent of their individual forms of dissatisfaction at the polls. Strikes were daily news. The intensity of discontent was shown not by the few sensational or violent strikes—the New York Streetcar strike or Chicago Haymarket Square riot of 1886, the Homestead affair or Coeur d'Alene mine strike of 1892, the Cripple Creek or Pullman strikes of 1894—but by the fact that the years from 1886 to 1894 averaged nearly six thousand strikes annually.

Before the war, the open farmlands of the West and the easy ability to form utopian, communistic societies—Charles Nordhoff counted seventy-two of them in 1875—had drawn off much of the excess of discontent. Now, however, the spread of railroads and rise of land values made the organization of such communities more difficult. As a substitute for such societies people turned, for instance, to the social security and status implied in the fraternal orders that proliferated after the War. Coincidently with the most intense period of labor discontent from 1880 to 1900, nearly five hundred secret fraternal societies were established, usually with names suggestive of compensatory aristocratic yearnings, such as the Knights and Ladies of the Golden Rule, the Royal Society of Good Fellows, and the Prudent Patricians of Pompeii.

In industrial terms, not secret societies but unions came to serve similar purposes by establishing for their members principles of order, identity, and security, and so helping to give relief from the chaos in society as a whole. Psychologically, the Knights of Labor stands close to the Knights of the Golden Rule in the social compensations it offered. Regularly opposing Protestantism in his speeches, Samuel Gompers of the AFL sought thereby to draw off religious devotion from church organizations to his gospel of unionism. Unionism sponsored its own martyrology in books like C. Osborne Ward's *The Ancient Lowly* (1888), and its own myth of success in the novels of social awakening that flourished in the '90s and on into the new century. The best known of these is undoubtedly Upton Sinclair's *The Jungle* (1905), which was greeted in the famous Socialist weekly, *The Appeal to Reason*, by young Jack London as "The 'Uncle Tom's Cabin' of wage slavery."[21] Between 1870 and 1901, W. F. Taylor has estimated, more than

19 Quoted in Merle Curti, *The Growth of American Thought* (New York, 1943), p. 617.
20 Quoted in *ibid.*, p. 607. 21 No. 520 (November 18, 1905 [Girard, Kansas]), 5.

250 volumes of economic fiction were published in the United States. In these, the worker became the new hero. Henry George dedicated *Progress and Poverty* "to those who, seeing the vice and misery that spring from the unequal distribution of wealth and privilege, feel the possibility of a higher social state and would strive for its attainment."[22] The myth of the noble workman replaced the myth of the noble savage. Not long after John Hay had expressed conservative fears by identifying organized labor with criminality in *The Breadwinners* (1884), Twain praised the Knights of Labor and said that the workingman "has before him the most righteous work that was ever given into the hands of man to do, and he will do it."[23] Reacting against the older image of the man with a hoe, an AFL pamphlet of 1892 declared that the union has transformed "the patient and sodden drudge into a manly and honest worker." Speaking for organized self-help, Herbert N. Casson announced somewhat later that "the unionist of today will be the statesman of tomorrow."[24] In short, the "tremendously effective repression of human aspiration and desire"[25] that Ordway Tead discovered in his investigation of working-class psychology (*Instincts in Industry* [1918]) found various nonrational, emotionally charged outlets for expression of general discontent during the period: in protest, fraternity, and unionism.

The most imaginatively powerful of the institutions containing these expressions of discontent was, however, the utopian novel. Intellectually it represented a commitment to make change result in plenitude; emotionally, it was a medium embodying wishes frustrated by experience. The utopian novel was vitalized by several factors: (1) the confusions brought about by rapid change and by general political, economic, and social discontent; (2) a new depth of concern with material life here-and-now (and thus with comfort, luxury, and elegance); (3) the mysticism and religious cultism resulting from the breakup of traditional religious uniformity; and (4) notions of promise and progress combined with millennial hopes and a faith in science to create the good life.[26] Obviously these elements mixed and reinforced one another, stirring the imagination. The first of these factors has been discussed, and the rest are here considered in order.

---

[22] P. v. [23] Quoted in Philip S. Foner, *Mark Twain, Social Critic* (New York, 1958), p. 173. [24] D. R. Weimer, "The Man With the Hoe and the Good Machine," quoting Dyer D. Lum, *Philosophy of Trade Unions* (1892) and Herbert N. Casson, *Organized Self-Help* (1901), in *Studies in American Culture, Dominant Ideas and Images,* ed. Joseph J. Kwiat and Mary C. Turpie (Minneapolis, 1960), pp. 67, 68. [25] *Instincts in Industry: A Study of Working-Class Psychology* (Boston and New York, 1918), p. x. [26] For most Americans, science and technology would *make* utopia. While the laboratory was still a popular symbol of mystery, the startling practical results of science drew national attention. Youmans's *Popular Science Monthly* was really popular, and science fiction tales—by Bellamy, among others—began to capture the public imagination. Leopold Eizlitz, the architectual partner of H. H. Richardson, gave one of the wisest analyses of contemporary life in his *Nature and Function of Art* (London, 1881). The American, he said, "denies what he cannot understand, and believes in other things because he cannot understand them. As much as he sneers at science, he is confident that at an early day science will teach us how to perform the labor of life by machinery, and give us a perpetual holiday thereafter" (pp. 17–19). Science would make a utopia of comfort. Preaching equality, the American nonetheless required an economy of superfluity.

MATERIALISM. In any event, the new utopia would make a religion of materialism. The Puritan Gospel of Work was distorted through and by the material concerns of frontier life[27] or life patterns developed in the recent war. Added to the American's inherited uneasiness with high culture and the growing ostentatiousness of the very rich, this combined to give Americans a materialistic definition of utopia. While, as many historians have remarked, this kind of utopia contrasts strikingly with the tradition of utopian ideals from Plato to More, it nonetheless follows the equally venerable and no less logical utopian tradition of the Earthly Paradise found in Lactantius,[28] Irenaeus, St. Brendon, Thomas Burnet, and Francis Bacon. In the formal comfort of the Pullman cars, in the popularity of books on interior decorating like Mrs. Stowe's and Charles Eastlake's, in the ostentation of the new imperial architecture (particularly in the stilted elegance of the bewildering rash of jigsaw ornament and mansard roofs) and in its overstuffed interiors, one can see the glitter of materialism that dazzled the American mind. To a large extent, the financier Russell Sage was unquestionably right in claiming that "if the truth were known, concentration of wealth is popular with the masses."[29]

American religions were redefined in material terms. In *American Notes* Rudyard Kipling described his visit to a Chicago church as "a revelation of barbarism complete." Fitted with "plush and stained oak and much luxury," it reminded him of a circus. The minister,

> with a voice of silver and with imagery borrowed from the auction room, . . .
> built up for his hearers a heaven on the lines of the Palmer House (but with
> all the gilding real gold and all the plate-glass diamond). . . . He was giving them
> a deity whom they could comprehend, in a gold and jewel heaven in which
> they could take a natural interest.[30]

S. S. McClure declined a biography of Jesus that he had commissioned from Elizabeth Stuart Phelps because he wanted, as he put it, "a more snappy life of Christ."[31] Progressive ministers translated such religious materialism into the Social Gospel movement. Its mystical supports weakened by scientific criticism, Protestantism redefined its role in terms of social action. Learned conservatives such as the Reverend G. Frederick Wright of Oberlin claimed that the demands of labor were caused by "the misguided sentimentalism and culpable cowardice of the ministry"[32] who had failed

---

[27] Samuel Bowles reported of the West in 1865: "When the Puritans settled New England, their first public duty was to build a church. . . . Out here, these degenerate sons begin with organizing a restaurant, and supplying Hostitter's stomachic bitters. . . . So the seat of empire, in its travel westward, changes its base from soul to stomach, from brains to bowels." (*Across the Continent*, pp. 201–202.)   [28] Compare, for instance, the familiar folk song "The Big Rock Candy Mountains" with Lactantius's description of Utopia, the Earthly Paradise: "The rocky mountains shall drop with honey; streams of wine shall run down, and rivers flow with milk. . . .In short, those things shall come to pass which the poets spoke of as being done in the reign of Saturnus." (*Divine Institutes*, VII, p. 24. Quoted in Ernest Lee Tuveson, *Millennium and Utopia: A Study in the Background of the Idea of Progress* [Berkeley and Los Angeles, 1949], p. 12.)   [29] Quoted in W. J. Ghent, *Our Benevolent Feudalism* (London and New York, 1902), p. 163.   [30] (New York, 1889), pp. 219–220.   [31] Quoted in W. W. Ellsworth, *A Golden Age of Authors* (Boston and New York, 1919), p. 130.   [32] Quoted in Aaron Ignatius Abell, *The Urban Impact on American Protestantism, 1865–1900* (Cambridge, Mass., 1943), p. 87.

to teach submission and subordination. But, according to the Social Gospel thinkers, not man, only his environment, required salvation. The poor, Frothingham said, "must have consolation in the present."[33] In Edward Eggleston's Lee Avenue Church (as in "the Church of the Best Licks" in *The Hoosier Schoolmaster*) gathered a large number of workmen to discuss questions of tariff, unionism, and the relations between capital and labor.[34] Bellamy was praising the Reverend Washington Gladden's *Working People and their Employers* (1876) while Lyman Abbott was discovering a common spirit in Christianity and Socialism, and approving both. The economist John R. Commons was recommending that a minister "devote one-half of his pulpit work to sociology," while Walter Rauschenbusch, the former pastor of a small German Baptist Church located on the edge of New York's Hell's Kitchen, declared:

> The Christian Church in the past has taught us to do our work with our eyes fixed on another world and a life to come. But the business before us is concerned with refashioning this present world, making this earth clean and sweet and habitable.[35]

The new social commitments of Protestantism were shown by the many adherents among clergymen to Bellamy's Nationalism and George's single-tax movement.

CULTISM. Such materialism encouraged the fadism and cultism that replaced the consolations of traditional religion. In many ways, the new kind of cultist spiritualism was associated with materialism. Commodore Vanderbilt, for instance, though shrewd in business, also absurdly sought information from a Staten Island seeress concerning the future course of the market, and once tried to establish contact with the ghost of Jim Fisk for celestial advice in his manipulations. A British visitor to Boston found "intense interest in the supernatural, the spiritualistic, the superstitious. Boston, of all places in the world, is, perhaps, the happiest hunting ground for the spiritualist medium, the faith healer and the mind curer. You will find there the most advanced emancipation from theological superstition combined in the most extraordinary way with a more than half belief in the incoherences of a spiritualistic séance."[36] This was true, of course, not only of Boston. D. D. Home, the spiritualist still remembered as the object of Browning's satire in "Mr. Sludge the Medium," was raised in America. Stimulants—from drugs to electricity—and Christian Science, Theosophy, hypnotism, and New Thought were flourishing. Mrs. Eddy's *Science and Health* (1875), Marie Corelli's novels, and R. W. Trine's *In Tune With the Infinite* (1897) were eagerly devoured. As a result of the kind of tensions of modernism that have been described in this chapter, the rate of physical

---

[33] Octavius Brooks Frothingham, *The Rising and the Setting Faith and Other Discourses* (New York, 1878), p. 82. [34] See George Cary Eggleston, *The First of the Hoosiers*, p. 354 and *passim*. [35] See Abbott, *Reminiscences* (Boston and New York, 1915), p. 408 and *passim*; quotations in Commons, *Social Reform and the Church, With an Introduction by Richard T. Ely* (New York and Boston, 1894), p. 19; and in Rauschenbusch, *A Rauschenbusch Reader,* ed. Benson Y. Landis, Introduction by Harry Emerson Fosdick (New York, 1957), p. 93. [36] Muirhead, *America: The Land of Contrasts,* pp. 17–18.

and mental breakdowns increased so sharply as to provoke public concern. Robert Herrick described Chicago as infested with "osteopaths, faith healers, mind healers, physical culturists, Swamis, Exodites, Introdites, masseurs... —prophets of the soul or of the belly."[37] In the career of Thomas Lake Harris—who, William James declared, was America's "best-known mystic" —can be read the dizzy connections among the various phenomena analyzed here. In rapid steps he moved from spiritualism to divine breathing, from Swedenborgianism to utopianism (he wrote a novel titled *The New Republic* [1891]), and at last to socialism.

Everywhere during the period one can detect this startling intermingling of mysticism and materialism, of the exotic and the economic.[38] An interesting mass analogue to Harris's career is the march of "Coxey's Army" upon Washington in 1894. On Easter Day—the symbolism is as planned and revealing as Thoreau's going to Walden on July 4—Jacob Coxey's "Commonwealth of Christ," as he called it, set out from Massillon, Ohio in a protest of the unemployed which combined the methods of revivalism and the traveling circus with Populist economics. Although the announced intent of the march was to support the Good Roads and Non-Interest-Bearing Bond bills then before Congress, less practical elements of the protest immediately asserted themselves. Like Coxey, Carl Browne, the actual leader of the march, held curious religious convictions. He called himself a theosophist, and taught that the spirit at death entered a reservoir "like a huge cauldron," which in turn provided souls for the newly born. Even the soul of Christ, Browne asserted, had gone into the amalgam; and from this reservoir he and Coxey had drawn extraordinarily large portions of Christ's soul. Coxey he called the "Cerebrum of Christ" and himself the "Cerebellum of Christ." On the banner which the "Army of Peace" triumphantly carried was a portrait of Christ painted by Browne and strikingly resembling its artist. Under this he inscribed: "Peace on Earth, Good Will to Men. He hath Risen, but Death to Interest on Bonds." The members of the Army who finally

---

[37] Quoted in Kenneth S. Lynn, *The Dream of Success: A Study of the Modern American Imagination* (Boston and Toronto, 1955), pp. 231–32. [38] The following striking mock-advertisements, for instance, appeared during the early 70's in *The Circular,* the official paper of the Oneida Perfectionists:

TO JEWELERS—A SINGLE PEARL OF GREAT PRICE. This inestimable Jewel may be obtained by application to Jesus Christ, at the extremely low price of "all that a man hath!"

TO BROKERS—WANTED—Any amount of SHARES OF SECOND COMING STOCK, bearing date A.D. 70, or thereabouts, will find a ready market and command a high premium at this office.

LEGAL NOTICE—Notice is hereby given that all claims issued by the old firm of Moses and Law were cancelled 1800 years ago. Any requirement, therefore, to observe as a means of righteousness legal enactments bearing date prior to A.D. 70, is pronounced by us, on the authority of the New Testament, a fraud and imposition.

The rhetoric is striking and instructive. Another, more conventional instance of such combination of the religious and the economic occurred in 1873 when, after the economic panic and the grasshopper devastation, Governor Pillsbury of Minnesota declared a day of prayer and issued a proclamation appealing for "divine mercy for sins." (See Nordhoff, *Communistic Societies,* pp. 266–67; Pillsbury quoted in Dorfman, *Thorstein Veblen,* p. 14.)

arrived in Washington were, despite their large share in Christ's soul, promptly arrested for walking on the grass.[39]

CATASTROPHISM AND APOCALYPSE. Appalled by the arrest of Coxey and Browne, the former governor of Kansas, Thomas A. Osborn, announced:

> I want to make this prediction, that there will be no overt act until the next election, then, simultaneous with the returns, flames will shoot into the air from the Atlantic to the Pacific and every palatial residence be destroyed in the uprising of the people.[40]

Certainly, the fear or hope of catastrophe was widespread during the period. Many predictions of apocalyptic revolution were made from the '70s onward. As if in local confirmation of Osborn's predictions, Governor Waite of Colorado told a Populist audience that it were "better to wade in blood to the horses' bridles than that the people's liberties should be destroyed."[41] A disciple of Henry George, William Godwin Moody, warned in *Land and Labor* (1883) that American capitalists "are as blind and as stubborn as the Bourbons of France, and it is a grave question whether the remedy that cured...similar evils in that country must not also be applied in this."[42] Ignatius Donnelly told his Midwestern readers that "the free man will exterminate any new aristocracy which may rise up...just as he blotted out the fierce creatures of prehistoric times."[43] With these and similar declarations in mind, Thomas Bailey Aldrich used the same metaphor of the French Revolution as an analogue for his day in declaring to a friend, "we shall have bloody work in this country some of these days, when the lazy *canaille* get organized."[44] More objectively, Henry Adams was transforming his and his age's anxiety about catastrophe into a principle of history by predicting, in an application of the Second Law of Thermodynamics, the dissipation of energy in the early twentieth century.

Of course, the sense of catastrophism recurs repeatedly in the history of consciousness, and the fear of the end of the world is an aspect of modern anxiety. But catastrophism had a particularly strong appeal in America through its association with the premillennial impulse which guaranteed a purposeful and fruitful catastrophe.[45] Irritated by Adams's insistence on degradation, for instance, William James pronounced the Second Law of

---

[39] Quotations concerning Coxey are in Donald L. McMurry, *Coxey's Army: A Study of the Industrial Army Movement of 1894* (Boston, 1929), pp. 37–39. [40] Quoted in *ibid.*, p. 274, from *The Weekly Iowa State Register* for May 4, 1894. [41] Quoted in *ibid.*, p. 8. [42] *Land and Labor in the United States* (New York, 1883), p. 73. [43] *The Bryan Campaign for the People's Money* (Chicago, 1896), p. 15. [44] Quoted in Brooks, *New England: Indian Summer*, p. 383. [45] One needs to distinguish carefully between the premillennial and postmillennial theories of the final catastrophe. The first notion assumes that the end of the world will be ushered in, and preceded by, a thousand-year period of utopia. The second assumes that this utopia will follow only after a violent world-apocalypse. The first treats signs of catastrophe optimistically, as evidences of the imminence of felicity; the second sees the growth of evil as evidence that a terrible, world-destroying second coming is about to take place. As will be indicated, both notions have influenced the American imagination. But the premillennial theory fit in well with the general tone of American optimism and belief in perfection during this period, and was the more readily seized upon.

Thermodynamics irrelevant to human history, asserting that, to the contrary, "there is nothing in physics to interfere with the hypothesis that the penultimate state might be the millennium."[46] So many other people thought during this period. The millennial hope was widespread. Norman Cohn and others have shown that throughout the Middle Ages social suffering was periodically expressed in "phantasies of a new Paradise on earth, a world purged of suffering and sin, a Kingdom of the Saints."[47] Now, in the midst of intellectual confusion, the yearning for material comfort, cultism, and social discontent in general, the millennial hope strongly reasserted itself in America. Most of the utopian books show directly the impact of millennial expectations. David Graham Phillips, himself despairing, wrote that the "Messiah-longing has been the dream...of the whole human race, toiling away in obscurity, exploited, fooled, despised."[48] And in *A New Moral World* (1885), for instance, James Casey offered a revolutionary system of education that he thought would "change the earth from hell to heaven and people it with saints."[49] Other novels like W. H. Bishop's *Garden of Eden, U.S.A.* (1895) and Jeff Hayes's *Paradise on Earth* (1913), hint in their titles at similar constellations of belief.

The postmillennial doctrine that Christ would appear only after a thousand years of peace was translated, by urgent psychic needs, into the premillennial conviction that catastrophe might occur at any moment, and Christ's appearance would usher in the thousand years of paradisal peace. Some men joyfully accepted the deterioration of their present condition as evidence, therefore, that the millennium was at hand. Thus, paradoxically, the frequent assertion of imminent catastrophe during this age suggests the desperate yearning for imminent peace. The acknowledgment of misery leads, in this dialectic, to the expression of delirious joy. A witness has described how at the first national convention of the People's party, in Omaha in 1892, after Donnelly had in his preamble passionately described the menaces of trust and corporation, "cheers and yells...rose like a tornado from four thousand throats and raged without cessation for thirty-four minutes, during which women shrieked and wept, men embraced and kissed their neighbors, locked arms, marched back and forth, and leaped upon tables and chairs in the ecstasy of their delirium."[50] It is like one of those sudden outbursts of frustration and expectation which occurred so frequently in the Middle Ages, and remained familiar in the Adventist and Millerite crazes that swept rural areas in eighteenth- and nineteenth-century America, when people, as Nordhoff said, seemed "to look forward with a quite singular pleasure to the fiery end of all things."[51]

Of the forty utopian novels which Vernon Louis Parrington, Jr. has analyzed, seventeen, he found, argued or implied that the world could be

---

[46] Quoted in Frederic I. Carpenter, *American Literature and the Dream* (New York, 1955), p. 92. [47] Cohn, *The Pursuit of the Millennium* (Fair Lawn, N. J., 1957), p. xiii. [48] Quoted in Lynn, *The Dream of Success*, p. 139. [49] *A New Moral World and a New State of Society* (Providence, 1885), p. 19. [50] Quoted in Dorfman, *Thorstein Veblen*, p. 88. [51] *Communistic Societies*, p. 349. The Millennial Church, or United Society of Believers, commonly called "Shakers," was organized at New Lebanon, New York, in 1787.

immediately reformed and regenerated. Such utopias assume a Damascus-like conversion of everyone. To cite two minor examples, Thomas Reynolds, in *Prefaces and Notes, Illustrative, Explanatory, Demonstrative, Argumentative, and Expostulatory to Mr. Edward Bellamy's Famous Book* (1890), was convinced that Bellamy's sweeping reforms could be instituted within six months; and Henry R. Everett, in *The People's Program* (1892), insisted that his scheme could be realized "almost immediately if the people choose to work in harmony. The author of this story believes in rushing."[52] Even the realistic Eugene Debs would write, in a circular letter of 1897: "The time has come to regenerate society—we are on the eve of a universal change."[53] Such notions of sudden regeneration reflect, essentially, the impulse of catastrophic millennialism translated into social terms.

Sixteen other books that Parrington writes of, however, offered utopias that would come only very slowly, and chiefly as the result of education. In these, traditional beliefs in chiliastic imminence merge with American faith in evolutionary amelioration. Officially committed to a philosophy of progress, and seeming to see it confirmed, many Americans tended unconsciously to assimilate their millennial hopes into the assumptions of evolution and progress. Both seemed to offer rational—even scientific—guarantees for the paradise to be regained in a more and more glorious golden age. Imperceptibly, Americans made their millennium (like their science, their philosophy, and their social thought) evolutionary. This is not to say that the basic impulses in American utopianism were rational, but that it is essential to understand the compulsions that made for utopianism in order to understand the character of the books which resulted. Certainly, utopianism became a kind of faith largely non-rational. Devastatingly aware of American myths, Chauncey Wright wryly noted: "Faith that moral perfectibility is possible...is a faith which to possess in modern times does not make a man suspected of folly or fanaticism."[54] But there were scores of others who were prepared to boom evolutionary progress. As early as 1874 John Fiske could tell a large audience that "the law of progress...will be found to be the law of history."[55] Darwin himself, making no distinction between nature, society, and morality, announced his conviction in *The Origin of Species*

---

[52] Quoted in Parrington, *American Dreams: A Study of American Utopias* (Providence, 1947), p. 129. [53] Quoted in Philip S. Foner, *Jack London: American Rebel* (New York, 1947), p. 43. The Socialist version of the millennial hope lay in the dream of a "general strike" by labor. For a good example of this, see Jack London's story "A Dream of Debs." [54] *Philosophical Discussions*, p. 70. [55] *Outlines of Cosmic Philosophy: Based on the Doctrine of Evolution...* (Boston, 1874), Vol. II, p. 195. Observe how quickly Fiske's historicism becomes evangelicism:

> Nay, if the foregoing exposition be sound, it is Darwinism which has placed Humanity upon a higher pinnacle than ever. The future is lighted for us with the radiant colors of hope. Strife and sorrow shall disappear. Peace and love shall reign supreme. The dream of poets, the lesson of priest and prophet, the inspiration of the great musician, is confirmed in the light of modern knowledge; and as we gird ourselves up for the work of life, we may look forward to the time when in the truest sense the kingdoms of this world shall become the kingdom of Christ, and he shall reign forever and ever, king of kings, and lord of lords.

(*The Destiny of Man Viewed in the Light of his Origin* [Boston and New York, 1884], pp. 48-9.)

(6th edition, 1880) that "as natural selection works solely by and for the good of each being, all corporeal and mental endowments will tend to progress towards perfection."[56] A convert to evolution, Henry Ward Beecher declared in 1885 that original sin was disproved by the divine decree that man would eventually mingle his with the divine life. Walter Rauschenbusch, too, was beginning to believe "the millennial hope [to be] the social hope of Christianity."[57]

All of these notions of millennial progress Henry George summed up as demonstrating the American's paradoxical but incurable "hopeful fatalism," a shrewd point that Herbert Croly would later develop into a philosophy of reform. The American found a golden future blissfully beckoning to him. Whatever would be, would be right. Refusing to exist in the present, emotionally or ideologically, he lived in a seething fever of hopeful expectation. For this reason, America presented the anomalous situation of unprecedented prosperity accompanied by extraordinary discontent.[58]

THE GOOD LIFE:
THE MYTH OF SUCCESS AND THE MESSAGE OF JESUS

This discontent was expressed in the proliferation of various compensatory versions of the good life. One version was in the Gospel of Wealth or the Success Myth. The other was in the utopian novels of social improvement written by Bellamy, Howells, and scores of others. We shall examine the first, the Myth of Success, only briefly. Russell Conwell's lecture on the ever-present chance of success, "Acres of Diamonds," was published only a year before Bellamy's *Looking Backward* (1888). Both met with equally astounding popular approval and, in the American mind, the prevailing and the dreamed orders, ideology and utopia, were momentarily but precariously balanced. The conservative ideological defense of business success reflected the categories of popular thought. Assuming the economic optimism shaped by earlier actualities of American life and catering to the traditional American commitment to individualism, conservative apologists for the business ethic used science, on the one hand, to support the Social Darwinist thesis of inevitable, immutable progress; and religion, on the other, to justify the accumulation of wealth in the name of Christian stewardship. In a period of confusion, men grasped at a philosophy in which scientific knowledge seemed to confirm the validity of traditional values. The famous story that the editor of the *North American Review* greeted Carnegie's article, "Wealth," as the best essay ever submitted to that journal suggests how desperate the American need was. Translated into the success stories of Horatio Alger and W. M. Thayer, Carnegie's gospel—an outcropping, W. J. Ghent would later say, of "the seigniorial mind"—tended both to stimulate the discouraged to greater efforts and to justify the prevailing order.

---

[56] (London, 1880), p. 428.   [57] See Beecher, *Evolution and Religion*, p. 83 and *passim ;* quotation in Rauschenbusch, *Christianity and the Social Crisis* (New York and London, 1916 [1907]), p. 106.   [58] For an excellent contemporary discussion of this paradox in American culture see Josiah Gilbert Holland, *Every-Day Topics: A Book of Briefs* (New York, 1876), p. 264.

Ghent, whose *Our Benevolent Feudalism* (1902) remains one of the best critiques of the conservative defense, saw that "the preaching of 'success' has become...a distinct profession, honored and well-recompensed."[59] Chronicling, almost litanizing and deifying success had become a leading journalistic activity. The success story appeared everywhere. During the Philadelphia Centennial, Franklin's *Autobiography* was revived to be used as a model of the success story. Inspired by *Moby Dick* to become a novelist, Horatio Alger brought his Ragged Dicks and Tattered Toms to fame and fortune while he himself failed to write the Melvillian epic that he really wanted to. Thayer, who had studied Wayland's economics at Brown, translated them into his log-cabin biographies of Franklin and Garfield. Men tended to take such stories seriously, as accurate analyses of business success. Indeed, Barnum's popular lecture, "The Art of Money-getting," inculcating the notion that "it is not at all difficult for persons in good health to make money," was incorporated into Freedley's *Practical Treatise on Business* (1888).[60]

The chief spokesman for business enterprise was Russell H. Conwell, who, like Alger and Thayer, was trained for the ministry; like them, too, he preached. His "Acres of Diamonds," originally conceived as a sermon and published by the Business Man's Association of Grace Baptist Church, was delivered on the lecture platform over 5,000 times. In his hands, religion was saved as a relevant institution by becoming a function of the business community. The responsibility of the preacher, Conwell contended, is "to make his congregation rich" by teaching them thrift, industry, and enterprise —virtues conventional in the Protestant ethic. If the members of his congregation "do not get larger salaries, obtain larger aggregate profits, dress better and occupy more comfortable homes because of the minister's teaching," Conwell declared, "then he should take the pew and let some good grocer or benevolent railroad conductor take his place." Defending the business order, Conwell was explicitly antiutopian. "Your riches are within your present reach," he insisted. "Yet every one thinks they could do better somewhere else. All look away—away to some imagined Eldorado or Isles of the Blessed, while the gems they seek are at their feet."[61]

Prophets aplenty followed Conwell's evangel. In the '90s, Orison Swett Marden, whose inspirational books were said to be on every fourth living-room table in America, updated Conwell's message with his own brand of the mysticism that by this time had replaced the moral principles of stewardship. Marden's "personal magnetism" and "mental control" were the new virtues which would eventuate into high-pressure salesmanship. In *Pushing to the Front* (1894) and in the several books that followed it, Marden taught

---

[59] See *Our Benevolent Feudalism*, p. 124. The disillusion rising out of deferred hopes led to the idealization of the past which is analyzed in the discussion of regionalism, in Chapter Three.   [60] See P. T. Barnum, *Life of P. T. Barnum, Written By Himself: Including His Golden Rules for Money-Making. Brought up to 1888* (Buffalo, 1888). p. xxxiii.   [61] *Acres of Diamonds: How Men and Women May Become Rich. The Safe and Sure Way to Amass a Fortune, Be a Benefactor, and Achieve Greatness. Advice and Examples Adapted to All Classes* (Philadelphia and St. Louis, 1890), pp. 202, 203, 204, 23–24.

this new "Law of Success." He consciously dedicated himself to uplifting the discouraged multitudes, "the boys and girls who long to be somebody and do something in the world, but feel that they have no chance in life."[62]

While Conwell and his fellow Success writers urged their audience to get rich, others, beginning in the late '80s, were appalled to find, as one minister put it, "that the church is a Pullman palace car," and so urged their fellows to spend their time in the service of humanity.[63] This was essentially the message of the Iowa minister George D. Herron, who became phenomenally popular in 1891 with his address, "The Message of Jesus to Men of Wealth." Pointing to the single tax, Nationalism, Populism, and socialism, Herron declared that God was at work in the world to establish the principle "that sacrifice and not self-interest is the social foundation, that the Golden Rule is natural law."[64] An obscure Kansas minister, C. M. Sheldon, would top even Herron's popularity with his novelized version of Christian regeneration, *In His Steps* (1897), which sold more than eight million copies. In their own terms, others asked: What would Jesus do? "Golden Rule" Jones became mayor of Toledo by making Sheldon's precepts his platform. Poets criticized "organized charity, scrimped and iced,/In the name of a cautious, statistical Christ," and began to declare the need for charity as a principle of human intercourse. Journalists like Jacob Riis and B. O. Flower, economists like Richard T. Ely, and politicians like J. P. Altgeld shared visions of society based on human brotherhood. Even Herbert Spencer bluntly repudiated his reputation as the philosopher of *laissez faire,* telling E. L. Youmans: "That is a persistent misunderstanding of my opponents. Everywhere...I have contended that in its special sphere, the maintenance of equitable relations among citizens, governmental action should be extended and elaborated." Such revisions as these of the conservative ideologies laid the foundation for the multifarious projection of utopia.[65]

Among numerous attempts to define utopianism, Karl Mannheim's is the most serious. "We regard as utopian," Mannheim says in *Ideology and Utopia* (1929), "all situationally transcendent ideas...which in any way have a transforming effect upon the existing historical-social order." Projected either spatially (for instance, into an Eden or a paradise) or tem-

---

62 *Pushing to the Front: Or, Success Under Difficulties: A Book of Inspiration and Encouragement to All Who Are Struggling For Self-Elevation Along the Paths of Knowledge and of Duty* (New York, 1897 [1894]), p. iii. See discussions of Marden in Alan Valentine, *1913: America Between Two Worlds* (New York, 1962) and Ralph Henry Gabriel, *The Course of American Democratic Thought* (New York, 2nd ed: 1956). 63 James McCosh, *et al., Problems of American Civilization: Their Practical Solution the Pressing Christian Duty of Today* (New York, 1888), p. 56. This volume richly documents the shift from conservative to Social Gospel Christianity in the late '80s. 64 *The New Redemption: A Call to the Church to Reconstruct Society According to the Gospel of Christ* (New York and Boston, 1893), p. 15. 65 John Boyle O'Reilly, "In Bohemia" in *In Bohemia and Other Poems* (Boston, 1886), p. 15. See Benjamin Orange Flower, *Civilization's Inferno; Or, Stories in the Social Cellar* (Boston, 1893), pp. 446ff.; J. P. Altgeld, *The Mind and Spirit of J. P. Altgeld: Selected Writings and Addresses,* ed. Henry M. Christman (Urbana, Ill., 1960), pp. 109ff.; Richard T. Ely, *Socialism: An Examination of Its Nature, Its Strength, and Its Weakness, With Suggestions for Social Reform* (New York and Boston, 1894), pp. 352–54. The remarks by Spencer are taken from *American Social History as Recorded by British Travellers,* ed. Allan Nevins (New York, 1923), p. 495.

porally (into a golden age in the future), ideology becomes utopian, according to Mannheim, when in the dialectical evolution of culture it condenses the "unrealized and the unfulfilled tendencies" of its age and so is able to burst the limits of the existing social order and reconstitute society. Before the nineteenth century, the radical nature of chiliastic millennialism had made intellectuals espouse its antithesis, a "conservative attitude of resignation" and a realistic view of politics. But with the beginnings of liberal humanism, chiliasm was largely (though, as we have seen, not completely) transformed into an aspect of evolutionary or historical progress.[66] In social suffering; in the confusion of values and the shifting ground of traditional ideas; in plans and panaceas; in the notions of millennium, either catastrophic or progressive —in these we can see a truly utopian mentality manifesting itself at all levels of American experience in the later nineteenth century.[67]

Combined with the regionalist impulse to locate bliss in a benign past, this utopian idealization of the future suggests a widespread flight from the systematization of a consciousness of the present. Essentially, however, the two impulses are contrary in character. The utopian element tends to shatter the prevailing order and to strive dynamically towards realizing a future, whereas the regional impulse merely seeks consolation for a lost past in finding its decayed symbols—rotting wharves, destroyed plantations, aging plainsmen. Regionalism seeks stasis; utopianism envisions the old orders broken and the old life regenerated. Generally speaking, as has been shown, regionalism involves a yearning for a lost Eden, for primitivity, innocence, and, in short, the state of nature. Quite to the contrary, utopianism, even when it uses a golden age as its vehicle, looks millennially towards the future where not nature but civilization creates perfection: the natural becomes the regulated, primitivity surrenders to knowledge and self to society; the simple gives way to the complex and innocence to law. For the one the ideal is an age of impulse, for the other the reign of contrivance. For the utopian, perfection means complication.

Although they insist upon the need for transcending reality, the utopias we remember are those that are nonethless so close to the unrealized needs of their age that they help to create a new reality in the image, not of the prevailing order, but of its deficiencies and dreams. Not unrelated in form or impulse to the archetype of metamorphosis which lies at the heart of most fairy tales, utopianism means transformation. So long as paradise remained outside life on earth the notion of world reform was ideological; but as the hope for Paradise tended to be assimilated into societal terms, this ideology became utopian and, shattering the medieval world-orders, has

[66] Quoted and summarized from Mannheim, *Ideology and Utopia: An Introduction to the Sociology of Knowledge,* Preface by Louis Wirth (New York and London, 1949 [1929]), pp. 185, 179, 192. [67] An interesting example of the conjunction and amalgamation of virtually all the myths and confusions that have been analyzed here is Frank Rosewater's novel, *The Making of a Millennium: The Story of a Millennial Realm, and Its Law.* (Omaha, Neb., 1908). Rosewater's book advocates the supposed panacea of Centrism, an extension of socialism, as the solution to class conflict and the labor problem. It includes chapters like "The Millennial Secret," "The Quest of Labor's Knighthood," "The Great Transition Era," "To Edenize the Outworld" (Centrism is Edenic), and "Where Art Thou, Adam?"

since periodically brought society to the crisis of change. Such a crisis came in 1888 with Edward Bellamy's *Looking Backward* and the utopian visions and revisions for which he was the catalyst.

Edward Bellamy

Edward Bellamy, grandson of the famous theologian and friend of Jonathan Edwards, Joseph Bellamy, remade the earlier religious hopes into social millennia. In this sense, the direction of his thought paralleled the thought of his time. "There is no better...literature," he said,

> than the splendid poems in which Isaiah and the other Hebrew seers foretold an era when war and strife should cease, when every man should sit under his own vine and fig-tree with none to molest or make him afraid, when the lion should lie down with the lamb, and righteousness cover the earth as the water cover the sea.... Did you suppose that because...[this] is called the millennium, it was never coming?

His nationalism he referred to as "a religion," "a Judgment Day," or "God's Kingdom of fraternal equality."[68]

Bellamy's *Looking Backward: 2000–1887* is important because in it he was able to give form and universality to the multitudinous and confused utopianism emerging in his time. Able to grasp, both intuitively and by design, the variety of millennia in the '80s, he fused these with traditional literary themes and so portrayed his society not as a wish, but as already accomplished. Although in 1889 Henry George announced his belief that Bellamy had drawn "a castle in the air with clouds for its foundation," others asserted with T. W. Higginson, an early Nationalist: "instead of believing that what...[Bellamy] says is too good to be true, [we] believe that it is too good not to be true."[69] Indeed, testimony to the power of the book to convince is abundantly conclusive. The Veblens, who read the book together, were deeply affected, Ellen believing that it helped to focus her husband's thinking at its "critical period before his life work began."[70] Calling Bellamy "The Great American Prophet," Dewey also praised him for first grasping and expressing "the *human* meaning of democracy."[71] From Paris, Peter Kropotkin remarked in *La Revolte* upon the power of the novel to win converts.[72] It is important first and last to insist upon the fact that *Looking Backward* is a novel, and only thus was able to wield a power to which Veblen, a better economist, Dewey, a better psychologist, and Kropotkin, a better sociologist than Bellamy, all paid tribute. Contrary to the usual claims for the "social vision" of the book, it is precisely by virtue of its fictive impact that it rises above and shoulders aside the scores

---

68 *Talks on Nationalism* (Chicago, 1938), pp. 66–7; *Edward Bellamy: Selected Writings on Religion and Society,* ed. Joseph Schiffman (New York, 1955), p. xxxvi. 69 Quoted in Gabriel, *Course of American Democratic Thought,* p. 221; and Syliva E. Bowman, *The Year 2000: A Critical Biography of Edward Bellamy* (New York, 1958), p. 119. 70 Quoted in Dorfman, *Thorstein Veblen,* p. 68. 71 "A Great American Prophet," *Common Sense,* III (April 1934), 6. 72 For Kropotkin's and other reactions abroad see Sylvia E. Bowman, *et al., Edward Bellamy Abroad: An American Prophet's Influence,* Preface by Maurice Le Breton (New York, 1962).

of utopias that surround it. Not without profit had Bellamy read and reviewed *The Gilded Age,* Holland's *Sevenoaks,* and DeForest's *Honest John Vane* in the '70s. Not without profit had he written two novels before he began *Looking Backward.*

Although his other work has been obscured by the enormous success of his utopian novel, it is perhaps from its vantage point that Bellamy is best approached. Howells found that in *Dr. Heidenhoff's Process* (1880), *Miss Ludington's Sister* (1884), and in the stories collected in *The Blindman's World* (1898), no less than in his utopian novel, Bellamy showed "a romantic imagination surpassed only by that of Hawthorne."[73] To the Hawthorne of "Dr. Heidegger's Experiment," "The Birthmark," "Rappaccini's Daughter," "The Celestial Railroad," and "Egotism," he does indeed bear a singular resemblance. The theme of his romances is the immorality of memory; retrospection Bellamy sees as destructive and vitiating. In *Dr. Heidenhoff's Process,* the heroine is tormented by the nemesis of her memory of her seduction. In a desperate effort to find peace and to return the hero's love, she pins her hopes upon a new cure, "The Extirpation of Thought Process," whereby one Dr. Heidenhoff has discovered how to extract painful memories.

This wish for the extirpation of memory and for the breakdown of time runs through all of Bellamy's work. In "The Blindman's World" a disembodied astronomer visits Mars, where he discovers men who, more maturely developed than those on Earth, can forsee the future, while having only a poorly developed, almost nonexistent power of memory, and despising the past. In "The Old Folks' Party" a group of teenagers throw a party— "a sort of ghost party," says one—in which they masquerade as their future selves—"ghosts of the future instead of ghosts of the past." They thus are able simultaneously to regard their present and future selves. So also, in "A Summer Evening's Dream," Bellamy begins with the situation of Mary Wilkins's "Two Old Lovers," but superimposes upon the interminable courtship of the two old lovers a pair of young lovers who help briefly to confuse past, present, and future with them by changing partners. Thus, for Mr. Morgan, "the two Miss Roods—the girl and the woman, the past and the present—were fused and become one in his mind. Their identity flashed upon him." Transforming the process of time, Bellamy portrays a remarkable group of shape-shifters who assume their several chronological identities simultaneously.

Julian West is precisely such a hero and *Looking Backward* such a romance of memory and anticipation. In an article published in *The Nationalist* for May, 1889, Bellamy discussed "How I Came to Write *Looking Backward.*" At the outset he had, he writes,

> no idea of attempting a serious contribution to the movement of social reform. The idea was of a mere literary fantasy, a fairy tale of social felicity. There was no thought of contriving a house which practical men might live in, but merely

---

[73] Howells, "Biographical Sketch" in Edward Bellamy, *The Blindman's World and Other Stories* (New York, 1898), p. xiii. The stories referred to below are in this volume.

of hanging in mid-air far out of reach of the sordid and material world of the present, a cloud-palace for an ideal humanity.[74]

Later, he changed his mind and wrote that he intended an intellectual protest from "the heart of all religion and the express meaning of Christ."[75] On another occasion, he told the readers of *The Ladies' Home Journal* that he had set out to solve the labor-capital problem. But his earliest description of his intention—merely to portray an ideal millennial world—is closest to the intentions of his earlier literary work. Certainly, it is clear that the publishers of *Looking Backward,* Houghton, Mifflin, at first directed the book toward the summer reading public's taste for light fiction. With Edward Bok gratuitously helping to alter the advertising, the novel leaped from 10,000 copies sold in its first year to an average sale of 40,000 copies a month through 1889.[76] So skillfully had Bellamy made his fantasy seem real that men, groping for principles of order, fastened onto the romance society his art made appear feasible.

The theme of the book is that of Bellamy's other novels and stories—transformation. Julian West's metamorphosis is dramatized by the large (and detailed) contrasts between the present and the future, the real and the ideal, the actual and the millennial, poverty and progress, sickness and health, self and society—in short, by the division in his identity between the chaotic, competitive nineteenth century and the harmoniously cooperative twentieth century. Julian himself is acutely aware of this "world-transformation," as he calls it, since he uniquely experiences its dramatic effects. Hypnotized in 1887, he lays in his fireproof underground vault until the year 2000 in a state of suspended animation—a device used earlier by a fellow romancer, Edgar Allan Poe, in "The Facts in the Case of M. Valdemar." In 2000 he is discovered and revived by Dr. Leete, who becomes his Dante's Virgil—while Edith Leete is his Beatrice—in the paradisal world that has been established in the interval. Indeed, to Julian's suggestion that he is in paradise, Dr. Leete replies: "Such is, in fact, the belief of some persons nowadays. . . . They hold that we have entered upon the millennium." The signs and symbols of transformation surround Julian's career in utopia. He has, throughout, a double identity. The Leete house is built on the former site of his own; Edith is the great-granddaughter of his betrothed Edith; his Boston is not quite unrecognizably altered. Caught between the past and the future, first the one then the other alternately seems unreal to him. In the pattern of this convention, then, he has to be born anew. The underground chamber in which Julian waits to assume his redefined, twentieth-century self is an obvious evocation of the womb. Julian's is the individual version of the social, collective bursting of the chrysalis of which the Reverend Barton speaks. Feeling early "a momentary obscuration of the

74 Quoted in Arthur E. Morgan, *Edward Bellamy* (New York, 1944), p. 224. 75 Quoted in Bowman *et al., Edward Bellamy Abroad,* p. 40. 76 Bok, *The Americanization of Edward Bok: The Autobiography of a Dutch Boy Fifty Years After* (New York, 1920), p. 118; and James D. Hart, *The Popular Book: A History of America's Literary Taste* (New York, 1950), pp. 170–71.

sense of one's identity"—the idea "that I was two persons, that my identity was double," Julian has moments much later, "when my personal identity seems an open question." He is a "waif from another century." His old life, Edith tells him, though "strangely cut off," will be returned to him in this new age. Confused and struck by his grotesque alienation from both past and future, Julian returns broodingly to his underground chamber, convinced that he "was neither dead nor properly alive." This is his return to the chrysalis preparatory to a new birth.

At last, then, he undergoes the drama of rebirth. Waking, he discovers that he has dreamed his utopia. Now, truly, he is torn between dream and reality; for his dream *qua* reality has enabled him (and as Bellamy hopes, the reader) to feel the terrors of his era, the social and industrial chaos of the late '80s. In scanning the newspaper headlines for the day, walking through the city, talking with laborers or his former friends, he finds confirmed that he has indeed been born anew—intellectually—and now is ironically alienated from his nineteenth-century world. He is overwhelmed by his simultaneous visions of the ideal and real. Wandering into the "festering mass of human wretchedness" in a tenement district, he looks, "horror struck, from one death's head to another, . . . affected by a singular hallucination. Like a wavering translucent spirit face superimposed upon each of these brutish masks, I saw the ideal, the possible face that would have been the actual if mind and soul had lived." At the moment of crisis, Julian awakens to find, however, that the *past* has indeed been abrogated—that his return to the past was a nightmare—and that his dream of the future *is* reality. Escaping from chaos with Julian, the reader is himself released into his dream of utopia, and embraces it with extraordinary relief. By adapting its patterns to social transformation, Bellamy gave new life and relevance to the recurrent literary theme of rebirth and metamorphosis.

In this cathartic sequence lay Bellamy's considerable hold upon the later nineteenth-century imagination. No vision of social felicity has ever possessed such power to compel response. More than a dozen books soon appeared— along with Bellamy's own sequel, *Equality* (1897)—to continue, counter, or modify Bellamy's book, while scores of others were electrified into being by the sudden revelation of this widespread utopian impulse. First of all, in dialectical fashion, Bellamy's vision of utopia produced visions of dystopia. Complaining that Bellamy's "temperament may be called the unmixed modern one, unhistoric and unartistic," and calling *Looking Backward* "a horrible Cockney dream," the English writer William Morris replied with his pastoral, pre-Raphaelite *News From Nowhere* (1890). In America, Arthur Dudley Vinton responded with *Looking Further Backward* (1890), which consisted of a series of lectures given by Julian West's successor in the Chair of History at Shawmut College, Professor Won Lung Li. By depicting a successful Oriental invasion, Vinton shows how unprotected Bellamy's America would be from foreign menace. In the same year the editor of the Chicago *Freie Presse*, Richard Michaelis, published *Looking Further For-*

ward: An Answer to Looking Backward. Continuing West's story after he
has supposedly uncovered the misrepresentations in Dr. Leete's rosy account,
Michaelis reconverts Julian to free enterprise. Mrs. M. A. Shipley, in *The
True Author of Looking Backward* (1890), attempts to discredit Bellamy's
social reforms by showing that he plagiarized August Bebel's *Die Frau und
der Sozialismus* (1883). That Bellamy's book could evoke response in Europe
as well as America and England was demonstrated by the appearance of
three German antiutopian novels in 1891. Translated into English as
Mr. East's Experiences in Mr. Bellamy's World, Konrad Wilbrandt's book
depicts the disastrous results of transplanting Bellamy's American utopia in
Berlin. Ernst Mueller's *Ein Rückblick aus dem Jahre 2037 auf das Jahr
2000. Aus den Erinnerungen des Herrn Julian West* reveals the corruption
and favoritism infesting the whole system, and returns the world to capitalism
by 2037. Last, Philip Wasserburg's *Etwas Später! Eine Fortsetzung von
Bellamy's Rückblick* converts Julian and Edith to Catholicism and brings
them to a new feudalistic, papal-monarchial Eden in Germany. In 1898
appeared the last dystopia directly drawing upon Bellamy. Provoked by the
appearance of *Equality,* George A. Sanders responded with *Reality, or Law
and Order vs. Anarchy and Socialism,* vitriolically reaffirming classical
economics.

Defenders and extenders of Bellamy's world-transformation, however, were
appearing as rapidly and writing as facilely as his detractors. Thomas
Reynolds's *Prefaces* (1890) is a series of fragmentary observations on
Bellamy's scheme. In the following year Ludwig Geissler enthusiastically supported Bellamy in *Looking Beyond. A Sequel to "Looking Backward"...and
an Answer to "Looking Further Forward" by Richard Michaelis.* In this
novel, the Nationalist, Mr. Yale, defeats Michaelis's Professor Forrest in
a debate on the new society. In 1890, Mrs. C. H. Stone attempted to prove
in *One of "Berrian's" Novels* that this utopia was intensely dramatic by
pretending to offer one of the romances of the novelist of the future referred
to by Bellamy. Attempting to answer similar criticisms concerning the
dullness of an achieved utopia like Bellamy's, Rabbi Solomon Schindler
showed the human and industrial conflicts which continue to stimulate
Julian's son to intense endeavor in *Young West* (1894). Schindler, who had
earlier translated *Looking Backward* into German, was New England's first
reform rabbi, a Nationalist and friend of Minot Savage. *Young West,* published by Benjamin Orange Flower's Arena Press, was radical even in design,
having yellow-, blue-, and green-bordered pages designed to prevent eye-
strain. Driven by a vision even more radical than Bellamy's, Schindler, as
Arthur Mann says, "talked himself right out of Judaism into an agnostic
socialist humanism."[77] In 1898, George Farnell attempted to solve the
thorny problems of the mode of transition to Bellamy's world, and in *Rev.
Josiah Hilton, the Apostle of the New Age* discovers the principle of regeneration to be in monetary reform. A novel interestingly combining Bellamy
with the spatial (as opposed to temporal) tradition of James Fenimore

[77] *Yankee Reformers in the Urban Age* (Cambridge, Mass., 1954), p. 57.

Cooper's utopian romance, *The Crater* (1847) or Howells's utopian novels, is the anonymous *Robinson Crusoe, Looking Upwards...The Up-Grade from Henry George Past E. Bellamy* (1892). These find utopia in a hidden place rather than in another time. Also anonymous were *Julian West, My After-dreams* (1900) and *Looking Ahead...Not by the Author of Looking Backward* (1902).

The mere listing of these books suggests the genuine crystalization of the utopian impulse during the two decades from 1880 to 1900. This is reinforced by the fact that many of these books were obviously often printed at their authors' expense out of compelling motives, and published in places as remote and as removed from each other in sectional needs or pecularities as Albany, New Orleans, Santa Rosa (California), Oklahoma City, Holstein (Iowa), Knoxville, Topeka, and Lewistown (Maine). In some senses, the utopian novel became for a brief time the true National Novel. The American discourse was conducted as the clash of alternate utopias, each asserting its right to shape the future.

Such utopianism helped to make Americans familiar with dreams, and thus able to envision and accommodate rapid social change. Providing the stable conventions of literary form, and thereby offering control over experience, the utopian novels helped Americans not merely to accept, but to direct change in this age of confusion. By ordering change, these books made it meaningful; preserving tradition where all traditional values seemed to be abrogated, they gave Americans a momentary respite from intellectual and emotional chaos. They manifested and helped to define the social consciousness that Americans were for the first time in their history developing. Appearing just after the terrifying Haymarket Square riots, *Looking Backward* helped Americans to readjust to social amelioration at a time when men advocating socialism were not only mocked but were sometimes in physical danger. Bellamy gave the confused social consciousness of his time not only justification, but life and wholeness. Being a skillful novelist working in a viable tradition, he was the most usable of utopians. Momentarily, he contained and controlled disaster.

Whatever the modifications of Bellamy's book, it remained the focus for utopian discourse, magnetizing a mixed group of enthusiasts. Progressives, unionists, Social Gospel writers, socialists, Populists, theosophists—these all discovered in Bellamy an evangel for the new life. Following Bellamy's vision of Nationalism, the Progressive found, as Louis Hartz has noted, his release in the sweet "dream of a trust so big that it absorbed all other trusts, so big that the single act of its nationalization collectivized all America."[78] Popular hopes for scientific millennia were as amply satisfied by Bellamy's mechanistic projections as by *Popular Science*. His ordering of American labor into an Industrial Army seems to have been the germ for the organization of Coxey's Army of laborers. His Religion of Solidarity anticipates the Social Gospel movement. Washington Gladden, among others,

[78] *The Liberal Tradition in America: An Interpretation of American Political Thought Since the Revolution* (New York, 1955), p. 233.

acknowledged Bellamy's influence. Socialists, too, welcomed Bellamy as one of their own. Laurence Gronlund ordered his agents to sell *Looking Backward* instead of his own *Co-operative Commonwealth* (1884). In 1896, Populists welcomed the Nationalists into the People's party as fellows. The *Labor Standard, Dawn* (the magazine of W. D. P. Bliss's Christian Socialists, with Hamlin Garland as one of its editors), Flower's muckraking *Arena, Lend-a-Hand*—the old-fashioned reform journal of Edward E. Hale—and *The Ladies' Home Journal* each in its own way boomed the book by offering it as a premium to new subscribers. Ignatius Donnelly welcomed the Nationalist delegates to the 1892 convention of the People's party rhetorically with: "Edward Bellamy—whom not to know is to argue one's self unknown"; Howells's claim that Bellamy "virtually founded the Populist Party" has some justification.[79] The Theosophists, too, apparently saw their hopes realized in *Looking Backward*. The Nationalist chapter of Boston was made up largely of Theosophists who, Cyrus Willard says in his unpublished autobiography, "believed with me that Nationalism was but the working out of the doctrines of human brotherhood as taught by Madam Blavatsky."[80] (Helen P. Blavatsky, whose influence on Yeats is well established, founded the Theosophical Society in New York in 1875, which remained essentially an American institution. The year after her *Isis Unveiled* [1877] appeared, she became an American citizen.) In similar manner, Francis E. Willard, who indefatigably stumped the country for women's rights, saw in Bellamy "an Evangel" and confided to a friend: "Some of us think that Edward Bellamy must be Edwardina—i.e., we believe a big-hearted, big-brained woman wrote the book. Won't you please find out?"[81]

William Dean Howells

The utopian energy which Bellamy released in the American people was sustained, ordered, and extended by the most influential of living American writers, Willian Dean Howells. We have come in recent years to recognize that Howells's interest in social—which for him meant ethical—reform was lifelong. Growing out of the Swedenborgian utopianism of his visionary father, it was widened and deepened by his sense of the transformation of the equalitarian America he knew in prewar Ohio into the industrial America that emerged after the War and every year more resembled hierarchical Europe. "I supposed we were so Europeanized already," one of the American leisure class says in *Through the Eye of the Needle* (1907), "that a European landing among us would think he had got back to his starting point." From the "Minor Topics" column which he wrote for Godkin's *Nation* in 1865 to the end of his life, Howells actively sought to direct the social change of his America.

As editor of the *Atlantic* and later of *The Cosmopolitan*, he encouraged fiction and essays concerned with social problems. He always preferred, for

---

79 Bowman, *The Year 2000*, p. 134. 80 Quoted in Morgan, *Edward Bellamy*, p. 264.
81 Quoted in Bowman, *The Year 2000*, p. 120.

instance, Crane's *Maggie: A Girl of the Streets* to his *Red Badge of Courage*. Not only Crane, but also Garland, Brand Whitlock, William Allen White, Robert Herrick, Harold Frederic, and David Graham Phillips profited from his help. Moreover, he accepted for the *Atlantic* perhaps the first genuine analysis of the predatory methods of capitalism, H. D. Lloyd's "The Story of a Great Monopoly," after it had been refused by several magazines. A study of the Standard Oil Company, this article was so sensational that it took the March, 1881 issue of the *Atlantic* (in which it held the leading place) into an unprecedented seven printings. Later, Lloyd expanded this into one of the basic texts for muckraking, *Wealth Against Commonwealth* (1894). As critic, also, Howells entered and provoked social controversy. From his "Editor's Easy Chair," he picked out for special notice the varied work of Bellamy, Abraham Cahan, Morris, Shaw, Tolstoy, Richard T. Ely, and Thorstein Veblen. The most influentially powerful of American critics, he brought fame to some of these—to Veblen, for instance—singlehandedly. Furthermore, as a serious essayist he wrote articles of social commentary, an aspect of his work which has been virtually ignored. His letter to the *Tribune* concerning the Haymarket Square affair is well known, of course; but such articles as "Are We a Plutocracy?," "Equality as the Basis of Good Society," "The Nature of Liberty," and "Who Are Our Brethren?"— published between 1890 and 1905—show the consistency and continuity of Howells's social conscience. In short, as America's most influential literary man, Howells was an effective publicist over several decades for reform ideas, establishing an acceptable popular context for Progressive and, later, New Deal legislation.

Certainly, in his novels he effectively dramatized the disparity between the ideal and real in America. Deeply concerned with social harmony, his oft-repeated theme involves family relations and the unity of the family. His novels, as Van Wyck Brooks notes, are "full of loyal households."[82] But the Maverings, the Marches, the Laphams and his other happy families are always threatened with familial dissolution through strife. Through *caritas* and generous understanding—the lack of which makes for the tragedy of *A Modern Instance*—such families cohere. In his economic novels, the metaphor is expanded as Howells compares the nation to a family, in which competition prevents harmony. The spirit of capitalism, he came to believe and to show, was inimical to the development of a unified nation, and, indeed, of complete individuals. Books as far distant as *The Rise of Silas Lapham* (1885) and *The Son of Royal Langbrith* (1904) studied the moral effects of competitive capitalism upon sensitive individuals. Deepening his portrayal of the millionaire, John Milton Northwick, in *The Quality of Mercy* (1892) beyond his sketch of Dryfoos in *A Hazard of New Fortunes* (1890), Howells established a literary type who would reappear in the work of other American writers—in lost souls like Norris's Shelgrim, Dreiser's Cowperwood, and Dos Passos's Charley Anderson. But in Howells's world, such hollow men are counterbalanced by other characters who vigorously symbolize social

[82] *New England: Indian Summer,* p. 221.

felicity. Basil, Conrad, and Lindau in *A Hazard of New Fortunes,* Brice Maxwell in *The Quality of Mercy,* and Reverend Peck in *Annie Kilburn* (1888) all symbolize alternatives to the competitive life. Howells's finest creation of this kind is perhaps David Hughes, the former member of Brook Farm, who in *The World of Chance* (1893) has gone on to establish his own utopian community based on equality and justice. Forced back into society, he and his followers dramatize the gulf between dream and reality in industrial America.

This gulf is the literal subject of Howells's two utopian romances, *A Traveler from Altruria* (1894) and *Through the Eye of the Needle* (1907). Like David Hughes, Aristedes Homos in the former novel acts "as a myth, . . . a thoroughly good myth." We take him at once as both a character and a symbol of the potentiality for ideals existing in the American tradition, and partially as realized in the pre-industrial West and Northeast. "America must imply Altruria," Mr. Homos says; and certainly the outline of Altrurian evolution which he gives toward the end of the novel indicates that the present state of America is the past of Altruria and so suggests the coming of another utopia here. Homos, in short, is the incarnation of the social dreamer. He is the Howells-as-social-critic of whom Mr. Twelvemough (Howells-as-romantic-novelist) asks in *A Traveler:* "Was he really a man, a human entity, a personality like ourselves, or was he merely a sort of spiritual solvent, sent for the moment to precipitate whatever sincerity there was in us, and show us what the truth was concerning our relations to each other?" Into the summer hotel which Howells uses as "a sort of microcosm of the American republic" flock specimens of an America of pomp and prejudice—stripped bare by the wise innocence and meek irony of Mr. Homos's questions. Momentarily penetrating cant with candor, the Altrurian reveals how fully selfish competition has eaten into the American community and resulted in fixed classes, the degradation of morality into business exigency, and a new and worse wage-enslavement of labor. If utopia is Altruria, America is "Egoria."

To be sure, Howells shows the terrible loss of the American dream for the lower classes, the Lindaus and the Camps. But he is chiefly concerned with the degrading effects of competitive capitalism upon the upper and middle classes. He reveals not only the human narrowing of men involved in merely commercial activity, but the predicament of their wives—doomed to useless lives of leisure—and their children, who too frequently inherit the frustrating and hopeless burden of reparation for the commercial sins of their fathers.[83] Rejecting the American myth of business success, Howells came to believe that the true rise of a man was the moral one illustrated in Silas Lapham's business failure. Silas, who will not sell his virtually worthless Western property to a group of "British dreamers" who wish to establish a "cummunity," symbolically affirms the relevance of their utopian ideal and thus, in the bankruptcy which results from his decision, achieves his success. But few

---

[83] It is interesting to note that *The Ivory Tower* (1917), which Henry James wrote after the renewal of his sense of America, is very Howellsian in its treatment of the tragic wound of money.

others achieve Silas's success. Most, like Mr. Makely, are "made" by the money they "make": they are mere reflex aspects of their possessions. At their most conscious they recognize their utter alienation, without an understanding of how to end it. Ansel Denton, in *The World of Chance*, for one, invents an engraving process which will at once make him rich and turn printers out of jobs. Committing suicide by swallowing the acid used in his invention, he enacts literally the deaths which all suffer emotionally, intellectually, and morally in a world where economy defies community. His is the tragic recognition of the contradiction in the condition of all.

Eveleth Strange, also, who suggests in her very name her alienation, tells Mr. Homos: "I loathe my luxury from the bottom of my soul, and long to be rid of it, if I only could, without harm to others and with safety to myself." So Mr. Homos reports in his letters to an Altrurian friend, which Howells wrote upon completing *A Traveler* and which were published in *The Cosmopolitan* in 1893–94.[84] Here Mr. Homos reveals to his friend that he and Eveleth had planned marriage, but that at the last moment she had found herself unable to accept the prospect of life in Altruria: in 1893 Egoria could not—the conclusion tragically implies—wed Altruria. But in 1907. in the midst of a flourishing progressivism, Howells resurrected these letters to form the first part of *Through the Eye of the Needle*. In the second, he reveals that Eveleth has changed her mind (or heart), has pursued the Altrurian on his homeward journey, and has married him. She is a new Eve, initiated into this future Eden where "we have the kingdom of heaven upon earth." What had appeared to be a tragedy Howells thus turned into a novel of transformation in which Eveleth documents by letters to her friend Mrs. Makely the stages of her regeneration.

How was America to be similarly transformed? The range and character of Howells's allegiances suggest a partial answer. In contemporary essays and reviews and in later books of reminiscence, Howells acknowledged the influence upon him of Gronlund, the Fabians, William Morris's tracts, and, above all, of Tolstoy. He praised Bellamy's *Looking Backward* and joined his Nationalist party. The cooperation and amalgamation of the Nationalists with the People's party he also approved. He lived near Henry George and visited him frequently. Many Social Gospel ministers were friends of his. Not only did he warmly praise Bliss's Christian Socialists, but he himself joined the Church of the Carpenter in New York. He had read widely in utopian literature, including Swedenborg's *New Jerusalem,* and reviewed such contemporary utopian novels as Edward Everett Hale's *Sybaris* (1869), *Ten Times Ten is One* (1870), and *How They Lived in Hampton* (1888). It is likely that Hale, in whom was incarnated both a retrospective and progressive Americanism, served as the spiritual model for Mr. Homos. In 1888, writing Hale in gratitude for his novels, Howells told him that conditions "cannot be bettered except through the unselfishness you enjoin, *the immediate altruism dealing with what now is.* . . . [The] best that is in men . . . cannot come out

[84] See Howells, *Letters of an Altrurian Traveler 1893–94,* ed. Clara M. Kirk and Rudolf Kirk (Gainesville, Fla., 1961).

till they all have a fair chance. I used to think that America gave this—now I don't."[85] Hale, who was a charter member with Howells of the Boston Nationalists, founded a Tolstoy Club in Cambridge, and served on the staff of *The Cosmopolitan* while Howells was writing his Altrurian pieces for it. From Hale's altruism to Homos's Altrurianism is only a short step.

Such varied affiliations suggest the intellectual diversity that prevented Howells's commitments from hardening (or softening) into dogmas. He declared unhesitatingly his belief in the millennium: "The millennium," he wrote, "the reign of Christliness on earth, will be nothing mystical or strange. It will be the application of [human cooperation]...to life."[86] Asked in 1898 what he considered the prospects for socialism in America, he told the editor of the *American Fabian:* "As to that, who can say? One sees the movement advancing all about him, and yet it may be years before its ascendancy. On the other hand, it may be but a short time.... A turn here or a turn there, and we may find our nation heading on the road to the ideal commonwealth."[87] Ready to welcome utopia, he was not prepared to prophesy it and thus could continue to imagine it. Bellamy, whose imagination was deadened by his need to defend *Looking Backward* in its successor, *Equality* (1897), had, privately congratulating Howells on *A Traveler*, warned him of this problem in 1893. "The responsibility upon us...to plead the cause of the voiceless masses," he wrote, "is beyond limit.... [The] trouble is the better a man does the better he has got to do. There is no discharge in that war."[88]

Howells never sought discharge. Looking neither forward nor backward, he knew that utopia was an ever-present possibility that lay in man's power to evoke as he willed. Undoubtedly he agreed with David Hughes, whom he made declare in *The World of Chance:* "The way to have the golden age is to elect it." Like Bellamy, Howells dreamed of that blissful election. But he knew, too, and demonstrated, the power of the environment to grapple and hold. He was a naturalist and realist even as a utopian. At the end of *The Quality of Mercy,* Putney says of Northwick: "His environment made him rich, and his environment made him a rogue. Sometimes I think there *was* nothing to Northwick, except what happened to him." Howells's realism helped him to imagine a usable utopia. Howells kept his mind open by keeping his novels open to possibility—the possibility of a utopia ever present, though not yet evoked; ever imagined, never realized. He might have his Altruria only as Hawthorne had his Blithedale, in sight but not within reach.

He wrote to Charles Eliot Norton of his uneasiness with his own utopia: "All other dreamers of such dreams have had nothing but pleasure in them; I have had touches of nightmare."[89] Howells, it is true, announced that he was for the smiling aspects of life; but following Hawthorne and Melville,

85 *Life in Letters of William Dean Howells,* ed. Mildred Howells (New York, 1928), Vol. I, pp. 418–19. Italics added. 86 Quoted in Robert L. Hough, *The Quiet Rebel* (Lincoln, Neb., 1959), p. 54. 87 Quoted in Kenneth E. Eble, *Howells: A Century of Criticism* (Dallas, Tex., 1962), p. 64. 88 Quoted in Bowman, *The Year 2000,* p. 140. 89 *Life in Letters,* Vol. II, p. 242.

and ready to accept Crane, Frederic, and Phillips as well as Zola, Ibsen, and Dostoyevsky, he took a certain pleasure in the kinds of heroism made possible by darker aspects. The ability to face and triumph over evil, the struggle against overwhelming forces, the assertion of the individual will, the conflict of social forces—in short, the strife that brings so much anxiety with it— also suggest certain kinds of vitality that would be lost in the harmonious, utopian world. With utopia, heroism ends. Such traditional virtues as bravery, constancy, self-denial, and self-assertion are useless, or even dangerous, in a regulated society. Inspired by the idea of progress, utopia nonetheless denies the dynamism involved in progress. Thus for Howells the vision of utopia inevitably brings with it the dystopian nightmare he vaguely felt. The abundance of utopias in the late nineteenth century has resulted, for this reason, in not only the existence, but even the popularity of the dystopia in our own day, of which Orwell's *1984* and Huxley's *Brave New World* are obvious examples.

Ignatius Donnelly

The nineteenth century produced immediate reactions to the blissful utopianism described here, going, in intensity, far beyond mere reaction to or commentary upon Bellamy's work. Visions of harmony frittered into prophecies of chaos. The idea of the cooperative commonwealths of industrial armies or of the commonwealths of Christ were racked by the war of classes, the general strike, and the reign of violence. Selling over a quarter of a million copies, Ignatius Donnelly's *Caesar's Column* (1889) was the most popular dystopia of all. It is a revelatory comment on the doubleness of the American mind, equally stirred by hope and fear, that this book and *Looking Backward*, published a year apart, should both have been sensationally popular. For Donnelly's book reverses the conventions of the utopian formula, presenting a vision not of regeneration, but of degeneration, the crumbling of the old orders and idols into insane confusion. The hope for progress, it would seem, involves the sinister fear that man has already taken irremediable steps toward insuring his almost total annihilation. Between Bellamy and Donnelly the utopian mind of the later nineteenth century was divided. For Bellamy, the world-order contains seeds of good that will flower in the natural processes of evolution; for Donnelly, it is infested with cankers which must be purged before millennial peace can reign. In short, Donnelly's utopia—only vaguely glimpsed at—entails riotous catastrophe as a necessary purgative initial stage. The conflict in religion between the post- and premillennialists; in geology between catastrophists like Clarence King and gradualists like O. W. Marsh; in historicism between Henry Adams and Herbert Adams; in sociology between the dynamics of Ward and the statics of Wayland; and in philosophy between Hegelians like Royce and Spencerians like Fiske—these define the impulses dividing Donnelly and Bellamy and splitting, in general, the American mind of this era.

Donnelly was possessed and driven by a vision of catastrophe. His first book, *Atlantis* (1882), combined a mythopoetic imagination with an erudite jumble of pseudo-science—a combination that so well agreed with the habit of the '80s to adapt religion to science and vice-versa that the book had gone into twenty-three editions in America (and twenty-six in England) by 1890. In it Donnelly "demonstrated" that Plato's myth of Atlantis was veritable history by gathering and analyzing the memories of catastrophe still preserved in the myths of the race, and concluding that the biblical story of the deluge refers to that sunken continent. Atlantis, he believed, achieved a golden age—a civilization only now being regained. Edward N. Beecher— the brother of Harriet and Henry—went even further than Donnelly in following out the implications of his *Atlantis*. In *The Lost Atlantis, or "The Great Deluge of All," An Epic Poem* (1897), acknowledging his indebtedness to Donnelly, Beecher declared: "Lost Atlantis was the Eden/Of which sacred history told."[90]

Donnelly himself had already turned by this time to other images of catastrophe and other symbols of the expulsion from Eden. He followed the success of *Atlantis* by publishing in the same year—apparently without feeling any contradiction between these books—*Ragnarok: The Age of Fire and Gravel*. Between the growing evil of the world and its climactic regeneration lay its "ragnarok," or, as Donnelly explains, "a world-convulsing catastrophe...quite out of the ordinary course of Nature's operations." In his conclusion, his prophecy and Populism mix as Donnelly declares the imminence of disaster and the need for reform:

> Build a little broader, Dives. Establish spiritual relations. Matter is not everything. You do not deal in certainties. You are but a vitalized speck, filled with a fraction of God's delegated intelligence, crawling over an egg-shell filled with fire, whirling madly through infinite space, a target for the bombs of a universe.[91]

Disappointed in the meager sales of this book, Donnelly urged his publisher, D. D. Appleton, to have it reviewed prominently in the company's magazine, *Popular Science Monthly*. Youmans, its editor, distinguishing (as Donnelly never could) between myth and science, replied with admirable irony: "The minds that are taken with that work are in a very unpromising condition to reason with.... What would you think of a man who would gravely reply to...the romancer Jules Verne?"[92]

A decade later, during the 1892 presidential campaign, Donnelly fused his romance of catastrophe with politics. In his famous "Populist Preamble," for instance, he predicted "terrible social convulsions, the destruction of civilization, or the establishment of an absolute despotism."[93] Supporting Bryan in 1896, he again warned capitalists of "an out-burst like the breaking forth of wild beasts. And the longer [the worker] is deceived and deluded the more terrible will be the catastrophe."[94] *Caesar's Column*, combining all of these elements, still retains an elemental power in its portrayal of the

---

90 (Cleveland, 1897), p. 53. 91 (New York, 1882), pp. 56, 441. 92 Quoted in Martin Ridge, *Ignatius Donnelly: The Portrait of a Politician* (Chicago, 1962), pp. 208–209. 93 "St. Louis Platform, February, 1892" in Hicks, *The Populist Revolt*, p. 436. 94 Donnelly, *The Bryan Campaign for the People's Money*, p. 184.

day of doom, when the world shaped by Social Darwinism, laissez-faire economics, hedonism, and machine technology is overwhelmed in the uprising of the masses. On the one hand, Gabriel, the hero, sees a vision of the hollow men and women in the dining hall of the (appropriately named) Darwin Hotel; then, in the slums, he is confronted by the equally horrible animality of the masses who have been degraded by "progress." The conventions established for the utopian world by Bellamy are all reversed; even Bellamy's benevolent sermon of the twentieth century (preached by the Reverend Barton) is distorted into the cruelly hedonistic sermon (preached by Professor Odyard) that Gabriel hears. Moreover, in his novel Donnelly predicts the nature of twentieth-century warfare: instead of ease and peace, technology has produced weapons—magazine rifles, the technique of blitzkrieg, poisoned gas, and so on. Not the utopian "Brotherhood of Justice," but the "Brotherhood of Destruction" will be the true result of the evolution which Donnelly reads from the character of his age.[95] Images of animal cunning or brute power—of rats, tigers, wolves, sharks, serpents, dragons, lizards, hornets, bloodhounds, lions, jackals, and vultures—dominate the imagery of the book and show how both classes are equally ripe for extermination. The deliberate parallels between the meetings of the "Plutocrats" and the "Brotherhood of Destruction"; between Prince Cabano and Caesar Lomellini; their equal involvement with the Demons—the destroying airships —all suggest the degradation infecting both sides.

Gabriel Weltstein, the reflector of all this, had, Donnelly wrote his publisher, "some reference to the Angel Gabriel.... Gabriel blows a trumpet to revive the sleeping nations."[96] Arriving in New York from an Africa that bears striking resemblances to Jeffersonian America (he will at one point praise "the honest yeomanry who had filled, in the old time, the armies of Washington and Jackson and Grant"), Gabriel watches the final upheaval of the corrupted orders. His is a vision of hell (Chapter 31 is entitled "Sheol") and the day of judgment in which, with the "Demons" everywhere, "civilization is gone, and all the devils are loose!" At the point of final chaos—"It was Anarchy personified," Gabriel declares—Gabriel and his beloved set out in an airship[97] for Africa, "The Garden in the Mountains," where they establish a New Eden, "a garden of peace and beauty, musical with laughter," while the rest of the world begins anew its long reemergence from savagery.

[95] The Constitution of the Boston Bellamy Club, adopted on January 8, 1889, declared the Nationalists committed foremost to "the Brotherhood of Humanity." (Bowman, *The Year 2000*, p. 125.) [96] *Caesar's Column*, ed. Walter Rideout (Cambridge, Mass., 1960 [1890]), p. 19n. [97] An interesting translation into modern terms of the myth of Noah's ark in the deluge, the "ship" is stocked not with animals but a library, printing presses, telescopes, and "electrical apparatus"—in short, with the achievements of civilization. "It may be," one character says, "that the ancient legends of the destruction of our race by flood and fire are but dim rememberances of events like that which is now happening." As yet unexplored and uncivilized, Africa inspired several utopian visions. Gabriel's party would have been near, on a literary map, to the citizens of Theodor Hertzka's *Freeland* (1889) and *Freeland Revisited: The New Paradise Regained* (1894). Hertzka actually organized a group of sixteen pioneers who set out for Uganda. Livingstone, of course, had revealed that in Africa he was searching for the Garden of Eden. Eden tends to exist just beyond the edge of the known, and so Africa began to take the place in the later nineteenth century of an America by then fully explored and exploited.

Jack London

Dear Comrades:

Here it is at last! The book we have been waiting for these many years! The "Uncle Tom's Cabin" of wage-slavery! Comrade Sinclair's book, "The Jungle!"

It is essentially a book of today. The beautiful theoretics of Bellamy's "Looking Backward" are all very good. They served a purpose, and served it well. "Looking Backward" was a great book. But I dare say that "The Jungle," which has no beautiful theoretics, is even a greater book.

It is alive and warm. It is brutal with life. It is written of sweat and blood, and groans with tears. It depicts not what man ought to be, but what man is compelled to be in our world, in the Twentieth Century.

So began a letter published in the November 18, 1905 issue of the *Appeal to Reason,* signed "Yours for the Revolution,/Jack London."[98] Thus London made explicit the need which ran through all of his books to abolish the mythical supports of conventional social, economic, and philosophical attitudes by confronting these with the actualities of human aspiration and frustration. Measuring prospects against realities, he wrote stories, novels, autobiography, articles, and reviews which even now appear remarkably free from contemporary myth-making.

London's work is usually discussed with Crane's and Norris's, although it bears little resemblance either to Crane's delineation of the agonized private sensibility or to Norris's romantic intermingling of the person and transpersonal forces. There was, moreover, no influence and little communication among these three writers. Essentially, London wrote in a philosophical tradition rather than a literary one. The books he carried to the Yukon with him were *The Origin of Species,* Haeckel's *Riddle of the Universe,* and—most precious of all—*Paradise Lost.* During a time when Melville was largely forgotten, London read *Moby Dick* again and again.[99] He read Franz Boas's pioneering anthropological studies and Frazer's *The Golden Bough;* in biology, Darwin, Huxley, and Wallace; among economists he studied Malthus, Ricardo, and Mill, as well as Kropotkin, George, DeLeon, Benjamin Kidd, Marx, and Engels; among philosophers, Aristotle, Hobbes, Locke, Hume, Hegel, Leibnitz, Spencer, and Nietzsche. The literature of reform, exposé, and unionism he consumed voraciously.

London's fiction grows naturally out of this tradition of ideas, and not essentially from his literary tradition or contemporaries. This distinction is, indeed, frequently the point of his novels. Humphrey Van Weyden, at the beginning of *The Sea Wolf* (1904), is said to have published an article on Poe in the *Atlantic,* and is interested only in romantic writers. This fact, in a sense, is a proof for London of Van Weyden's inadequacy. For the Wolf

[98] No. 520 (Girard, Kansas), 5. [99] Laying the keel for his *Snark,* he recalled: "When I was a small boy I read a book of Melville's called *Typee....*I resolved...when I had gained strength and years I too would voyage to Typee." Making the extremely difficult crossing from Hawaii to the Marqueses, London explored the valley of Hapaa and wrote his own "Typee," recording the violation of the garden where Melville's strong tribe had been gutted and degraded by leprosy, elephantiasis, and consumption. Richard O'Connor discusses London's reading of Melville in *Jack London: A Biography* (Boston, 1964), pp. 39, 46–7, 263–65.

Larsen to whom he must go to school in order to conquer has read not only Poe and DeQuincey, but also Darwin and Spencer. Like Larsen's mind, London's resounds with ideas. In this and other ways London, who possessed an imagination driven and vitalized by intellect, resembled D. H. Lawrence.[100] Beginning with material as various as those of the Yukon, the South Seas, the London slums, or the San Francisco waterfront, he made all alike embody the similar excitement of the life of the mind. Halting and careless in mere narration, frequently rhetorical and posturing in dialogue, his style shows, when engaged in the play of mind, the conscious craftsmanship which might have been predicted of the author who, at the age of twenty-three, had published two articles, one on language and the other on the use of verbs, in the *American Journal of Education*. He was able to tranform dogmatic ideology into general ideas and ideas into action.

Having marched with Kelly's tramp army from Oakland in 1894—deserting it in Twain's Hannibal—he was impatient with the Oakland Socialist local, where intellectuals casually argued theory on evenings really devoted to beer and music. Nor was he any more satisfied with the Oakland Theosophists, from whom the romantic Joaquin Miller got the utopian and Nationalist impulse for his *Building of the City Beautiful* (1893). In the working class, rather, London found (he says in "What Life Means to Me") "keen-flashing intellects and brilliant wits."[101] In his fiction ideas are translated into and assessed by their results in action. To the end of his life he retained this intellectual vitality. The decline in his work coincided with the decline of Socialism and Progressivism, when his intellectual tradition lost popular relevance and left his books mere money-makers without an intellectual *raison d'être*. "I loathe the stuff [i.e., fiction]..." he wrote to Upton Sinclair in 1911. "[If] I could have my choice about it I never would put pen to paper—except to write a Socialist essay to tell the bourgeois world how much I despise it."[102]

At his best, in his books London entertained imaginatively the imperatives of life for the individual and for society, and the clashes between them. Unfortunately for his reputation London's work has been misrepresented. Tracing the permutations of his literary popularity, James Hart, for instance, has contended that London's thousands of readers "translated his Nietzschean doctrine into terms of their own lives, dreaming of rugged-individualistic successes."[103] But London's work did not enact Roosevelt's Strenuous Life or Nietzsche's Superman. When Avis Everhard describes her husband in *The Iron Heel* (1907) as " a blonde beast such as Nietzsche has described," London appends the ironic footnote from the point of view of achieved socialism: "Friedrich Nietzsche, the mad philosopher of the nineteenth century of the Christian Era, who caught wild glimpses of truth, but who, before he was done, reasoned himself around the great circle of human

---

100 London was so excited by *Sons and Lovers* that upon finishing it he cabled his congratulations to the then unknown Lawrence. 101 *Essays of Revolt*, ed. Leonard D. Abbott (New York, 1926), p. 88. 102 Quoted in *Jack London, American Rebel: A Collection of His Social Writings...*, ed. Philip S. Foner (New York, 1947), p. 110. 103 *The Popular Book*, p. 215.

thought and off into madness." In "The Class Struggle" (1903), London insisted that the present generation should refuse to be "the 'glad perishers' so glowingly described by Nietzsche."[104] Rather, they should reinterpret or reject the concepts of the struggle for the survival of the fittest. His program for reinterpretation he had already outlined in "Wanted: A New Law of Development" (1902). There he declared that "all the social forces are driving man on to a time when the old selective law will be annulled."[105] Finding in Spencer's cosmic synthesis justification for his own compulsions, London saw development pointing toward the triumph of group over individual strength; of cooperation over primitive competition.

So also, in his novels, socialism is the health of the state and the cure for the alienated individual. *Martin Eden,* he wrote to Upton Sinclair, "was an attack on individualism." On the flyleaf of a copy he added in 1910: "This is a book that missed fire with a majority of the critics. Written as an indictment of individualism it was accepted as an indictment of socialism. . . . Had Martin Eden been a socialist he would not have died." To Mary Austin he continued in 1915: "At the very beginning of my writing career, I attacked Nietzsche and his super-man idea. This was in *The Sea Wolf.* Lots of people read *The Sea Wolf,* no one discovered that it was an attack upon the super-man philosophy." His last literary note before his suicide in 1916 dealt with "Martin Eden and Sea Wolf, attacks on Nietzschean philosophy, which even the Socialists missed the point of."[106] Martin Eden, the book makes clear, finds his individual success empty; lacking social conviction, and thus alienated, he commits suicide. In *The Sea Wolf,* Wolf Larsen inhabits a world where individualism lacks opportunity for achievement and leads to physical decline and madness. To be sure, as London wrote in "How I Became a Socialist" (1903), he *had* celebrated the strong individual. He had been "dominated by the orthodox bourgeois ethics" of success before he experienced the horrors of the Social Pit and became a convert to socialism.[107] This celebration of individual force remained an implicit aspect of his imagination—and, in equilibrium with his social commitments, provided his books with the basic tension of the tragedy in psyche and society which he repeatedly portrayed.

In *The Iron Heel,* then, London projects the clash of the selfish and social within himself into a war of classes. Like the utopian novels of Bellamy and Howells, London's novel has as its basic theme the transformation and regeneration of its narrator, in this case Avis Everhard, who moves from self- to social-concern. Her metamorphosis anticipates and symbolizes the eventual rejuvenation in her society. She buries "the old Avis Everhard beneath the skin of another woman whom I may call my other self." But unlike the metamorphoses of Bellamy's Julian West or Howells's Eveleth Strange, hers is accomplished in a world inimical to reformation. Thus, for her and Ernest Everhard (her husband, and a great Socialist leader), as

---

[104] In Foner, ed., *Jack London,* p. 459. [105] In *ibid.,* p. 433. [106] Quoted in Irving Stone, *Sailor on Horseback* (Boston, 1938), p. 259, and Foner, ed., *Jack London,* p. 104. [107] In Foner, ed., *Jack London,* pp. 362–65.

well as for John Cunningham, Bishop Morehouse, and others, the formulas of utopian success are reversed. Aspiring to bring "lasting peace and happiness upon the earth," they cause incredible "carnage and destruction" in the war of the "Plutocrats" against the masses. Seeking to make manifest a benevolent socialism, they bring a brutal feudalism into being to oppose them.[108] Ernest, who appears "transfigured, the apostle of truth, with shining brows and the fearlessness of one of God's own angels," is a Christ figure who issues forth the catastrophic Chicago Commune instead of millennial peace. Virtues like honesty, integrity, love, fidelity, and humanitarianism are opposed by a society consecrated to predatory materialism. As Ernest remarks, "Times have changed since Christ's day." Replacing the utopian vision of the "City Beautiful" inhabited by regenerated man, then, is London's dystopian revelation of the degraded animality of the "people of the abyss":

> It was not a column, but a mob, an awful river that filled the street, the people of the abyss, mad with drink and wrong, up at last and roaring for the blood of their masters. . . . It surged past my vision in concrete waves of wrath, snarling and growling, carnivorous, drunk with whiskey from pillaged warehouses, drunk with hatred, drunk with lust for blood—men, women, and children, in rags and tatters, dim ferocious intelligences with all the godlike blotted from their features and all the fiendlike stamped in, apes and tigers, anaemic consumptives, and great hairy beasts of burden, wan faces from which vampire society had sucked the juice of life, bloated forms swollen with physical grossness and corruption, withered hags and death's-heads bearded like patriarchs, festering youth and festering age, faces of fiends, crooked, twisted, misshapen monsters blasted with the ravages of disease and all the horrors of chronic innutrition, the refuse and the scum of life, a raging, screaming, screeching, demoniacal horde.

With the masses thus blunted and broken and the "impassive and deliberate. . .Oligarchy" triumphantly regnant at the book's conclusion, seven centuries of imperial, capitalist persecution are required before socialism is achieved and the Everhard manuscript edited and published as one of its historic documents.

Although both Donnelly and London wrote dystopian novels in answer to Bellamy's sweet dream of peace, Donnelly is much closer ideologically to Bellamy than to London. Both Bellamy and Donnelly rely for their ideological assumptions on the Darwinian concept of evolution. The difference is that one sees felicity evolving from elements present in American culture, while the other sees elements present that will bring chaos as a preliminary to the social utopia. London, to the contrary, subscribes to the Marxian dialectic. Thus, whereas Donnelly warns his nineteenth-century

---

[108] It was Ghent's *Our Benevolent Feudalism* (1902) which objectified for London his disillusionment with the progress of reform. Ghent ironically showed how the oligarchy was reestablishing for the machine age patterns of belief and action similar to those of feudalism. London reviewed Ghent's book favorably in the *International Socialist Review* and recommended it to socialists who believed that capitalism would give way to socialism at the drop of a ballot. The tone of the unimpassioned footnotes in *The Iron Heel* call to mind both Ghent's and Veblen's ironic styles.

audience that a war may develop as a way of reforming the present, London
sees the class war as inevitable and necessary. He writes no lesson for the
times. He is confident only in the future, when the synthesis of social
felicity will issue into the millennium. He is concerned not with Darwinian
evolution, but with Marxian revolution.

In 1905, speaking at Yale on "Revolution," London told his audience that
the Socialists demand "all that you possess. . . . We are going to take your
governments, your palaces, and all your purpled ease away from you, and
on that day you shall work for your bread even as the peasant in the field
or the starved and runty clerk in your metropolises." "The revolution," he
announced in concluding, "is a fact. It is here now."[109] For a decade he
remained of two minds concerning the possibility of such revolutionary
success. If *The Iron Heel* envisions militant capitalism and the suppression of
the masses, "The Dream of Debs" (1909) describes the successful effects of a
general strike in immediately establishing a utopia of social justice. If
"Goliah" portrays a socialist state made possible by science, *The Scarlet
Plague* (1913) portrays the reversion of man to primitive conditions after
a plague has destroyed civilization. Finally, in 1916, London resigned from
the Socialist Party, which, he felt, had lost its energy by denying the
primacy of the class struggle. He wrote to his Oakland local: "I believed
that the working class, by fighting, by never fusing, by never making
terms with the enemy, could emancipate itself."[110] At the age of forty he
faced a period of social compromise in which his own revolutionary formula-
tions would lack significance. No longer able to imagine how his ideas could
issue into action, he lost interest in the ideas and began to buy story plots
from Sinclair Lewis, George Sterling, and others. Believing in social transformation—committed to the drama of catastrophe—he was disillusioned
by the compromising triumphs of reform. London was the first important
American writer to close his letters with the Socialist formula. He was also,
perhaps, the last to do so meaningfully. His career spans the years of the
socialist hope for utopia. His letter of resignation from the Socialists he
pointedly signed "Yours for the Revolution,/Jack London."

Jack London was perhaps the last of the writers whose work was vitalized
by the remarkable efflorescence of utopian ideas in the nineteenth century.
From Charles Francis Adams's excited discovery of Mill and Comte in 1865
to London's desperate affirmation of the need to realize principles is a long
way. But Charles and Henry Adams—whose family history Francis Galton
used as his first example in *Hereditary Genius*—were among the first to
understand the shape of things to come. As modern men, they were anticipating in 1865 what London would be. London's very life and mind is a demon-

---

109 In the poster advertising his appearance, London is pictured in a red sweater, "and
in the background [is] the lurid glare of a great conflagration." (Charmian London,
Jack London [London, 1921], Vol. II, p. 123.) At Yale he was interviewed for the
Yale Daily News by Sinclair Lewis, who later sold London several story plots (at prices
from $2.50 to $15.00) in order to earn enough money to try writing independently.
Quotations are in Foner, ed., *Jack London,* pp. 490, 504.   110 Quoted in *ibid.,* p. 123.

stration of the multiplicity of the modern mind that they had predicted. The illegitimate son of an astrologer father and spiritualist mother (born in Coxey's Massillon); alternately a utopian and dystopian; blond beast and Socialist— mingling, harmonizing, or confusing Marx, Darwin, Spencer, and Nietzsche; trapped into clichés of racial or national superiority, yet proclaiming himself a comrade to workers everywhere; paralleling the muckraking movement with his analysis of the London slums, *The People of the Abyss* (1902), but with no faith in reform movements; continuing the heroic tradition of Melville in *The Sea Wolf,* but also of the Beadle pulp tradition in *The Mutiny of the Elsinore* (1914); restless and ever traveling, the last of the first lost generation that Adams initiated—Jack London fittingly concludes the attempt to control the world by controlling ideas, and so to write utopia into existence.

SIX

The Visible and Invisible Cities

But the real appeal, unmistakably, is in that note of vehemence in the local life [of New York],... for it is the appeal of a particular type of dauntless power.

The aspect the power wears then is indescribable; it is the power of the most extravagant of cities, rejoicing, as with the voice of the morning, in its might, its fortune, its unsurpassable conditions, and imparting to every object and element, to the motion and expression of every floating, hurrying, panting thing, to the throb of ferries and tugs, to the plash of waves and the play of winds and the glint of lights and the shrill of whistles and the quality and authority of breeze-borne cries—all, practically, a diffused, wasted clamour of detonations— something of its sharp free accent and, above all, of its sovereign sense of being "backed" and able to back.

—Henry James, *The American Scene* (1907)

In the early autumn of 1893, Aristides Homos, the Altrurian traveler, briefly left "the ugliest city in the world," New York, to visit the World's Columbian Exposition in Chicago. "The Fair City," he declared, "is a bit of Altruria." Throughout his visit he was haunted by the illusion that Egoria had begun its metamorphosis into Altruria. In any event, the Exposition's "White City" would remain, he thought, "in the hearts of [the American]...people. An immortal principle, higher than use, higher even than beauty, is expressed in it, and the time will come when they will look back upon it, and recognize in it the first embodiment of the Altrurian idea among them, and will cherish it forever in their history as the earliest achievement of a real civic life."[1] Between New York and the White City Howells found contrasted the principles of competition and cooperation. Against the Babylon of New York, the White City was a New Jerusalem; against the City of Man and Mammon was this City of God—a dialectic familiar to Howells from his boyhood, when his father had read Swedenborg's *New Jerusalem* aloud to his family.

Not Howells alone, but countless people all over the country found in the White City the fulfillment of the promises of metropolitanism.[2] It

[1] William Dean Howells, *Letters from an Altrurian Traveler*, pp. 21, 34. [2] Writing to the Swedenborgian artist Howard Pyle, Howells made explicit the extent to which the

served Americans as a symbol of the solution to the problems of urbaniza-
tion. Writing in *Scribner's*, W. H. Gibson found the "hopeful, faithful fancy
of so many sons of Adam" in the "Heavenly City" or the "New Jerusalem"
realized at the Fair.[3] For the children in Frances Hodgson Burnett's *Two
Little Pilgrims' Progress: A Story of the City Beautiful* (1895), the White
City was the modern version of the Heavenly City toward which Bunyan's
Christian had striven. "Sell the cook stove if necessary and come," Hamlin
Garland wrote to his parents in North Dakota. Garland had visited the
Exposition in June and immediately decided that it established Chicago as
the cultural capital of the Middle Border. Contrary to J. P. Morgan's blunt
assertion that the French exhibits in the Palace of Fine Arts "seemed to have
been picked by a committee of chambermaids," Garland found there evidence
"of the immense growth of impressionistic or open-air painting" and, cor-
relating this with his own veritism, produced *Crumbling Idols* (1894).[4]
Coinciding with the leisure enforced by the depression of 1893, the Fair
resulted in the burgeoning of "study groups," "art clubs," and "cultural
societies" throughout the Midwest.[5] "For the first time," Garland's friend
Henry Blake Fuller said, "art was made vitally manifest in the American
consciousness."[6] Even the artists were impressed. The sculptor Augustus
Saint-Gaudens thought the Exposition the greatest winnowing of talent since
the Renaissance. The architect Henry Van Brunt believed Americans to be
"in the most receptive mental condition of their history, . . . intent on the
possibilities of their higher development." And the painter Elihu Vedder
found the White City "a dream indeed, never to be forgotten," as he paused
briefly in America before returning to the Eternal City.[7]

Everyone went to the Fair. While Theodore Dreiser wandered obscurely
among the crowds, reporting the Fair for a St. Louis paper, Richard Harding
Davis rejoiced at being "tumultuously cheered" by crowds who mistook
him for the Prince of Wales.[8] Nearly two decades before she would start
Poetry, Harriet Monroe, learning that all the arts but poetry were to be
represented at the Fair, presented herself as the laureate for the White City.
On Dedication Day, her "Columbian Ode" was read by a famous actress to
an appreciative audience of 125,000 and, in the critics' momentary enthusiastic response, was declared to have excelled Lanier's earlier "Centennial

---

White City had stirred his utopian imagination. Daniel Burnham, the chief architect of
the Fair, Howells reported to Pyle, told him that when he told his mother of the
magnificent consensus of will and aims in the capitalists and artists who created its
beauty, she saw in it a vision of the New Jerusalem, and a direct leading of the Lord
toward "the wonder that shall be," when men all work in harmony, and not in rivalry.
(*Life in Letters of William Dean Howells*, Vol. II, p. 40.)   [3] W. H. Gibson, "Foreground
and Vista at the Fair," *Scribner's*, XIV (July 1893), 29.   [4] *A Son of the Middle Border*,
p. 458; See also *Crumbling Idols*, p. 121.   [5] Lynes, *The Tastemakers*, pp. 148ff.   [6] Quoted
in Dorfman, *Thorstein Veblen*, p. 98.   [7] Henry Van Brunt, "The Development and
Prospects of Architecture in the United States" in *The United States of America: A
Study of the American Commonwealth, Its Natural Resources, People, Industry, Manufactures, Commerce, and Its Work in Literature, Science, Education, and Self-Government*, ed. Nathaniel Southgate Shaler (New York, 1894), p. 1091; Elihu Vedder, *The
Digressions of V . . .*(Boston and New York, 1910), p. 491.   [8] Langford, *The Richard
Harding Davis Years*, p. 132.

Meditation of Columbia."[9] At the Exposition, Henry Adams "found matter of study to fill a hundred years, and his education spread over chaos." Standing on the steps of Richard Morris Hunt's Administration Building as he had stood at Ara Coeli, Adams brooded on this latest rupture in historical continuity. "Chicago," he concluded with little confidence, "was the first expression of American thought as a unity."[10] If there had been a former unity, that indeed was broken, as one could tell equally from the ragtime music that Americans first heard on the Midway Plaisance or from the giant Ferris Wheel—the world's largest—that dominated the scene.

Rather than memorializing the Old, the Fair celebrated the New, the vision of the urban future. In its dazzling monumentality of architecture, its abundance of exhibits, its emphasis on the artistic and the international, the White City embodied the utopian impulses of the whole generation that had combined to create and celebrate it. There was no more sublimely pathetic instance of this than Henry George's bemused satisfaction that the People had accomplished this—and Charles Nolan's correction: "No, most of the money was subscribed by rich men. The people had nothing to do with designing the buildings." Anyhow, the people were enjoying it, George sighed.[11] Others were equally stirred by their vision of this Heavenly City and their awarenesses of its significance for American culture. Howells's friend Burnham told Frank Lloyd Wright: "I can see all America constructed along the lines of the Fair, in noble, dignified, classic style."[12] Though he declined the offer to join Burnham's firm, Wright was no less affected by the urban-utopian contagion and devoted a lifetime to offering an alternate urban plan to the White City in his vision of Broadacre City. But for the moment, Burnham was certainly right. With the firm of McKim, Mead[13] and White, he revived and helped to execute the L'Enfant plan for Washington as the first step in the transformation of America into the New (metropolitan) Jerusalem.

But the White City was not the solution to the problems of metropolitanism bothering Americans. It was an illusion through and through. Made of staff, a kind of plaster, the monuments of the White City were constantly crumbling and in need of repair. Moreover, with the exception of Hunt's Administration Building, they were mere classic masks—their steel girders were unconcealed in the interiors, where exhibits were laid out in irregular rows across the vast floors. It was a City of Illusion—for some, a Vanity Fair—in which Veblen found an illustration for his theory of the dominance of pecuniary over aesthetic considerations in middle-class taste.[14] Behind the illusion of affluence in the Fair, furthermore, lay the fact of severe urban depression. The aging socialist Thomas Morgan told an audience that the unemployed "assemble peacefully on the lake front, begging for work, and with the strong arm of the law are driven back into their tenement houses, [so] that the visitors who come to see the White City might not see the

---

9 Carlin T. Kindilien, *American Poetry in the Eighteen Nineties: A Study of American Verse 1890–1899*... (Providence, 1956), p. 174. 10 *The Education of Henry Adams*, pp. 339, 343. 11 Quoted in Beer, *The Mauve Decade*, p. 378. 12 Quoted in James Marston Fitch, *American Building: The Forces That Shape It* (Boston, 1948), p. 123. 13 W. R. Mead and the sculptor Larkin Mead, both represented at the Fair, were Howells's brothers-in-law. 14 See *The Portable Veblen*, ed. Max Lerner (New York, 1948), p. 171.

misery of the Garden City which built it."[15] Around the statue of Columbus, William Hope Harvey, the author of *Coin's Financial School* (1894) wrote, the unemployed daily gathered. Just after the Fair closed, in November, 1893, W. T. Stead summoned a conference in the Central Music Hall with the cry, "If Christ came to Chicago!" Municipal corruption, vagrancy, and prostitution were, he proclaimed, flourishing beneath the mask.[16] While a descendant of Kate Chopin was exhibiting, for a fee, the Place-du Bois cabin that was supposed to have belonged to the model for Uncle Tom, Stead and others were announcing the advent of a new, industrial slavery.

Perhaps, after all, the Fair was really the expression of the new American seigniorial mind, as Louis Sullivan believed. In the "bigness, organization, delegation, and intense commercialism" which Burnham impressed on the Fair, Sullivan saw the reflection of the increasing mergers, combinations, and trusts in the industrial world. "The White Cloud of the Fair," he wrote, "is the feudal idea." In it he watched Root's, Wright's, and his own hopes for a truly democratic architecture falter. His varicolored, romanesque Transportation Building, with its famous golden door, was a sensational, though not completely successful, democratic and romantic protest against the imperial implications of the White City. Against the Gold Medal of the Institute of British Architects which Hunt won—the first American so honored—for his imitation of St. Paul's Cathedral, Sullivan could set the award given him by the Beaux Arts. Against the architecture of imperialism, of Wall Street, of commercialism, he set the architecture of nature, expressed beautifully in his delicate, filiform designs.[17]

Ward McAllister, adviser to New York's Four Hundred, unwittingly corroborated Sullivan's assessment of the imperial appeal of the Fair by declaring that Chicago society proved in the Fair that it was "moving in the right direction, and should be encouraged in every way."[18] Next to the Fair grounds, visible from the Ferris Wheel, rose the Gray City of Rockefeller's University of Chicago, to which Charles T. Yerkes—later to serve as Dreiser's model for Cowperwood—donated the world's largest telescope in the year of the Fair. "It is much better for people like Mr. Yerkes," W. T. Stead commented wryly, "that the scrutinizing gaze of the public should be turned to the heavens, than to the scandalous manner in which he neglects his obligations to the people."[19]

Perhaps, in the final analysis, both Howells and Sullivan were wrong. For the Fair was really neither Altrurian nor Feudal: it was, rather, the catalyst for the expression of the contradictions, the hopes, and the fears of American culture itself. It was the first attempt of Americans to create their ideal city. There was the feudal, to be sure, but even Aristides Homos

---

[15] Quoted in Dorfman, *Thorstein Veblen*, p. 100. [16] See W. T. Stead, *If Christ Came to Chicago* (Chicago, 1894). [17] See Louis Sullivan, *The Autobiography of an Idea* (New York, 1924), pp. 314ff. The sense of nature was expressed elsewhere at the Fair in the marine decorations on Henry Ives Cobb's Fisheries Building, in the Davy Crockett log cabin built by an obscure New Yorker named Theodore Roosevelt, and in the colonies of Javanese, Esquimaux, or Samoans. The autobiography of Sullivan's Democratic Idea ends appropriately with the triumph of the Feudal Idea in the Fair. [18] Quoted in Wayne Andrews, *Architecture, Ambition, and Americans* (New York, 1955), p. 220. [19] Stead, *op. cit.*, p. 115.

happily consumed a bottle of Rhenish wine in the Old Vienna restaurant. If there was a German Castle—and, even more sinister, a Krupp Gun Exhibit at the Fair—there were also the ethnological exhibits of American Indians, and Frederick Jackson Turner also appeared and rendered the West relevant again by reading a paper called "The Significance of the Frontier in American History." (This was delivered on Exposition grounds to the same meeting of the American Historical Association that elected Henry Adams its president.) If a modern battleship appeared to be moored at the basin—built on piles, it too was an illusion—so also, replicas of Columbus's ships were there, along with a Viking craft and the Venetian gondolas that skimmed the lagoon. Robert Herrick in *The Web of Life* (1900) and Meyer Levin in *The Old Bunch* (1937) used the ruined buildings left deserted after the Fair was over to suggest the hollowness of modern values; but in those deserted buildings—the photo-shops, the stores, the restaurants— Chicago's artist colony established itself.[20] While Dr. Gunsaulus, the popular preacher and President of the new Armour Institute of Technology, was spreading the gospel of affluence to vast crowds, the first Parliament of Religions was being held at the Fair. If the dynamo was there, so was the Virgin.

The problem of multiform metropolitanism, first confronted in America in the White City, was becoming progressively significant. Josiah Strong's declaration that "the new civilization is certain to be urban; and the problem of the twentieth century will be the city"[21] echoed in many minds, and made necessary a reevaluation of the American pattern of agrarian ideals. Bellamy, who had written in his notebook "cities are always pagan,"[22] had filled his future Boston with parks and gardens, denying to it specifically urban qualities. But the city of steel and concrete was already a fact and raised many real questions. How would the shift from agrarian to urban values affect an America whose pride and past were in agrarianism? How would Americans emotionally and intellectually accommodate the city, when the American intellectual tradition was to a certain extent anti-urban? For the most part, Americans refused to consider the implications of these questions, believing, as Bryan said in his "Cross of Gold" speech, that the country, not the city, demanded the focus of attention. "The great cities rest upon our broad and fertile plains," he said. "Burn down your cities and leave our farms, and your cities will spring up again as if by magic; but destroy our farms and the grass will grow in the streets of every city in the country."[23] Others—among them the thousands who moved to cities each year[24]—were less sure. Frank Parsons's basic contention in *The City for*

---

[20] The history of this colony is given in Albert Parry, *Garrets and Pretenders: A History of Bohemianism in America* (New York, 1933); see, in particular, p. 187. [21] *The Twentieth Century City* (New York, 1898), p. 53. [22] Quoted in Morgan, *Edward Bellamy*, p. 94. [23] William Jennings Bryan, "The Cross of Gold" in *The Speeches of William Jennings Bryan, Revised and Arranged by Himself* (New York, 1909), Vol. I, p. 248. [24] Richard Grant White contended as early as the '70s that the American dream was to "ascend to a mansion in the Fifth Heavenue." If the businessman was the new American hero, as Howells insisted, his example drained the countryside of boys devoted to finding their earthly reward in "Fifth Heavenue." (White, *The Chronicles of Gotham* [New York and London, 1871, 1872], p. 73.)

the People (1900), that the city is "the aggregation of all that is best in civilization and all that is worst in the remnants of barbarism," accurately reflected the division and indecision in the American mind concerning increasing urbanization.[25]

During the depression of 1893–96, increasing dissatisfaction with the business ethic reinforced fear of the city. While Americans earlier had seen in the structure of Darwinian ethics an image of their own fruitfully competitive economic world—and thus saw the successful entrepreneur as the culmination of economic evolution—they now began tentatively to reject the ruthless dream of individual conquest, and consequently to find in commerce a predator blocking social evolution. Hitching his parlor car, The Duchess, to the Flying Devil and roaring down the tracks with Jim Wood at the throttle, Commodore Vanderbilt had been superbly romantic. His famous assertion, "the law...goes too slow for me"—like Cowperwood's motto "I satisfy myself"—was admired and applauded as the economic counterpart of this adventurousness. Indeed, even as late as 1917, Elbert Hubbard, convinced that "business will eradicate poverty, disease, superstition and all that dissipates and destroys,"[26] could title a book *The Romance of Business.* But in the '90s the public attitude was definitely shifting. In fiction the critical portrait of the businessman, begun by Twain and Warner and continued in Josiah Gilbert Holland's portrayal of Jim Fisk in *Sevenoaks* (1875), gained momentum with Howells's Dryfoos and Brander Matthews's Ezra Pierce (the "Bandit of Broad Street"), and culminated in a deluge of anti-business novels.[27] Veblen's phrases, "predatory emulation" and "conspicuous consumption," passed into the language. By 1900 the conventional attitudes toward business success had been so reversed that Barrett Wendell, in reply to a lady who complained that the flowers at Collis Huntington's funeral were stifling, inquired: "But the smell of sulphur wasn't noticeable?"[28]

The revolt against the business ethic was largely of middle-class origin. Believing himself to represent the real strength of the country, the middle-class citizen nevertheless was rapidly becoming, as William Graham Sumner said, the "Forgotten Man." Caught in the dialectic of progress and poverty, he felt himself about to be swept away. On the one hand lay the possibility of enormous wealth; but contemporary observers were pointing out that 95 per cent of all capitalist enterprises failed.[29] On the other hand lay the Social Pit —the inferno of poverty. Believing with Henry Demarest Lloyd that "the striking feature of our economic condition is our poverty,"[30] and fearing the poverty that appeared only too likely to be the lot of the losers in the struggle for existence, the middle-class man sent his journalists into the social cellar to expose and thus to remove the sufferings of the populous

---

[25] Philadelphia, p. 5. [26] *The Romance of Business* (East Aurora, New York, 1917), p. 11. [27] It should be made clear that during the period of shifting attitudes towards the businessman, Howells's *Silas Lapham,* James's *The American,* and Dreiser's Cowperwood trilogy—all portraying the businessman merely as the representative, not the ideal, American—were more truly accurate portraits than the pro- or anti-business books which surrounded them. [28] Quoted in Beer, *The Mauve Decade,* p. 83. [29] See Kirkland, *Dream and Thought,* p. 8. [30] *Wealth and Commonwealth,* ed. Charles C. Baldwin, Foreword by John Chamberlain (Washington, D.C., 1936 [1894]), p. 336.

slums. Whitman's epithet for New York—the "City of Orgies"—was being confirmed by studies of both rich and poor. Jacob Riis, for instance, revealed in 1890 that the East Side, with an average of 290,000 persons per square mile, was "the most densely populated district in all the world, China not excluded."[31] This was within walking distance of Wall Street. Shantytown, running parallel to the mansions along the East Side as far North as 110th Street, was inhabited by Irish squatters living in shacks with their goats and pigs.

Such sentimental and sensational contrasts as Riis's were characteristic of muckraking journalism and vividly expressed the fears of the middle class, which was irrevocably (but unwillingly) committed to urban conditions. The portrayal of urban poverty, corruption, and business rapacity alternately delighted and disgusted, but always compelled and fascinated middle-class readers. Yearning for the simpler conditions of country life, the muckrakers and their audience nevertheless returned repeatedly to the complexities of the metropolis. One of the best known muckrakers, for instance, was Ray Stannard Baker, whose "Railroads on Trial" series of 1905 helped establish public support for the Interstate Commerce Commission eight years later. He was equally famous, however, as David Grayson, the charming, contented farmer who wrote such books as *Adventures in Contentment* (1907). His "deepest and truest thoughts and feelings," he would write in his autobiography, were David Grayson's.[32] Similarly divided personalities are evident in the work of Lincoln Steffens and Ida Tarbell. Alongside *The Shame of the Cities* (1904) one must put Steffens's idyllic account of his California childhood; Steffens said that he felt about the ghetto the way other boys felt about the romance of the Wild West. Alongside Miss Tarbell's *History of the Standard Oil Company* (1904) must be placed her friendly biography of Judge Gary of U. S. Steel and her article "The Golden Rule in Business" (1914), wherein she expressed her belief that commercial enterprise had shifted from Darwinian to Christian ethics.[33]

Such magazines as *The Forum* (founded in 1886), *Cosmopolitan* (1886), *The Arena* (1889), *Munsey's* (1889), and *McClure's* (1893), provided ready vehicles for the literature of exposé. That these and lesser magazines existed for and on muckraking led to the extremes that prompted Roosevelt to compare journalists of exposure to Bunyan's man with the muck-rake and thus to introduce the term "muckraker." Roosevelt's warning to McClure in 1905—"we must not confine our hostility to the wealthy, nor feel indignant only at corruption. There are other classes just as guilty, and other crimes as bad"[34]—was largely unheeded, for the muckraking formula was designed precisely for sensational targets, and extended no farther. From 1901 to about 1912, the literature of exposure dominated the middle-class imagination by giving the vague feelings of hostility and frustration a focus

---

[31] *How the Other Half Lives: Studies Among the Tenements of New York* (New York, 1890), p. 10. [32] Baker, *Native American: The Book of My Youth* (New York, 1941), p. 236. [33] See Henry F. May, *The End of American Innocence: A Study of the First Years of Our Own Time, 1912-1917* (New York, 1959), p. 131. [34] *The Autobiography of Theodore Roosevelt* in *Centennial Edition...Supplemented by Letters, Speeches, and Other Writings*, ed. Wayne Andrews (New York, 1958 [1913]), pp. 247–48.

in the evils of the new metropolitanism. By 1914 the formula of exposure had hardened into a stereotype and inured the public to revelations of corruption, no matter how sensational. David Graham Phillips and others had begun to rely upon emotional rather than documentary exposures by using mysterious and magical phrases like "the system," "the interests," and "the syndicates." By 1914, this had gone so far that even Mr. Dooley was satirizing the corruption of "the McClure gang." Then, too, around this time returning prosperity for the middle class made progress look more likely than poverty and quieted the fears that had given exposure its compelling emotional appeal.

Disguised as social analysis or statistical, scientific investigation, the muckraking movement became the literary outlet of American naturalism. If Crane's *Maggie* was unacceptable in fiction, Jane Addams' *A New Conscience and an Ancient Evil* (1912) and G. K. Turner's influential article, "The Daughters of the Poor" (1909), were widely praised and influential in provoking legislation. Within the still moral and rationalistic literary conventions of the time, the naturalistic portrayal of what Edward Albion Ross called "Sin and Society" was acceptable only when performed for ethical, reforming, or scientific purposes. The naturalistic techniques which James and Howells had developed and sponsored in fiction were used by the muckrakers, then, to make vivid and sensational their portrayals of metropolitan degradation. But if James, Howells, Norris, and Crane had revealed metropolitan evil, they had also seen in the city a rich and various metaphor of human experience. In the later nineteenth century it was they who continued the tradition—which includes Franklin, Melville (*Pierre* and *Redburn*), Hawthorne (*The Marble Faun*), Emerson, and Poe—wherein the city is portrayed as the principle not merely of exchange, but of change, for good or evil, in the social and personal orders. Man is involved in and tested by his capacity to meet, adjust to, or sometimes alter urban change. "If I were to preach any doctrine to the world," Theodore Dreiser began a philosophical essay, "it would be love of change, or at least lack of fear of it."[35] With little intention to reveal or reform, these writers kept their visions open to the varieties of urban experience. For all these writers, the city provided the context and possibility for both good and evil. In it they set characters who richly demonstrated their capacities for both. Accepting the city as a fact, these writers transformed it into a fiction, and so provided the means whereby their contemporaries might adjust themselves to the conditions and opportunities of metropolitan regionalism. These had shown the City of God and the City of Man inextricably intermingled, and refused to let their dramas stiffen into moral formulas. This was the distinction Dreiser made when he declared: "The things called property interests were...beyond me. My mind was too much concerned with the poetry of life to busy itself with such minor things as politics."[36] If the muckrakers explored the documentation of life in the city, it was the literary tradition of Howells, James,

[35] "Change" in *Hey Rub-a-Dub-Dub: A Book of the Mystery and Wonder and Terror of Life* (New York, 1920), p. 19. [36] Quoted in F. O. Matthiessen, *Theodore Dreiser* (New York, 1951), p. 24.

Crane, and Norris that created metropolitan poetry. But from 1905 to 1912, with Crane and Norris dead and Howells and James ignored, the muckrakers cornered the techniques of literary naturalism to polarize good and evil, the simple and complex, the country and the city. They thus offered placebos for America's fears and frustrations. Momentarily they severed the tradition of American adjustment to the city.

The Continuity of Naturalism— Henry Blake Fuller and Frank Norris

Despite the overwhelming ascendancy of the muckrakers, a faint line of the naturalistic absorption of the new patterns of metropolitan life ran from Howells to Henry Blake Fuller, expanded in Norris's *McTeague* (1899), and emerged in the twentieth century with Dreiser's *Sister Carrie* (1900). Fuller did not begin as a naturalist. His first novel, *The Chevalier of Pensieri Vani* (1890), written out of his Italian travels and his love of the medieval, was warmly received in autumnal Boston by Charles Eliot Norton, James Russell Lowell (who had similarly established Howells with his review of *Venetian Life*), and by Howells himself. Much as Howells had written a second travel book, *Italian Journeys* (1867), to solidify his first success, so Fuller responded to their praise with *The Chatelaine of La Trinité* (1892). In both, the innocent male or female American is initiated, by travel and European acquaintance, into—as the names of the three companions in the second volume have it—Fin-de-siècle, Zeitgeist, and Tempo Rubato.

In 1893, however, Fuller abruptly abandoned the medieval revival just then gaining momentum in New England and, in *The Cliff-Dwellers,* perceptively analyzed the imperial myths spawned by the Chicago metropolis. There is reason to believe that Fuller's interests were deflected in that year from recrudescent Europe to contemporary Chicago by the World's Columbian Exposition. Indeed, he had written several articles for the *Chicago Record* on "World's Fair Architecture," "Mural Painting," and similar subjects, recognizing in the invasion of Chicago by Europe the reverse of James's transatlantic theme. In *The Cliff-Dwellers* Fuller shows conclusively how completely the city had come to embody American hopes for the future. The tall buildings by Root, Holabird and Roche, and Sullivan that had created "Chicago Architecture" served Fuller as his central symbol. In the Clifton, the skyscraper wherein the various fortunes of the Cliff-Dwellers are enacted, Fuller summarized the city's ruthless and impersonal but energetic forcefulness. Although the Easterner satirizes the brash self-assertion of Chicago—"I see, if you can only be big you don't mind being dirty"—the Chicagoan believes that his city will "give the country the final blend of the American character and its ultimate metropolis." This "ultimate metropolis," as Fuller shows it, has elicited a myth of hope and satisfaction as strong as the agrarian, regional, or utopian myths with which it contended for a place in the American imagination. The city summons faithful commitment. "To the Chicagoan," Fuller writes,

...the name of the town, in its formal, ceremonial use, has a power that no other word in the language quite possesses. It is a shibboleth, as regards its pronunciation; it is a trumpet-call, as regards its effect. It has all the electrifying and unifying power of a college yell.

In 1928 Theodore Dreiser wrote:

I find the usually well-informed H. G. Wells speaking of Stephen Crane as not only the pioneer but the most brilliant of all the early realists of this generation. Stuff and nonsense! Crane was not the pioneer nor even the equal in any sense of the man who led the van of realism in America. That honour—if any American will admit it to be such—goes to to Henry B. Fuller of Chicago, who [wrote, in]...*With the Procession,* as sound and agreeable a piece of American realism as that decade, or any since, produced.[37]

With the Procession (1895) studies the overwhelming drive in the metropolis to maintain economic and social pace, and thus violently to accelerate change. Again Fuller uses the skyscraper as his chief symbol. David Marshall, an early settler and symbol of frontier Chicago, is persuaded to build a new office building and a new house. When both his business and personal hopes crumble, Marshall, unable to keep up with the procession, dies. But at the same time, the involvement of others in the procession of force raises them to new types of heroism. Fuller's view is essentially paradoxical, much like Henry Adams's. The dynamo that destroys the old also creates a new and, in its own way, better order of man.

From the very first Howells admired Fuller's delicately objective analyses of good and evil in the metropolis. "I wish you would write of Chicago whether you like it or not," he advised Fuller in 1893. Fuller followed consciously in the tradition of Howells and James. His early admiration for Dickens was superseded by his veneration for *Silas Lapham*—"the great representative novel of American manners," he termed it—and for his favorite novel, *The Portrait of a Lady.* Imitating the methodical dialectical objectivity of these novels, Fuller attempted, he later wrote Howells, "to raise this dirt pile [i.e., Chicago] to some dignity and credit." His success is suggested by the fact that while Howells retained reservations about even Crane and Norris, to Fuller he wrote in 1909, when he himself, at seventy-two, was wearying of his craft: "It came over me that it was past the time with me to write fiction....Can't you see it is your duty to write, hereafter, my novels for me?" Fuller was clearly Howells's successor and Dreiser's ancestor, and intermediary between the two.[38] But after his two early Chicago novels, Fuller's metropolitan studies appeared only at wide intervals—in *Under the Skylights* (1901), *On the Stairs* (1918) and posthumously in *Not on the Screen* (1930).

Frank Norris more spectacularly continued, though only briefly, the Howells tradition. *McTeague* (1899), begun in 1892 while Norris was attending the University of California at Berkeley, originated in his studies of the

---

[37] Introduction to Frank Norris, *McTeague* (Garden City, 1928 [1899]), p. viii. [38] In this paragraph is quoted the correspondence between Fuller and Howells in Constance M. Griffin, *Henry Blake Fuller: A Critical Biography* (Philadelphia, 1939), pp. 45–6.

San Francisco poor. Uninterested in Zola or the Impressionists when he was an art student in Paris, and still writing romantic poetry after his return to America, Norris now felt the influence of the naturalism inherent in American life. Turning to Zola as his justification for writing a naturalistic fiction, he stalked conspicuously across the California campus carrying French editions of Zola's work, ready passionately to defend the Experimental Novel. Back-trailing east in the familiar pattern of the American realist—Howells, Garland, and Dreiser, among others, pursued the same path—Norris continued *McTeague* at Harvard; eventually he would dedicate the novel to his Professor in English there. After he had completed the final three chapters in the Sierras in 1897, he again returned east and became a staff writer for *McClure's*. Working in the same office with Tarbell, Steffens, and Baker, he remained hardly touched by the muckraking stereotypes.[39] Emphasizing always the fictional possibilities of experience, he wrote to one critic of the forthcoming *McTeague*—which he was then calling "The People of Polk Street"—

> I have great faith in the possibilities of San Francisco and the Pacific Coast as offering a field for fiction. Not the fiction of Bret Harte, however, for the country has long since outgrown the "red shirt" period. The novel of California must be now a novel of city life.[40]

The life of the city fills *McTeague*. In McTeague's day-long observation of the changing scene on Polk Street, Norris suggests the fluctuating varieties of mixed metropolitan life. Particularly in his vivid evocation of metropolitan odors, Norris delineates the specific surface of urban life. Largely unaware of their environment, never for themselves analyzing their surroundings, the characters are subjected to what one reviewer called "a study in stinks"—of "bedding, creosote, and ether," ink, the "choking odors" of Zerkow's junk shop, of "salt, tar, dead seaweed, and bilge" on the beach, of stale cigars, flat beer, orange peels, gas, sachet powders, and cheap perfume in the theatre; of coffee and spices, popcorn, photographer's chemicals, of oil stoves, of cooking, of paint—and finally, the smell of blood when McTeague murders Trina. Norris's San Francisco anticipates Eliot's London of the "Preludes" by two decades. Through the odors and other sense-impressions of scraps and fragments of the city, Norris conveys sensuously the character of McTeague's city—or any city; for, as he wrote, although the novel is set in San Francisco, it "could have happened in any big city, anywhere."[41] He learned from Zola and Balzac, but also from his own life in several cities, that the metropolis is properly defined not by the romantic curiosities it contains—as Davis and O. Henry would define it—but by its abundant embodiment of mass, surface life, which agitates (and finally dulls) man's senses.

In the city the business ethic of success ruled and allured. Ragged Dicks

---

[39] It is perhaps significant that the selfish, greedy Marcus Schouler, who informs the authorities that McTeague lacks a dental degree, is the one character in that novel who attacks "the capitalists, a class he pretended to execrate. It was a pose which he often assumed, certain of impressing the dentist [McTeague]." [40] *Letters*, p. 23. [41] *Ibid.*, p. 30.

abounded and, "blessed" by log cabins in their backgrounds, waited for their chance. While Henry George was finding in cities the best evidence for his dialectic, a whole generation saw only the glitter of opportunity. This success ethic defeats McTeague. His mother was "filled with the one idea of having her son rise in life and enter a profession." Her ambition for him fired by a traveling charlatan, she sends McTeague away with him to learn dentistry. When, much later, he opens his "dental parlors" he "felt that his life was a success." But he is not without further desire. His ambitions are summarized in his yearning to possess "a huge gilded tooth, a molar with enormous prongs" as a sign for his office. Later, after his marriage, he "began to have ambitions—very vague, very confused ideas of something better." In his rise he takes to wearing a silk hat and Prince Albert coats; he likes to smoke "Yale mixture"; he even joins the "Polk Street Improvement Club." Other characters are similarly caught up in this whirlwind of success. The mad Maria Macapa has a fantasy that her family had been immensely wealthy in Central America. From "dim memories of the novels of her girlhood," Miss Baker convinces herself that Old Grannis was the "younger son of a baronet," cheated of his title by his stepfather. Norris's chief case of the ironies of success is Trina's winning $5,000 in a lottery. As the lottery agent describes it, the lottery symbolizes the American ideal of success. "Invariably it was the needy who won, the destitute and starving woke to wealth and plenty, the virtuous toiler suddenly found his reward in a ticket bought at a hazard; the lottery was a great charity, the friend of the people, a vast, beneficent machine that recognized neither rank nor wealth nor station." But Norris reveals the degradation of that ideal in his novel. In her "success" Trina passes from thrift to parsimony, to a paranoic love of money for itself alone. Under the weight of their rise, both Trina and McTeague fall to the depths of personal and social degradation. The commercial success ethic, Norris suggests, debases true human ethics.

The gilded cage that imprisons McTeague's canary suggests, in short, how appearances have duped them all. Images of gold flash throughout the narrative—not only McTeague's enormous gold sign, but also, gold fillings, Maria's fantasy of a gold dinner service worth a million dollars, Zerkow's greed for gold, light appearing like golden dollars, and finally, McTeague's discovery of gold in the desert when, ironically, it is useless, for he is now being pursued by the authorities for murdering Trina. Trina, of course, is insanely obsessed by gold. Money replaces McTeague as the object of her sexual energy. She plays with her money "by the hour," putting "the smaller gold pieces in her mouth, and [jingling] them there. . . . She would plunge her small fingers into the pile with little murmurs of affection, her long, narrow eyes half closed and shining, her breath coming in long sighs." Later, when her love of money has destroyed every other affection, "one evening she had even spread all the gold pieces between the sheets, and had then gone to bed, stripping herself, and had slept all night upon the money, taking a strange and ecstatic pleasure in the touch of the smooth flat pieces the length of her entire body."

Engaged in the fanatical effort to become wealthy, all become subhuman grotesques, progressively animalistic. In their masochism Trina and Maria are as degraded as the violent and brutal Zerkow and McTeague. The latter is variously described as elephantine, a dog, an ape, a bull, and a horse. In the typical regressive pattern of naturalistic fiction, under pressure McTeague reverts to his animal self. Only his canary and the "six lugubrious airs" that he plays on his concertina suggest the higher but feeble possibilities which his nature also contains. Trina too—who carves the Noah's ark animals for toy sets but, ironically, cannot carve the people—becomes more and more animal-like. She fights McTeague, at the last, with the "strength of a harassed cat."

Using the violent animal imagery of the Darwinian struggle, then, Norris associates it with the rise to dominance—symbolized by gold—in the achievement of success. Dramatizing the Social Darwinist's absorption of the principles of biological into social patterns, he reveals the brutality and injustice of the assumptions underlying Social Darwinism. Nonetheless, Norris remained essentially committed to city life. His next novel, *Blix,* appearing in the same year as *McTeague,* provides his affirmation of the smiling aspects of urban life, and so serves as an appropriate counterbalance to *McTeague.* Less than a decade after Turner announced the closing of the Frontier, Norris declared that trade, and thus the spread of cities, already constituted the New Frontier.[42] Portraying the diversity and varying possibilities of city life, Norris was beginning to modify the structure of Howells's National Novel by giving it a focus not in travel, but in an elucidation of the multiform character of a metropolis. "I have traveled much in Walden," Thoreau wrote. A whole generation was now discovering that in a literal sense they could travel much in the cities that the new shape of America provided.

Theodore Dreiser

In 1900, after his novel had been refused for serialization by *Harper's Weekly* and for book publication by Harper and Brothers, Theodore Dreiser, one year Norris's junior, sent *Sister Carrie,* his own novel of city life, to Doubleday, Page and Company. This new firm—which had formerly included McClure—had published *McTeague*; and Dreiser hoped, apparently, that such a house might give favorable consideration to his naturalistic novel. Fortunately, and appropriately, it was assigned to Frank Norris, who had recently become a manuscript reader for the house. Norris read the manuscript with enthusiasm, and to the two junior partners, Walter Hines Page and Henry Lanier, insisted, "It *must* be published." To the author he generously wrote: "I said [in my report] it was the best novel I have read in M.S. since I had been reading for the firm, and that it pleased me as well

---

42 To be sure, Turner himself called, in 1925, for "an urban reinterpretation of our history," a fact too often forgotten. At his death he was planning an essay to be entitled "The Significance of the City in American Civilization." (See *Frontier and Section: Selected Essays of Frederick Jackson Turner,* ed., Ray Allen Billington, pp. x, 8.)

as any novel I have read in any form, published or otherwise."[43] In the absence of Frank Doubleday, Norris's enthusiasm prevailed and the house signed a binding contract to publish 1,000 copies of this first novel in the fall of 1900. But, shocked and disgusted with the proof sheets when he returned from Europe, the senior partner sought to terminate the agreement. "Crushed and tragically pathetic," as Lanier described him, Dreiser followed Norris's angry advice and insisted on his legal right to publication. Of the 1008 copies bound, Norris sent 129 out for review—the novel was widely, but unfavorably, reviewed—and 465 copies were sold. The book was not advertised, although it was listed, according to the contract, in the publisher's catalogue. After five years 414 unsold copies were remaindered. Norris had been insistent, however, on the greatness of *Sister Carrie;* and, as an English publisher said, "more eager for [it]...to be read than his own novels," he helped arrange an English edition in 1901. In England (like Whitman and Crane earlier and Frost and Pound somewhat later), Dreiser received his first enthusiastic reviews and began to acquire a subterranean reputation. But it would be eleven years before he would regather the emotional strength to attempt a second novel.[44] In some ways he would never again write as good a novel as this first one, *Sister Carrie.*

Theodore Dreiser, who resigned from the staff of the *Broadway Magazine* when editorial policy began to emphasize the muckraking formula, intuitively rejected its singleminded stress on the shame of cities. "A big city," he wrote in 1914, "is not a little teacup to be seasoned by old maids.... Removing all the stumbling stones of life, putting to flight all the evils of vice and greed, and all that, makes our little path a monotonous journey."[45] He himself had arrived in New York City "very much afraid," just at the time that Steffens was beginning his exposés of municipal corruption and while James Gibbons Huneker, on the other hand, was beginning to hope New York might rival the cities of Europe as an artistic center. But, as F. O. Matthiessen has remarked, Dreiser came to neither Steffens's nor Huneker's New York, but to his songwriting brother Paul Dresser's "city of actors and sports, the Broadway of the Martinique and the Metropole, of Muldoon the famous wrestler and Tod Sloan the jockey, of Tony Pastor's and Niblo's and Weber and Fields."[46] In this New York he found what he had found earlier in the White City of Chicago—illusion. Stirring vague emotions of wonder, hope, and fear, betraying and perpetually changing, the city was above all—in one of Dreiser's favorite images—an Arabian Nights' enchantment, illusory and ultimately deceptive. In their inarticulate ineptitude in the face of the metropolis his characters render the tragedy—but also the romance—of the city, for whose immensity and impenetrability they can find no words. "Woe to him who places his faith in illusion," Dreiser wrote, "—and woe to him who does not. In one way lies disillusion with its pain, in the other way regret."[47] Carrie, Jennie Gerhardt (of *Jennie Gerhardt*), Cowperwood (of

[43] *Letters,* p. 61. [44] For a full account of this period see W. A. Swanberg, *Dreiser* (New York, 1965). [45] Dreiser, quoted in the *Chicago Journal,* March 18, 1914; quoted from Robert Elias, *Theodore Dreiser: Apostle of Nature* (New York, 1949), p. 173. [46] Matthiessen, p. 43. [47] *The Titan* (New York, 1914), p. 389.

The Financier, The Titan, and *The Stoic*), Eugene Wilta (of *The Genius*), and Clyde Griffiths (of *An American Tragedy*)[48] are all caught and defeated by a web of urban illusion. But all gain stature and remain important to us by virtue of the readiness and power with which they embrace the illusions that, although ultimately defeating, are momentarily comforting and even ennobling.

Preserving this richness of dialectic, Dreiser continued the tradition of the urban novel into the twentieth century. Outside of the genteel tradition in origin, training, and temperament; antipathetic to muckraking; hardly aware of the older egalitarian America which his regional contemporaries strained to remember; and unable to envision the wholly regenerated society conjured up by the utopians—possessing imaginatively neither a past nor a future, but incredibly receptive to the fluctuations of the present—Dreiser was able to rescue the city for fiction by presenting it undistorted by literary or ethical conventions. He restored the city to the uses of the American imagination by attempting, as Floyd Dell remarked, "to see [neither] the badness of the city, nor its goodness," but rather, "its beauty and its ugliness," and to find "a beauty in its ugliness."[49] Like John Sloan and Everett Shinn—to some degree the artistic prototype for his otherwise autobiographical hero Eugene Witla—Dreiser treated the city not as a moral, but an aesthetic aspect of experience. Appropriately, then, late in his career Dreiser would complain of the lack of "exaltation" in the new generation of realists who wanted "to indict life, not picture it in its ordinary beauty."[50]

In the late '90s, Dreiser's fellow Indianans apparently cornered the reading public for romance. Besides James Whitcomb Riley, there appeared such romantic, sentimental writers as Charles Major with *When Knighthood Was in Flower* (1898), Booth Tarkington with *The Gentleman From Indiana* (1899), and Maurice Thompson with *Alice of Old Vincennes* (1900). But Dreiser refused to sentimentalize urban life. While another Indianan, Eugene Debs, cried for reform, Dreiser was writing in *Demorest's* of breadlines of the unemployed in the mid-'90s depression.[51] Here too, however, he remained dispassionate and objective. "The individuals composing this driftwood," he concluded, "are no more miserable than others."[52] Pain, he judged from his own experience, and in spite of his great attraction to beauty, was the human condition. In his massive objectivity his writings resemble the camera that Alfred Stieglitz was at the same time turning on the city. Indeed, interviewing Stieglitz for Orison Swett Marden's *Success,* Dreiser praised his "endless patience" with detail, the very quality that marks his own work.[53]

During the later nineteenth century, the modern psyche was being made. This mind is characterized by an enormously increased receptivity to the

---

[48] Convinced that "life is a complete illusion or mirage which changes and so escapes and chides one at every point," Dreiser used as his working title for the story of Clyde the single word: *Mirage.* (Matthiessen, *Theodore Dreiser,* p. 185.)   [49] Quoted in Matthiessen, p. 73. Dell reviewed *Jennie Gerhardt* on November 3, 1911 in the *Chicago Evening Post* and wrote on Dreiser in "American Fiction," *Liberator,* II (September 1919) and "Talks with Living Authors," *Masses,* IX (August 1916).   [50] Quoted in Matthiessen, p. 188.   [51] It is interesting to note that both Debs and Dreiser were born in Terre Haute.   [52] "Curious Shifts of the Poor," *Demorest's Family Magazine,* XXXVI (November 1899), 26.   [53] Matthiessen p. 49.

data of surface occurrences and an increase in the power and dominance of the senses, particularly of sight, in response to a world which seemed to *contain* more than ever before, whose surface was agitated by fact, whose events came more rapidly. This increase in receptivity was accompanied by an equally significant decline in valuation and discrimination. In the rush of fact, order seemed impossible—the fact was all. Such a transformation of the mind and its faculty to judge was particularly accelerated by the rise of the city. In his famous analysis of "The Metropolis and Modern Life," the sociologist Georg Simmel has shown that the *"intensification of neurotic agitation* which results from the swift and uninterrupted change of outer and inner stimuli" in the metropolis necessitates in urban man various kinds of emotional indifference: "He reacts with his head instead of his heart. In this an increased awareness assumes the psychic prerogative."[54] By emphasizing surfaces, techniques, details—in short, by attempting to integrate one's personality with metapersonal order—one preserves his psyche (but thus often, in another sense, loses the humanness of his psyche) by withdrawing from fully responsive involvement in his environment. Dreiser is the first of our writers to reflect, as the principle of his fiction, this transformation in the American urban mind. In many senses his much discussed naturalism—obviously different from Zola's or Norris's in lacking a real base in scientific experimentation—is in reality the reflection of the state of his own psychic involvement with the life of the city. He has told, for instance, how as a newspaperman in St. Louis he witnessed, in the aftermath of a spectacular train wreck, several people horribly killed by the explosion of an oil tank, while he was thinking only of how he would describe the scene effectively. Briefly swept away by pity at the morgue, he was soon vainly imagining how everyone would read his vivid account in the morning *Globe-Democrat*.[55]

Dreiser's novels are shaped like his mind. Various critics have commented with surprise on how little his career as writer and editor for popular magazines touched his fiction. Included for his journalism in the first compilation of *Who's Who* in 1899, the year before *Sister Carrie* appeared, from 1903 to 1910 he worked for a succession of magazines, eventually rising to the direction of the Butterick trio—*The Designer, The New Idea Woman's Magazine,* and *The Delineator*—all issued primarily to advertise Butterick dress patterns. Grasping perfectly the traditions of magazine literature, he sounds very much like a later and lesser Gilder or Stedman in gently, but firmly, reproving misguided contributors. To one he wrote, for instance:

> We like realism, but it must be tinged with sufficient idealism to make it all of a truly uplifting character. Our field in this respect is limited by the same limitations which govern the well-regulated home. We cannot admit stories which deal with false or immoral relations. . . . The fine side of things—the idealistic— is the answer for us, and we find really splendid material within these limitations.[56]

[54] In *Images of Man: The Classic Tradition In Sociological Thinking,* ed. C. Wright Mills (New York, 1960), pp. 437, 438. [55] See Dreiser's account of this in *A Book About Myself* (New York, 1922), pp. 156–68. [56] Quoted in Matthiessen, p. 204.

Working steadily at this editorial formula, he rose to a salary of $25,000 a year and appeared—so the young Sinclair Lewis, seeing him in *The Delineator* office, felt—"more like a wholesale hardware merchant than a properly hollow-cheeked realist."[57] But his awareness of commercial considerations and the conventions of periodical literature were on a surface level of his consciousness. At a deeper, separate level lay his intuitive, personal sense—what Ernst Jünger well terms the "second, colder consciousness"— of the profoundly inexplicable tragedy and romance of the human condition. Between these two psychic levels there was no influence. Existing on a level wholly apart from his surface editorial concerns, this colder consciousness provided the context and conventions for his fiction. As a novelist he projected stories and novels which as an editor he would have immediately dismissed. With a mind divided in this way, he wrote out of a consciousness uniquely free from genteel convention, but vigorously informed by metropolitan actuality.

Dreiser had written pageants of success about Armour, Carnegie, and Marshall Field for Marden.[58] But when he turned to fiction, he described the terrible parade of failure, or failure-in-success, in *Sister Carrie* and the Cowperwood trilogy. As he could finally describe Carrie as "a harp in the wind"—without his knowledge using the same words with which Melville had described himself in *Battle Pieces*—so he instinctively spoke of himself frequently as "an Ishmael, a wanderer."[59] Carrie, too, is a wanderer. She is called a "half-equipped little knight," a "soldier of fortune," a "pilgrim," and—allegorically—the journeying Spirit who, though seeking the Heavenly City, nevertheless is "turned as by a wall." Confronted by the Walled City, she is a "waif amid forces," a "wisp in the wind," and an "outcast." "It must be glow and shine everywhere," she thinks when she comes to New York, "...and she was out of it all."

Her drifting condition is characterized, moreover, by sea imagery and metaphors of voyage. She is a seeker who revises the Columbiad of American discovery. She comes from Columbia City, as a later Carrie, Jennie Gerhardt, comes from Columbus, Ohio. In a comparison that would have come naturally to Dreiser from the World's Columbian Exposition, she is a Columbus resailing the sea trails West to East—an innocent, like Twain's, engaged, however unconsciously, on the exploration of her own Atlantics. She thus assumes a series of new identities as signs of her self-discovery. Like Huck Finn earlier and Jay Gatsby later, she takes new names to express her sense of perpetual metamorphosis. Caroline Meeber has already been "half affectionately" called "Sister Carrie" by her family up to the time when she boards the train leaving home. In the city the factory foremen looks "her over as one would a package," "never so much as inquiring her name." Once in the city, she loses her family name along with her sense of

[57] Lewis, "Editors who Write," *Life*, L (1907), 414. [58] Dreiser's interviews so perfectly expressed the success formula that Marden reprinted them—unchanged and without acknowledgment—as his own work in the popualr compilations, *How They Succeeded* (1901) and *Little Visits With Great Americans* (1903). [59] Quoted in Matthiessen, p. 34.

relatedness. She never again mentions her family. She is only "Sister Carrie." To Drouet she becomes "Cad"; Hurstwood first meets her as "Mrs. Drouet"; later she believes she is "Mrs. Hurstwood," but is known as "Mrs. G. W. Murdock" in Montreal and "Mrs. Wheeler" in New York. Finally, for the stage she becomes "Carrie Madenda."

The character and imagery of the theatre embody Dreiser's sense that in the modern city Carrie must be a player of parts. Her desire for life is translated into "having a part" in a play: "Oh, if she could have such a part, how broad would be her life! She too could act appealing." With Minnie at first and with Hurstwood at last, she is frustrated by not being able to go to the theater to watch romantic dramas and engage in the illusion of playing a part. In life, as on the sage, she assumes a series of parts, all illusory, swiftly fading and changing. Referring repeatedly to fairy-tale states and characters in his chapter titles (for instance, "The Machine and the Maiden: A Knight of Today," "A Witless Aladdin," and "An Hour in Elfland"), Dreiser writes a novel in which, as in fairy tales, such metamorphoses are natural and assumed. Each stage of her upward progress opens a freshly enticing vision of felicity and mingles desire and frustration with achievement. A sense of the past is entirely lacking in her—only the present and the future rushing to become present are meaningful. After her stage success near the end of the book, "she thought of going down and buying a few copies of the paper [with her picture in it], but remembered that there was no one she knew well enough to send them to."

Dreiser found the appropriate metaphor for this illusory movement within the larger context of motionlessness in the simultaneous stasis and incessant motion of the rocking-chair, instinctively recalling for us Whitman's "Out of the Cradle Endlessly Rocking." Carrie's rocking chair is a larger kind of cradle, in which she—and even Drouet and Hurstwood—seek solace in times of distress. The rocking chair is the equivalent to the imagery of sea-drift in the novel. Both are characterized by directionless motion. Together they make Dreiser's symbol of the human tragedy. After her first disappointment at the bareness of her prospective life with Minnie, she "drew the one small rocking-chair up to the open window, and sat looking out upon the night and streets in silent wonder." With no money, she nightly watches the city she cannot enjoy from her rocking-chair. Later, her first real dissatisfaction with Drouet occurs when she is taken for a drive along the mansions on North Shore Drive through Lincoln Park. That evening, contrasting her three rooms to those mansions, she "thought it over, rocking to and fro,... too pensive to do aught but rock and sing." After her success in an amateur theatrical performance, again "she sat down in her rocking-chair by the window to think about it." Separating herself from Drouet, fleeing with Hurstwood, meeting Ames, perplexed by her stage career—at each stage of her transformation or transplantation she consults the illusory movement of her chair for comfort. In agitation and confusion she seeks the cradle and endlessly rocks. Concluding his Balzacian epilogue, Dreiser directly addresses Carrie:

It is when the feet weary and hope seems vain that the heartaches and the longings arise. Know, then, that for you is neither surfeit nor content. In your rocking-chair, by your window dreaming, shall you long, alone. In your rocking-chair, by your window, shall you dream such happiness as you may never feel.

Associated with the symbol of the rocking-chair, Dreiser's sea images similarly suggest illusory movement. There is no real movement—only change. Dreiser repeatedly characterizes Carrie's apparent movement as mere "drift" in the rocking ebb and flow of tides or as similar to the ceaseless reappearance of waves. Carrie is "a wisp on the tide." Later, with Hurstwood, she "was getting into deep water. She was letting her few supports float away from her." Breaking indecisively with Drouet, she resembles "an anchorless, storm-beaten, little craft which could do absolutely nothing but drift." Nevertheless, unlike Hurstwood (who is "an inconspicuous drop in an ocean like New York") she thrives on change—it is the principle of her existence—and "seemed ever capable of getting herself into the tide of change where she would be easily borne along."

It must not be supposed that Dreiser was unconscious of the literary effects he was creating, as many critics seem readily to assume. In his portrait of Dreiser, Ford Madox Ford provides a note which offers a healthy corrective to the view that Dreiser's style was the bumbling expression of his confused thought. Ford, one of the shrewdest of twentieth-century English stylists, writes:

> On the occasion of my first meeting with the author of the *Titan* we had for a period of three or four hours talked of nothing but words and styles and Mr. Dreiser had been so completely in agreement with me that I had taken him to be a larger and gentler Conrad. . . . Indeed, Mr. Dreiser, even on the surface, seemed to know quite as much of the technique of writing as I did. . .and I gave him mental credit for knowing a little more.

Struck by "the extraordinary readableness of his books," Ford was convinced that "Dreiser knew what he was about and was trying after effects hitherto unessayed."[60] Certainly, it is true that far more than most American writing, Dreiser's style seems contrived. Like Melville's and Whitman's, and later, Henry Miller's, his speech is made from the shoddy clichés of his time. Contrasting Dreiser to Hawthorne, Thoreau, and Emerson, Lionel Trilling has made his distance from their colloquial tradition clear. "If we are to talk of bookishness," Trilling observed, "it is Dreiser who is bookish."[61] Ordering, even twisting and contriving his speech, Dreiser—in this way, much like James—was willing to chance artificiality to achieve art. His bumbling clichés embody everyday experience. On one level of his mental experience he was so close to the archetypes of the early twentieth-century mind that the very force of the experience bursts through the artificiality of the language. In one sense, we are forced by Dreiser to an awareness of the intensity of his experience by seeing how life breaks through language.

---

60 Quotations are in "Portrait of Dreiser" in *The Stature of Theodore Dreiser*, ed. Alfred Kazin and Charles Shapiro (Bloomington, Ind., 1955), pp. 29–30 and p. 30.   61 "Reality in America," in *ibid.*, p. 141.

His symbols arise out of the life of the novel itself, as the accumulation of his response to reality. Not in themselves, but in the recurring of his characters' feelings about clothes, rooms, warmth, and so on, these things come cumulatively to represent the nature of their lives. The impact of the experience in the book thus seems almost to come directly, unconveyed by any technical resources. Dreiser's triumph as a novelist is his ability to convince the reader that his experience is so strong it cannot be conveyed by his words. By using the flowers of rhetoric and the paste gems of genteel speech he creates a verbal situation in which the powerful life of his narrative must overrun the false life of his speech. Thus he impresses us all the more with the power of his experience, as it apparently shatters the bonds of literary convention. The facts and details which engage his narrative come not from the clichés of language, but from the commonplaces of life. It is the phenomena of rooms, warmth, and light; food, resturants, and bills of fare; clothes and department stores, that concern him.

Dreiser's vitally commonplace details should not be confused with his clichéd language. Brunetiere's defense of Balzac—*"Mal ecrire est une condition de la representation de la vie"* ("Bad writing is necessary to represent life accurately")—does not really apply to Dreiser. The accumulation of detail vitalizes his language. His is the kind of fact which the genteel had refused to acknowledge. Dreiser brings the genteel cliché back into contact with the basic needs of physical life, and so refreshes both that language and the sense of life it conveys. His style has force and power—not, surely, in its rough ungainliness, but in Dreiser's adept and unashamed insistence on the repetitive character of ordinary circumstance. Man's primary needs and emotions—love, death, hope, wonder, helplessness, self-assertion—fill the narrative and are as fully conveyed as if Dreiser were confronting these for the first time. Dreiser observes and describes the common real as if it were the rare. His style glitters with the wonder of details, and as a result he was the first man to accept and reveal, in all its massive incomprehensibility, the modern city. The surface of life is thus rendered incandescent. Dreiser endures, then—as the muckrakers and progressives and novelists of the city like Phillips or Upton Sinclair have not endured—because he filled his books with the clutter and imperatives of ordinary human circumstance. Now, therefore, when concern with the ephemeral social context has largely disappeared as a factor in our reading of his books, we can see that the historical occasion merely provoked his imagination to render lovingly the eternal news of everyday life.

The Financier (1912), *The Titan* (1914), and *The Stoic* (1947) taken together form what Dreiser called a "Trilogy of Desire." All of his books, indeed, have longing, aspiration, or desire at their emotional center. By providing the natural equivalents of his plot in the images of the rocking chair and the tide of change, Dreiser was responding instinctively to the predicament of his characters. In her rocking chair, Carrie "longed and longed and longed." Incredibly receptive to the surface of life, she defines her existence in terms of the masks it wears. Dreiser symbolizes this in her longing for fine clothes. "A woman should someday write the complete philosophy of clothes. No matter how young, it is one of the things she wholly comprehends," Dreiser remarked. The permutations in Carrie's life are dramatized as the longing for and putting on of new clothes—new disguises, as it were, although the disguise is always offered as the reality. Her rise is signalized in terms of the clothes she wears, just as Hurstwood's moral fall is accentuated by the difference between his former "new and rich clothes"—the Scotch plaid vest, "set with a double row of round mother-of-pearl buttons," his silken cravat, his calf shoes—and the ragged coat and vest he stuffs under his flophouse door to keep in the fatal gas fumes. Equally as commonplace and likewise achieving cumulative relevance as symbols are the associations of pleasure and increase in wealth with images of light and warmth; and conversely, of degradation and diminishment with images of darkness and cold. Drouet "radiates"; Carrie appears "in a fine glow" or, as a successful actress, "dawns on the audience"; she "blazes" in the "shine of fashion," where glittering crystal, jewels, and candles are abundant. She goes to conventional romantic plays like *Under the Gaslight* and *A Gold Mine*, titles of real dramas that Dreiser chooses for their symbolic fitness. Images of gold—particularly of illusory gilt—fill the book. On the other hand, Hurstwood, who is originally associated with the sun—"he shone upon [Carrie] as the morning sun," Dreiser writes—is seen after his theft and deception of Carrie in increasingly darkened rooms, reflecting his dimmed moral lustre. Dreiser's description of Hurstwood's suicide in a cold, lightless room—his clothes used as instruments of death rather than life—brings all of these images together brilliantly.

Asked by an interviewer in 1901 about his intentions, Dreiser responded: "I simply want to tell about life as it is. Every human life is intensely interesting. . . . [These] are the things I want to write about—life as it is, the facts as they exist, the game as it is played!"[62] Again, in *A Traveler at Forty* (1913) he emphasized his open-ended immersion in the varieties of existence. "For myself," he wrote, "I accept now no creeds. I do not know what truth is, what beauty is, what love is, what hope is. I do not believe anyone absolutely and I do not doubt anyone absolutely."[63] Instinctively rejecting the experimental naturalism of Zola, he expressed, even more clearly than Norris had, the naturalism that was imbedded in the structure of the American mind. He was affected by the American tendency to naturalize concepts, in understanding the mind, as E. L. Youmans put it, as "inextricably interwoven with corporeal actions."[64] Translating idea into act, philosophers like James or jurists like Holmes believed, as Holmes wrote, that "the final test of . . . [intellectual] energy is battle in some form—actual war—the crush of Arctic ice—the fight for mastery in the market or the court."[65] This tendency was Dreiser's by heritage.

Dreiser shared, too, the fierce rejection of the supernatural, nowhere more

---

[62] Interview in the *New York Times Review of Books,* (June 15, 1907), p. 393. [63] *A Traveler at Forty* (New York, 1913), p. 4. [64] "On the Scientific Study of Human Nature" in E. L. Youmans, *et al., The Culture Demanded by Modern Life. . .* (New York, 1867), p. 394. [65] Quoted in Commager, *The American Mind,* p. 384.

emphatic than in the Middle West and best represented there by Robert Ingersoll—the "general in the war of ideas for freedom," as Edgar Lee Masters called him.[66] Ingersoll influenced a whole generation of Americans, including Dreiser, Masters, Sandburg, and Clarence Darrow. Stumping towns and cities across the country in the '70s and '80s with lectures on *The Gods* (1872) and *Some Mistakes of Moses* (1879), Ingersoll translated middle-class uneasiness into religious rebellion. Personally in rebellion against his Catholic father, Dreiser early found in Ingersoll the apologist who generalized his revolt. Not until *The Bulwark* (1946) and *The Stoic* (1947) would he dramatize the saving power of the supernatural—even then finding value only in Oriental or pietistic worship, far removed from conventional middle-class mores.

Walt Whitman—who had declared in his preface to the first two editions of *Leaves of Grass* (1855, 1856), "There will soon be no more priests. Their work is done. . . . A new order shall arise and they shall be the priests of man, and every man shall be his own priest"[67]—also gave expression to a naturalistic aesthetic, the spirit of which influenced Dreiser. While Whitman frequently expressed his admiration for Ingersoll, yet Whitman's naturalism was larger than Ingersoll's. "The Colonel and I," Whitman remarked shrewdly, "are not directly at issue even about God and immortality: I do not say yes where he says no: I say yes where he says nothing."[68] Beginning with Ingersoll's repudiation of supernaturalism, Dreiser went on to the affirmation of Whitman's transcendental naturalism. Fascinated and delighted with the facts of material life, celebrating the body electric and preserving, by listing, the actualities of the metropolis and life en masse, Whitman had proclaimed the transcendental character of this life. He found in the city what Emerson had concluded in *Nature*—that the natural world is supremely important in the hints that it gives of the spiritual. The Material is the symbol of the Spiritual; physical laws reveal spiritual absolutes in translation, the transcendentalists insisted. In *A Hoosier Holiday* (1916) Dreiser spoke of Whitman along with Christ and St. Francis as dreamers who appeared in times of distress to mitigate injustice with idealism. Later, in an extended introduction to a collection of Thoreau's writings, he echoed and reaffirmed Thoreau's insistence that "Man is related to all of nature."[69] Dreiser read not only Democritus but also Einstein, and knew that matter was energy. In short, he accepted Darwinian mechanics while insisting that implicit in matter is beneficence, spirit, and control.

Art should show, he asserted accordingly, "not only the concentrated filth

---

[66] Edgar Lee Masters, "Robert G. Ingersoll" in *The Great Valley* (New York, 1916), p. 77. [67] Walt Whitman, *Leaves of Grass: The First* (1855) *Edition,* ed. Malcolm Cowley (New York, 1959), p. 22. [68] "Ingersoll is a man," he said, "whose importance to the time could not be overfigured." Whitman's father had deeply admired Thomas Paine, to whom Ingersoll swore allegiance in one of his best-known lectures, and to the young Walt had given Paine's *The Age of Reason* for study. Later, in 1877, Whitman publicly defended Paine at Philadelphia's Lincoln Hall. (See Horace Traubel, *With Walt Whitman in Camden* [New York, 1906], Vol. I, pp. 82, 114.) [69] Dreiser, ed., "Presenting Thoreau" (Introduction) in *The Living Thoughts of Thoreau* (New York, 1939), p. 23.

at the bottom but the wonder and mystery of the ideals at the top."[70]
As Cowperwood yearningly watched the stars from his prison window, so
Dreiser kept his double-minded, penetrating gaze fixed upon nature, and
revealed its possibilities for both beauty and terror. His portrayal of Cowperwood, for instance, is hardly the attack on the businessman that several
historians have wished to see in it. Indeed, Dreiser carefully chose Yerkes
as a model for Cowperwood; unlike the puritanical Rockefeller or lascivious
Fisk, Yerkes was characterized by a vigorous love for beauty—in art as
well as women—and by a daring forcefulness, which point to the energy
of both his spirit and his desire. Summoning his characteristic imagery of
blazing light and total darkness, Dreiser wrote in 1914 of the hero of his
trilogy: "A rebellious Lucifer this, glorious in his sombre conception of
the value of power. A night-black pool his world will seem to some....To
the illuminate it will have a very different meaning."[71] The massive force
of his details shattered stereotypes. If, beginning in the '90s, the rapacious
businessman had become a stock figure in the gallery of American men—
as witness Barrett Wendell's remark on Collis Huntington—Dreiser presented Yerkes "unidealized and uncursed." Whereas in the literature that
followed Dugdale's study of *The Jukes* (1877) the poor had been portrayed
stereotypically as degraded by their heredity and environment, Dreiser
presented Carrie, Jennie, and Clyde supported and sustained by the desire
to rise. In a period when Americans seemed either to be gloriously optimistic
or (like Henry and Brooks Adams) sensationally disenchanted, Dreiser
created characters whose hope and despair were mingled and equally
justified. He returned our world to us in all its vast, irregular complexity.

Inevitably and inconsolably alienated from the older American systems
of values and emotional attachments, Carrie, Jennie, Cowperwood, and the
rest of Dreiser's characters reflect his own alienation from the American
scene. On his fiancée's Missouri farm in 1894, Dreiser felt himself briefly
in touch with an America never his and already tragically vanishing. He
wrote:

> To me it seemed that all the spirit of rural America, its idealism, its dreams,
> the passion of a Brown; the courage and patience and sadness of a Lincoln,—
> the dreams and courage of a Lee or a Jackson, were all here. The very soil
> smacked of idealism and faith, a fixedness in sentimental and purely imaginative
> American tradition, in which I, alas! could not share. I was enraptured. Out
> of its charms and sentiment I might have composed an elegy or an epic, but
> I could not believe that it was more than a frail flower of romance. I had seen
> Pittsburgh. I had seen Lithuanians and Hungarians in their 'courts' and hovels.
> I had seen the girls of that city—walking the streets at night. The profound
> faith in God, in goodness, in virtue and duty that I saw here in no wise squared
> with the craft, the cruelty, the brutality and the envy that I saw everywhere
> else.[72]

[70] Dreiser, quoted in the New York *Evening Sun,* Sept. 28, 1912; quoted from Elias,
Theodore Dreiser, p. 171. [71] New York *Evening Sun,* June 18, 1914; quoted in *ibid.,*
pp. 175–76. [72] Quoted in Matthiessen, pp. 36–7.

Personally his by heritage and training, estrangement was as well the experience of his age. With Henry James, Emily Dickinson, and Henry Adams, with the late Twain and with Howells after the Haymarket Square riots, Dreiser shared the plight and passion of the outsider. Presenting characters whose success is meaningless because they neither possess nor envision an environment where true human success is possible, Dreiser projected into his books the depression and frustration that sent him to a mental sanitarium in 1903, midway through the slough of despond between *Sister Carrie* and *Jennie Gerhardt*. To express his own sense of his alienation from meaningfulness he titled his book of philosophical essays *Hey-Rub-a-Dub-Dub* (1920), suggesting that "life—like the title. . .is without meaning and has no objective."[73] His subtitle, *A Book of the Mystery and Wonder and Terror of Life*, expresses the outsider's passive awareness of the incomprehensible, but nonetheless strangely attractive, character of existence. Up to the end of his life, when he simultaneously embraced Christianity and Communism, Dreiser sought to find meaning in life with a desperation that eventually spoiled his last books.

Edith Wharton

Edith Wharton felt the pain of alienation perhaps more deeply than any other of Dreiser's contemporaries. In many ways Mrs. Wharton's and Dreiser's personal senses of isolation are so similar that it will be wise to hold off speaking further of Dreiser's autobiographical works, *A Book About Myself* and the others, until we can examine Wharton's *A Backward Glance*. These two writers—whose subject matter is so different—both wrote naturalistic novels derived from the similar collective, American, and personal experiences which they shared. Like Dreiser, Edith Wharton lived most of her life in a kind of essential solitude. Inheriting a secure social position, she was nevertheless personally so shy that she terrorized many people (including Bernard Berenson) by her protective, imperiously cold aloofness. Descended from "the Schermerhorns, Joneses, Pendletons, on my father's side, the Stevenses, Ledyards, Rhinelanders on my mother's, the Gallatins on both,"[74] whose Gothic mansions bracketed the Hudson, she however, was convinced that she was the illegitimate child of a man—perhaps her brothers' tutor—of intellectual qualities; and she apparently made discreet inquiries on this matter in England.[75] Of distinguished American ancestry (her great-grandfather, Ebenezer Stevens, appeared in one of Trumbull's historical portraits), she nonetheless expatriated herself in Paris, where she lived from 1910 until her death. She wrote in *A Backward Glance* that her first memory concerned a walk on Fifth Avenue; but her first published story, "Mrs. Manstey's View" (1891), has a dingy tenement as its setting. Hers was a mind divided.

---

[73] Quoted in *ibid.*, p. 183. [74] *A Backward Glance* (New York, 1934), p. 11. [75] Illegitimacy, of course, would be the subject of *The Old Maid* (1924), the second of her *Old New York* series.

By heritage and marriage part of a group that refused to take literature seriously, she formally acquiesced to this attitude to such a degree that Bernard Berenson wrote: "She never fussed about her work, never made you feel that it obsessed her."[76] Yet she produced more than twenty novels (the first not published until she was thirty-eight), six books of travel, ten volumes of short stories, a classic in the history of interior decoration, a distinguished memoir, and three volumes of poetry—altogether forty-seven books. Still, her view of the artist remained an outsider's, as she proved in her portrayal of such artists as Vance Weston in *Hudson River Bracketed* (1929) and its sequel, *The Gods Arrive* (1932). Although she ignored and scorned the Bohemian vagaries of the Left Bank, she could be remarkably frank in matters of sordid fact—as when Scott Fitzgerald, slightly drunk, attempted to shock her by declaring that when he and Zelda first came to Paris they had lived for two weeks in a brothel. Instead of registering shock, Mrs. Wharton responded to the suddenly hesitant young man, "But, Mr. Fitzgerald,...You haven't told us what they did in the bordello." "They beat me, they beat me, they beat me," Fitzgerald told Zelda when he arrived home. When Fitzgerald subsequently confided to her friend that one of his three great aspirations was to gain Mrs. Wharton's friendship, he was advised to drink less. Following the tea at the Pavilion Colombe, she had written after his name in her diary: *"horrible."*[77]

Edith Wharton published her first volume, *Verses,* in 1878 in the manner of Longfellow and with his encouragement. After an interruption of more than a decade, she resumed writing with Balzac, Tolstoy, Flaubert, and George Eliot as her models. As she would show in *The Writing of Fiction* (1925), she had turned forcefully away from the American literary tradition. She puts Poe and Hawthorne "outside of the classic tradition," for example, and speaks of "the joyous clatter" of the "novels of adventure" by Herman Melville, grouping him with Marryat and Stevenson.[78] Her instructions in the art of fiction she summarizes and exemplifies with an admirable essay on Marcel Proust. To Theodore Roosevelt, who offered to rearrange Mrs. Wharton's first novel, *The Valley of Decision* (1902), "in conformity with his theory of domestic morals and the strenuous life," she "pointed out that these ideals did not happen to prevail in the decadent Italian principalities."[79]

Such was the double life and mind of Edith Wharton. If her tradition, her parents, and her America had early consecrated and confined her to the approved models—if, as her friend and Henry James's Percy Lubbock says, "she was pleased with her place, well content to keep and adorn it, and never had the least inclination to flaunt the law under which she was born" —she was also bent on enlarging her models and deliberately, though subtly, rejecting her tradition. The ferocity of that rejection is nowhere better sug-

[76] Quoted in Blake Nevius, *Edith Wharton* (Berkeley and Los Angeles, 1953), p. 21. [77] The full account of Fitzgerald's relation to Mrs. Wharton is given in Arthur Mizener, *The Far Side of Paradise: A Biography of F. Scott Fitzgerald* (Boston, 1951), pp. 154, 170, 183–85. [78] See *The Writing of Fiction* (New York, 1925), p. 34. [79] *A Backward Glance,* p. 312.

gested than by Lubbock's remark on her two beings: "She was all that was right and regular in her smooth clan-plumage," he wrote reminiscently, "but the young hawk looked out of her eyes."[80] Against the cumlative force of society and tradition the young hawk gathered strength. Alien from, or at the least uncomfortable with, her social peers, her colonial heritage, her family, and her literary tradition, Edith Wharton instinctively wrote her own savage hawk-like version of the novel of estrangement.

Perhaps it was only by projecting her estrangement into fiction that she saved herself. Dreiser had been cured in a sanitarium by the Spartan regimen of the retired wrestler Muldoon—lovingly portrayed in *Twelve Men* (1919) as "Culhane, the Solid Man." In Mrs. Wharton's case, it was S. Weir Mitchell —the model for the nerve specialist in Howells's *Shadow of a Dream* and himself a distinguished novelist—who advised Edith Wharton to write for therapeutic reasons. But this was a solution that she herself had already undertaken. By 1892, before her prolonged illness of 1894–95 (although even then she complained of flu, earaches, and eye trouble), she had already written several of the tales that would appear in *The Greater Inclination* (1899). Prompted by Mrs. Wharton's own account, Edmund Wilson has suggested that her marriage was responsible for generating the tensions that required release in fiction; and Blake Nevius has written, "I would not be surprised to learn someday that her health improved suddenly beginning about 1914, the year which followed her divorce."[81] Nonetheless, it is clear that the restrictions that marriage imposed on her only made concrete in a personal way the chafing of the young hawk under the limitations of family, national, or literary tradition.

"Balzac says that he wishes to paint men, women and things," Zola remarked. "I count men and women as the same, while admitting their natural differences, and subject men and women to things."[82] In her recognition of the devastating influence of *things*—rooms, homes, and landscapes—over man, Edith Wharton is allied closely to the naturalistic tradition. Discussing Italian devotional painting of the early Renaissance in *Italian Backgrounds* (1905), she distinguished between the conventionalized foreground personages and the background, where "the artist finds himself free to express his personality. Here he depicts not what someone else has long since designed for him, in another land and under different concepts of life and faith, but what he actually sees about him."[83] She was quick to reflect influences from such varied writers as James, Balzac, Turgenev, Flaubert, Thackeray, George Eliot, and Hawthorne. But these influences nevertheless remained superficial, affecting only the conventionalized foreground of characterization, symbolism, and allusion in her work. To her strikingly original backgrounds, however, she subjects her characters and plots and thus makes them her own. Set against the dumb, uncomprehending, impersonal landscapes of brutal nature or indifferent society, her characters are tragically isolated. Unable to mix

---

[80] *Portrait of Edith Wharton* (London, 1947), p. 23. [81] *Edith Wharton,* p. 16. [82] Quoted by Malcolm Cowley in *Evolutionary Thought in America*, ed. Stow Persons (New Haven, 1950), p. 314. [83] New York, pp. 173–74.

satisfactorily with their physical or human environments, unable to find meaning (and thus fulfillment) in things, they either are wedged in by or drift aimlessly among the objects of an alien world.

Mrs. Wharton writes two distinct versions of the naturalistic novel, corresponding to her double vision of the possibilities of human tragedy. In her first kind of novel, "things" encumber the individual, binding him to a permanently indifferent universe. Fundamentally a novel of self or psyche, this version delineates the tragedy of aspiration. Inevitably held and defeated by his alien surroundings, the protagonist nonetheless aspires, imaginatively and intellectually, to strike through the bondage of things into the personal freedom and fulfillment that he can only suppose might be his. In this genre, Wharton's chief works are the novella *Bunner Sisters* (1891), *Ethan Frome* (1911), and *Summer* (1917).

In her second kind of novel not the natural, but the human "things" of a hollow society are so devoid of meaning that the individual drifts aimlessly among them. People are defined by their clothes or houses; they are spoken of, usually, in terms of the machine culture that they mentally exemplify, as "a screw or a cog in the great machine." One of her characters, Judy Trenor, is "suggestive, with her glaring good-looks, of a jeweller's window lit by electricity." Another, Mrs. Spragg, resembles "a wax figure in a show-window." In the midst of a society filled with human automata, Mrs. Wharton sets seekers after human fulfillment. Here she writes a picaresque novel of manners in which the individual seeks satisfaction in collectives as far apart as vulgar parvenu parties and "republics of the spirit." Again and again, however, he is alienated by the indifference or emptiness of society; he can find no satisfactory way of penetrating social things, and so wanders vaguely across the changing surface of society. Wharton's major novels in this group are *The House of Mirth* (1905), *The Custom of the Country* (1913), and *The Age of Innocence* (1920). The last novel, written after her divorce and her charitable warwork, shows an unwillingness to pursue the logic of alienation, and suggests, perhaps, the growing appeasement of the young hawk that would lead to the sentimentality of her later books. "Things," she finds, have, after all, the previously unglimpsed benignity which would make her autobiography, *A Backward Glance*, an apologia:

> When I was young, [she writes] it used to seem to me that the group in which I grew up was like an empty vessel into which no new wine would ever again be poured. Now I see that one of its uses lay in preserving a few drops of an old vintage too rare to be savoured by a youthful palate; and I should like to atone for that unappreciativeness by trying to revive that faint fragrance.

Bunner Sisters, written in 1891, suggests how far from this view she began. The title refers not to *the* Bunner sisters, Ann Eliza and Evelina, but to the business sign—"merely 'Bunner Sisters' in blotchy gold on a black ground" —that tenuously preserves their identity in a neighborhood that "as it stretched eastward, rapidly fell from shabbiness to squalor, with an increasing frequency of projecting sign-boards." Like the London of Eliot's "Preludes," the New York of *Bunner Sisters* is a city of scraps and fragmented lives: its "fissured pavement formed a mosaic of colored hand bills, lids of tomato-cans, old shoes, cigar-stumps and banana skins, cemented together by a layer of mud." In the narrow lives of the sisters, the smallest events assume extraordinary significance. Ann Eliza's brief encounter with a lonely German clock-maker so stirs her latent discontent that "for the first time in her long years of drudgery she rebelled at the dullness of her life." After Ann Eliza has refused Mr. Ramy's business-like proposal, her sister, still seeking a meaningful relation, marries him. Later Evelina returns home, disillusioned and dying. Then, for the first time, Ann Eliza sees that her self-sacrifice has been in vain:

> Hitherto she had never thought of questioning the inherited principles which had guided her life. Self-effacement for the good of others had always seemed to her both natural and necessary; but then she had taken it for granted that it implied the securing of that good. Now she perceived that to refuse the gifts of life does not ensure their transmission to those for whom they have been surrendered; and her familiar heaven was unpeopled. She felt she could no longer trust in the goodness of God, and that if he was not good, he was not God, and there was only a black abyss above the roof of Bunner Sisters.

Her ethical and cosmic order sundered, Ann Eliza is buffeted by more personal estrangements. From her sister, who has become a Catholic, she feels "an exile"; Evelina dies, "a stranger in her arms." She feels "that the shop and the back room no longer belonged to her." As she leaves the surroundings familiar to her for years, "she looked at it all as though it had been the scene of some unknown life, of which the vague report had reached her." The story concludes as she wanders from store to store, "looking for another shop window with a sign in it." Without employment she lacks the only kind of identity (that is, a new sign) she can hope—hopelessly—to achieve in a modern world dominated by "things."

Although Nature in *Ethan Frome* is far more beautiful than Ann Eliza's New York, it is no more benign than are the buildings among which she wanders. Both surround the individual with essentially the same "granite outcroppings" that Mrs. Wharton found in the heart of the New England (and human) character.[84] Ethan's village—the decaying, deserted New England hill town familiar from the stories of Rose Cooke and Mary Wilkins—is appropriately named Starkfield. Here, as in *Bunner Sisters,* Mrs. Wharton portrays an individual imprisoned by his environment. The snow that winterlong buries and desolates the potentially beautiful landscape suggests the circumstances blocking Ethan's aspirations for a meaningful life. He attended college briefly and "has always been more sensitive than the people about him to the appeal of natural beauty"; he feels stirrings of imaginative life and, to the end, "inarticulate flashes" of joy; as a young man he fitted up a study in his bare house, nailing up shelves for books, and hanging an engraving of Abraham Lincoln beside a calender with "Thoughts from the Poets."

---

84 See "Introduction" to *Ethan Frome* (New York, 1922: "With an Introduction Written for this Edition"), pp. i–v.

He has been to Florida—the memory of which later serves his imagination as a symbol of release from his prison-like confinement in New England—and he wants "to live in towns, where there were lectures, and big libraries and 'fellows doing things.'" Yet these meager aspirations are brutally defeated. Unable to escape his alien environment because of his marriage and his own fatalism, his very qualities of imagination, sensitivity, and endurance intensify his tragedy. Each day he passes the family graveyard: "For years that quiet company had mocked his restlessness, his desire for change and freedom. 'We never got away—how should you?' seemed to be written on every headstone." At last, just before his attempted suicide with Mattie Silver, he achieves a full recognition of the malign indifference of the universe: "The inexorable facts closed in on him like a prison warden's handcuffing a convict. There was no way out—none." Like Ann Eliza, he has no place to go. Lionel Trilling has found demonstrated in *Ethan Frome* "the idea . . . that moral inertia, the *not* making of moral decisions, constitutes a large part of the moral life of humanity."[85] Yet the degrading tragedy of both Ann Eliza and Ethan is not that they are morally inert, but rather that their world is so constituted that their morality can find no expression. The sophisticated narrator of *Ethan Frome* feels that Ethan "lived in a depth of moral isolation too remote for casual access." The natural and human "things" of this world never engage his moral sense. Much as he desires to choose (and thus to act morally), he can only waver until his minimal life flickers painfully out.

Mrs. Wharton's later novel, *Summer,* in which she portrays the terrible psychological process wherely her heroine, Charity Royall, stumbles toward consciousness of the higher levels of civilization above her, shocked and pained Mrs. Wharton's contemporaries. Not far from Ethan's Starkfield, her village is even more desolate than his. It lies on the edge of "The Mountain," from which Charity was taken as an infant and where a colony of the half-human dregs of New England's decline herd promiscuously together. Her instinctive yearning for culture is stirred by the appearance of a young architect who is sketching the decaying rural houses. She stands poised between culture and primitive anarchy. The more she is stirred by "the vision of vague metropolises, shining super-Nettletons, where girls. . . talked fluently of architecture to young men with hands like Lucius Harney's," the more strongly does she feel her bondage to the Aeschylean inevitability of "The Mountain." For while she can only dream of super-Nettletons—Springfield, Massachusetts is her city of the sun—she comes to know the terrible reality of her mountain origin. Not since John DeForest's depiction of backwoods Southerners in *Kate Beaumont* (1872) had human brutalization been so viciously rendered by an American. Charity, finding that she is pregnant by Lucius, is confusedly drawn to the mountain for the first time—only to find her mother dead there:

> She seemed to have fallen across her bed in a drunken sleep, and to have been left lying where she fell, in her ragged disordered clothes. One arm was

---

[85] "The Morality of Inertia" in *Edith Wharton: A Collection of Critical Essays,* ed. Irving Howe (Englewood Cliffs, N.J., 1962), p. 143.

flung above her head, one leg drawn up under a torn skirt that left the other bare to the knee: a swollen glistening leg with a ragged stocking rolled down about the ankle. . . . There was no sign in it of anything human: she lay there like a dead dog in a ditch.

Like Clyde Griffiths, Charity "felt herself too unequally pitted against unknown forces": in the levels of life that spiral above her she feels "a terror of the unknown, of all the mysterious attractions. . .and of her own powerlessness to contend with them." A waif amid these forces, she is saved from the mountain, but deserted by Harney and barred from civilization. After all her pitifully ineffectual struggles, then, she remains at last imprisoned in North Dormer, where she began, no longer possessing even her original energy of hate. With no meaningful alternatives, she marries Lawyer Royall, the town's conspicuous failure. Mrs. Wharton perfectly renders Charity's dulled acquiescence to the ceremony:

> She was so busy trying to understand the gestures that the clergyman was signalling her to make that she no longer heard what was being said. After another interval the lady on the bench stood up, and taking her hand, put it in Mr. Royall's. It lay enclosed in his strong palm and she felt a ring that was too big for her being slipped on her thin finger. She understood then that she was married.

This is the morality of inertia with a vengeance. But in a world where both nature and man are fundamentally inhuman, no other kind of morality is possible. Briefly in their flashes of imagination, Ann Eliza, Ethan, and Charity conceive of a natural and social world where they might find meaning. They are, in this sense, martyred picaros, saints of the imagination.

Translated into the quest for meaning by physical movement across the surface of society—in a picaresque of manners—their situation and theme is essentially reproduced in *The House of Mirth* and *The Custom of the Country*. "The heart of fools is in the house of mirth," Mrs. Wharton quotes from Ecclesiastes. Her heroine, Lily Bart, passes through a number of such houses, which reminds one that Mrs. Wharton's second book had been *The Decoration of Houses* (1897). At first slow, but soon dizzying, Lily's fall through the levels of society is thus defined by the successive houses at which she is a guest; for indeed, the people who share her world are no better characterized than by the houses they can, by taste or wealth, manage to encase themselves in. Lily, the perpetual guest, is in her turn defined by the houses to which she is invited. If she is ultimately unable to remain in the house of mirth, it is because she has aspired—but without real conviction or guidance—to what her friend Lawrence Selden calls "the republic of the spirit." In her alternate flickering between these two principles lies the structural principle of the book, suggested on the first page: standing irresolutely in Grand Central Station, "in the act of transition between one and another of the country-houses which disputed her presence after the close of the Newport season," Lily encounters the lawyer Lawrence Selden and stops at his genteel, shabby, and vaguely artistic apartment for tea. Between her destination (the palatial Gus Trenor's Bellomont at

Rhinebeck) and Selden's flat lies the kind of choice by which Lily, unwilling to choose at all, will be paralyzed and finally defeated. It is, as Lily severally puts it to herself, a choice on the grossest level between wealth and "dinginess"—her word for poverty—between freedom and servitude, or luxury and discontent.

But essentially, as it turns out, it is the conflict between her artificial calculations and natural inclinations. "What she craved, and really felt herself entitled to," Mrs. Wharton says, "was a situation in which the noblest attitude should also be the easiest." But in her world necessity and desire never seem to match, and she is thus reduced to ineffectual vacillations between them. On the one hand she knows "she was not made for mean and shabby surroundings, for the squalid compromises of poverty." On the other, she would not have cared "to marry a man who was merely rich." Her longing for "the claims of an immemorial tradition," satisfied neither by the dully puritanical standards of old New York—typified by her aunt, Mrs. Peniston—nor by Selden's passive vision of "the republic of the spirit," will repeatedly reduce her to fruitless activity or ineffectual drifting. Though her travels range from Alaska to Europe, the range of her possibilities is essentially as limited as those of Ethan's or Charity's. Wandering purposelessly, morally indecisive, merely set loose upon the swell of experience, she defines the fundamental hollowness of the world in which her intentions can never correspond to her inclinations. Her seal— "a grey seal with *Beyond!* beneath a flying ship"—points strikingly to both the romance and the irony of her aspirations. Unsatisfied with the here, she is ever flying toward a *Beyond!* that dazzles, but disintegrates at a touch. For all the confidence of her symbol, she is better symbolized, so Mrs. Wharton later puts it, as "the castaway who has signalled in vain to fleeting sails"; she is, in the brutal sea imagery of Mrs. Wharton's (like Dreiser's) metaphor for society, "an organism as helpless...as the sea-anemone torn from the rock"; or, later, "a stray uprooted growth [swept] down the heedless current,...mere spindrift of the whirling surface of existence, without anything to which the poor little tentacles of self could cling before the awful flood submerged them."

In her unimpeded descent, she briefly clings to the following houses of decreasing mirth: (1) the Trenor's, rich and still preserving slight traces of an inherited order; (2) the Dorset's, connected to the past only enough to be unhappy with the present; (3) the Wellington Bry's, on their way up and longing desperately to be accepted; (4) the Sam Gormer's, possessing only wealth and still in the process of formulating a social credo; (5) Norma Hatch's overheated hotel world, "Oriental [in] indolence and disorder"; (6) the genteel apartment of Gerty Farish; (7) Mme. Regina's drab millinery establishment; (8) Nettie Struther's tenement flat; and, at last (9) "the solitude of a hall bedroom in a house where she could come and go unremarked among other workers." She goes, in terms of the decorative symbolism, from the richness of Bellomont to the ugly "peacock-blue parlour" of her final home, a room decorated with dried bunches of pampas grass, blotchy wallpaper, sentimental steel engravings, and Rogers's groups. Dazzled by success, she nevertheless from the first declines imperceptibly toward failure: "If she slipped she recovered her footing, and it was only afterward that she was aware of having recovered it each time on a slightly lower level." Thus, while she is set adrift on the surface of society, she is also confined to it by her lack of moral—or even immoral—continuity. This Mrs. Wharton makes clear repeatedly in the novel. Lily had, for instance, once happened upon a translation of *The Eumenides* and had since defined the inevitability of her own predicament in terms of their pursuit.[86] So completely is she the victim of her civilization that, as Selden remarks, "the links of her bracelet seemed like manacles chaining her to her fate." Lily, always wiser than Selden because less morally inert than he, knows better. For if she too recognizes her imprisonment in the "great gilt cage" of society, she knows as well that "in reality...the door never clanged: it stood always open." But the cage has its own allurement; not until the end—and even then only ambiguously—does Lily manage to step out of her cage: and then only into death.

Against Lily's increasingly accelerated descent from social grace Mrs. Wharton counterpoises the astonishing ascent of Undine Spragg in the later novel, *The Custom of the Country* (1913). Undine is Lily's anti-self. Beginning in the hotel world where Lily found Norma Hatch, Undine undergoes a rapid series of initiations and transformations. Innocent where Lily was wise, yet instinctively wiser than Lily, she sloughs off the background of her hometown, Apex, disposes of her parents, and in turn marries Ralph Marvell, a member of the old New York aristocracy; is calculatingly seduced by but fails to marry Peter Van Degen, one of the new rich; marries Raymond de Chelles of the Faubourg Saint-Germain; and finally, marries the railroad king Elmer Moffat, to whom, the reader at last, yet not surprisingly, discovers, she had been married briefly in Apex. Like her, he has risen rapidly, from town loafer to millionaire. They are the male and female versions of the ferociously predatory American—the "Invaders," Ralph Marvell calls them. Always ambivalent toward Lily, Mrs. Wharton entirely withdraws her sympathy in depicting Undine. Named after a hair-waving lotion which her father had marketed, she is essentially a product. The imagery of gilding, of light, of money, jewels, of unopened books, and of the surfaces and textures of objects—particularly the reflection which Undine always seeks in her omnipresent mirrors—declare and define her externality.

"Fiercely independent and yet passionately imitative," Undine takes on the coloration of her successive environments—for "it was instinctive with her to become...the person she thought her interlocutors expected her to be." But at each level of her social rise, her tentative glimpse of "something beyond" leaves her dissatisfied with her new identity and achievement. Thus she is ever alien from the society that, as she supposed, would give

---

[86] To Lily's repeated references to *The Eumenides*, compare Dreiser's personal affirmation: "I acknowledge the Furies. I believe in them. I have heard the disastrous beating of their wings." (*Dawn* [New York, 1931], p. 6.)

her fulfillment. The achievement that brings knowledge also brings discontent. To be sure, this is an old theme in literature, as in life; but Mrs. Wharton so vividly portrays Undine's terrible, tenacious energy of aspiration and frustration that Undine, though not nearly so fine a character as Lily, nevertheless possesses a brutally memorable character. Though she learns and in moments knows that "success may be as fatiguing as failure," she pursues her predatory course through four marriages. Even at the conclusion of her ironically triumphant career, although "she had everything she wanted, . . . she still felt at times, that there were other things she might want if she knew about them." The perpetual need to rise brings with it the torment of achievement and, as the book ends, she determines that "the one part she was really made for," a diplomat's wife, is one she can never attain.

Against the Spraggs, the Elmer Moffats, the Millard Blinches, and the Indiana Frusks of the new American world, the Lawrence Seldens or the Ralph Marvells—their names tell their story—are helpless. The shadow of the crudely new falls ominously upon the children of light, who manage to preserve their world only at the tragic cost of hollow inactivity. Ever tempted by the new, the unfeeling, the showy, and the loud, they are driven to affirm the nostalgic, the primacy of inarticulate traditions, and of contemplative sensibility. All of Mrs. Wharton's men are made increasingly hollow by the new. Raymond de Chelles sums up their feelings of impotence in his indictment of Undine:

> You come among us speaking our language and not knowing what we mean; wanting the things we want, and not knowing why we want them; aping our weaknesses, exaggerating our follies, ignoring or ridiculing all we care about, . . . and we're fools enough to imagine that because you copy our ways and pick up our slang you understand anything about the things that make life decent and honourable for us!

So, likewise, at the end of *The Age of Innocence* (1920) Mrs. Wharton puts into striking perspective the true relevance of the struggle in morals and manners that Newland Archer has gone through. His son, Dallas, is the updated version of an innocence that believes itself receptive to all experience. "What's the use of making mysteries?" he asks. "It only makes people want to nose 'em out." Confident of his knowledge, spontaneous in his enthusiasms, self-assured because without the rudiments of hesitation or reserve, Dallas belongs "body and soul to the new generation." Largely unconcerned with the sensitivities of the previous generation, he yet knows and reveals what Newland had not known—that Newland's wife, May, all the while had known how near he had come to leaving her for Ellen:

> ". . . But mother said—"
> "Your mother?"
> "Yes: the day before she died. . . . [she] said she knew we were safe with you, and always would be, because once, when she asked you to, you'd given up the thing you most wanted."
> . . . At length, [Newland] said in a low voice: "She never asked me."
> "No. I forgot. You never did ask each other anything, did you?"

If Dallas has achieved the freedom from convention whereby to marry Fanny Beaufort, he has lost the ability to understand the responsibilities to traditions that both prevented Newland from fleeing with Ellen Olenska and simultaneously dignified his moral choice. Transfigured by tradition, human waste becomes spiritual wealth. Newland shows the relevance of his tradition by his recognition and acceptance of the essential human rightness of the choice toward which it guided him. In the "hieroglyphic world" of old New York, the suffering which Newland prevents compensates for the suffering he undergoes. Set by the self-sufficient, external Dallas—who could neither willingly accept suffering nor realize that he might inflict it on others—Newland illustrates the continuing relevance of tradition. It is the principle of his heroism—and his wife May's. Described in terms of radiance, transparency, and pure light as a superficial being, May is only at the last, in Dallas's revelation—the "crucial instance" of this book—shown to have depths of inarticulate but indescribably passionate love that Newland never guessed were there. Not the pink and white surface, but her torn and muddy wedding dress stands finally forth as the appropriate symbol for May. "How rich in suffering and incommunicable love must have been her buried life!" Louis Coxe has written.[87] Precisely because they are willing to bury their lives to preserve others', May and Newland transcend and so preserve their own lives.

From giving the irresponsible pleasure-seeking of the characters in *The House of Mirth* dramatic significance by implying what sort of heritage its frivolity destroys, Mrs. Wharton moved in *The Age of Innocence* to a more direct rendering of the value salvaged through tradition in the face of personal and social disintegration. In her four-volume series of 1924[88] she rendered even more directly, but certainly with less skill, the transition from the pre-Civil War and commercial to the postwar, industrial New York. Finally, her autobiography, *A Backward Glance* (1934), in effect resumes where *Old New York* (1924) leaves off. There were obviously strong compulsions for Mrs. Wharton to move from a fictive and historical to a personal affirmation of tradition. Her autobiography was an extension and completion of the impulses which drove her fiction. Considering her writing as a whole, it is clear that she used literature as a means of preserving, establishing, and even of creating her ideals for culture and civilization. Her early book, *The Decoration of Houses* (1897), for instance, is the codification of the eclectic principles of the World's Columbian Exposition, just as Harriet Prescott Spofford's *Art Decoration Applied to Furniture* (1877) earlier celebrated the popular triumph of genteel taste encouraged by Philadelphia's Centennial Exposition in 1876. Settling upon Italian Renaissance decoration as best adapted to modern use, Mrs. Wharton repeatedly inculcates the necessity for steadfast allegiance to fixed and formal style in life as in art. Later, in her Italian and French travel books, in her work on technique in fiction, and her interpretative *French Ways and their Mean-*

---

[87] "What Edith Wharton saw in Innocence" in *Edith Wharton: A Collection of Critical Essays*, p. 160.   [88] *False Dawn (The 'Forties), The Old Maid (The 'Fifties), The Spark (The 'Sixties),* and *New Year's Day (The 'Seventies).*

ing (1919), she set forth the manners and morals of the European scene, against which her fictional studies of New York—not concluded until her posthumous final volume, *The Buccaneers* (1938)—must be projected to be understood.

Seen in this context, *A Backward Glance* is Edith Wharton's ultimate strategy of affirmation. Unable sooner or later to depend wholly on the external, imposed forms of the tradition that in the later nineteenth century seemed to be so rapidly breaking up that one almost supposed it never to have existed, American writers wrote, first or last, autobiography. Knowing personally what Tocqueville had observed about the rapidity of change in America, they guaranteed social order by tying it to the individual consciousness and testifying to its continuance in their own beings. To Henry James's complaint that there was little material for the novelist in a rudimentary social order like America's, Howells replied emphatically: "We have the whole of human life remaining."[89] Thus have many Americans replied to their fears; and turning to human nature, they turned naturally to themselves. Lacking confidence in the external orders of tradition, they made theirs the tradition of the selfhood emerging from within.

Mrs. Wharton's ability to find solace in the orders of art, decoration, morals, and manners is well testified to by the series of books that have been discussed. Even as the Indiana Frusks and Undine Spraggs sweep away the old, she could fasten briefly and lovingly upon a room, a street, a house, or a family to incarnate the valued antique. But by the 1930s the relics of that age were past, or passing. Its rooms, streets, and houses had been demolished or defaced. Its representative men were dead. Only a chosen few remained, and old New York lived only in their memory. "If anyone had suggested to me, before 1914, to write my reminiscenses," Edith Wharton remarked,

> I should have answered that my life had been too uneventful to be worth recording. Indeed, I had never even thought of recording it for my own amusement, and the fact that until 1918 I never kept even the briefest of diaries has greatly hampered this tardy reconstruction. Not until the successive upheavals which culminated in the catastrophe of 1914, had "cut all likeness from the name" of old New York, did I begin to see its pathetic picturesqueness.[90]

Abandoning the fiction which evokes the old by focusing upon its symbols, she makes a symbol of herself—makes her own consciousness representative— through the meditations of *A Backward Glance*. Her persona is the "assiduous relic-hunter" who collects the "smallest fragments...before the last of those who knew the live structure are swept away with it."[91] She is the reverential archaeologist of an Atlantis-like New York. Preserving a past by preserving her self through memory, she solves the problem of isolation. Remembering a past into existence, she finds her place.

[89] "James's Hawthorne," *Atlantic Monthly* (February, 1880), reprinted in *Discovery of a Genius: William Dean Howells and Henry James,* ed. Albert Mordell (New York, 1961), p. 96. [90] *A Backward Glance,* p. 6. [91] P. 7.

Like Edith Wharton, Theodore Dreiser redeemed the past through memory and thus relieved his alienation from an inimical present. Knowing only a City of Man, he contrived to recall a City of God. Without Wharton's inherited and temperamental ability to situate value in traditional orders, he turned sooner, more naturally, and more insistently to autobiography.

In *A Traveller at Forty* (1913), Dreiser set forth on his pilgrimage to Europe. Reversing the American westward journey, he is—only on first consideration surprisingly—in the literary tradition of such earlier travelers as DeForest, Taylor, Twain, Howells, and Mrs. Wharton herself. Everywhere impressed, while yet indubitably faithful to his Americanism, he seeks out our English, French, and German cousins, seeing resemblance at every turn of the tour. Charmed in France by "the very medieval air," finding the marble yellowed by age in Pisa "gloriously satisfying," feeling "at home" in London "for the first time in almost any great city," Dreiser makes the obedient American bow to a past which he suddenly seems to have without paying for. Seeking out the romance of this past, he comes as close as Mrs. Wharton to realizing the way tradition energizes the imagination:

> I was seeing things which, after all, I thought, did not depend so much upon their exterior beauty or vast presence as upon the import of their lineage or connections. They were beautiful in a low, dark way, and certainly they were tinged with an atmosphere of age and respectability. After all, since life is a figment of the brain, built-up notions of things are really far more impressive in many cases than the things themselves.... It is almost impossible any more to disassociate the real from the fictitious or, better, spiritual. There is something here which is not of brick and stone at all, but which is purely a matter of thought. It is disembodied poetry; noble ideas; delicious memories of great things; and these, after all, are better than brick and stone.[92]

Quarreling with democracy throughout the book, he follows the conventional dialectic of the American tourist by at last asserting faith in the future of American civilization. He learns to have both present and past, America and Europe, himself and tradition.

"Of dreams and the memory of them is life compounded."[93] With these words Dreiser concluded his reenactment of the westward march in his second autobiographical account, *A Hoosier Holiday* (1916). While *A Traveller at Forty* is much like Mark Twain's *Innocents Abroad*, *A Hoosier Holiday* is Dreiser's *Roughing It*.[94] He recounts ambivalently his return to the scenes of his boyhood on an auto trip from New York. He is uncompromisingly aware of the dullness and stupidity, the hypocritical morality, and the ruined lives in Indiana. He recalls the intensity of his own suffering and relives his hatred for his father. He feels anew his desire to escape this alien environment.[95] But he still silvers over his birthplace, Terre Haute,

---

[92] New York. Quotations on pp. 207, 311, 79, 58. [93] Dreiser, *A Hoosier Holiday* (New York and London, 1916), p. 513. [94] Dreiser, who worked in St. Louis, wrote in *A Book About Myself* that "Mark Twain had idled about here for a time, drunk and hopeless," and he was well aware of Twain as his literary forebear. (p. 88.) [95] "All the world was outside and I, sitting on our porch...all alone, used to wonder and wonder. When would I go out into the world? Where would I go? What would I do? What see?" (*A Hoosier Holiday*, p. 77.)

with the romance of dreams, not the less appealing because illusory. Dreiser had written *Jennie Gerhardt* and the first two Cowperwood books during the five years previous to this return. These had been tough-minded portrayals of the tragedy that lay deeply at the heart of man's life, dramatizing existence as endless and inexplicable flux. But now, in *A Hoosier Holiday*, he moved in the opposite direction and rendered the continuing idyll of youth in the country: of contentment as against desire, of dream as against disillusion. Now he sees this Middle Western region as "holy Granges— Mecca, Medina—the blessed isles of the West":

> You have no idea what a charm these places have—what a song they sing— to one who has ever been of them and then gone out into the world and changed and cannot see life anymore through the medium—the stained glass medium, if you will—of the time and the mood which we call our youth. . . .
> How good it all tasted after New York! And what a spell it cast. I can scarcely make you understand, I fear. . . . The intervening years fizzled away and once more I saw myself quite clearly in this region, with the ideas and moods of my youth still dominant.

Unhesitatingly, he wishes to "restore it all"—the pain, the suffering, the poverty—but also, as he now sees it, the ecstatic, hopeful joy of youth.[96] To the cities of his novels he contrasts the countryside of his youth; to defeat, illusion; to experience, revived innocence. To be sure, because Dreiser always knew that city and country merely symbolize different aspects of the same human condition, he remains ambivalent. But, saying with Whitman, "I am the man. . . .I suffered. . . .I was there," he momentarily constructs as actualities the aspirations of his personal dreaming.

Polarizing Europe and America in his autobiographies, Dreiser, like Twain, made clear the extent to which his travels East and West were merely symbols of his inward exploration by emphasizing the personal equation of the inward journey in *A Book About Myself* (1922). Here, restricting the account of his interior life to a history of his newspaper days, he traces the evolution of his consciousness in contact with newspapers, the gathering of fact and detail that characterizes the state of the modern consciousness. In Chicago, St. Louis, Cleveland, Pittsburgh, and New York, he traces the development within himself of indifference, a deep malaise. Much as in *A Book About Myself*, in *The Color of a Great City* (1923) he lets the metropolis take and shape his mind. In both books he shows his self becoming a reflection of the city's impersonal machine-like brutality, but also of its romance; and in the structure of his consciousness he makes no distinction between these polarities.

In particular, *A Book About Myself* is an account of Dreiser's growing understanding of the actualities of metropolitan existence. By learning how to report the news of the city he understands how to dispel its myths. He comes to recognize "the pagan or unmoral character [of reporting], as contrasted with the heavy religionistic and moralistic point of view seemingly prevailing in the editorial office proper." In the city newsroom,

[96] Quotations on pp. 256, 260–61, 309.

he wrote, "the mask was off."[97] His newspaper work thus comes to symbolize the stripping away of social, political, and economic myths in the pursuit of personal truth. Dreiser early specialized in the interview. Interviewing the theosophist Annie Besant, the fighter John L. Sullivan, Henry Stanley, and Paderewski, Dreiser asked each the same question: "What did they think of life, its meaning?" Taught by the city room to drive through the mask, he put shams aside with his essential question. His progress in the course of *A Book About Myself* from paper to paper, city to city, then, represents an intellectual progress whereby he stumbles toward truth. Not Dreiser alone, but several of his contemporaries had found their imaginations stimulated by this abrupt revelation of the gulf between the ideal and real. Twain, Howells, Bierce, Crane, and Harold Frederic all were touched and moved by the disillusioning experience of the city room. In this sense, Dreiser makes his increasing awareness representative of a significant aspect of the American imagination. Buffeted and beaten by his agonized consciousness, he is increasingly ineffectual as a reporter. But his failure to harden his sensibilities allows him at last to become the writer he vows to become as the book ends.

If Edith Wharton, though inheriting a usable tradition, had nevertheless to guarantee its continuing actuality by asserting it autobiographically, Dreiser, who lacked such a past (as he makes clear in *Dawn*), had repeatedly to rewrite his autobiography in order to *make* a past, one centering upon what he personally had seen, done, and learned.[98] Carrie, Clyde, Cowperwood, and Witla have no pasts, or at least are repeatedly compelled to shed them. But to project the tragedies of their alienation Dreiser himself sought a personal sense of the past. His repeated need to reconduct this search suggests how completely the rootlessness of his characters reflected his own. The only pasts he could have were those that he could find (as in Europe) or refind (as in Indiana) or recreate (as in his account of his newspaper days). Hesitating and tentative, they were nevertheless all he needed.

THE INVISIBLE CITY

Joseph Hudnut, a recent analyst of city life, has made clear that modern man is a city dweller, not essentially from economic necessity or for metropolitan pleasures,

> but by a hunger which transcends both practical and sensuous experience, a hunger seldom revealed by appearances, seldom acknowledged in our consciousness. We are held in the city by our need of a collective life; by our need of belonging and sharing; by our need of that direction and frame which our individual lives gain from a larger life lived together.

[97] Quotations on pp. 151, 152. [98] In addition to the personal accounts discussed above, Dreiser intended to treat his literary career in *A Literary Apprenticeship* and *Literary Experiences*, both incomplete and unpublished at the time of his death. *Dawn* (1931) is an account of his youth in Indiana up to the time when *A Book About Myself* begins. A final travel book is *Dreiser Looks at Russia* (1928).

There are city habits and city thoughts, city moralities and loyalties, city harmonies of valuations which surround us in cities with an authority and system which, whatever may be the turmoil in which they exist, are yet friendly to the human spirit and essential to its well being. Beneath the visible city... there lies an invisible city laid out in patterns of idea and behavior, which channels the citizen with silent persistent pressures and, beneath the confusion, noise, and struggle of the material and visible city, makes itself known and reconciles us to all of these.[99]

Such satisfactions as the city would offer for the twentieth-century American were brought into question in the late nineteenth century by the reformers' emphasis on the shame of cities and the agrarian's insistence that true virtue resided only in nature. The earlier and wiser recognition, by Americans from John Adams and Franklin to Emerson and Hawthorne, that the American identity was eradicably marked by metropolitanism, was threatened by these stereotypes of urban worthlessness. The beneficence of the invisible city was submerged by the insistence on the evils of the material metropolis. It is certainly true, as Ralph Ellison has brilliantly shown in his novel *Invisible Man* (1952), that the individual can be made invisible by the mass collective life of the modern city. But he may be invisible anywhere. The new architecture of urban expansion, monumental demonstrations like that in the Columbian Exposition of the connection between the city and civilization, the paintings of John Sloan and his followers (Glackens illustrated Dreiser's *A Traveller at Forty*), and city planners like Frederick Law Olmsted have all proved that the value of the invisible city is to help man to be visible again by reviewing himself. But it was chiefly by the writers who have been discussed here that a vital sense of the uses of the city was preserved, enlarged, and transmitted. Using the techniques of literary realism, they stripped away the economic struggle and blasé pleasures of metropolitan life to reveal beneath these the permanently satisfying nature of the invisible city. Unwilling to be trapped by the extreme alternatives of progress or poverty, they knew and showed that these were not exclusive, and were hardly the basic choices of modern man. Norris, balancing *McTeague* with *Blix*; Fuller, setting his studies of energetic Chicago life against an enervated, though benign, Europe; Dreiser, solving the problem of metropolitan alienation in a series of volumes which finally affirm metropolitan community; and Edith Wharton, salvaging out of the chaos of the new the ancient invisible city, preserved by being remembered— each in his own way helped to rewrite the news of the city for the American imagination.

[99] *Architecture and the Spirit of Man* (Cambridge, 1949), pp. 159–60.

SEVEN

The Apocalypse of the Mind

Whether nature enjoy a substantial existence without, or only in the apocalypse of the mind, it is alike useful and alike venerable to me.

—Emerson, *Nature* (1836)

He was to go without many things, ever so many—as all persons do in whom contemplation takes so much the place of action; but every-where...he was to enjoy more than anything...wondering and dawdling and gaping: he was really, I think, much to profit by it. What it all appreciably gave him...would be difficult to state; but it seems to him...an education like another: feeling, as he has come to do more and more, that no education avails for the intelligence that doesn't stir in it some subjective passion, and that on the other hand, anything that does so act is largely educative....Strange, indeed, furthermore, are some of the things that have *stirred a subjective passion....*

—Henry James, *A Small Boy and Others* (1913)

Walt Whitman's Specimen Man and the "Genteel Little Creatures"

Speaking of Pfaff's, the famous bar that was the center of New York Bohemianism, Richard Henry Stoddard confessed: "Once I walked down the steps and stood at the door. I saw Walt Whitman and others inside, but...I did not enter."[1] This is a pathetic scene—Stoddard pressing his face momentarily against the window to a gay Bohemianism he had to reject—but revelatory of the state of poetry in the post-Civil War era. Neither Stoddard nor his fellow idealists—Stedman, Taylor, Aldrich, or Gilder—could enter Whitman's Pfaff's.[2] They were unwilling to dedicate their art to the exploration of the protean guises of the self, though society never more needed individual self-understanding than in the period of self-evasion following the War. Instead, like their audience, they made a cult of evasion, a myth and literature from the guises they could adopt. Stoddard and Taylor liked

[1] *Recollections,* ed. Ripley Hitchcock (New York, 1903), p. 66. [2] Whitman, as usual, had the last word. Asked his opinion of Stedman, he smiled and said: "Stedman is, after all, nothing but a sophisticated dancing master." Sadakichi [Hartman], *Conversations With Walt Whitman* (New York, 1895), p. 17.

279

to pretend that they were Keats and Shelley reincarnate; and their peers similarly felt themselves part of a previous age. Bent on preserving literature from the crass materialism that they saw everywhere, they declared themselves champions of Ideal Poetry. In their gentle insistence on the primacy of beauty, their conviction that art was allied to polite morality, their devotion to the feminine and exotic, and their fear of science they offered a romanticism which, not surprisingly, attracted large followings of convinced disciples; for their Ideality provided convenient forms to disengage the mind from experience. This was a refuge that Americans readily elevated into a national literary doctrine so fixed that in the '90s, Howells, even after the accomplishments in literary realism of James, Twain, and himself, could ruefully lament: "I perceive now that the monstrous rag-baby of romanticism is as firmly in the saddle as it was before the joust began, and that it always will be, as long as the children of men are childish."[3]

The Ideal became the official code of, and gave the countersigns to, the genteel tradition. Much earlier, even before the War, Hawthorne had complained about "the damned mob of scribbling women"[4] who produced and sustained the literature of ideality. Certainly from the '40s on, popular literature was bedewed with the cheerful tears of sentimental indulgence. Associating Beauty and Culture with the Antique—even Hawthorne half desired the picturesque country of shadow, antiquity, and mystery— Americans fled the forms of newness. The Genteel surreptitiously put modern plumbing into the romantic Grecian villas, Gothic cottages, and Italian mansions that Alexander Jackson Davis and others had constructed. The official philosophical programs of academic Genteel thought were no less antiquated. In short, after the War—perhaps largely accelerated by though not necessarily in reaction to it—there was an increasing split in America between folk and Genteel culture, between naturalism and ideality, self and romance. T. W. Higginson acutely remarked in 1871 that for years

> the people of our Northern States were habitually in advance of their institutions of learning, in courage and comprehensiveness of thought. There were long years during which the most cultivated scholar, so soon as he embraced an unpopular opinion, was apt to find the college doors closed against him, and only the country lyceum—the people's college—left open. Slavery had to be abolished before the most accomplished orator of the nation could be invited to address the graduates of his own university. The first among American scholars was nominated year after year, only to be rejected, before the academic societies of his own neighborhood.[5]

Yet at the same time, Theodore Parker, Wendell Phillips, William Lloyd Garrison, and Ralph Waldo Emerson were enthusiastically demanded by the rural lecture associations. The professor had ceased to be Man Thinking, content with being Man Maintaining. Comte, Mill, Fourier, and even Hume

---

[3] Quoted in Harper, *The House of Harper*, p. 323. [4] Quoted in Caroline Ticknor, *Hawthorne and His Publisher* (Boston and New York, 1913), p. 141. [5] *Atlantic Essays* (Boston, 1871), p. 61.

were made to seem academically respectable by the moral philosophers. Not until Sumner, James, and Dewey injected the implicit naturalism of American life into academic thought did it begin to swing away from the defense of philosophical ideality.

As the War and its aftermath revealed the widening divergence between the offical defenders of ideality and its critics, the idealists closed ranks in positions more and more extreme. Their aesthetics—summarized in Stedman's *The Nature and Elements of Poetry* (1892), for instance—now seem hollow and unconvincing. A double standard for American and European literature began to emerge whereby foreign authors—as reflections of a decadent Europe—were allowed, even encouraged, to indulge in the revelations of corruption forbidden to Americans and the American scene. Louisa May Alcott, for one, found *Anna Karenina* and *Pere Goriot* exciting, but warned the author of *Huckleberry Finn:* "If Mr. Clemens cannot think of something better to tell our pure-minded lads and lasses, he had best stop writing for them."[6] Similarly, Theodore Dreiser tells in *A Book About Myself* of two friends who, wanting to write a sordid tale of American life, naturally placed the scene in Paris. In short, publishers, critics, editors, and academics defended an ideality which, reacting more and more violently to American life, was progressively attenuated. Henry Wells's formulation—"as industrial society grew uglier the personal life grew more refined"[7]—suggests how the romantic cultivation of sensibility as a sign of distinction led to the development in the later nineteenth century of high-strung, over-sensitive reactions. Offended by their brash world, the idealists insisted all the more on a romantic one, less and less usable as a guide to action. Gentle with their rosy initiates, they estranged or exiled James, Dreiser, Twain, Mrs. Wharton, Henry Adams and a score of others whose shattered, lonely lives testify to the official power of the idealists to reject and deny.

Such writers as these had severely criticized ideality by testing it in their own experience. All wrote autobiographies almost by necessity; but, more important, all clearly wrote from an urgency for self-knowledge. Certainly, in the later nineteenth century, the quality of a writer's life assumed increased importance. Cooper, Poe, Hawthorne, Emerson, Lowell, and their contemporaries wrote no autobiographies but adjusted their psyches to convention in various other ways. But, following in Whitman's tradition, almost every important writer who emerged after the War was compelled to become increasingly *aware*, to move in art toward self-revelation. Necessarily, much of the result of this remained private literature. Henry Adams printed all of his later books privately and provided that *The Education* be released only after his death. During her life-time, Emily Dickinson published only a few poems, all anonymously. Curiously resembling Henry Adams and Emily Dickinson in this respect, even such an ostensibly public writer as Mark Twain wrote hundreds of pieces never

---

6 Quoted in Beer, *The Mauve Decade*, p. 25.   7 *Introduction to Emily Dickinson* (New York, 1947), p. 173.

intended for publication. His comment on one essay—"I will leave it behind and utter it from the grave"[8]—applies to the practice of all three writers in private self-revelation. By striking out for new territories of self-understanding, they banished themselves from the older social territories, and were thus exiled from society. Estranged from the official conventions, they published the conventions of the soul. "One may set out with the best will in the world to talk of more important matters," Howells wrote, "but one ends in talking mainly about oneself."[9]

Self-revelation had been sanctioned and encouraged by several intellectual strains in America. Puritanism, as has been widely noted, used the "Personal Narrative"—Jonathan Edwards's phrase—as a guide to spiritual introspection and self- as well as social-evaluation. Moreover, the Scottish Common Sense philosophy, which retained a hold on American philosophy until the 1870s, was essentially psychological (in contrast to Kantian epistemology, which dominated philosophical method in Europe). The leading Scottish philosophical opponent of Hume, Thomas Reid, insisted that the philosopher is basically an anatomist of the mind, "for it is his own mind only that he can examine with any degree of accuracy and distinctness."[10] Several generations of Americans were thus taught that philosophy and introspection were identical. Transcendentalism, obviously, continued this psychological tradition. In his Journal for 1833, Emerson wrote: "Wherever we go, whatever we do, self is the sole subject we study and learn."[11] Thoreau's famous comment—"I, on my side, require of every writer, first or last, a simple and sincere account of his own life"[12]—translates Emersonianism into aesthetics. Finally, Darwinian (and eventually Freudian) psychology read the history and future of man in the involved matrix of his consciousness.

Toward the end of his life, Howells decided that no matter was more important to him than autobiography, and began talking openly and freely about himself in a series of volumes. Sooner or later agreeing with him, American writers have sent their egos out into a hostile universe in perpetual reassessment of the history of experience. Offering their personalities as paradigmatic, turning their historicity into archetype, the American has made a myth of the self, ever going forth like Whitman's child, ever terrorized and tormented by confronting the not-self wherein resides the experience he requires. Restating Whitman's "Camerado, this is no book; /Who touches this touches a man"—willing to stand thus exposed—the American artist is, as Pound observed, "ready to endure personally a strain which his craftsmanship would scarcely endure."[13] Nowhere better is the pathetic tragedy of the confrontation of the Me by the Not-Me (Emerson's terms, adopted later by Whitman) characterized than in one of Edward Bellamy's notebook entries:

8 Quoted in Paine, *Mark Twain*, Vol. II, p. 724. 9 Quoted in Harper, *The House of Harper*, p. 327. 10 Reid's *Inquiry into the Human Mind on the Principles of Common Sense* in *Selections from the Scottish Philosophy of Common Sense*, ed. G. A. Johnston (Chicago and London, 1915), p. 13. 11 *Journals of Ralph Waldo Emerson 1820–1872*, ed. Edward Waldo Emerson and Waldo Emerson Forbes (Boston and New York, 1910), Vol. III (1833–1835), p. 28. 12 *Walden* (New York, 1951 [1854]), ed. Basil Willey, pp. 17–18. 13 *Patria Mia*, p. 63.

I must write me a fable of man that shall present him under the similitude of a genius doomed to walk the earth in banishment, toil, bitterness, misery, until he learn the secret of his own shape and form, and to this end seeking everywhere a mirror and finding only fragments too small or too blurred to render back a full reflection. Poor genius, I am sorry for thee, even if thou wert not my self.[14]

Vainly seeking the world in broken bits of mirrors, the writer made the search itself, not its resolution, his subject.

This had been Whitman's theme from the beginning and, predictably, as he observed in the essay, "A Backward Glance O'er Travel'd Roads" (1888), "I have not gain'd the acceptance of my own time."[15] In this Whitman attempted to briefly set down the personal and cultural conditions that made his self-investigation not only desirable but necessary.[16] His poems, he says in writing the prose revelation of his poetic exploration, have

mainly been the outcropping of my own emotional and other personal nature— an attempt, from first to last, to put *a Person*, a human being (myself, in the latter half of the Nineteenth-Century, in America) freely, fully and truly on record.

His extended prose counterpart to *Leaves of Grass* was *Specimen Days* (1882), in which he depicted himself as the specimen, archetypal man of his age, commanded to write autobiography in the fullness of self, and responding vigorously to worlds within and worlds without. Never before so filled, body and soul, with the mandate of self to set down the specimens of his ego, he obeys the happy hour's command to write "the most wayward, spontaneous, fragmentary book ever printed."[17] But it is a waywardness that, much like Whitman's 8,000-mile walk across America during 1851–53, goes variously outward only to plunge intensely inward. Writing his book as a journey through life, Whitman asks, as the Idealists could not, the crucial questions of the extent and limits of identity:

What is the fusing explanation and tie—what the relation between the (radical, democratic) Me, the human identity of understanding, emotions, spirit, etc., on the one side, of and with the (conservative) Not Me, the whole of the material objective universe and laws, with what is behind them in time and space, on the other side?

Without doubt, this is the question that he learned from Emerson's *Nature* (1836); but a half century had made a difference in both the terms and the urgency of the answers. A decade before Whitman's death, in 1882, when he was sixty-three, and at a time when self was evaded, Whitman set down for himself and his age the elements of his own "simple separate person," as well as the nature of its relation to the "Democratic En-Masse,"

[14] Quoted in Arthur E. Morgan, *Edward Bellamy,* pp. 180–81. [15] Quotation from "A Backward Glance O'er Travel'd Roads" in *November Boughs* (Philadelphia, 1888), where it serves as the preface. This essay was later used as the conclusion to the authorized 1891–92 edition of *Leaves of Grass.* [16] It is not without significance that among those writers emerging between the wars, Edith Wharton, virtually the last of them living, should in 1935 turn to Whitman for the title of her own autobiography. [17] In this chapter the quotations from *Specimen Days* are in *Specimen Days and Collected Writings* (Philadelphia, 1882–83).

by attempting to "symbolize two or three specimen interiors, personal or other, out of the myriads of my time, the middle range of the nineteenth-century in the New World."

Specimen Days, then, is a bridge—between the Me and the Not-Me that it understands and absorbs, between literature and life, and Whitman and his fellows. Repeatedly Whitman employs bridging images in his book—streets, boats, ferries, great avenues, and railroads. But more important is the way in which he makes his book a report on how he himself can bridge the abysses between man, society, and nature through the power of sympathy and sensibility. He had been one of the first to record the dominance of the will to power over moral sensibility in his earlier *Democratic Vistas* (1871), no less satirical than the books of Twain, DeForest, and Adams, which appeared at about the same time. In *Specimen Days* Whitman uses the War to symbolize the lucid and absurd indifference to life that he detected in the early '80s.[18] His book, exerting a contrary influence, is a way of restoring the balances by proving the possibility of responsiveness. Emerson had challenged man to go forth and, becoming a "transparent eyeball," dissolve the Not-Me in the Me. "Somehow," Whitman says, "I seemed to get identity with each and everything around me, in its condition." In this "Adamic air bath," "Nature was naked, and I was also." In the book, Whitman, calling himself a "good walker," daily invites nature and society to be transfigured in him, as he steps literally and imaginatively from place to place. He meditates upon the "lucky" minutes that bring "in a brief flash the culmination of years of reading and travel and thought," and makes his wayward book from scores of such epiphanies. In returning to familiar places, enjoying past and present delights, responding to war and peace, to city crowds or rural rambles, cataloging the various fragments of beauty, social and natural—all calling us to love the world—"receiving impressions," as James would say, Whitman demonstrates the continuing possibilities of man even in the depths of the brown decades.

Specimen Days is also Whitman's history as a poet. Having nearly brought *Leaves of Grass* to its final form by 1882, he writes in *Specimen Days* a book reporting on both the poetry that he had gathered in his volume and the raw materials of life that he had failed to transform into verse—those jottings that are "never to be possibly said or sung" except as they can sing now in his prose. He is unwilling to falsify the immediacy of his responses and so gives them unaltered as notes-in-progress, since he aims not at factual truth but at "the deepest veracity of all." His plans for *Leaves of Grass;* his comments on Poe, Longfellow, Emerson, Bryant, and Whittier; his lists of the titles he proposed for his autobiography; his remarks on the nature of poetry and poetic symbolism; his theory

---

18 In the massacre of seventeen Confederate prisoners Whitman understood the trans-formation of modern man:

I was curious to know whether some of the Union soldiers, some few (some one or two at least of the youngsters), did not abstain from shooting on the helpless men. Not one. There was no exultation, very little said, almost nothing, yet every man contributed his shot.

of the American epic—these all make *Specimen Days* a life of Whitman's art within the art itself of his life. Conrad Aiken writes in one of his poems: "We need a theme? then let that be our theme."[19] Whitman makes his autobiography the joyful discovery of themes. For he recognized—as the "genteel little creatures" who opposed him could not—that in an age of public evasion the poet who could thus insist upon self was the true hero, the Specimen Man of later nineteenth-century America.

Emily Dickinson

For nearly thirty years, Emily Dickinson projected her consciousness into a world devastatingly hostile to the self. Her more private America was no less chaotic than the one Whitman or Adams confronted, and her personal cosmos was ruled by terror and alienation. "She died all her life," Conrad Aiken wrote, "she probed death daily."[20] And out of the daily loss she sent back the triumph of life and poetry. Writing no fewer than 1,775 poems—perhaps as many as 366 of them in 1862—she composed a natural history of the self by plumbing its subterranean secrets. "The soul must go by Death alone, so, it must by life, if it is a soul./If a committee — no matter,"[21] she wrote to Mrs. Josiah Gilbert Holland. Making its own conventions, selecting its own society (as she herself put it), her soul never conformed to collectives, but went alone. While Henry Adams made a drama of the failure of the public self, she made a tragic poetry of personal solitude. That solitude was partly her own construction—an aspect of the needs of her art—and partly a condition of her New England circumstance.

In *Mercy Philbrick's Choice* (1876), her friend Helen Hunt Jackson portrayed a "unique and incalcuable" poetess whose unwillingness to publish resembles Emily's. "Truth, truth, truth, was still the war-cry of her soul," Mrs. Jackson writes of her heroine. The daughter of an Amherst professor, Mrs. Jackson understood in the fragmentation of the New England community and the dissipation of the Puritan heritage the sources of physical and mental isolation:

> In the ordinary New England town, neighborhood never means much: there is a dismal lack of cohesion to the relations between people. The community is loosely held together by a few accidental points of contact or common interest. The individuality of individuals is, by a strange sort of paradox, at once respected and ignored. This is indifference rather than consideration, selfishness rather than generosity.... Our people are living, on the whole. the dullest lives that are lived in this world, by the so-called civilized....[22]

We have already explored the disintegration of the New England myth that provided tragic material for Mary Wilkins, Sarah Jewett, Robinson,

[19] *Time in the Rock,* "II" in *Collected Poems* (New York, 1953), p. 666. [20] "Emily Dickinson" in *A Reviewer's ABC: Collected Criticism of Conrad Aiken, 1916 to the Present* (New York, 1958), p. 162. [21] *The Letters of Emily Dickinson,* ed. Thomas H. Johnson and Theodora Ward (Cambridge, Mass., 1958), Vol. II, p. 455. The verselike arrangements of Emily Dickinson's letters are indicated with slash-marks. [22] Boston, pp. 13, 283–84.

Frost, and others. Emily Dickinson came to adulthood during the time when New England was just beginning to feel this sapping of vitality. She came to consciousness just as Puritanism and Transcendentalism were seeming less and less satisfactory as world-views. Her emotional life was blooming just as the War was demonstrating how costly emotions could be. She was, in short, part of the tragic material that the regionalists would later explore.

In this context, biographical questions concerning her love life or psychic wound lose some of the importance usually assigned to them. She may indeed have been passionately in love with the Reverend Charles Wadsworth; but it is equally clear that she compensated for the breakup of a relevant public community by forming passionate private attachments to a whole series of individuals—among women, Abiah Root, Jane Humphrey, Louisa Norcross, Elizabeth Holland, Susan Gilbert; and among men, Benjamin Franklin Newton, Vaughan Emmons, Thomas Wentworth Higginson, Samuel Bowles, Josiah Gilbert Holland, and Judge Otis Lord. She may indeed have more and more assumed mannerisms that strike one as essentially psychopathic—wearing white gowns throughout the year[23]; talking to visitors from behind a screen or from another room; speaking of herself as King Charles, Sancho Panza, Herod, King of the Jews, Jeremy Bentham, or "your mad/Emilie."[24] But these, clearly, were all devices by which she preserved her sensitivity, by protecting herself from the inconsequential facts of daily life that would otherwise have drained her emotional responses in her highly tense personal and local atmosphere. They were the ways she remained brilliantly sane.

Certainly her life was daily fraught with tension. Her father she described as "pure and terrible." Higginson called him "evidently a man of the old type, *la vieille roche* of Puritanism."[25] Lonely, rigorous, and remote, her father strengthened the reticence that was hers by Puritan heritage and personal inclination. She did not learn to tell time, she says, until she was fifteen, since she was afraid to confess to her father that she did not understand his explanation when he had attempted to teach her much earlier. Only by "limiting her sources of stimulus,"[26] as Theodora Ward puts it, could she preserve her emotional responsiveness for her poetry. Her biography confirms the connection between poetry and solitude. The beginning of her self-imposed seclusion coincided with the earliest overflow of her emotion into poetry in 1858. By the end of 1865, by which time she had written nearly a thousand poems, her seclusion was complete and irremediable. She knew at what cost she had saved herself—writing, in 1865, "The Missing All — prevented Me/From missing minor Things"[27] and she

---

[23] This was not until 1874. A decade afterward, Mark Twain, too, began to affect white suits.   [24] Jay Leyda, *The Years and Hours of Emily Dickinson* (New Haven, 1960), Vol. I, p. 262; *Letters,* Vol. II, p. 324.   [25] *Letters,* Vol. II, p. 528.   [26] *The Capsule of the Mind: Chapters in the Life of Emily Dickinson* (Cambridge, 1961), p. 72. [27] Quotatious from the poems of Emily Dickinson are in *The Poems of Emily Dickinson,* ed. Thomas H. Johnson (Cambridge, Mass., 1955), 3 Vols. They will be identified by the numbers assigned to them by Johnson, also used in *Final Harvest,* ed. Thomas H. Johnson (Boston, 1961). "The Missing All..." is J. 985.

understood her commitment. Even so, a few years before her death she had an attack diagnosed by her doctor as "a revenge of nerves."[28] Wisely, "I do not cross my father's ground to any house or town," she told Higginson.[29]

Her basic theme, appropriately, is the alienating dissolution of the social community: "I see–New Englandly," she wrote.[30] Her disintegrating New England could not provide the relevant community which might have kept her responses public. It is important to remember, however, that from a distance she was deeply engaged in the larger community of American ideas—a fact that the clichés about her seclusion tend to make us forget. Her mind was never secluded. Daily she read Samuel Bowles's *Springfield Republican,* a fact reflected in her references to Jay Cooke and the Molly Maguires, for instance. The family subscribed as a matter of course to *Scribner's,* which Holland had founded and edited, and to *Harper's.* Her father, a well-known public man, could claim a wide acquaintanceship with people as different as Frederick Law Olmsted and Frances Hodgson Burnett. Emerson visited her brother's house in 1857 and eight years later gave six lectures at Amherst. She was, moreover, exposed to the freshest of ideas. B. F. Newton, her earliest "Master," had given her Emerson's *Poems* while Emerson's thinking was still considered dangerous. Later, in 1877, Emily herself sent a copy of *Representative Men* to Mary Higginson, the wife of another of her masters. Among the other lecturers she heard were Park Benjamin, Wendell Phillips, Henry Ward Beecher, Higginson, and Mark Twain. Harriet Beecher Stowe spent her summers in Amherst to be near her daughter and Calvin Stowe occasionally preached there.

She knew the literature of the best of her literary tradition and of her contemporaries. We must remind ourselves of the breadth of her reading. In letters she refers to Keats, Ruskin, the Brownings, Sir Thomas Browne, Bunyan, Henry Vaughan, Milton, the Brontës, Coleridge, Tennyson, and Cowper. She knew Shakespeare, Dickens, and George Eliot thoroughly. Among Americans she read Hawthorne, Irving, Holmes, Whittier, Longfellow, Theodore Parker, and Horace Bushnell. She ordered a copy of James's *The Europeans* in 1878, and was soon quoting James's stern Mr. Wentworth to inquire of a correspondent: "Where are our moral foundations?"[31] Austin Dickinson read *Huckleberry Finn* aloud to the family as each installment appeared in *The Century.* Clearly, she followed Howells's career with interest: one of her gifts to her sister-in-law, Sue, in 1867 was Howells's recent *Italian Journeys.* She referred to both *A Fearful Responsibility* and *The Undiscovered Country* in letters. With few exceptions—one being her conviction that *Reveries of a Bachelor* was "a great book"[32]—her taste was as unerring, though not as wide, as Howells's. In short, she was widely acquainted with the literature of the '60s and '70s. The dissolution of her social community brought with it frustration and isolation; but it also made possible her compensatory release into this community of the imagination.

---

[28] Quoted in Clark Griffith, *The Long Shadow: Emily Dickinson's Tragic Poetry* (Princeton, 1964), p. 207. [29] *Letters,* Vol. II, p. 460. [30] J. 285. [31] *Letters,* Vol. II, p. 647. [32] *Ibid.,* Vol. I, p. 178.

She could live in art, finding community enough in reading the work of her contemporaries and responding to them, however silently, in her own poetry. She had only a community of one—the poet in the act of writing poetry.

Still, there is no question but that her social isolation was real and almost complete. If she had no vital social community, neither did she really feel the communal guaranties of a stable religion—the kind of community of belief that had, in New England, long served as the basis of the community of man. Not until the general "Awakening" of Western Massachusetts in 1850 did she understand fully the fact and consequences of her isolation. "I am standing alone in rebellion, and growing very careless," she wrote.

> Abby, Mary, Jane, and farthest of all my Vinnie have been seeking, and they all believe they have found; I can't tell you *what* they have found, but *they* think it is something precious. I wonder if it *is?*

"I am alone–all alone" is the reiterated cry of her correspondence during this winter. *She* could not acquiesce:

> The path of duty looks very ugly indeed – and the place where *I* want to go more amiable – a great deal – it is so much easier to do wrong than right – so much pleasanter to be evil than good, I don't wonder that good angels weep – and bad ones sing songs.

In the time of revival the religious community achieved sufficient social coherence to make Emily feel her isolation in a social as well as a spiritual way. From choosing not to attend the missionary Sewing Society, she was "set down as one of those brands almost consumed — and my hardheartedness gets me many prayers."[33] What institutions of spiritual community remained from the Puritan past were closed for Emily. Even the inner beatitudes of the community of the elect she could not accept. Like Harriet Beecher Stowe she never accepted Calvinism. As late as 1880 she pointedly juxtaposed these two comments on a scrap of paper: " 'All liars shall have their part (in the lake that burneth with fire and brimstone)' — Jonathan Edwards — 'And let him that is athirst come' — Jesus."[34]

By 1862, when she told Higginson that the members of her family "are religious — except me — and address an Eclipse, every morning — whom they call their Father — "[35] she was confirmed in her theological isolation and had already begun to translate it into poetry. Rejecting the Puritan past, she wrote down poems in theological revolt—with fear of God and trembling, but also with witty or withering scorn for Him. He is a God arbitrarily indifferent. She put this in an early poem (1862):

[33] The quotations in this paragraph are from *Letters*, Vol. I, pp. 82, 83, 84, 94. [34] Leyda, Vol. I, p. 325. [35] *Letters*, Vol. II, p. 404.

Of Course – I prayed –
And did God Care?
He cared as much as on the Air
A Bird – had stamped her foot –

  * * *

'Twere better Charity
To leave me in the Atom's Tomb –
Merry, and Nought, and gay, and numb
Than this smart Misery.[36]

And in a later (1882) poem:

Those – dying then,
Knew where they went –
They went to God's Right Hand –
That Hand is amputated now
And God cannot be found – [37]

"I don't like Paradise" she writes, and imagines herself running away "From Him – and Holy Ghost – and All – ."[38] Translating the Bible into secular terms, she jests about notions of biblical authority:

The Bible is an antique Volume –
Written by faded Men
At the suggestion of Holy Spectres –
Subjects – Bethlehem –
Eden – the ancient Homestead –
Satan – the Brigadier
Judas – the Great Defaulter –
David – the Troubadour –
Sin – a distinguised Precipice
Others must resist – [39]

 Lacking a divine defense against chaos, she seized upon a secular one. To the divine "No in thunder"—the commandments, the condemnations, and the prohibitions of Puritanism—she could thus speak a "Yea" to the freedom of nature, a "Yea" in symbolic birds and flowers. Loving birds, she wrote, "is economical. It saves going to Heaven."[40] In her verse she imitates the hymn meters of her Puritan heritage; but her poems remain secular hymns. "In the name of the Bee–/And of the Butterfly–/And of the Breeze – Amen!"[41] she concludes one of her earliest poems. In these fragile aspects of the natural world her vision resides. For, as with Emerson, through nature one glimpses oneself, the nature within. "Gethsemane – /Is but a Province – in the Being's Centre," she insisted.[42] Celebrating her own creation and crucifixion, she is the self-contained Emersonian:

[36] J. 376. [37] J. 1551. [38] J. 413. [39] J. 1545. [40] *Letters*, Vol. II, p. 550. [41] J. 18.
[42] J. 553.

> Some keep the Sabbath going to Church –
> I keep it, staying at Home –
> With a Bobolink for a Chorister –
> And an Orchard, for a dome – [43]

But at other times her commitment to a purely secular affirmation stops her short of the *Divinity School Address*. She moved from the Christian argument by design exemplified for the period by Edward Hitchcock's *The Religion of Geology* (a popular manual written by the president of Amherst) to the more naturalistic *First Principles of Chemistry* by Benjamin Silliman and the physiology of J. C. Cutter. In both of these scientific texts, she was, she declared, "much interested."[44] This was in 1848; thirty years later she had not retreated from her commitment to scientific realism. Essentially naturalistic and tough-minded in temperament, she followed the new currents in science very carefully. "We thought Darwin had thrown 'the Redeemer' away,"[45] she told a friend who had spoken of God. A poem in 1860 turns such revolt against theology into aphorism:

> "Faith" is a fine invention
> When Gentlemen can *see* –
> But *Microscopes* are prudent
> In an Emergency.[46]

Against the faith which had become suitable for the tender-minded gentleman, Emily pressed the intensity of her imprudent despair—"that White Sustenance,"[47] as she called it, of the ego self-made in rebellion. She felt the necessity, before any of her contemporaries except Melville, of achieving and expressing this wholly secular defense. Thus, when her poems were finally published in 1890 they were immediately popular and, despite the official hostility of academic reviewers, her first volume went into sixteen printings within eight years. Her reputation, like Melville's and Adams's, increased steadily in the new century when her defense of self was desperately needed by a public only then, fifty years later, arriving in general at her predicament.[48]

Whereas Emerson could leave the Church, or Thoreau the community, and yet find divinity in nature or the self, Emily Dickinson's world—with its daily news of war, sorrow, and death—was populated by terror. For her there was no final peace but the act of mind, the act of writing poetry. All else was chaotic and insecure. Even nature, although incredibly beautiful —like the hummingbird in "A Route of Evanescence," for instance— provides both snakes and occasions for "Zero at the Bone."[49] "Nature is a stranger yet," she remarks. More mysterious the more studied, it is a haunted house whose ghost no man has "simplified."[50] To suggest the

---

[43] J. 324. [44] *Letters,* Vol. I, p. 59. [45] Leyda, Vol. I, p. 368. [46] J. 185. [47] J. 640.
[48] The poets of the twentieth century might almost be grouped according to their response to Emily Dickinson's work. Those who followed Pound and Eliot in seeking stability in tradition almost completely ignored her. Those who, like Conrad Aiken, William Carlos Williams, and Hart Crane, sought salvation in self-awareness admired her intensely. [49] J. 1463, J. 986. [50] J. 1400.

essential terror in nature she alters Marvell's Edenic "green shade" to make it a "Green Chill":

> There came a Wind like a Bugle –
> It quivered through the Grass
> And a Green Chill upon the Heat
> So ominous did pass
> We barred the Windows and the Doors
> As from an Emerald Ghost –
> The Doom's electric Moccasin
> That very instant passed – [51]

But human nature is no less inimical than physical nature. She knew the terrors of her self. "Nature is a Haunted House –" she wrote Higginson, "but Art – a House that tries to be haunted."[52] Both nature and the self provide what Emily Dickinson characterizes as the simultaneously gay, ghastly, numbed world which her poems reflect. In the self Emily Dickinson finds not the Oversoul, but "funerals"; "Gnomes" who are "never gone"; "a Goblin with a Gauge" and with threatening "Paws"; "Gibbets, and the Dead":

> The Soul has Bandaged moments –
> When too appalled to stir –
> She feels some ghastly Fright come up
> And stop to look at her –
>
> Salute her – with long fingers –
> Caress her freezing hair –
> Sip, Goblin, from the very lips
> The Lover – hovered – o'er – [53]

Following Poe and anticipating the metaphors that Freud would use to describe the mind possessed, she insisted: "One need not be a Chamber – to be Haunted –/ . . . The Brain has Corridors."[54] She wrote poems as her only defense against disorder. Her work was her secular salvation.

Isolated first by circumstance from a social community; and by will from a declining spiritual one, she isolated herself by desire from the community of public literature, and so preserved her self-possession intact. Because Emily Dickinson published so little, critics have too hastily assumed that she kept her poems a secret. Far from unwilling to have her poems read, she sent out hundreds of them with or in letters. A famous literary visitor to the Dickinson house in 1880 has described how "in the midst of luncheon there was brought to me from Miss Emily Dickinson a strange wonderful little poem lying on a bed of heartsease in a bow."[55] But only seven of her poems were published during her life time: all were anonymous, and all but two appeared in Bowles's *Springfield Republican*.

Her famous letter of 1862, in which she asks Higginson to be her "Master"

[51] J. 1593. [52] *Letters*, Vol. II, p. 554. [53] Three poems are referred to successively: J. 298, J. 414, J. 512. [54] J. 670. [55] Leyda, Vol. II, p. 322.

and audience combined, obviously was related to the question of publication that must have been troubling her that year, since within the previous year she had had two poems published. Less than a month after "Safe in their Alabaster Chambers" had appeared in the "Original Poetry" column of the *Republican,* Emily would have read in Holland's section on "Books, Authors, and Art":

> The *Atlantic Monthly* for April is one of the best numbers ever issued.... Its leading article. T. W. Higginson's Letter to a Young Contributor, ought to be read by all the would-be authors of the land.... It is a test of latent power. Whoever rises from its thorough perusal strengthened and encouraged, may be reasonably certain of ultimate success.[56]

The phrases "latent power" and "ultimate success" would have dazzled Emily's imagination. She must have eagerly studied Higginson's advice when the *Atlantic* appeared in early April. There she found a confirmation of her own practices and inclinations: "Often times a word shall speak what accumulated volumes have labored in vain to utter," Higginson observed.

> There may be years of crowded passion in a word, and half a life in a sentence. Such being the majesty of the art you seek to practice, you can at least take time and deliberation before dishonoring it.[57]

Enclosing her recently published poem and three others, along with her name penciled on a card, she wrote to Higginson on April 15: "Are you too deeply occupied to say if my Verse is alive?/The Mind is so near itself – it cannot see, distinctly – and I have none to ask." Evidently Higginson ventured some gentle criticism in reply, but asked to see more poems, since she thanked him for his "surgery"—"it was not so painful as I supposed," she says—and sent three poems in response. In his second letter, calling her verse "spasmodic" and "uncontrolled," he suggested that she regularly submit her verse to a "friend," himself. But he also advised her against publication. "I smile when you suggest that I delay 'to publish' – that being foreign to my thought, as Firmament to Fin," she responded, asking him to be her "Preceptor." In her next letter she was already signing herself "Your Scholar."[58]

Inevitably one wonders why she chose Higginson as her preceptor. To be sure, in common with the other men she admired he possessed a definite aggressive masculinity. And by 1862 he had established himself as a public man-of-letters, one of the most frequent contributors to the *Atlantic,* and a popular lecturer. But he had published only a few inferior verses; and his best prose work, *Army Life in a Black Regiment* (1870) and *Cheerful Yesterdays* (1898), had not appeared. It is strange that she did not write to one of the more celebrated New England worthies. What of Oliver Wendell Holmes, whose *Poems* Emily was given in 1849, and who was

---

[56] "Books, Authors, and Art," *Springfield Republican* (March 29, 1862), in Leyda, Vol. II, p. 50. [57] Quoted in *ibid.,* Vol. II, pp. 50, 52. [58] *Letters,* Vol. II, pp. 403, 404, 408–409.

known to be receptive to young writers? Or Longfellow, also approachable? Whittier, who gathered together a bevy of women (Ceclia Thaxter, Sarah Orne Jewett, and Lucy Larcom among them) was in the neighborhood. Emerson, whom she obviously admired, had already visited her brother Austin in 1857. Between these two poets there might surely have been a kinship. When her poem, "Success," was printed anonymously in *A Masque of Poets* (1878), Emerson was generally thought to be the author. Moreover, Emily would have known of Emerson's cordial reception to Whitman, and might have supposed that his vision would be sympathetic to her own. What of Lowell, who greeted Howells so enthusiastically? Indeed, what of Howells himself? Howells published volumes of poetry in 1860 and 1869, and after the war would have been at least officially receptive to her manuscripts in his role as Assistant Editor of the *Atlantic*. Reviewing her *Poems* in 1890 with enthusiasm and insight—when idealistic critics like Aldrich were coldly contemptuous—Howells showed that he would have been (as he *was* for Mark Twain) the best of preceptors.

The fact that she chose none of these as preceptor suggests that she sought not sympathy but surgery. Higginson's was the public voice of literary convention. Popular and acceptable everywhere, asked to speak and to write on nearly every topic, he epitomized the public mind. His was the general mind that gave her, in himself, a mass audience. Against him she could measure the extent and daring of her self-assertion. Her frequent references to him in the impersonal pronoun suggest, perhaps, how far he had become a symbol in her imagination. In 1867 she reopened correspondence with him by asking: "Bringing still my 'plea for Culture,'/Would it teach me now?"[59] From him she learned what her culture was—in this sense alone he was her master. Curiously proud, she never pretended that his experience reached the depth of her own. He was merely the public man. When his wife died, she made this pointedly clear. "The Wilderness is new—to you," she wrote—saying all with her dash—and continued: "Master, let me lead you."[60] But on the public green he was leader. Her idiosyncrasy remained ever Scholar to his conventionality. Pushing against the culture he offered, she learned how to be and preserve herself.

We must take very seriously, then:

> Publication – is the Auction
> Of the Mind of Man –
> Poverty – be justifying
> For so foul a thing
>
> Possibly – but We – would rather
> From our Garret go
> White – Unto the White Creator
> Than invest – Our Snow – [61]

She was concerned, essentially, with maintaining the kind of inner integrity

59 *Ibid.,* Vol. II, p. 457. 60 *Ibid.,* Vol. II, p. 590. 61 J. 709.

that would allow her to continue writing. She used Higginson's public voice, therefore, as her renunciatory defense against the yearning to publish. In his early suggestion that she "delay to publish" was her protection. He helped to shape her mask of isolation by emphasizing a romantic notion of the inspired poet: "It isolates one anywhere to think beyond a certain point or have such luminous flashes as come to you," he wrote in 1869.[62] Fifteen years after his "Letter" appeared, she quoted the final paragraph of it back to him as her defense against an "entreaty" to publish. Her poems were in fact fairly well known, and she was variously entreated. Elizabeth Stuart Phelps wrote from her position as editor in 1871, requesting a contribution. Helen Hunt Jackson insisted four years later: "You are a great poet—and it is a wrong to the day you live in, that you will not sing aloud." When Mrs. Jackson entreated her to place a poem in *A Masque of Poets*, Emily turned inevitably to Higginson: "I would regret to estrange her" she wrote, "and if you would be willing to give me a note saying you disapproved it, and thought me unfit, she would believe you."[63] Later, she pointedly ignored Mrs. Jackson's request to be named her literary executor. Finally, Thomas Niles, editor of Roberts Brothers, wrote in 1882 asking her to assemble "a volume of poems" for publication by that house.[64] Throughout, Higginson was appealed to for disapproval. From the very beginning, he was the public whom she could not convince, and did not try to overcome.

Instead, in private poems, she concentrated upon exploring and revealing her own ego. Implicit in her poetry are her ultimate defenses against the auction of her mind. In an age of oratory—her father was a well-known public speaker—she was brief and aphoristic, even gnomic. Few of her poems run over thirty lines and none over fifty. In an age of happily mellifluous verse, her syntax was willfully irregular. While most American poetry was intent upon resolving verse to statement, she seems to have begun with the sensuous patterns that word combinations make, and so ended with obvious logical inconsistencies between her poems. Jay Leyda has spoken of the "omitted center" as one of the major devices of her poetry.[65] Assuming the obvious and concentrating on the peripheral—insisting, "My Business is circumference"[66]—she communicated only to an imaginary initiate. Concerned with evoking the epiphany of self-revelation, she practiced and advised obliquity:

> Tell all the Truth but tell it slant –
> Success in Circuit lies
> Too bright for our infirm Delight
> The Truth's superb surprise[67]

Concentrating intensely on individual words, she incarnated in her verse the truth in Higginson's clichéd remark that a word may speak whole

---

[62] *Letters*, Vol. II, p. 461. [63] *Ibid.*, Vol. II, pp. 545, 563. [64] *Ibid.*, Vol. III, p. 726. [65] Leyda, "Introduction," Vol. I, p. xxi. [66] *Letters*, Vol. II, p. 412. [67] J. 1129.

volumes. Knowing as instinctively as the child that words are no less than acts, she compiled long lists from which she selected her words carefully. "This loved Philology,"[68] as she calls the possibilities of language in one poem, she rendered in a series of explosive instants, each of which carries its own revelation. Her poems are deliberately meant to appeal, then, directly to the intuitive, nonrational faculties. Her famous definition of poetry is clearly the formulation of her own aspiration:

> If I read a book [and] it makes my whole body so cold no fire ever can warm me I know *that* is poetry. If I feel physically as if the top of my head were taken off, I know *that* is poetry. These are the only ways I know it. Is there any other way?[69]

Emily Dickinson made for herself, in poetry, a mask of solitude and heroic renunciation. In private poetry she celebrated her loss of a public usefulness in her own time. But always, she was sustained by her personal myth of final victory—not of salvation as a person, but of eventual recognition as a poet. "If fame belonged to me," she early told Higginson with a certain pride, "I could not escape her – if she did not, the longest day would pass me on the chase."[70] In a sense she gave herself private publication: after her death Emily's sister, Lavinia, discovered forty-nine "volumes" —Lavinia's phrase—of her poetry among her possessions. Beginning in 1858, Emily had assembled her poems into gatherings of letter paper sewn together as pamphlets. Each "volume" contains about twenty fair copies or semifinal drafts of poems. All of the poems of her great creative period are in such packets; other gatherings were made intermittently, in 1866, 1871, and 1877. These forty-nine volumes were Emily's publication without auction. Making her own books, she could remain anonymous and yet leave a legacy to the fame which she never wanted to escape. Unwilling to compromise the self while she lived and could write, she provided, as she thought, aids to communication with the future: her method of punctuation in these manuscript volumes shows conclusively how public her ultimate intentions were. Working generally from Noah Webster's *Rhetorical Reader* or some other elocution book, she punctuated so as to explain her poems by showing how they must be spoken. From Webster's pointing for oration she took the slash (/) to indicate rising inflection; the reversed slash (\) for falling inflection; the circumflex (∼) for a rise and fall joined; the vertical line (|) for caesural pause; and the dash (–) to indicate a monotone delivery.[71] Mark Twain, for one, marked his manuscripts for platform reading with the same signs. In this way Emily returned the private utterance to public recitation. To the irregularities of her syntax she provided the key of voice. On the private poem she superimposed, in shorthand, the public response. To her own voice—whispering—she counterpointed the collective voice, Man Speaking.

Corresponding with Sue in 1862 about an early version of "Safe in their

68 J. 1651. 69 *Letters*, Vol. II, pp. 473–74. 70 *Ibid.*, Vol. II, p. 408. 71 See Edith Perry Stamm, "Emily Dickinson: Poetry and Punctuation," *Saturday Review of Literature*, XLVI (March 30, 1963), 26–27, 74.

Alabaster Chambers," she wrote: "Could I make you and Austin – proud – sometime – a great way off – 'twould give me taller feet."[72] Her fame was still a long way off—too long for Sue or Austin—but it was secure. She had calculated shrewdly. The figure that has emerged from the myth of Emily Dickinson—the face behind the mask she herself created—is universal rather than idiosyncratic. In the best sense a popular rather than private poet, she delineates the experiences that are the ever-important common-places of conscious intellectual and imaginative life. Not the precious little Tippler, but the deeply engaged woman has emerged. For us *she* has become Preceptor.

Henry Adams

Like a wry Arnold winking at a dithering Shelley, T. S. Eliot wrote of Henry Adams in his review of *The Education of Henry Adams* (1918): "He was seeking for education, with the wings of a beautiful but ineffectual conscience beating vainly in a vacuum jar."[73] To Eliot, who saw in him the expression of cultural decline, Adams was useful as a symbol, and became the model for his Gerontion:

> History has many cunning passages, contrived corridors
> And issues, deceives with whispered ambitions,
> Guides us by vanities.

Adams was like Eliot's Tiresias, "throbbing between two lives"[74]—which Adams himself identified as unity and multiplicity. And Eilot was not alone in understanding Adams as a particularly revelatory figure in the transition between the old and new Americas. Others of Eliot's generation found in Adams's overt insistence on alienation a reflection of their own lostness, and made *The Education* a best seller in the 1920s. Adams had himself matter-of-factly adumbrated the notion of artistic alienation in his brief memoir, *The Life of George Cabot Lodge* (1911), perhaps the first piece of literary criticism in which the isolation of the twentieth-century artist is the central principle. In Lodge's early death Adams read the incredible tensions which society puts on the poet. Born into a Boston "which commonly bred refined tastes, and often did refined work, but seldom betrayed strong emotions," Lodge, Adams says, could only assert his "suppressed instinct" for poetry in "a reaction against society"—one that, consuming all his energy, left him none for poetry. Each literary effort, Adams's analysis suggests, alienated Lodge (or any poet) still further from society, until at last the gulf between act and acceptance became unbridgable. He was "talking and singing in a vacuum that allowed no echo to return."[75]

[72] *Letters,* Vol. II, p. 380.   [73] "A Sceptical Patrician," *The Athenaeum,* XCII (May 1919), 362.   [74] Eliot, "Gerontion," *Complete Poems and Plays 1909–1950* (New York, 1952), p. 43; *The Waste Land,* p. 80.   [75] *The Life of George Cabot Lodge* (Boston and New York, 1911), p. 145.

Eliot, then, was focusing Adams's own earlier analysis of Lodge's situation as representative poet upon Adams himself. But the Henry Adams who could write not simply a memoir analyzing alienation, but also an autobiography illustrating it, was obviously not in the same predicament as the ineffectual Lodge. By the time he wrote this memoir Adams had, after all, endured the personal and historical shocks of seventy years and was to survive until the age of eighty, from first to last conspiring against the society which could confound but not wholly alienate him. He had disguises sufficiently strong to protect himself. To understand the sources and sustenance of Adams's resiliency, let us remind ourselves of the lines of force in his career.

In his first two books those lines were already drawn. *Chapters of Erie and Other Essays* (1871), written with his older brother Charles, Jr., is the earliest and shrewdest indictment of the corruption and decline of idealism that followed the Civil War. Political and social life in America, Adams wrote, "are gloriously rich and stink like hell." Already taking a position outside social conventions, he hoped to become an influential commentator on American morals and manners and believed that *Chapters of Erie* would help to regenerate American life. He wrote in 1869 to his brother Charles that "the return in public horror and disgust will, I hope, make me a 'degenerate son,' and a...'person whose career is closed before it has begun.' "[76] Certainly, *Chapters of Erie* ended Adams's attempts to establish himself as a power in the journalism of the capital. It was his first step outside society, a testimony to disillusionment. The primary assumption of Adams's early thought, in line with the liberal Republicanism of the '60s and '70s, was that the triumph of Union and the defeat of slavery implied, as Lincoln put it, "a new birth of freedom" and a stepping forward in political evolution. But Adams, returning to America in 1868, saw a decided reaction against democratic idealism in Americans' widespread tolerance of political rings and conspiracies involving even the highest government officials. Far from requiring the reform tradition that Adams represented, Americans were tolerantly acquiescing to the decline of their ideals.

By the time *Chapters of Erie* appeared, Adams had officially ended his Washington experiment by assuming the Assistant Professorship of Medieval History recently held at Harvard by John Fiske. From his graduate seminar at Harvard came his second book, *Essays in Anglo-Saxon Law* (1876), containing the doctoral dissertations of three of his scholars and his own monograph, "Anglo-Saxon Courts of Law." *Chapters of Erie* had been largely history-as-narrative; now Adams was concerned with the sequence of document and fact. Deeply engaged—as narrator and commentator—in the first book, he withdrew so far from the second that he composed an ironical epigraph for himself in it as "a master of barbarian lore."[77] In

---

[76] *Letters of Henry Adams,* ed. Worthington Chauncey Ford (Boston and New York, 1930), Vol. I (1858–1891), p. 150. [77] Printed in Latin in *The Education of Henry Adams,* this is translated into English by J. C. Levenson in his book, *The Mind and Art of Henry Adams* (Boston, 1957), p. 50.

the first book he analyzed the "degradation" (as his younger brother Brooks would later put it) of the "democratic dogma"; tracing out the development of the Anglo-Saxon "hundred court" in the second, he believed that he had discovered the germ of the modern ideal of democracy. Concerned in the first with disorder and chaos, in the second he followed the orderly path of law "safely and firmly back until it leads him out upon the wide plains of Northern Germany."[78] From the present American multiplicity he turned to contemplate the past Anglo-Saxon unity of belief.

In this balancing of past order and coherence with contemporary chaos, Adams immediately established the poles of his thought. But he was committed to both poles. He resisted both the regionalist tendency to idealize the past and his own personal inclination to venerate his family, although either of these retreats into the past would have easily provided an escape for the self from the world that tormented it. Knowing that the debased present which he castigated in *Chapters of Erie* was somehow continuous with the American past—that the past, no less than the daily decision, was responsible for the present—he set out to assess, by writing, his national history.

As a historian, Adams was the natural heir to the great tradition of Boston scholars. His answer to Henry Cabot Lodge's query about "the historico-literary line" as a profession reveals his own hopes:

> Now if you will think for a moment of the most respectable and respected products of our town of Boston, I think you will see at once that this profession does pay. No one has done better and won more in any business or pursuit, than has been acquired by men like Prescott, Motley, Frank Parkman, Bancroft, and so on in historical writing.... With it, comes social dignity, European reputation, and a foreign mission to close.[79]

As early as 1858 Adams had himself written prophetically from Berlin: "I shall get most pleasure and (I believe) advantage, from what never entered into my calculations: Art."[80] But even then, already learning the techniques of historiography in Germany, he was about to inherit the techniques and principles of an age of science. He would make an art of scientific history. Inheriting von Ranke, he was disinherited of Prescott, Parkman, and Motley: his endeavor to become a scientific historian involved the bare intention to "state facts in their sequence," and "to give a running commentary on the documents in order to explain their relation"[81] —an aspiration far removed from the romantic reconstructions of Parkman or Prescott or the historical nationalism of Bancroft. Adams definitively asserted the wide differences coming between these and himself in complaining to Lodge: "I *cannot* read Bancroft's two volumes, though the Appendices are very entertaining."[82] Becoming a scientist, he lost the social prestige

---

78 "The Anglo-Saxon Courts of Law" in *Essays in Anglo-Saxon Law* (Boston and London, 1876), p. 1. 79 *Letters*, Vol. I, p. 228. 80 *Ibid.*, Vol. I, p. 5. 81 *History of the United States of America During the Administrations of Jefferson and Madison* (New York, 1891 [1889]), p. 45; *Henry Adams and His Friends: A Collection of His Unpublished Letters*, ed. Harold Dean Cater, (Boston, 1947), p. 548. 82 *Letters*, Vol. I, p. 342.

of the literary historians. And since he was unwilling to follow in their tradition, he was denied the public honors which they had taken as by right. Again, Adams's step forward meant alienation, the closing of another public career.

As if to establish at once that he would not be Bancroft's successor in the romanticizing of New England, Adams began his career as an Americanist by editing a volume entitled *Documents Relating to New England Federalism, 1800–1815* (1877). While other Bostonians were embalming their Federalist ancestors in laudatory histories and biographies, Adams presented, with little comment, a sequence of documents that showed that the leading Federalists had contemplated secession in 1804, if not thereafter as well. This, of course, was far from what his audience called for. It is ironical, but instructive, that Lodge, whose nationalistic history the *Documents* refuted, would go on to achieve the political power and rewards that Adams hoped for but could never approach.

In 1879, having resigned his Harvard post, Adams published the next volume in his analysis of American culture, *The Life of Albert Gallatin*. In his life of Gallatin, Jefferson's Secretary of the Treasury, Adams wrote his first of several versions of the themes that would finally coalesce in *The Education*. Gallatin, Adams shows, set out as a practical statesman to enact Jefferson's humanitarian theories by paying the national debt—"the great dogma of the Democratic principle,"[83] as Adams calls it. But, despite his intentions, Gallatin had to watch as this dream was shattered by the War of 1812. Eminently among his fellows Gallatin embodied the best of the democratic dogma. His failure, then, signifies the degradation of the democratic dream. Adams says of Gallatin, in effect, what he would later say of himself: that an eighteenth-century education could not provide adequate insight into a drifting world in which "circumstances must by their nature be stronger and more permanent than men."[84]

In his biography of *John Randolph* (1882), Adams completes his analysis of American failure. Adams's biographies make a kind of condensed American *Plutarch's Lives*—not of great heroism, but of great failure. An emiment Jeffersonian like Gallatin, Randolph provided Adams with a complementary instance—of noble aspirations defeated not by circumstances but by personal inadequacy, in Randolph's case by the love of power. Adams never tired of insisting that political power personally corrupts. The post-Civil War reaction against liberalism had left his reform ideals without force or influence and conclusively proved to him the power of circumstance over ideals. He was, he told Lodge, "struck by the remarkable way in which politics deteriorate the moral tone of everyone who mixes in them."[85] This is the point of his biography of Randolph. Great as the Virginian might have been, he was corrupted by power and so for Adams stood as a symbol of the degradation of American ideals. Gallatin's and Randolph's careers exemplify alternate perils of American politics. Adams's projected biography

[83] *The Life of Albert Gallatin*, Philadelphia, p. 270.   [84] *Ibid.*, p. 379.   [85] *Letters*, Vol. I, p. 331.

of Aaron Burr would have presented the final possibility of the degradation of democracy by modern man; for in Adams's view, Burr was the complete scoundrel, lacking even the noble intentions that made the other two seem heroic in their defeats.

Burr, like a stage villain in whom Adams showed little human interest, played this role in Adams's nine-volume *History of the United States of America During the Administrations of Jefferson and Madison* (1889–91). Applying the method outlined in his earlier *Essays in Anglo-Saxon Law*— where he had followed out the historiographic assumptions of the germ theory of history—to a study of America on a large scale, Adams slowly put together the documents testifying to the beginnings of the democratic decline. This decline, of course, was obvious to all by the late 1860s, when the accumulated evidence of corruption on all levels of American life meant that such a book as *Chapters of Erie* could be written. But Adams now assailed the past with all the tools of his scientific historiography in order to discover the germ of decay inherent in the beginnings of American culture. What was it in the past that made this debased present? he asks. He was writing, in short, the history of national failure. This was the point of his later insistence that two books—his *History* and Nicolay and Hay's *Abraham Lincoln: A History*—comprised the whole history of America. For, according to Adams, after Lincoln the decline of democracy was too obvious to require documentation. This is the ironical point, too, of the quizzical conclusion to the *History*:

> They were intelligent, but what paths would their intelligence select? They were quick, but what solution of insoluble problems would quickness hurry? They were scientific, but what control would their science exercise over their destiny? They were mild, but what corruptions would their relaxations bring? They were peaceful, but by what machinery were their corruptions to be purged? What interests were to vivify a society so vast and uniform? What ideals were to ennoble it? What object, besides physical content, must a democratic continent aspire to attain?[86]

The democratic experiment that he traced had ended only in a multiplicity of questions—but ones which pointed inevitably toward Jay Gould, Fisk, Vanderbilt, and Grantism.

Personally the end point of this historical process—a modern man needing to understand the sources of value in a world where these appeared to have been lost—Adams conceives of his profession of history as an act of self-understanding. He learns the true shape of his present by understanding the shape of the past. Thus his nine-volume account, drawing the historical lines from Jefferson to himself, is an act of self-creation. Making his past, he makes himself. But at the end of his *History* lay only disillusionment. This work, he told a friend, was his Emma Bovary. As painfully as Flaubert, he insisted on drawing forth the naturalistic lesson from his labor. Jefferson and Madison, then, he sees finally as merely "grasshoppers...kicking and

86 *History*, Vol. IX (1891 [1890]), pp. 241–42.

gesticulating"[87] futilely in the stream of history. "All my wicked villains," he wrote to John Hay the night before finishing his last volume, "will be rewarded with Presidencies and the plunder of the innocent; and my models of usefulness and intelligence will be fitly punished, and deprived of office and honors."[88] Little wonder that when he arrived in Paris in 1891 he read Zola, Flaubert, Stendhal, Balzac, and swallowed "a volume of Maupassant with [his] roast."[89]

Adams, this is to say, was the earliest of American naturalistic historians. He grew up as a naturalist. He was one of the earliest defenders of Darwinism in this country. In 1868 he wrote a thirty-five page review of Lyell's *Principles of Geology.* Moreover, he was a close friend of several of the members of the Cambridge Metaphysical club. He learned from William James, C. S. Peirce, and Chauncey Wright the logic of chance and pluralism, and he embedded this into his accounts of historical change. Adams's thinking is perhaps closest of all to Chauncey Wright's. Wright's "naturalistic empiricism" has been summarized by Philip Wiener as implying: (1) an emphasis on particular observations and experiments; (2) the freedom of the investigator from a priori metaphysical or theological systems; (3) evolution as a cosmic generalization; (4) the conception of such naturalism as a pluralistic methodology, "rather than as a positive doctrine or peculiar mode of intuitive knowledge."[90] The laws of matter replaced the law of morals. This is the obvious philosophical analogue to Adams's scientific historicism and suggests how fully Adams's work was an aspect of the upsurge of naturalism around Cambridge immediately following the War. Howells and Henry James were the literary counterparts of the same impulse. By the end of the century, of course, such naturalism would become so integral to the American imagination that readers of Norris, Crane, Herrick, Edith Wharton, and Dreiser would turn to Adams with nothing less than the shock of recognition.

But unlike the Americans at the century's end, Adams had also been brought up on John Stuart Mill and Tocqueville and led to assume that history was truly unity merely disguised as pluralism. Left emotionally dissatisfied by the tendency of his *History*—although he had sternly suppressed the "patriotic glow" that his brother Charles had detected in the early volumes—he increasingly sought refuge in travels to primitive areas as he neared the end of his work. The sense of history weighed too heavily upon him. In Cuba, in the Rocky Mountains, in the Carolina wilderness, and at last in the South Seas, Adams sought escape from his vision of degradation. He found, instead, that in primitive nature "another Paradise opens its arms to another son of Adam."[91] It was inevitable that such

---

[87] Quoted in William H. Jordy, *Henry Adams: Scientific Historian* (New Haven, 1952), p. 274. [88] *Letters,* Vol. I, p. 391. [89] Max Baym, *The French Education of Henry Adams* (New York, 1951), pp. 177, 179. Adams owned thirteen volumes by Maupassant, six by Flaubert, a set of forty-four volumes by Balzac, Stendahl's *La Chartreuse de Parme,* and six books by "the amiable Zola." See Baym's chapter, "Belles Lettres," pp. 108–182. [90] Wiener, *Evolution and the Founders of Pragmatism,* pp. 56–7. [91] *Letters,* Vol. I, p. 523. He continues, tragically, "but the devil of restlessness, who led my ancestor to the loss of my estate, leads me."

traveling would be reflected in his work. The imaginative equivalents to these journeys were the peregrinations on which he set his characters in two novels, *Democracy* (1880) and *Esther* (1884). Dissatisfied with the villains and heroes of fact, he projected his search for political and spiritual order into two women, Madeleine Lee and Esther Dudley.

His refusal to sign the name of the historian Henry Adams to these books affirms symbolically the emergence of a self in opposition to the naturalistic empiricist, a double determined to find meaning where the historian can find none. Indeed, in his letters he had begun to speak out against himself as a historian. He spoke of "the weariness of self—self—self"[92] to a female correspondent and consistently tried to refuse the honors offered to him for his historical work. He decisively rejected President Eliot's offer of a Harvard degree; he found pressing business in Mexico when he was called upon to deliver the presidential address to the American Historical Association in 1894; he declined Columbia University's Loubat Prize for "reasons, personal and literary, which led me to lay aside the [historicist's] career, and which will probably preclude my resuming it."[93]

Adams, then, was divided by what history he knew and what ideals he longed to know realized—by the historian and the poet. As early as 1862, he had confusedly sensed the existence of a double within. He had, he wrote Charles, discovered himself to be a "humbug," and continued:

> How is this possible? Do you understand how, without a double personality, *I* can feel that *I* am a failure? One could think that the *I* which could feel that, must be a different *ego* from the *I* of which it is felt.[94]

Now, after the *History,* in his correspondence he began to talk simultaneously about the death of his old self and the resurrection of his "double." "I am as dead as a mummy myself," he wrote Gaskell, "but don't mind it. As a ghost I am rather a success in a small way, not to the world, but to my own fancy."[95] Later, he spoke of "my happy home at Rock Creek [Cemetery] where I can take off my flesh."[96]

Democracy: An American Novel was the product of Adams's double, and it is significant that he published it anonymously. To be sure, there were public reasons for anonymity. Portraying James G. Blaine satirically, the book was Adams's *succès de scandale,* and was attributed to Clarence King, John Hay, and John DeForest, among others. But there is reason to believe that Adams had even more private reasons for masking the true author of the novel than the mere desire for anonymity. In the midst of the public controversy over the authorship, Adams wrote to Hay: "My ideal of authorship would be to have a famous *double* with another name, to wear what honors I would win."[97] The double that the historian had created was, of course, the novelist, the anonymous Henry Adams. For a time he jokingly spoke of Hay as his double, attributing *Democracy* to him, while speaking of Hay's novel, *The Breadwinners,* as his own.

---

92 Quoted in Levenson, p. 221. 93 *Letters,* Vol. II, p. 44. 94 In *A Cycle of Adams Letters,* ed. Worthington Chauncey Ford (Boston and New York, 1920), Vol. I, p. 113. 95 *Letters,* Vol. I, p. 401. 96 *Ibid.,* Vol. II, p. 317. 97 *Ibid.,* Vol. I, p. 337.

He made a more personal double serve as the author of his second novel. *Esther* was published under the pseudonym Frances Snow Compton in the same year that the first two volumes of the *History* were printed. Eventually Adams would be able to put his double's revolt against the scientific historian aphoristically—"The mind resorts to reason for want of training," he insisted—while for the moment in his pseudonym he disguised this revolt in an elaborate pun that may be read: "Francis [the middle name of his father and brother] is no Comtian." Auguste Comte, of course, is the French positivistic philosopher whose *Cours de philosophie positive* (1830–42) had had a decisive impact upon Adams's own empirical view of history. William Jordy, indeed, has argued persuasively that the *History* itself "revealed its Comtian inspiration in both subject matter and conception, [and]...also disclosed a Comtian basis in its method."[98] But, "the light had gone out"[99] in the last two volumes of the *History,* and the Comtian historicist had gone out with it. His place was taken by the anti-positivistic novelist, Frances Snow Compton. Rejoicing in a newspaper attack on his *History,* Adams told Elizabeth Cameron:

> I feel that the history is not what I care now to write, or want to say, if I say anything. It belongs to the *me* of 1870; a strangely different being from the *me* of 1890. There are not nine pages in the nine volumes that now express anything of my interests or feelings; unless perhaps some of my disillusionments. So you must not blame me if I feel, or seem to feel, morbid on the subject of the history. I care more for one chapter, or any dozen pages of *Esther* than for the whole history, including maps and indexes....[100]

The double was assuming control. In fact, he came into power in Adams's two novels.

Democracy is the imaginative counterpart to Adams's search in his lives of *Gallatin* and *Randolph* and in the *History* for a viable democratic dogma, affected neither by circumstances nor egoism. "Devoured by ambition, and... eating her heart out because she could find no one object worth a sacrifice," the new hero Madeline (Mrs. Lightfoot) Lee sets out for Washington,

> to see with her own eyes the action of primary forces; to touch with her own hand the massive machinery of society; to measure with her own mind the capacity of the motive power. She was bent on getting to the heart of the great American mystery of democracy and government.

What she wanted, in short, was "POWER," the nineteenth-century version of salvation. She learns, however, that the energy of the age organizes power only for corruption. But her insight into the nature of power leads only to her recognition of the degradation of political morality in the age in general and of the personal moral blindness of Senator Ratcliffe in particular; she is left drifting as aimlessly at the end as at first.

Esther is a richer novel than *Democracy,* though it has been less popular. In this novel Adams wrote the up-to-date version of Hawthorne's "Legends

[98] Jordy, p. 118. [99] *Letters,* Vol. I, p. 458. [100] *Ibid.,* Vol. I, p. 468.

of the Province House," which ends as Old Esther Dudley, who for years has kept the key to the house in anticipation of the return of the Royal Governor, hands the key accidentally—but significantly—to Governor John Hancock. Hawthorne points out the symbolism: "Your life has been prolonged until the world has changed around you... [You, Hancock tells Esther,] are a symbol of the past. And I...represent a new race of men—living no longer in the past, scarcely in the present—but projecting our lives forward into the future."[101] For the heroine Esther Dudley of Adams's second novel this conflict between the past and present is overwhelming. On the one hand she is emotionally attached to the Reverend Stephen Hazard, whose cere-monial medievalism Adams modeled on Phillips Brooks's. On the other, she is intellectually committed to the opinions of George Strong, whose catholic, scientific objectivity is based on Clarence King's. Immobilized between the two, Esther, like Adams, is racked between religion and science, stability and evolution, faith and technology, unity and multiplicity. It is a conflict that she was not alone in feeling during the '80s and '90s. Andrew D. White's *Warfare of Science with Theology* (1896), one of Twain's favorite books, was a textbook for the age. In *Esther*, only the artist Wharton—modeled after John La Farge—embodies both the inspirations of the past and the techniques of the present. Wharton remains, however, not a symbol of Esther's solution, but the reflection of her vacillation. If her endeavor to discover moral certitude is more important and more serious than Mrs. Lee's attempt in *Democracy* to plumb the mysteries of political power, Esther succeeds no better. Politically or spiritually the sensitive individual, Adams concludes, preserves himself only by rejecting the subtle—but no less real and decisive—compromises that modern faith requires. But such rejec-tion leads only to public powerlessness. The self is preserved only by losing its influence, and ends in inertia. Thus, as Mrs. Lee ends her search drifting on the Nile, Esther surrenders to the eternal flood of Niagara Falls. Both heroines remain immersed with Adams himself in the tide of change—like Sister Carrie—without moorings.

Adams significantly derived some of the details for the story of *Esther* from the construction of Trinity Church in Boston, which, built during Adams's tenure at Harvard, began a vogue for Romanesque architecture and placed H. H. Richardson first among American architects. An undergraduate friend of Adams, Richardson spent the War years at the Beaux Arts in Paris, where Adams occasionally sought him out in his Rue du Bac atelier. Cut off by War from his native Louisiana and designing his major buildings in traditionless American cities, he turned naturally for his inspiration to the placid twelfth-century buildings of Southern France. Adams was deeply affected by the same need to find a stable past, and was thus undoubtedly influenced by Richardson's mind and work. Not only did Adams discuss the construction of Trinity Church in all its stages with Richardson and

101 "Old Esther Dudley" in *Twice Told Tales* in *The Works of Nathaniel Hawthorne* (Boston and New York, 1882), Vol. I, pp. 340–41.

La Farge—who designed the stained-glass windows—but the turn which Richardson's romanticism thus gave to Adams's personal revolt against his own historical naturalism was conclusive. Both literally and symbolically, Adams lived in the Romanesque house that Richardson had completed for him in 1885, just before his death. Through Richardson's example, Adams eventually found his way from his house to what it implied, *Mont-Saint-Michel and Chartres* (1904). In 1899 he told a friend:

> I am now all eleventh and twelfth century, and you will find a gay library of twelfth-century architecture [collected by Adams] whenever you get back to your ancestral property. I caught the disease from dear old Richardson who was the only really big man I ever knew; and as I grow older, the task becomes a habit, like *absinthe*, and I crave my eleventh-century Norman arch.[102]

In *Mont-Saint-Michel and Chartres* Adams's restless traveling during the previous two decades provides a structural principle for his imagination. Writing near the conclusion of the great age of American travel literature, Adams conceived of this study as an uncle's guidebook for an interested niece, or for "nieces in wish." The book is the report of this traveler's gentle and audacious instructions to the young girl who is equipped only with a Kodak. She has no sense of history, but only a camera, a sense of the surface of life. He, Adams suggests, will give her a guided history lesson in historylessness. Thus his book is a pilgrimage that moves rapidly inward, where the Kodak is of no use, until at last the uncle, the antiself of Adams-the-historian, declares: "For us the poetry is history, and the facts are false."[103] He now writes the natural history of the imagination and demonstrates its power by imaginatively recreating the sundered unity of the medieval mind.

In his *An Artist's Letters from Japan* (1897), La Farge had remarked that "A——'s historic sense amounts to poetry, and his deductions and remarks always set my mind sailing into new channels."[104] The artist had completely replaced the scientist. Now Adams spoke of his scientific work on Anglo-Saxon law as "a *tour-de-force* possible only to my youth,"[105] as an example of his intellectual blindness. La Farge's work with stained glass had provided the bridge for Adams that Wharton's work could not give to Esther. Upon the same metaphor of the bridge that Hart Crane would later use as the center of his epic of America, Adams builds his own recreation of a usable past. The church door, Adams's "uncle" declares to the "niece" early in their travels, is

> the *pons seculorum,* the bridge of ages, between us and our ancestors. Now that we have made an attempt...to get our minds into a condition to cross the bridge without breaking down in the effort, we enter the church and stand face to face with eleventh-century architecture.[106]

Repeatedly Adams and his audience cross the bridges of time and space— the progress from Mont-Saint-Michel to Chartres involves both—in order to

---

102 *Letters*, Vol. II, p. 240. 103 *Mont-Saint-Michel and Chartres*, ed. Ralph Adams Cram (Boston and New York, 1913 [1904]), p. 226. 104 New York, p. 25. 105 *Letters*, Vol. II, p. 332. 106 *Mont-Saint-Michel and Chartres*, p. 5.

revisit and thus restore the past—*their* past, because the past of their ancestors. Not the Anglo-Saxon, but the Norman, Adams declares, is his ancestor; not the German—that is, science—but the French—that is, poetry—is his parent. *Mont-Saint-Michel*, then, is the document of this transformation of the Historian to the Aesthetician. Politically, scientifically, philosophically, and spiritually it achieves effortlessly the harmony that Adams had earlier sought and failed to find in his novels. *Mont-Saint-Michel and Chartres* is his choosing of the proper guides for modern man.

In *The Education*, the double, now well in control, depicts the Henry Adams who, like his Jefferson and Madison, kicked and gesticulated ineffectually. With the new ideals that *Mont-Saint-Michel* provided him he sternly portrays the ineffectuality of the old ones. In an "Editor's Preface" that Adams himself wrote for the signature of Henry Cabot Lodge—thus compounding his disguise—Adams quotes himself to explain this transformation:

> This volume [was] written in 1905 as a sequel to the same author's "Mont-Saint-Michel and Chartres.". . . [Man] as a force must be measured by motion from a fixed point. Psychology helped here by suggesting a unit—the point of history when man held the highest idea of himself as a unit in a unified universe. Eight or ten years of study led Adams to think he might use the century 1150–1250, expressed in Amiens Cathedral and the Works of Thomas Aquinas, as the unit from which he might measure motion. . . . From that point he proposed to fix a position for himself which he could label: "The Education of Henry Adams: A Study of Twentieth-Century Multiplicity."[107]

His historical self, which Adams had begun to reject cotemporaneously with the appearance of his *History*, now becomes, as Adams called him in the "Editor's Preface," a "manikin on which the toilet of education is to be draped."[108] Obviously reminiscent of Carlyle's *Sartor Resartus* and Swift's *Tale of a Tub* as well as Augustine, Rousseau, and Franklin, *The Education of Henry Adams* is simultaneously a satire and a confession chronicle. Dismissing his protagonist as irrelevant except insofar as he provides a model for testing the varieties of educational experience, Adams defines his hollow man in terms of what he learns. And, as he predicts, the garment of modern man—his fragmented consciousness—is many-colored, patched, and not entirely serviceable.

The two closest models for Adams's *Education* are Rousseau and Franklin's autobiographies. As an undergraduate Adams had written, of an anecdote concerning Rousseau, "Self-conceit is an admirable weakness, and we should not dare to find fault with it under any circumstances,"[109] a remark that is strikingly similar to Franklin's justification (against the Puritan ethic) for autobiography: "Perhaps I shall a good deal gratify my own *vanity*," Franklin wrote early in his autobiography.

---

107 "Editor's Preface," p. vii. 108 P. x. 109 "ΚΑΤΟΙΗΣΙΣ ΚΕΙΤΛΣΙΑ" in *Harvard Magazine*, III (December 1857), 404.

Most people dislike vanity in others, whatever share they have of it themselves; but I give it fair quarter whenever I meet with it, being persuaded that it is often productive of good to the possessor.[110]

Adams, to the contrary, reverts in *The Education* to the Puritan version of self-analysis, or introspection, as a searching out of faults. *The Education* is not autobiography; there is no self-conceit. On the contrary, its major theme consists in the demonstration of personal and cultural failure. As early as 1883 Adams realized that autobiography somehow involved destroying "the last vestige of heroism" in one's life, and concluded: "I object to allowing mine to be murdered by any one except myself."[111] *The Education* is his own self-castigation. His insistence on the failure of Henry Adams as the representative twentieth-century man has been spoken of variously by critics as (1) a recapitulation of European romanticism under American conditions; (2) a narrative principle; (3) an implicit assertion of superiority or "a device to redeem his wounded vanity"; and (4) a satire on the society whose hollowness provided no context for success.[112] Unquestionably all of these elements are involved. As we have seen, moreover, the narrative that reversed the success story—so dear to the prewar mind, but continuing through Conwell and Marden to exert influence into the new century—was one of the pervasive themes in fiction from the '90s on. Howells, James, Dreiser, Norris, Crane, and Mrs. Wharton all wrote the kind of fiction of failure that gives life to Adams's presentation of the tattered coat on his paltry stick man. Rejecting the beliefs of his eighteenth-century manikin— in the morality of government; in progress, reform, and purposeful historical change; in the ability of scientific investigation to attain certitude—Adams writes the internal chronicle of failure. In *Mont-Saint-Michel and Chartres* Adams had provided a guidebook to the thirteenth-century unity of intellect; there, in method he, like Edith Wharton (long Adams's friend), proceeded from the external inward, from architecture to states of mind. Now, in *The Education* he begins his tour already within and writes of the mental travels of one Henry Adams, historian, deceased. His Washington, London, Paris, Rome, and Chicago are thus the symbols of his restless wandering in search of education. Not what they are as cities—so also, not what the War, or the dynamo, or the motor car were—but what they teach him— how they are internalized—is all important.

"Failure," R. P. Blackmur wrote of Adams, "is the expense of greatness." Precisely by the enormous variety of experience that Adams attempts to unify, or by the incredible variety of responses that he strives to elicit, he must necessarily fail. Deliberately touching on "every possible level of experi-

---

[110] *The Autobiography of Benjamin Franklin*, ed. Leonard Labaree, Ralph L. Ketcham, *et al* (New Haven, 1964), p. 44. The usual practice of indicating the date of first publication has been departed from here, since Franklin's book was printed first in Paris in 1791 as *Memoires de Vie Privée de Benjamin Franklin*. The first complete edition, edited from the original manuscripts, was published in 1868 by John Bigelow as *The Autobiography of Benjamin Franklin*. [111] *Letters*, Vol. I, p. 347. [112] Alluded to, successively, are Baym, p. 224; George Hochfield, *Henry Adams* (New York, 1962), *passim;* and Jordy, p. 257.

ence,"[113] however, he restores us once more to the vast complexity—to the *opportunity* for complexity—of our twentieth-century condition.[114] He refuses to let us remain eighteenth-century men. To match the acceleration of physical energy, Adams told Gaskell, just after finishing *The Education* in 1906, society must double its "mind-capacity" by a more perfect "consciousness of complex conditions."[115] Privately, he was optimistic about this mental evolution; publically, he sent forth *The Education,* itself meant to aid in the acceleration of consciousness. "The sole tragic action of humanity is the Ego," he wrote in his memoir of Lodge, "—the Me—always maddened by the necessity of self-sacrifice."[116] In the tragedy of *The Education* is our modern comedy; in his self-sacrifice is our salvation. He called himself, with an ironic twist of self-assertion, "the champion failer of all."[117] The expense of his failure is our success.

In terms of the narrative technique of *The Education* the failure of the historian is the expense of the aesthetician. The double thus generalized his revolt against empiricism into a principle of literary structure. Similarly, in a late poem—almost a confessional—Adams wrote:

> But we, who cannot fly the world, must seek
> To live two separate lives; one, in the world
> Which we must ever seem to treat as real;
> The other in ourselves, behind a veil
> Not to be raised without disturbing both.[118]

In *The Education* the worldly Henry Adams—already a mask, as the poem suggests—becomes a symbol for modern man. Adams formulated this principle in 1902 as: "What I am the mass is sure to become."[119] Consciously he makes himself a Representative Man, at last in the best tradition of the New England Sage. He was, he told Henry James, the *"Type-bourgeois-bostonien."*[120] As James had portrayed the representative man in his biographies of Hawthorne and Story, so in *The Education* Adams employed something of James's manner to investigate himself. He combines James's analytical *William Wetmore Story and his Friends* (1903) with the reminiscent *Notes of a Son and Brother* (1914). In its ambiguity and irony, its playing upon shades of opinion, its focusing of the "burning-glass... on alternate sides of the same figure" (as Adams himself well defined James's style), his own *Education* has the qualities of James's late manner. Responding to William James's baffled praise of *The Education,* Adams wrote, "Harry tries such experiments in literary art daily, and would know instantly what I mean."[121]

This literary Henry Adams lurks just behind the veil. In the joyous vitality of his memories and reactions, the vigor of his consciousness, the

---

[113] R. P. Blackmur, "The Expense of Greatness," *Virginia Quarterly Review,* XII (1936), 414. [114] *Ibid.,* 414. [115] *Letters,* Vol. II, p. 469. [116] *The Life of George Cabot Lodge,* p. 109. [117] *Letters,* Vol. II, p. 490. [118] "Buddah and Brahma," *Yale Review,* V (1915), 88. This follows a brief introductory letter by Adams to John Hay, dated April 26, 1895. [119] *Letters,* Vol. II, p. 386. [120] *Ibid.,* Vol. II, p. 414. [121] *Ibid.,* Vol. II, p. 490.

fidelity of his self-revelations, he peers out serenely, Brahma-like, at his agitated, gesticulating historian, and at us. As we come to recognize his actuality we watch our lost unity restored to us. For out of the jumble of a life, he could write a book that is itself the unity for which he was searching. This was Henry Adams's education, and ours.

EIGHT

Henry James: The Wings of the Artist

Art is the resurgent form of human activity. The artist or producer is the only regenerate image of God in nature, the only living revelation of the Lord on earth.

—Henry James, Sr.. *Substance and Shadow* (1863)

We have passed through the fiery furnace and profited by experience.

—Henry James, "Charles Baudelaire" (1878)

As the forces that were to generate the First World War were gathering, Henry James thought back to that other war, the Civil War, in which—because of an "obscure wound" suffered in "twenty odious minutes" almost simultaneously with the firing on Fort Sumter—he had failed to take part. Between the public rupture and the private wound, he says in his *Notes of a Son and Brother* (1914), he had "felt from the very first an association of the closest." His personal sense of disaster was, first and last, interlaced with the public conflagration as "a single vast visitation":

> One had the sense...of a huge comprehensive ache, and there were hours at which one could scarce have told whether it came most from one's own poor organism...or from the enclosing social body, a body rent with a thousand wounds and that thus treated one to the honour of a sort of tragic fellowship. The twenty minutes had sufficed...to establish a relation—a relation to everything occurring round me not only for the next four years, but for long afterward—that was at once extraordinarily intimate and quite awkwardly irrelevant.

The intensified duration of the War—in a sense James's first vital contact with the American experience—was for him, as he thought back fifty years, "a more concentrated and sustained act of living, in proportion to my powers and opportunities, than any other homogeneous stretch of experience." Not only did his two younger brothers see combat, but Henry, who spent 1862–63 at the Harvard Law School, could even years later recall the names and fates of his classmates. Even those he had never known personally, he wrote in 1914, "have lived for me since just as communicated images." These, the

310

fallen ones, or the ones, like his wounded brother Wilky, brushed by the great disaster, were for James the outward equivalents of his private sense of his own hidden and complex disaster. The concentrated, intense time of the Civil War stirred both his imagination and his heart. In his personal sense of being both alien to and, simultaneously, a part of the War experience, James found one of the richest symbols by which, in his autobiographies, he could convey the history and character of his sensibility.[1]

In his three volumes of autobiography—*A Small Boy and Others* (1913), *Notes of a Son and Brother* (1914), and *The Middle Years* (1917)—James attempted to write what he calls early in the first volume "the history of my fostered imagination,"[2] or as he again, but more fully, puts it toward the -end of the second volume, "the personal history...of an imagination."[3] He had, to be sure, begun *A Small Boy* as a commemoration of his brother William, who had died in 1910. But he soon saw that writing biography meant, for the biographer, the freeing of his own perceptions to respond to the memory of his brother, and so, in effect, invoking, by his imagination, the whole abundant store of impressions that it contained. Seeking William, he had to, as he saw, find himself. And thus he asks the central questions of self-knowledge: "What was *I* thus, within and essentially, what had I ever been and could I ever be but a man of imagination at the active pitch?"[4] Needing to answer the questions, What can I tell? and To what can I testify? he must also ask, What do I remember? and thus, essentially, Who am I? He felt himself, on the one hand, irredeemably alienated from ordinary relations—always alone in contemplation—but he also saw very soon the advantage that this gave him. He could thus possess a richly overflowing inner life, fed with the impressions gathered by what he calls his "visiting mind."[5] Able to visit so freely, because unattached, his imagination is tragic in its solitude, but heroic in the abundance and range of the appearances and impressions it gathers. Unable ever fully to be the public man, he reconstructs the nature of his inward career as artist. In this sense the images that he could sharply recall—and there were for him, as for Mark Twain, many—become crystal and timeless symbols of the artist's ability to restore them from the past to the present, in his memory and on the printed page, and so, as well, to give them to the future.

His recollections, then, are both reconstructions of, and testimonies to, the growth of his artistic consciousness. In three volumes—the third still incomplete at his death—James explores the history of the small boy becoming the man-as-artist. It is precisely in his ability to remain open to impressions that James sees his triumph. Such open-ness was a natural condition of his mind. His was perhaps the perfection of the mind of the James family. The psychic collapses of his father and William are well documented. Both experienced, in their young manhood, a feeling of "vastation," a terror for the extinction of self and life—the quintessential fear and trembling. Both

---

[1] The quotations above are from *Notes of a Son and Brother* in the collection, Henry James, *Autobiography*, ed. F. W. Dupee (New York, 1956), pp. 415, 414, 414–15, 415, 382, 429. [2] P. 65. [3] P. 454. [4] *Notes*, p. 455. [5] *A Small Boy*, p. 16.

recovered by finding absolutes—Henry Sr. in Swedenborgianism, and William in medicine and physiology. But Henry would be strong enough to need no absolutes. Commenting on his father's progress from despair to confidence, Henry wrote, "I felt how the *real* right thing for me would have been the hurrying drama of the original rush"—the time when despair was complexly intermingled with the dawning of confidence, the eminently *human* state of a few days when the hopes and fears of the personality could be most intense.[6] Neither science nor mysticism contented him, only the rich confusion of the visiting mind. His only absolute would be the act of art, the varying responses to the terrors of experience without guide or certitude. In this sense, Henry lived his whole life in a state of vastation—in the terrors of "the thing hideously behind" that several of his tales, from "A Passionate Pilgrim" to "The Turn of the Screw" and "The Jolly Corner," would reveal. In his autobiographies he gives his sense of his growth from boy to artist in terms of his ability to relate imaginatively to things, to have "impressions" rather than knowledge. *Not,* finally and conclusively, *to know*—this is his achievement; his imagination refuses to be closed by either the mind or the affections. This is the point of the theme of his abortive education[7] that runs through the first two autobiographical volumes. Continuously educated, he claims to be uneducable, for he never has his mind closed to the continuing stream of impressions. In this sense he followed his father's dictate that *any* profession was spiritually narrowing. In literature—in "going in for impressions," as he puts it—he found the way to turn his open-ness to advantage.[8] No impression was wasted, no discussion, venture, excursion, or relation lost on the self that could variously respond to each and thus be perpetually redefined and enlarged. "Nothing," he would write in response to a reviewer of *An International Episode* (1879), "is my *last word* about anything."[9]

Henry James's essential theme, then, was the exploration of his own ego in the wide-ranging exploration of other selves. Aspiring to make a literature possessing a range of facts as wide as of Balzac's, Zola's, and Trollope's, yet as personally intense as Turgenev's, he exposed his visiting mind to the varieties of human experience, drawing its wayward elements together in the focusing glass of his imagination. It is not only to the War that he feels an intense and personal relation, but to the whole of the public world. He arranges his autobiographies to suggest the increasingly wide range of public facts that he gathers, thereby testifying to the contemporaneous intensification of the ego that thus joyfully gathers. He moves from the solitude of his self—being merely a small, unconnected boy—toward "others," which is to say, toward the first tentative reachings out of that solitary self. He goes from being a brother to being a son: he learns his patrimony. And simultaneously he begins to take in the world outside his family—to be educated in different ways: by a boyhood friend like Louis De Coppet, or

6 *Notes,* p. 340.   7 It is instructive, and no accident, that the autobiographies of both James and Henry Adams have similar basic themes.   8 On the question of a profession see *A Small Boy,* p. 126; on going in for impressions, *Notes, op. cit.,* pp. 253–54; "What we were to do instead was just to *be* something..." (p. 268).   9 Quoted in Leon Edel, *Henry James: The Conquest of London* (New York, 1962), p. 316.

later ones, like John La Farge (who, with William, studied under William Morris Hunt, and painted a memorable portrait of the young Henry), Chauncey Wright, and T. S. Perry. He learns to be a son and an American. Both his personal patrimony, in the largest sense, and his public relation come together in the discovery that he abruptly makes, during the War, of his America. And, at last, toward the end of *Notes of a Son and Brother,* and particularly in *The Middle Years,* he discovers the world of Art—necessarily, in this progressive exfoliation, larger than the American world, and thus bringing in the European world as well. Literature, to use his own symbol, is inevitably best summarized in the *Revue des Deux Mondes,* and in Browning as well as in Hawthorne, in Balzac and Matthew Arnold, in Turgenev no less than in Emerson. Coming thus, in a kind of Yeatsian sense of widening gyres, to know the worlds of family, nation, and art above him, he penetrates the worlds within; discovering the increasingly complex outer world, he becomes ever more simple—learns, that is, to unify his impressions, "to feel them related and all harmoniously colored." This, as he concludes in *Notes,* "*was* positively to face the aesthetic, the creative, even, quite wondrously, the critical life and almost on the spot to commence author."[10]

What these impressions were *of,* to be sure, early dominated what they were *for.* If James would at last discover, as William said of him, that "he is a native of the James family, and has no other country,"[11] he at first gave his impressions for their public value, and made a literature out of his travels. No doubt this was an aspect of the character of his age—its own collective movement toward widened experience taking the simple form of an enlarged experience of the world. Like Howells and Twain, James gained his earliest reputation as a travel writer. Like them he was, in Howells's phrase, a traveler before he was a noveler. He had seen N. P. Willis in his father's New York house, and later breakfasted, at Howells's, with Bayard Taylor; along with scores of others he crossed and recrossed the familiar paths of literary wanderings and wanderers. If he followed Irving, Cooper, and Hawthorne, and was contemporaneous with Howells, Hay, DeForest, Adams, and Twain, the greater intensity of his commitment to the alienated, and therefore visiting, mind was prophetic of the characteristic displacement of modern writers—not only of Americans like Edith Wharton, Eliot, Pound, Aiken, Fitzgerald, and Hemingway, but of Europeans like Malraux, Mann, and Lawrence as well. The "grasping imagination" that he developed in order to redeem his alienation through art anticipates the scores of later writers whose drifting work largely reflected their own emotional and mental displacement.

From the first James's literary "impressions" of foreign parts attracted attention. The letters that he sent back to his family during his travels in England, France, and Italy in 1869–70 were, William told him, in danger of being pirated and published. Emerson, to whom Henry James, Sr. had taken some of these letters, asked whether he might keep and study them:

10 *Notes,* p. 253. 11 Quoted in Ralph Barton Perry, *The Thought and Character of William James* (Boston, 1935), Vol. I, p. 412.

"Emerson does nothing but talk of your letters," William told Henry. And Ruskin, to whom Charles Eliot Norton showed a letter, greatly admired Henry's skill at catching unique impressions.[12] Knowing the way in which his letters would be thus easily shown around, he was already writing, if warily, for a public. It was only a question of enlarging his audience when, in 1870, he engaged to write a series of American travel sketches for *The Nation*. Taking the American journey north—as Howells's Marches would, to Niagara Falls and Quebec—James paused at Saratoga, Newport, and Lake George, already showing his characteristic predilection for scenes rich in historic and cultural ambiguity. These travel sketches, published in *The Nation* during 1870–71 (although not collected until 1883, in *Portraits of Places*), no doubt helped to convince Godkin that James might well be the ideal European correspondent for his magazine.

Thus, when Henry returned to Europe in 1872, it was with an arrangement to chronicle his travels in a series for the *Nation*. It was with singular foresight that in the same year he reviewed Hawthorne's newly published French and Italian *Journals*; for he himself would need, inevitably, to take account of these in confronting the European experience—just as he would eventually need to take account of Hawthorne as a novelist in coming to understand his American background. His was a special kind of travel writing. The articles written for the *Nation* he would collect into his first book, *Transatlantic Sketches* (1875). But he never was able to write successfully for the mass audience to whose unexpressed desires Twain had so brilliantly given form in *Innocents Abroad*. James's attempt to write for the audience of Whitelaw Reid's *Tribune* ended, after twenty letters, in James's feeling that "if the letters have been 'too good,'...they are the poorest I can do."[13] Nevertheless, he was recognized as their kind of traveler by the same magazine audience that had acclaimed Howells's *Venetian Life*. In book form, *Transatlantic Sketches* sold regularly and well, and gave James a permanent place on the shelves of a select public and in the travel departments of such periodicals as the *Galaxy* and the *Atlantic*. His career in the art of impression had begun.

The earliest aspect of James's characteristic theme, then, was his exploration of the scenery of his own mind in its response to the national and human landscapes of America and Europe. The two personae he adopted—of the Europeanized American aware of the barreness of the American scene (who could comment on the lack of salient details in Saratoga[14]), and of the American wary of Europe (he called himself in 1878 "an observant stranger" in London)—both gave him the objectivity of perspective by which he could

12 The quotation is from Edel, p. 30; see also F. W. Dupee, *Henry James* (New York, 1951), p. 75. 13 *The Selected Letters of Henry James*, ed. Leon Edel (New York, 1955), p. 68. 14 "Saratoga: 1870" in *Portraits of Places* (London, 1883), pp. 324–337. This whole piece is interesting for its illustration of how far the typical Howells scene was strange to James. He tried out his hand at Howells's theme: "They [the hotel boarders] suggest to my fancy the swarming vastness—the multifarious possibilities of our young civilization....I seem to see in their faces a tacit reference to the affairs of the continent." (p. 328). But *his* national novel had to be international in scene. Europe was to James what a hotel could be for Howells.

turn his visiting mind inward. By remaining lovingly alien to mere scenes he could test his essential attachments. The American, he knew, "*must* deal, more or less, even if only by implication, with Europe."[15] But he must, in a deeper sense, deal with himself, and thus remain apart from both Europe and America. This is the reiterated claim of James's journals and letters. He could be at home nowhere, in neither America nor Europe. To the Paris where he lived for a year (1875–76) he was, he wrote, "an eternal outsider."[16] After two years in London, where he settled in 1876, he again wrote: "I am still completely an outsider here."[17] One must recognize, however, that he remained outside "things" so that he could penetrate their "beings" all the more.

Equivalent to his travel sketches were his reviews and critical articles, wherein he explored the geography of the literary world. It is important to understand that for James this geography—the visitable scenery of literature—was as real as the natural, social world. Equally at ease in either, he explored the rich or deficient scene in nature as well as in art. All that constituted the world beyond self he set out to understand and possess. James made four collections of his literary criticism.[18] In the first of these he praised George Sand, Turgenev, and Balzac, while reviewing Baudelaire unfavorably, calling him "a sort of Hawthorne reversed."[19] During his lifetime he would test his own work against his responses in critical articles to George Eliot, Maupassant, D'Annunzio, Emerson, Arnold Bennett, and others as different, as well as by writing books on Hawthorne and William Wetmore Story. In all he used what he called the method of "literary portraiture," a method geared to understanding the author sympathetically in terms of his culture and personality and the interaction in his art between these. He insisted always that literature was the product of conscious art and therefore analyzable, but was not to be confused with doctrine or belief. "Morality is hot," he told Vernon Lee (a pseudonym for Violet Paget), "—but art is icy."[20] Yet he also argued that the artist shared his consciousness with others—a fact that, concerning his own mind, he would insist upon in a title of his autobiography—and so must be considered in relation to the phenomena of his family, country, and time. His essays show the artist implicated, as it were, in these, struggling toward or bursting into speech as he transcends them in the perfected work of art. In this way James reconnected the artist with the social scene. For others, as for himself, he knew that his traveling and his imagining were one and the same—that taking "impressions," as he puts it in *Notes of a Son and Brother,* might be a science, and that science literature. This sense of the inextricable connections between knowledge and art, like Taine's, would lead to his famous comments, in *Hawthorne* (1879), concerning the "elements of high civilization...absent from the texture of

---

15 Quoted in F. O. Matthiessen, *Henry James: The Major Phase* (New York, 1944), p. 2. 16 *The Notebooks of Henry James,* ed. F. O. Matthiessen and Kenneth B. Murdock (New York, 1947), p. 26. 17 *The Letters of Henry James,* ed. Percy Lubbock (London, 1920), Vol. I, p. 60; see also Edel, *Conquest,* p. 279. 18 *French Poets and Novelists* (1878), *Partial Portraits* (1888), *Essays in London and Elsewhere* (1893), and *Notes on Novelists* (1914). 19 "Charles Baudelaire" in *French Poets and Novelists* (London, 1878), p. 78. 20 *Selected Letters,* p. 207.

American life." "No State... [no] sovereign, no court, no personal loyalty, no aristocracy, no church, no clergy, no army, no diplomatic service," he begins, and runs through a catalogue of institutions that, in America, Hawthorne lacked as material.[21] The Civil War had, to be sure, as James would say, made "a great deal of history" of the kind that Hawthorne had lacked; and Americans did attain a degree of self-awareness after it. And even in Hawthorne's time, he knew, there was something left in the American scene to compensate for that appalling lack of the possibility of social implication for the artist.[22] But from James's point of view, Howells's response (in echo of Tocqueville's remarks in *Democracy in America*), that "simply the whole of human life" was still left to be written about,[23] begged the question in not considering what a human life so impoverished would be. At least, for James, the mind needed implication. He would not cry Simplify! with Thoreau, but rather, Complicate! He would not reduce his life, but instead, with his grasping imagination, enrich it; not discover its essence, but its attachments, and declare abundance of relation to be its essence. Henry found his own idea that society is the best form of self confirmed in his father's *Society: The Redeemed Form of Man* (1879). Perhaps, indeed, he had absorbed this principle unconsciously from his father. "The finiting principle in human life, the evil principle," Henry, Sr. wrote, "is invariably that of selfhood or private personality; while the infiniting principle, the good principle consequently, is invariably that of society, or the broadest possible fellowship, equality, brotherhood."[24] In his travel writing or in

[21] London, p. 43. [22] What remained—the American's "secret, his joke, as one may say"—James had suggested brilliantly in an earlier and little noticed essay on Howells's *A Foregone Conclusion*. Howells, he remarks,

> reminds us how much our native-grown imaginative effort is a matter of details, of fine shades, of pale colors, a making of small things do great service. Civilization with us is monotonous, and in the way of contrasts, of salient points, of chiaroscuro, we have to take what we can get. We have to look for these things in fields where a less devoted glance would see little more than an arid blank, and, at the last, we manage to find them. All this requires and sharpens our impressions, makes us in a literary way, on our own scale, very delicate, and stimulates greatly our sense of proportion and form.

The American's "secret," then, was his gain of imagination and perceptivity. It was appropriate that an English critic would later speak of *Daisy Miller* as "a very exquisite and typical specimen of the American suggestiveness of style."

James's review appeared in *The Nation* (January 1875), and is reprinted in Henry James, *Literary Reviews and Essays on American, English, and French Literature*, ed. Albert Mordell (New York, 1957), pp. 211–215. The quotation is on p. 214. The comment on *Daisy Miller* is by James F. Muirhead, *America: The Land of Contrasts*, p. 170. [23] This review, originally appearing in *The Atlantic Monthly* in 1880, is reprinted and discussed in Albert Mordell, ed., *Discovery of a Genius: William Dean Howells and Henry James* (New York, 1961), pp. 57–9, 92–7. James replied to Howells in a letter: "It is on customs, manners, usages, habits, forms, upon all these things matured and established, that a novelist lives—they are the very stuff his work is made of." But he also added:

> I applaud and esteem you highly for not feeling it; i.e., the want. You are certainly right—magnificently and heroically right—to do so, and on the day you make your readers...do the same, you will be the American Balzac. That's a great mission—go in for it!

In fact, both James and Howells were already going in for it, each seeing the "paraphernalia" only in slightly different ways. See *Letters*, Vol. I, pp. 72, 73–4. [24] *Society: The Redeemed Form of Man, and the Earnest of God's Omnipotence in Human Nature: Affirmed in Letters to a Friend*, Boston, p. 314.

criticism Henry James the son wrote on this principle, by investigating the variety of relations that his visiting mind could establish in the geography of the intertwined worlds of nature, society, and art.

From the first James saw himself as a passionate pilgrim to experience. His consciousness, under the influence of his father's Swedenborgianism, began ("quaintly," he said) with the *inward* life. Unlike Thoreau's, then, all his pilgrimages were outward, to mix the self in the "thicker civility"[25] of public life. Appearing in the same year as *Transatlantic Sketches* (1875), indeed, was his first volume of stories, all concerned with the theme of the American adventurer in Europe, and appropriately entitled *A Passionate Pilgrim*. The title story—which, even forty-five years later, Howells would reprint as one of *The Great Modern Short Stories* (1920)—is James's early version of the International Theme: the American adventurer in England. Twain, of course, would later adopt precisely this theme in *The American Claimant* (1892), making it the occasion for both comedy and tragic longing. Clement Searle, James's claimant, has for years held and been held by a tenuous claim to an English estate. He is one of the wandering figures of James's displaced generation, dissatisfied in America, but unable, as an American, to possess Europe. "I should have been born here [in England], and not there," he laments. In England at last, he finds his Doppelgängers in a tramp, the portrait of a distant ancestor, and at last in an economically reduced graduate of Wardham College. Tragically alien, he finds psychic comfort in the hallucination that he is a kind of reincarnation of the past— that his ancestor's spirit "has lived, homesick, these forty years [in my body], shaking its rickety cage, urging me...to carry it back to the scenes of its youth." He becomes, in this sense, the ghost that haunts himself—for he seeks and finds, as Spencer Brydon in "The Jolly Corner" will many years later, the ghostly self that he might have been.

Arnold Bennett once remarked lightly that James had never "felt a passion, except for literature."[26] Certainly literature was his passion, as his writing in all its aspects shows. His passion for literature was essentially for a more subtle and intense life than mere civility could provide. If that was his only passion, it would be, in the decades to come, sufficient.

JAMES AND THE AMERICAN QUESTS FOR EUROPE

Made self-conscious by the War—during which James discovered his vocation as a writer—Americans turned naturally to the richer social and imaginative life of Europe. There they sought the selves they had dreamed of possessing. Europe—which, as James said, was "vast, vague, and dazzling"[27]— would give James's heroes the glorious object for their passions that America seemed unable to provide after the War. From a world they had not made, they come, like James himself, as passionate pilgrims to one which they could not quite enter. T. S. Eliot has remarked of James:

[25] *A Small Boy,* p. 34. [26] Quoted in Matthiessen, p. 4. [27] Quoted in Dupee, *Henry James,* p. 3.

He was possessed by the vision of an ideal society; he *saw* (not fancied) the relations between the members of such a society. And no one, in the end, has ever been more aware—or with more benignity, or less bitterness—of the disparity between possibility and fact.[28]

Certainly James was never beguiled into offering Europe as the redeemed society for the American man: his American expatriates in *The Portrait of a Lady* and *Daisy Miller* live hollow lives. But he did attempt to suggest the yearning and possibilities for a universal human society by treating in his books the varying dialogue between America and Europe. The "great good place" was neither Europe nor America, but the promise of a true society that underlay both. As Louis Leverett, speaking for James in the early story "A Bundle of Letters," put it, "I am much interested in the study of national types, in comparing, contrasting, seizing the strong points, the weak points, the point of view of each." How pitiful the American's need was to make his intelligence adequate to his innocence James showed repeatedly in *Daisy Miller, The Portrait of a Lady, Washington Square* and the last great trilogy of *The Ambassadors, The Wings of the Dove,* and *The Golden Bowl.* How equally pitiful was the European's opposite need to make his innocence equal to his intelligence he depicted as frequently—directly in *An International Episode, The Europeans, The Awkward Age,* and *The Sacred Fount,* and indirectly in the scores of Europeanized Americans populating his novels who have lost their innocence in a mere partial gain of intelligence. Herbert Croly—who, like James, and in similar ways, was concerned with the promise of American life—commented in 1905 that in their America, "social forms are confused and indefinite; its social types [are] either local or evasive or impermanent," and in this way justified James's emphasis "on his individual—as compared to the national—intellectual outlook."[29] Lacking a society to sustain him, but therefore projecting a vision that his countrymen needed, James, as Croly wisely concluded, of necessity had "to live with his conception." His International Theme, in short, is the theme of the pilgrim passionately in search of a society—the ideal society that will be the source of his secular redemption.

The dialogue that James attempted to keep up between America and Europe, present and past, innocence and knowledge, and freedom and attachment was strongly opposed by several tendencies of his age. As was suggested earlier, the period following the War at first seemed to have publically abandoned the American prewar tradition of the rebellion of ideals against restraints, and to have substituted the love of magnitude for the love of transcendence. Conditioned by the vast scale of operations in the War, American thinking became essentially quantitative. In business, education, and politics, the American remedy for inadequacy seemed to be in number. The American was interested, as Henry Steele Commager has pointed out, in

---

28 "A Prediction" in *Henry James: A Collection of Critical Essays,* ed. Leon Edel (Englewood Cliffs, N. J., 1963), p. 56. 29 "Henry James and His Countrymen" (1904) in *The Question of Henry James: A Collection of Critical Essays,* ed. F. W. Dupee (New York, 1945), pp. 32, 34.

"population statistics, skyscrapers, railroad mileage, production records, school and college enrollment figures,"[30] the Great Lakes, the Mississippi River, Niagara Falls, Texas, trusts, combines, and giant corporations. In contrast to such a figure as Thoreau, the American cheerfully acceded to the principle of the tyranny of the majority. He believed that he could supply, by sheer organization, the institutions that James lamented were missing for Hawthorne, and would have seen little essential difference between James's' list and the vast number of educational, religious, and civic clubs and societies that he soon created.

Moreover, the American was sure that intelligence and virtue had traveled with empire westward: and, following his manifest destiny toward California and the Pacific, he kept his face resolutely turned away from Europe. Conceiving of his westward march as a perpetual rejuvenation at the limits of civilization, he developed a cult of newness that minimized the historic contributions of European culture to his civilization and discouraged permanency in intellect, affection, or art. Concerned with interior development, American investors boomed railroads and manufactures. As a direct result of the War and of the resulting dominance of capital and industry over Southern planting, maritime commerce disintegrated. This shift of interest from the East—or Europe and the Far East—to the West made the '70s and '80s the most provincial period in American history. The new audience no longer quite understood what writers like Hawthorne had meant by speaking of England as *Our Old Home* (1863). Instead, they took to calling California the American Italy, or Colorado the American Switzerland. They were calling for a literature that, beginning with *Mr. Barnes of New York* (1887), and continuing on through *The Princess Aline* (1895) and *Graustark* (1901), depicted Americans saving kingdoms, winning the hearts of princesses, and reorganizing a decaying Europe on American principles. With the hero of *Graustark,* McCutcheon's enormously popular book, they told themselves that

> every born American may become ruler of the greatest nation in the world—the United States. His home is his kingdom, his wife, his mother, his sisters are his queens and princesses; his fellow citizens are his admiring subjects if he is wise and good.[31]

Worried by Max Nordau's sensational revelations of the degeneracy of modern European society, they sent their reporters to Paris to interview him and were relieved to learn that he did not view America as degenerate.[32] They felt complacent enough to applaud Mr. Dooley's sharp remarks concerning what they considered the Eastern Anglomania of the "dilute Englishman, the dudes around New York," and "the enfeebled literary men around Cambridge and New Haven."[33]

Simultaneously, to be sure, there were those who were feeling the inade-

---

[30] *The American Mind,* p. 7. [31] George Barr McCutcheon, *Graustark: The Story of a Love Behind a Throne* (Chicago, 1901), p. 442. [32] Grant C. Knight, *The Critical Period in American Literature* (Chapel Hill, 1951), p. 75. [33] Quoted in Van Wyck Brooks, *The Confident Years,* p. 187.

quacies that foreign visitors frequently remarked in the American scene. Bryce, for one, noted "a certain commonness of mind and tone, a want of dignity and elevation in and about the conduct of public affairs" resulting in "a certain apathy among the luxurious classes and fastidious minds, who find themselves of no more account than the ordinary voter."[34] The new rich—and their sons, daughters, and wives—were vividly aware of the opportunities abroad for ostentatious spending and social diversion. The manners that they adopted and imported almost at once created a demand among the middle and lower classes for more and newer manuals of etiquette, nearly three hundred of which appeared between 1865 and 1914.[35] Just as the War created the first tramp class on the lowest level of society, it also heralded the first widespread appearance of American colonists abroad. We have already seen how American artists and writers—who by the very nature of their activity had from the beginning of American history been culturally in advance of their society—were drawn to Europe. Those who speak of James's rootlessness tend to forget that it was the Westerner—Twain or Bret Harte in real life, Elmer Moffat or Christopher Newman in literature—who populated the American colonies on the Continent. West as well as East, economic and political power had arisen unaccompanied by a corresponding rise of cultural centers. These latter remained, for the American, London, Paris, and Rome. Expatriation to an American colony abroad was the symbol of this disorder between economy and culture. Thus made alien to changes in America, these colonists tended to deny the relevance of time and environment altogether and so to lose the vital sources of their imaginations. "The master stands in no relation to the moment at which he occurs," Whistler declared in his *Ten O'Clock* lecture.[36] Just as Whistler had invented an aristocratic past, stating under oath that he had been born in St. Petersburg, Russia, so an American like Henry Harland, editor of the aesthetic *Yellow Book,* claimed a high but irregular birth, hinting at the paternity of the Austrian emperor Franz Joseph and alleging that he had received a Catholic education in Rome.[37] Resolutely rejecting their American past, artists created a European one. Such loss of a feeling for place was a result, essentially, of the dangerous experiment that Americans were making of separating life from culture.

Americans generally either ignored or, more often, scorned their expatriates. Even Emerson said contemptuously in 1878:

> They who find America insipid—they for whom London and Paris have spoiled their own homes, can be spared to return to those cities.... They complain of the flatness of American life; America has no illusions, no romance. They have no perception of its destiny. They are not Americans.[38]

---

[34] *American Commonwealth,* Vol. I, p. 452. [35] Americans were asking the question, as O. B. Frothingham put it in 1878, "What shall the American gentleman be like?" (*The Rising and the Setting Faith and Other Discourses* [New York, 1878], p. 239.) [36] James McNeill Whistler, *Mr. Whistler's "Ten O'Clock": Together with Mr. Swinburne's Comment and Mr. Whistler's Reply* (Chicago, 1904 [1885]), p. 28. [37] Whistler was born in Lowell, Massachusetts; Harland in New York; Harland's godfather was the poet and stockbroker Edmund Clarence Stedman and his father an American who lived on Beekman Place. Edith Wharton too appears to have believed her true patrimony to have been English. [38] *The Fortune of the Republic: A Lecture,* Boston, p. 33.

It is well known that James's reputation has suffered from suspicions concerning his continuing expatriation. As late as 1925, in Van Wyck Brooks's *The Pilgrimage of Henry James,* James's later work was virtually dismissed because James, according to Brooks, had lost contact with his native soil. For Europe continued to exist in the American collective unconscious as a symbol of evil. Especially in the '70s, the middle and lower classes began widely to fear what they understood as a kind of new feudalism controlling men politically and economically. They defined their fears for the present, that is to say, in terms of their sensationalistic stereotypes about the feudal European past. "The principle of monarchy," as Bryce said, "banished from Government, reasserted itself in industry and finance."[39] Now the fear of a revived feudalism became a serious matter. Thomas Nast's most famous cartoon depicted the Tweed gang in 1871 seated in the imperial enclosure of the Roman Colosseum watching the Tammany Tiger crush the Republic. As early as 1873, Edward Bellamy wrote an article called "Feudalism of Modern Times," arguing that "the analogies between the old political and modern commercial feudalism are many."[40] H. D. Lloyd spoke of industrial and corporate Caesars. Vanderbilt, Charles Francis Adams, Jr. said, "had introduced Caesarism into corporate life"; Americans, his brother Brooks added, were "passing from contract to servitude." Shortly before Morgan's announcement of the formation of U.S. Steel, even the conservative President Hadley of Yale was predicting that if trusts were not regulated, the country could expect "an emperor in Washington within twenty-five years."[41]

To a large extent businessmen, seeking comparisons and standards for their new power, were themselves responsible for spreading the feudal image. Finding an equivalent for their position in Renaissance and, more covertly, in Roman imperial power, business began to question democratic values. "I expect no Caesar," the Reverend Roswell D. Hitchcock said after the strikes of 1877.

> But then I expect to see this communistic madness rebuked and ended. If not, . . . I shall have to say, as many a sad-eyed Roman must have said nineteen hundred years ago, *I prefer civilization to the Republic.*[42]

Partially in compensation for their increasing individual powerlessness within corporate structures, businessmen spread the feudal myth of the Captain of Industry. While Veblen was pointing out that the Captain of Industry had no more relevance to contemporary life "than the Crown, the Country Gentleman, or the Priesthood," businessmen demanded of their architects suitably imperial symbols for their new imperialism, and McKim, Mead and White complied with imitations of Roman and Renaissance buildings. Tiffany's, for instance, was clearly adapted from the Palazzo Cornate and

---

[39] *American Commonwealth,* Vol. I, p. 576. [40] Quoted in Morgan, *Edward Bellamy,* p. 108. [41] Referred to successively are: Lloyd, *Wealth Against Commonwealth,* ed. Charles C. Baldwin (Washington, D.C., 1936 [1894]), p. 2; Charles F. Adams, Jr. and Henry Adams, *Chapters of Erie,* p. 12; Brooks Adams, "Law Under Equality: Monopoly" in *Centralization and the Law: Scientific Legal Education: An Illustration* (Boston, 1906), p. 134; and Arthur Twining Hadley, quoted in Frederick Lewis Allen, *The Lords of Creation* (New York and London, 1935), p. 33. [42] Quoted in Aaron Ignatius Abell, *The Urban Impact on American Protestantism* (Cambridge, Mass., 1943), p. 60.

the New York *Herald* Building from the Palazzo del Consiglio. "The right way to adapt a French Chateau for an American house," the architect Joy Wheeler Dow explained,

> is really to make believe to restore one, pretending for the nonce that one is M. Pierre Lescot, M. Claude Perrault, or M. Gabriel, and that the king or some grand seigneur has commanded one's services for the purpose.

In Richard Morris Hunt's Vanderbilt House, reminiscent of the Chateau de Blois, was held the famous ball that the broker Henry Clews pronounced superior "from every essential standpoint" to the entertainments given by Alexander the Great at Babylon, or by Cleopatra or Louis XIV. When in 1904, the painter Philip Burne-Jones mingled with New York's Four Hundred, he was convinced by them, he reported, that "the middle classes accept them cheerfully as the best available substitute for the dukes and duchesses whom, in their heart of hearts, the Americans love so well."[43]

In short, for Americans "Europe" (like the West, or the ante-bellum plantation South) was a myth, infinitely variable in meaning. It represented the hopes of artists and the wealthy for culture, but labor's fears of feudalism. It evoked the nostalgia for the old, but the hatred of tradition. It stood for a life of the mind, but bondage for the body; a way of violently rebelling against America, or a way of blindly affirming it; a possibility of escape, or a threat of entrapment. The myth of Europe was used and abused by James's contemporaries until it threatened to lose meaning altogether.

THE GREAT INTERNATIONAL NOVEL

In his richly varied series of International Novels, James attempted to sift the myth of Europe through the reality of human character and action, and thus to restore to the American mind and retain in American practice a true sense of European actuality. Only by expelling myth, as he saw it, could Americans come to understand themselves by truly understanding others. In an age politically and economically isolationist, James saw that the American mind was inextricably involved with the mind of Europe. Elihu Vedder, the American artist, remarked: "Had there been two of me made exactly alike, I most certainly would have had one go home while I waited [in Rome] to see how he turned out."[44] As early as "A Passionate Pilgrim" (1875) and as late as his last, unfinished novel, *The Sense of the Past* (1917), James dramatized this fantasy drama of the double consciousness. He knew, as George Santayana said, that "to be an American is of itself almost a moral condition, an education, and a career."[45] Lacking roots in the land and the historical restraints of traditional institutions—all that, in the European

[43] Referred to in this paragraph are: *The Portable Veblen*, ed. Max Lerner (New York, 1948), p. 378; Wayne Andrews, *Architecture, Ambition, and Americans*, pp. 190–91; Dow, quoted in Lynes, *The Tastemakers*, p. 168; Clews quoted in Andrews, p. 179; and Burne-Jones in *American Social History as Recorded by British Travellers*, ed. Allan Nevins (New York, 1923), p. 439. [44] *The Digressions of V....Being a Portrait of Himself...* (Boston, New York, and London, 1910), p. 308. [45] *Character and Opinion in the United States* (New York, 1921), p. 168.

sense, goes to make a nation—Americans, James saw, might take their patrimony from the planet, borrowing widely, and in all directions. Learning to make foreign ideas their own, Americans might create, he knew, the first international consciousness. "The American," as Jean Paul Sartre has said, "makes no distinction between American reason and ordinary reason. . . . The peculiarity of the American. . .is the fact that he regards his thought as universal."[46]

James saw that he might make a literature based, as American life was, on wide contacts and the drama of unity emerging from the flux of diversity. Aware that American life had been enriched by this kind of multiform interrelatedness, he sought to create a literature in which American innocence could similarly survive, improved, the rush of experience. If, as E. L. Godkin said in the '90s, American "social thinking [was] growing more verbose and less dignified every day,"[47] James sought, in the remarkable application and development of his vision and style, to order and reduce this verbosity and so restore to the mind its true dignity. In an age of confusion, an awkward age, he represented intelligence, purpose, and felicity. Instinctively recognizing the ways in which the human cravings for knowledge, order, and allegiance were being starved in the Gilded Age and afterward, he dramatized a world, and created a sensibility, for which these were intensely possible. Insofar as he could enable his audience to inhabit and live in that world, James was making possible the universal society that remained his particular version of utopia.

He discovered very soon that the drama of the double—of the doubled, mirrored, ambiguous sensibility—would provide him with the richest field for the exploration of the infinite possibilities of consciousness. That this need not involve the dialectic of Europe and America he showed at once in his first novel, *Watch and Ward* (serialized in 1871, but not published in book form until 1878). An admirer of Balzac's attempt to depict the whole of French society—calling him "the father of us all"—James set out in *Watch and Ward* to begin his own delineation of the entire American scene.[48] Howells had generously (and hopefully) predicted in 1866 that James was "gifted enough to do better than anyone has yet done toward making us a real American novel."[49] *Watch and Ward,* which in 1871 began serialization in the *Atlantic* a month after *Their Wedding Journey,* was indeed James's attempt to write the Great American Novel, a subject that was on his mind as well as on Howells's, as his travel sketches of the same year for the *Nation* show. A description of a Lake George scene he reserves from these sketches "for its proper immortality in the first chapter of the great American novel." At Newport he imagines an observer like himself "dreaming momentarily

[46] Quoted in Eric Larrabee, *The Self-Conscious Society* (Garden City, N.Y., 1960), p. 22.
[47] Quoted in Thomas Beer, *The Mauve Decade,* p. 203.   [48] Speaking of the period of his early novels, James remarked: One "nestled, technically, in those days, and with yearning, in the great shadow of Balzac; his august example, little as the secret might ever be guessed, towered for me over the scene." ("Preface" to *Roderick Hudson* [New York, 1907: "The New York Edition of the Novels and Tales"], p. xi. See also Edel, *Conquest,* p. 196.)   [49] *Life in Letters of William Dean Howells,* Vol. I, p. 116.

of a great American novel."[50] Somewhat thin and, like Howells's early novels, detachedly cold and ironical, *Watch and Ward* is of interest chiefly in its foreshadowings of James's fiction to come. It is cleverly based on the drama of the relations of Roger Lawrence to several people: his ward Nora Lambert, Isabel Morton, the Peruvian Dona Teresa, and the American equivalent of the French novelist, Miss Sands; and to his cousin Hubert Lawrence. To whom can he relate—whom marry? is James's dramatic question, and leads to the more essential question of Roger's truthfulness to himself.

Around the same time that Howells was announcing his allegiance to common life as the basis of his program for the American Novel, James similarly in *Watch and Ward* was satirizing the conventions of romance. In response to an ironical description of a conventional romance, one character observes:

> I very seldom read a novel, but when I glance into one I am sure to find such stuff as that! Nothing irritates me so as the flatness of people's imagination. Common life,—I don't say it's a vision of bliss, but it's better than that.

James knew that the commonplace real, closely observed and properly understood in all of its manifold interrelatedness, possessed the power of the strange, and he was preparing already to go beyond *Watch and Ward,* which he did not print in book form until 1878.

In the meantime, the book that he later took to calling his first novel, *Roderick Hudson* (1875), appeared. Still following Howells's lead in now writing the international version of the National Novel, but at once surpassing him, James here gathers the themes and modes that before he had projected separately. *Roderick Hudson* is a summary of James's literary preparation, in travel writing, criticism, and literary psychology. From his familiarity with the European travel sketch he draws the scene and much of the action—inner and outer—of the novel. From his experiments in literary portraiture he invents the novel concerned with the situation and character of the artist-as-hero. And from *Watch and Ward* and "A Passionate Pilgrim" he takes and continues the theme of sensibility deeply implicated in the search for ideal social and imaginative interrelatedness. Essentially romantic in plot, the novel portrays the consequences for the artist, Roderick Hudson, of Rowland Mallet's attempt to provide him a richer milieu for his art by taking him from Northhampton, Massachusetts to Europe. Almost immediately after his first impressive successes, Roderick dissipates his art in self-indulgence: he loses his innocence in abandoning his intelligence. Roderick shows, indeed, as large a capacity for ruin as for accomplishment.

The book deals, then, with Rowland's involvement in Roderick's capacity for both. The preface to *Roderick Hudson,* which James wrote for the 1907 "New York Edition" of his novels and tales is particularly revealing in this respect, for *Roderick Hudson* is the first volume in that collection. There he speaks of being in this (as in successive) books "led on by 'developments.' " These, James says, pointing to one of the basic principles of his art,

---

[50] "Lake George," *The Nation,* XI (August 1870), 119–120; "Newport: 1870" in *Portraits of Places,* p. 344.

are the very essence of the novelist's process, and it is by their aid, fundamentally, that the idea takes form and lives, ... the painter's subject consisting ever, obviously, of the related state.... To exhibit these relations, once they have all been recognized, is to "treat" his idea.

"Relations," he concludes, "stop nowhere, and the exquisite problem of the artist is eternally but to draw by a geometry of his own, the circle within which they will appear to be so."[51] The circle of the artist's geometry expressed in the form of the novel is the circle of the perceiving consciousness at the center of the book, constituting the point of view by which the narrative proceeds as the idea is treated. James's great triumph in *Roderick Hudson* was in drawing his circle about Rowland Mallet. To him, rather than to Roderick, all of the characters relate. He is a character who, like Roger Lawrence, seeks to live in his protégé, but finds that precisely in this attempt at minimizing the variety and depth of his relatedness he is implicated beyond help in the whole series of relations that grow out of his undeniably intimate relation to his ward. Corresponding to the outward, scenic drama of Roderick's decline—symbolized in his restless wandering from place to place and from project to project—is the inner drama of Rowland's expanding consciousness, the moral exfoliation of his self in coming to understand and accept the implications of his initial acceptance of responsibility. "What happened to him," James wrote, "was above all to feel certain things happening to others." But in recognizing his responsibility for what all these others feel Rowland makes their responses his own, and thus contains the collective consciousness of the novel.

Like Lambert Strether at the beginning of *The Ambassadors* or, better, John Marcher in "The Beast in the Jungle," Rowland appears doomed to be (as the short story has it) "the man to whom nothing on earth was to have happened." The son of a frigid Puritan, educated "with exaggerated simplicity" at great expense, having served in the Civil War "if not with glory, at least with a noted propriety," he lacks any clear outlet for the essential, but hidden, energy of his character. After the War, "he felt a deep disinclination to take up again the harsh and broken threads [of a business career]. He had no desire to make money, he had money enough.... His was neither an irresponsibly contemplative nature, nor a sturdily practical one." His mission, he comes to believe, will be in vigorous action on behalf of a noble idea—so far has his American and Puritan heritage influenced him—but he has not yet found an idea quite fully worthy of his life. Rowland is preparing to go abroad, a fictional James Jackson Jarves (and an early Adam Verver), with the vague fancy of collecting "certain valuable specimens of the Dutch and Italian schools," and presenting them to an American city such as Northampton, Massachusetts, where he is visiting his cousin. But this fancy immediately vanishes in his discovery that a young sculptor, apparently of genius, is living in that very town. Not, then, to bring art objects to America, but to bring the artist to Europe at once, precipitously, becomes the fancy galvanizing all of Rowland's hitherto unexpressed energy of decision and action. He decides to bring Roderick to

[51] "Preface," *Roderick Hudson*, pp. vi–viii.

Rome—the "original, *ab*original American artist" (as Roderick had called himself) to the antique world and traditional ideals.

The consequences of this, for either himself or Roderick, Rowland cannot, of course, see. But the possibilities are already clearly symbolized in the first statue of Roderick's that he sees—of a naked youth drinking from a gourd. "Why, he's youth, you know," the sculptor explains; "he's innocence, he's health, he's strength, he's curiosity." But the cup, "is knowledge, pleasure, experience!" The youth, Rowland remarks, is "drinking very deep." Both Rowland and Roderick—the one thirsting in his postwar lassitude, the other languishing in a provincial Massachusetts town—will also drink deep. Both— as their names suggest, essentially romantic—will engage the real; both innocents will plumb experience. Roderick's great statue is of Adam, and his career is Adamic. Late in the book, standing among his works beside his life-size Adam, he summarizes his career for his mother: "If I hadn't come to Rome, I shouldn't have risen, and if I hadn't risen, I shouldn't have fallen."

Rowland moves essentially in the opposite direction. His original decision to bring Roderick to Rome constitutes his fall—from his perfectionist ideals of action into a hopelessly ambiguous experience and, at last, to the tragic knowledge that in providing the opportunity for Roderick's self-knowledge he has allowed the possibility for his self-indulgence, the dissipation of his genius, and his suicide. His one grand act of decision has ironically made for his one irremediable failure. Not, however, in its tragic consequences, but in his decision lies his salvation, his rise. The man to whom nothing had ever happened sees, standing beside Roderick's body, "how up to the brim, for two years, his [Rowland's] personal world had been filled." Roderick had fallen from genius to hollow vacancy, but Rowland had risen from fancy to knowledge. He is the man to whom, essentially, everything has happened.

From the tragic rise and fall of Roderick Hudson James turned, in *The American* (1877) and the series of sketches with which he followed it, to the comic aspects of his "Americano-European legend," as he came to call it. An essential part of this would be the particular *légende* of the American-Adam-as-Westerner-and-entrepreneur, Christopher Newman. "Oh, you have your *légende*," the duchess tells him.

> What is that about your having founded a city some ten years ago in the great West. . . . You are exclusive proprietor of this flourishing settlement, and you are consequently fabulously rich, and you would be richer still if you didn't grant lands and houses free of rent to all new-comers who will pledge themselves never to smoke cigars. At this game, in three years, we are told, you are going to be made president of America.

The American is James's *Innocents Abroad*. As Twain had sent his comic tramp back to his human origins, through Europe to Jerusalem, from the consequence to the creation, from civilization to Eden in a second pilgrim's progress, so the equally comic and restless Chriptopher Newman, in whom "innocence and experience were singularly blended," has come to Europe to test his genius for both. He is the Western Barbarian, the archetypal new man who, named for Christopher Columbus, now sets out to resail his journey, eastward, to discover the India of Europe. Like Rowland Mallet, he is suddenly, and with "mortal disgust," disengaged from business—which he had treated merely as an "open game"—by the intuition that "the more a man knows the better." What his acquired knowledge will mean for his old being becomes the concern of the novel. What he feels and belives, how he encounters and treats this expansion of his consciousness, is the subject of the book.

The book, then, is the tragicomic account of Newman's metamorphosis. Reversing the American myth of the westward march of civilization, he seeks his newly forming self in Europe. "I seemed to feel a new man inside my old skin, and I longed for a new world," he says. As he comes to define this in literal terms, he means to marry. He has come to Europe to find the perfect wife. Writing in the tradition of the novel bringing harmony from diversity, James used, ironically, here as elsewhere, the conventional romantic plot of love presumably leading to marriage as the vehicle for his symbolism.[52] In Claire de Cintré Newman discovers, as he supposes, his ideal. "You will even find my sister a little strange," Claire's brother tells Newman, who replies: "Very good...; that's the sort of thing I came to Europe for. You come into my programme." But from the first this innocent abroad, though believing that "Europe was made for him," and highly civilized and morally delicate though he is—this Western Barbarian is a helpless outsider in Europe. Oscar Cargill's suggestion that in *The American* James was satirizing *L'Etrangère*, a play by Alexandre Dumas, *fils*, may very well help to explain James's discovery here of the condition of the outsider, of strangeness, in modern life. The distance international—and human—relations had come since the War is hinted at in Madame de la Rochefidèle's comment that the last American she had seen was "the great Dr. Franklin.... He was received very well in our monde." Between Franklin and Newman, who is at last expelled from the foreign *monde*, lies nearly a century of change. Morally disgusted with his American life, he cannot yet enter the life of Europe. He possesses, to sustain him in the end, only his American qualities: first, his humor (he had "sat with Western humorists...and seen 'tall' stories grow taller"); and second, the powerful Puritan energy of his final renunciation of revenge. These, only, remain. He is deprived of both innocence and experience, "like a man talking to himself in the mirror for want of better company." Indifferent to business, but with no inner or outer pleasure in his leisure, he is the man without qualities. His hollow life is symbolized in the house the vast gilded rooms of which stand ever waiting for him in Paris; and his utter alienation

---

[52] How rigidly the novelist was confined to this situation is suggested by Anthony Trollope's account of the composition of *Miss Mackenzie* (1865):

Writing this book, with a desire to prove that a novel may be produced without love....I took for my heroine a very unattractive old maid..., but even she was in love before the end of the book.

James's triumphs in fiction are, as here, in probing and deepening the suggestiveness of conventions in the novel. (Trollope quoted in Oscar Cargill, *The Novels of Henry James* [New York, 1961], p. 15.)

is summarized in the image of his standing helplessly outside Claire's convent, staring at the "pale, dead, discolored wall."

James had found, as Twain had, that the American comedy ends in tragedy. Newman gazing at the blank and pitiless convent wall or Twain's pilgrims waiting at the edge of the Sea of Galilee for a boat that will never return—these images equally depict the fatal alienation of the American innocent. Immediately after the publication of *The American,* Howells, however, was already asking James for a book with a "cheerful ending" to assuage the readers disappointed by the melancholic conclusion to what had promised to be a comic novel. Howells had himself so far surrendered to popular taste as to forestall the tragic conclusion of the American-European dialectic by making his European figures really only Europeanized Americans, ready at the crucial moment of tragedy to reassert their American essence. Ferris in *A Foregone Conclusion* (1875), for instance, finally resolves his national and personal doubts, goes home to fight in the war, and marries Florida Vervain.

This use of the Europeanized American was the solution by which James managed to conclude *The Europeans* (1878) with four marriages. The Baroness Eugenia is a less complex Claire de Cintré and her brother Felix Young a simplified version of Valentin de Bellegarde as artist. But they are also cousins to the New England Wentworths. To the New England conscience—embodied in Mr. Wentworth, who looked "as if he were undergoing martyrdom, not by fire, but by freezing"—they bring the warmth of gay wit, generous fancy, and charming conversation. They test the American on his own grounds. And at last it is only the duplicity of Eugenia that New England cannot understand. All the other couples marry. But even New England at its most cosmopolitan in Robert Acton exhibits no real power of action. His gain of knowledge has merely enlarged his capacity, as F. W. Dupee has written, for being suspicious. "She is a woman who will lie," he so repeatedly murmurs to himself that he at last lets Engenia return to Europe and makes a virtue of his moral limitations by marrying "a particularly nice young girl." Acton has only given the appearance of knowledge; in reality he has invented a convenient image of Europe, like Bessie Alden in *An International Episode* (1879), James's next book. The point of that novella is precisely that Bessie has never really seen Lord Lamberth, but instead adapts him to her ideal of a marquis, "as you might attempt to fit a silhouette in cut paper upon a shadow projected upon a wall." She preserves her innocence, this is to say, by overworking her imagination, even so far that she finally refuses to marry him rather than set her silhouette beside the real face.

James had subtitled *The Europeans* "A Sketch," and *An International Episode* was obviously a similarly rapid rendering. Both are valuable not for their depth, but for the sparkle and improvisational charm of their surface. Conceived from the first as *"A Study,"* *Daisy Miller* (1879) is perhaps the brightest creation of this group of long tales, all comic examinations of the International Theme. Daisy became, indeed, James's best known heroine, and even had, a historian of American manners has written, "an effect on American canons of behavior" by becoming a "stock example of what American girls should not be and do."[53] James's audience was quicker and more willing than he himself to adopt the European point of view. For, certainly, it is not Daisy, but the Europeanized American Winterbourne whose deficiencies the novel exposes and ridicules. Clinging stubbornly to her innocence, making a conscious point of her Americanism in Europe, as Americans tend to do, Daisy becomes a reflector—James calls her "an elegant image of free light irony"—in which Winterbourne detects that he has lived in Europe "so long as to have got morally muddled; he had lost the right sense for the young American tone." Unable to understand the cunning contrivances of her innocence, he contents himself in human affairs with the simple innocence of conventional knowledge and is, at the end as at the beginning of the novella, reported to be "much interested in a very clever foreign lady." He is too innocent—or too guilty, in the essential humanistic sense—to understand the open character of American experience.

JAMES'S PORTRAIT OF THE AMERICAN

In these early books James variously explored the real and symbolic implications of his own relatedness to America and Europe. He came to think of himself, it can be said, as *creating* in his novels the kind of subtle perceptions and range of reactions, the kind of sensibility, that would give the American mind the inner equivalents to the public institutions the lack of which he had lamented in *Hawthorne* and would even more fully record in *William Wetmore Story and His Friends* (1903). After James, Hawthorne's formless society would be impossible, for James would give its consciousness form in his novels and tales. Doing this, he would not make, as he said Story had, "a beautiful sacrifice to a noble mistake,"[54] but rather a passionate sacrifice of self for art and the ideal society he envisioned. James had seen, and seen around, the parochialism of his age. "It's a complex fate, being an American," he wrote in a letter of 1872, "and one of the responsibilities it entails is fighting against a superstitious valuation of Europe."[55] From European, no less than from American narrowness, he remained free. He had seen, in his Paris year, that the French were as provincial as Americans; and in London he would declare himself aghast at the limits of the English imagination. In common with Turgenev (who had preceded him on the international scene) he understood that the French were interested in no affairs but their own. *He* knew French literature intimately—better than most of the members of Flaubert's circle—while they neither knew nor cared anything of his, and showed almost as profound an indifference toward George Eliot, for instance, as English writers did toward Baudelaire.

[53] Arthur M. Schlesinger, *Learning How to Behave: A Historical Study of American Etiquette Books* (New York, 1946), p. 45.   [54] *William Wetmore Story and His Friends: ...Letters, Diaries, and Recollections* (Boston, 1903), Vol. II, p. 224.   [55] *The Letters of Henry James*, Vol. I, p. 13.

James would write perceptively on both. Deeply concerned to see literature in universal rather than in national terms, James created the figure of the International Man. If Americans lacked a clergy, a military, or an aristocracy, he could supply them with the sense of what all these meant to the essential self. Late in his life, then, writing an essay on Henry Harland, he remarked that the time had come for "looking more closely into the old notion that, to have a quality of his own, a writer must need to draw his sap from the soil of his origin."[56] If he could tell Edith Wharton that her proper subject lay in "*our* native and primary material,"[57] it was because in the thirty-five years since the War he, his co-workers, and disciples had created an American sensibility sufficiently rich to fertilize and sustain the twentieth-century artist. He helped to make his own kind of expatriation an unnecessary condition for the success of others.

We have seen how James managed, toward this end, to redefine and deepen his work through successive novels. His first great success, the triumphant conclusion and summary of his early work, came in 1881 with *The Portrait of a Lady*. Here, in a novel twice as long as any he had written up to that time, James showed how well he had learned from his travel sketches to invoke with precision the vaguest of atmospheres. In his characterization of Isabel Archer he focused all of his skill in literary portraiture. But novels as great as this are never merely reintegrations of earlier habits or lessons. Without that preparation, of course, they do not come; but no effort of will can bring them about on that basis alone. In this portrait of the woman who, as James wrote in his notebook, "has dreamed of freedom and nobleness" but "finds herself in reality ground in the very mill of the conventional,"[58] he suggests not that the death (as Poe said), but that the agony of a beautiful woman is one of the richest themes for literary treatment. No less passionate a pilgrim than Clement Searle or Rowland Mallet, Isabel Archer also comes to discover that people, as well as houses, may be haunted.

In the largest sense, James built *The Portrait* upon the contrast between states of interrelatedness—dramatized in terms chiefly of marriage—and states of independence or freedom. The book is rich in characters who demonstrate the inadequacy of either dependence or freedom alone. The characters who show their independence all prove to have sharply limited senses of the richness of human possibility, personal or national. Mrs. Touchett, Isabel's first protectress, is virtually a caricature of the independent self-willed woman. She keeps separate apartments and travels extensively, living much of the year in Florence. Her husband dryly says of her: "She likes to do everything for herself and has no belief in any one's power to help her. She thinks of me as no more use than a postage-stamp without gum." Their son, Ralph, exhibits the tragedy of independence from the nation of his birth. Unlike his father, whose emotional ties to America remain strong, he possesses a vital allegiance only to his house. Slowly dying of

---

56 "The Story Teller at Large: Mr. Henry Harland," *Fortnightly Review,* LXIX (April 1898), 650–54.   57 *Letters,* Vol. II, p. 58.   58 *Notebooks,* p. 15.

consumption there, he has nowhere else to go: his house is his only country. So valuable does independence seem to both Mrs. Touchett and Ralph that the mother brings Isabel to Europe, and it is the son who convinces his father to change his will so as to make Isabel independent of marrying "for a support." Arranging to have half of his legacy made over to her, Ralph begins an experiment with Isabel's desire for independence that will have fatal consequences. In love with her, he has too little relation to life to consider marriage. He is tragically independent. The comically independent figure is Isabel's friend, the woman journalist Henrietta Stackpole, who has made a virtue for newspaper journalism out of Daisy Miller's willful self-assertiveness against convention. She speaks of Ralph as "the alienated American": "There's a great demand just now for the alienated American," she remarks as she begins an article on him—but she herself is equally an outsider to human contact. She is well described in terms of the imagery of the newspaper whose impersonal stamp she has taken. "She doesn't care a straw what men think of her," Isabel comments. Her masculine counterpart, one of Isabel's lovers, is the American businessman, a humorless Newman named Caspar Goodwood. In the social sense as well as the financial, he is the stereotype of the passionately solitary captain of industry. Surrounding these characters is a teeming society with no interest or purpose —particularly the American colonists in Europe. Once American expatriates had sat in the Tuileries and counted the royal carriages that passed; but now, as Mr. Luce laments, "Paris is much less attractive than in the days of the Emperor; *he* knew how to make a city pleasant." Having escaped republican America, they remain, discontented, in republican France. They find pleasure, perhaps, only, as Ned Rosier does, in their relation to their *bibelots,* devoting their lives to gathering a few good pieces.

The question of relatedness running simultaneously through the book is chiefly expressed and symbolized in terms of the marriage state. As F. W. Dupee perceptively remarks, marriage figures "as a condition of existence" in *The Portrait.*[59] Lord Warburton in particular suggests the danger of marriage as a substitute for finding a basis in self for relatedness. Although a professed radical in politics, he has, as Isabel can see, no sense of the consequences of his radicalism; for his traditional habits of coherence and continuity restrict his imagination. "He's trying hard to fall in love," Ralph says of him. Marriage will be merely his personal enactment of the habit of the security of relatedness. In response to Ralph, Warburton agrees: "I'll lay hands on [a wife] as soon as possible and tie her round my neck as a life preserver." Refused by Isabel, he later briefly considers marrying Pansy—who also wants nothing more than marriage—and he at last weds "a member of the aristocracy"—"Lady Flora, Lady Felicia," Henrietta calls her. Isabel's betrayer, Madam Merle, is again ironically, slavishly, and miserably related to Osmond, the man Isabel will marry. Madam Merle is tied to him through the child, Pansy, whom she has illegitimately borne him. Moreover, her need to provide for Pansy's future by securing a rich

[59] *Henry James,* p. 122.

dot for her is the motive for her contriving Isabel's marriage to her former lover.

Between the millstones of freedom and dependence Isabel is crushed. From the first she resolutely, perhaps even defensively, asserts her independence: "I'm not a candidate for adoption," she tells Ralph. "...I'm very fond of my liberty." Like Daisy Miller, she does as she pleases. Impoverished, she has nonetheless refused Caspar Goodwood, and presently, as quickly, rejects Lord Warburton. She remains, throughout the book, as F. O. Matthiessen has remarked, "essentially virginal," fearful of sexual possession. "Deep in her soul," James writes, "—it was the deepest thing there—lay the belief that if a certain light should dawn she could give herself completely; but this image on the whole was too formidable to be attractive." Yet, at the same time, she has a deep need for relatedness—as her instant attachments to houses, places, and people show. Her relationships to her Aunt, Ralph, Serena Merle, Pansy, and Osmond—even to Ned Rosier —begin with a predilection to favor that rapidly develops into real sympathy. She has an enormous capacity for and inclination toward the kind of love which will yet leave uncommitted the final reserve of her freedom. As that freedom is enlarged by her inheritance, so her acquiesence to relation develops proportionately. She becomes imtimately attached to Madam Merle and, although she had rejected two rich suitors when she was poor, now she precipitously accepts a poor one, even against her own counsels.

Her marriage is empty. Osmond, she comes to realize, married her only for her money and in order to deepen his own feelings of association with the ideals of elite civilization. It is not until three years after her marriage that she comes at last to fully comprehend the tragedy of her exclusion, the tragedy, basically, of selfhood. For Osmond has no self apart from society, and so hates the last reserve of freedom that remains at the untouched core or her being. Sitting in a cold, dark room, she achieves her finest moment of knowledge. Osmond, she sees,

> was unable to live without [society], and...had never really done so.... His ideal was a conception of high prosperity and propriety, of the aristocratic life, which she now saw that he deemed himself always, in essence at least, to have led.... Her notion of the aristocratic life was simply the union of great knowledge with great liberty.... But for Osmond it was altogether a thing of forms, a conscious, calculated attitude. He was fond of the old, the consecrated, the transmitted; so was she, but she pretended to do what she chose with it. He had an immense esteem for tradition; he had told her once that the best thing in the world was to have it, but that if one was so unfortunate as not to have it one must immediately proceed to make it.

The deep but narrow devotion of his relatedness excludes all human life, including his wife's. He pleads the cause of servitude, she of freedom—as James wryly puts it, "quite another ideal." As James summarizes her circumstance: "They were strangely married, at all events, and it was a horrible life."

Although she had given him a child, Osmond has never loved Isabel;

the child, symbolically, has died. Only at the end, in the violent overflowing of Goodwood's frustrated passion does Isabel understand that "she had never been loved before." What Goodwood offers is complete freedom: "Why shouldn't we be happy?" he demands. "What have you to care about?... We can do absolutely as we please.... The world's all before us—and the world's very big." But what her contrary mind is able to perceive, through the anarchic strength of this plea, is that the world—the world of the self, of fidelity to oneself—is very small; and that the irresponsible freedom that Goodwood offers and understands is as limiting and pernicious as Osmond's servitude to tradition. It was Henrietta who, momentarily reaching below the surface of her breezy Americanism to the core of her own renunciations, had midway through the book formulated the lesson that Isabel now understands: "You can't always please yourself," she told Isabel; "you must sometimes please other people....[But] there's another thing that's still more important.... you must be prepared...to please no one at all—not even yourself." Henrietta's is the last word, literally and figuratively, in the novel. Pleasing no one, Isabel at last goes back to Rome, to Osmond. Like Newman she has been walled out of life. Her gilded *salon* has become a prison. She is also walled in, no less so than Poe's doomed heroes, and with no less terror. She realizes, in suddenly discovering that Osmond and Serena Merle have been lovers, that she has been imprisoned by the liberty of her decision to marry impetuously. The walls of her house "were to surround her for the rest of her life." But within these walls, the tomb of self, what a wild, incandescently rich, hidden life Isabel accepts and lives. She had come to Europe from Albany to collect "specimens" of European life. These, as for Newman, had been in her "programme." But she is driven from casual observation to intense involvement. Her ultimate freedom is in the luxury of renunciation.

There are, R. P. Blackmur has written, two states of society that demand dramatization by balance and contrast—by mutual criticism: first,

> the society of Europe where the vital impulse has so far run out that all its meanings are expressed by the deliberate play of conventions and their refinements; and second, the society of America where the original convictions and driving impulse have not yet matured in conventions adequate to express them on high levels.[60]

In *The Portrait of a Lady* James focuses these two states on the soul and sensibility of Isabel Archer. As in no earlier novel, his style becomes luminous and alive, analytic and accurate in depicting states of consciousness and abundantly dramatizing them in clusters of images vibrating with significance. The detailed epic journey of Isabel through Europe in the first part of the novel is a kind of elaboration of the methods and themes of his earlier work; but as the second part becomes more and more concentrated upon and in her soul—as that whole abundantly superfluous

---

[60] "Henry James," in Spiller *et al., Literary History of the United States,* Vol. II, p. 1046. See Blackmur's entire essay on James, pp. 1039–1064, for a brilliant brief view.

world narrows to the bare antagonism of equally unrewarding forces within her[61]—James's fineness of style and mind reaches depths and intensities nowhere approached in his earlier work. Moving from the fiction of international states of action to that of complex being, he wrote a novel so good that for the next decade he would dissipate his art in trying to equal it.

"THE AGE OF THE MISTAKE"

In the other work that James published around the same time as the large, "public" novels that follow *The Portrait*—*The Bostonians* (1886), *The Princess Casamassima* (1886), and *The Tragic Muse* (1890)—are clues to the sense of incompleteness that hovers about these three. For the other volumes that James published during this time were made largely of either continuations of the theme of the international state of action (as in *The Pension Beaurepas* and *The Point of View* [1883], *The Reverberator* [1888], and *The Patagonia* [1889]), or they were made of travel stories and sketches (as *Portraits of Places* [1883], *Tales of Three Cities* [1884], and *A Little Tour in France* [1885]). A professional writer, with increasing needs for money, but also needing to feel the public responsive to his work—who could imagine a Balzac or a Turgenev ignored by *his* nation?—James unquestionably hoped to repeat the popular success of *The Portrait* with these novels of social or public concern. He wrote in his notebook that *The Bostonians,* for instance, was intended to be "very national, very typical."

> I wished to write a very American tale, a tale very characteristic of our social conditions, and I asked myself what was the most salient and peculiar point in our social life. The answer was: the situation of women, the decline of the sentiment of sex, the agitation on their behalf.

The book, as he wrote to J. R. Osgood, his publisher, would be "as local and American as possible, and as full of Boston: an attempt to show I *can* write an American story."[62] In no earlier novel had he been so indebted to Hawthorne as in this, where one is reminded repeatedly of *The Blithedale Romance.* As Hawthorne had attacked the provincial and playful utopianism of his Brook Farm colony, so James here satirizes the social and intellectual diseases of the ebb tide, as Brooks Adams described it, "of all those humanitarian impulses which, at an exceptional hour and at the hands of exceptional men, had assumed such elevated if rather fantastic forms, and had now lost themselves in fatuity and petrification."[63] The sexual disorders of the sterile Olive Chancellor and her oversexed sister Mrs. Luna; the emasculation of Burrage and of the reporter Matthias Pardon—these, set

[61] It has been suggested by one critic, W. B. Stein, that James was influenced in this book by Henry Adams's concept of *Vis Inertia* and force. Oscar Cargill, moreover, has seen something of Clover Hooper (Mrs. Henry Adams) in Isabel, which suggests the interesting possibility of James's application of Adams's ideas to his wife's character. Possibly, in *The Bostonians,* James drew upon Adams's notions concerning the beginnings of the profound disturbances in American sexual life. [62] *Notebooks*, p. 47. [63] Quoted in Van Wyck Brooks, *The Pilgrimage of Henry James* (New York, 1925), p. 35.

against the possessive sexual egoism of Basil Ransom, in a world guided by mystics, magicians, faith healers, and fakirs, divide the allegiance and soul of Verena Tarrant, who by training has been made the champion of feminine freedom, but by nature is capable of deep and spontaneous sexual arousal. The novel parallels the disorders of mind and body in Boston to the disorientation of American society as a whole. James writes, here, the reverse of Howells's Great American Novel—a novel of disintegration, of the falling apart of diversities into chaos, of the immediate and ultimate breakdown of the society Howells was envisioning.[64] Verena can hardly make a social or personal choice between Olive's hysterical lesbianism and Basil's equally hysterical over-masculine aggressiveness; she cannot even, as Isabel could, choose herself. James can only conclude his novel:

> "Ah, now I am glad," said Verena when they reached the street. But though she was glad, [Basil] presently discovered that...she was in tears. It is to be feared that with the union, so far from brilliant, into which she was about to enter, these were not the last she was destined to shed.

She is the first of James's innocent victims, unlike Isabel Archer trapped irredeemably, without ever making a personal choice.

In the mid-'70s James had expressed doubt concerning the patient note-taking of the French naturalists. He amusedly told Howells of Zola's collection of the working-class argot, of Edmond Goncourt's research on "a whorehouse *de province*," and of Flaubert's omnium-gatherum of the "dictionary of accepted ideas" for *Bouvard et Pècuchet*. Now, a decade later, he wrote T. S. Perry, "I have been all the morning at Milbank prison (horrible place) collecting notes for a fiction scene. You see I am quite the Naturalist. Look out for the same—a year hence."[65] Little more than a year later, *The Princess Casamassima* appeared, the result of James's assiduous collections. Included among his characters is the only major character that James ever revived for an important place in a later novel, Christina Light, the Princess herself, who had indulged Roderick Hudson's self-destructive impulses in that earlier book. To a large extent, Hyacinth Robinson, whom she now takes up, is an artist figure *manqué* (whose initials accidentally reverse Roderick's) but who has no Rowland Mallet to make the attempt to save him.

Hyacinth who, ironically, like the Princess herself, is illegitimate, is emotionally suffocated by the tragic knowledge that his mother had killed his father and by the agonizing memory of visiting his dying mother in prison. Carrying this dark personal burden of consciousness he is put by

---

[64] Howells, as has been said, certainly showed himself more and more disillusioned with America. His *Doctor Breen's Practice* (1881), from which James took several details, has Grace Breen, pressed into the cause of women's rights, personally freeing herself and marrying happily, in the conventional scheme of Howells's novel of reconciliation. But in 1910 he would have the last word *for The Bostonians* and *against* his own vision. That novel, he told James, was "one of the masterpieces of all fiction ..., avouching you citizen of the American cosmos." (*Life in Letters of William Dean Howells*, Vol. II, p. 279.) [65] Quoted in Edel, *Henry James: The Middle Years* (Philadelphia and New York, 1962), p. 148. Moreover, James cautioned himself in his notebook: "*À la Maupassant* must be my constant motto. I must depend on the collective effect." (*Notebooks*, p. 92.)

James into the mass life of an abundantly detailed London—of revolutionists and bookbinders, strikers and shopgirls, of public riots, intrigues, and political derangements, as well as private scandals, divorces, and adultery. No novel better shows James attempting to surpass his early master, Turgenev, in imbuing his fiction with incredibly detailed and suggestive pictorial qualities. But none, therefore, better shows how different his talents really were. For all its social machinery, the book remains, like James's other novels, interesting primarily for its intense and accurate exploration of a consciousness.

Hyacinth Robinson's conflicts are at the center of the novel. Like Verena Tarrant, Hyacinth is divided between his temperamental inclination toward restraint or civilization, and the heritage of radical resentment that, as Christina does, he turns against society. He has, significantly, two mothers —his real one, who has rebelled against society in killing her lover; and his foster mother Miss Pynset, who epitomizes romantic adulation for aristocratic society and for the traditions which support it. He also has two fathers—his real father, the conservative Lord Frederick, and Paul Muniment, his revolutionary father, from whom he accepts the burden of his anarchism. Moreover, he has two loves, the Princess and Millicent Henning, a working girl, both of whom are equally unfaithful to him. He is, on the one hand, a bookbinder, a preserver of the continuity of the civilized mind—at least in its literature and handiwork; and he also receives a small inheritance from his foster mother that allows him to travel briefly in France and Italy, the scenes Christina has rejected and left. But he also has joined a conspiratorial group of anarchists, one which James modeled after the Bakunin circle with which Turgenev had been associated. He agrees to perform an as yet undetermined act of violence when necessary; but very soon he understands how incapable of and disinclined to social violence he is. Precisely in his working out of the implications of his contrary allegiances he becomes, like Verena Tarrant, a victim of the conflicting forces of his chaotic social world, which, impinging itself upon him socially, will not allow him to order his contrary mind and thus become himself. He must remain divided. Whereas Isabel could determine to be true to her own renunciation, to live richly only in the intensity of her buried life, Hyacinth has social involvements so demanding that he must either destroy them or be destroyed by them. Attempting to be true to himself, he is betrayed by society—by his father and his mother; by the Princess, who uses him to gain access to the conspirators; by Paul Muniment's social anarchism and personal coldness; and at last by Millicent Henning, who is faithless to him with the hollow Captain Sholto. As he kills himself, he rids the world, so it seems to him, of its last flicker of faith.

IN THE COUNTRY OF THE BLIND—

By 1888, when it was apparent that James had failed, in his public novels, to hold and increase the audience that *The Portrait of a Lady* and *Daisy*

Miller had won him, he told Howells: "I have entered upon evil days." Far from beginning to assume the place in the American consciousness that the deaths of Emerson and his peers were making vacant, he saw the popular interest in his work diminishing. "I am still staggering," he continued to Howells,

> a good deal under the mysterious and (to me) inexplicable injury wrought— apparently—upon my situation by my last two novels, ... from which I had expected so much and derived so little. They have reduced the desire, and the demand, for my productions to zero.[66]

To the contrary, as Howells pointed out to him, he was entering a new phase of both creativity and critical regard. James, however, could not yet be wholly satisfied by either his own art alone or the appreciation, however acute, of critics. He felt himself the legitimate inheritor of the New England Sages, and desired to affect as large a popular following. The problem of the mass audience was continually to obsess him for the next decade. It was no accident that beginning in the '80s James wrote a score of stories concerned with the problems of the artist in modern society. These show his need to understand (and perhaps redefine) the peculiar role of the artist in the modern world. In his "New York Edition" (1907–1909) he would bring several of these (but by no means all) together in two of his volumes, including "The Lesson of the Master," "The Death of the Lion," "The Next Time," "The Figure in the Carpet," "The Coxon Fund," "The Author of Beltraffio," "The Middle Years," "Greville Fane," and "Broken Wings." There were, of course, other stories in which the question of art or the artist was of major concern. To name "The Story in It," "The Private Life," "The Beldonald Holbein," and "The Abasement of the Northmores" is not to mention all. There had been *Roderick Hudson,* and there was now published, in 1888, *The Aspern Papers.* And there was soon to be raised in the last of his social novels, *The Tragic Muse,* the very same questions of the possibilities of art that his stories were raising in fragments. All essentially question whether a truly popular but also truly fine art was possible in an age when, as James saw in *The American Scene* (1907), literature meant sentimental tales, mostly by ladies, about and for children; or sensational romantic stories—both "having mass appeal."[67]

His stories of writers appeared at the moments in his career of his greatest self-doubt—around the same time as his first large novel, *Roderick Hudson,* then during the years (1886–1890) when his hope for the success of his social novels was shattered. "The Next Time" is perhaps the most

---

66 *Letters,* Vol. I, p. 136.   67 James's shrewd recognition of the demands on mass media in the United States was authoritative:

> The nation is almost feverishly engaged in producing, with the greatest possible activity and expedition, an "intellectual" pabulum after its own heart, and...not only the arts and the draughtsman...pay their extravagant tribute, but...those of the journalist, the novelist, the dramatist, the genealogist, the historian, are pressed as well, for dear life, into the service.

(*The American Scene* [London, 1907], p. 458.)

lucidly transparent allegorizing of both his vague hopes and his very real self-doubts. He explored his own ego in those of his artists and writers. "The Next Time," he wrote in his notebook, came from the overflowing into his consciousness of "all the little backward memories of one's frustrated ambition." In this tale James contrasts the facile Mrs. Highmore (the popular novelist who yearns for once to write "an exquisite failure") to her brother-in-law Ralph Limbert, who had produced one "shameless merciless masterpiece" after another in a futile, lifelong effort to sell his novels. For both, the next time will only repeat the past: Mrs. Highmore is as fatally doomed to success as Ralph is to failure. Surely, this was James's psychic and artistic defense aginst his own failure to sell. By 1895, when he wrote this tale, he had prepared himself to accept Ralph Limbert's fate as his own. But in 1888, when he was agreeing to write a new serial for the *Atlantic,* the problem of the artist vibrated in his mind. The title of his unwritten book, he told Aldrich (who had replaced Howells as editor of the *Atlantic*) would be *The Tragic Muse.* In *The Bostonians* he had dealt consciously with the social subject that seemed most crucial in America, the problem of women; and in *The Princess* with the problem of anarchism, then much a social issue in Europe. Now, in his next novel, he would deal with the social problem most pressing upon his own consciousness—the problem of the artist himself.

In *The Tragic Muse* James treats two ideas, a political "case," as he calls it, and a theatrical one. He holds these together in terms of the choice that in each case must be made between social success or renunciation of certain success for art. The political case involves Nicholas Dormer, son of a deceased member of Parliament, who aspires to paint. Nick, however, has made his father a death-bed pledge that he will continue the family political tradition; he feels, as well, a responsibility to recoup the family fortune. It appears, moreover, that his favorable relations with the wealthy Julia Dallow and the political veteran Carteret will allow him to fulfill both his political and financial ambitions—and in short time. He is even elected to represent the constituents of Harsh. Thus, "James arrays against Nick Dormer's artistic inclinations," as Leon Edel has written, "all the forces which, in such circumstances, could destroy volition in any young man—family, father, tradition, maternal strength, political friendship and even public demand."[68] James's second, theatrical "case" involves Miriam Rooth, who is, or will be, the Tragic Muse. Like Nick's, her case involves a division between art and politics, the inner and outer lives. Peter Sherringham, who wishes to marry her, has no notion of choice; marriage must be on his terms: she must give up her career in the theater, by no means, at this point, assuredly to be a successful one. His politics cannot accommodate her art.

Both Nick and Miriam, of course, ultimately choose art, and thus choose the careers which might at last raise their inner selves to public value. James does not make their choices easy, however. The book is not his apology, but his meditation. The full, rich world, the great dazzling scene

---

68 "Introduction" to *The Tragic Muse* (New York, 1960), p. x.

of London—the antique dignity that, in political office, Mr. Carteret has achieved—the worlds of wealth, fashion, pleasure, security, status, power, and position—these all call temptingly to both Nick and Miriam. The social doors are open. The tragedy and triumph for them both is the way they refuse to enter the pleasure dome. They do not, even by their self-sacrificing choices, earn each other, as romantic conventions, and even their own inclinations, suggest they might. Life is short, but art is long; and they must ultimately choose. "The truth is," Nick says, "painting people is a very absorbing, exclusive occupation." "Yes," she replies—this is their last real "scene" together, and they say less than they mean— "it's a cruel honour." Miriam, who has yearned for "five years of hard, all-around work, in a perfect company, with a manager more perfect still," marries, for the sake of her career, an actor who becomes a theater manager and organizes a repertory company. Quite calmly they close the door to the public scene, and to each other. Nick perhaps, as Miriam suggests, goes to the finer ultimate triumph; for he goes utterly alone. His great, intense moment is precisely as she shuts the door to his studio, and the consciousness of his descision burns with a hard, gem-like flame in Nick. "It was lonely," James writes of Nick's vision of his complex fate:

> and yet it peopled with unfriendly shadows (so thick he saw them gathering in winter twilights to come) the duller conditions, the longer patiences, the less immediate and less personal joys. His late beginning was there, and his wasted youth, the mistakes that would still bring forth children after their image, the sedentary solitude, the clumsy obscurity, the poor explanations, the foolishness that he foresaw in having to ask people to wait, and wait longer, and wait again, for a fruition which, to their sense at least, would be an anti-climax.

In the supreme sacrifice, all there and already known in its consequences, is his moment of justifying passion. And that is his deliverance. The victim has become the hero.

—AND THE COUNTRY OF THE BLUE

But James was not yet, in his own career, quite ready to follow the logic of Nick's heroism. Before he had even finished *The Tragic Muse,* he was laying plans—not to recapture the audience he had lost for his novels in abandoning the International Theme, but to attract a whole new audience by writing plays. To be sure, his income had been somewhat reduced, while his expenses were increasing, and he told friends that he needed to earn a good deal more money. "I simply *must* try," he noted, "to produce half a dozen—a dozen, five dozen—plays for the sake of my pocket, my material future."[69] But it was quite clear that what he wanted as much if not more than the money was the popular success—the cry of "Author! Author!"— the direct contact with an audience that had, after all, remained largely anonymous for him. He had never, surely, been able to predict with certitude,

---

[69] *Notebooks,* p. 99. See the comprehensive essay by Leon Edel, "Henry James: The Dramatic Years," introductory to *The Complete Plays of Henry James* (Philadelphia and New York, 1949).

as Mark Twain could, the sales of his successive books.[70] At best, his relations with his audience had always been tentative and unsure. Now he might hear the applause. And in return he was now reduced to a willingness —one he had expressly denied concerning his *Tribune* letters—to make his plays as bad as they needed to be in order to ensure that success. The novelist, like the painter, he had taught himself in *The Tragic Muse,* works alone; but the dramatist is busy with the affairs of life, of the company, the rehearsals, the tryouts, the noisy success. Fifty-years-old and apparently rejected by the audience that he had cultivated for twenty years, he demanded success at any cost. Unwilling to risk a repetition of his failure at the novel, indeed, he seemed *determined* to make his plays bad, to be sure of success.

He made them, in fact, too bad through fear of making them too good. After five years, from 1890 to 1895, only two of his plays were performed: a mildly successful adaption of *The American* (to which he gave the happy ending he had earlier refused his magazine audience) and *Guy Domville,* produced in 1895. The story of the personal catastrophe with which the first performance of this play closed has been frequently told. Arriving late, and unaware that the play had been badly received, James was led forth from the wings at the end of the play by its actor-producer, George Alexander. Then, as H. G. Wells, who was in the audience, says, "the pit and gallery had him." For fifteen minutes the house resounded, James told his brother William, "with the hoots and jeers and catcalls of the roughs, whose *roars* [were]...like those of a cage of beasts at some infernal 'zoo.' "[71] The applause he had bargained for had turned into scorn. He had himself become literally the artist-as-victim of a brutal society.

He had the lesson of Nick Dormer yet to learn, the knowledge of his conclusion in *The Tragic Muse* that Nick's triumph was precisely in his turning his victimization and solitude into the self-reliance necessary for the artist to create the lasting artifact. He had, also, to learn to deserve the ending of "The Next Time," written in 1895, after *Guy Domville*'s failure: Ralph Limbert, after years of trying to write a best seller, at last contents himself with the unabashed masterpiece:

> He had floated away into a grand indifference, into a reckless consciousness of art. The voice of the market had suddenly grown faint and far. He had come back at the last, as people so often do, to one of the moods, the sincerities of his prime. Was he really, with a blurred sense of the urgent, doing something now only for himself? We wondered and waited—we felt he was a little confused. What had happened, I was afterwards satisfied, was that he had quite forgotten whether he generally sold or not. He had merely waked up one morning again in the country of the blue and had stayed there with a good conscience and a great idea.

This "country of the blue" was James's great good place, symbolizing his sense that the artist could be free from a public. It is the country of his private imagination. And unlike Ralph Limbert, in whose death James surely expresses one of the fears of his own artistic awakening—he was fifty-two—James would not die just at the moment of self-knowledge. He would write his masterpieces by finding his salvation, not in politics, and not even in a Miriam, a Tragic Muse, but in Nick's human comedy; not in the world, but in the self. He recognized, as Emily Dickinson so calmly had, that he could not fail ultimately to succeed. He had made his attempt for the immediate sign of recognition and had failed. And he was now determined that there would be no next time.

When Edmund Gosse called on Henry the morning after his hideous humiliation at the St. James Theatre, expecting to find him in despair, Gosse "was astonished to find him perfectly calm."[72] *Guy Domville* was James's Damascus. Suddenly (and almost joyfully) he was emptied of hope for popular success of any kind. Seventeen days after the play's opening, James announced to Howells: "I hope to write six immortal short [novels]—and some tales of the same quality."[73] But it was in his notebook that he best expressed his vivid sense of his lifelong commitment to a career of popular failure. There is hardly a passage in all literature that better expresses the moral grandeur of the artist thus dedicated:

> I take up my *own* old pen again—the pen of all my old unforgettable efforts and sacred struggles. To myself—today—I need say no more. Large and full and high the future still opens. It is now indeed that I may do the work of my life. And I will.[74]

Earlier, when he had aspired to write the public novel, he had despised the "petty" aesthetic concerns of Flaubert's circle, its almost religious dedication to questions of art and artifice. But he had come more and more to admire the truly intense intelligence and artistic life of Flaubert, Maupassant, and their circle.[75] Taking up his own old pen again, he would follow their example. He would have the strength to see himself in terms of the myth of the artist-as-hero that he was creating in his stories of artists and writers. Now he would make his novels interesting precisely in his experimental restriction in them of point of view. In fiction he would conduct experiments in the intense geometry of consciousness. His novels would serve art and shape the future of the audience only by making the novel of the future. The American writer, James had early seen and said, had as his secret the ability to penetrate the surface vivacity of forms, to see into areas of social sensibility and private sense where the continental artist would find little to interest him. James contrasted his own novels to the "loose, baggy monsters" of Tolstoy, Dickens, and Thackeray—those

---

[72] Gosse, *Aspects and Impressions* (New York, 1922), p. 34. [73] *Letters,* Vol. I, p. 238. James admonishes himself in this same letter to "Produce again—produce; produce better than ever, and all will yet be well." (p. 237.) [74] *Notebooks,* entry dated January 23rd, 1895, p. 179. [75] James's later comment on Flaubert was becoming more and more true of himself: "His complications were of the spirit, of the literary vision, and though he was thoroughly profane he was yet essentially anchoretic." ("Gustave Flaubert," [the title of James's critical introduction to *Madame Bovary*] [London, 1902], p. x.)

novels, as Stephen Crane was then putting it, that go "on and on like Texas."[76] He had failed to win popular regard by crowding his own writing in his social novels. Now, suddenly—and with exhilaration—he discovered that he might be free to create the American novel as it would, for modern man, inevitably have to be—the novel not of facts but of awareness, dealing not with society but with self, exploring not people but perceptivity.

THE NEW AMERICAN NOVEL

James ignored henceforth, then, the notion that the National Novel would have to deal with American subjects; for he now saw that it was not the character of the American physical and social scene that would make a book, but rather the American's inner geography—his ability to see, to feel, and to understand more deeply than the European. He came fully to understand that in exploring his own deeply American imagination he could write novels, whatever their setting, about the essential America—the country of the blue, the American mind itself. Using London and its surroundings as his symbol for the modern world, he would write the distinctive American novel. In the six years after the failure of *Guy Domville* in 1895, he used this abruptly gained freedom to write a series of remarkable books, including *The Spoils of Poynton* (1897), *What Maisie Knew* (1897), *In the Cage* (1898), *The Awkward Age* (1899), and *The Sacred Fount* (1901). His experiments in these would give his work the fineness and subtlety of texture and the intensity of emotional response that would at last allow him to write his final great books.

The Spoils of Poynton and *In the Cage* are kinds of prefaces to the longer and greater studies. In these James analyzes the effects of ideas lodged in sensitive minds. In each he deliberately surrounds the innocent (or innocence itself) with the possibilities of its corruption. In them James has returned, one might say, to the second, more intense, part of *The Portrait of a Lady* without enmeshing his characters in the first. That whole rich world that Isabel so long entertains in the first half of the novel before, in the second half, she sees it as all she must renounce—this is all absent. Only the renunciation remains. And renunciation is from the first a condition for the intensity of sensibility that the central characters have achieved. James is concerned with the "moral sense" only in its widest meaning, as an aspect of self. Essentially it is the pursuit of consciousness that occupies him. His characters attain in his books a sensibility finer than ordinary; in that attainment they find their satisfactions. Like the little telegraphist in *In the Cage*, they have "winged intelligences" and "winged wits."

The question these books raise, then, is what it means for such cramped and confined winged intelligences to be exposed to an enormous range of experience, but to understand as well that the quite natural temptation to

[76] Quoted in Beer, *Stephen Crane*, p. 143.

act upon this life would close fatally their fine ability to understand it. To be or to act is their choice: to follow public conventions but be ignorant of self, or to indulge the individual yearning for self-knowledge at the cost of public powerlessness. James knew that the "mass of mankind are banded, probably by the sanest of instincts, to defend themselves to the death against any...vitiation of their simplicity."[77] But he knew also that one who had had, like the telegraphist, "a certain expansion of her consciousness," might equally hold on to that and defend it fiercely against degradation by the mass. "To criticise," James said, "is to appreciate, to appropriate, to take intellectual possession, to establish in fine a relation with the criticised thing and make it one's own." Defending their knowledge against the mass, these characters all imitate the condition of the artist as James was (at about the same time) defining it in his tales. That the artist who renounces life for art should find in art a more intense life was the theme of "The Lesson of the Master," "The Figure in the Carpet," and, best of all, of "The Story in It," where James makes a story out of the denial that there could be a story in such renunciation. By renunciation one achieves meditation, and thus the self; literally, gaining the world means losing the self. James's is a christianity of consciousness. In as violent an image as he could summon, he would suggest in *In the Cage* that being caged within was really to *cage out* the teeming, bestial life of the modern mass metropolitan world. The prison was a protection.

This is the logic of Fleda Vetch in *The Spoils of Poynton*. When this story was serialized, James had pointedly titled it "The Old Things." The question for Fleda is how to have things while not losing her moral intelligence; how to possess them while not being possessed *by* them. The novel originated in James's revulsion against the English custom of dispossessing the mother for the sake of the bride. Essentially, as he saw, this might be symbolic of his own discovery of Emerson's belief that material things were in the saddle. Mrs. Gereth is a woman with exquisite taste who has collected together a household of lovely and loved things, and Fleda Vetch a young girl who has studied painting in France and, by nature even more than art, understands, perhaps even better than Mrs. Gereth, the beauty of her old things. Certainly she understands them better than does Mrs. Gereth's son, Owen, who is "all nature in a pair of boots." Mona Brigstock, the mindless young woman whom Owen plans to marry, demands possession of the house, Poynton, complete with all the things, and the eviction of Mrs. Gereth, not because she wants the things themselves, but only because they legally belong there. As Mrs. Gereth suggests,

> she would simply say, with that motionless mask: "It goes with the house." And day after day, in the face of every argument, of every consideration of generosity, she would repeat, without winking, in that voice like the squeeze of a doll's stomach: "It goes with the house—it goes with the house."

When Mrs. Gereth withdraws to Ricks, a smaller house, taking all of the spoils of Poynton with her, Mona demands their return before the

[77] "Preface" to *In the Cage*...(New York, 1908: "The New York Edition"), p. xix.

marriage. Fleda and Owen are left together as intermediaries between the two women whose imaginations have been equally corrupted by their devotion to things.[78] Mrs. Gereth had implied that she would surrender the things to Fleda who, if married to Owen, would continue to "appreciate" them and render her devotion to them. And, in fact, Fleda is in love with Owen, as he comes rapidly to be with her. Deeply passionate, aesthetically and sexually, she yet knows (in what James speaks of as her "intense consciousness") that to accept Owen on his terms is to surrender her will to things. The absolute moral condition that she faces up to Owen—"the great thing is to keep faith"—is such that either she will have him without the question of the things, or not at all. And the constitution of Owen and the world is such that they are unequal to her ego. She has nothing, but therefore herself. At the last a kind of sublime spirit enfolds and protects her. When she so far compromises herself as to agree to accept, in remembrance, "the thing in the whole house that's most beautiful and precious"— but thus, symbolically, to accept them all, to *take* the *things* as a compensation for *missing Owen*—the house, with all its things, is consumed by fire. She is preserved by a divine cosmic busk. She is saved in having nothing. She remains unspoiled by the spoils of Poynton.

Whereas Fleda Vetch is just barely saved from losing the fine consciousness of her renunciation in gaining only one thing, in Maisie Farrange, the child whose developing consciousness is at the center of *What Maisie Knew*, James dramatized the possibilities in the logical consequences of Fleda's compromise. Surely in no other novel, not excluding *The Golden Bowl*, does James so terrifyingly imagine the possibilities of corruption, and the defenses of the self against it. Maisie is involved in watching a ballet of copulation. The novel opens as her divorcing parents agree to share her custody, chiefly as a way of punishing each other. Before long her mother remarries, and only shortly thereafter her father marries Maisie's governess, whom he had already made his mistress. Soon afterward her new stepfather, Sir Claude, and her stepmother begin an affair for which Maisie offers an obvious pretext. With her mother and father she meets an odd assortment of lovers, including a gentle captain and a remarkable American "countess." The question, in the first place, is, of course, what *does* Maisie understand of this sexual dance? Quite clearly the answer is that she sees a good deal, and eventually understands it all. "It was to be the fate of this patient little girl," James writes, "to see much more than she had at first understood, but also even at first to understand much more than any little girl,

---

[78] Mrs. Gereth early reveals her own hollowness in her complete devotion to the "things":

> Yes,...there are things in this house that we almost starved for! They were our religion, they were our life, they were us! And now they're really me.... They are living things to me; they know me, they return the touch of my hand.

Again, at the end of the book, James remarks: "It was absolutely unselfish—she cared nothing for mere possession. She thought solely and incorruptibly of what was best for the things." Her "ruling passion," James concludes, "had in a manner despoiled her of her humanity."

however patient, had perhaps even understood before." Very early she learns the trick of feigning innocence she no longer possesses, assuming this guise as a way of learning more and more. She clearly understands her mother's compulsive love affairs, Sir Claude's shallow weaknesses for sexual affairs, her father's adulterous relation to the Countess, and the varieties of coupling in the book. Moreover, she unquestionably uses her knowledge to attempt to achieve some relatedness for herself with other persons—with her father and Mrs. Beale, with her mother or Sir Claude—in a series of scenes at the conclusion of which she is repeatedly rejected. She understands the character, if not all the details, of the corruption surrounding her personal life and the life of her society. She has, in short, as all the characters agree, no moral sense whatsoever. Her father had put this to her, concerning the affair of Mrs. Beale and Sir Claude:

> "You're a jolly good pretext."
> "For what?" Maisie asked.
> "Why, for their game. I needn't tell you what that is."
> The child reflected. "Well then that's all the more reason."
> "Reason for what, pray?"
> "For their being kind to me."
> "And for you're keeping in with them?...Do you realize, pray, that in saying that you're a monster?"

Both Sir Claude and Mrs. Beale assume that Maisie lacks a moral sense, and hope, in the end, to take advantage of this. It is especially Mrs. Wix, her governess, however, who takes with intense seriousness the question not of what Maisie knows of the affairs, but of what she knows of the moral sense itself, "the thing that...Maisie absolutely and appallingly had so little of."[79]

The reader is able, certainly, to catch Maisie in the act of feigning a moral sense to Mrs. Wix. Her governess, however, is not fooled, and finally concludes that Maisie has none whatsoever. Mrs. Wix, of course, is right. In *What Maisie Knew,* James wrote his naturalistic version of *Huckleberry Finn.* There, too, and told similarly from the child's point of view, the question of Huck's moral sense had come to be the central one of the novel. Huck says of his own conscience that it has no more sense than a yaller dog; yet at first he feels obliged to follow its dictates. At last coming to the crucial decision concerning Jim, he begins:

> The more I studied about this the more my conscience went to grinding me, and the more wicked and lowdown and ornery I got to feeling. And at last... it hit me all of a sudden that here was the plain hand of Providence slapping me in the face and letting me know my wickedness was being watched.... Well, I tried the best I could to kinder soften it up somehow for myself by saying I was brung up wicked, and so I warn't so much to blame....

[79] It seems clear that in this story James quite reverses the question of *The Turn of the Screw.* There the moral ambiguity centers about the governess, here about the child, with no question of Mrs. Wix's position.

Huck determines finally, of course, to reject conscience in order to follow the impulses of his nature, to "take up wickedness again, which was in my line, being brung up to it." Ridding himself of conscience he earns his self; learning to be evil in the social sense, he is good in the private one.

Twain's conclusion, widely criticized in the mid-'80s, is James's conclusion as well. For it is, in various ways, the *moral sense* that Sir Claude, Mrs. Beale, Ida Farrange, and Beale Farrange all possess. It drives them, never satisfied, from one love affair to another. Theirs is a restless, rootless inhuman society of cabs and trains and boats—hopelessly, for all its movement, without direction. The moral sense that it claims is itself, as in *Huckleberry Finn,* a thing of evil. It has led only to the chaos and corruption that Maisie has understood so well. Only by lacking the corrupting moral sense can Maisie retain her innocence. Like Huck, she has been "brung up evil," and by this chance is able to see the hollowness of a society that pretends to be good. To remain completely good she must lack wholly the moral sense that will fatally implicate her in her immoral society. To be good she must, from the point of view of society, be unutterably evil—a monster, as her father has said. James's first word on her was his last. She was, he wrote at the beginning, "a ready vessel for bitterness, a deep little porcelain cup in which biting acids could be mixed." If the porcelain seems to have no color, it has the ability to resist corruption from the bitter acid of its environment. Thus Maisie resists. Her conditions are as absolutely honest as Fleda Vetch's. Like Huck—but with how much less than he, in a sensuous way, to justify and support her!—she is saved, James writes at Maisie's great moment, because "she knew what she wanted. All her learning had made her at last learn that." What she wanted was the opposite of what she had learned her society to consist of and thrive on. She wanted truth, love, faith, peace. "She made her condition...the only right one," Sir Claude declares ecstatically. But Maisie's demands, like Fleda's and Huck's, are too absolute for her degraded society. When, at the last, she is again rejected, she, like Huck, lights out. "She's free—she's free," Sir Claude repeats, sensing perhaps a little of the freedom he has long ago lost. Maisie is free. Out of her knowledge she has saved her innocence. It is no accident that as Huck's great good place is removed from society, sailing down the Mississippi, so the last we see of Maisie is on the steamer, "in mid-channel, surrounded by the quiet sea." Hers is a triumph so great that we can hardly begin to say what, and how well, Maisie knew.

What the territory to which she, this innocent, will go, should be like, is James's concern in *The Awkward Age.* In the late '90s he was writing at so feverish a pace that the residue of one book was spilling over into the next. The problems raised in *Maisie* required an *Awkward Age* to resolve them. As he reversed the conditions of *Maisie* in "The Turn of the Screw," so, in *The Awkward Age* he reconsidered the question, left unanswered, of how the Maisie-figure might continue into adulthood with knowledge untouched by corruption. Mitchett of *The Awkward Age* ironically phrases the difficulty: "Why, my moral beauty, my dear woman...is precisely my

curse. What on earth is left for a man just rotten with goodness?" In
The Awkward Age the question fundamentally concerns another young girl,
Nanda Brookenham, just ready to "come downstairs" into her mother's,
Mrs. Brook's, worldly (and, in some of its denizens, utterly corrupt, even
perverted) society. As yet unmarried, Nanda raises the question of how
far she may be exposed to this society without being personally degraded and
thus made socially undesirable for a good Victorian marriage. It is, as
James puts it in his preface, a "case of the account to be taken, in a circle
of free talk, of a new and innocent, a wholly unacclimatised presence." Indeed,
Nanda has already been thrown dangerously upon the hospitality of a
discontented and foolish young married woman, Tishy Grendon. Mrs. Brook
has tried to save her daughter within the conventions of her corrupt
society by trying to marry her to Mitchett, whose personal concern for his
moral beauty suggests him as a possible compromise. But Nanda has been
so far exposed to the world that she herself will marry only Vanderbank, her
mother's lover and the one person Mrs. Brook herself desires.

Working with much the same debased world as in *What Maisie Knew,*
James here conducts an experiment in virtuousity. As he had in its companion
piece confined our fragmentary sense of the world wholly to Maisie's limited
consciousness, so now his point of view is wholly in the disparate, outer,
social fragments. From Maisie's consciousness we had to construct the world
about her; now, from Mrs. Brook's world, we must guess at Nanda's consciousness. From the French comic writer Gyp and the witty Henri Lavedan,
James adopted the form of the *roman dialogué,* modifying and easing its
formalism by eliminating the paraphernalia of stage directions, but otherwise
writing a novel largely in dialogue. In the rapid moves from one scene to
another, as in a play, James mirrors and symbolizes his fragmentary society.
The Awkward Age has all of the overtones absent in *Maisie,* then—all of the
surface glitter and agitation that the earlier book lacks. It is the undertone,
the consciousness—of Nanda chiefly, but also, in various degrees, of the other
characters—that remains secret. *Maisie* is all undertone. In the figure of
Longdon, alone, James provides a symbolic reflector to suggest the inward
nature of Nanda's salvation from this chaotic society that James shows falling
apart from person to person and scene to scene. Longdon, who has been living
in the country for the last quarter of a century, has managed to preserve,
uncorrupted by the passage of time, a sense of the past. He can thus be
an accurate social and moral critic of the new age, which, abruptly coming
into Mrs. Brook's circle, he suddenly confronts. Certainly he symbolizes the
sense of the past itself. A kind of mythical figure of ancient wisdom, he
speaks of himself as Rip Van Winkle, as "disinterred—literally dug up from
a long sleep," and as having a "fresh, . . . uncorrupted ear." Nanda herself
seems physically to have reincarnated her grandmother, with whom Longdon
had been in love. In this society she alone suggests contact with the past. Even
little Aggie, kept perfectly innocent "for consumption"—in marriage—by the
debauched duchess, will be contaminated by her society immediately upon
entering it. Nanda, Longdon declares, is "more like the dead than the living."

He will reinitiate her into the past. As Maisie's lack of a moral sense preserves her innocence, so for Nanda to die to the awkward age is to be reborn to the age of grace. Her refusal to marry and her final consignment of Van to her mother's foolish needs—"She's so fearfully young," Nanda says—show her superior to her society while simultaneously the opposite of innocent regarding its degeneration. Like Maisie, she knows everything, but in learning as well Mr. Longdon's sense of the past, she is tainted by nothing. In the final lesson she speaks the voice of eternality:

> It was all obviously clearer to her than ever yet. And her sense of it found renewed expression; so that she might have been, as she wound up, a very much older person than her friend [Longdon]. "Everything's different from what it used to be."
>
> "Yes, everything," he returned with an air of final indoctrination. "That's what [Van] ought to have recognized."
>
> "As *you* have?" Nanda was once more—and completely now—enthroned in high justice. "Oh he's more old-fashioned than you."
>
> "Much more," said Mr. Longdon with a queer face.
>
> "He tried," the girl went on—"he did his best. But he couldn't."

Fleda Vetch, Maisie Farrange, and Nanda all suffer—deeply and irredeemably—in having the power to see, to understand all. Like actors who for a time have stepped off the stage to constitute an audience, they can no longer be touched by the action of disintegration. But the burden of their innocence carries it all. It will help in understanding James's method to understand that these characters, fated to see all but helpless to change anything, are the forerunners of Eliot's Tiresias, the ominipresent consciousness of *The Waste Land* who "foresuffered all." In his notes, Eliot wrote, "What Tiresias *sees*, in fact, is the substance of the poem."[80] The greatness of James's art was that in naturalistic, rather than mythical terms, he could understand and show the multiform expansion of consciousness in these figures, and so invest real people with the magic and heroism of mythical ones.

This difficult art he worked once more in *The Sacred Fount* (1901). This is the adult version of the earlier novels. But now one sees that the Narrator (who earns no Christian name) has too long remained in the modern England of Mona Brigstock, Beale Farrange, or Fanny Cashmore, and has himself become a moral vampire preying upon its evil. His only morality can be in feeding upon the immorality of others. He is not merely, and helplessly, exposed to corruption; he actually organizes an entertainment, at a country house, to seek out corruption by trying to discover which couples are having illicit relations. He thrives on degradation. James was obviously coming more and more to rely upon symbols or symbolic situations.[81] If the "Sacred Fount"

---

80 *Complete Poems and Plays*, p. 52. 81 For instance: the fire at Poynton; the temptation of the (false) Maltese Cross; the "golden virgin" beside which, inviolable, Maisie offers to wait for Sir Claude; Mr. Longdon himself. Even the titles of his books have moved from an emphasis on *seeing*, as in *The Portrait of a Lady*, to that on *understanding* the core of meaning: expressed symbolically in *The Sacred Fount, The Wings of the Dove, The Golden Bowl,* and *The Ivory Tower.* These all obviously point to a symbolic core of renunciatory meaning in these novels.

is the wellspring of life, to which all the characters, futilely, seek access in sex, the Sacred Terror, the Narrator, is the least alive. He only detects the futile energy of others. He himself is personally associated in the novel with a symbolic picture of "a young man in black. . .with a pale, lean, livid face and a stare, from eyes without eyebrows, like that of some whitened old-world clown." In his hands he holds a mask, made of "some substance not human," which, the Narrator suggests, he has just taken off. It is he who has taken off the Mask of Life, the Mask of Innocence. Thus bared, he shows (as in *The Picture of Dorian Gray,* for as a character he is much like Wilde) the pale, livid face of death beneath. He is a Tiresias who has lost his eternality—symbolized in the enamel mask—in his surrender to the corruption of his society. Thus he is abruptly stripped to the bare bone of the death's-head. Unlike Maisie, he has lost his knowledge of what innocence wants and has become a grotesque caricature of what evil society wants.

In *The Spoils of Poynton, What Maisie Knew, The Awkward Age,* and *The Sacred Fount,* then, James showed a world at last in chaos. Two decades before Yeats's "Second Coming," James's novels provided definitive evidence that "the ceremony of innocence" had been degraded in all but the few individuals who could establish, with "passionate intensity," the small bright circle of their consciousness. In these books James anticipated the novels and poems of apocalypse that reflect a significant aspect of the twentieth-century mind. In an essay that James wrote only a few months before his death he makes clear how far and how clearly he saw the essential corruption of the age beneath its gilded, confident surface:

> I measure the spread as that of a half a century—only with the air turning more and more to the golden as space recedes, turning to the clearness of all the sovereign exemptions, the serenity of all the fond assurances, that were to keep on and on, seeing themselves not only so little menaced but so admirably crowned. This we now perceive to have been so much their mistake that as other periods of history have incurred, to our convenience, some distinctive and descriptive name, so it can only rest with us to write down the fifty years I speak of, in the very largest letters, as the Age of the Mistake.[82]

In the novels that have been discussed James freed himself from the superficiality of this age. These novels have been largely ignored. But it is certain that without them James could not have written the novels that follow. He had taught himself, in his parables of the varieties of experience, what the International Theme really meant in terms of the geography of the mind. He had created a style adequately and abundantly rich in overtone and suggestion to convey this new sense. And he had learned to give over, to some extent, his portraiture to the sense of the drama that he had salvaged from his failure in the theater. He had learned, most of all, that it was in art that he would preserve his own self, in the beatific dedication to response and responsibility. He had written these novels out of the blessed sense of the grace the very doing had bestowed upon him. He

[82] "The Founding of the 'Nation': Recollections of the 'Fairies' That Attended Its Birth," *Nation,* CI (July 8, 1915), 45.

learned to believe in his art: "The thing I want will come," he said in one of the memorable passages in his notebooks,

—will come in its glory: the quiet, generous, patient mornings will bring it. . . . Oh, soul of my soul—oh sacred beneficence of *doing! Ohne Hast, Ohne Rast!* Consider many things and open the hospitable mind![83]

It was this sense of majesty that had given him these novels. Only the sense of experimentalism—a consequence of his acquired private dedication to art—that hovers about these books keeps them from being, as in all other ways they are, part of what is usually called his "major phase."

THE "MAJOR PHASE"

The Ambassadors largely continues the theme, the possibilities of life in a lifeless world, that all these books share. It is, in particular, the other side of the coin of *The Sacred Fount*. In almost every sense, Lambert Strether is James's alternate "case" to the degeneration of the Observer of that novel.[84] Strether too is playing the game of spying, in his case on the illicit love affair between Chad Newsome and Mme. de Vionnet. He seeks to find, as the Observer puts it in *The Sacred Fount*, "the woman in the case." James returned to his earliest use of the International Theme in taking an innocent American—a man, like Rowland Mallet, to whom nothing had ever happened—and setting this adult Maisie on the journey toward the world of European experience. Strether almost from the first realizes that he is a man in danger: that he will either be saved, by saving himself, as Maisie and Nanda have, or become the degraded spy of *The Sacred Fount*. He is a faceless man, as it were, who must of necessity assume either the Mask of Life or the Mask of Death. Strether, of course, is saved. His dead life will bloom; he will put on the Mask of Life and make it his.

James declares in his preface that the subject of *The Ambassadors* is concentrated,

for the reader's benefit, into as few words as possible—planted, or "sunk," stiffly and saliently, in the centre of the current, almost perhaps to the obstruction of traffic. Never can a composition of this sort have sprung straighter from a dropped grain of suggestion.[85] . . . The whole case, in fine, is in Lambert Strether's irrepressible outbreak to little Bilham. . . . The remarks to which he gives utterance contain the essence of "The Ambassadors."[86]

[83] *Notebooks*, p. 158. [84] James would leave *The Sacred Fount* out of "The New York Edition," feeling perhaps that the sequence of the salvation of the child (Maisie), the adolescent (Nanda), and the adult (Strether) made a kind of unity that the threat posed in *The Sacred Fount* disturbed. [85] This essential germ of the tale came from a story James had heard of how William Dean Howells advised a young man "to live." Using Howells himself (or, more exactly, Howells's projection of himself in Basil March) as the prototype for Lambert Strether, James was perhaps unconsciously announcing his triumphant and confident return to the American Novel. His novel was his declaration of supremacy—that, as he had said of both Flaubert and Ruskin, for instance, he could see "all around" Howells in the matter of the life of the novel. [86] "Preface" to *The Ambassadors* (New York, 1909: "The New York Edition"), p. v.

At this critical moment of the book Strether, feeling the moment to be a crisis—the same kind we have seen in *What Maisie Knew*—reveals that he also knows what he wants: neither to discover Chad's weakness nor to succeed as an intermediary, but merely (and supremely) to live:

> "Live all you can [Strether insists]; it's a mistake not to. It doesn't so much matter what you do in particular, so long as you have your life. If you haven't had that what have you had?...What one loses one loses; make no mistake about that.... [One] lives, in fine, as one can. Still, one has the illusion of freedom; therefore don't be, like me, without the memory of that illusion. I was either, at the right time, too stupid or too intelligent to have it; I don't quite know which."

But this is early in the book. Declaimed in Gloriani's garden (evocative of Eden), Strether's speech reveals the full extent of his innocence. Unlike Maisie, he has seen much, yet understood nothing. He has not yet even perceived, though he perhaps begins dimly to sense it here, that he may yet live—that there is yet "time for reparation," and that the resultant freedom is not an illusion. James planned this progressive deepening of Strether's consciousness very carefully. His protagonist, he early states in his notebook, would be a man who had lived "only for duty and conscience."[87] He has existed, this gentle, clever, literary man, on the fringes of the moral sense all his life, doing neither good nor evil. Now, at fifty-five, he had been sent to Paris by the wealthy Mrs. Newsome to fetch her son Chad back to the family business at Woollett, Massachusetts. Upon his successful return, he knows, he will marry Mrs. Newsome, thus becoming literally, as he will have been symbolically, Chad's father. He will be the father, the representative of civilization—the instrument of the same New England conventionality whose hollowness Mary Wilkins was portraying—who will bring out Chad's moral sense and "save" him from Paris. He is sent to be the widow Douglas of Woollett. Instead, however, he discovers that he himself has no moral sense and discerns that he must stay in Paris to learn to live, to accept life, and to keep the sacred flame glowing in Chad, who unexpectedly develops the incipient moral sense that he inherited from Woollett and is prepared to go back just at the moment that Strether is unwilling to allow him to do so.

On this turn of events James builds from the theme of the hero-as-victim that he had adumbrated in earlier books. Strether has been faced at once not only with the threat to his potential growth in sensibility that he may yet take refuge in his New England conscience and spy on life instead of living it; but also with the threat that his very presence in Paris, as a manifestation of the moral sense that Chad believes him to represent, will in fact awaken that very faculty in Chad. The eventuality that he had supposed would constitute his success now promises to be, even if he saves himself, his defeat. While he himself is blossoming so miraculously, Chad is promising to become a Strether. They have changed roles; and Strether must

---

[87] *Notebooks*, p. 226.

now, to save the beauty of his own transformation, make Chad again as he had been.

Strether's own moral difficulty is further complicated by his growing understanding of Chad's mistress, Marie de Vionnet. He had at first supposed Chad to have a mistress "out of the streets." But fooled by his own naïveté, Maria Gostrey's silence, and little Bilham's lie ("a technical lie," he admits later), Strether comes to believe, in succession, that Chad has no mistress; that Chad is innocently in love with Marie's daughter Jeanne de Vionnet; and last, that Chad is merely devoted to Marie in gratitude for the transformation she has wrought in his character. Thus beguiled, Strether himself unconsciously falls in love with Marie: originally thinking Marie ordinary upon seeing her in Gloriani's garden, he increasingly sees in her all that he has learned is meant by living intensely.

Ironically, it is just after his belated discovery that Chad and Marie are lovers that Marie, realizing Chad is tiring of her (and that she now needs the superior presence of Strether to keep him faithful) holds out the possibility to Strether that they might become lovers when Chad—it is inevitable —finally deserts her. But Strether's moral conditions are as absolute as Fleda Vetch's. Were he to accept even that possibility of love with Marie, he would have proved his transformation to have been cankered at its root. He can gain the triumph of his insight into the truths of self only by giving up the world that would ever threaten it. He must take no spoils. His ambassadorship will be unsullied by moral graft, as he tells Maria Gostrey, only if he returns home, "not, out of the whole affair, to have got anything for myself." The Puritan conscience with which he had arrived in Paris would have cautioned him, in Cotton Mather's famous title phrase, *to do good.* But he finally sees that in a world where the garden has been violated, a world alluringly corrupt, all he can have permanently, undeceptively, is *to be right.* He has lost everything—Mrs. Newsome, Marie de Vionnet, Maria Gostrey, comfort, position, love—but he has gained himself. Maria, whose avocation is initiating Americans into Europe and then sending them home, understands: "But with your wonderful impressions," she tells Strether, "you'll have got a great deal." With, and to that, after all, he goes home.[88]

"We shall never be again as we were"—Kate Croy's final words in *The Wings of the Dove* leave the reader with the same problem that all of James's novels, beginning with *The Spoils of Poynton,* have raised at

---

[88] It is entirely possible to see James expressing in Strether's ambassadorship an analogue to his own literary career. James had taken such ambassadorship as his theme, and had, like Strether, been accused of faithlessness to the American woman; as Sarah Pocock reports Strether morally abandoned to Europe, so critics like Higginson had reported James. Like Strether, of course, James had gotten nothing out of his efforts to be right. (Even *The Ambassadors,* ironically, was virtually rejected by the reader for *Harpers,* Henry Mills Alden.) Perhaps, then, he is suggesting here, as he did in the score of stories about artists, that as Strether has his "impressions," *he* has his art, and that too, as we have come to know, was a great deal.

their conclusions: how the sensitive individual may preserve himself in a world desperately demanding and gloriously alluring, how he may keep himself from surrendering to beauty, wealth, and power, while yet not becoming indifferent to them; by what cunning, in short, we may gain the world without being lost in it. Early in the book James, employing the Christian mythology with whose grief and grace he fills his novel, furnishes the perfect image for Milly Theale's paradoxical situation, living richly with the knowledge of her impending death. Sitting calmly—but precariously—on a slab of rock looking over "gulfs of air"—she is, her companion thinks, "in a state of uplifted and unlimited possession. . . .She was looking down on the kingdoms of the earth."

In no character better than in Kate Croy does James dramatize the power of that world's attraction. She possesses extraordinary beauty, a dazzling, but hard, gem-like beauty that burns constantly before all the characters in the book—certainly for Merton Densher and Lord Mark, who both love her, and for her Aunt Maud, and for Milly Theale herself. Moreover, she is emotionally changeable and, much like Mrs. Brook in *The Awkward Age,* even in some ways morally tender and beautifully understanding: sharing her small income with her sister, she is prepared to defy her wealthy Aunt Maud by going to live with her disgraced father; she loves the poor journalist Merton Densher and discourages her aunt's choice of Lord Mark for her. Possessing such brilliant allure, however, she is essentially the symbol of that corrupt and vicious English society— Milly thinks her the "London girl in person"—that James castigated in four of his five previous novels. She is that world at its most attractive and its most debased. Her inhuman insensitivity, not only toward Milly but toward Densher confirms this. Knowing that Milly will soon die, and suspecting that she loves Densher, Kate proposes to him that he marry Milly in order to inherit her immense fortune after her death, and thus enable him to marry her, to which he replies:

> "Since she's to die I'm to marry her?"
>
> It struck him even at that moment as fine in her that she met it with no wincing nor mincing. She might, for the grace of silence, . . . have only answered him with her eyes. But her lips bravely moved. "To marry her."
>
> "So that when her death has taken place I shall in the natural course have money?"
>
> . . ."You'll in the natural course have money. We shall in the natural course be free."

The incredible strength of her will to power raises her character sublimely, almost to the heights of heroism, while it plunges her, Ahab-like, to the depths of moral madness.

The strength of Kate's will, moreover, creates in her a defect of the imagination. Even Densher, at first rather unimaginative, represents for her "what her life had never given her[:] . . . all the high dim things she lumped together as of the mind." Her great error of imagination lies in misunderstanding Milly's and her own lover's natures. Both she regards as victims, as innocents whose wills her stronger will can easily mold. "You're a dove," she early tells Milly. Densher, whom she regularly treats like a lamb, at one point is himself described as a passive, dove-like bird. In his varied education, we are told, "he had passed...through zones of air that had left their ruffle on his wings." No doubt the reader is misled into accepting Kate's mistaken judgment—that both Densher and Milly are helplessly in her power—by the very authority with which she seems to deal with life, as well as by Milly's own self-deprecations. But it soon becomes clear that Milly has the wisdom of the dove. At Aunt Maud's, for instance, Milly at once sees straight through Lord Mark and singles out Kate as the only complex figure in the group. She resigns herself to being thought dull—which, the narrator remarks, *"protected her wish to keep herself...in abeyance"* (italics added)—in order that she might study England by studying its symbol in Kate. Already aware that she is dying, Milly has no time for self-assertion. She must, as Strether similarly saw, above all *live*. She keeps "herself in abeyance," then, in order to live, in her observation of others, in her relatedness to them, as deeply as possible. She falls in easily, then, with Kate's facile assumption that she is easy prey. Assuming the guise of the dove, she invites pursuit.

How false Kate's notion of Milly's helplessness is suggests itself in the kinds of images by which Susan Stringham—a writer of New England tales[89] —defines her. Susan is not, like Kate, misled by desire, and for her, therefore, Milly is the opposite of dove-like. From first to last she regards Milly as a powerful princess, and associates her with fairy-tale grandeur. As Milly assumes the guise of the dove for Kate's benefit, so she plays the commanding princess for Mrs. Stringham in Venice, where she rents an enormous palace and scores of retainers. She is great, for Susan, not only in her wealth, but chiefly in her emotions. Milly appears to her at one time to be a great steamer in whose wake her own little boat bobs. On another James describes her feeling similarly: "Odd though it might seem that a lonely girl, who was not robust and who hated sound and show, should stir the stream like a leviathan, her companion floated off with a sense of rocking violently at her side." Mrs. Stringham sees the kind of inner greatness in Milly that Kate's calculations have altogether missed. This greatness, it becomes clear, is in the intensity of Milly's consciousness—her great joy, her sensibility, "almost too sharp for her comfort," her sense "that her doom was to live fast," and thus her crowding of her consciousness proportionately, in one violent effort to touch, to see, to understand all. "Since I've lived all these years as if I were dead, I shall die," she declares, stating the paradox on which the book is based, "...as if I were alive."

Milly, then, appears to be either a dove or a fairy-tale figure only because she has concentrated all her public, human perceptions and attitudes into one inward-burning point of consciousness. She is quiet on the surface in proportion to the agitation of her depths—such water images run throughout the book. Kate has not calculated the possibility that Milly would be

[89] It has been suggested that Mrs. Stringham is modeled after Sarah Orne Jewett.

not the dove of innocence, but the holy dove of knowledge—the spirit that would bless Densher at last and raise him from Kate's corruption. Not until the eighth book, at the party that Milly gives in Venice, does Kate appear to Densher to be "wanting in lustre," her black dress in striking visual and symbolic contrast to Milly's white one. It is only now that he begins to see through Kate's view of Milly's innocence. When Kate, commenting on Milly's pearls, remarks, "She's a dove," Densher sees for the first time what inner spiritual power of grace the metaphor suggests. James imagines Densher's assent:

> Milly was indeed a dove; this was the figure, though it most applied to her spirit.... [This] was a power, which was a great power, and was dove-like only so far as one remembered that doves have wings and wondrous flights.

In this realization Densher possesses at once the life for which he had longed. He is caught up in the wings of the dove, in his memory of Milly, and so can give up, much as Strether had done, everything else but the consciousness of *that*. And having that he needs neither Milly's money nor Kate. To him, we sense in the last great scene, Milly has imparted her intensity for life. Kate, brilliant to the end, remains unchanged. Referred to as an "offered victim" in James's preface, Milly is offered here for Densher's transformation; between him and Milly there is a "fusion of consciousness." Densher—in this sense truly Milly's heir—will never again be as he was.

James had frequently spoken of his work as attaining the condition of poetry. As early a piece as *Daisy Miller* he called "pure poetry." *The Wings of the Dove* he thought of as similarly invigorated by a kind of poetry. In *The Golden Bowl,* at last, he claimed the role of poet for himself fully. Not in writing verse, he notes in his preface, but insofar as artists "passionately cultivate the image of life and the art, on the whole so beneficial, of projecting it," are they poets. The seer and oracle speaking "under the descent of the god is the 'poet,' whatever his form."[90] Certainly *The Wings of the Dove* and *The Golden Bowl* are the novels in which the god most nearly descended to James. Milly Theale surrounded by the glittering beauty of Venice; or the Ververs, in Rome or amid Adam's gathering treasures— all live in a rich splendor of sheer sensuous loveliness.

Both books are touched, too, by a halo of moral beauty raised almost to ecstasy by the corruption or possibilities of corruption that encircle it. This beauty is not "innocence," surely, in the ordinary sense that critics usually employ that term in speaking of James's books. R. W. B. Lewis has sharply defined its character by speaking of it as "aggressive innocence," the result of James's sense "that innocence could be cruel as well as vulnerable; that the condition prior to conscience might have insidious overtones."[91] There is no doubt that the quality possessed by the heroes

[90] "Preface" to *Daisy Miller*...(New York, 1909: "The New York Edition"), p. viii; and "Preface" to *The Golden Bowl* (New York, 1909: "New York Edition"), p. xviii.
[91] *The American Adam: Innocence, Tragedy and Tradition in the Nineteenth Century* (Chicago, 1955), p. 154.

of James's later books is aggressive—even dangerous. But if that quality eventually attained by Fleda, Maisie, Nanda, Strether, and Milly may be called innocence, it is an innocence that is ultimately in them so all-seeing and all-knowing, so reveling in the very fact of its knowledge, and making of that knowledge so much in the way of practical results, that "innocence" seems hardly the proper term to describe it. Perhaps it may be described as the very opposite, indeed, of innocence, if innocence is a state of pre-knowledge. This state of awareness *appears* to be innocence, in fact, only in that it constitutes a kind of divine post-knowledge, a seeing around and into society by virtue of having entered and fully transcended it. No longer, in this sense, are these characters *aware* primarily of society. They have "lost" the social world by discovering the self, and they thus treat the world merely as providing the materials for art—the art of ·the consciousness. These heroes strike us as innocent, then, only insofar as we fail to make, with and through them, their divine ascension into a state beyond good and evil.

In *The Golden Bowl,* James projects, in Adam Verver and his daughter Maggie, this same ascension to the innocence that comes after knowledge. Adam, like his namesake before the Fall, has already, as Milly had, achieved this innocence. From this he cannot be dislodged, except perhaps by a great disaster befalling his daughter, just as Milly's innocence was for the moment splintered by the sudden revelation to her of Kate's plot. Adam is secure in his knowledge. Certainly, there is no evidence that his wife Charlotte's unfaithfulness (which Adam certainly knows about and has perhaps even anticipated under the circumstances) affects his joy in life or, indeed, in his marriage. "It's a good deal for me," he tells his daughter, "to have made Charlotte so happy, to have perfectly contented her. ...What she does like [he finally says]...is the way it has succeeded." "Your marriage?" Maggie responds. "Yes—my whole idea. The way I've been justified. That's the joy I give her." When, in conclusion, Adam and Charlotte go to America, Maggie's husband, Prince Amerigo, insists that Charlotte will be happy. At the end, the Ververs are "conjoined for a present effect as Maggie had absolutely never seen them." Adam's mission has become Charlotte's—to represent "the arts and graces to a people languishing, afar off [in America], in ignorance." In contrast to Maggie, Adam has no flawed pieces in his collection. His passion is for "perfection at any price."

If Adam is, like Milly, inviolable, Maggie is a Strether who moves from a state of pre-knowledge to one of post-knowledge. Although, ironically, she literally becomes a princess early in the book, she is not a princess in the same sense as Milly had been until near its conclusion. In this connection, it is important to understand the symbolism of the Golden Bowl. It is not Maggie's marriage that is symbolized by the flawed Golden Bowl. Charlotte, who had thought, ironically, to buy the flawed bowl, does not finally choose it for a wedding present after all. And her marriage is not, like the bowl, shattered. Rather, it is Maggie herself who is flawed—it is she who buys the bowl—in allowing her innocence to be corrupted—not, like Adam's, perfected—by knowledge. In her suspicions, her fears, her turmoil of emotions, she is losing herself. It is she who has become unfaithful, as Prince Amerigo never has, by imagining his infidelity. She is in danger of becoming as corrupted as the Narrator of *The Sacred Fount* by her belief in corruption. " 'If I'm jealous, don't you see? I'm tormented,' [she tells Fanny Assingham]...'and all the more if I'm helpless....Only now,...here I am fairly screaming at you....I go about on tiptoe, I watch for every sound, I feel every breath....'" Moreover, the suggestion is clear—it has been posed not only by Fanny, but by Maggie's father—that, although suspecting Amerigo of unfaithfulness, she has herself been unfaithful to him in a deeper way, by still centering her life upon her father instead of her husband. There had certainly been, as Adam remarks, some "immorality" in this. For these reasons, Maggie's existence, as Fanny says, is surely poisoned.

But it is at this point, in her conversation with Fanny—at the moment when she is most in danger of being consumed by her passion—that we have the first hint of her release from torment. After her hysterical outburst, she suddenly declares herself "surprisingly mild." "I can bear anything," she says:

"Oh, 'bear'!" Mrs. Assingham fluted.
"For love," said the Princess.
Fanny hesitated. "Of your father?"
"For love," Maggie repeated.
It kept her friend watching. "Of your husband?"
"For love," Maggie said again.

Refusing to qualify her moral absolute by tying it to mere persons, Maggie begins, perhaps confusedly, her transformation. The shattering of the Golden Bowl—the final revelation of its flaw—suggests both how her own flaw has been exposed, and how she can now begin to reshape herself. At the end the brilliance of her deception, in sparing Charlotte by refusing to recognize her adultery with the Prince, makes, as Amerigo suggests, Charlotte's deceit stupid. Wise, Maggie is willing to appear a fool. Her knowledge is the power of her innocence. Her innocence is the expense of her wisdom. Prince Amerigo—whose ancestor gave his name to America—had early in the book lamented his utter lack, as he thinks it, of the moral sense. He appeals to Fanny to guide him by her New England conscience: "Your moral sense," he brightly says, "works by steam—it sends you up in a rocket. Ours is slow and steep and unlighted...." But in the end it is Maggie who instructs him with her immoral (in society's terms) sense. For in her suppression of pride, of moral outrage, she preserves the lives of the two couples. She knows, as Oscar Cargill has said, "that she could not claim any revenge upon her rival without spreading destruction among all she knew."[92] To save herself, she must spare the others. She too, then, at last knows what she wants—not the revenge, the humiliation, the hate, the distrust that society conventionally demands, but the forgiveness, the confi-

92 *The Novels of Henry James,* p. 418.

dence, (above all) the love that the self requires. The precious Golden Bowl of her all-enfolding love—this, flawless, preserves them all.

At first discontented, even tormented, Maggie reminds one of no character in James more than Christina Light, who had also become a princess, the Princess Casamassima, and who had out of her pain destroyed Roderick Hudson in one novel and Hyacinth Robinson in another. In learning how not to destroy, learning to enfold, Maggie, however, ceases to be merely the real but hollow Princess, Christina, and becomes the essential Princess, Milly Theale. Finally, James had succeeded in bringing together the inner and outer, actual and essential princesses. In this respect *The Golden Bowl* constitutes a new stage in James's art. For Maggie's triumph in making her inner grandeur match her outer signifies that for her no renunciation is necessary. Fleda has only memory; Maisie will be poor; Nanda retreats to Longdon's country house; Strether returns to America with nothing; and Milly literally dies, as Densher dies imaginatively, to the world. All renounce society in order to retain themselves. But Maggie manages to possess both world and self, to live the life of a princess while continuing, inwardly, to *be* a princess.

JAMES'S SUMMING-UP:
THE TWENTIETH-CENTURY SAGE

James had first begun to project his fable of renunciation soon after his failure as a popular novelist and dramatist led him to feel that he had to seek his success in his art itself. By 1904, when *The Golden Bowl* was published, an increasingly large group of devotees had gathered about him. Partly because he had given his age the instrument of analytical criticism, he was now receiving, if not popular, at least intelligent critical attention. His correspondence became increasingly rich in letters from young men eager to take lessons from the "Master." He had taken, in 1898, a house at Rye, Sussex and now, after years of being a guest, began to entertain. H. G. Wells was nearby; Joseph Conrad or Harold Frederic, also expatriates, might appear; and Stephen Crane, miraculously, would turn up. Crane too had read James. James developed a particularly close relation with Edith Wharton although she failed to appreciate his late fiction. In America during 1904 and 1905, James would be taken to the White House by Secretary of State John Hay to visit President Theodore Roosevelt, and would deliver his lectures on *The Lesson of Balzac* and *The Question of Our Speech* to huge audiences in several American cities. As a final evidence of a change in climate, *The Golden Bowl*, to everyone's astonishment, sold out four printings in America within a year. All this suggests, one might say, that in *The Golden Bowl* James significantly altered the patterns of his novel of renunciation in response to his own sense that now, at last, he might have the world and his art both, without compromise. He too had made his absolute conditions. And they had been met.[93] *The Golden Bowl,* then, is the conclusion to the whole series of novels following *The Spoils of Poynton,* in the sense that it provides the ultimate vision of absolute knowledge reentering and thus redeeming the world. But it is also obviously as much the beginning of a whole new kind of novel, for the age of renunciation was ended.

Now James, as he himself said, redreamed his career in three works or collections that have as their very theme and *raison d'être* the public revelation of the private character: his prefaces to "The New York Edition of the Novels and Tales of Henry James" (1907–1917)[94]; his *The American Scene,* the result of his trip to America in 1904; and his volumes of autobiography, appearing between 1913 and 1917. These three undertakings unquestionably make for a kind of summing-up of the several aspects of his life and mind—in the prefaces, of the art that went into his books; in *The American Scene,* of the country that gave him his mission in the largest sense; and in the autobiographies, of the personal life that shaped him to accept his American mission to be an artist. These are James's public testaments to a world that he had rediscovered. At his crisis in the late '90s, he had identified the situations of his heroes with that of the artist, tainted by and driven out of society. But as he now felt himself, in all the royal panoply of his art, to have been "claimed" by society, so he was able, first in *The Golden Bowl,* and afterward in these works, to bring that art to the service of society. It was fitting that on his seventieth birthday a large group of friends presented him with a golden bowl. For that, as book and as symbol, constituted his rebirth into society.

F. W. Dupee's remark that in his prefaces "James selects [and] revises... almost exclusively from his viewpoint as...author of *The Golden Bowl*"[95] thus suggests more than Dupee meant. For it was that vision that gave him the ability to write the prefaces at all, hard as he found this task to be. Taken together, as James intended them to be, the prefaces are fundamentally a discourse by James on his way with fiction. All have essentially the same form: by what means the germ of the story came to him; the permutations of its development once lodged in his mind (and notebooks); his seeing more and more deeply into its implications; the problems of composition and technique (with much talk of the complex attempts to manage point of view); and his sense of his own relative success in solving, by seeing into, these questions. Thus, each preface is a sort of self-portrait of the artist himself, each a veritable dramatization of the creative process of his whole life. In the preface to the first volume of "The New York Edition" *Roderick Hudson,* James remarked pointedly:

---

93 As early as 1893, in *The Middle Years,* James had forecast precisely this possibility in Dencombe's encounter with Doctor Hugh:

> He enjoyed this gushing modern youth and felt with an acute pang that there would still be work to do in a world in which such odd combinations were presented. It wasn't true, what he had tried for renunciation's sake to believe, that all the combinations were exhausted.

94 It would perhaps have been a melancholy satisfaction to James that even Howells, for all his popularity and acute business sense, had not had the collected edition for which he had hoped. 95 *Henry James,* p. 278.

These notes represent, over a considerable course, the continuity of an artist's endeavour, the growth of his whole operative consciousness and, best of all, perhaps, their own tendency to multiply, with the implication, thereby, of a memory much enriched.[96]

In the leisurely but controlled flow of these prefaces, in the pleasure James shows in lingering on a detail or a theme and testifying to the abundance of his memory, in the wonder he expresses at the marvelous connections between things, James depicts himself as a kind of benevolent literary father-seer for his audience. He envisioned his prefaces, he told Howells, as forming "a sort of comprehensive manual...for aspirants in our arduous profession,"[97] and as educating their audience by teaching Americans criticism, discrimination, and appreciation. James enfolds his audience in the wings of his art.

"I am hungry for Material," James wrote to Howells as he was making plans to come to America. He had been away for twenty-one years and was expecting "quite [to] thrill with the romance of elderly and belated discovery."[98] Surely he had been away so long that America had come to hold the same romantic fascination for him that Europe had in the '70s. With this fascination was mingled James's reawakened sense of his relatedness to his American audience and to the place of his birth and the scenes of his childhood. Lecturing, and supported by arrangements to write a book out of his American travels,[99] James first visited his brother William and his family in New Hampshire, in the autumn of 1904. He traveled to Boston, Cambridge, Concord, Salem, and Newport; Christmas he spent in New York; then he moved southward, to Philadelphia, Washington, Virginia, Richmond, Charleston, and Florida during the next two months. In March, he moved westward, pausing at Indianapolis, Chicago, St. Louis, and finally ending in California. It was an amazing journey, one that saturated James with impressions of his America as never before.

As could be expected, he found America strange from the first, "a great monster"; but he also confessed "feeling, how agreeable it is, in the maturity of age, to revisit the long neglected and long unseen land of one's birth."[100] In the book he produced, surely the best book of American travel ever written by an American, James responds variously in both directions, to his revulsion and to his wonder. He detects everywhere the evidences of vulgarity and power that symbolize the new America for him. But he discovers as well the compensating possibilities of a life of the imagination, of life for the arts. Prevented from calling the book *The Return of the Native* by Hardy's title, but perhaps sensing how much he was not merely a native but also a writer, he improved this to *The Return of the Novelist*. That at last his book emerged as *The American Scene* suggests how he had ultimately decided to treat it as largely "other," reserving his personal responses for a small late group of remarkable stories.

[96] P. vi. [97] *Letters*, Vol. II, p. 99. [98] *Letters*, Vol. II, pp. 9, 21. [99] A traveler to the end, James published not only *The American Scene,* but also *English Hours* (1905) and *Italian Hours* (1909). [100] *Letters*, Vol. II, p. 20.

What he had felt personally is brilliantly evoked, however, in the opening scene of the book, depicting the return of the passionate pilgrim to an America that he fears he may have lost:

> Conscious that the impressions of the very first hours have always the value of their intensity, I shrink from wasting those that attended my arrival, my return after long years.... They referred partly, these instant vibrations, to a past recalled from very far back; fell into a train of association that receded, for its beginning, to the dimness of extreme youth. One's extremest youth had been full of New York, and one was absurdly finding it again, meeting it at every turn, in sights, sounds, smells, even in the chaos of confusion and change; a process under which, verily, recognition became more interesting and more amusing in proportion as it became more difficult, like the spelling out of foreign sentences of which one knows but half the words.[101]

This feeling of strangeness—held in abeyance while he is in New Hampshire —grows increasingly pronounced as James discovers that the English Claimant has been robbed of his American properties: the America he knew has been seized by change.

After *The American Scene* James's fiction continued, as always, to record the lessons of his life. "A Round of Visits" and "Crapy Cornelia," two of the most striking stories in *The Finer Grain* (1910) would show the influence of his multiplied sense of the ambiguous character and potentialities of the American scene. The same is true of one of his most famous stories, "The Jolly Corner." These stories, together with his uncompleted novels, *The Ivory Tower* and *The Sense of the Past,* show James, stirred deeply by his renewed confrontation with the American environment, returning specifically to the themes of *The Passionate Pilgrim.* Whatever his disillusionment with the actualities of that return, the wonder of his pilgrimage had been revitalized in him. James spoke of "The Jolly Corner" (written in 1909), for instance, as a "finished fantasy."[102] In that story Spencer Brydon, returning to the New York of his youth in order to oversee the disposition of one of his houses, comes to feel that his past, his American ghostly double who has been growing all these years in terms of his own American potential, inhabits a jolly corner of the house that is being renovated. The living man, like Clement Searle in "A Passionate Pilgrim," is haunted by the self he never quite possessed. But when he at last "corners" his American ghost—it is *he* who has been haunting *it*—he finds that "the face was the face of a stranger," covered at first with a mutilated hand. Only at the last, in love, can he understand how this "evil, odious, blatant, vulgar," businessman—with a million a year—is himself; and yet how far he has freed himself, in having gone to Europe, from this potentiality. Only then, this is to say, can he, like James, finally accept the life he *has* lived.

The Ivory Tower (1917) was left incomplete by James and published posthumously under the supervision of Percy Lubbock. This is his first

---

101 *The American Scene,* p. 1.   102 "Preface" to *The Altar of the Dead...and Other Stories* (New York, 1909: "The New York Edition"), p. xxiv.

specifically American novel since *The Bostonians* and, like that book, satirizes the ways in which older American aspirations—of reform or of business success—have been corrupted by change and are corrupting man in the present. Gray Fielder is another of those "exposed and assaulted, active and passive" characters passionately engaged in the search for self-knowledge through his relations with others. Like Milly Theale, Strether, and Maggie Verver, however, he is sent forth on his moral journey through a ruthless, blighted, immoral society by inheriting a large fortune from his half-uncle, Mr. Betterman. Gray must, to preserve himself, cut through the deceptive appearances of American society; for, no less than the Hollywood that Nathanael West would portray in *The Day of the Locust,* James's America is a world made of illusion: although Betterman has been a perfectly "ruthless operator," Gray at first believes him to have been "a model of every virtue"; Gray's friend Horton Vint, whom Gray trusts to manage his fortune, is corrupted by money; Cissy Foy, whom Gray becomes interested in romantically, is in reality Vint's mistress. All is illusion. Contaminating money has overwhelmed and blighted all, even the Newport that James had earlier loved. But this degradation—as for Henry Adams, violent and soon apparent—provides an education for Fielder. He is the sole character to escape from the Ivory Tower of Illusion. Buffeted by one disillusionment after another, he is the only one ultimately undeceived. All the others, in their devotion to money or sensuality, remain webbed in their delusive power, in the Ivory Tower.

Just before he died, James began to revise the work he had done on *The Sense of the Past* (1917), a novel first begun as early as 1899, a decade after Twain's *A Connecticut Yankee in King Arthur's Court,* the book which it so curiously resembles. Like Hank Morgan, James's Ralph Pendrel is a kind of international ghost, an American Claimant who has become stranded in the English past. Out of admiration for a slim volume titled "An Essay in Aid of the Reading of History," which Ralph has written, an English relative wills him an old English house—a veritable part of the past that Ralph has been hoping, by historiography, to preserve. Longing for the antique world, he is another Clement Searle who this time, however, becomes successful in his claim upon it. For the eighteenth-century house that he inherits is a kind of naturalistic time machine. In it he is transported backward more than a hundred years, while his Doppelgänger steps down from a portrait to assume his role in the present. But, much like Twain's Camelot, the past London that Ralph Pendrel comes thus to possess in the past is no less debased, he learns, than the present which James depicts in *The Ivory Tower.* Moreover, Ralph is forced to act in the past without complete knowledge of it; and so, in continually exposing his modernity, he proves himself tragically alien from both past and present. He becomes a ghost from the present, haunting the past, as much as the past had haunted Clement Searle.

These two novels and "The Jolly Corner" suggest, it can be argued, that in returning to America in 1904 (and later in 1910), James became, as never before, painfully aware of the changes in society and sensibility wrought in America by a collective machine technology. Other writers would soon begin to respond vigorously to this feeling. Only a few years after James's death, Sherwood Anderson would publish *Winesburg, Ohio* (1919) and *Poor White* (1920); Randolph Bourne was writing his radical essays at about the same time; Eliot and Pound were in England, reviewing James's unfinished books; F. Scott Fitzgerald, influenced by James and Edith Wharton, began to satirize his own age—the "Jazz Age"—in 1920; Dos Passos's *Manhattan Transfer* would appear in 1925, less than a decade after James died; Mencken and Lewis were beginning to satirize the "boobgeosie." This is to say that the fable of *The Sense of the Past* and *The Ivory Tower* are "A Passionate Pilgrim" made new and different by James's lifelong development—within his works and for his followers—of a modern sensibility.

For while James knew that the machine technology was corrupting to the individual, he knew as well that one could not find a resort in the past: while the past haunts the individual in his sense of the incompleteness of the present, the past itself, he knew, was incomplete. Either for good or bad, one was locked in the present. When William published *Pragmatism* in 1907, Henry told him that he himself had always thought pragmatically. He had understood, that is, how the past (as William had said) was irretrievable, but how the present might preserve the continuity from it to the future of eternal human impulses and values. His autobiographies, therefore, moving from the past into the present, showed both devotion and irony toward the past. These, written during the same period as his unfinished novels, were statements, essentially, of how he had discovered his vocation in a life of art. In them he was concerned with the very process whereby they themselves could ultimately, as summaries of a life so lived, come into being. The sensibility achieved and the books that flowed from it justified the past. His sense of the past could at last, like Ralph Pendrel's, give him a sense of the ineluctable present.

James was never more alive to the present and the past simultaneously than when, on July 28, 1914, the Central Powers declared war on Serbia. Only a week after this, writing to Howard Sturgis, he summed up his vivid sense of how the whole period between the Civil War and the First World War had been a betrayal of the present:

> The plunge of civilization into this abyss of blood and darkness by the wanton feat of those two infamous autocrats is a thing that so gives away the whole long age...that to have to take it all now for what the treacherous years were all the while really making for and meaning is too tragic for any words.[103]

This was the day after Britain went to war, August 4, 1914. James had lived his whole life as a novelist undeceived, without an Ivory Tower wherein he could find refuge in illusions. He had castigated English, American, and international society. Now, in scores of letters, he wrote to friends of the ultimate illusion of a Europe only apparently civilized, a world at last

103 *Letters*, Vol. II, p. 398.

blatantly revealing the moral and cultural degradation that James had described in nearly all of his novels. He had seen the Civil War at the beginning and the First World War at the close of his career, and understood both as personal and public betrayals. In "the look of everything, especially in that of people's faces, the expressions, the hushes, the clustered groups, the detached wanderers" during the early days of World War One he recalled "so many impressions long before received [during the Civil War] and in which the stretch of more than half a century had still left a sharpness." He also felt a compensating exhilaration for the involvement that he had missed earlier, as he now participated in the war effort through the American Volunteer Motor-Ambulance Corps in France and Edith Wharton's *Accueil Franco-Belge*. The only writing he could concentrate on were essays concerned with war issues, collected posthumously in *Within the Rim* (1918). Essentially he came to see the two wars as one and the same. His second, like his first great war, he spoke of as an American War, even before the United States had entered it. The Allies, he told an interviewer for the New York *Times*, "are fighting to the death for the soul and the purpose that are in *us*, for the defense of every ideal that has most guided our growth and that most assures our unity."[104] To the end America was in his mind. He dictated the first part of the autobiographical *The Middle Years* in the autumn of 1915 and only the night before his stroke on December 1st, finished his last piece of writing. This was a memorial to a young British soldier, Rupert Brooke, already dead, whose book *Letters from America* James introduced. He wished, he said in this piece, that he could have shown America to Brooke, helped him to understand it. James had come full circle round. The age was preparing to begin the enormous task of incorporating into the evolution of consciousness the complex and subtle sensibility he had willed it. On February 28, 1916, in "great serenity of spirit," Henry James died. An age was over, and one that he and his peers had helped to make was ready to begin.

---

[104] Quoted in Leon Edel, "Henry James: The War Chapter 1914–1916," *University of Toronto Quarterly*, X (January 1941), 133.

Index

Entries in capital and small capital letters are of American writers
and other important figures who were active from 1865
to 1914 and receive more than passing mention.
Page numbers in italic type (e.g., *241*) indicate major discussions.
Titles of books, articles, etc. and subjects of treatment are
listed under individual authors' names.

f = discussion continued on the following page   n = reference to a footnote
ff = discussion continued on several following   q = author is quoted
    consecutive pages

Abbott, Lyman, 9q, 211
Accueil Franco-Belge, 364
ADAMS, BROOKS, 22q, 262, 298, 321, 334q;
  Civilization and Decay, 83n
Adams, Charles Francis, Sr., 176
Adams, Charles Francis, Jr., 7q, 27, 202q,
  238, 301q, 302, 321q; *Chapters of Erie,*
  2q
Adams, Clover Hooper, 334n
ADAMS, HENRY, 5, 8, 9, 17, 27, 43, 79n,
  84q, 95, 155, 176q, 178, 213, 231, 238,
  239, 242q, 244, 249, 262f, 284f, 290,
  296ff, 313, 362; and America, studies of,
  299ff; on *Ancient Society,* 199fq; "Bud-
  dha and Brahma," 308q; *Chapters of
  Erie,* 2q, 176f, *297ff,* 300; *Democracy,*
  35, 177, *302ff; Documents Relating to
  New England Federalism,* 299; *Education,* 11, 78q, 176, 182, 199, 281, 296,
  306ff; Essays in Anglo-Saxon Law,
  297f, 300; *Esther,* 302, *303ff; Gallatin,*
  299, *303;* and historicism, 298, 300;
  History, 180, *300ff,* 302, 303, 306; and
  Henry James, 312n; and journalism,
  297; *Life of George Cabot Lodge,* 296q,
  308; and medievalism, 304ff; *Memoirs
  of Arii Taimai,* 79n; *Mont-Saint-Michel,*
  71, 90, *305ff,* 307; and naturalistic history, 300, 301n, 303; and psychology,
  47q; *Randolph,* 299, 303; and shifts in
  attitude, 306ff; split personality of,
  302ff; thought, poles of, 298; and Mark
  Twain, 176ff; *Vis Inertia,* and the concept of, 334n; and Zola, 71n
Adams, Herbert, 231
Adams, John, 278

Addams, Jane: *A New Conscience,* 247
Afterdreams, My, 225
Agassiz, Louis, 9q
Agrarianism, 83; and farmers' protest
  movements, 110; and Garland, 126f, 128,
  135
Aiken, Conrad, 50, 290n, 313; *Brown-
  stone Eclogues,* 162n; on Emily Dick-
  inson, 285q; *Time in the Rock,* 285q;
  Ushant, 200
Alcott, A. Bronson, 14
Alcott, Louisa May, 21, 281q; *Jo's Boys,*
  59; *Little Men,* 59, 185; *Little Women,*
  59, 185
Alden, Henry Mills, 47n, 352n
ALDRICH, THOMAS BAILEY, 5, 42, 153,
  178, 213q, 279, 293, 338; *An Old Town
  by the Sea,* 135q; *Story of a Bad Boy,*
  59, 185; on travel, 78q, 79n; "Twelve
  Memorable Murders" (with Howells),
  165f
Alexander, George, 340
Alexis, Grand Duke of Russia, 106f
ALGER, HORATIO, 216f
Alienation, 296f; in James, 314f, 327f; in
  Edith Wharton, 263ff
Alta Californian, 168
Altgeld, J. P., 27q, 41, 218
American dream, 13, 42
American Economic Association, 206
American exploration, 80
American Fabian, 230
AFL, 208f
American Historical Association, 244, 302
American Journal of Education, 235
American Psychical Society, 132

American Publishing Company, 166
American Volunteer Motor-Ambulance Corps, 364
Ancestral societies, 83n
Anderson, Sherwood: *Poor White*, 4, 363; *Winesburg, Ohio*, 4, 363
Andover Seminary, 134
Anglo-Catholicism, 84
Anson, Adrian C., 86nq
Apocalypse: *see* Millennialism
Appeal to Reason, 208, 234
Appleton Co., D. D., 232
Arena, 236, 246
Aristotle, 234; and evolution, 85
Armour, Philip D., 256
Armour Institute of Technology, 244
Arnold, Matthew, 296, 313
Associated Press, 26
Astor, John Jacob, 82
Astor, Mrs. William, 3n
Atchison Globe, 120
Atlanta Constitution, 92, 96, 100
Atlantic Monthly, 35f, 41, 49, 53, 92, 108, 140, 172, 175n, 186, 194, 226f, 234, 292f, 314, 323, 338
Auden, W. H., 193q
Augustine, St., 306
Austin, Mary, 236
Autobiography, 1; in Henry Adams, *306ff*; American backgrounds, 282f; in Dreiser, *275ff*; Howells on, 282q; in Henry James, *310ff*, 312n, 363f; and self-investigation, *279ff*; in Twain, *197ff*; in Edith Wharton, 263, *273ff*; in Whitman, *281ff*

Bacheller Syndicate, 56, 60
Bacon, Francis, 210
Badeau, Adam, 22q
BAKER, RAY STANNARD (David Grayson, *pseud.*): *Adventures in Contentment*, 246; *Native American*, 246q; "Railroads on Trial," 246
Bakunin, Mikhail A., 76, 336
Baldwin, James Mark, 204q; on the child, 184q; *Senses and Intellect*, 205
Balzac, Honoré de, 250, 257, 259, 264f, 301, 312f, 315, 323f, 323n; *Pere Goriot*, 281
Bancroft, George: Henry Adams on, 298q
Bangs, J. K., 175n
Barlow, Joel: *Columbiad*, 95
BARNUM, P. T., 3, 9, 23ff, 168n; "The Art of Money Getting," 217q; *Humbugs of the World*, 23
Bates, Arlo, 160
Baudelaire, Charles, 153, 315, 329; "Calumet de Paix," 13n; *Les Fleurs du Mal*, 13n
Baxter, Sylvester, 179
Beadle Dime Novels, 239
Beard, Charles, 206n
Beauregard, General Pierre G. T., 29

Beaux Arts, 243
Bebel, August: *Die Frau und der Sozialismus*, 224
Beecher, Catherine, 139
Beecher, Edward N.: *The Lost Atlantis*, 232q
BEECHER, HENRY WARD, 3, 9, 18, 30, 168n, 216, 287; *Evolution and Religion*, 10q; and Tilton trial, 22; on wealth, 72q
Beecher, Thomas K., 169
Belasco, David: *Heart of Maryland*, 26
Bellamy Club, 233n
BELLAMY, EDWARD, 20n, 209n, 211, *220ff*, 227, 230q, 233, 236f, 244q, 282, 283q; "The Blindman's World," 221; *Dr. Heidenhoff's Process*, 221q; *Equality*, 223f, 230; "Feudalism of Modern Times," 321q; "How I came to write *Looking Backward*," 221q; *Looking Backward*, 178, 216, *222ff*, 226, 229, 230f, responses to, *223ff*, Twain on, 179q; *Miss Ludington's Sister*, 221; "The Old Folks' Party," 221q; "A Summer Evening's Dream," 221q
Bellamy, Joseph, 220
Benjamin, Park, 287
Bennett, Arnold, 315, 317q
Berenson, Bernard, 263, 264q
Berlin, University of, 176
Berryman, John, 57q
Besant, Annie, 277
Beyle, Henri (Marie Stendahl, *pseud.*), 301
BIERCE, AMBROSE, 17, 51, 88, *121ff*, 277; "Affair at Coulter's Notch," 123; "Chickamauga," 123q; "The Coup de Grâce, 123; *Devil's Dictionary*, 121, 122q; *Fiend's Delight*, 122; and Hamlin Garland, 124f; "An Imperfect Conflagration," 122q; on James and Howells, 124q; "Oil of Dog," 122q; "One Summer Night," 122q; and Satanism, 122; as satirist, 123f; and violence, 122; *The Wasp*, 121
"Big Rock Candy Mountains, The," 210n
Bigelow, Sturges: *The Soul of the East*, 79n
BILLINGS, JOSH: *see* Shaw, Henry Wheeler
Bishop, W. H.: *Garden of Eden, U.S.A.*, 214
Bixby, Horace, 167, 189
Björnson, Björnstjerne: on Howells, 47fq
Black, William, 153
Blackmore, Richard, 153
Blackmur, R. P., 307q, 333q
Blaine, James G., 22, 302
Blair, Walter, 194q
Blake, William, 95; *The Marriage of Heaven and Hell*, 122
Blavatsky, Helen P.: *Isis Unveiled*, 226
Bliss, W. D. P., 226, 229
Boas, Franz, 234
Bohemianism, 14, 244, 279

Bok, Edward, 222; *Americanization,* 13q
Bond, J. Wesley, 111q
Boone, Daniel, 109
Booth, General William, 86
Boston Advertiser, 36
Boston Evening Transcript, 75
Boston Globe, 20
Bourne, Randolph, 363
BOWLES, SAMUEL, 26q, 286f, 291; *Across the Continent,* 80q, 210n
Boyesen, H. H., 102q
Brace, Rev. John Pierce, 139
Bradford, William, 121, 170
Brendan, St., 210
"Broadacre City," 242
Broadway Magazine, 253
Brockett. L. P., 107q
Brontë, Charlotte, 287
Brontë, Emily, 287
Brooke, Rupert: *Letters from America,* 364
Brook Farm, 228, 334
Brooks, Phillips, 84, 304
Brooks, Van Wyck, 55, 136q, 227q, 321; on Howells, 50q
Brown, Alice, 159f
Brown, Charles Brockden, 30
Browne, Carl, 213
BROWNE, CHARLES FARRAR (ARTEMUS WARD, *pseud.*), 28, 107
Browne, Sir Thomas, 287
Browning, Elizabeth B., 287
Browning, Robert, 108, 287, 313; "Mr. Studge the Medium," 211
Browning Societies, 19
Brown University, 205, 212, 217
Brunetiere, Ferdinand, 259q
BRYAN, WILLIAM JENNINGS, 86, 110; "Cross of Gold," 244q
BRYANT, WILLIAM CULLEN, 18, 284; *Iliad* and Spanish mystics, translation of, 12; *Picturesque America,* 17; *Poems,* 17
Bryce, Sir James, 82, 83nq, 106q, 320q, 321q
Buckle, Henry Thomas, 15
Buddhism, 79n
Buffalo Express, 170
Bulfinch, Thomas: *Age of Chivalry,* 93
Bull, Ole, 7
Bulwer-Lytton, Sir Edward George, 21
Bunyan, John, 4, 241, 246, 287; *Pilgrim's Progress,* 128
Burke, Edmund, 13n
Burlinghame, J. W., 96
Burne-Jones, Philip, 322q
Burnet, Thomas, 210
BURNETT, FRANCES H., 287; *Little Lord Fauntleroy,* 59; *Two Little Pilgrims' Progress,* 241
BURNHAM, DANIEL, 241n, 242q
Burroughs, Edgar Rice: *Tarzan,* 87
Burroughs, John: *Notes on Walt Whitman,* 36nq
Business Man's Association of Grace Baptist Church, 217

Cabell, James Branch, 90q
CABLE, GEORGE WASHINGTON, 7, 88, *100ff,* 137, 147, 167; *The Cavalier,* 111, 151; "The Due Restraints and Liberties of Literature," 101q; "The Freedman's Case in Equity," 101; *The Grandissimes,* 85, 100, *102ff,* 111; on Howe, 116q; "Literature in the Southern States," 101q; *Lover of Louisiana,* 92q; *The Negro Question,* 28, 101; "The Silent South," 101; in Southern fiction, 101; *Strange True Stories of Louisiana,* 111
Cahan, Abraham, 50, 227
California, University of (at Berkeley), 72n, 249
Calvinism, 72
Cameron, Elizabeth, 303
Cameron, James Donald, 27
"Captain of Industry," 321, 331
Carey, Henry C., 206, 206n
Cargill, Oscar, 327, 334n, 357
Carleton, Will, 7
Carlyle, Thomas, 14n, 19; *Sartor Resartus,* 306
Carman, Bliss, 15
CARNEGIE, ANDREW, 7, 14, 74, 94, 256; *Triumphant Democracy,* 5q; "Wealth," 216
Carpet Bag, The, 172
Casey, James: *A New Moral World,* 214q
Casson, Herbert N., 209q
Catastrophism, 8, 110, 178; *see also* Millennialism
Cather, Willa, 143, 156n
Catherine, St., 84
Centennial Exposition of 1876 (Philadelphia), 28f, 79n, 83, 217, 273
Century, The, 71, 116, 175n, 193, 287; "War Series," 29, 60
Century Club, 115
Century Company, 97
Chambers, Robert: *Book of Days,* 84; *Vestiges of the . . . Creation,* 202
Change, 307
Channing, William Ellery: translation of Dante, 12
Chapman, George: *Eastward Ho!,* 106q
Chateaubriand, François René, 106
Chaucer, Geoffrey, 92
Chautauqua, 7
Chicago, University of, 243
Chicago Daily News, 151
Chicago Freie Presse, 223
Chicago Inter Ocean, 19
Chicago Record, 248
Child: figure of, 184f; children's literature, 142f, 185
CHOPIN, KATE, 147, 243
Christian Science, 181, 211
Christian Socialists, 226, 229
CHURCHILL, WINSTON: *Richard Carvel,* 26, 83n
Church of the Carpenter, 43, 229
Church of the Christian Endeavor, 115, 211

Circular, The, 212nq
City, *3ff,* 184n, 189, *240ff;* Crane's view, 62; depiction of, 148f; Howells's view, 57; population increase, 4
Clapp, Henry, 168
Clarke, James Freeman: *Ten Great Religions,* 205
Clemens, John Marshall, 172
Clemens, Olivia L., 194
Clemens, Orion, 171f, 176
CLEMENS, SAMUEL LANGHORNE: see Twain, Mark
Clemens, Susy, 197
Cleveland, Grover, 27
Clews, Henry, 322q
Cobb, Henry Ives: Fisheries Building, 243n
Codman, Ogden, Jr., 3q; *Decoration of Houses,* 269, 273
Cody, William F. ("Buffalo Bill"), 65f, 74, 106
Coeur d'Alene strike, 208
Coffin, R. P. Tristram, 136q
Cohen, Morris, 206n, 214q
Coleridge, Samuel Taylor, 287
Colfax, Schuyler, 80
Collens, T. Wharton: *The Eden of Labor,* 105q
Colonial Dames, 83n
Columbia University, 302
Columbus, Christopher, 106
Commager, Henry Steele, 203, 204q, 318, 319q
Commons, John R., 211q
Common Sense Philosophy (Scottish), 203f, 282
Comte, Auguste, 202, 238, 280; *Cours de philosophie positive,* 303
Condivi, Ascanio: *Life of Michelangelo,* 84
Congregational . . . Publishing Society, 140
Conrad, Joseph, 70, 358
Consciousness, 1, 3, 7, 11f, 16, 21, 84, 122, 158, 254ff, 282, 290n, 308, 329, 341
CONWELL, RUSSELL H., 307; "Acres of Diamonds," 7, *216ff*
Cooke, Jay, 287
COOKE, JOHN ESTEN, 88; *Stories of the Old Dominion,* 89q; *Surrey of Eagle's Nest,* 105; *Virginia,* 89; *Virginia Comedians,* 89
COOKE, ROSE TERRY, 137, 139n, 142, 144, 148, 155, 160, 267; "Amandar," 146q; "Cal Culver and the Devil," 141q; "Clara's Question," 140; "The Deacon's Week," 140; "Eben Jackson," 141; emotional compulsions, 139; fiction, kinds of, 139ff; "Freedom Wheeler's Controversy with Providence," 141, 190n; *Happy Dodd,* 139f; *Huckleberries . . . ,* 190n; "John Carter's Sin," 140; "Miss Beulah's Bonnet," 141; "Miss Lucinda," 141, 150; "Mrs. Flint's Married Experience," 141fq; *No,* 140q,

142q; *Poems,* 156n; *Rootbound,* 140; "Saint the First," 140; "Saint the Second," 140; "Some Account of Thomas Tucker," 141; *Somebody's Neighbors,* 141; "The Sphinx's Children," 140q, 141q; "Too Late," 141q; "West Shetucket Railway," 141
Cooper, James Fenimore, 19, 21, 30, 75, 113, 281, 313; *The Crater,* 225; *Excursions in Italy,* 52
Cooper, Peter, 208q
Cooper Union, 167
Corelli, Marie, 211
Corliss engine, 28
Corruption, 82f, 176ff
Cosmopolitan, The, 20, 226, 229f, 246
Cosmos Club, 9
Cowper, William, 153, 287
Coxe, Louis, 273q
Coxey's Army, 78, 110, *212ff,* 225, 239
Crabbe, George, 153
Cranch, C. P.: translation of Virgil, 12
Crane, Hart, 15, 290n, 305
CRANE, STEPHEN, 4f, *55ff,* 77, 149, 231, 234, 247ff, 253, 277, 301, 307, 342q, 358; *Active Service,* 56; alienation, 61; American life, 58ff; anti-romanticism, 58f, 63; "The Blue Hotel," 56, *65ff;* "Billy Atkins Went to Omaha," 61; "The Bride Comes to Yellow Sky," *65ff;* "A Christmas Dinner Won in Battle," 61; and city, 62; "A Dark Brown Dog," 59; and John DeForest, 55; "An Experiment in Luxury," 56, 61; "An Experiment in Misery," 56, 61; "George's Mother," 59, 64f; Hemingway on, 65; "Horses—One Dash," 63q; Howells, influence of, 56f, interview of, 59; impressionism, 63f; initiation, novel of, 65; "In the Depths of a Coal Mine," 61; and H. James, 70q; journalism, 60ff; "The Little Regiment," 60; on the long novel, 70nq; *Maggie: A Girl of the Streets, 57ff,* 63ff, 83, 148, 184n, 227, 247; "The Men in the Storm," 61; "The Merry-go-Round," 56; *Midnight Sketches,* 56; "Mr. Binks' Day Off," 61q; and National Novel, 55; "Nebraskans' Bitter Fight for Life," 62q; "A Night at the Millionaire's Club," 60q; Norris on, 71q; "An Ominous Baby," 59, 184n; "The Open Boat," 56, 64, 65, 68f, 71; the personal, emphasis on, 69f; and realism, 56; recapitulation theory, 57f; *Red Badge of Courage,* 35, *55ff, 62ff,* 65, 71, 77, *227,* sources of, 60; Revolutionary War, novel on, 56; style, 64; *Third Violet,* 56, 70; "Tramps and Saints," 56; travel writing, 56; "The Veteran," 65n; war, theme of, 62f; *Whilomville Stories,* 59; *Wounds in the Rain,* 60
Crawford, F. Marion, 153
Crédit Mobilier scandal, 22
Crèvecoeur, Hector St. John, 5

Cripple Creek Strike, 208
Crockett, Davy, 109
CROLY, HERBERT, 216; on H. James, 318q;
  Promise of American Life, 6nq
Crothers, Samuel McC., 79q
Crouse, Nellie, 65
Crystal Palace, 167
Cultism, *211ff*, 217, 319; *see also* Mysticism
Cummings: *Enormous Room*, 12n
Curti, Merle, 16
Curtis, George William, 22q
Custer, General George A., 106f
Cutter, J. C., 290

D'Annunzio, Gabriele, 315
Dante, 4, 12, 36f, 128
Darrow, Clarence, 261
Darwin, Charles, 8, 10q, 16, 47, 85f, 95,
  108, 205, 234ff, 290; *Descent of Man*,
  188; *Origin of Species*, 215f, 216q, 234
Darwinism, 8ff, 184, 202, 245f, 252, 261,
  282, 301; acceptance of, 8
Daudet, Alphonse, 19, 153
Davis, Alexander Jackson, 280
DAVIS, REBECCA HARDING, 2q, 6q, 18, 54;
  "Grey Cabins of New England," 135q,
  136q; "Life in the Iron Mills," 53q;
  Silhouettes of American Life, 53
DAVIS, RICHARD HARDING, 4q, 18, 51,
  53ff, 241q, 250; *About Paris*, 54; *The
  Congo and the Coasts of Africa*, 54;
  Our English Cousins, 54; and Hemingway, 54f; and Norris, 72; *The Princess
  Aline*, 55, 319; *Soldiers of Fortune*, 55;
  Three Gringos . . ., 54; travel writing,
  54f; *Van Bibber and Others*, 54; *The
  West from a Car Window*, 65
Dawn (journal of the Christian Socialists), 226
DeBow's Review, 16
Debs, Eugene, 41, 215q, 254, 254n
Deere, John, 109
DEFOREST, JOHN, 17, 29ff, 50, 53, 55, 87,
  167, 175, 275, 284, 302, 313; *The Bloody
  Chasm*, 35, 78; and Stephen Crane, 55;
  "The Great American Novel," 30fq;
  Honest John Vane, 35, 221; and
  Howells, 39; *Irene the Missionary*,
  35q; *Kate Beaumont*, 35q, 268; *A
  Lover's Revolt*, 87; National Novel, 32,
  34f; *Overland*, 34; *Playing the Mischief*, 177; *Miss Ravenel's Conversion*,
  31ff, 77, theme of experience in, 33f;
  Witching Times, 87
DeLeon, Daniel, 234
Delineator, The, 255f
Dell, Floyd, 254q, 254n
Delmonico's, 72
Democratic Review, 85
Democritus, 261
Demorest's, 254
Depression of 1893–96, 242, 245
DeQuincey, Thomas, 235

Derby, G. H. (John Phoenix, *pseud.*), 119
Designer, The, 255
DeVoto, Bernard, 183q, 195q, 196, 198
DEWEY, JOHN, 162q, 199, 202q, 203f, 281;
  "The Great American Prophet," 220q;
  Psychology, 205
Dialect speech, 28
Dickens, Charles, 18f, 21, 153, 249, 341
Dickinson, Austin, 287
DICKINSON, EMILY, 12, 20n, 92, 134, 137q,
  263, 281, *285ff*, 341; and Higginson,
  292f; isolation, 288ff; literary tastes,
  237; naturalism, 290f; *Poems* (1890),
  49f, 293; poems quoted, J. 18, 289q;
  J. 185, 290q; J. 298, 291q; J. 324, 290q;
  J. 316, 289q; J. 413, 289q; J. 414, 291q;
  J. 512, 291q; J. 553, 289q; J. 640,
  290q; J. 670, 291q; J. 709, 293q; J. 985,
  286q; J. 986, 290q; J. 1129, 294q;
  J. 1400, 290q; J. 1463, 290q; J. 1545,
  289q; J. 1651, 295q; private and public
  poetry, 294; secular imagination, 289;
  terrors of self, 291
Dickinson, Lavinia, 295
Dickinson, Sue, 287, 295
Disraeli, Benjamin: *Tancred*, 8q
Dodge, Mary Mapes, 142
Donne, John, 20n
DONNELLY, IGNATIUS, 178, 226, *231ff*, 237;
  Atlantis, 232q; *Bryan Campaign*, 3nq;
  Caesar's Column, 232ff; *Ragnarok*,
  232q; "St. Louis Platform," 110q, 214q,
  232q
DOOLEY, MR.: *see* Dunne, Peter Finley
Dos Passos, John, 35; *The Big Money*,
  227; *Manhattan Transfer*, 363
Dostoyevsky, Fydor, 19
Doubleday, Frank, 253
Doubleday, Page, and Co., 252
Dow, Joy Wheeler, 322q
Doyle, Arthur Conan, 132
Draper, J. W.: *Conflict Between Religion and Science*, 7, 176
DREISER, THEODORE, 3f, 12, 55, 59, 149,
  167, 200, 241, 247q, 250, *252ff*, 270,
  275ff, 278, 281, 301, 307; alienation,
  262f; *An American Tragedy*, 254, 269;
  autobiographical writing, 275; *A Book
  About Myself*, 263, 275n, *276ff*, 277n,
  281; *The Bulwark*, 261; "Change,"
  247q; *The Color of a Great City*, 276;
  Cowperwood novels, 227, 243, 245q,
  245n; "Culhane, the Solid Man," 265;
  Dawn, 271nq, 277, 277n; *Dreiser Looks
  At Russia*, 277n; and Eggleston, 115n;
  fiction, view of, 260ff; *The Financier*,
  254, 259; *The Genius*, 254; *Hey-Rub-
  a-Dub-Dub*, 263; *A Hoosier Holiday*,
  261, 275, 275n; imagery, 262; *Jennie
  Gerhardt*, 253, 256, 263, 276; *A Literary Apprenticeship*, 277n; *Literary Experiences*, 277n; naturalism 260ff; *Sister Carrie*, 58, 61, 248, *252ff*, 263, 304;
  The Stoic, 254, 259, 261; style, 258f;
  The Titan, 254, 259; *A Traveler at*

Forty, 260q, 275q, 278q; and Twain, 275, 275n; *Twelve Men,* 265
Dresser, Paul, 253
Dudley, Thomas, 138
DUGDALE, RICHARD: *The Jukes,* 136, 262
Dumas, Alexandre, *fils: L'Etrangère,* 327
DUNNE, PETER FINLEY (MR. DOOLEY, *pseud.*), 4, 247q, 319q
Dupee, F. W., 328, 331q, 359q
Duyckinck, Everett: *Literary World,* 29
Dystopia, *231ff; see also* Millennialism

"Earthly Paradise": and reform, 6; tradition of, 210; two versions of, 43; *see also* Eden; Millennialism; Progress
Eastern myth of Eden, 128, 136, 171; *see also* New England
Eastlake, Charles, 210
EDDY, MARY BAKER, 181; *Science and Health,* 211
Eden, myth of, 8, 89, 93, 171, 179, *232ff;* in Howe, 117f; of West, 105ff
Edison Institute of Technology, 84
Edwards, Jonathan, 138, 220; "Personal Narrative," 282
Education, *6ff;* scientific, 7f
EGGLESTON, EDWARD, 20q, 82q, *111ff,* 126, 152q; *Beginners of a Nation,* 115, 152; *The Circuit Rider,* 114fq; dialect, use of, 112; and Dreiser, 115n; *End of the World,* 114, 149; *The Faith Doctor,* 20, 115; *The Graysons,* 116; grotesque, 113f; *Hearth and Home,* 142; as historian, 115f; *Hoosier Schoolmaster,* 87, 111, *112ff,* 152, 211; as minister, 115; *Mystery of Metropolisville,* 114fq; personal restlessness, 111f; *Roxy,* 115; "Wild Flowers of English Speech," 116
EGGLESTON, GEORGE CARY, *A Rebel's Recollections,* 16q, 26q; *Recollections,* 183nq
Einstein, Albert: "Special Theory of Relativity," 204n, 261
Eizlitz, Leopold: *Nature and Function of Art,* 209nq
Eliade, Mircea, 85f, 86q
Eliot, Charles W., 302
Eliot, George, 19, 21, 95, 264f, 287, 315, 329
Eliot, T. S., 12n, 15, 20n, 290f, 297, 313, 317, 318q, 363; on H. Adams, 296q; "Baudelaire," 49; "Gerontion," 269q; "Preludes," 250, 266; *Waste Land,* 114, 296q, 348q
Ellet, Mrs. E. F., 29
Ellis, W. R., 2
Ellison, Ralph: *Invisible Man,* 278
ELY, RICHARD T., 206, 218, 227
Embargo Act of 1807, 143
EMERSON, RALPH WALDO, 3, 11q, 12f, 13n, 36, 82q, 106, 125, 134, 137, 203, 247, 258, 278, 280f, 284, 287, 289f, 293, 313ff, 320q, 337, 343; character in Crane sketch, 60; *Divinity School Address,* 290; *Journals,* 282q; *Nature,* 261,

283, 284q; *Poems,* 287; *Representative Men,* 287; translation of Dante, 12
Emigration, 27, 77f
Emmons, Vaughan, 286
Engels, Frederick, 234
Enlightenment, 203
Euripides, 154
Europe, *78ff;* and American literature, 152; American view of, *317ff*
European literature, 16, *19ff*
Everett, Henry R.: *The People's Program,* 215q
Evolution, 82n, 85, 216, 237f, 245; Twain on, 182q
Expatriation, 320f

Fabianism, 229
Failure, theme of, 154, 285, 307
Family, breakdown, 59
Farmers' Alliance, 110
"Farmers' Declaration of Independence, The," 207, 208q
Farnell, George: *Rev. Josiah Hilton,* 224
Faulkner, William, 35; and Howells, 47n; *Sartoris,* 105q
Federalism, 172, 229
Fenollosa, Ernest, 79n
Feudal metaphor, 321f; *see also* Europe; Medievalism
Field, Cyrus W., 78
Field, Eugene, 151q
Field, Marshall, 256
Fields, Annie, 139, 142q, 143
Fields, James T., 36, 49
FISK, JIM, 177n, 211, 245, 262, 300
FISKE, JOHN, 8f, 13, 72, 82n, 85, 130, 203, 215q, 231, 297; on child, 184q; *Cosmic Philosophy,* 10; *Destiny of Man,* 9q, 215n; *Myths and Myth-Makers,* 47
Fitzgerald, F. Scott, 264q, 313, 363; *Great Gatsby,* 256
Fitzgerald, Zelda, 264
Flaubert, Gustave, 19, 147fq, 264f, 300f, 329, 341, 350n; *Bouvard et Pècuchet,* 335; James on, 341q; *Madam Bovary,* 19
Fletcher, John Gould, 50
FLOWER, BENJAMIN ORANGE, 132, 218, 226
Force Bill (1890), 27
Ford, D. R., 171
Ford, Ford Madox, 70q, 258q
Ford, Henry, 84
Ford, Paul L.: *Janice Meredith,* 83n
"Forgotten Man," 245
Forum, 246
Foster, C. H., 137q, 138q
Foster, Stephen, 27
Fourier, F. M. Charles, 280
France, Anatole, 19
Frank, Joseph: "Spatial Form in Modern Literature," 200q
Franklin, Benjamin, 105, 217, 247, 278, 306; *Autobiography,* 217

Franz Joseph, Emperor of Austria, 320
Fraternal societies, 208f
Frazer, Sir James G.: *Golden Bough*, 205, 234
FREDERIC, HAROLD, 50, 227, 231, 277, 358
Freedley, Edwin T.: *Practical Treatise on Business*, 217
Fresh-Air Funds, 184n
Freud, Sigmund, 11, 199, 291; Freudianism, 282
Froissart, Jean: *Chronicles*, 72
FROST, ROBERT, 50, 55, 141, 159ff, 253, 286; "Acquainted with the Night," 163q; "Birches," 161; "The Birthplace," 161; "The Black Cottage," 160; "My Butterfly . . . ," 159; "Death of the Hired Man," 163f; "Directive," 159q; "A Drumlin Woodchuck," 161; "The Fear," 161; "For Once, Then, Something," 163q; "Ghost House," 161q; "The Hill Wife," 160; "Home Burial," 163q, 164; "The Lone Striker," 160; "The Mountain," 160; New England doubleness, 159; "An Old Man's Winter Night," 160; "The Pasture," 161q, 162; "Pauper Witch of Grafton," 160; "From Plane to Plane," 163f, 164q; and pragmatism, 162f; and regionalism, 159; resolution of solitude, 160; "The Road Not Taken," 163q, 164; on Robinson, 153q; "The Self-Seeker," 160; "A Servant to Servants," 160; "Snow," 160; "Subverted Flower," 160; "A Winter Eden," 161; "The Witch at Coös," 160
FROTHINGHAM, OCTAVIUS BROOKS, 7, 205, 211q; *Rising and Setting Faith*, 43q
Fry's Army, 78
FULLER, HENRY BLAKE, 50, 131f, 241q, 248ff, 278; *The Chatelaine of La Trinité*, 248; *The Chevalier of Pensieri Vani*, 248; *The Cliff-Dwellers*, 248f,; "The Downfall of Abner Joyce," 125q; "Mural Painting," 248; *Not on the Screen*, 249; *On the Stairs*, 249; *Under the Skylights*, 249; *With the Procession*, 249; "World's Fair Architecture," 248
Fundamentalism, 86
Funk and Wagnalls, 17

Galaxy, The, 171, 314
Gallatin, Albert, 299
Galton, Francis: *Hereditary Genius*, 238
GARFIELD, JAMES A., 13, 217
Garibaldi, Giuseppe, 176
GARLAND, HAMLIN, 54, 56f, 57q, 62, 87q, 88, 111, 116q, *124ff*, 135ff, 140, 151q, 152q, 179q, 226f, 241q, 250; "Altruism" (*Prairie Songs*), 129q; *Back-Trailers from the Middle Border*, 131q; and Bierce, 124f; *Boy Life on the Prairie*, 129, 132, 142, 185; *The Captain of the Grey Horse Troop*, 130; *Cavanagh*,
130; critic of the West, 128; *Crumbling Idols*, 126q, 129, 241q; "A Day's Pleasure," 128; *The Eagle's Heart*, 130; *My Friendly Contemporaries*, 131q; *Forty Years of Psychic Research*, 132; "God's Ravens," 128; *Her Mountain Lover*, 130; *Hesper*, 130; Howells, lecture on, 57; "The Joys of the Trail," 131; *Main-Travelled Roads*, 126q, 127, 149, 158; *Mystery of the Buried Crosses*, 132q; *Other Main-Travelled Roads*, 127; *Prairie Folks*, 127; "A Prairie Heroine," 126, 127n, 128, 128q, 129; realism, 126; "The Return of a Private," 127f; "Mrs. Ripley's Trip," 126f; *Roadside Meetings*, 127; *Rose of Dutcher's Coolly*, 130; *The Shadow World*, 132; *Trail of the Goldseekers*, 130q; *The Tyranny of the Bark*, 132; "Vanishing Trails," 131q; "Under the Lion's Paw," 126, 127q; "Up the Coulee," 126, 128q; writer of romance, *129ff*
GARRISON, WILLIAM LLOYD, 6, 280
GARY, ELBERT H., 94, 246
Gaskell, Charles Milnes, 302
Gaughin, Paul, 79n
Geissler, Ludwig: *Looking Beyond*, 224
"Genteel tradition," 254, *279ff*; criticism of, 281f
Geoffrey of Monmouth, 92
Geology, 231
GEORGE, HENRY, 76, 127, 211, 213, 216q, 220q, 229, 234, 242q, 251; *Progress and Poverty*, 206q, 206n, 209q
GHENT, W. J., 216q; *Our Benevolent Feudalism*, 109q, 217q, 237q
Gibson, Charles Dana, 54
Gibson, W. H., 241q
Gide, André, 13q
Gilbert, Susan, 286
GILDER, RICHARD WATSON, 14, 71, 97, 153, 255, 279
Giotto, 84
Glackens, William, 278
GLADDEN, WASHINGTON, 10q, 41, 225f; *Who Wrote the Bible?*, 205; *Working People and their Employers*, 43, 211
GLASGOW, ELLEN: *The Descendant*, 105; *Virginia*, 105
Glasgow, University of, 13n
GODKIN, E. L., 5, 13n, 22, 226, 314, 323q
Gold Mine, A, 260
Goldsmith, Oliver: *Letters from a Citizen of the World*, 171
Gompers, Samuel, 208
Goncourt, Edmond, 335
"Good Roads and Non-Interest Bearing Bond Bills," 212
"Gospel of Work," 210; *see also* Protestant Ethic
Gosse, Edmund, 153, 341q
Gough, John B., 7
GOULD, JAY, 13, 82, 177n, 300
Gower, John, 92

GRADY, HENRY W., 92, 96, 98ff
Grange songs, 83n, 110
GRANT, ULYSSES S., 80, 82, 159, 300;
Memoirs, 22q, 26q, 166
GRAYSON, DAVID: *see* Baker, Ray Stannard
"Great American Desert," 34, 107
"Great American Novel": *see* National Novel
Greco-Turkish War, 56
Greeley, Horace, 22
Greenback Party, 110; and Labor Party, 208
Greenfield Village, 84
Greenwood, John, 186n
GRONLUND, LAURENCE: *Co-Operative Commonwealth*, 226, 229
Guilbert, Yvette, 54
Guiney, Louise Imogen, 15, 151q
Gunsaulus, Frank W., 244
Gyp (Sibylle de Riquetti de Mirabeau), 347

Hadley, Arthur Twining, 321q
Haeckel, Ernst H.: *Riddle of the Universe*, 234
Haight, Gordon, 46
HALE, EDWARD EVERETT, 226, 229f; *How They Lived in Hampton*, 229; *A New England Boyhood*, 185; *Sybaris*, 229; *Ten Times Ten is One*, 229
HALL, G. STANLEY, 85q; *Adolescence*, 184n, 185q
Hamilton, Alexander, 60
Hancock, John, 304
Hanna, Mark, 99
Hannibal *Journal*, 172
Hardy, Thomas, 19, 21, 152f
HARLAND, HENRY, 320, 330
Harper and Brothers, 168, 252
Harper, J. Henry: on C. F. Woolson, 53q, 137q
Harper's, 17, 20, 22, 168, 175n, 287
Harper's Weekly, 252
Harper's Young People, 185
Harris, George Washington: *Sut Lovingood*, 91
HARRIS, JOEL CHANDLER, 20n, 28, 87, 91, 96ff, 117, 120, 139, 142, 151; and Howe, 116q; as journalist, 96f; *Life of Henry W. Grady*, 96q; "Mark and Mack," 99; "Mr. Billy Sanders Discourses . . . ," 99q; "The Night Before Christmas," 98q; *Nights With Uncle Remus*, 98, origin of, 98, *personae*, 99; "Philosophy of Failure," 100q; "Santa Claus and the Fairies," 100q; *Sister Jane*, 97; "Southern Literature," 100q; split personality, 96ff; "Story of the Deluge," 99; *Uncle Remus*, 96ff; *Uncle Remus's Magazine*, 100
Harris, Thomas Lake: *The New Republic*, 212
HARRIS, W. T., 204

Hart, James D., 235
HARTE, BRET, 88, 107, 320
Hartford Female Seminary, 139
Hartford Wits, 29
Hartt, R. L., 135, 136q
Hartz, Louis, 101, 225q
Harvard, 37, 84, 156n, 184n, 204, 250, 297, 299, 302, 304
Harvard Law School, 310
Harvard Monthly, 156
Harvey, William Hope: *Coin's Financial School*, 243
Hauptmann, Gerhart, 47
HAY, JOHN, 77q, 79n, 79nq, 108q, 301f, 313, 358; *Abraham Lincoln*, 300; *The Breadwinners*, 61, 209, 302
Hayes, Jeff: *Paradise on Earth*, 214
Hayes, Rutherford B., 208
Haymarket Square riot, 6, 208, 225, 227, 263; Howells on, 41f
Hayne, Paul Hamilton, 17, 92q
Hawthorne, Nathaniel, 21, 30, 36, 75, 134, 136, 143, 155f, 258, 264f, 278, 280q, 281, 287, 308, 313ff, 319; "The Birthmark," 221; *Blithedale Romance*, 230, 334; "The Celestial Railroad," 221; as character in Crane sketch, 60; "Dr. Heidegger's Experiment," 221; "Egotism," 221; French and Italian *Journals*, 314; "Legends of the Province House," 303, 304q; *Marble Faun*, 247; *Our Old Home*, 319; "Rappaccini's Daughter," 221; *Scarlet Letter*, 133; "The Unpardonable Sin," 134
HEARN, LAFCADIO, 19, 104; *Ghombo Zhebes*, 103
Hearst, Randolph, 121
Hearth and Home, 113
Hegel, Georg W. F., 234; Hegelianism, 8, 204, 231
Hemingway, Ernest, 35, 86n, 313; on Stephen Crane, 65q; and Richard H. Davis, 54f; and Norris, 71; *Old Man and the Sea*, 69
Henley, W. E.: "Invictus," 157
Henry, Joseph, 205
Hentz, Caroline Lee, 21
Hero: artist as, 296f, 349f; businessman as, 244n, 245n, 337ff; worker as, 209, 235
HERRICK, ROBERT, 50, 212q, 227, 301; *The Web of Life*, 244
HERRON, GEORGE D.: "The Message of Jesus to Men of Wealth," 218q
Hertzka, Theodor: *Freeland*, 233n; *Freeland Revisited*, 233n
Higginson, Mary, 287
HIGGINSON, THOMAS WENTWORTH, 6q, 27, 90, 134, 153, 220q, 280q, 286q, 287, 288, 291, 294; *Army Life in a Black Regiment*, 292; *Cheerful Yesterdays*, 292; and Emily Dickinson, 292f; on Howells, 37q; "The Monarch of Dreams," 164q; translation of Epictetus, 12

Hill, James J., 94
Hinman, Wilbur F., 60
Historical romance, 137, 151
History, fear of, 82ff; method, 231
Hitchcock, Edward: *Religion of Geology,* 290
Hitchcock, Rev. Roswell D., 321q
Hobbes, Thomas, 234
HODGE, CHARLES: *What Is Darwinism?,* 9q
Hoffman, Daniel G., 191q
Hofstadter, Richard, 94q
Holabird and Roche (architectural firm), 248
Holland, Elizabeth, 285f
HOLLAND, JOSIAH GILBERT, 29, 286f; "Books, Authors, and Art," 292q; *Every-Day Topics,* 14n, 216n; *Seven-oaks,* 221, 245
Holmes, Mary J., 21
HOLMES, OLIVER WENDELL, Jr., 207, 260q
HOLMES, OLIVER WENDELL, Sr., 12ff, 21, 30, 37, 138, 149, 287; and R. H. Davis, 54; *Elsie Venner,* 134; on Howells, 49q; *Poems,* 292
HOLT, HENRY, 9q, 202q
Home, D. D., 211
Homestead strike, 208
Houghton, Mifflin Co., 20n, 222
Hovey, Richard, 15; translations, 20
Howard, Bronson: *Shenandoah,* 26
HOWE, EDGAR WATSON, 20n, 87, 111, 116ff, 125, 140; *Anthology of Another Town,* 117; *The Blessings of Business,* 120; *Country Town Sayings,* 117, 120q, critical responses to, 117; and Harris, 97; *A Moonlight Boy,* 152; *Plain People,* 116nq, 117, 120q; split personality, 117, 120; *Story of a Country Town,* 116ff; travel writing, 120; *Ventures in Common Sense,* 120
Howe, Julia Ward: "Battle Hymn of the Republic," 54
Howells Medal for Fiction, 152
HOWELLS, WILLIAM DEAN, 1, 4, 6, 12, 17, 19, 20n, 21, 31, 35ff, 52f, 55ff, 59, 71, 75, 80, 87, 92, 108, 125, 126q, 132q, 134, 142, 147, 150, 153, 167, 172, 174q, 175f, 178ff, 186, 197, 216, 225f, 226ff, 236, 241n, 242n, 243, 244n, 247ff, 263, 274, 277, 282q, 293, 301, 307, 313f, 314n, 316q, 323q, 324, 335, 337, 341, 350n, 359n, 360; *Annie Kilburn,* 41, 48, 228; "The American James," 50; on American literature, 50; "Are We a Plutocracy?," 227; autobiographies, 49; Basil March as *persona,* 40f; on E. Bellamy, 221q; *Between the Dark and the Daylight,* 47; on *Bostonians,* 335nq; *A Boy's Town,* 37, 185; *A Chance Acquaintance,* 39, 48, 175nq; *Choice Autobiographies,* 198; and city, 57; Crane, influence on, 56f, interviewed by, 59; crucial experiences, 41f; Dante, lectures on, 12; and Davis, 54; and DeForest, 39; on DeForest, 35q; *Dr. Breen's Practice,* 48, 335n; "An East-Side Ramble," 57; "Editor's Easy Chair," 227; "Equality as the Basis of Good Society," 227; *A Fearful Responsibility,* 287; fiction and travel writing, 37; fictive "world," 47n; *The Flight of Pony Baker,* 49; followers of, 50ff; *A Foregone Conclusion,* 48, 175, James on, 316nq, 328; on Frost, 159; genius of, 49; *Great Modern Short Stories,* 317; on Haymarket Square incident, 41; *A Hazard of New Fortunes, 42ff,* 48, 175, 227f, 245; *Heroines of Fiction,* 77; "A Hoosier's Opinion of Walt Whitman," 36q; on Howe, 117q; *Indian Summer,* 48; *Italian Journeys,* 13n, 37, 248, 287; "Italian Poets of Our Century," 37; and Italy, 36; and H. James, 47n; *Kentons,* 48; *Lady of the Aroostook,* 48; *Landlord at Lion's Head,* 48; *Leatherwood God,* 38; *Letters from an Altrurian Traveler, 1893–4,* 229q, 240q; *Literary Friends and Acquaintances,* 49; *Literary Passions,* 49; on *Maggie,* 57; *Minister's Charge,* 41, 48; "Minor Topics," 226; *A Modern Instance,* 48, 116, 227; *Mrs. Farrell* ("Private Theatricals"), 48; *My Mark Twain,* 175n; and National Novel, 45, 49; "The Nature of Liberty," 227; *New Leaf Mills,* 37, 49; "Niagara Revisited," 40; on Norris, 77q; Norris on, 74n; on *Octupus,* 75q; *An Open-Eyed Conspiracy,* 40; "personal equation," 45; on psychology, 46q; *Quality of Mercy,* 48, 227f, 230q; *Questionable Shapes,* 47; *A Ragged Lady,* 58; *Rise of Silas Lapham, 42n,* 48, 227, 245n, 249; on romance and realism, 46; and sage, tradition of, 36, 49f; *Shadow of a Dream,* 40, 45ff, 49, 265; *Shapes that Haunt the Dusk,* 47nq; social conscience, 41ffq, 226f; and social gospel, 43; *Son of Royal Langbrith,* 48, 227; *Story of a Play,* 48; *Suburban Sketches,* 37; Swedenborg, influence of, 41; *Their Silver Wedding Journey,* 40; *Their Wedding Journey,* 37, 38ff, 41, 44, 48, 323; *Through the Eye of the Needle,* 45, 226q, 228, 229ff.; on Tolstoy, 41q; *Traveler from Altruria,* 48, 228ff, 230; Twain on, 175nq; "Twelve Memorable Murders," 165f; *Undiscovered Country,* 115, Garland on, 130q, 287; *Venetian Life,* 36, 248, 314; "Who Are Our Brethren," 227; *World of Chance,* 228f, 230q; *My Year in a Log Cabin,* 49; *Years of my Youth,* 13q, 37f, 49, 185
Howells, Winifred, 197
Hubbard, Elbert, 10q, 84; *Romance of Business,* 245q
Hudnut, Joseph, 277, 277fq
Hume, David, 234, 280, 282

Humphrey, Jane, 286
Huneker, James Gibbons, 253
HUNT, RICHARD MORRIS, 322; Administration Building, 242
Hunt, William Morris, 313
HUNTINGTON, COLLIS P., 76, 121, 245, 262
Huxley, Aldous: *Brave New World*, 231
Huxley, T. H., 8, 9n, 10, 95, 234
Huysmans, J. K., 19
Hypnotism, 211

Ibsen, Henrik, 47, 231
Ideal Poetry, 280f
Illusion, 253f, 254n, 362f
Immigrants, 3, 5f, 133ff
Immigration Restriction League, 5
Impressionism, 250
Independent, The, 115, 159
Industry, disillusion with, 82
INGERSOLL, ROBERT, 261; *The Gods*, 261; *Some Mistakes of Moses*, 261
Initiation, theme of, 146, 191
Institute of British Architects, 243
"Instrumentalism," (Dewey's), 162, 204
International Copyright Law, 16ff
International Novel: of Howells, 80; of James, *322ff*; theme, 318f, 328ff, 339, 349f
International Socialist Review, 237n
Interstate Commerce Act, 27
Interstate Commerce Commission, 246
Irenaeus, 210
Irving, Washington, 19, 30, 287, 313

JACKSON, HELEN HUNT: *Mercy Philbrick's Choice*, 285q, 294q
Jacksonianism, 172
James, Garth Wilkinson, 311
JAMES, HENRY, 1, 12, 17, 19, 20n, 24q, 35, 37, 41, 45, 47, 50, 53, 55f, 65, 75, 77, 80, 87, 92, 104q, 147, 150, 153, 175f, 181, 188, 247, 263ff, 274, 281, 284q, 301, 307f, *310ff*; "Abasement of the Northmores," 337; alienation, 314f; *Ambassadors*, 318, 325, *350ff*, 356, 358, 362; America, return to, 359ff; *The American*, 78, 245n, 320, *326ff*, 331, 333, as drama, 340; *The American Scene*, 337q, 337n, 359, *360f*; Artist-as-hero, theme of, 337; *Aspern Papers*, 337; "Author of Beltraffio," 337; autobiographies, 310f, 359, 363f; *Awkward Age*, 318, 342, *346ff*, 348f, 350, 350n, 353, 356, 358; basic theme, 312f; "Beast in the Jungle," *325q*; "Beldonald Holbein," 337; *Bostonians*, 6, *334ff*, 338, 362; "Broken Wings," 337; "A Bundle of Letters," 318q; "Coxon Fund," 337; and Crane, 70; "Crapy Cornelia," 361; *Daisy Miller*, 316n, 318, *328f*, 331f, 336f, 355; "Death of the Lion," 337; declining popularity, 336f; "Double," theme of, 322f; dramatic experiment, *339ff*; *Europeans*,

287q, 318, *328f*; "Figure in the Carpet," 337, 343; *The Finer Grain*, 361; *Golden Bowl*, 78, 318, 325, 344, *355ff*, 358f, 362; "Greville Fane," 337; *Guy Domville*, *340ff*; *Hawthorne*, 315q, 329; on Howells, 41q, 47n, 49q; ideal of society, 318; *International Episode*, 312, 318, 328q; international novels, *322ff*; *In the Cage*, *342f*; *Ivory Tower*, 228n, *361f*, 363; "Jolly Corner," 312, 317, 361fq; *Lesson of Balzac*, 358; "Lesson of the Master," 337, 343; literary portraiture, 315ff; *Little Tour in France*, 334; "The Middle Years," 337, 359nq; *The Middle Years*, 311, 313, 364; "New York Edition," 324, 337, *359f*; "The Next Time," 337fq, 340q; *Notes of a Son and Brother*, *310ff*, 313, 315; "Passionate Pilgrim," 79, 312, 317, 322, 324, 330, 361, 363; *The Patagonia*, 334; *The Pension Beaurepas*, 334; "The Point of View," 334; *Portrait of a Lady*, 78, 249, 318, *330ff*, 334, 336, 342, Crane on, 70; *Portraits of Places*, 314, 334; *Princess Casamassima*, 334, *335ff*, 338, 358; "Private Life," 337; *The Question of Our Speech*, 358; Renunciation, theme of, *342ff*; *The Reverberator*, 334; *Roderick Hudson*, *324ff*, 327, 330, 335, 337, 350, 358; "Preface," 359q, 360q; "A Round of Visits," 361; *The Sacred Fount*, 318, 342, *348f*, 350, 350n, 357; "Saratoga: 1870," 314nq; *The Sense of the Past*, 84q, 322, 361, 362f; *A Small Boy*, 1, *311ff*; *Spoils of Poynton*, 342, *343f*, 346, 348f, 352, 356, 358; "The Story in It," 337, 343; summing up, *358ff*; symbolism, 348; *Tales of Three Cities*, 334; *Tragic Muse*, 44, 334, 337, *338ff*, 340; *Transatlantic Sketches*, 314; travel writing, 313; "Turn of the Screw," 312, 345n; victimization, theme of, *335ff*, 339f, 351, 353; *Washington Square*, 318; *Watch and Ward*, *323f*; *What Maisie Knew*, 342, *344ff*, 347ff, 350, 350n, 351, 356, 358, Crane on, 70q; *William Wetmore Story and His Friends*, 308, 329q; *Wings of the Dove*, 52, 318, *352ff*, 356, 358, 362, and C. F. Woolson, 52; "wise innocence," theme of, 355; *Within the Rim*, 364; and C. F. Woolson, 53q
JAMES, HENRY, SR., 84n, 204f, 312f; *Society the Redeemed Form of Man*, 316q
JAMES, WILLIAM, 10, 24, 45, 62, 95n, 162f, 199, 204f, 212ff, 214q, 260, 281, 301, 308, 311ff, 313q, 314q, 340, 360; on Howells, 44q; *Pragmatism*, 162fq, 363; *Principles of Psychology*, 44, 205, Howells's review of, 45f; on Robinson, 153q; *Varieties of Religious Experience*, 47
Jarves, James Jackson, 325
Jefferson, Thomas, 3, 83, 105, 143, 178, 203, 299f

JEWETT, SARAH ORNE, 88, 137, 139q, 141, *142ff*, 148, 152f, 155, 156n, 159, 285, 293, 354n; *Betty Leicester's Christmas*, 142; *Country of the Pointed Firs*, 142, 143f, *145ff*, 154, 160; *Deephaven*, 142; "doubleness," 145ff; "A Dunnet Shepherdess," 162n; emotional compulsions, 139; "King of Folly Island," 145q; literary precepts, 147; *The Normans*, 147; *Play Days*, 142; "The Queen's Twin," 143q; "River Driftwood," 142q; *Tory Lover*, 151; *Verses*, 156n; "A White Heron," 144q, 145, 151
Johns Hopkins University, 7f
Jones, John P., "Golden Rule," 218
Jordy, William, 303q
Julian West, 225
Jünger, Ernest, 22, 256
Jurisprudence, 206ff

Kahler, Erich, 219
Kantian epistemology, 282
Keats, John, 84, 95, 280, 287
Kelly's Army, 78, 235
Kennedy, John Pendleton, 30
Kerr, Orpheus C.: *see* Newell, Robert Henry
Khayyam, Omar: *Quatrains*, 79n
Kidd, Benjamin, 234
KING, CLARENCE, 8, 79n, 231, 302, 304; *Mountaineering in the Sierra Nevada*, 80q, 109
King, Edward: *The Great South*, 29
KING, GRACE: *Memoirs of a Southern Woman of Letters*, 151, 152q
Kipling, Rudyard, 188; *American Notes*, 27q, 210q
KIRKLAND, JOSEPH, 60, 111
Knights of Labor, 208f
Knights and Ladies of the Golden Rule, 208
Kropotkin, Peter, 220, 234; *Mutual Aid*, 94
Ku Klux Klan, 89

Labor Standard, 127, 226
Lactantius, 210, 210nq
Ladies' Home Journal, 222, 226
LA FARGE, JOHN, 79n, 304f, 313; *An Artist's Letters from Japan*, 305q
Lakeside Library, 19
Lamarckianism, 8
Langdon family, 108
Langland, William, 92
LANIER, SIDNEY, 17, 29, 88, 91, *92ff*, 142, 252, 253q; *Boy's Froissart*, 92, 92fq; *Boy's King Arthur*, 92; *Boy's Mabinogion*, 92; *Boy's Percy*, 92; "Centennial Meditation of Columbia," 241f; chivalry, 92f; "Corn," 95, 96q; *The English Novel*, 71n; "Hard Times in Elfland," 91n; "The Jacquerie," 71, 93ff; "The New South," 91q, 95; "Psalm of the West," 91, 95; *Shakspere and His Forerunners*, 93q; "The Symphony," 93, 94q; trade, critique of, 93ff; on Whitman, 106nq
LARCOM, LUCY, 148, 160, 293; *A New England Girlhood*, 185
Lawrence, D. H., 68q, 235, 313; *Sons and Lovers*, 235n
LeConte, Joseph, 9
LeConte brothers, 95
Lecture series, 7, 85
Lee, Robert E., 27
Lee, Vernon: *see* Paget, Violet
Leibnitz, Gottfried W., 234
Lend-a-Hand, 226
L'Enfant plan for Washington, 242
Levedan, Henri, 347
Levin, Meyer: *The Old Bunch*, 244
Lewis, R. W. B., 355q
Lewis, Sinclair, 132, 238, 238n, 256q, 363; on Richard H. Davis, 54q; *Main Street*, Garland on, 131q
Leyda, Jay, 294q
Liberator, The, 6
Life, 54
Lincoln, Abraham, 2q, 8q, 14, 77, 167, 176, 267, 297q
Lindsay, Vachel, 50
Linson, Corwin: on Crane, 61nq
Lippincott's, 98
Liszt, Franz, 13n
Litchfield Academy, 139
Literature, 175n
Literature, distribution of, 16ff
Living Age, 20
Livingstone, David, 87, 233n
LLOYD, HENRY D., 245q, 321; "The Story of a Great Monopoly," 227
LOCKE, DAVID ROSS (PETROLEUM V. NASBY, *pseud.*), 119, 120q
Locke, John, 178, 234
LODGE, GEORGE CABOT, 15q, 155, 296f
LODGE, HENRY CABOT, 5, 298f, 306
LONDON, JACK, 208q, *234ff;* "The Class Struggle," 236q; "A Dream of Debs," 215n, 238; "Goliah," 238; "How I Became a Socialist," 236q; *The Iron Heel*, 62, 235q, *236ff.; Martin Eden*, 236; *The Mutiny of the Elsinore*, 239; *People of the Abyss*, 239; philosophical tradition, 234; "Revolution," 238q; *The Scarlet Plague*, 238; *The Sea Wolf*, 234ff, 239; "Wanted: A New Law of Development," 236q; "What Life Means to Me," 235q
LONGFELLOW, HENRY WADSWORTH, 13, 36, 49, 79n, 205, 264, 284, 287, 293; Dante, translation of, 12, 37; *Golden Legend*, 13n; *Hiawatha*, 13n
Longstreet, Augustus Baldwin: *Georgia Scenes*, 90
Looking Ahead . . ., 225
Lord, Otis, 286
"Lost Generation," 77ff
Loubat Prize, 302

Lovell's Popular Library, 19
Lowell Institute, 37
LOWELL, JAMES RUSSELL, 5, 12, 14, 20n, 24q, 27q, 49, 94, 108, 136, 144q, 248, 281, 293; *Bigelow Papers,* 112; on Howells, 37q
Lubbock, Percy, 264q, 265q, 361
Lyceum, 85
Lyell, Charles: *Principles of Geology,* 8, 301

MCALLISTER, WARD, 3, 243q
Macauley, Thomas B., 13n
MCCLURE, S. S., 5, 210q, 252
McClure's Magazine, 61, 71, 73, 246, 250
McCormick's reaper, 26
MCCOSH, JAMES, 9, 203f
MCCUTCHEON, GEORGE BARR: *Graustark,* 319q
McGuffey's Reader, 184nq
McKim, Mead, and White (firm), 3, 242, 321
McKinley, William, 99
McLean, Sally Pratt, 160
McVickar, John: *Outlines of Political Economy* (1825), 94
Madison, James, 300
Maeterlinck, Maurice, 47
Magazines, significance of, 29
Maine, Sir Henry, 106q; *Ancient Law,* 207q
MAJOR, CHARLES: *When Knighthood Was in Flower,* 84, 254
Mallarmé, Stéphane, 19, 153
Malory, Sir Thomas, 92
Malraux, André, 313
Malthus, Thomas, 76, 205f, 234
Mann, Arthur, 224q
Mann, Thomas, 313
Mannheim, Karl: *Ideology and Utopia,* 218fq
MARDEN, ORISON SWETT, 307; *Pushing to the Front,* 217q, 218q; *Success,* 254; *How They Succeeded,* 256n; *Little Visits With Great Americans,* 256n
MARKHAM, EDWIN: "The Man With a Hoe," 76, 82
Marryat, Frederick, 264
Marsh, O. W., 231
Marshall, John, 172
Marvell, Andrew, 291
Marx, Karl, 206n, 234, 237ff
Masque of Poets, A, 293f
Mass audience, 87, 337, 337n
Masters, Edgar Lee, 50; "Robert G. Ingersoll," 261q
Materialism, 209, 210ff, 343f
Mather, Cotton, 352
MATTHEWS, BRANDER, 245q
Matthiessen, F. O., 253q, 332q
Maupassant, Guy de, 19, 301, 315
Maximilian, Emperor of Mexico, 78, 89
Mead, Larkin, 242n
Mead, W. R., 242n

Medievalism, 84; in H. Adams, 304ff; *see also* Feudal metaphor
MELVILLE, HERMAN, 134q, 134n, 170, 181, 230, 239, 258, 264, 290; *Battle Pieces,* 2q, 24, 256; *The Confidence Man,* 106, 156; Howells on, 509; "The March Into Virginia," 65q; *Moby Dick,* 5, 217, 234, 353; *Pierre,* 247; *Redburn,* 247; *Typee,* 234n
Mencken, H. L.: on Richard H. Davis, 54q, 363
Meredith, George, 21, 152
Meredith, Owen: *Tannhäuser,* 16
Mere Marie of the Ursulines, 84
Merk, Frederick, 133q
MERRILL, STUART, 19
Metaphysical Club, 10, 207, 301
MICHAELIS, RICHARD: *Looking Further Forward,* 223f
Middle class, 246f, 261
Mill, John Stuart, 16, 202, 234, 238, 280, 301
Millennial Church ("Shakers"), 214n
Millennialism, 209, 213n, 213ff, 219, 225, 230, 238, 349
Miller, Henry, 258
MILLER, JOAQUIN, 130; *Building of the City Beautiful,* 235
Milton, John, 287; *Paradise Lost,* 146, 234
Mission, myth of, 133, 136, 147, 170
Mr. Barnes of New York (novel by Archibald C. Gunter), 319
MITCHELL, C. WEIR, 30, 47, 153, 265; *Hugh Wynne,* 83n
Mitchell, Donald Grant (Ik Marvel, *pseud.*): *Reveries of a Bachelor,* 287
Molly Maguires, 287
Monroe, Harriet: "Columbian Ode," 241
MOODY, DWIGHT L., 72, 86
MOODY, WILLIAM GODWIN: *Land and Labor,* 109q, 213q
Moody, William Vaughan, 158
Moore, Arthur K., 110q
More, St. Thomas, 210
MORGAN, J. P., 241q, 321
MORGAN, LEWIS HENRY, 206n; *Ancient Society,* 10, Henry Adams on, 199fq
Morgan, Thomas, 242q
Morley, Christopher: *Walt,* 53n
Morris, William, 84, 227, 229; *News from Nowhere,* 223q
Motley, John Lothrop, 298
Muckraking, 5, 73, 227, 245ff, 253f, 259
Mueller, Ernst: *Ein Rückblick,* 224
Muirhead, J. F., 23q
Mumford, Lewis, 55
Munsey's, 246
Museums, 86
Mussel Slough Affair, 75
Mysticism, 209; *see also* Cultism
Myth: and American character, 85; of Casey Jones and John Henry, 11; and literature, 86f; patterns, exemplary, 86; *see also* Hero

Napoleon III, 78
NASBY, PETROLEUM V.: *see* Locke, David Ross
NAST, THOMAS, 7, 22
Nation, 5, 13n, 20, 30, 36, 79q, 135, 176, 226, 314, 323
National Banking Act, 3
"National Novel," 16, *25ff*, 29, 35, 45, 50f, 81, 84n, 87, 175f, 225, 316n, 323f, 327, 335, 342, 350n; of Crane, 55; of Davis, 55; Howe on, 116nq; and Howells, 49; of Norris, 55, 71; *see also* International Novel
Nationalism (Bellamy's), 124, 179, 208, 211, 218, *220ff*, 229, 230
Nationalist, The, 221
Naturalism, *247ff*, 250, 255, 261, 281, 348; of Adams, 301; of Emily Dickinson, 290f; of Dreiser, 260ff; of James, 335f; of Wharton, 265f
"Natural Selection," 9f
Neff, Emery, 156n
Neider, Charles, 198
Neill, Rev. E. O., 111q
Neue Sachlichkeit, 124
Nevins, Allan, 78q
Nevius, Blake, 265q
New Deal, 227
Newell, Robert Henry (Orpheus C. Kerr, *pseud.*), 28
New England: conscience, 357; economic decline, 135, 153f, 351; myth, 133, 285f; regionalism, *133ff*, 156, 267; Sage tradition, *11ff*, 35, 49f, 175n, 308, 337
New Idea Woman's Magazine, The, 255
Newspapers: during civil war, 16f; foreign language, 5; writing, 277
"New South," 91f, 96f
New Thought, 211
Newton, Benjamin Franklin, 286f
New York Herald, 28; *Herald* Building, 322
New York Press, 61
New York Times, 59, 176, 364
New York Tribune, 8, 9n, 41, 57, 82, 168, 227, 314, 340
New York World, 9
Nicolay, John G.: *Abraham Lincoln*, 300
Nietzsche, Friedrich, 8, 234f, 239; *Ecce Homo*, 16q
Niles, Thomas, 294
Nitchie, George, 159
Noah's Ark myth, 233n
Noble, David, 189
Noble Savage, 184f, 209
Nolan, Charles, 242q
Norcross, Louisa, 286
Nordau, Max, 319
NORDHOFF, CHARLES, 208; *Communistic Societies*, 108q, 109q, 214q
Norris, Frank, 4, 50, 56, 59, 65, *70ff*, 149, 234, 247, 249, *249ff*, 252f, 255, 260, 301, 307; and an American epic, 74ff; "An American School of Fiction?," 74q; *Blix*, 71q, 252, 278; and chivalric literature, 72f; and Crane, 71; and De-Forest, 77; "Epic of the Wheat" trilogy, 71, 75, 77; evolutionary transcendentalism, 72; failure, theme of, 73; "The Frontier Gone at Last," 74; "The Great American Novelist," 74q; "The Green Stone of Unrest," 71; and Hemingway, 71; influences upon, 72f; *McTeague*, 71, 248, *249ff*, 252, 278; and National Novel, 55, 71, 76; "National Spirit as it Relates to 'The Great American Novel.' " 75q; naturalism and romanticism, 71; "A Neglected Epic," 74q; "The Novel With a 'Purpose,' " 73fq, 74q; *The Octopus*, 73, *75ff*, 227; *The Pit*, 47n, 72, 74n, 75, 75n; *The Responsibilities of the Novelist*, 74f; travel writing, 71f; unfinished plans, 77; "The Wolf: A Story of Europe," 71, 77; *Yvernelle*, 71; and Zola, 71n, 72n
North American Review, 7f, 36, 176, 216
Norton, Charles Eliot, 5, 36f, 84q, 230, 248, 314; translation of Dante, 12
Norton, Sara, 142
Nott, C. C., 135q
NYE, EDGAR WATSON (Bill Nye, *pseud.*), 7, 120q; *Comic History of the United States*, 119

Oberlin College, 210
O. HENRY: *see* Porter, William Sydney
OLMSTED, FREDERICK LAW, 278, 287
Oneida Perfectionists, 212n
O'REILLY, JOHN BOYLE, 5, 5nq; "In Bohemia," 218q
Orient: and America, 74, 79n
Orwell, George: *1984*, 231
Osborn, Thomas A., 213q
OSGOOD, JAMES R., 189, 334
Outlook, The, 152, 154

Paderewski, Ignace Jan, 277
PAGE, THOMAS NELSON, 18, 88; *Marse Chan*, 90q, 193; Santa Claus myth, use of, 91n
Page, Walter Hines, 96q, 252
Paget, Violet (Vernon Lee, *pseud.*), 315
Paige typesetter, 180, 195, 197
PAINE, ALBERT BIGELOW, 186q, 198, 200
Paine, Thomas, 176; *Age of Reason*, 261n
Panic of 1873, 107
Parker, Theodore, 280, 287
PARKMAN, FRANCIS, 39, 176, 298; on *Silas Lapham*, 42nq
Parliament of Religions (1893), 244
Parrington, V. L., Jr., 214f
Parsons, Frank: *The City for the People*, 244, 245q
Parsons, Rev. Willard, 184n
Past: idealization of, 87; in Sarah Jewett, 146; and regionalism, 89, 152; in Harriet Stowe, 138; *see also* Regionalism
Paulding, James Kirke, 30
PEABODY, JOSEPHINE PRESTON, 15, 84q
Peck, George W., 119

Peck, Harry Thurston: on the new rich, 54q
PEIRCE, CHARLES SANDERS, 10, 82n, 95n, 204q, 207, 301
Peixotto, Ernest, 75
Pennell, Joseph, 104
People's Party: *see* Populism
Perry, T. S., 313, 335
Pfaff's, 168, 279
PHELPS, ELIZABETH STUART, 134, 210, 294; *Gates Ajar*, 27
Phelps, William Lyon, 155
Philadelphia Press, The, 53
PHILLIPS, DAVID GRAHAM, 214q, 227, 247, 259
PHILLIPS, WENDELL, 6, 280, 287
Philosophy, *204ff*, 231, 280ff
Phoenix, John: *see* Derby, G. H.
Pillsbury, John Sargent, 212nq
Pilot, The, 5
Plato, 210, 232
Plutarch's Lives, 299
Poe, Edgar Allan, 16, 234f, 247, 264, 281, 284, 291; "Facts in the Case of M. Valdemar," 222
Poetry: A Magazine of Verse, 241
Popular Science Monthly, 209n, 225, 232
Populism, 100, 110, 124, 208, 212ff, 218, 225f, 229, 232
Porter, Noah, 8, 204
PORTER, WILLIAM SYDNEY (O. HENRY, *pseud.*), 3, 250
POUND, EZRA, 12n, 15, 55, 85q, 160, 253, 282q, 290n, 313, 363; *Cantos*, 79n; Greek, translations from, 50; *Patria Mia*, 28nq
POWELL, JOHN WESLEY, 9
Pragmaticism (Peirce's), 204
Pragmatism, 162f, 204
Prescott, W. H., 298
Princeton Review, 9, 17
Princeton University, 9, 204
Progress, 8f, 82n, 83f, 86, 209, 215f, 231, 247, 307; Twain on, *178ff*
Progressivism, 155, 162, 225, 227, 235, 259
"Promised Land" myth, 170; and immigration, 5
Protestant Ethic, 118, 141f, 210, 217, 306; *see also* Success myth
Protest parties, 208, 225
Proust, Marcel, 264; *Remembrance of Things Past*, 34
Prudent Patricians of Pompeii, 208
Psychology, 184, 282
Publisher's Weekly, 18
Pullman cars, 210; workers' strike, 27, 208
Puritanism, 133ff, 140, 148, 156, 282, 286ff, 307, 325, 327, 352
Pyle, Howard, 240n, 241n

Railroads, 11, 26, 109, 208; and farmers, 83; Norris's use of, 75; publicity campaigns, 107; strike of 1877, 27, 208

Ranch, symbol of expansive life, 108
Randolph, John, 299
Ranke, Leopold von, 298
Ransom, John Crowe: *Captain Carpenter*, 155
Rauschenbusch, Walter, 211q, 216q
Recapitulation theory, 57f, 184, 184n
Reconstruction, 27f, 51
Reese, Lizette Woodworth, 201q
Reform, 6, 128, 307
Regionalism, *81ff*, 217n, 254, 298; irony in, 88; literature of, 25, Bierce on, 124fq; New England, *133ff*; Southern, *88ff*; and Mark Twain, 185f; and utopia, 219; Western, *105ff*
Reid, Thomas, 282q
REID, WHITELAW, 8, 31, 81q, 314
Religion, *7ff*, 288; decline in fervor, 133
Religion of Humanity, 43, 205
Religion of Solidarity, 225
Repplier, Agnes, 84
Revivalism, 86
Revolte, La, 220
Revolutionary period, 83n, 84
Revue des Deux Mondes, 313
Reynolds, Thomas: *Prefaces and Notes*, 215
Ribot, Théodule Armand: *Diseases of Personality*, 45
Ricardo, David, 205, 234
RICHARDSON, H. H., 90, 209n, 304f
RIIS, JACOB, 5, 62, 218, 246q
Riley, James Whitcomb, 254
Rimbaud, Arthur, 153
Roberts Brothers, 294
ROBINSON, EDWIN ARLINGTON, 50, 55, 141, *152ff*, *285;* "Aaron Stark," 156q; "Benwick Fenzer," 158; *Captain Craig*, 153, 156ff, 159; *Cavendar's House*, 158; "Charles Carville's Eyes," 156n; "Chorus of Old Men in Aegeus," 154; "Cliff Klingenhagen," 156n; consciousness, theme of, 158; "The Dead Village," 154q; disaster, experience of, 153ff; "Flammonde," 158; "Fleming Helphenstine," 156n; "The House on the Hill," 154q; "John Brown," 158; *King Jasper*, 159; *Lancelot*, 158; "Luke Havergal," 153f; "The Man Against the Sky," 158; *Merlin*, 158; "Miniver Cheevy," 158; "Mr. Flood's Party," 160; and 19th century taste, 153; "optimistic desperation," 155; prose fiction, attempts at, 156, 156n; "Rembrandt to Rembrandt," 158; "Reuben Bright," 156n; "Richard Cory," 156n; *Roman Bartholomew*, 158; solitude, resolution of, 155f; *The Torrent and the Night Before*, 153; *The Town Down the River*, 158; *Tristram*, 158
Robinson, Rowland E., 160
Robinson Crusoe, 225
Rockefeller, 262; on wealth, 72
Roman dialogué, 347
Romanticism, 221

ROOSEVELT, THEODORE, 154q, 235, 246q, 264, 358; at Exposition of 1893, 243n; "New Nationalism," 26q; "The Strenuous Life," 107q
Root, Abiah,286
Root, John Wellborn, 243, 248
Rosewater, Frank: *The Making of a Millennium,* 219n
Ross, EDWARD ALBION, 62; *Sin and Society,* 247
Rourke, Constance, 18q
Rousseau, Jean Jacques, 306
Royal Society of Good Fellows, 208
ROYCE, JOSIAH, 231; *The Feud of Oakfield Creek,* 121
Roycrofters, 84
Ruskin, John, 19, 84, 287, 314, 350n

Sacramento Union, 168
Sage, Russell, 210q
SAINT-GAUDENS, AUGUSTUS, 79n, 241
St. James Theatre, 341
St. Louis Evening News, 167
St. Louis Globe-Democrat, 225
St. Nicholas, 142, 185
Sanborn, Frank, 29
Sanborn, H. F., 135q
Sand, George, 315
Sandburg, Carl, 261
Sanders, George A.: *Reality . . . ,* 224
San Francisco Chronicle, 71
San Francisco Examiner, 121
SANKEY, IRA DAVID, 86
SANTAYANA, GEORGE, 155, 203, 322q
Sartre, Jean-Paul, 323q
Saturday Press, 35, 168
SAVAGE, MINOT J., 9, 132, 224; *Evolution and Religion,* 9nq
SCHINDLER, SOLOMON: *Young West,* 224
Schlesinger, Arthur M., Sr., 4
Schmoller, Gustav F., 206
SCHURZ, CARL, 22, 78q
Schuyler, Montgomery, 28q
Science, 7, 209, 298, 307
Scopes trial, 86
Scott, Sir Walter, 18f, 21, 92, 95, 129; *Ivanhoe,* 89
Scribner, Charles, 18, 21q
Scribner's, 20, 29, 96, 241
SCUDDER, HORACE, 117q, 139
Scudder, Vida, 84
Sears, Roebuck Co., 17
Seaside Library, 19
Seligman, Edwin R. A., 206
Serra, Fr. Junipero, 84, 132
Shakespeare, William, 287
Shaw, George Bernard, 131, 227
SHAW, HENRY WHEELER (JOSH BILLINGS, *pseud.*), 28, 120q; *Farmers Allminax,* 119
SHELDON, REV. CHARLES M.: *In His Steps,* 140, 218
Shelley, Percy B., 280, 296
Sheridan, General Philip, 106
Sherman, General W. T., 168n

Shinn, Everett, 254
Shipley, M. A.: *The True Author of Looking Backward,* 224
Sill, Edward Rowland, 107
Silliman, Benjamin: *First Principles of Chemistry,* 290
Simmel, Georg: "The Metropolis and Modern Life," 255q
SIMMS, WILLIAM GILMORE, 17, 19, 30, 88
SINCLAIR, UPTON, 235f, 259; *The Jungle,* 208, London on, 234q
"Single-tax," 206, 211, 218
SLOAN, JOHN, 254, 278
Slosson, Annie Trumbull, 148, 160
Smith, Adam, 13n, 94q, 205
SMITH, F. HOPKINSON: *Colonel Carter,* 89f; *Gondola Days,* 90q
Smith, Harry deForest, 156
Smith, Henry Nash: *Virgin Land,* 108q, 109q, 115q
Social Darwinism, 3, 42, 73f, 94, 205, 216, 233, 252; and Norris, 72f
Social Gospel, 43, 210f, 225, 229
Socialism, 82n, 208, 211, 215n, 218, 225f, 230; Crane on, 62q; and J. London, 234ff
Society of Colonial Wars, 83n
Sociology, 231
Sons of the American Revolution, 83n
Sophocles, 154
Southern Literary Messenger, 16
Southern myth, 81f, *88ff,* 167n
Southworth, Mrs. E. D. E. N., 21
Spanish-American War, 56, 70
Spencer, Herbert, 3, 8, 10q, 14n, 16, 72, 82n, 95n, 203, 205, 218q, 231, 234ff, 239; *First Principles,* 8, 202, sales of, 8n
SPOFFORD, HARRIET PRESCOTT, 134, 139q; *Art Decoration Applied to Furniture,* 273
Sports, 86, 86n
Springfield Republican, 80, 287, 291f
Standard Oil Company, 227
STANLEY, HENRY M., 7, 56, 87, 277
Stead, W. T., 14n, 132, 243q
STEDMAN, EDMUND CLARENCE, 14, 43, 155, 255, 279, 279n; *American Anthology,* 153; *Complete Pocket-Guide to Europe,* 79q; *Nature and Elements of Poetry,* 15, 281
STEFFENS, LINCOLN, 73, 250, 253; *Shame of the Cities,* 246
Stein, Gertrude, 15
Stein, W. B., 334n
Steinbeck, John, 83
Stendahl, Marie: *see* Beyle, Henri
Sterling, George, 238
Stevens, Ebenezer, 263
Stevenson, Robert Louis, 18, 21, 111, 264; *Across the Plains,* 110q
Stewart, William, 176
STICKNEY, TRUMBULL, 155f
Stieglitz, Alfred, 254
Stoddard, Charles Warren, 107
Stoddard, Elizabeth: *The Morgesons,* 134

Stoddard, John L., 7
STODDARD, RICHARD HENRY, 13n, 15, 153, 279q
Stone, C. H.: *One of Berrian's Novels,* 224
STORY, WILLIAM WETMORE, 308, 315
Stowe, Calvin, 139, 143, 287
STOWE, HARRIET BEECHER, 28, *137ff,* 143f, 148, 152, 155, 210, 287f; compulsions, emotional, 138; *Key,* 138; *Minister's Wooing,* 133, 134q, 137f; *Oldtown Folks,* 137fq, 138nq, 139; *Pearl of Orr's Island,* 138, 143; *Poganuc People,* 138; and Puritanism, 134, 137f; *Sam Lawson's Oldtown Fireside Stories,* 138, 139q; *Uncle Tom's Cabin,* 30, 98, 138
Strikes, 208, 215n, 231
Strindberg, August, 47
Strong, Josiah, 244q
Sturges, Howard, 363
Success myth, 155, 208f, 216f, 250f, 307; revolt against, 245
Sullivan, John L., 277
SULLIVAN, LOUIS, 248; *Autobiography of an Idea,* 243q; Transportation Building, 243
Sumner, Charles, 82q
SUMNER, WILLIAM GRAHAM, 22, 72, 94, 245q, 281; *Folkways,* 186, 205q
Sunday, Billy, 86
"Survival of the fittest," 95n, 236
Swedenborgianism, 41, 47n, 212, 226, 240n, 312; *New Jerusalem,* 229
Swift, Jonathan: *Tale of a Tub,* 306
Swinburne, Algernon, 153
Symons, Arthur: *Symbolist Movement in Literature,* 20

Taft, Lorado, 132
Taine, Hippolyte, 152, 315; *Philosophy of Art in the Netherlands,* 114
Tammany Hall, 22, 82
TARBELL, IDA, 73, 250; "The Golden Rule in Business" 246; "History of the Standard Oil Company," 246
TARKINGTON, BOOTH: on Richard H. Davis, 54q; *Gentleman from Indiana,* 254
Tate, Allen: *The Fathers,* 34, 89; "A Southern Mode of the Imagination," 105q
TAYLOR, BAYARD, 30, 36, 54, 79n, 107q, 275, 279, 313; *By-Ways of Europe,* 167; Faust, translation of, 12
Taylor, Frederick Winslow, 82
Taylor, Walter Fuller, 130q, 208fq
Tead, Ordway: *Instincts in Industry,* 209
Technology, 10, 26, 233, 363
Tennyson, Alfred, 19, 153, 287
Thackeray, William M., 19, 21, 95, 100, 153, 265, 341; *Henry Esmond,* 89
THAXTER, CELIA, 143, 148, 293
THAYER, W. M., 216f
Theosophy, 211f, 225f, 235

Thompson, Charles Miner, 148q
Thompson, Maurice: *Alice of Old Vincennes,* 254
Thoreau, Henry David, 122q, 137, 258, 261q, 290, 316f, 319; *Walden,* 11, 252q, 282q
Ticknor and Co., 20n
Tiffany Building, 321
Timrod, Henry, 17
Tocqueville, Alexis de, 2, 204, 274, 301; *Democracy in America,* 316
Tolstoy, Leo, 19, 41, 60, 62, 70n, 227, 229, 264, 341; *Anna Karenina,* 281
Tolstoy Club, 230
TOURGÉE, ALBION W., 27, 51f, 55; "American Historical Novels" series, 51; *Bricks Without Straw,* 51; *Figs and Thistles,* 51; *A Fool's Errand,* 51; *Hot Plowshares,* 51, 51q; *John Eax,* 51, 52q; *A Royal Gentleman,* 51, 51q; "The South as a Field for Fiction," 90
Tramp armies, 59, 78
Transatlantic cable, 78
Transcendentalism, 203, 261, 282, 286
Translation, 12
Traubel, Horace, 153
Travel writing, 56, 80, 128, 275, 305, 313ff
Trilling, Lionel, 258q, 268q
Trine, R. W.: *In Tune With the Infinite,* 211
Trinity Church, Boston, 90, 304
Trollope, Anthony, 312; *Miss Mackenzie,* 327nq
Trumbull, John, 263
Truth, 60
Tucker, Benjamin R. J., 16q
Tufts, James H., 203q
Turgenev, Ivan, 19, 108, 265, 312f, 315, 329, 334, 336; *Fathers and Sons,* 14n
TURNER, FREDERICK JACKSON, 26q, 74, 108q, 252; "The Significance of the City in American Civilization," 252n; "The Significance of the Frontier in American History," 65, 244
Turner, George Kibbe: "The Daughters of the Poor," 247
TWAIN, MARK, 1, 7, 10, 12, 17, 19, 20q, 21, 35, 56, 59, 65, 70, 75, 88, 89, 92, 97, 108, 117, *165ff,* 209q, 235, 275, 277, 281f, 232q, 284, 287, 293, 295, 304, 311, 313, 320, 328, 340, 340n; "Adam family papers," 182f; Adam myth, 169f; and H. Adams, *176ff;* alienation, 196f; *An American Claimant,* 181, 197, 317; "Around the World," 170f; *Autobiography, 197ff;* "The Autobiography of a Damn Fool," 198; "The Awful German Language," 174; "Boy's Manuscript," 186f; *Captain Stormfield's Visit to Heaven,* 199, 199n; career, 168; child, view of, *184ff; A Connecticut Yankee in King Arthur's Court,* 58, 84, 177n, 178, *179ff,* 186, 189f, 197, 362; "The Curious Republic of Gondour," 172q; "The Dandy Frightening the Squatter,"

172; *The Death of Jean,* 199; "double-ness," 181; and Dreiser, 275, 275n; drift, theme of, *193ff;* "Eddypus Cycle," 181; Eden myth, 171ff; "enchanted sea wilderness . . . ," ms., 195q; "Eve's Autobiography," 183q; and evolution, 182f; "Extract from Methuselah's Diary," 182q; "Facts Concerning the Recent Carnival of Crime," 188q; *Following the Equator,* 174, 191, 197; *The Gilded Age* (with Charles Dudley Warner), 35, 165, *177ff,* 221, 245; "Goldsmith's Friend Abroad Again," 171; "Greetings from the 19th to the 20th Century," 183; and History, *175ff.; Huck Finn and Tom Sawyer Among the Indians,* 195; *Huckleberry Finn,* 59, 166, 181, *190ff,* 193ff, 256, 281, 287, 345f, 351; human development, view of, 187; *Innocents Abroad,* 165, 167, *168ff,* 171, 173, 175n, 194q, 275, 314, 326; *Is Shakespeare Dead?,* 199; "Jim Smiley and His Jumping Frog," 168; *Life on the Mississippi,* 167, 186, *189ff,* 191, 194; "The Man that Corrupted Hadleyburg," 172; "Mark Twain's (Burlesque) Autobiography," 177n; and mass mind, 165f; *The Mysterious Stranger,* 122, *196f,* 198; and National Novel, 175f; *New Adventures of Huckleberry Finn,* 195; "Noah's Ark Book," 169; "Old Times on the Mississippi," 186, 193; "On Progress, Civilization, Monarchy, etc.," 179q; "Open Letter to Commodore Vanderbilt," 166n, 177nq; *Personal History of Joan of Arc,* 182q, 197; popularity, decline of, *196f; Prince and the Pauper,* 181f; "The Private History of a Campaign that Failed," 29, 167; progress, view of, *178ff; Pudd'nhead Wilson,* 193, 197; "Pudd'nhead Wilson's New Calendar," 174; recapitulation theory, 57; and reform, 178; and regionalism, 185f; restlessness, 167; *Roughing It,* 116, *171ff,* 191, 194q, 275; satan figure, 196; as satirist, 171; sequels to *Huckleberry Finn,* 194f; "A Serio-Humorous Lecture . . . ," 167; "Some Rambling Notes . . . ," 194q; on *Story of a Country Town,* 116q; "Stupendous International Procession," 196; suppressed romanticism, 186; *Tom Sawyer,* 59, *186ff,* 190f, 194q, 195q; *Tom Sawyer Abroad,* 194q, 195; *Tom Sawyer, Detective,* 195; "Tom's Conspiracy," 195; *A Tramp Abroad, 173ff,* 194q; travel writing, *167ff;* "Universal Suffrage," 172; wealth, attitude toward, 166, 166n; *What Is Man?,* 166, 183, 197; "Whittier Birthday Dinner Speech," 60; "Young Satan," 196

TWEED, WILLIAM M., 22, 82, 321

TWICHELL, J. H., 174, 178, 186, 190n, 194

Tyndall, John, 16, 95

Under the Gaslight (Augustin Daly), 260

Unionism, 208f, 211, 225, 234

Unitarianism, 84

United States Geological Survey, 8, 80

United States Steel, 246, 321

Utopianism, 41, 78, 92, 178f, *202ff,* 209, 241n, 242, 254

VAN BRUNT, HENRY, 10q, 241q

VANDERBILT, CORNELIUS, 13, 211, 245, 300, 321

Vanderbilt, William H., 79n

Vanderbilt house (Hunt's), 322

Van Winkle, Rip, 347

Vaughan, Henry, 287

Veblen, Ellen Rolfe, 220q

VEBLEN, THORSTEIN, 60f, 95q, 206, 206n, 220, 227, 242, 245q, 237n, 321q

VEDDER, ELIHU, 79nq, 322q

"Veritism," 125f

VINCENT, REV. JOHN H., 7q

Vinton, Arthur Dudley: *Looking Further Backward,* 223

Virginia City Territorial Enterprise, 176

"Virgin Land," 181

Voltaire, François, 176

Wadsworth, Rev. Charles, 186

Wagner, Adolf H. G., 206

Wagner, Richard, 29

Waite, Davis Hanson, 213q

Walcutt, Charles Child, 64fq

WALKER, FRANCIS, 206q

Wallace, Alfred Russell, 82n, 234

WARD, ARTEMUS: *see* Browne, Charles Farrar

Ward, C. Osborne: *The Ancient Lowly,* 208

WARD, LESTER, 203, 231; *Dynamic Sociology,* 94, 203

Ward, Theodora, 286q

WARNER, CHARLES DUDLEY: *Being a Boy,* 285; *Gilded Age* (with Mark Twain), 35, 165, *177ff,* 221, 245; ". . . Mr. Froude's 'Progress,'" 178q; *The Relation of Literature to Life,* 165q; "Studies in the South," 96q; *Their Pilgrimage,* 26q

Washington, George, 60

Wasserburg, Philip: *Etwas Später!,* 224

Watson, Thomas Edward, 100

Wayland, Francis, 94, 203; *Elements of Political Economy,* 205q, 206, 217, 231

Wealth, rise of, 2ff, 216, 320

Weaver, Raymond M.: *Herman Melville,* 50

Webster, Noah: *Rhetorical Reader,* 295

Wells, Henry, 281q

Wells, H. G., 60, 340q, 358

WENDELL, BARRETT, 245q, 262

West: in Crane, 65ff, disillusion with, 109; myth of, 80, 121, 132, 171, 319,

327; regionalism, 82, *105ff;* tours of, 80, 106; Western humor, 119f, 168, 174
West, Nathanael: *Day of the Locust,* 362
Western Union Co., 26
WHARTON, EDITH, 4, 59, 200, *263ff,* 275, 277f, 281, 283n, 301, 307, 313, 330, 358, 364; *Age of Innocence,* 266, *272f;* A *Backward Glance,* 263, 266q, *273ff.;* The *Buccaneers,* 274; *Bunner Sisters, 266ff;* *Custom of the Country,* 266q, 269, *271ff,* 320; *Decoration of Houses* (with Ogden Codman, Jr.), 3q, 269, 273; *Ethan Frome,* 266, *267ff,* 270; *French Ways and Their Meaning,* 273f; *The Gods Arrive,* 264; "The Great American Novel," 31; *The Greater Inclination,* 265; *House of Mirth,* 174, 266q, *269ff,* 273; *Hudson River Bracketed,* 264; *Italian Backgrounds,* 265q; literary productivity, 264; literature as therapy, 265; "Mrs. Manstey's View," 263; naturalism, 265f; *The Old Maid,* 263; *Old New York Series,* 263n, 273, 273n; *Summer,* 266, *268ff,* 270; *Valley of Decision,* 264; *Verses,* 264; *Writing of Fiction,* 264q
WHISTLER, JAMES A. MCNEILL: *Ten O'Clock,* 320q
WHITE, ANDREW A., 37, 176; *Warfare of Science with Theology,* 304
WHITE, RICHARD GRANT: *Chronicles of Gotham,* 244n; *Fall of Man,* 9q
White, William Allen, 227
WHITLOCK, BRAND, 227; *The 13th District,* 83
WHITMAN, WALT, 3, 14, 17, 25, 35, 49, 51, 69, 77, 84q, 106q, 125q, 127, 153, 168, 170, 246q, 253, 258, *279ff,* 285, 293; "A Backward Glance O'er Travel'd Roads," 283q; "Chanting the Square Deific," 122; *Democratic Vistas,* 15q, 284; on Richard H. Davis, 53; drama by Morley, 53n; on Ingersoll, 261q; "On Journeys Through the States," 168q; *Leaves of Grass,* 5, 14, 30, 147, 261q, 284, 3rd edition, 36; and National Literature, 36; *Notes on Walt Whitman,* 36n; "Out of the Cradle," 257; *Specimen Days, 283ff;* and Wharton, 283n
Whitman fellowship, 14, 35
WHITTIER, JOHN GREENLEAF, 6, 12, 14, 29, 49, 94, 205, 284, 287, 293; "Among the Hills," 134, 156n; *Margaret Smith's Journal,* 156n; *Snowbound,* 18
Who's Who (1899), 255
Wilbrandt, Konrad: *Mr. East's Experiences,* 224
WILKINS, MARY E., 88, 137, 141f, *148ff,* 154f, 159f, 267, 285, 351; children's literature, 148; "A Conflict Ended," 149q; "A Conquest of Humility," 151; critic of New England, 148; *Decorative Plaques,* 156n; "Gentian," 149; *The Hearts Highway,* 151; "A Humble Romance," 148q, 149q, 151; *Jerome,* 152q;

By the Light of the Soul, 152q; "A New England Nun," 148, 150f, 158; "A New England Prophet," 149; *Once Upon a Time,* 156n; "One Good Time," 151; pathetic comedy, 149; *Pembroke,* 149q, 151; *The Portion of Labor,* 152, 160; portrait of a solitary, 150; "The Revolt of 'Mother,'" 149, 151; romanticism, 151f; *Six Trees,* 151; "A Solitary," 150; "Two Old Lovers," 149q, 221; *Understudies,* 151; "A Village Singer," 149, 151; *The Wind in the Rose Bush,* 151
Wilde, Oscar: *Picture of Dorian Gray,* 349
Willard, Cyrus, 226q
Willard, Frances E., 226q
William of Prussia, 78
Williams, William Carlos, 15; *Paterson,* 162n, 290n
Willis, N. P., 313
Wilson, Edmund, 265
WILSON, WOODROW: *The State,* 207q
Winters, Yvor, 162
Winthrop, John, 138
Witherspoon, John, 203
Wood, Jim, 245
WOOLSON, CONSTANCE FENIMORE, 51, *52f,* 55; *Castle Nowhere,* 52; and Europe, 52f; "The Front Yard," 52; J. Henry Harper on, 53q; H. James on, 52fq; *Jupiter Lights,* 53; and National Novel, 53; *Rodman the Keeper,* 52; and South, 52; "The South Devil," 52nq; "A Transplanted Boy," 52f; travel writing, 52
Wordsworth, Dorothy, 144f
Wordsworth, William, 95, 144f, 153
World's Columbian Exposition (1893), 167, *240ff,* 248, 253, 256, 273, 278
WRIGHT, CHAUNCEY, 8, 10, 86q, 95nq, 215q, 301, 313; and H. Adams, 301; *Philosophical Discussions,* 10q
WRIGHT, FRANK LLOYD, 242f
Wright, Rev. G. Frederick, 210q

Yale Daily News, 238n
Yale University, 8, 204, 238, 238n, 321
Yeats, William Butler, 160, 226, 313; "All Soul's Night," 150; "The Second Coming," 144, 349
Yellow Book, The, 320
"Yeoman farmer," 91
YERKES, CHARLES T., 243, 262
YOUMANS, EDWARD LIVINGSTON, 9, 209n, 218, 232q, 260q
Young, Brigham, 173
Young, Philip: *Ernest Hemingway,* 65q
Yukon Gold Rush of 1898, 130

Zola, Émile, 19, 60, 62, 70n, 71, 71n, 73, 153, 231, 250, 255, 260, 265q, 301, 312, 335; *Nana,* 19